T0238545

Communications
in Computer and Information Science 330

S.G. Ponnambalam   Jussi Parkkinen
Kuppan Chetty Ramanathan (Eds.)

Trends in Intelligent Robotics, Automation, and Manufacturing

First International Conference, IRAM 2012
Kuala Lumpur, Malaysia, November 28-30, 2012
Proceedings

 Springer

Volume Editors

S.G. Ponnambalam
Jussi Parkkinen
Kuppan Chetty Ramanathan
Monash University Sunway Campus, 46150 Malaysia
E-mail: {sgponnambalam, jussi.parkkinen, kuppanchetty.ramanathan}@monash.edu

ISSN 1865-0929   e-ISSN 1865-0937
ISBN 978-3-642-35196-9   e-ISBN 978-3-642-35197-6
DOI 10.1007/978-3-642-35197-6
Springer Heidelberg Dordrecht London New York

Library of Congress Control Number: 2012952290

CR Subject Classification (1998): I.2, I.4, F.1, H.3, I.5, H.4

Typesetting: Camera-ready by author, data conversion by Scientific Publishing Services, Chennai, India

Printed on acid-free paper

Springer is part of Springer Science+Business Media (www.springer.com)

Preface

The Organizing Committee of the First International Conference on Intelligent Robotics, Automation and Manufacturing (IRAM 2012) aimed to facilitate interaction among researchers in the field. Through this conference, the committee intended to enhance the sharing of individual experiences and expertise in the areas of intelligent robotics automation and manufacturing with particular emphasis on technical challenges associated with varied applications.

IRAM 2012 was successful in attracting 102 full-paper submissions, from more than 15 different countries, addressing state-of-the-art developments in robotics, automation, and manufacturing. After a rigorous peer-review process, the Program Committee selected 64 deserving papers for inclusion in this CCIS volume. The selected papers were presented at IRAM 2012, held at Monash University Sunway Campus, Kuala Lumpur, Malaysia, during November 28–30, 2012. The contribution of the Technical Program Committee and the referees is deeply appreciated. Most of all, we would like to express our sincere thanks to the authors for submitting their most recent work. Special thanks to Monash University Sunway Campus for their support.

We sincerely hope that this volume will prove to be an important resource for the scientific community and informative to readers.

Our particular thanks are due to Mr. Alfred Hofmann and the editorial staff of Springer-Verlag for enthusiastically supporting the project.

September 2012

S.G. Ponnambalam
Shamsudin Hj. Mohd Amin

Organization

General Chair

S.G. Ponnambalam — Monash University Sunway Campus, Malaysia

Co-chair
Shamsudin Hj. Mohd Amin — Universiti Teknikal Malaysia, Malaysia

Program Chair

Kuppan Chetty Ramanathan — Monash University Sunway Campus, Malaysia

Co-chair
A. Senthil Kumar — National University of Singapore, Singapore
Mohd Rizal Bin Arshad — Universiti Sains Malaysia, Malaysia

Publications

Jussi Parkkinen (Chair) — Monash University Sunway Campus, Malaysia
Velappa Ganapathy — Universiti Malaya, Malaysia
Liyanage C. De Silva — UBD, Brunei

Finances

Tan Chee Pin (Chair) — Monash University Sunway Campus, Malaysia
Deborah Cheah — Monash University Sunway Campus, Malaysia

Registration

Parasuraman (Chair) — Monash University Sunway Campus, Malaysia
Khoo Boon How — Monash University Sunway Campus, Malaysia
Mark Ng Kok Yew — Monash University Sunway Campus, Malaysia

Publicity and Local Arrangements

Madhavan (Chair) — Monash University Sunway Campus, Malaysia
Narayanan Ramakrishnan — Monash University Sunway Campus, Malaysia
Yogeswaran Mohan — Monash University Sunway Campus, Malaysia

Steering Committee

Anthony Guo (Chair)	Monash University Sunway Campus, Malaysia
Y. Narahari	Indian Institute of Science, India
M. Singaperumal	Indian Institute of Technology Madras, India
Rainer Leisten	University of Duisberg Essen, Germany
Michael Wang	The Chinese University of Hong Kong, Hong Kong
Parasuraman	Monash University Sunway Campus, Malaysia
S.G. Ponnambalam	Monash University Sunway Campus, Malaysia
Prahalad Vadakepad	National University of Singapore, Singapore
Tetsunari Inamura	National Institute of Informatics, Japan
Kuppan Chetty Ramanathan	Monash University Sunway Campus, Malaysia

International Advisory Committee

Mingcong Deng	Tokyo University of Agriculture and Technology, Japan
Marcelo Ang Jr.	National University of Singapore, Singapore
Marzuki Khalid	Unversiti Teknologi Malaysia, Malaysia
Chung Myung Jin	KAIST, Korea
Hongai Liu	University of Portsmouth, UK
Mohamed Kamel	University Waterloo, Canada
Nilesh J. Vasa	Indian Institute of Technology Madras, India
Angappa Gunasekaran	University of Massachusetts Dartmouth, USA
V.S.S. Yadavalli	University of Pretoria, South Africa
F.T.S. Chan	The Hong Kong Polytechnic University, Hong Kong

Technical Program Committee

A. Elaya Perumal, India
A. Noorul Haq, India
Abdul hamid, Malaysia
Abdul Rashid Hussain, Malaysia
Alpha Agape Gopalai, India
Amir Akramin Shafie, Malaysia
Antonios Tsourdos, UK
Asan Gani Abdul Muthalif, Malaysia
B.K. Panigrahi, India
C.S. Shankar Ram, India
Danilo De Rossi, Italy
Darwin, Malaysia
Devadasan, India
Elizabeth Rufus, India

Farazila Binti Yusof, Malaysia
Gandhinathan, India
Huei-Yung Lin, Taiwan
I.A. Palani, India
I. Rajendran, India
Jawaid I. Inayat Hussian, Malaysia
John Billingsley, Australia
K. Prakasan, India
Kanagaraj, Malaysia
Kang Li, Australia
Kauko Leiviskä, Finland
Kin Keung Lai, Hongkong
Koh Keng Huat, Malaysia
Kuppan Chetty, Malaysia

Kuang Ye Chow, Malaysia
L.A. Kumaraswamidhas, India
Lingxue Kong, Australia
Loo Chu Kiong, Malaysia
Low Sew Ming, Malaysia
Lucia Pallottino, Italy
Madhavan, Malaysia
Mahapatra, India
Maki K. Habib, Egypt
Mark Ng Kok Yew, Malaysia
Mukund J., Malaysia
Muralidhara, India
Murugappan, Malaysia
Myong K. Jeong, USA
N. Jawahar, India
Nilesh J. Vasa, India
Nachiappan Subramaniam, India
P. Asokan, India
P.V. Manivannan, India
P.V. Mohanram, India
Parasuraman, Malaysia
Pasupathi, India
Paulraj Murugesapandian, Malaysia
P.D.D. Dominic, India
Peter Xu, New Zealand
Prahalad Vadakepat, Singapore
Ponnamblam, Malaysia

Pooria Pasbakhsh, Malaysia
Rajendran Parthiban, Malaysia
Rajendran, India
Ramakrishnan Narayanan, Malaysia
Rini Akmeliawati, Malaysia
S. Kumanan, India
S. Subha Rani, India
S. Venakataramaniah, India
S. Vinod, India
S. Narayanan, India
Santhakumar, India
Simon G Fabri, Malta
Singaperumal, India
Somasundaran Kumanan, India
Sundar D.L., India
T. Asokan, India
T. Nagarajan, Malaysia
Tan Chee Pin, Malaysia
Tsai-Yen Li, Taiwan
Veeraragavan, Malaysia
Victor Raj, India
Vineetha Kalavally, Malaysia
Wang Xin, Malaysia
Yangmin Li, Macau
Yogeswaran Mohan, Malaysia
Yuh Min Chen, Taiwan

Web Administration

Yogeswaran Mohan, Malaysia
Janardhanan Mukund Nilakantan, Malaysia

Table of Contents

Intelligent Robotics

Automation

Manufacturing

A Heuristic Approach towards Path Planning and Obstacle Avoidance Control of Planar Manipulator

R.M. Kuppan Chetty and S.G. Ponnambalam

Monash University Sunway Campus, Bandar Sunway, Selangor, Malaysia
{kuppanchetty.ramanathan,sgponnambalam}@monash.edu

Abstract. This paper addresses the development and application of heuristic control strategy to plan collision free configurations of a 5 D.O.F. planar robot manipulator, to position its end effector at the desired target with minimal error and convergence time, while avoiding the obstacles in the workspace. Four variants of Particle Swarm Optimization (PSO) technique is used as the heuristic approaches to solve the above problem. The efficiency and performance of the proposed approaches is investigated through both simulation and experimental studies. It is found out that the variant of PSO-W produces better results in terms of convergence and positional in scenarios such movements in environment with free obstacles, with one obstacle and two obstacle respectively with error less than 2.3% overall. Results revealed that the heuristic methods based on the search algorithms is a viable alternative over the traditional approaches for solving redundant manipulator problems constrained with nonlinearities and obstacles.

Keywords: Particle swarm optimization, redundant manipulator, obstacle avoidance, robot arm, heuristic approaches.

1 Introduction

For industrial robot manipulator to perform tasks such as pick and place in the shop floor, the ability of robot's end-effector to reach the desired points with minimal error is utmost important for quality performance. During its operation, the capability to avoid operational singularities and evading obstacles that subsist in its environment is required to guarantee the efficacy of robot's operation. It is common to cluster multiple robot manipulators in a workspace for the purpose of higher space occupancy. Kinematic redundancy [1-4, 6-7] is a feasible approach to address all three requirements above. Kinetic redundancy in robot manipulators can be achieved by allocating one or more extra degree of freedom (DOF) than required to arrive at a certain position in the workspace. Additional DOF enables the robot manipulator to better avoid obstacles and operation singularities with its increased flexibility.

There are two common approaches for controlling such robot manipulators: forward kinematics and inverse kinematics. Forward kinematics approach can be better realized in joint space where the changes in joint angle values would immediately affect end-effector position. In contrary, inverse kinematics can be

S.G. Ponnambalam et al. (Eds.): IRAM 2012, CCIS 330, pp. 1–11, 2012.

viewed as Cartesian space mapping problem where exact joint angle values are required to be computed according to the input of desired end-effector position. Study on redundant robot manipulator problem with a wide range of approaches starting from the use of Fuzzy Logic with suitable fuzzy rule base function [1], Adaptive Fuzzy Logic Control [2], Genetic Algorithm [3] Neural Network based algorithms [4] has also been reported in the literature.

As a further development, in 2008, significant improvement in solving trajectory planning problem (TPP) was observed in particle swarm optimization (PSO) [5, 8]. A Simplex Algorithm (SA) based PSO was compared against A* Algorithm by Huang et al. [6]. Their study revealed that SA-PSO was able to produce more accurate solution and SA has displayed its feature in preventing the PSO being trapped in local optima. In 2010, Guo et al. [7] introduced Quantum-PSO (QPSO) that is capable to devise a collision-free trajectory for planar redundant manipulator. In QPSO, the particles were initialized using chaotic sequence and to move in a quantum style. It was shown that QPSO converges faster than GA while preserving the accuracy of solution.

In this paper, the potential of PSO in robot manipulator problem is further investigated by employing a hybrid algorithm of PSO and QA. Two hybrid algorithms namely qPSO-W and qPSO-C are created by hybridizing QA with PSO-W (PSO with inertia weight) and PSO-C (PSO with constriction factor) respectively which are addressed in [9]. The performance of the algorithms is compared in the following scenarios: i) free-space, ii) environment with one obstacle, and iii) environment with two obstacles; in both simulation and experimentation.

2   Problem Statement

The following assumptions are made and utilized throughout this work while formulating the control laws for the variants of PSO's.

- 2 dimensional Cartesian coordinate representation is considered.
- 5 D.o.F. Planar manipulator is considered as the redundant robot.
- Obstacles present in the workspace are considered as static regular polygons with known geometrical patterns and postures.
- Orientation of the end effector is not given and could have any free orientation in the workspace.
- Workspace is considered to be a semicircular with the radius of 0.37m and the robot motion is constrained with the presence of obstacles in the workspace.
- Links of robots are identical with equal length and the individual joints are constrained to work within the range of $-\pi/2 \leq \theta_i \leq \pi/2$.

Based on the above assumptions, the problem could be defined in detail as, to devise a heuristic control strategy to plan collision free configurations that positions the end effector of the planar robot at the desired target posture from its initial position, with maximized accuracy, by making the positional error asymptotically zero, within minimum amount of time. In this regard, it is necessary to estimate the individual joint angles of the planar manipulator with the use of the heuristic approaches to position its end effector accurately.

3   Methodology

Purpose of any optimization problem is to minimize or maximize the objective function subject to several constraints that are related to the applications. Therefore, the major objective in this problem is to position the end effector of a planar robot manipulator at the target locations constrained by the static obstacle in the workspace with minimal error. Therefore, this paper details the use of variants of PSO's to solve this problem.

3.1   Kinematic Model

The kinematic model of a 5 D.o.F planar robot in a 2D Cartesian space, which is considered as the system of interest in this work is shown in Fig. 1. It consists of 5 identical links of equal length connected by intermediate rotary joints. Use of forward kinematics will be an easiest way in deriving the end effector position of such planar manipulator. Therefore, a systematic approach based on the Denavit - Hartenberg (DH) convention is used to derive the forward kinematic equations.   This DH convention allows the generation of minimal representation on the entire robot kinematics with the center geometric concept of common normal between successive links such that the axes are located at the distant ends of the link and the joint i is located at coordinate i-1.

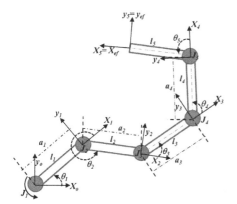

Table 1. represents the DH table for the manipulator shown in Fig. 1

i	α_{i-1}	a_{i-1}	d_i	θ_i
1	0	0	0	θ_1
2	0	l_1	0	θ_2
3	0	l_2	0	θ_3
4	0	l_3	0	θ_4
5	0	l_4	0	θ_5
6	0	l_5	0	0

Fig. 1. Kinematic Model of 5 D.o.F Planar Robotic Manipulator

Where, i represents the number of joints, α_i represents the angle about common normal from old 'z' axis to new 'z'axis, a_i is the length of the link about the common normal, d_i is the offset along the previous 'z' axis at common normal and θ_i is the joint angle (variable of interest) about previous normal. Therefore, based on this convention, the homogenous transformation matrix T_i is given by the following relationship.

$$
{}^{i-1}_{i}T = \begin{bmatrix}
c\theta_i & -s\theta_i & 0 & a_{i-1} \\
s\theta_i c\alpha_{i-1} & c\theta_i c\alpha_{i-1} & -s\alpha_{i-1} & -s\alpha_{i-1}d_i \\
s\theta_i c\alpha_{i-1} & c\theta_i c\alpha_{i-1} & c\alpha_{i-1} & c\alpha_{i-1}d_i \\
0 & 0 & 0 & 1
\end{bmatrix} \tag{1}
$$

The transformation matrix of the individual joints is then obtained by substituting the parametric details from the DH table into equation 1.

As a result, the coordinate position of the manipulator end effector (x,y) is given as the function of the joint angles θ_1, θ_2, θ_3, θ_4 and θ_5 and can be determined by having the product of the transformation matrices of the individual links and it is given by

$$
\begin{bmatrix} x \\ y \\ z \\ 1 \end{bmatrix} = {}^{0}_{5}T \cdot \begin{bmatrix} l_5 \\ 0 \\ 0 \\ 1 \end{bmatrix} \tag{2}
$$

Therefore, the transformation matrix ${}^{0}_{5}T$, which is used to derive the end effector position with respect to the global reference frame and it is the jacobian matrix which is given by

$$
{}^{0}_{5}T = \begin{bmatrix}
c_{12345} & -s_{12345} & 0 & l_4c_{1234}+l_3c_{123}+l_2c_{12}+l_1c_1 \\
s_{12345} & c_{2345} & 0 & l_4s_{1234}+l_3s_{123}+l_2s_{12}+l_1s_1 \\
0 & 0 & 1 & 0 \\
0 & 0 & 0 & 1
\end{bmatrix} \tag{3}
$$

Consequently, the end effector position and the orientation could be obtained as given by the following equations

$$
\begin{aligned}
x = &\, l_5 \cos(\theta_5 + \theta_4 + \theta_3 + \theta_2 + \theta_1) + l_4 \cos(\theta_4 + \theta_3 + \theta_2 + \theta_1) \\
&+ l_3 \cos(\theta_3 + \theta_2 + \theta_1) + l_2 \cos(\theta_2 + \theta_1) + l_2 \cos\theta_1
\end{aligned} \tag{4}
$$

$$
\begin{aligned}
y = &\, l_5 \sin(\theta_5 + \theta_4 + \theta_3 + \theta_2 + \theta_1) + l_4 \sin(\theta_4 + \theta_3 + \theta_2 + \theta_1) \\
&+ l_3 \sin(\theta_3 + \theta_2 + \theta_1) + l_2 \sin(\theta_2 + \theta_1) + l_2 \sin\theta_1
\end{aligned} \tag{5}
$$

$$
\theta = \theta_5 + \theta_4 + \theta_3 + \theta_2 + \theta_1 \tag{6}
$$

In this case, it is necessary to estimate the individual joint angles θ_i, to make the robot to reach the desired position with minimal positional error, by satisfying the constraints related to the collision free movement with the obstacles. Therefore, heuristic approaches finds a better solution in a simplistic manner rather than the traditional inverse kinematic approach, since the later yields two sets of solutions which are computationally complex in nature. Consequently, the control law is derived based on the variants of Particle Swarm Optimization techniques as detailed in [9].

3.2   Control Algorithm

The individual joint angles of the planar manipulator determine the position of the end effector to reach the target postures. Therefore, it is necessary to find out the global best joint angles of the individual joints, that minimized the error between the position of the end effector and the target, asymptotically zero. In addition, it is also necessary to consider the constraints (positions of the obstacle) while estimating the joint angles to have a collision free configuration of the manipulator. Fig. 2 shows the flowchart of the search algorithm which determines the collision free joint angles from the search space. Here the joint angles are the particles in a 2D solution space.

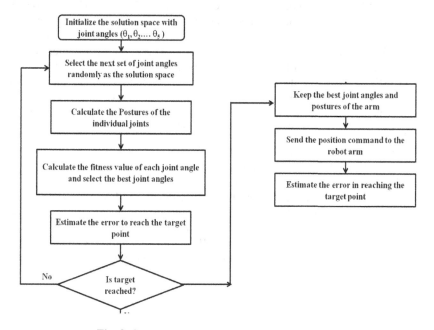

Fig. 2. Control Algorithm of heuristic search approach

The best joint angles are selected, when the end effector position reaches the target without collision and with minimum positional error. Therefore, the positional error between the robot current position (x_c, y_c) and the target position (x_t, y_t) is estimated as

$$P_e = \sqrt{\left((x_T - x_c)^2 + (y_T - y_c)^2\right)} \tag{7}$$

and the objective function or fitness function (F_s) which is used to select the global best joint angles is given by

$$F_s = F_o * P_e + 0.1 * \sum_{k=1}^{5} \theta_k + C_l \tag{8}$$

where, C_i is an penalty value which is introduced to recognize the collision and carries a huge value of 900,000 incurred to the particles that are colliding with obstacles and F_o is the fitness coefficient 100,000.

3.3   Experimental Setup

In order to prove the efficiency of the proposed methods it is necessary to investigate through real time implementation along with the simulation studies. Therefore, there is a need to develop an experimental platform with 5 degrees of freedom in planar configuration as shown in the kinematic model. Figure 3 shows the diagram of such a manipulator developed in house, with links of similar lengths equal to 7.5cm making the total length of 37.5cm in its initial condition (fully extended). The links are built primarily on Aluminum brackets connected by means of 5 High precision Hitec HS485B servo motors as angular joints of the robot. This servo motor has the resolution of 0.123°, with the operating range of $0 \leq \theta_i \leq \pi/2$ (count of 0 to 1463), is used as the actuator and provides the necessary joint motion to the robot. Moreover, these servo motors have the inbuilt rotary potentiometric sensor to provide the feedback of the joint angles to the control algorithms. These motors are interfaced to the PC running the variants of PSO's as control algorithms in MATLAB engine, through an SSC32 servo controller. The SSC32 servo controller and the PC are serially interfaced through UART communication standards. A Pulse width modulated (PWM) signal with the pulse duration of 0.5ms to 2.5ms, with 1.5 ms as center, positions the joint between the ranges of $\frac{-\pi}{2}, 0$ and $\frac{\pi}{2}$ respectively. These PWM signals are repeated at the pulse repetition rate of 20ms in order to hold the joints in the desired positions. Therefore, in general, an increase or decrease in the pulse width corresponds to the motion in CW or CCW direction. Fig. 3 shows the block diagram of the experimental platform and its interface illustrating the flow of the present study. The individual joints are commanded to move from its initial position based on the joint angles and velocities that are computed by the variants of PSO's and given by equations 4 to 8. A simple PID controller, inbuilt in the controller takes the potentiometric feedback from the servos and positions the servo at the commanded joint angles.

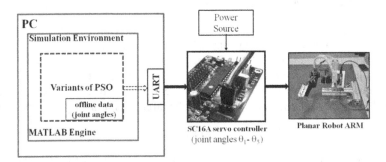

Fig. 3. Block Diagram of the present study

The pulse duration with respect to the corresponding global joint angles are estimated by the following empirical relationship given as

$$P_s = (1.367 \mu s * N) + 0.5ms \tag{9}$$

Where, N is the count value given by the relationship

$$N = \left(N_0 - \frac{\theta}{R} \right) \tag{10}$$

Where, N_0 is the value of count that corresponds to the center position of the servo, which is 732 (in this case), R is the resolution of the servo's which is 0.123° equivalent to 1.367μs duration and 0.5ms is residual duration of the pulse which positions the servo at 0°.

4 Results and Discussion

The performance of the four variants of the PSO's applied to such robotic control problem is investigated and demonstrated through both simulation and experimentation. The main parameters that are used in both simulation and experimentation are given in the following table 2.

Table 2. Experimental parameters

Workspace size	$0.25m^2$
Solution Space	Joint Angles
Population Size	40
Co-efficient of weights	
w	0.9, linearly decreased to 0.4 linearly
w_1 and w_2	0.7 and 1.0 (PSO-W); 5.8 and 2.8 (PSO-C); 0.3 and 0.3 (hybrid PSO's)
No. of. Iterations	400
Convergence	<0.1cm

With these parameter selections, the global best joint angles are estimated and the simulation and experimental studies are carried out for three scenarios as mentioned in previous sections, to evaluate the performance of the proposed methods.

Experimental Results
The experiments are carried out on a real planar robot as shown in Fig. 3, built at the Mechatronics laboratory of Monash university Sunway campus, similar to the one illustrated in kinematic model. The details regarding the specifications and design methods are already given in section 3. These experimental investigations are aimed to bridge the gap between the computer based simulations and actual real time implementations, towards estimating the efficiency and positional error of the robot end effector, by different variants of PSO algorithms detailed in previous sections.

Figure 4 (a) and (b) illustrates the configuration and end effector positions obtained for the various PSO variants, for the first set of experiments as in simulation studies i.e. robot moved in environment without obstacles. It could be observed from the results that the PSO-W variant positions the robot end effector at the target position of (15, 15). Further it could also be observed from table 4 that the PSO-W has minimal positional error of less than 1.5% within area of 2cm when compared to its simulation counterpart. Therefore, it is evident that the PSO-W performs better than the other variants.

Similarly, Fig. 5(a) and (b) illustrates the configuration and position of the end-effector obtained while avoiding an obstacle in the workspace of interest. The obstacle is positioned similar to the simulation studies and the variant of PSO-W positions the robot end effector at the target position of (16, 22), with the minimal error of less than 2.15% as given in table 4, complimenting the simulation results.

Similarly, Fig. 6(a) and (b) illustrates the robot configuration and the position of the end effector obtained while avoiding two obstacles in the workspace of interest, for all the four variants of PSO's in both simulation and experiments. As such in the

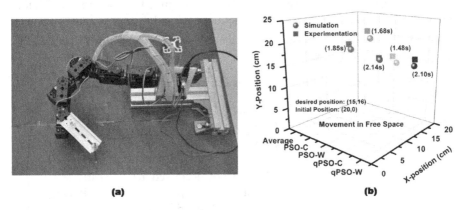

Fig. 4. (a) Robot manipulator reaching point (15, 15) in free-space. (b) Comparison between simulated end-effector position and measured value in free-space.

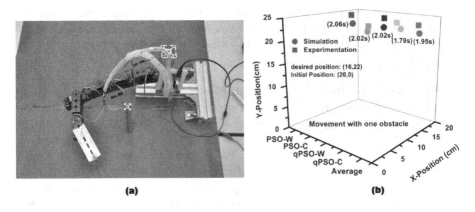

Fig. 5. (a) Robot manipulator reaching point (16, 20) with an obstacle in workspace. (b) Comparison between simulated end-effector position and measured value.

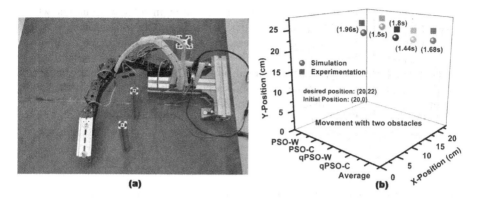

Fig. 6. (a) Robot manipulator reaching point (20, 22) with an obstacle in workspace. (b) Comparison between simulated end-effector position and measured value.

previous studies, the obstacles are positioned similar to the simulation environment and the target position is fixed as 20, 22. Agreeing to the simulation results, the once again the PSO-W provides a better results when compared to the other variants of PSO's, with the positional error less than 2.4% as given in table 3. In this case the positional error slightly increased from 2cm to 2.3cm.

Table 3. Positional error between simulation and experimental results

Environment	PSO Variants	Simulation [9]		Experimentation		Positional Error
		X	Y	X	Y	%
Free-Space (15,15)	PSO-W	14.92	14.92	14.8	15.2	1.51
	PSO-C	16.91	18.18	16.0	19.3	2.54
	qPSO-C	13.96	16.07	13.7	16.5	3.28
	qPSO-W	14.61	15.81	14.4	15.8	2.2
Environment with One Obstacle (16,22)	PSO-W	16.01	22.03	15.6	22.2	2.15
	PSO-C	16.01	20.49	16.2	20.80	3.64
	qPSO-W	16.02	22.01	16.1	24.1	2.99
	qPSO-C	16.00	22.13	14.6	23.7	3.54
Environment with Two Obstacles (20,22)	PSO-W	19.99	22.02	19.3	22.7	2.27
	PSO-C	21.15	24.12	21.0	25.3	3.33
	qPSO-W	19.99	22.01	20.4	24.0	2.80
	qPSO-C	20.05	22.16	20.02	24.4	3.75

It is evident from the experimental results, the variant of PSO-W proves to be a better heuristic algorithm in terms of both positional accuracy and convergence time for all the scenarios as depicted in these investigations. The positional accuracy of the proposed variants of PSO's are within the limit of 4% especially less than 2% in PSO-W when compared to the existing methods that are reported in literature.

Moreover, the PSO-W guarantees the optimal solution in all the scenarios when compared to its counter parts and appears to be computationally simplistic and easy to be used by the operator. Even though the search space is complex with discontinuities and nonlinearities such as obstacles, the PSO-W does not fall in local optima, but as an alternative, it usually finds nearly global optimal solutions. Therefore, this is an important aspect which has to be taken into account when compared to the other techniques such as the simulated annealing, GA's etc., since they usually end up in local optima for such kind of problems.

5   Conclusion

The path planning and control of redundant planar manipulator problem is studied and an effective solution based on heuristic search approaches to the problem is presented in this paper. Variants of PSO's are used as the methods of heuristic approaches to solve such constrained optimization problem, with the major objective being the minimization of positional error while avoiding obstacles in the workspace of interest. The search for better approach is refined by narrowing the selection of PSO variants namely PSO-W, PSO-C, qPSO-W and qPSO-C , with various trials. The performance of these variants is compared in terms of positional error, convergence time and cycle to converge. The efficiency of these algorithms is demonstrated through three scenarios in both simulation and real time implementations on a 5 D.O.F planar robot. These algorithms promise the collision free movement of the planar robot with a reasonable positional error. However, out of these four variants, PSO-W produces better results in terms of the convergence and positional error in all the three scenarios with the error less than 2.3% overall. Moreover, it guarantees an optimal solution in all the scenarios when compared to its counter parts and appears to be computationally simplistic and easy to be used by the operator. It must be noted that the heuristic methods based on the search algorithms is a viable alternative for the traditional inverse kinematic solutions for solving redundant manipulator problems constrained with nonlinearities and obstacles. Further studies is aimed fully utilize the advantages of PSO-W in developing an dynamic algorithm with proper sensing strategies as a feedback mechanism to provide the information about static and dynamic obstacles in the environment having an online path planning solution for redundant manipulator.

References

1. Kim, S.W., Lee, J.J.: Resolved motion rate control of redundant robots using fuzzy logic. In: Proc. of the IEEE International Conference on Fuzzy Systems, vol. 2, pp. 333–338 (1993)
2. Beheshti, T.: Obstacle avoidance for kinematically redundant robots using an adaptive fuzzy logic algorithm. In: Proceedings of the American Control Conference, pp. 1371–1375 (1999)
3. Nearchou, A.C.: Solving the inverse kinematics problem of redundant robots operating in complex environments via a modified genetic algorithm. Mechanism and Machine Theory 33, 273–292 (1998)

4. Zhang, Y.N., Wang, J.: Obstacle avoidance for kinematically redundant manipulators using a dual neural network. IEEE Transactions on Systems, Man, and Cybernetics, Part B: Cybernetics 34, 752–759 (2004)
5. Eberhart, R.C., Kennedy, J.: A new optimizer using particle swarm theory. In: Proceeding of the International Symposium on Micromachine and Human Science, Nagoya, Japan, vol. 6, pp. 39–43 (1995)
6. Huang, G., Li, D.H., Yang, J.: A research on particle swarm optimization and its application in robot manipulators. In: Proceedings of the IEEE Pacific Asia workshop on Computational Intelligence and Industrial Applications, pp. 377–381 (2008)
7. Guo, J.C., Wang, X.J., Zheng, X.W.: Trajectory planning of redundant robot manipulators using QPSO algorithm. In: Proceedings of the 8th World Congress on Intelligent Control and Automation, Beijing, China, vol. 8, pp. 403–407 (2008)
8. Zahiria, S.H., Seyedin, S.A.: Swarm intelligence based classifiers. Journal of the Franklin Institute 344, 362–376 (2007)
9. Goh, S.C., Ponnambalam, S.G.: Obstacle avoidance Control of Redundant robots using variants of Particle Swarm optimization. Robotics and Computer Integrated Manufacturing 28, 147–153 (2012)

A Nonlinear Disturbance Observer Based Adaptive Control Scheme for an Underwater Manipulator

Santhakumar Mohan

Discipline of Mechanical Engineering, School of Engineering,
Indian Institute of Technology Indore, Madhya Pradesh, India
santhakumar@iiti.ac.in

Abstract. A new nonlinear disturbance observer based tracking control scheme for an underwater manipulator is presented in this paper. This observer overcomes the disadvantages of existing disturbance observers, which are designed or analyzed by the linear system techniques. The performance of the proposed tracking control scheme is demonstrated numerically by the payload compensation and interaction effects compensation for a two degrees of freedom vertical underwater manipulator.

Keywords: underwater manipulator, disturbance observer, tracking control, adaptive control, nonlinear estimation.

1 Introduction

The underwater manipulator, as an important piece of equipment for underwater vehicles, plays a crucial role in underwater applications. With the increased interest in the development of undersea intervention technology in the fields of offshore oil, military, and ocean scientific investigation, many approaches have been presented to improve undersea intervention capability of an underwater manipulator attached to the vehicle [1-4]. Currently, the state of art of the underwater manipulator is represented by remotely operated vehicles with manipulators through master/slave schemes by human pilots [1]. This human-piloted scheme causes several operational difficulties, inaccurate trajectory tracking and force control, time delay in the man-machine control loop, and fatigue and performance of the human operator [1]. Some of the above mentioned difficulties can be overcome by the use of autonomous manipulation, which considered the nonlinear and coupled dynamics between the underwater vehicle and manipulator systems. For developing a control scheme considering the nature of the system, a detailed mathematical model of the system is required. A summary of the recent developments and researches of modelling and control of an underwater manipulator can be found in the [1-4]. However, most of these schemes required the exact knowledge of the UVMS dynamics whose hydrodynamic parameters generally have large uncertainties. Also, the manipulator total mass including its working payload can vary, which can lead to an additional uncertainty.

S.G. Ponnambalam et al. (Eds.): IRAM 2012, CCIS 330, pp. 12–19, 2012.

Moreover, handling the disturbance in motion control is one of the important and difficult tasks and the better approach to overcome is using a disturbance observer. In this paper, it presents a non-regressor nonlinear disturbance observer based tracking control scheme for the underwater manipulator system. The disturbance observer is widely used as an interdisciplinary tool (either linear or nonlinear) where the system states and external influences (disturbances) are not measurable [5]. The disturbance observer regards the difference between the actual output and the output of the nominal model as an equivalent disturbance applied to the nominal model. The equivalent disturbance can be removed by the disturbance observer, and then as asymptotically stable feedback control loop can be constructed around the nominal model. The proposed scheme is very simple in structure and computationally efficient. By carefully selecting the observer gain function and controller gain matrices, it will be shown that global convergence is guaranteed based on Lyapunov direct method. The effectiveness of the proposed control scheme is demonstrated with numerical simulations.

The reminder of this paper is organized as follows: The dynamic modelling of a two degrees of freedom underwater manipulator is derived in Sec. 2. In Sec. 3, a nonlinear controller for the underwater manipulator based on nonlinear disturbance observer is discussed. Detailed performance analysis of the underwater manipulator with different operating conditions is presented in Sec. 4. Finally, Sec. 5 holds the conclusions.

2   Dynamic Modeling of the Underwater Manipulator

The dynamic model of an underwater manipulator is developed through the recursive Newton-Euler algorithm [6]. In this work, it is assumed that the underwater manipulator is build-up of cylindrical element. Here, the links are considered as cylindrical shape because such shape provides uniform hydrodynamic reactions and is one of the primary candidates for possible link geometry for underwater manipulators. Although it is cylindrical, our mathematical framework does not depend on any particular shapes, it can be easily accommodated any other shapes. Indeed, cylindrical underwater manipulators are available in the present market. The effect of the hydrodynamic forces on circular cylindrical elements are described in the section, which are mainly consist of added mass effects, frictional forces (such as linear skin friction, lift and drag forces), munk moments (due to current loads) and buoyancy effects. For the sake of clarity the present study is restricted to a two degrees of freedom planar manipulator on the vertical plane, that is, the manipulator mounted vertically, as shown in Fig. 1 along with the establishment of the link coordinates system. The force and moment interaction between two adjacent links are expressed as [4, 6]:

$$
\begin{aligned}
{}^k\mathbf{f}_k &= \mathbf{R}_k^{k+1\,k+1}\mathbf{f}_{k+1} + \mathbf{F}_k - m_k\mathbf{g}_k + \mathbf{b}_k + \mathbf{p}_k \\
{}^k\mathbf{t}_k &= \mathbf{R}_k^{k+1\,k+1}\mathbf{t}_{k+1} + \mathbf{d}_{k/k+1} \times \mathbf{R}_k^{k+1\,k+1}\mathbf{f}_{k+1} \\
&\quad + \mathbf{d}_{k/kc} \times (\mathbf{F}_k - m_k\mathbf{g}_k + \mathbf{p}_k) + \mathbf{T}_k + \mathbf{d}_{k/kb} \times \mathbf{b}_k
\end{aligned}
\tag{1}
$$

where

$$\mathbf{p}_k = \mathbf{F}_{Lk} + \mathbf{F}_{Dk} + \mathbf{F}_{Sk}$$

$$\mathbf{F}_{Sk} = \mathbf{D}_s^k{}^k\mathbf{v}_k, \mathbf{F}_{Dk} = \left|{}^k\mathbf{v}_k\right|^T \mathbf{D}_D^k{}^k\mathbf{v}_k, \mathbf{F}_{Lk} = \left|{}^k\mathbf{v}_k\right|^T \mathbf{D}_L^k{}^k\mathbf{v}_k$$

$$\mathbf{F}_k = \mathbf{M}_k \left({}^k\mathbf{a}_k + {}^k\boldsymbol{\alpha}_k \times {}^k\mathbf{d}_{k/kc} + {}^k\boldsymbol{\omega}_k \times ({}^k\boldsymbol{\omega}_k \times {}^k\mathbf{d}_{k/kc})\right)$$

$$\mathbf{T}_k = \mathbf{I}_k{}^k\boldsymbol{\alpha}_k + {}^k\boldsymbol{\omega}_k \times (\mathbf{I}_k{}^k\boldsymbol{\omega}_k)$$

(2)

$$^{k+1}\boldsymbol{\omega}_{k+1} = \mathbf{R}_{k+1}^k{}^k\boldsymbol{\omega}_k + \mathbf{z}^T\dot{q}_{k+1}$$

$$^{k+1}\boldsymbol{\alpha}_{k+1} = \mathbf{R}_{k+1}^k\left({}^k\boldsymbol{\alpha}_k + {}^k\boldsymbol{\omega}_k \times \mathbf{z}^T\dot{q}_k\right) + \mathbf{z}^T\ddot{q}_{k+1}$$

$$^{k+1}\mathbf{v}_{k+1} = \mathbf{R}_{k+1}^k{}^k\mathbf{v}_k + {}^{k+1}\boldsymbol{\omega}_{k+1} \times {}^{k+1}\mathbf{d}_{k/kc}$$

$$^{k+1}\mathbf{a}_{k+1} = \mathbf{R}_{k+1}^k{}^k\mathbf{a}_k + {}^{k+1}\boldsymbol{\alpha}_{k+1} \times {}^{k+1}\mathbf{d}_{k+1/k} + {}^{k+1}\boldsymbol{\omega}_{k+1} \times \left({}^{k+1}\boldsymbol{\omega}_{k+1} \times {}^{k+1}\mathbf{d}_{k+1/k}\right)$$

(3)

where $\mathbf{R}_k^{k+1}$ is the rotation matrix, k is the corresponding join axis, $\mathbf{f}_k$ is the resultant force vector, $\mathbf{t}_k$ is the resultant moment vector, $\mathbf{p}_k$ is the linear and quadratic hydrodynamic friction forces, $\mathbf{F}_{Sk}$ is the linear skin friction force vector, $\mathbf{F}_{Dk}$ is the quadratic drag force vector, $\mathbf{F}_{Lk}$ is the quadratic lift force vector, $\mathbf{D}_s^k$ is the linear skin friction matrix, $\mathbf{D}_L^k$ is the diagonal matrix which contains lift coefficients, $\mathbf{D}_D^k$ is the diagonal matrix which contains drag coefficients, $\mathbf{g}_k$ is the gravity force vector, $\mathbf{b}_k$ is the buoyancy force vector, $\mathbf{d}_{k/kb}$ is the position vector from the center of buoyancy to the kth link frame, $\mathbf{d}_{k/kc}$ is the position vector from the center of gravity to the kth link frame, $\mathbf{d}_{k/k+1}$ is the position vector from the joint axis k to the axis k+1, i.e., position vector between the kth link frame to the k+1th link frame. $\mathbf{F}_k$ is the vector of total forces acting at the center of mass of link, $\mathbf{T}_k$ is the vector of total moments acting at the center of mass of link, $\mathbf{a}_k$ is the linear acceleration vector of the, $\boldsymbol{\alpha}_k$ is the angular acceleration vector, $\mathbf{v}_k$ is the linear velocity vector, $\boldsymbol{\omega}_k$ is the angular velocity vector, m_k is the mass of the link, $\mathbf{M}_k$ is the mass and added mass matrix of the link (located at the center of mass), $\mathbf{I}_k$ is the moment of inertia and added moment of matrix of the link (located at the center of mass). $\mathbf{z} = \begin{bmatrix} 0 & 0 & 1 \end{bmatrix}^T$ is the unit vector along the z-axis. The joint torques of each axis is represented as below [4, 6]:

$$\tau_k = \mathbf{z}^T{}^k\mathbf{t}$$

(4)

The iterative Newton-Euler dynamics algorithm for all links, symbolically it yields the equations of motion for the underwater manipulator. The result of the equations of motion can be written as follows [4]:

$$\mathbf{M}(q)\ddot{\mathbf{q}} + \mathbf{C}(q,\dot{q})\dot{\mathbf{q}} + \mathbf{D}(q,\dot{q})\dot{\mathbf{q}} + \mathbf{g}(q) = \boldsymbol{\tau} + \mathbf{f}_{dis}$$

(5)

where q is the vector of joint variables and $\mathbf{q} = \begin{bmatrix} q_1 & q_2 \end{bmatrix}^T = \begin{bmatrix} \theta_1 & \theta_2 \end{bmatrix}^T$, θ_1 and θ_2 are the joint angles of the corresponding underwater manipulator links, $\mathbf{M}(q)\ddot{\mathbf{q}}$ is the vector of inertial forces and moments of the manipulator, $\mathbf{C}(q,\dot{q})\dot{\mathbf{q}}$ is the vector of Coriolis and centripetal effects of the manipulator, $\mathbf{D}(q,\dot{q})\dot{\mathbf{q}}$ is the vector of damping effects of the manipulator, $\mathbf{g}(q)$ is the restoring vector of the manipulator, $\mathbf{f}_{dis}$ is the vector of total disturbances. $\boldsymbol{\tau} = \boldsymbol{\tau}_c - \hat{\mathbf{f}}_{dis} = \begin{bmatrix} \tau_1 & \tau_2 \end{bmatrix}^T$ is the input vector, $\boldsymbol{\tau}_c$ is the control input vector and $\hat{\mathbf{f}}_{dis}$ is the estimated disturbance vector.

3   Tracking Control Scheme of the Underwater Manipulator

In this paper, a non-regressor nonlinear disturbance observer is proposed to estimate the unknown disturbances along with a direct adaptive controller based on feedback linearization principle. The block diagram that corresponds to the proposed controller is shown in Fig. 2.

The proposed system has measurement systems which will give joint positions and velocities of the manipulator, through the help of joint position sensors (i.e., potentiometer) and motor encoders, respectively. In this work, one of the tasks is to design an observer such that the estimated disturbance obtained from the observer exponentially converges to the actual disturbance under any system states and time. The actual disturbance vector ($\mathbf{f}_{dis}$) can be expressed as follows:

$$\mathbf{f}_{dis} = \mathbf{f}_{idis} + \mathbf{f}_{edis} \tag{6}$$

where $\mathbf{f}_{edis}$ is the vector of external disturbances such as disturbances due to underwater current, waves, etc. $\mathbf{f}_{idis}$ is the vector of internal disturbances such as disturbances due to system uncertainties, sensor noises, etc., it can be expressed as:

$$\mathbf{f}_{idis} = \Delta\mathbf{M}(q)\ddot{\mathbf{q}} + \Delta\mathbf{C}(q,\dot{q})\dot{\mathbf{q}} + \Delta\mathbf{D}(q,\dot{q})\dot{\mathbf{q}} + \Delta\mathbf{g}(q) + \upsilon \tag{7}$$

where, $\Delta\mathbf{M}(q)\ddot{\mathbf{q}}$, $\Delta\mathbf{C}(q,\dot{q})\dot{\mathbf{q}}$, $\Delta\mathbf{D}(q,\dot{q})\dot{\mathbf{q}}$ and $\Delta\mathbf{g}(q)$ are the components which represent the variation of the actual system model from the nominal model (variations due to parameter uncertainties). υ is the vector of internal disturbances due to the system process noises and the measurement noises.

The observer is designed with the help of an auxiliary variable (η), which is defined as follows:

$$\eta = \hat{\mathbf{f}}_{dis} - \kappa(q,\dot{q}) \tag{8}$$

where, $\kappa(q,\dot{q})$ is the designed observer function vector, which is determined later.

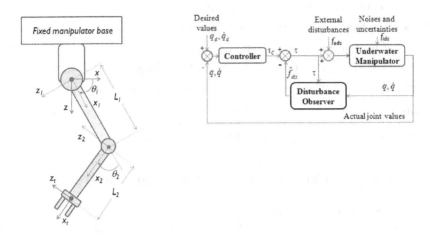

Fig. 1. Establishing link coordinate systems of the manipulator

Fig. 2. Block diagram of the proposed control scheme for an underwater manipulator

Let the function $\Gamma(q,\dot{q})$ is defined in the following nonlinear function as given:

$$\Gamma(q,\dot{q})\mathbf{M}(q)\ddot{\mathbf{q}} = \left[\frac{\partial\kappa(q,\dot{q})}{\partial\mathbf{q}} \quad \frac{\partial\kappa(q,\dot{q})}{\partial\dot{\mathbf{q}}}\right]\begin{bmatrix}\dot{\mathbf{q}}\\\ddot{\mathbf{q}}\end{bmatrix} \tag{9}$$

The proposed disturbance observer is as given:

$$\dot{\hat{\mathbf{f}}}_{dis} = -\Gamma(q,\dot{q})\hat{\mathbf{f}}_{dis} + \Gamma(q,\dot{q})\left(\mathbf{M}(q)\ddot{\mathbf{q}} + \mathbf{C}(q,\dot{q})\dot{\mathbf{q}} + \mathbf{D}(q,\dot{q})\dot{\mathbf{q}} + \mathbf{g}(q) - \boldsymbol{\tau}\right) \tag{10}$$

No explicit acceleration information is assumed to be provided to the observer and it is difficult to construct the acceleration signal from the velocity signal by differentiation due to measurement noises. Although, this proposed observer not implement directly, it provides a basic formulation for the further development. Moreover, there is no prior information about the derivative of the disturbance therefore it is assumed that the disturbance varies slowly, that is: $\dot{\mathbf{f}}_{dis} = 0$. However, it will be illustrated by simulations that the observer can track some fast time-varying disturbances as well.

Differentiate the auxiliary variable η with respect to time, it yields:

$$\dot{\boldsymbol{\eta}} = \dot{\hat{\mathbf{f}}}_{dis} - \frac{d\kappa(q,\dot{q})}{dt} = \dot{\hat{\mathbf{f}}}_{dis} - \left[\frac{\partial\kappa(q,\dot{q})}{\partial\mathbf{q}} \quad \frac{\partial\kappa(q,\dot{q})}{\partial\dot{\mathbf{q}}}\right]\begin{bmatrix}\dot{\mathbf{q}}\\\ddot{\mathbf{q}}\end{bmatrix} \tag{11}$$

Therefore, the proposed nonlinear disturbance observer is given as follows:

$$\begin{aligned}\dot{\boldsymbol{\eta}} &= -\Gamma(q,\dot{q})\boldsymbol{\eta} + \Gamma(q,\dot{q})\left(\mathbf{M}(q)\ddot{\mathbf{q}} + \mathbf{C}(q,\dot{q})\dot{\mathbf{q}} + \mathbf{D}(q,\dot{q})\dot{\mathbf{q}} + \mathbf{g}(q) - \boldsymbol{\tau} - \kappa(q,\dot{q})\right)\\\hat{\mathbf{f}}_{dis} &= \boldsymbol{\eta} + \kappa(q,\dot{q})\end{aligned} \tag{12}$$

Choosing a control input of the form as expressed as:

$$\tau = \mathbf{M}(q)(\ddot{\mathbf{q}}_d + \mathbf{K}_P\tilde{\mathbf{q}} + \mathbf{K}_D\dot{\tilde{\mathbf{q}}}) + \mathbf{C}(q,\dot{q})\dot{\mathbf{q}} + \mathbf{D}(q,\dot{q})\dot{\mathbf{q}} + \mathbf{g}(q) - \hat{\mathbf{f}}_{dis} \tag{13}$$

will lead to the manipulator tracking position and velocity errors tending to zero asymptotically. i.e., the underwater manipulator will follow the given desired trajectory. Here, K_D and K_P are symmetric positive definite (SPD) design matrices. $\tilde{\mathbf{q}} = \mathbf{q}_d - \mathbf{q}$ is the vector of position tracking errors. $\dot{\tilde{\mathbf{q}}} = \dot{\mathbf{q}}_d - \dot{\mathbf{q}}$ is the vector of velocity tracking errors. $\dot{\mathbf{q}}_d$ and $\mathbf{q}_d$ are the vectors of desired joint velocities and joint positions, respectively. $\mathbf{e}_{dis} = \mathbf{f}_{dis} - \hat{\mathbf{f}}_{dis}$ is the observer error.

4   Performance Analysis

To explore the tracking performance of the proposed control scheme, widespread computer based numerical simulations have been accomplished and the scheme is verified with the help of real-time experiment as well. The manipulator used for this study consists of a two degrees of freedom vertical manipulator (refer Fig. 1). Hydrodynamic parameters of the manipulator are estimated using empirical relations based on strip theory. Some parameters like inertia, centre of gravity, centre of buoyancy are calculated from the geometrical design of the manipulator.

A simple pick and place operation is considered for the analysis. This is for the reason that most of the underwater intervention tasks involve this type of task in the spatial trajectory. The manipulator initiated its motion from its home position and it reaches the picking position. At the picking point the manipulator picks an unknown mass object (for the simulation it is considered 10% of total manipulator mass), and the manipulator tip point reaches the placing position and drops the object, and finally back to its home position. In the above mentioned task, an unknown ocean current is added in the simulation by properly considering the relative velocity of the in the dynamic model. It is assumed as an irrotational current, constant in the inertial frame and the value of the current is considered as: $\mathbf{v}_c = \begin{bmatrix} 0.3 & 0.2 & 0 \end{bmatrix}^T$ m/s and the system parameters uncertainties are assumed to be 15% from its original values.

4.1   Results and Discussions

The proposed controller performances are compared through numerical simulations i.e., with and without disturbance compensation (through disturbance observer). Detailed simulation results are presented in Figs. 3-5. In Fig. 3, both desired and actual task space trajectories of the manipulator tip are plotted, and from these results it is observed that the proposed controller is good in adapting the uncertainties and disturbances. The time histories of the tracking errors both joint and task spaces are presented in Fig. 4. From the results, it is observed that the proposed controller compensated the external disturbances and parameter uncertainties well. These tracking errors are well below in the proposed controller performance. The time histories of the estimated disturbances are presented in Fig. 5.

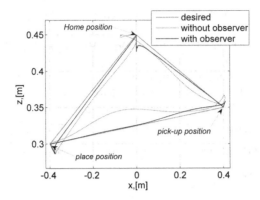

Fig. 3. Comparative task space (xz) trajectories of the manipulator tip

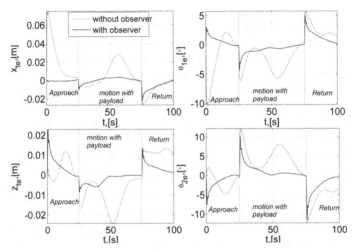

Fig. 4. Tracking errors of the manipulator tip trajectory and tracking errors in manipulator joint positions

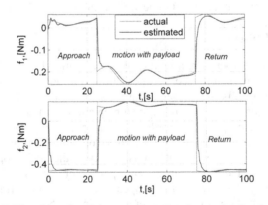

Fig. 5. Time histories of the estimated disturbances by the observer

From the results, it is noted that the observer performance is quite satisfactory in estimating disturbances. Compared with the tracking performance of the proposed controller without disturbance compensation, the performance is greatly improved disturbance observer and the steady state tracking errors disappear.

The focus of this paper is the dynamic modelling, disturbance observer and subsequent adaptive control scheme for the underwater manipulator. The primary task is assumed to be one of controlling the motion of the end effector in a given desired manner with respect to the external environment. In order to fulfil the primary task, the secondary task is assumed to be estimating the effects of the external and internal disturbances, and compensating these effects to achieve the desired task. The simulation results illustrate the capabilities for simultaneously estimating the disturbances and controlling the motion of the manipulator with the interaction effects between the manipulator and the environmental interaction effects. It is also demonstrated the ability of the proposed control scheme to follow complex end-effector trajectories with a natural preference given to the tracking performance.

In overall, it is observed that the proposed controller is good in adapting the uncertainties, system dynamic changes and external disturbances. In this work, numerical simulation results are provided to investigate the performance and to demonstrate the effectiveness of the proposed control scheme. These results are intuitive, promising and point out the prospective of the proposed approach.

5   Conclusions

This paper has presented a nonlinear observer based tracking control for an underwater manipulator. Applicability of this scheme is tested for a two-link planar manipulator. The effectiveness of the scheme is demonstrated and verified using numerical simulations. The simulation is performed to show the effectiveness of the nonlinear observer in the presence of underwater current, and the performance in particular, the steady-state performance is significantly improved.

References

1. Cui, Y., Sarkar, N.: A unified force control approach to autonomous underwater manipulation. Robotica 19, 255–266 (2001)
2. Antonelli, G.: Underwater Robots Motion and Force Control of Vehicle-Manipulator Systems. Springer Tracts in Advanced Robotics. Springer, Berlin (2006)
3. Yuh, J., Zhao, S., Lee, P.M.: Application of adaptive disturbance observer control to an underwater manipulator. In: Proceedings of the IEEE International Conference on Robotics and Automation, Seoul, Korea, pp. 3244–3248 (2001)
4. Santhakumar, M.: Proportional-derivative observer based backstepping control for an underwater manipulator. In: Mathematical Problems in Engineering 2011, pp. 1–18 (2011)
5. Chen, W.H.: Disturbance observer based control for nonlinear systems. IEEE/ASME Transactions on Mechatronics 9, 706–710 (2004)
6. Craig, J.J.: Introduction to Robotics: Mechanics and Control. Addison Wesley, Boston (1986)

Obstacle Avoidance Using Multi-Point Potential Field Approach for an Underactuated Flat-Fish Type AUV in Dynamic Environment

Saravanakumar Subramanian[1], Thomas George[2], and Asokan Thondiyath[3]

[1,3] Robotics Laboratory, Department of Engineering Design,
Indian Institute of Technology Madras, Chennai, India-600036
[2] Department of Mechanical Engineering, Indian Institute of Technology Hyderabad,
Hyderabad, India-502205
{srsaravanakumar,thomasgeorge2571766}@gmail.com,
asok@iitm.ac.in

Abstract. This paper presents a multi-point potential field (MPPF) method for obstacle avoidance of Autonomous Underwater Vehicles (AUV) in a 2D dynamic environment. In this method, an arc of predefined radius on a semicircle in the positive x-axis around the bow of an AUV is discretized into equiangular points with centre as the current position. By determining the point at which the minimum potential exists, the vehicle can be moved towards that point in 2D space. Here the analytical gradient of the total potential function is not calculated as it is not essentially required for moving the vehicle to the next position. The proposed obstacle avoidance algorithm is interfaced with the dynamic model of an underactuated flat-fish type AUV. The obstacle avoidance algorithm generates the path elements to the trajectory planner and the vehicle tracks the trajectory. The details of the algorithm and simulation results are presented.

Keywords: AUV, dynamic model, obstacle avoidance, potential field, trajectory planning.

1 Introduction

A great amount of research work has been carried out in the field of autonomous underwater vehicles (AUVs) over the last two decades. AUVs play a major role in exploration and exploitation of underwater resources [1]. But the development of guidance and navigation strategy in unknown dynamic environment is a major challenge for underactuated AUVs. An underactuated AUV cannot track a random path due to less controllable degrees of freedom (DOF) than movement DOF and hence the trajectory generation methods cannot be directly used to navigate it through unknown environments. Also, underactuated AUVs cannot take the "stop-then-turn-around" strategy like most autonomous ground vehicles [2]. Hence the real-time path planning and obstacle avoidance is a complex task in dynamic unknown environment. Road map, cell decomposition, optimal control and potential field methods are used

S.G. Ponnambalam et al. (Eds.): IRAM 2012, CCIS 330, pp. 20–27, 2012.

for developing obstacle avoidance schemes. Among them potential field method is mostly used for obstacle avoidance due to its simplicity and computational elegance.

Artificial potential field method for obstacle avoidance was initially proposed by [3]. The potential field methods and their inherent limitations are discussed in [4]. A path planning method using virtual potential field concept for AUV is proposed in [5]. Several types of potential field method are presented in the past. A superquadric potential function is proposed by Khosla and Volpe [6] to model the obstacles and avoid local minimum. Harmonic potential method was suggested by Kim and Khosla [7]. To address the goal non reachable with obstacle nearby (GNRON) problem, Ge et al. [8] presented a method in which the positive scaling factors present in the potential functions are properly chosen to avoid local minimum problem. In most cases, the potential field methods are used for mobile robots. The potential of an obstacle is calculated at only one point and the gradient of the potential function is calculated analytically for driving the mobile robot. But the analytical gradient is essentially not required for moving the vehicle to the next position. In this paper, we propose a simple and improved obstacle avoidance strategy to address this. The obstacle avoidance can be improved by discretizing both the periphery of the obstacle and an arc of radius around the AUV into equiangular points. The potential fields due to each point on an obstacle can be calculated and integrated to obtain a strengthened potential field for that particular obstacle. By determining the point at which the minimum potential exists, the vehicle can be moved towards that point in 2D space. The developed algorithm is interfaced with the dynamics of AUV in order to study the performance of the algorithm and the response of the vehicle. The mathematical modeling of AUV is presented in Section 2 and the obstacle avoidance methodology is explained in the next section. Section 4 presents the implementation of the developed algorithm with the vehicle dynamics and simulation results are discussed in Section 5.

2   Mathematical Modeling of AUV

In order to simulate the system dynamics, the mathematical model of the AUV is developed. It is developed based on Newton-Euler's formulation. Two reference frames such as body-fixed frame {B} and inertial frame {I} are used to describe the kinematics. These frame assignments are shown in Fig. 1. It can be seen that, the origin of the body fixed frame coincides with the centre of the mass. The 6 DOF kinematic equation can be given as [9]:

$$\dot{\eta} = J(\eta)v,$$ (1)

where, $J(\eta)$ is the Jacobian transformation matrix and it can be given as

$$J = \begin{bmatrix} J_1(\eta_2) & 0_{3x3} \\ 0_{3x3} & J_2(\eta_2) \end{bmatrix}$$ (2)

The dynamic equation of an AUV in 6 DOF can be given as [9]:

$$M\dot{v} + C(v)v + D(v)v + g(\eta) = \tau,$$ (3)

where $M \in \Re^{6\times6}$ is the inertia and added inertia matrix, $C(v) \in \Re^{6\times6}$ is the coriolis and centripetal matrix including added mass terms. $D(v) \in \Re^{6\times6}$ contains hydrodynamic damping and lifting forces and moments. $g(\eta) \in \Re^{6}$ is the vector of gravitational and buoyancy forces and moments. $\tau \in \Re^{6}$ is the vector of control input forces and torques in the body reference frame.

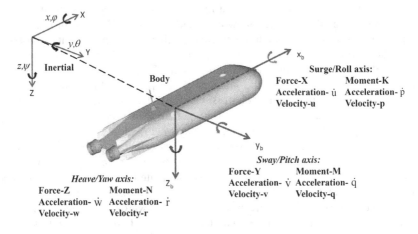

Fig. 1. Frame assignment of an underactuated flat-fish type AUV

The AUV considered here for analysis has a length (L) of 4.5 m, width (b) of 1.46m and height (h) of 0.634m. The vehicle is underactuated i.e the number DOF is lesser than the number of actuators. It has two propulsion thrusters and three vertical maneuvering thrusters. The various parameters of the vehicle that are used in the dynamic model are as follows: m=1462kg is the mass of the vehicle and I_x=498.63Nms^2, I_y=1850.34Nms^2 and I_z=2348.97Nms^2 are the moments of inertia about the body fixed x_b, y_b and z_b axes respectively. The centre of gravity vector (r_G) is (-22,0,0)mm, the centre of buoyancy vector (r_B) is (-22,0,-15)mm. The buoyancy force is 14391N. The detailed description of the vehicle parameters and their values can be found in [10].

3   Obstacle Avoidance by Multi-Point Potential Field Method

The objective of the obstacle avoidance algorithm is to find an obstacle free path by avoiding the obstacles so that the vehicle can reach the desired goal position without collision. The main idea of the potential field method is to generate attraction and repulsion potentials for the target and the obstacles. The target has an attraction potential and the obstacles have repulsion potential. Here, multi-point potential field method is used for developing the obstacle avoidance algorithm. In this method, the total potentials are generated at multiple points. By determining the point at which the minimum potential exists among the total potentials, the vehicle can be commanded to that point. The proposed method has been developed for 2D dynamic environment.

The methodology for the implementation of the obstacle avoidance algorithm is shown in Fig. 2. The following steps give the methodology of the obstacle avoidance algorithm. More details about the methodology can be found in [11].

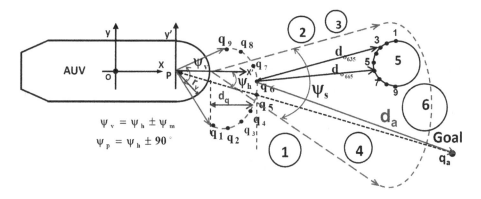

Fig. 2. Methodology for the implementation of 2D obstacle avoidance algorithm

- Discretize the arc of radius r around the AUV into N points ($q_i : 1 = 1,2,...N$) over a range of interest defined by a span angle of ψ_v. Here $\psi_v = \psi_h \pm \psi_m$, where ψ_h is the heading angle of the vehicle and ψ_m is the maximum turning angle in horizontal plane (Refer Fig. (2)).
- Compute the attractive potential U_{att} at these points. The attraction influence tends to pull the vehicle towards the target position. The most commonly used attractive potential field is of the form [8]:

$$U_{att_{(i)}}(q) = \frac{1}{2}\xi(d_{a_{(i)}} + u)^2, \tag{4}$$

where $d_{a_{(i)}} = |q_i - q_a|$ is the distance between q_i [th] point around the vehicle and the goal point q_a. ξ is an adjustable constant. u is the forward speed of the vehicle.

- Define another region of interest to model the obstacles in the AUV path. This region is defined by the detection range and horizontal span of the sonar sensor. The obstacles with in this region are only selected. Obtain the location and size of the obstacle from the sonar data and discretize the semicircular area on the periphery of the obstacle that is facing the bow of the vehicle into K points($p_j : 1 = 1,2,...N$).
- Compute the repulsive potential U_{obs} at q_i due to the obstacle point p_j. The repulsion influence tends to push the vehicle away from the obstacles. The repulsive potential at q_i due to the obstacle point p_j is given as [8]:

$$U_{obs_{(i,j)}}(q) = \begin{cases} \dfrac{1}{2}\eta\left(\dfrac{1}{d_{o_{(i,j)}}} - \dfrac{1}{d_t}\right)^2 d_{a_{(i)}}^2, & \text{if } d_{o_{(i,j)}} \le d_t \\ \\ 0, & \text{if } d_{o_{(i,j)}} > d_t \end{cases} \qquad (5)$$

where $d_{a_{(i,j)}} = |q_i - p_j|$, is the distance between q_i [th] point around the vehicle and p_j [th] point on the periphery of the obstacle, d_t is the influence distance, η is an adjustable constant.

- Compute the actual repulsive potential U_{rep} at q_i due to the obstacle

$$U_{rep_{(i)}}(q) = \sum_{j=1}^{K} U_{obs_{(i,j)}}(q) \qquad (6)$$

- Compute the total potential U_{tot} at each point around the vehicle. The total potential at a point around the vehicle is represented as a sum of attractive potential and all the repulsive potentials. Here the repulsive potential results from the superposition of the individual repulsive potentials generated by the obstacles.

$$U_{tot_{(i)}}(q) = U_{att_{(i)}}(q) + \sum_{m=1}^{R} U_{rep_{(i,m)}}(q), \qquad (7)$$

where m=1,2...,R. R is the number of obstacles, $U_{att_{(i)}}(q)$ represents the attractive potential and $U_{rep_{(i,m)}}(q)$ represents the repulsive potentials generated by the obstacle m. In this way, obtain the total potential for all the points around the vehicle and predict the next one step by determining the minimum potential $U_{min tot}$.

$$U_{min tot} = min(U_{tot}) \qquad (8)$$

- Represent the minimum potential point in Cartesian space.
- Command the vehicle to the position calculated in the previous step.
- Repeat the above steps till the goal is reached.

4   Implementation of Obstacle Avoidance Strategy

The developed obstacle avoidance algorithm is interfaced with the dynamic model that was discussed in Section 2. In the outer loop, the user input and sensor data are fed to the obstacle avoidance algorithm. The inner loop consists of the AUV dynamics, a trajectory planner, a controller and actuators (thrusters and control planes). Figure 3 shows the Simulink model of the integrated system. The obstacle avoidance algorithm is executed at a time interval 'T' that is proportional to the velocity of the vehicle. Once the user inputs are given, this block gets the sensor data for every time, T and then it defines the next one-step position as path elements to the trajectory planner. The present positions are delayed and given as past input to the trajectory planner in order to calculate the desired yaw angle. Upon receiving the data, the desired trajectory is generated. As the forward speed of the vehicle is too slow and is taken as constant, a straight line trajectory in Cartesian space is implemented. The desired trajectory information is given to the PID controller and the controller outputs are shown in Fig.3. Finally, the manipulated variable (total force) is obtained from the actuator and is given to the vehicle dynamics. The blocks in the inner loop are executed with a time interval 't' of the step size specified in the solver. The current states of the vehicle are given to the controller and the obstacle avoidance algorithm till the vehicle reaches the target.

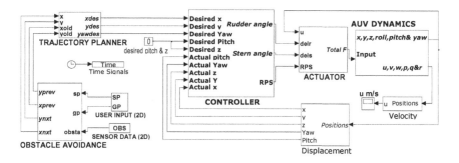

Fig. 3. Simulink model of the integrated system

5   Results and Discussion

In order to verify the performance of the proposed method, numerical simulations are performed. The obstacles in circular shape of various sizes with random velocities are taken. The forward speed (u) of the vehicle is fixed to a constant value of 1m/s. It is assumed that the velocity of the obstacle is lesser than the velocity of the vehicle. As the environment is a 2D space, the pitch and depth values are taken as zero. Simulations are carried out for two different cases.

In case-1, static obstacles are only considered with the given starting and goal point of (30,20) and (170,170) respectively. The results of the simulation are presented in Figs. 4 and 5. It has been observed from Fig.4 that the obstacle avoidance algorithm is able to find a collision free path by avoiding the obstacles and the vehicle is able to track the path. The corresponding tracking errors are shown in Fig.5. The vehicle reached the goal point with the position errors in surge (xe) and sway (ye) axes of 0.05m, -0.1m respectively and a yaw error (ψe) of 3° which are in the acceptable limits. In the next case, both static and moving obstacles at various locations are considered. The starting and goal points are taken as in the previous case and the results are shown in Figs. 6 and 7. It has been seen from Fig. 6 that the obstacle avoidance algorithm is able to generate a smooth path by avoiding both static and moving obstacles. As the path elements are generated at every 1s and the trajectory is planned for every 1m, the minimum potential is calculated based on the current position of the moving obstacles at every 1s. It is found that the vehicle is able to follow the desired path at a safe distance from the moving obstacles. The vehicle reached the goal point at t=220s with negligible position and orientation errors as shown in Fig. 7.

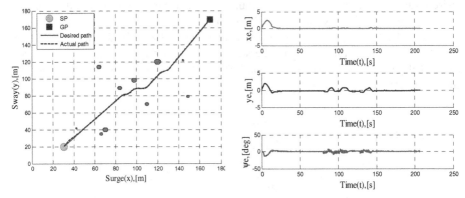

Fig. 4. 2D scenario of the multi-point potential field method in static environment

Fig. 5. Position tracking errors in 2D static environment

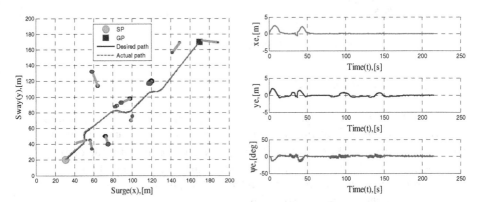

Fig. 6. 2D scenario of the multi-point potential field method in dynamic environment

Fig. 7. Position tracking errors in 2D dynamic environment

The significance of multi-point potential field method is studied by comparing it with a single point potential field (SPPF) method as shown in [5]. The value of repulsion potential in both methods are compared and has been found that the SPPF method generates a repulsive potential of 0.4 whereas MPPF generates repulsive potential of 3.06. Hence it can be said that the vehicle is always moving at much safer distance from the obstacles.

6   Conclusions and Future Work

An obstacle avoidance algorithm using multi-point potential field approach for an underactuated flat-fish type AUV is developed by improving the basic potential field approach. Both static and dynamic environments in 2D space are considered. The simulation results show that the algorithm helps the vehicle to avoid the obstacles and reach the target successfully. It has also been observed that the position tracking errors are very minimal and the path generated by the method is smooth. In order to implement the developed obstacle avoidance algorithm for real-time applications, hardware in the loop (HIL) simulations are carried out to validate the algorithm. It has been observed that the algorithm can be implemented to the actual vehicle to control it in real-time scenarios like repair and rescue operations, formation control, and obstacle avoidance. The proposed method is being improved to address the issues of local minima as well as dynamic environments in 3D space.

References

1. Repoulias, F., Papadopoulos, E.: Planar Trajectory and Tracking Control Design for Underactuated AUVs. J. Ocean Eng. 34, 1650–1667 (2007)
2. Xu, H.L., Feng, X.S.: An AUV Fuzzy Obstacle Avoidance Method under Event Feedback Supervision. State Key Laboratory of Robotics. Shenyang Institute of Automation, China (2009)
3. Khatib, O.: Real-time Obstacle Avoidance for Manipulators and Mobile Robots. Int. J. Robotic Research 5, 90–98 (1986)
4. Koren, Y., Borenstein, J.: Potential Field Methods and their Inherent Limitations for Mobile Robot Navigation. In: IEEE Conference on Robotics and Automation, pp. 1398–1404 (1992)
5. Fu-Guang, D., Peng, J., Xin-Qian, B., Hong-Jian, W.: AUV Local Path Planning Based on Virtual Potential Field. In: IEEE International Conference on Mechatronics and Automation, Niagara Falls, Canada, pp. 1711–1716 (2005)
6. Khosla, P., Volpe, R.: Superquadric Artificial Potentials for Obstacle Avoidance and Approach. In: IEEE Conference on Robotics and Automation, Philadelphia, PA, pp. 1778–1784 (1988)
7. Kim, J.O., Khosla, P.K.: Real-time Obstacle Avoidance using Harmonic Potential Functions. IEEE Trans. Robot. Automat. 8, 338–349 (1992)
8. Ge, S.S., Cui, Y.J.: New Potential Functions for Mobile Robot Path Planning. IEEE Trans. Robot. Automat. 16, 615–620 (2000)
9. Fossen, T.I.: Guidance and Control of Ocean Vehicles. John Wiley and Sons Ltd., Chichester (1994)
10. Asokan, T.: Mathematical Modeling and Simulation of Autonomous Underwater Vehicle. Technical report, Department of Engineering Design, Indian Institute of Technology Madras, Chennai, India (2007)
11. Saravanakumar, S., Asokan, T.: Waypoint Guidance based Planar Path Following and Obstacle Avoidance of Autonomous Underwater Vehicle. In: 8th International Conference on Informatics in Control, Automation and Robotics, Noordwijkerhout, The Netherlands, pp. 191–198 (2011)

Synchronizing Multi-robots in Switching between Different Formations Tasks While Tracking a Line

Ibrahim M.H. Sanhoury, Shamsudin H.M. Amin, and Abdul Rashid Husain

Centre of Artificial Intelligence and Robotics, Material and Manufacturing Research Alliance,
Universiti Teknologi Malaysia, 81310 Johor Bahru, Malaysia
sanhoury124@yahoo.com, {sham,rashid}@fke.utm.my

Abstract. This paper extends the synchronization approach for formation control of multiple mobile robots in switching between different time-varying formations tasks while the entire system moving in a line. Each robot in the group is controlled to track its desired trajectory while synchronizing it is motion with the two adjacent robots to maintain a time-varying desired formation. The proposed controller guarantees the asymptotic stability of both position errors and synchronization errors. Simulation results show the effectiveness of the proposed synchronous controller in maintaining formation tasks.

Keywords: Formation Control, Multiple Mobile Robots, Synchronization.

1 Introduction

During the previous decades, researchers give increased attention to multiple mobile robots to cooperatively work together to efficiently accomplish a specific task. Multi-robot systems have several advantages over a single powerful robot in achieving complicated tasks. First, the task complexity is hard to accomplish by a single robot. Second, the task is naturally distributed. Third, constructing many limited robots is cheaper and simpler than a single powerful one. Fourth, multiple mobile robots can work in a decentralized manner, and the task time will be reduced through using the parallelism. Finally, multi-robot system is more robust and consistent through redundancy.

Multi-robot cooperation is one of the significant topics in robotics. Formation control of robots draws relevant attention in recent years. The applications of Multi-robot formation contain search and rescue, landmine deduction, space exploration, control of satellites groups, multiple Unmanned Aerial Vehicles (UAVs), and multiple Autonomous Underwater Vehicles (AUVs). Exploiting the formation control can enhance robustness, flexibility, feasibility, accuracy, and energy efficiency.

Several control approaches have been reported throughout the literature to solve the formation control task. From these methods, the behavior-based approach [1, 2], virtual structure approach [3-5], and the leader-following approach [6-10] are considered as the three main methods for formation control for the multi-robot

S.G. Ponnambalam et al. (Eds.): IRAM 2012, CCIS 330, pp. 28–36, 2012.

system. Other approaches for formation control include artificial potential [11], graph theory [12], and recently synchronization approach [13, 14].

In the synchronization approach, the control goal is developed according to the desired formation. In this method, the motion control for each robot is separated into two parts: the first part will force the robot to move along the desired path to achieve the tracking control goal. The second part will synchronize the movement for each robot with the two adjacent robots. Therefore, all the robots in the formation will be synchronized, which reduces the complication of the system to achieve the synchronization goal. Synchronization error is used to measure how multiple mobile robots achieve the desired formation task. The synchronization method can be designed in a decentralized manner; also, it is suitable for time-varying formation, besides the controller is simple and scalable. However, this approach still needs more research effort for different types of the mobile robot's dynamics model to carry out formation task efficiently.

This paper is an extension to our previous work [14], where a switching between formations shapes of multiple mobile robots by utilizing synchronization approach was conducted.

This paper is an extension to our earlier results [14], in which the center of the formation shape is moving in a straight line; while each robot in the group will track it is desired trajectory in the shape, and concurrently synchronizing its motion with the two nearby robots to maintain the desired time-varying formation. This study differed from [15], where the robots changing their formation shape twice in a time-varying manner whiles the center of the shape is moving in a straight line. These results help the robots to navigate in an indoor environment while maintaining a time-varying formation.

2   Formation Control via Synchronization Method

Fig. 1 shows wheeled mobile robot (WMR), in which $q=[x_c,y_c]^T$ denotes the position coordination of the robot in the x-y plane, and ϕ represents the heading angle measured from the x-axis. The dynamic for each robot is given by;

$$\mathbf{M}_i \ddot{\mathbf{q}}_i + \mathbf{V}_i \left(\mathbf{q}, \dot{\mathbf{q}} \right) = \tau_{qi} \tag{1}$$

$$I_{ddi} \ddot{\phi}_i = \tau_{\phi i} \tag{2}$$

where $\mathbf{M}_i = \begin{bmatrix} M_{di} & 0 \\ 0 & M_{di} \end{bmatrix}$, $\mathbf{V}_i \left(q, \dot{q} \right) = \begin{bmatrix} 2m_{wi}d_i I_{di} \dot{\phi}_i^2 \cos\phi_i \\ 2m_{wi}d_i I_{di} \dot{\phi}_i^2 \sin\phi_i \end{bmatrix}$, $\tau_{qi} = \begin{bmatrix} \tau_{qxi} \\ \tau_{qyi} \end{bmatrix}$,

$\ddot{\mathbf{q}}_i = [\ddot{x}_{ci} \quad \ddot{y}_{ci}]^T$, $I_{di}=I_i-4(m_{wi})^2 d_i^2$, $M_{di}=m_i I_{di}$, $m_i=m_{ci}+2m_{wi}$, $I_i=I_{ci}+2m_{wi}b_i^2+2I_{mi}$, b_i the distance between each driving wheel and the axis of symmetry, m_{ci} the mass of the WMR without the driving wheels and the rotor of the motors, m_{wi} the mass of each driving wheel with the rotor, I_{ci} the moment of inertia of the WMR without the driving wheels and the rotor of the motors about the vertical axis through P_c, I_{wi} the moment of inertia of each wheel and the rotor of the motor about the wheel diameter, P_o the intersection of the axis of symmetry with the driving wheel axis, P_c the center

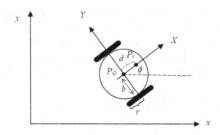

Fig. 1. Wheeled Mobile Robot

of the mass of the WMR, and d_i is the distance from P_o to P_c along the driving axis (X-axis).

A time-varying desired shape $S(p,t)$ is introduced for each robot, where p denotes 2-D position vector and t the time. The target position q_i^d for each robot in the group should be situated in the curve as $\partial S(q_i^d,t)=0$. The aim is to propose a control inputs for the dynamics (1) and (2), in order for each robot to converge towards its desired pose q_i^d while maintain its position in the desired shape $S(p,t)$. The desired heading ϕ_i^d for each robot is defined such that the robot orientation is always facing towards its desired position q_i^d.

The position and orientation errors of the ith robot are defined as: $e_i=q_i^d-q_i$ and $\Delta\phi_i=\phi_i^d-\phi_i$, correspondingly. Each robot should accomplish a translational control goal of $e_i\to0$ and $\Delta\phi_i\to0$ as $t\to\infty$, in addition to achieve a formation control aim to sustain the robots on the desired curve. The following example explains how the synchronization control goal is determined based on the desired formation.

Example: Consider that n robots are required to maintain in an ellipse curve during the motions, while the center of the ellipse moving in straight line. The coordinates q_i of the each robot should meet the following restrictions:

$$q_i(t)=\begin{bmatrix}\cos\varphi_i(t)\\\sin\varphi_i(t)\end{bmatrix}\begin{bmatrix}a(t)\\b(t)\end{bmatrix}+\begin{bmatrix}x_{cent}(t)\\y_{cent}(t)\end{bmatrix}=A_i(t)\begin{bmatrix}a(t)\\b(t)\end{bmatrix}+\begin{bmatrix}x_{cent}(t)\\y_{cent}(t)\end{bmatrix} \quad (3)$$

where a and b stand for the longest and the shortest radii of the ellipse, respectively, $\varphi_i=\tanh(b\sin\alpha_i/a\cos\alpha_i)$, with $\alpha_i=\tanh[y_i/x_i]$, represents the angle of the robot located on the ellipse with respect to its center, and $(x_{cent}(t),y_{cent}(t))$ denotes the center of the ellipse with respect to the time. Suppose that the robots are not situated in the longest or the shortest axis of the ellipse such that the inverse of A_i exists. The synchronization constrains to q_i can be derived as:

$$A_1^{-1}(q_1-C_r(t))=A_2^{-1}(q_2-C_r(t))=\cdots=A_n^{-1}(q_n-C_r(t))=\begin{bmatrix}a & b\end{bmatrix}^T \quad (4)$$

where $C_r(t)=[x_{cent}(t),y_{cent}(t)]^T$. From (4), the synchronization constraints can be represented as follows:

$$c_1(q_1-C_r(t))=c_2(q_2-C_r(t))=\cdots=c_n(q_n-C_r(t)) \quad (5)$$

where c_i denotes the coupling parameter for the robot i, and its inverse exits based on (4). Moreover, (5) can be hold for the entire desired coordinate q_i^d,

$$c_1\left(q_1^d - C_r(t)\right) = c_2\left(q_2^d - C_r(t)\right) = \cdots = c_n\left(q_n^d - C_r(t)\right) \tag{6}$$

Subtracting (5) from (6), gives up the formation control goal as follows;

$$c_1\mathbf{e}_1 = c_2\mathbf{e}_2 = \cdots = c_n\mathbf{e}_n \tag{7}$$

Equation (7) represented the control goal implicitly, which can be divided into n sub goals of $c_i e_i = c_{i+1} e_{i+1}$. Note that, when $i=n$, $n+1$ is represented as 1. Furthermore, the synchronization errors can be defined as a subset of all possible pairs of two adjoining robots as follows;

$$\begin{aligned}
\varepsilon_1 &= c_1\mathbf{e}_1 - c_2\mathbf{e}_2 \\
\varepsilon_2 &= c_2\mathbf{e}_2 - c_3\mathbf{e}_3 \\
&\vdots \\
\varepsilon_n &= c_n\mathbf{e}_n - c_1\mathbf{e}_1
\end{aligned} \tag{8}$$

where ε_i is the synchronization error for the ith robot. Notice that, if the synchronization error $\varepsilon_i = 0$ for all the robots, $i=1,\ldots,n$, the control goal (7) can be achieved automatically. The essential condition for the formation shape is that it must be represented mathematically, such that the synchronization constraints (5) can be achieved.

3   Synchronous Controller

To converge the position errors and synchronization errors to zero, a coupled position errors $\mathbf{E}_i$ that links these errors is introduced as follows:

$$\mathbf{E}_i = c_i\mathbf{e}_i + \beta\int_0^t\left(\varepsilon_i - \varepsilon_{i-1}\right)d\zeta \tag{9}$$

where β is a diagonal positive gain matrix. Notice from (8) and (9) that the coupled position errors for the ith robot feeds back the data from the two adjacent robots i-1 and i+1, respectively.

Differentiating $\mathbf{E}_i$ with respect to time, yields;

$$\dot{\mathbf{E}}_i = \dot{c}_i\mathbf{e}_i + c_i\dot{\mathbf{e}}_i + \beta\left(\varepsilon_i - \varepsilon_{i-1}\right) \tag{10}$$

In order for both $\mathbf{E}_i \to 0$ and $\dot{\mathbf{E}}_i \to 0$, a control vector $\mathbf{u}_i$ that directs to a combined position and velocity error is introduced as follows:

$$\mathbf{u}_i = c_i\dot{q}_i^d + \dot{c}_i\mathbf{e}_i + \beta\left(\varepsilon_i - \varepsilon_{i-1}\right) + \Lambda\mathbf{E}_i \tag{11}$$

where Λ is a diagonal positive gain matrix. The following position/velocity vector is defined based on $\mathbf{u}_i$ as:

$$\mathbf{r}_i = \mathbf{u}_i - c_i \dot{\mathbf{q}}_i = c_i \dot{\mathbf{e}}_i + \dot{c}_i \mathbf{e}_i + \beta(\varepsilon_i - \varepsilon_{i-1}) + \Lambda \mathbf{E}_i = \dot{\mathbf{E}}_i + \Lambda \mathbf{E}_i \qquad (12)$$

Then, the translational controller is designed to drives $\mathbf{r}_i$ to zero, such that the coupled errors $\mathbf{E}_i$ and $\dot{\mathbf{E}}_i$ converge to zero as well. The input torque that controlling the robot dynamic (1) is designed as follows:

$$\tau_{qi} = M_i c_i^{-1} (\dot{\mathbf{u}}_i - \dot{c}_i \dot{\mathbf{q}}_i) + K_{ri} c_i^{-1} \mathbf{r}_i + c_i^T K_\varepsilon (\varepsilon_i - \varepsilon_{i-1}) + \mathbf{V}(q, \dot{q}) \qquad (13)$$

where K_{ri} and K_ε are positive feedback control gains. The last term in (13) is introduced to compensate for the centripetal and Coriolis effect of the WMR.

Substituting (13) into the robot dynamic (1), yields the closed-loop dynamics of the system as follows:

$$M_i c_i^{-1} \dot{\mathbf{r}}_i + K_{ri} c_i^{-1} \mathbf{r}_i + c_i^T K_\varepsilon (\varepsilon_i - \varepsilon_{i-1}) = 0 \qquad (14)$$

To proof the asymptotic stability for the closed-loop system (14) readers can refer to our former work [14].

To control the robot's orientation, a general computed torque method is used as:

$$\tau_{\phi i} = I_i \left(\ddot{\phi}_i^d + k_{vi} \Delta \dot{\phi}_i + k_{pi} \Delta \phi_i \right) \qquad (15)$$

where k_{vi} and $k_{pi} k_{pi}$ are computed torque control gains. The desired orientation ϕ_i^d is defined such that the ith robot is always oriented towards its desired position.

4   Simulation Results

Simulation is performed to validate the efficiency of the proposed synchronous control law. In this work, a generalized super ellipse with varying parameters while its center is tracking straight line was selected to represent different formation curves

$$\begin{cases} x_i = \pm a \, \cos^m \varphi_i + x_{cent} \\ y_i = \pm b \, \sin^m \varphi_i + y_{cent} \end{cases} \qquad (16)$$

where m denotes the exponent index, a, b, and φ_i are defined as in (3), and (x_{cent}, y_{cent}) denotes the center of the formation shape. The parameters m, a, and b assumed to be a time-varying.

In this study, four WMR are positioned in an ellipse curve shown in Fig 2, and the parameters for each robot are given in [14]. Throughout the simulation, the center of the formation shape will move in a straight line, while the formation shape is switched from an ellipse curve $m_o = 1$ to a rounded rectangle shape $m_f = 1/8$ at the beginning of the simulation. Furthermore, the parameters a and b will also change from their initials values of $a_o = 40$ and $b_o = 80$ to their final desired value of $a_f = 120$ and $b_f = 30$. In this case, the formation shape parameters are changed as follows:

$$m(t) = m_0 + (m_f - m_0) \left(1 - e^{-t} \right) \qquad (17)$$

$$a(t) = a_o + (a_f - a_o)\ (1 - e^{-t}) \tag{18}$$

$$b(t) = b_o + (b_f - b_o)\ (1 - e^{-t}) \tag{19}$$

Moreover, after the first 20 second of the simulation, again the formation shape will switch from a rounded rectangle $m_f = 1/8$ to an ellipse curve $m_L = 1$. Also, a and b will vary from their current value to $a_L = 30$ and $b_L = 90$. During this second switch, the formation shape parameters are changing in the following way:

$$m(t) = m_f + (m_L - m_f)\ (1 - e^{(20-t)}) \tag{20}$$

$$a(t) = a_f + (a_L - a_f)\ (1 - e^{(20-t)}) \tag{21}$$

$$b(t) = b_f + (b_L - b_f)\ (1 - e^{(20-t)}) \tag{22}$$

The center of formation shapes with respect to time is given as follows;

$$x_{cent}(t) = 2t; \quad y_{cent}(t) = 2t \tag{23}$$

The desired trajectory for the ith robot is given by:

$$q_i^d(t) = \begin{bmatrix} x_i^d(t) \\ y_i^d(t) \end{bmatrix} = \begin{bmatrix} \cos^{m(t)}\varphi_i \\ & \sin^{m(t)}\varphi_i \end{bmatrix} \begin{bmatrix} a \\ b \end{bmatrix} + \begin{bmatrix} x_{cent} \\ y_{cent} \end{bmatrix} = A_i(t) \begin{bmatrix} a \\ b \end{bmatrix} + \begin{bmatrix} x_{cent} \\ y_{cent} \end{bmatrix} \tag{24}$$

The coupled parameter matrix is defined as follows:

$$c_i(t) = A_i^{-1}(t) = \begin{bmatrix} \cos^{m(t)}\varphi_i \\ & \sin^{m(t)}\varphi_i \end{bmatrix}^{-1} \tag{25}$$

The sampling time for this simulation was set to 0.005 second. The synchronous controller parameters were selected for each robot as: $\beta = diag\{514,510\}$, $\Lambda = diag\{147,140\}$, $k_\varepsilon = diag\{4,3\}$, $k_{ri} = diag\{1000,1000\}$, $k_{pi} = 10$, and $k_{vi} = 15$. The initial heading for the four robots are selected to be at zero degree.

Fig. 3 shows the position errors in the x- and y-directions, while Fig. 4 illustrates the synchronization errors. Notice from the figures that the values of both position errors' and synchronization errors' increases to finite amount and consequently, converged to zero until reaching the desired shape and position. Furthermore, both the position and synchronization errors slightly increased again and converge faster towards zero though achieving the final desired shape and location during the switching between the formation shapes at $t = 20$ sec. From the simulation, notice that, both position errors and synchronization errors are maintained at zero, which indicated that an enhanced formation is accomplished.

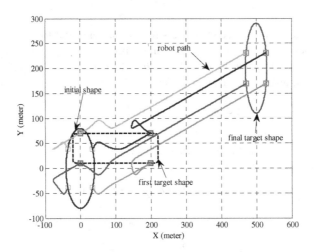

Fig. 2. Switching between different formation shapes while moving in a line

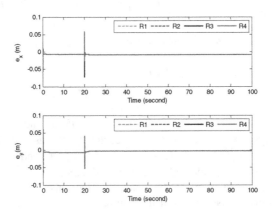

Fig. 3. Position errors in x- and y-direction e_x, e_y respectively

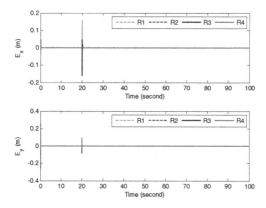

Fig. 4. Synchronization errors in x- and y-direction E_x, E_y respectively

5   Conclusion

The paper presents switching between different time-varying formations shapes while the centers of the formation curve following a predetermined line. The proposed synchronous controller guarantees asymptotic stability of both position errors and synchronization errors. The simulation results show the effectiveness of the synchronization method to allow a group of robots to track a desired trajectory while maintaining a switching between different time-varying formations shapes. The future work will focus on combining the synchronization method with path planning and navigation to accomplish better performance in real time applications.

Acknowledgments. The authors would like to thank MOHE and UTM for the Research University Grant (RUG) Tier 1, under the vot no. Q.J130000.2501.02H72 on multi-robotics formation control.

References

1. Parker, L.E.: ALLIANCE: an architecture for fault tolerant multirobot cooperation. IEEE Transactions on Robotics and Automation 14, 220–240 (1998)
2. Balch, T., Arkin, R.C.: Behavior-based formation control for multirobot teams. IEEE Transactions on Robotics and Automation 14, 926–939 (1998)
3. Lewis, M.A., Tan, K.-H.: High Precision Formation Control of Mobile Robots Using Virtual Structures. Autonomous Robots 4, 387–403 (1997)
4. Egerstedt, M., Hu, X.: Formation constrained multi-agent control. IEEE Transactions on Robotics and Automation 17, 947–951 (2001)
5. Ren, W., Beard, R.W.: Formation feedback control for multiple spacecraft via virtual structures. In: IEE Proceedings - Control Theory and Applications, vol. 151, pp. 357–368 (2004)

6. Desai, J.P., Ostrowski, J.P., Kumar, V.: Modeling and control of formations of nonholonomic mobile robots. IEEE Transactions on Robotics and Automation 17, 905–908 (2001)
7. Das, K., Fierro, R., Kumar, V., Ostrowski, J.P., Spletzer, J., Taylor, C.J.: A vision-based formation control framework. IEEE Transactions on Robotics and Automation 18, 813–825 (2002)
8. Tanner, H.G., Pappas, G.J., Kumar, V.: Leader-to-formation stability. IEEE Transactions on Robotics and Automation 20, 443–455 (2004)
9. Takahashi, H., Nishi, H., Ohnishi, K.: Autonomous decentralized control for formation of multiple mobile robots considering ability of robot. IEEE Transactions on Industrial Electronics 51, 1272–1279 (2004)
10. Tran, V.H., Lee, S.G.: A Stable Formation Control Using Approximation of Translational and Angular Accelerations. International Journal of Advanced Robotic Systems 8, 65–75 (2011)
11. Sam, G.S., Fua, C.-H., Lim, K.W.: Multi-robot formations: queues and artificial potential trenches. In: 2004 IEEE International Conference on Robotics and Automation, New Orleans, IA, pp. 3345–3350 (2004)
12. Fax, J.A., Murray, R.M.: Information flow and cooperative control of vehicle formations. IEEE Transactions on Automatic Control 49, 1465–1476 (2004)
13. Sun, D., Wang, C., Shang, W., Feng, G.: A Synchronization Approach to Trajectory Tracking of Multiple Mobile Robots While Maintaining Time-Varying Formations. IEEE Transactions on Robotics 25, 1074–1086 (2009)
14. Sanhoury, I.M.H., Amin, S.H.M., Husain, A.R.: Switching between formations for multiple mobile robots via synchronous controller. In: 2012 IEEE 8th International Colloquium on Signal Processing and its Applications (CSPA), Melaka, Malaysia, pp. 352–357 (2012)

Reconfigurable Stewart Platform for Vibration Isolation

G. Satheesh Kumar[1] and Thirumalaiswamy Nagarajan[2]

[1] Department of Mechanical Engineering, Indian Institute of Technology Madras, India
[2] Department of Mechanical Engineering, Universiti Teknologi Petronas (UTP)
human_flag@yahoo.com,
tnaga@iitm.ac.in

Abstract. Stewart platform in real time for reconfigurable applications has been a problem due to the lack of an efficient methodology for determining the optimum geometry for a given task. The authors extend the solution from their previous work (Satheesh et al., 2009) to encompass all the possible design constraints that generally might occur in scenarios with varying task requirements. This paper attempts to characterize the parameters for active vibration isolation applications through the same approach. The output of simulation shows a better performance for the 3-3 configuration over 6-6 configuration for active vibration isolation applications. Overshoot diminishes with a reduction in η. The effective active range of the dimensionless parameter joint vector η, is observed to be 2.0-0.5. This methodology thus becomes established encompassing all constraints to build a complete set of design tool for reconfiguration of any new reconfigurable Stewart platform..

Keywords: Modularity, Reconfigurable systems, Stewart platform, Vibration isolation.

1 Introduction

Among many, the potential direction for future work is the alternative kinematic configurations and improved modularity/configurability (Wavering, 1998). In a flexible automation approach to batch or job-shop production, the re-configurability of the elements of a manufacturing system has proved to be important. A key element for reconfigurable manufacturing systems is the reconfigurable machine tools (RMT). The conceptual design of this type of machine is introduced, and the detailed configurations of potential structures were shown by Dan Zhang and Zhuming Bi (2006). The results illustrated that this type of reconfigurable kinematic machine can achieve a large workspace without a void or a hole, and it has no interference among the system components. Added to this characteristic the reconfigurability of the system permits a seamless integration into the complex task requirements that are in great demand in the market off late (Jian Dai, 2009; Mekid, 2007; Valsamos and Aspragathos, 2009). It stands to fulfill the industrial needs of adaptability and reconfigurability in the manufacturing and robotics sector.

S.G. Ponnambalam et al. (Eds.): IRAM 2012, CCIS 330, pp. 37–45, 2012.

1.1   Reconfigurable Stewart Platform

Stewart platforms have unique features allowing for re-configuration. The two main approaches that have been proposed for the reconfiguration of Stewart platforms are modular design and a variable geometry. From a different perspective there are two more categories namely hardware and software reconfiguration. This paper addresses the fundamental issues associated with hardware reconfiguration through the variable geometry approach. Modular design is a trial-and-error methodology to re-configuration, where the idea is to develop an inventory of standardized leg modules and customized mobile and base platforms, so that a modular Stewart platform can be custom-configured, be portable and easy to repair. The original problem being the development of a re-configurable platform suitable for various applications; two applications chosen are contour generation and vibration isolation for this study. The choice of these applications is justified since the problem becomes more interesting because of the opposing nature of the operating principles. The difference in operation principle for these applications is shown in Fig. 1. K. Ma and M. N. G. Nejhad (2005), presented an adaptive control scheme for simultaneous precision positioning and vibration suppression of an intelligent structure viz, active composite panel. This still does not cater to the demand placed on the stiffness if the isolator is used in other applications.

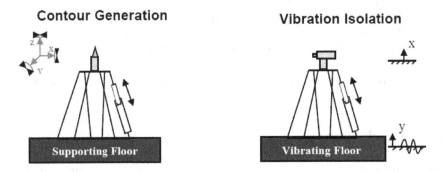

Fig. 1. Variation in Principles

2   Parameters of Modularity

Among the multitude of parameters available for the study of Stewart platform the parameters considered important for this research are presented below:

1. Configuration
2. bi - position vector of the joints in the moving platform
3. p - position vector of the origin of the moving platform coordinate
4. λ - angle between the moving platform and the legs
5. γ - angle between the legs
6. Control law
7. Work volume

6-6 and 3-3 configurations are chosen for this study owing to their common usage in industries for their simplicity in design. The symmetry of the legs allows equal distribution of load to all the legs. Fig. 2 represents the parameters λ and γ which are directly dependent on bi (called as joint vector from now on) and so an explicit study on them is avoided. p is chosen as the fixed parameter (refer Fig.3 for other parameters) for both the applications. Control law is also held constant for Vibration isolation studies for the ease of initial studies. Other parameters do not come under the scope of this research.

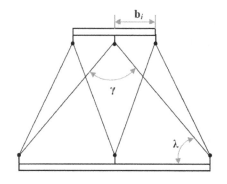

Fig. 2. Modular Parameters

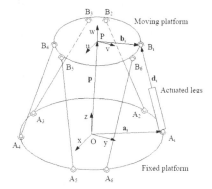

Fig. 3. General Stewart platform

3   Simulation Results and Discussion

The purpose of simulation is given below:

- To prove the validity of the proposed stiffness algorithm
- Perform stiffness analysis, for identifying the trajectory with maximum stiffness
- Perform kinematic analysis for trajectory with maximum stiffness
- Study the results obtained for characterizing the behavior of the platform.

The first parameter chosen for analysis is configuration. Four different configurations of Stewart platform are studied for different trajectories. Kinematic comparisons are made between Tsai6-6 and Tsai3-3 and for PeilPOD6-6 and PeilPOD3-3 configurations. PeilPOD3-3 is the platform developed for conducting experimental investigations on the parameters mentioned. PeilPOD6-6 configuration is obtained numerically. More information on Tsai6-6 configuration can be obtained from Tsai, (1999) and Tsai3-3 configuration is obtained numerically. The reason to choose these platforms for analysis: the displacements obtained are in the range of centimeters in Tsai platforms and for PeilPOD it is in millimeters.

4   Effect of Parameters

Since for this research the optimal geometry for the mechanism to generate multiple DOF anti-vibration forces is important, 'configuration' and 'joint vector' are the parameters chosen to be studied for active vibration isolation. Workspace required for this application is very minimal and hence an extensive study involving it is avoided. The control law is chosen to be a constant parameter for the purpose of simulation.

4.1   Influence of Configuration

3-3 and 6-6 configurations are the configurations studied in time domain. Tsai3-3 and Tsai6-6 platforms are simulated for the sinusoidal input of 70 Hz, a frequency that is less than half of minimum natural frequency found from the experiments performed on the test rig. A block diagram showing the control-loop with displacement (x) and velocity as feedback is shown in Fig. 4. The input signal with maximum force amplitude of 300 N is provided to the fixed platform.

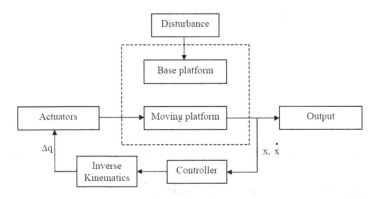

Fig. 4. Schematic representation of the control-loop

The initial conditions taken for simulation are $t0 = [0.1, 0.0, 0.3]T$ m and $\Theta0 = [0.0, 0.0, -0.2]T$ m and by applying the control law the displacement of the moving platform is brought to zero represented by $t = [0.0, 0.0, 0.0]T$ m and $\Theta0 = [0.0, 0.0, 0.0]T$ m. The results obtained are plotted for without control along with the plots with control, in pairs. Figs. 5a and 5b provide the comparison of linear displacement of Tsai 3-3 and Tsai 6-6 platforms without and with control respectively, in z direction. It is observed that 3-3 configuration has a settling time of 10 ms lesser than the 6-6 configuration for the z direction. The overshoot observed in Fig. 5a necessitates a derivative control to be included in the control algorithm and so a PD control law is chosen to control the vibration. The steady state error if any could be neglected since it is not included under the scope of this research.

Since the disturbance is produced in z-direction alone the displacements obtained in other directions is lesser than that obtained in the z-direction. Figs. 6a and 7a provide linear displacement for the y and z directions without control respectively. Figs. 6b and 7b represent the same with control. It is observed that 3-3 configuration provides a better performance than the other configuration as expected from the literature. Figs. 8a, 9a and 10a provide the angular displacements for z, x and y direction respectively without control. And the angular displacements obtained with control are presented in Figs. 8b, 9b and 10b. Here too it is observed that the PD control gives better performance for the 3-3 configurations.

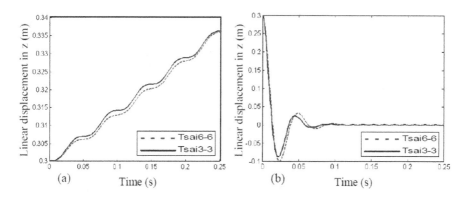

Fig. 5. (a) & (b) Linear displacement of the platform in z-direction

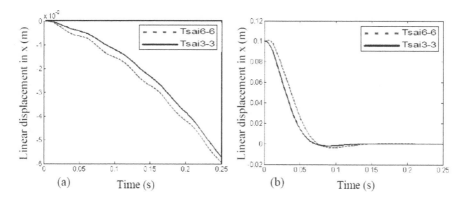

Fig. 6. (a) & (b) Linear displacement of the platform in x-direction

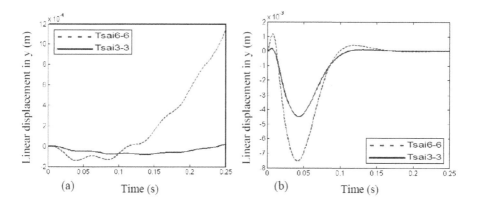

Fig. 7. (a) & (b) Linear displacement of the platform in y-direction

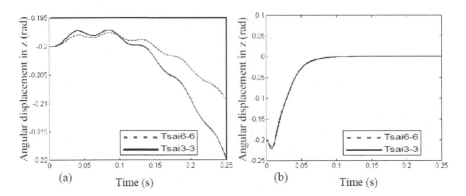

Fig. 8. (a) & (b) Angular displacement of the platform in z-direction

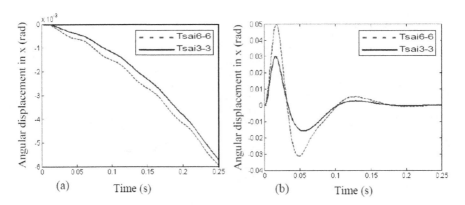

Fig. 9. (a) & (b) Angular displacement of the platform in x-direction

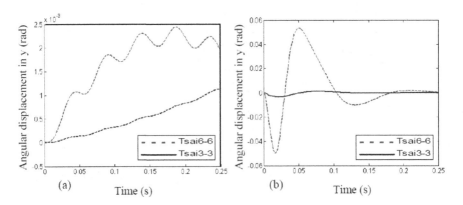

Fig. 10. (a) & (b) Angular displacement of the platform in y-direction

The overshoot in each case is considerably reduced for 3-3 configuration. The results presented are for Tsai platforms and similar results are obtained for other platforms like PeilPOD3-3 and PeilPOD6-6 too. Stiffness algorithm and dynamics could be referred from Satheesh et al., 2009.

4.2   Influence of Joint Vector

As in the case of stiffness study, the joint vector is simulated only for the 3-3 configurations of Tsai and PeilPOD, and results are presented for Tsai platform. The dimensionless parameter η, the ratio R/r, is varied from 0.5 to 3.0. Though an angle of 90o between legs is preferred for vibration isolation, the advantages offered is to be studied by analyzing the effect of this parameter for modular systems. The effective active range of η is observed to be 0.5 to 2.0. An increase or decrease beyond this range introduces a highly unstable behavior into the system which is beyond the control of the applied PD control law. Fig. 11 provides the plot for linear displacement in z-direction for different η. As η is increased from 0.5 to 2.0 the settling time is increased. The overshoot also reduces with reduction in η.

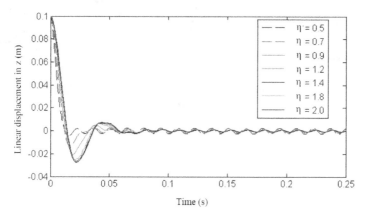

Fig. 11. Angular velocity of the platform in y-direction

5   Natural Frequency

Experiments were also conducted to quantify the natural frequency of the test-rig in order to establish the frequency at which the simulation is to be performed for vibration isolation application. Fig. 12 shows the developed Stewart platform, a 3-3 configuration with spherical joints at the top and the bottom platform. An accelerometer is mounted at the centroid of the moving platform as shown in Fig. 13. The platform is held at nominal height and an impulse is produced on the moving platform and the natural frequency is found from the output obtained from the accelerometer. At the same height the position of the accelerometer is shifted and natural frequency is recorded for all those positions. The same procedure is repeated at different heights of the mobile platform. The experimentally obtained frequencies are plotted against the heights of the mobile platforms and a polynomial curve is fitted. The lowest point in Fig. 14 gives the natural frequency of the developed Stewart platform. The natural frequency of the system is found to be 166 Hz which is sufficiently higher than the frequency of 70 Hz used in simulation. Apart from this experiment, error analysis is to be performed on the developed Stewart platform and will be compensated for. Then the joint vector effect is to be studied on the vibration isolation performance of the platform. However, experimentations that are suggested in this section do not come under the scope of this paper and has been submitted as another paper.

Fig. 12. PeilPOD3-3 (Developed in-house)   **Fig. 13.** Experimental setup for Natural frequency

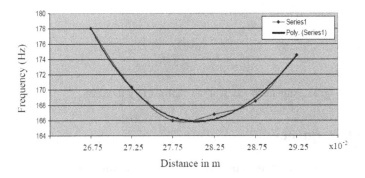

Fig. 14. Natural frequency of the developed Stewart platform

6   Conclusions

In the time domain Tsai3-3 and Tsai6-6 platforms are simulated for the sinusoidal input of 70 Hz and maximum amplitude of 300 N. Kinematic and dynamic analysis of the developed Stewart platform is incorporated through Newton-Euler's formulation and PD control law is implemented for active vibration control using position and velocity. It is observed that 3-3 configuration has a settling time of 10 ms lesser than the 6-6 configuration for z direction. Since the disturbance produced is in the z-direction alone displacement obtained in other directions is lesser than that obtained in the z-direction. The output of simulation shows a better performance for the 3-3 configuration over 6-6 configuration for active vibration isolation applications in all the directions. The overshoot in each case is considerably reduced for 3-3 configuration.

The effective active range of the dimensionless parameter joint vector η, the ratio R/r, is observed to be 2.0 to 0.5. An increase or decrease beyond this range introduces a highly oscillatory behavior into the system which is beyond the control of the applied PD control law. As η is decreased, the settling time decreases. The overshoot also reduces with reduction in η. A similar performance was observed for the Peil POD too. This parameter would serve as a design tool to choose between the isolation and the corresponding dimensions of the top and bottom platforms. An experimental test rig developed integrating sensors for original problem was presented along with its kinematic analysis on simulation. The natural frequency of the system is found to be 166 Hz which is sufficiently higher.

References

1. Wavering, A.J.: Parallel Kinematic Machine Research at NIST: Past, Present, and Future. In: First European-American Forum on Parallel Kinematic Machines: Theoretical Aspects and Industrial Requirements, Italy, pp. 1–13 (1998)
2. Kumar, S.G., Nagarajan, T., Srinivasa, Y.G.: Characterization of Reconfigurable Stewart Platform for Contour Generation. Robotics and Computer Integrated Manufacturing 25, 721–731 (2009)
3. Dasgupta, B., Mruthyunjaya, T.S.: The Stewart Platform Manipulator – A Review. Mechanism and Machine Theory 35, 15–40 (2001)
4. Zhang, D., Bi, Z.: Development of Reconfigurable Parallel Kinematic Machines using Modular Design Approach. In: CDEN 2006, International Design Conference, University of Toronto, Ontario, Canada, pp. 1–6 (2006)
5. Mekid, S., Schlegel, T., Aspragathos, N., Teti, R.: Foresight formulation in innovative production, automation and control systems, vol. 9(5), pp. 35–47. QEmerald Group Publishing Limited (2007) ISSN 1463-6689
6. Valsamos, H., Aspragathos, N.: Determination of Anatomy and Configuration of a Reconfigurable Manipulator for the Optimal Manipulability. In: IEEE ASME ReMAR 2009 Conference, London, England, pp. 497–503 (June 2009)
7. Hauge, G.S., Campbell, M.E.: Sensors and Control of a Space-based Six-axis Vibration Isolation System. Journal of Sound and Vibration 269(3-5), 913–931 (2004)
8. Ma, K., Ghasemi-Nejhad, M.N.: Adaptive Simultaneous Precision Positioning and Vibration Control of Intelligent Composite Structures. Journal of Intelligent Materials Systems and Structures 16, 163–174 (2005)
9. Dai, J.S.: International Conference on Reconfigurable Mechanisms and Robots.asp. King's College of London, London (2009),
   http://www.cyberneticsnews.com/research/
10. Tsai, L.W.: Robotic Analysis: The Mechanics of Serial and Parallel Manipulators. John-Wiley & Sons, New York (1999)

Posture Estimation Strategy for Multi Robot System Based on Visual Perception and Optical Pointer

G. Rishwaraj, R.M. Kuppan Chetty, and S.G. Ponnambalam

School of Engineering, Monash University Sunway Campus, Malaysia
{rishwaraj.gengarajoo,kuppanchetty.ramanathan,
sgponnambalam}@monash.edu

Abstract. The key objective of this research work is to develop and improve the posture estimation of the robots relative to each other using a combination of visual perception and optical (laser) pointers. The two critical parameters that are estimated in this work are the linear separation between the robots and the orientation angle of the robots. An empirical model is developed for linear separation estimation while five different models are developed towards the estimation of orientation related to the distance. Performance of the developed models are investigation through simulation studies and the results shows that the linear model exhibits an average error of 5.19% while the angular estimation model exhibits an error of 13.9% at a predetermined distance.

Keywords: Multi robots system, Posture estimation, Visual perception, Image processing, Wheeled Mobile Robots.

1 Introduction

In recent years, the usage of multi robot systems in a coordinated fashion has garnered an extensive attention in research due to its diverse application fields [1]. Some of the applications include exploration, surveillance, environment mapping, warehouse package transporters, industrial transportation etc., which requires robots to work in a tightly coupled formation. In most of the existing literatures in multi robot applications, one of the robots is classified as leader and other robots are assigned as followers [1-8]. In such application, the follower robots are designated to track the leaders by estimating their posture through various means of sensory perception [2-6] in order to maintain the formation and work coherently while achieving tasks. According to the literatures, one of the major challenges in formation control is the posture estimation of the neighbouring robots in the group to accomplish a given task without deviating from the formation. In such applications, various methods such as visual perception [1, 4, 8-10], traditional sensor based perception using Sonars, Laser range finders etc.; multi-sensor fusion [1] and also through inter-robot communications [2-7] have been used for estimation of posture's of the robots.

A study utilizing a vision based sensor on follower robot has been reported in [1], for posture estimation of leader robot in sustaining a desired formation. A better posture estimation with the use of an omnidirectional camera as vision sensor has

S.G. Ponnambalam et al. (Eds.): IRAM 2012, CCIS 330, pp. 46–56, 2012.

been reported in [4], for such applications. A panoramic camera (an omnidirectional camera) has been used in [8] for the estimation of leader's posture employed in a tightly coupled formation. Instead of having a fixed camera, a video camera with pan mechanism is also used as a vision sensor in [9], in order to track the object along with its posture estimation. Albeit being robust methods, most of the above visual perception based sensor studies have their own drawbacks. The prominent setback is the complex structure of the feature extraction and processing techniques that are involved in the estimation process. These methods are not advisable especially where user-friendliness is concern. Postures of the neighbouring robots were also estimated through an explicit Inter-robot communication [4, 6-7] where the information is transferred through a communication network. Further study of inter-robot communication has been reported in [2] detailing the use of wireless Ethernet network in preserving the multi-robot cooperation explicitly.

Most recently, a combination of vision and laser range finder (laser sensor) have been proposed in [1], for the posture estimation of objects and localization. Other study using laser emitters that are mounted on a robot to estimate its distance from possible obstacles and also for location of the target have been proposed in [11]. In these methods, the distance is estimated in terms of pixel values and this was further used to estimate the relative distance between the robot and the obstacle. However, the major drawback of this method is that it lacks the estimation of angular orientation of the robots and also to predict the turn directions of the robot during fly.

Even though, most of the above studies focus on robots working in a formation while maintaining visual or sensory proximity within each other, an error in the posture estimation may lead to the loss of formation and coordination between the robots. However, there are drawbacks in the above methods such as the inter-robot communication relies heavily on the availability of communication network and lacks in ensuring the cooperation of the mobile robots when the communication system fails during fly. Although the method involving laser range finder provides good posture estimation, the current cost of the laser range finder is too expensive making it difficult to adopt in most cases. Moreover, the complexity of signal processing and extracting the features makes it difficult to adopt.

Inspired from the above literatures, the major objective of this work is to develop a posture estimation strategy through a vision system coupled with optical (LASER) pointers projected on a target board. This research further improves the method in [11] by employing two laser pointers for a better posture estimation as well as developing a simple vision based posture estimation algorithm which is used to estimate both the relative separation between the robots as well as the angular orientation of the robots. The major challenge addressed in this work is the development of empirical models which are necessary for estimating the relative distance and the orientation angle of the robots from the perspective of the follower robot during fly.

2   Methodology

2.1   Modelling Method

Considered the situation where two robots are required to estimate each other's posture while moving in a tightly coupled formation in an inline topology.

These robots were arranged where the leader robot is called R_L, while the follower robot is called R_F as shown in Fig. 1. It also illustrates the kinematic model for this typical leader follower formation setup of R_L and R_F. During the fly, it is necessary for the robot R_F to remain in the desired angular separation (Θ^d) and linear separation (l^d) with respect to the R_L, in order to maintain the in line column formation by minimizing the separation distance asymptotically zero. To achieve this goal, the robot R_F has to determine the current linear separation distance (l) w.r.t R_L and the current orientation angle (φ) of the R_L to estimate the desired position that it needs to position itself. Therefore, this problem reduces as a posture estimation problem of the follower robots. In order to achieve this feat, a simple technique which utilizes the combination of webcam along with two laser pointers positioned in equidistance on either side of the webcam. In addition, the robot R_L is equipped with a rectangular target board that is viewed by the sensory system positioned in R_F. The laser pointer is made to point its beam on the target board and the value of l and φ is estimated by analysing the position of the blobs in the image captured by the webcam.

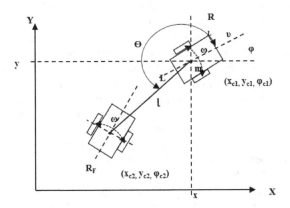

Fig. 1. Typical setup in a leader follower formation

Fig. 2 illustrates the schematic diagram of the laser beam points on the target board as viewed by the webcam from a top angle view. This design is a modified version of visual perception addressed in [12], which originally uses a single laser pointer to estimate only the linear distance. However, in this proposed design, the use of two laser pointers provide a more robust approach in determining the angular orientation of the target robot along with the linear separation distance. The value of H is the distance between the laser pointer and webcam in the proposed design, which is fixed at 75mm. The value of l varies according to the distance of R_L w.r.t R_F as it denotes the linear separation between the two robots, while α is the viewing angle of the webcam. Considering the perception system, the variable α could be estimated by equation 1 and 2.

$$\tan \alpha = \frac{H}{l} \tag{1}$$

$$\alpha = pfc * R + rad \tag{2}$$

where,

pfc   = No. of pixel between the laser beam point (blob) and the center of target board

R   = radians per pixel pitch

rad   = radian compensation for alignment error

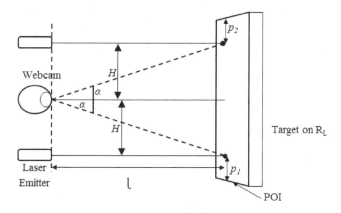

Fig. 2. Webcam and Laser Emitter setup

Since the linear separation (l), i.e. the relative distance between the robot (follower) and its target (leader), cannot be determined directly, the value could be estimated by substituting equation 2 into 1, and rearranging the terms provides an empirical relationship as

$$l = \frac{H}{\tan(pfc*R+rad)} \qquad (3)$$

Therefore, the current linear separation between the robots is determined by using equation (3). Next step is to derive a model which could determine the angle of turn which is the orientation of the leader from the observed image. As R_L turn towards a direction, the value of 'p' varies, according to the turn direction and the orientation angle of the robot. The value of p is the pixel distance between the laser beam points to the Point of Interest (POI), which is the edges of the rectangular target board positioned on R_L (ref Fig. 4a). For an ease of understanding, the value of 'p' could be represented by 'p_1' and 'p_2' representing the distance on both ends of the target board as shown in Fig. 2. According to the hypothesis, for example, the value of 'p_1' reduces and 'p_2' increases, when the target robot turn towards the left and vice versa when it turns toward the right. Therefore, the orientation angle and turn directions of the target robot is estimated through an empirical relationship that is derived by attaining the value of 'p' from the captured image using simple image processing technique. Therefore, the devised empirical model depicts the relationship between the orientation angle of the robot and the value of 'p', which is our major contribution addressed in this manuscript. The next section details the set of image processing technique which are used to extract the values of 'p' and pfc from the captured image for the estimation of both 'l' and 'φ'.

2.2   Algorithm

The webcam carried by the follower robot (R_F) is connected to a notebook that runs the image processing algorithm used for posture estimation of the robots. The purpose of the algorithm is to find the location of the red laser beam points in the target board with respect to the Point of Interest (POI) which is the either edge of the target board. The generic structure of the algorithm used to process the captured image is illustrated as flowchart in Fig. 3. The developed algorithm is implemented utilizing the image processing toolbox in Matlab R2011b.

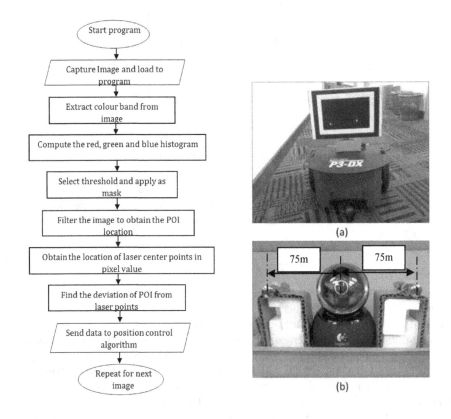

Fig. 3. Flow Chart of the generic structure of the image analysis algorithm

Fig. 4. (a) Rectangular board on R_L and (b) laser pointers with webcam setup on R_F

The objective of the image analysis is to estimate the pixel distance from the laser beam points (p) to the center of the target board image and between the laser beam points to the POI. The first data is used to estimate the linear separation between the robots by analysing the change in position of the laser beam with the observed distance. The center of the target board a prefixed value since the target board is at the center view of the webcam. The second one is used analyse the change in pixel distance between the POI and laser beam points at different angular orientation of the target.

Therefore, the analysis starts with the image captured from the camera and then the image is loaded to the image processing algorithm towards further analysis. At first, the captured image is segmented into three separate colour bands: red, blue and green for analysis of the colour component. Based on this segmentation, a histogram is computed for individual colour band and the peak value of the colour band is used as a mask to filter out the lower intensity objects. Then, the low and high threshold value of the image is computed from the histogram, is allocated for individual colour band. The low and high threshold value is selected considering that any pixel level lower or higher than the laser beam is filtered out. Therefore, once the threshold and the mask are applied to the image, the filtered image is the red laser beam points in addition to the pixels with similar intensity levels. As a next step, this image is converted into binary (black and white) form where the only one out of two values; 1 or 0 is assigned to each and every pixel that is present in the image to assist in further analysis. The prominent objects evident are the white rectangular border of the target, laser beam points and some minor background image. The rectangular border is represented in a bounding box and the analysis of this box returns the pixel coordinates at x-axis of POI. For calculating the axis of the laser beam points, all other pixels apart from the laser beam points are inverted resulting in an image with only the laser beam blobs. Each pixel in the blob is evaluated at the x-axis and taking the average of those values computes the center coordinates of the blobs.

2.3   Experimental Setup

Two Pioneer 3DX robots were employed in this experiment. They are positioned in in-line with the linear separation distance of 600mm between their axes. As mentioned in previous section, the robot R_L has the rectangular target board and the sensory and optical pointer system is positioned on R_F as shown in Fig. 4. The dimension of the target board is 222mm x145mm x20mm. The Point of Interest (POI) is the inner edge of the inside white rectangle of the board as shown in Fig 4 (a).

The black background of the board nullifies the immediate effect of external lighting and makes it easier to observe the changes of the POI relative to the laser points' positions. The target board is placed on a highly precise angular tilt for observing the changes of the POI with respect to the laser beam points at different angles. The angles investigated in this experiment are zero to twenty degree with the increments of two degrees for the right turn as well as for the left turn.

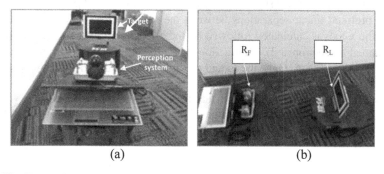

(a)   (b)

Fig. 5. Experimental setup of the robots: (a) view from R_F and (b) view from top

A Logitech Quickcam Sphere with focal length of 3.7mm is used as the visual perception system along with two red laser pointers of 650nm wavelength positioned at an equidistance of 75mm on both sides of the camera, resembling the devised sensory system shown in Fig. 2. In addition, it is also ensured, that the laser pointers are placed at a height parallel to the axis of the webcam lens which is at 117mm from the base. The real time implementation of the devised system is shown in Fig. 4 (b). During fly, the two laser point falls on the board which is captured by the webcam and subsequently analysed to extract the distance 'p' relative to the laser points and POI. Images were captured at an interval of 10 frames for a continuous posture observation. The complete experimental system is illustrated in Fig. 5. In order to get the preliminary data, the images of the laser points are observed at a prefixed linear separation of 600mm, 700mm, 800mm and 900mm between the target and the follower robot.

3   Results and Discussions

3.1   Model Analysis

In order to attain the linear separation between the robots directly from relationship given in 3, the two unknowns R and rad that are present in the model has to be determined. Therefore, initial calibrations have been conducted to obtain these values. This is done by applying the known values of l and H from the initial set of images which are used as reference. With this, the value of α is determined and thus equation 3 forms as a simple simultaneous equation given by

$$l = \frac{H}{\tan (\text{pfc}*6.793 \text{x} 10^{-4}+0.00724)} \qquad (4)$$

The value of pfc is calculated by subtracting the x-axis coordinate of the laser beam point (obtained from section 2.2) with the fixed x-axis center coordinate of the image. Observation shows that the value of pfc decreases with the increase in the linear separation between the two robots. Therefore, equation 4 gives the estimate of the relative distance of R_L with respect to R_F by determining the value of pfc from the captured image during the fly.

As for the development of a model for estimating the angular orientation of the target, the image analysis is started by calculating the distance of p w.r.t to POI at four different prefixed linear separations between the robots. First, the center of the laser beam in the x-axis is calculated followed by the x-axis coordinate analysis of the POI (as explained in section 2.2). Subtraction of these two values gives the resulting p value as shown in Fig. 6. Once the p_1 and p_2 values are calculated for the data sets (as explained in section 2.3), the average of the p values are computed. A graph displaying the orientation angles and the corresponding average of the p values at each angle are plotted for every investigated angle. From Fig. 7, it is observed that the p value reduces as the orientation angle increases. A basic curve fitting method is

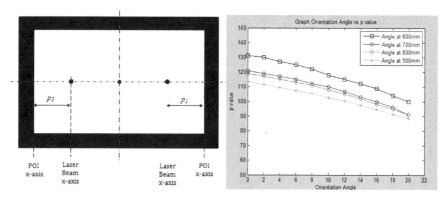

Fig. 6. p value calculated by subtracting the POI x-axis with Laser Beam x-axis

Fig. 7. Orientation Angle (deg) vs average p value at four linear separation

employed to derive the empirical relationship that best fits the plotted graphs. Table 1 provides the empirical models that are developed for estimating the orientation angle, φ of R_L at four different linear separations.

Table 1. Models developed for orientation estimation at different linear distance

Linear Separation, mm	Model	Equation. No
600	$z = (p - 117.55)/10.501$ Angle $= -0.7843z^2 - 6.792z + 10.713$	(5)
700	$z = (p - 107)/9.333$ Angle $= -0.929z^2 - 6.31z + 11.836$	(6)
800	$z = (p - 106.73)/9.3284$ Angle $= -0.954z^2 - 6.87z + 10.867$	(7)
900	$z = (p - 102.05)/8.323$ Angle $= -0.663z^2 - 6.748z + 10.602$	(8)

3.2   Model Discussion

The laser pointers were used to determine the posture of the leader robot through the analysis of center points of the lasers in the captured image in a simulated environment. With the objective to minimize the separation error in the in-line formation, the analysis provides the probable error in estimating the current linear separation and the orientation angle (angle of turn) of the leader robot. The analysis was done at 600mm, 70mm, 800mm and 900mm (equations 5, 6, 7 and 8 respectively) for the angle estimation while four trials were done for the linear distance estimation. With the linear separation model, a total of five developed models were analysed. These models were tested with a set of images to determine the error in its posture evaluation. The results of the analysis are shown below (see Fig. 8 and 9).

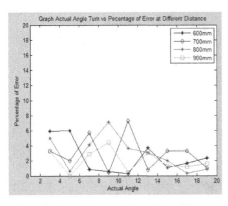 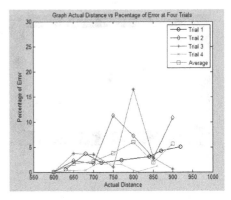

Fig. 8. Actual Angle (°) vs Percentage of Error

Fig. 9. Actual Distance (mm) vs Percentage of Error

The initial analysis shows that the highest error detected as 7.21% in the orientation angle estimation, while for the linear separation estimation is 16.50%. For the linear separation estimation model, the average errors of the four trials are 3.01%, 5.19%,4.03% and 0.75% respectively and have an overall error of 3.25%.

As for the angular estimation model at 600mm, 700mm, 800mm and 900mm linear separation distance, the average recorded error of the models are 2.49%, 3.02%, 2.97% and 2.03% respectively. This shows that the model has a low possibility to estimate the posture incorrectly. When comparing these models with study done in [5], this technique provides equal and in some cases a much better pose estimation. In the linear separation estimation, the highest error in the model is 16.5% or 133mm. This means that the 800mm linear separation is perceived by the model as 667mm. The error in [5] is almost 200mm in some extreme cases, while averaging at 100mm while the errors from the model here ranges from 50mm to 100mm in extreme cases and averaging lower than 50mm of estimation error in others. In order to further test the reliability of the system, an online simulation was carried out using Matlab to mimic the condition of robots moving in formations. As per the actual scenario, images are captured by the webcam at stipulated intervals and immediately analysed by using the model. In this case, the robots are set to be at 800mm apart. The results are shown in the Table 2. The result from the online simulation is fairly accepted as

Table 2. Error in the online simulation at 800mm for turn angle prediction

Estimated Angle, °	Actual Angle, °	Error, %
4.07	4.00	1.75
5.85	6.00	2.50
8.36	8.00	4.5
11.31	10.00	13.90
12.1	12	0.83
14.08	14	0.57
17.93	18	0.39

the error reading is relatively low except at one instant. However, this could be contributed by the odometry error or a misreading of the image due to poor lighting condition instead of error with the model itself. The online simulation of the angle estimation shows the highest error being 13.90% with deviation of 1.31° or in different term 0.02 rad. In the study of [5], the highest recorded error was 0.2 rad. Although the error in [5] eventually reduces, the model developed here shows a much lower error in the angle estimation.

4   Conclusion

In this paper a simple robust posture estimation strategy based on combination of visual perception and optical (LASER) pointers is addressed. Two critical parameters that are estimated are the linear separation between the robots and orientation angle of the target relative to the robots. An empirical relationship is developed for the estimation of the above parameters in terms of follower robots perspective during the fly. Performance of the developed models has been investigated through simulation studies. The model exhibits maximum average percentage error of 5.19 in estimating the linear distance between the robots and a maximum error of 13.9% in estimating the angular distance of the target robot. The results obtained are quite promising when compared to the results that are presented in [5] and this method could be a viable alternative method for such applications. Apart from the presented investigations, our future work is to investigate the robustness of the addressed model and to implement it as a posture estimation method in multi robot formation control applications.

References

1. Lang, H., Wang, Y., de Silva, C.W.: Mobile Robot Localization and Object Pose Estimation Using Optical Encoder, Vision and Laser Sensors. In: Proceedings of the IEEE International Conference on Automation and Logistics, pp. 617–622 (2008)
2. Carelli, R., Soria, C.M., Morales, B.: Vision – Based Tracking Control for Mobile Robots. In: ICAR 2005, Proceedings. 12th International Conference on Advanced Robotic, pp. 148–152 (2005)
3. Chaimowicz, L., Sugar, T., Kumar, V., Campos, M.F.M.: An Architecture for Tightly Coupled Multi – Robot Cooperation. In: Proceedings 2001 ICRA. IEEE International Conference on Robotics and Automation, vol. 3, pp. 2992–2997 (2001)
4. Das, A., Fierro, R., Kumar, V., Ostrowski, J., Spletzer, J., Taylor, C.: A Framework for Vision Based Formation Control. IEEE Transactions on Robotics and Automation 18(6), 813–825 (2001)
5. Ha, Q.P., Ha, H.M., Dissanayake, G.: Robotic Formation Control using Variable Structure System Approach. In: Distributed Intelligent Systems: IEEE Workshop on Collective Intelligence and Its Applications, pp. 37–42 (2006)
6. Kanjanawanishkul, K.: Formation Control of Omnidirectional Mobile Robots using Distributed Model Predictive Control. In: Proceedings of the 2nd International Conference on Robotic Communication and Coordination, pp. 1–7 (2009)

7. Kuppan Chetty, R.M., Singaperumal, M., Nagarajan, T.: Distributed Formation Planning and Navigation Framework for Wheeled Mobile Robots. Journal of Applied Sciences 11(9), 1501–1509 (2011)
8. Mariottini, G.L., Pappas, G., Prattichizzo, D., Daniilidis, K.: Vision-based Localization of Leader-Follower Formations. In: 44th IEEE Conference on Decision and Control, and the European Control Conference, pp. 635–643 (2005)
9. Maya-Mendez, M., Morin, P., Samson, C.: Control of a Nonholonomic Mobile Robot Via Sensor-based Target Tracking and Pose Estimation. In: Proceedings of the 2006 IEEE/RSJ International Conference on Intelligent Robots and Systems, pp. 5612–5618 (2006)
10. Renaud, P., Cervera, E., Martinet, P.: Towards a Reliable Vision Based Mobile Robot Formation Control. In: International Conference on Intelligent Robots and Systems, vol. 4, pp. 3176–3181 (2004)
11. Shojaeipour, S., Haris, S.M., Shojaeipour, A., Shirvan, R.K., Zakaria, M.K.: Robot Path Obstacle Locator using Webcam and Laser Emitter. Physics Procedia 5, 187–192 (2010)

Fuzzy Membership Scaling Mechanisms for Mobile Robot Behaviours

Jon Liang Loh and S. Parasuraman

School of Engineeering, Monash University, Sunway Campus, Malaysia
{loh.jon.liang,s.parasuraman}@monash.edu
http://eng.monash.edu.my

Abstract. Fuzzy behaviours are commonly used in reactive mobile robot navigation strategies, where sensory information is either uncertain or incomplete. However, the complexity of such controllers usually grow exponentially with the number of fuzzy input partitions and rules in the rule base. Furthermore, attempts to reduce the number of input partitions will typically erode the performance of the controllers. This work investigates several membership function scaling mechanisms as an avenue for improving the performance of fuzzy behaviours based on minimal rule base controllers. The configurations are based on the closely-related concepts of linguistic hedges and non-linear scaling. The scaling parameters for the goal seeking and obstacle avoidance behaviours are tuned in simulation via a genetic algorithm optimisation process. The results show that the controller configuration based on input membership function scaling consistently outperforms simple fuzzy logic controllers with the same number of fuzzy input partitions and rules.

Keywords: Mobile robots, fuzzy logic, membership function, fuzzy hedges, genetic algorithm.

1 Introduction

Fuzzy logic controllers (FLCs) are commonly used in mobile robot navigation, particularly in the area of behaviour-based reactive strategies [1,2,3]. The approximate reasoning capabilities of FLCs are especially suitable for robot navigation applications where information is typically uncertain or unknown. Furthermore in sensor-based approaches [4,5] the tight coupling between perception and actuation enables a robot to react to unexpected events in a timely manner, akin to reflex action in biological systems.

The hurdle of controller complexity in the fuzzy behaviour approach to robot navigation is not well explored in the literature. The larger the controller rule base, the more expensive (in terms of computation and time) it is to produce the output, and the more difficult or time-consuming it is for the designer to construct the rules in the rule base. If we assume that, for completeness, every permutation of the antecedent fuzzy set labels is accounted for in the rule base, the number of rules grows exponentially with the number of input domains

S.G. Ponnambalam et al. (Eds.): IRAM 2012, CCIS 330, pp. 57–66, 2012.

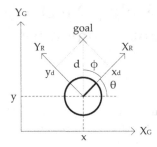
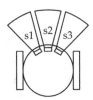

(a) The robot frame relative to the global frame.

(b) The ultrasonic sensor configuration.

Fig. 1. Robot base configuration

and labels. This is compounded by the fact that behaviour-based architectures usually consist of multiple controllers, each of which has a unique rule base tailored to the subtask to be solved, and that the reduction of the number of fuzzy partitions on the input domains usually results in eroded performance. The number of rules that has to be designed and computed in real-time therefore quickly becomes unmanageable.

One of the aims of this work is to propose a means to construct fuzzy logic controller-based behaviours with the minimum possible number of rules while maximising performance. This paradigm is similar to that of research under the umbrella of "interpretability versus accuracy trade-off" in the field of linguistic fuzzy modeling [6], in which researchers attempt to balance the contradictory requirements of high interpretability and high accuracy in linguistic fuzzy rule base systems. Techniques for achieving this include tuning of the membership functions' parameters or shapes, weighting the rules in the rule base, rule base reduction, linguistic modifiers, or a combination of the above [6].

In the field of mobile robotics, similar strides towards this goal were demonstrated in the work performed by Samsudin et al. [7]. A fuzzy logic controller for obstacle avoidance behaviour based on the ordinal structure model was designed using a GA optimisation process. In their work, only 17 rules were needed for successful demonstration of obstacle avoidance behaviour.

2   Preliminaries

A differential-drive robot constrained to planar motion can be represented in terms of its reference frame affixed to the mid-point of its axle, as shown in Figure 1a. The pose of the robot is defined as the vector $\mathbf{p} = [x \ y \ \theta]^T$, where (x, y) are the Cartesian coordinates of the robot frame origin in the global frame, and θ is the heading angle. The kinematics are expressed as

$$\dot{\mathbf{p}} = \begin{bmatrix} \dot{x} \\ \dot{y} \\ \dot{\theta} \end{bmatrix} = \begin{bmatrix} \cos\theta & 0 \\ \sin\theta & 0 \\ 0 & 1 \end{bmatrix} \begin{bmatrix} v \\ \omega \end{bmatrix}, \tag{1}$$

where $\dot{x}$, $\dot{y}$ and $\dot{\theta}$ are the velocity components of the robot in the global frame, and $v \in [-1, 1]$, $\omega \in [-4, 4]$ are the robot's linear and angular velocities respectively. The minimum and maximum velocities are arbitrarily chosen for the purposes of this simulated work. In a practical application they would have to be measured from the robot base on which the controllers are to be ultimately applied. The Euclidean distance $d = \sqrt{x_d{}^2 + y_d{}^2}$, $d \in [0, 2]$ and angle to the goal $\phi \in (-180°, 180°]$ relative to the robot frame are taken as inputs to the goal seeking behaviour. The activations of the three frontal ultrasonic sensors $s_1, s_2, s_3 \in [0, 1]$ representing the sensor range readings are the inputs to the obstacle avoidance behaviour (see Figure 1b). Each of these sensors has a beam width of 30°, collectively forming a 90° wide frontal perceptive cone.

3   Behaviour Design

Any desired behaviour can be implemented as a Mamdani-type fuzzy inference system described by a linguistic rule set, the semantic meanings of which are defined by fuzzy set definitions. Each FLC will produce a recommendation on the desired output based on the subtask that it is designed to solve. The output of the rule base is computed by aggregation of the individual rule outputs and defuzzification via the centroid method.

The scope of this work is limited to the design of two specific behaviours: Goal seeking (GS) and obstacle avoidance (OA). The input and output fuzzy sets of the behaviours are shown in Figure 2. The OA behaviour is only activated when an obstacle is detected within 1 m of the robot's frontal perceptive region.

The inputs, outputs and basic rule bases of the behaviours are given in Table 1 and 2. Note that these rule bases are *minimal* in the sense that the fewest possible number of fuzzy sets are defined in the input domains for proper operation so as to reduce the number of rules that needs to be constructed.

In this work four different approaches based on the idea of membership function scaling are explored. Each configuration scales the membership function of a fuzzy set A in the input domain X with a non-linear scaling factor, α:

$$A \triangleq \int_X \frac{(\mu_A(x))^\alpha}{x}. \tag{2}$$

The choice of values for α and the manner in which the input membership functions are scaled are detailed in Sections 4 and 5.

4   Linguistic Hedge-Based Approaches

Linguistic hedges are operators on the linguistic labels in a rule base that either emphasizes or relaxes the meaning of the labels. In fuzzy set theoretic terms, a hedge term appended to a primary term in the rule base scales its membership function according to its associated scaling factor.

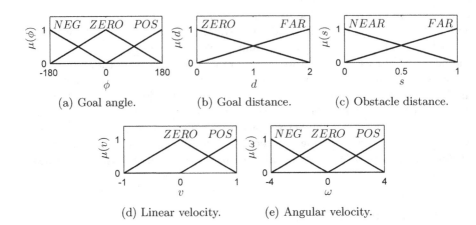

(a) Goal angle.   (b) Goal distance.   (c) Obstacle distance.

(d) Linear velocity.   (e) Angular velocity.

Fig. 2. Fuzzy set definitions for the goal seeking and obstacle avoidance behaviours

Table 1. Fuzzy control rules for the goal seeking behaviour

	Inputs		Outputs	
Rule	ϕ	d	v	ω
1	NEG	ZERO	ZERO	NEG
2	NEG	FAR	ZERO	NEG
3	ZERO	ZERO	ZERO	ZERO
4	ZERO	FAR	POS	ZERO
5	POS	ZERO	ZERO	POS
6	POS	FAR	ZERO	POS

The simplest way of applying hedges to the existing rule base is by modifying the antecedent linguistic labels. Each primary term in the antecedent is concatenated with a single hedge term, which scales the membership function with its associated hedge value. The hedge terms used are *slightly, more or less, minus, empty-hedge, plus, more, much more, very* and *absolutely* with associated hedge values h defined as 0.25, 0.5, 0.75, 1, 1.25, 1.5, 1.7, 2 and 4 respectively. The choice of linguistic hedges and their associated values are consistent with other work done in this area [8]. This method is referred to as the LH configuration in this work.

In the PLH configuration, hedge operations are applied to the membership functions in a piecewise manner. The methodology behind this approach is detailed in Liu et al.'s work [8]. In brief, each input membership function is partitioned into slices. The unique hedge values, h_i applied to each partition i are described in a hedge combination vector, **h**:

$$\mathbf{h} = \begin{bmatrix} h_1 & h_2 & \cdots & h_n \end{bmatrix}, \tag{3}$$

Table 2. Fuzzy control rules for the obstacle avoidance behaviour

Rule	Inputs			Outputs	
	s_1	s_2	s_3	v	ω
1	FAR	FAR	FAR	POS	ZERO
2	FAR	FAR	NEAR	POS	POS
3	FAR	NEAR	FAR	POS	POS
4	FAR	NEAR	NEAR	ZERO	POS
5	NEAR	FAR	FAR	POS	NEG
6	NEAR	FAR	NEAR	POS	ZERO
7	NEAR	NEAR	FAR	ZERO	NEG
8	NEAR	NEAR	NEAR	ZERO	NEG

Table 3. Hedge combination vectors

Vector	n	Behaviour	Input	Fuzzy set
$\mathbf{h}_{ganp}$	18	GS	ϕ	NEG, POS
$\mathbf{h}_{gaz}$	18	GS	ϕ	ZERO
$\mathbf{h}_{gdz}$	10	GS	d	ZERO
$\mathbf{h}_{gdf}$	10	GS	d	FAR
$\mathbf{h}_{lron}$	10	OA	s_1, s_3	NEAR
$\mathbf{h}_{lrof}$	10	OA	s_1, s_3	FAR
$\mathbf{h}_{fon}$	10	OA	s_2	NEAR
$\mathbf{h}_{fof}$	10	OA	s_2	FAR

where n is the number of membership function partitions. In this work, eight hedge combination vectors are defined (see Table 3), one for each unique fuzzy set defined in the input domains of the behaviours.

5 Non-linear Scaling Approaches

The linguistic hedge approach can be generalised by allowing the scaling factors to vary over a continuous range of values. This increases the flexibility of the membership function definitions at the cost of linguistic interpretability, since the choice of scaling factors are no longer tied to any linguistic meaning in the rule base. This trade-off is acceptable in this application as the information that the hedge terms add to the rule base is rarely useful to the designer.

Given that the minimum and maximum hedge values defined are $h_{min} = 0.25$ and $h_{max} = 4$ respectively, the shape of the membership functions can be tuned directly with nonlinear scaling factors $\eta \in [h_{min}, h_{max}]$ according to Equation 3. This configuration will be referred to as the NS configuration. The same upper and lower bounds are used in this work so that comparisons can be readily made with the hedge-modified controllers defined previously. In practice, η may vary over arbitrarily defined domains since it is not tied to any linguistic meaning in the rule base.

The PNS configuration is a generalization of the PLH, in which the hedge values in the hedge combination vector are replaced with scaling factors η_i, $i = 1, 2, \ldots, n$:

$$\eta = \begin{bmatrix} \eta_1 & \eta_2 & \cdots & \eta_n \end{bmatrix} \tag{4}$$

6 Optimisation by Genetic Algorithm

Some form of tuning process is required to ensure optimality in the controllers' performance, however due to the large number of search parameters, manual tuning will be laborious and time-consuming. It is for this reason that fuzzy logic researchers resort to automatic tuning or learning processes such as genetic algorithms (GA) and artificial neural networks (ANN) to optimize their fuzzy systems. Liu's original formulation of the LHFLC [8] utilized a simple GA process to tune the hedge combination vector. A similar GA tuning process is used to tune the controllers in this work.

6.1 Chromosome Representation

Each individual is uniquely defined by its chromosome, which is represented by a string of parameters. In this application, the chromosome consists of a concatenation of the hedge or non-linear scaling factor combination vectors defined for each fuzzy set. The parameters for the controllers that use discrete hedge values are integer encoded, while the non-linear scaling factors are directly represented in the chromosome as real values.

6.2 Genetic Operators

In addition to the standard single-point crossover and uniform mutation commonly used in the GA community, a specialised set of operators specifically designed for real-coded genetic algorithms (RCGA), namely the BLX-α operator [9] and Michalewicz's non-uniform mutation [10], is also utilised in this work to improve the convergence of the nonlinear scaling factor configurations. Configurations tuned with these operators are appended with the suffix "+RO" (e.g., PNS+RO). Individuals are selected by roulette wheel selection, where the probability of being selected is proportional to the fitness of the individual.

6.3 Fitness Function

The performance of the tuned robot behaviour hinges on the choice of an appropriate fitness function. The fitness function used in this implementation is composed of four weighted terms that represent the performance criteria:

$$F = w_{dg} \left(\frac{1}{d_{goal} + 1} \right) + b_{goal} \left(w_{dt} \frac{d_{shortest}}{d_{travelled}} + w_{lv} \frac{\text{mean}(v(t))}{\text{max}(v(t))} \right.$$
$$\left. + w_{av} \left(1 - \frac{\text{mean}(|\omega(t)|)}{\text{max}(|\omega(t)|)} \right) \right) \tag{5}$$

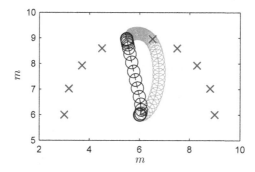

Fig. 3. Performance of the simple fuzzy controller (blue) and the tuned PNS controller (black) seeking a goal

The first fitness term is inversely proportional to the distance between the robot and the goal, d_{goal} at the end of the simulation. The second fitness term is the ratio of the shortest distance between the initial position of the robot and the goal, $d_{shortest}$, to the total distance travelled, $d_{travelled}$. This term rewards shorter routes. The third fitness term encapsulates the need for the robot to travel at high linear velocities, v, while the fourth fitness term is maximised as the average angular velocity of the robot, ω is minimised. Both velocities are normalised over their respective maximum values.

The binary value b_{goal} takes on a value of 1 if the robot has reached the goal within the simulation time limit, 0 otherwise. This provides a measure of fitness for sub-performing individuals in order to prevent the process from degenerating into purely random selection during the initial generations.

The weights w_{dg}, w_{dt}, w_{lv} and w_{av} are derived empirically. The purpose of the weights is to ensure that each fitness term contributes meaningfully to the total fitness. Additionally, a linear scaling operation is performed on the raw fitness values to improve convergence.

6.4 The Tuning Process

The fitness of a particular candidate solution is evaluated in a simulated environment. Optimisations for specific behaviours are performed in specially-designed virtual behaviour training environments. In the GS training courses, the robot starts from a known starting position and moves towards a single goal location in an obstacle-free environment. Figure 3 illustrates the goal locations of all ten virtual GS courses and the robot starting position.

Similarly, the OA training course involves the robot starting from a known starting location and moving towards the goal location in an obstacle-laden environment. There are twenty-two different configurations of such obstacles. In both cases, the main idea is to ensure robustness by designing training environments that cover the input spaces of the behaviour in training so that all possible contingencies are accounted for.

Table 4. Fitness values for the GS and OA behaviour training

	Fitness	
Configuration	GS	OA
LH	39.901089	78.492683
PLH	38.405203	86.712051
NS	39.498143	86.809951
PNS	37.580772	86.528802
PLH+S	40.253967	86.534865
PNS+S	39.835109	87.269635
PNS+S+RO	40.507373	87.048719

Since both the PLH and PNS controllers have high-dimensional search spaces, two additional configurations that attempt to improve convergence are included. By seeding the initial population of the PLH and PNS controllers with the final generations of the tuned LH and NS configurations respectively, the search can be localised to a smaller search area at the cost of exploratory ability. These configurations are appended with the suffix "+S" in this work (e.g., PLH+S).

In all cases, the two fittest individuals in each generation are preserved and carried over to the next generation as a form of elitism. The population consists of a constant size of 100 individuals, and the tuning process is performed for 60 generations.

7   Results

The results for the GS and OA training are given in Table 4. The table lists the fitness values of the best performing solution in each configuration.

In general, the LH and NS configurations converge more readily to higher fitness levels than the PLH and PNS configurations due to their lower dimensionality. The performance of the PLH and PNS configurations are slightly improved by introducing the initial population seeds. The similarity in the fitness levels indicate that any of the configurations introduced in this work are viable techniques for improving FLC performance, however in general the best performance is achieved with the PNS controller–particularly when it is tuned with the seed and RCGA operators.

Figure 3 illustrates the performance of a simple fuzzy controller and the tuned PNS controller seeking a goal at $+100°$ relative to its starting position. The simple controller used here is defined by the behaviour described in the rule base in Table 1, with no scaling performed on the fuzzy set definitions. The trajectory of the robot with the simple fuzzy controller illustrates a fundamental issue with the controller, in that the robot is unable to reach the goal under the time limit of the simulation. In contrast, the performance of the tuned PNS GS controller introduced in this work shows that the robot is able to consistently converge to

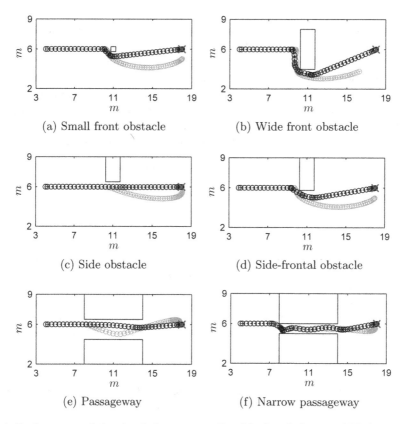

(a) Small front obstacle

(b) Wide front obstacle

(c) Side obstacle

(d) Side-frontal obstacle

(e) Passageway

(f) Narrow passageway

Fig. 4. Performance of the simple fuzzy controller (blue) and the tuned PNS controller (black) in selected OA training courses

each goal location. The simulation results also indicate that the robot achieves higher linear velocities and travels across shorter distances on average.

Figure 4 illustrates the differences in performance between the simple and the PNS controller in the OA training courses. The robot trajectories show that the PNS consistently outperforms the simple FLC, in that the robot is able to reach the goal location under the simulation time limit in all cases. Figure 7 and 7 in particular show that the simple FLC is too sensitive to obstacles in the periphery of its perceptive region.

The results show that membership function scaling mechanisms provide an avenue for designers to improve the performance of simple FLCs for fuzzy mobile robot behaviours without further partitioning of the fuzzy input domains or inclusion of new rules.

8 Conclusions

This work has shown that input membership function scaling allows a designer to construct fuzzy logic controllers for demonstrably operational robot navigation behaviours with very small rule bases. Three of the four proposed techniques offer large performance gains over the basic FLCs they operate on, in that they allow the robot to complete all the training courses. Of the three, piecewise non-linear scaling offers the largest performance gain by a small margin, subject to the efficiency of the optimisation process. Future work can be done in this area by considering other tunable aspects of the controller, such as the membership function parameters or rule weighting.

References

1. Saffiotti, A.: The Uses of Fuzzy Logic in Autonomous Robot Navigation. Soft Computing 1(4), 180–197 (1997)
2. Aguirre, E., González, A.: Fuzzy Behaviours for Mobile Robot Navigation: Design, Coordination and Fusion. International Journal of Approximate Reasoning 25(3), 255–289 (2000)
3. Parasuraman, S., Ganapathy, V., Shirinzadeh, B.: Mobile Robot Navigation Using Alpha Level Fuzzy Logic System: Experimental Investigations. In: 2008 IEEE International Conference on Systems, Man and Cybernetics, Singapore, pp. 1878–1884 (2008)
4. Maaref, H., Barret, C.: Sensor-Based Navigation of a Mobile Robot in an Indoor Environment. Robotics and Autonomous Systems 38, 1–18 (2002)
5. Yang, X., Moallem, M., Patel, R.: A Sensor-Based Navigation Algorithm for a Mobile Robot Using Fuzzy Logic. International Journal of Robotics and Automation 21, 129–140 (2006)
6. Alcalá, R., Alcalá-Fdez, J., Casillas, J., Cordón, O., Herrera, F.: Hybrid Learning Models to Get the Interpretability-Accuracy Trade-Off in Fuzzy Modeling. Soft Computing 10(9), 717–734 (2005)
7. Samsudin, K., Ahmad, F., Mashohor, S.: A Highly Interpretable Fuzzy Rule Base Using Ordinal Structure for Obstacle Avoidance of Mobile Robot. Applied Soft Computing 11(2), 1631–1637 (2011)
8. Liu, B., Chen, C., Tsao, J.: Design of Adaptive Fuzzy Logic Controller Based on Linguistic-Hedge Concepts and Genetic Algorithms. IEEE Transactions on Systems, Man, and Cybernetics, Part B: Cybernetics 31(1), 32–53 (2001)
9. Eshelman, L., Schaffer, J.: Real-Coded Genetic Algorithms and Interval-Schemata. Foundation of Genetic Algorithms 2, 187–202 (1993)
10. Michalewicz, Z.: Genetic Algorithms + Data Structures = Evolution Programs. Springer, London (1996)

Adaptive Speed Control for Autonomous Mobile Robot Using Fuzzy Logic Controller

Hamzah Ahmad*, Wan Nur Diyana Wan Mustafa, and
Mohd Rusllim Mohamed

Faculty of Electrical & Electronics Engineering,
Universiti Malaysia Pahang 26000 Pekan, Pahang,
Malaysia
{hamzah,rusllim}@ump.edu.my, wandiyanamustafa@gmail.com,
http://fkee.ump.edu.my/

Abstract. This paper deals with the development of an adaptive speed controller for autonomous mobile robot using a fuzzy logic controller.The analysis of performance between a system applying triangular membership and a system using gaussian membership is compared to distinguish their differences. The results have shown that the gaussian membership method has improved the tracking performance for the mobile robot to reach its target. This also suggest the same behavior even when a different mobile robot movements is assigned. This paper considers three, five and seven memberships for both techniques to determine their effectiveness and effects to the system performance. The investigation has leads to the conclusion that the gaussian membership has competently surpassed the triangular membership performances even when the robot has different movements to achieve its target.

Keywords: Fuzzy Logic, speed control, mobile robot, membership.

1 Introduction

Navigation always comes as the main issue in pursuing a real autonomous mobile robot behavior. Solving the navigation problem also means that mobile robot can move effectively to achieve its assigned task even if the environment is unknown or has unpredictable conditions. Navigation includes a simple task where a mobile robot only identifies itself location in an environment to a higher degree of complexity where a mobile robot is required to localize itself and maps its surrounding simultaneously such as reported in various research[1–3].

In deciding how to control a mobile robots effectively, a number of approaches have been proposed by using artificial intelligence system such as neural networks, fuzzy logic, and genetic algorithm. Between those techniques, fuzzy logic can be the best candidates for navigation[4–7] as it requires less computational cost, do not need training or iterations and have almost the same performance to any of available methods. Hence, the processing time can be shorten.

---

* Corresponding author.

S.G. Ponnambalam et al. (Eds.): IRAM 2012, CCIS 330, pp. 67–74, 2012.
© Springer-Verlag Berlin Heidelberg 2012

The research on fuzzy logic for mobile robot has been immensely proposed since two decades ago. Vamsi et al.[8] have developed a fuzzy logic controller to control the robot motion along a predefined path. They found that if the Fuzzy Logic is appropriately being designed, then it could give better performance of convergence. Another work were reported by M.K Singh et al. whose proposed a fuzzy control scheme that considered two inputs of the mobile robot which are the heading angle and the relative distance between mobile robot and any landmark. The study considered three different scenario of environment, and are analyzed both by simulation and experiments to determine the consistency of their proposed technique. A study on the effect of different fuzzy sets membership to the mobile robot navigation also has been proposed by R.Rashid et al[9]. They suggested the designer must choose the fewer membership in the fuzzy logic controller to achieve better and faster time reaching a target. They used triangular membership function to demonstrate their results as it is the commonly applied membership used for analysis. This result is acceptable as if fewer membership are applied then the processing time will be reduced which finally result in faster time of task completion.

Regarding the membership type used in Fuzzy Logic, other choices than the triangular membership are available such as the gaussian membership, trapezoid membership or sigmoid membership. As explained above, researcher usually applies the triangular membership as it is seems to be easier than other membership. Even if this is the factor, there were also some other findings that discovered very interesting results as shown by V.O.S Olunloyo et al.[10]. Based on their findings, the triangular membership can exhibit linguistic error as it may not defines properly the real system conditions. As a result, the gaussian membership can be the best membership to describe any practical system for most engineering application. Moreover, gaussian membership may surpassed triangular membership function if better tracking performance is being prioritized[11].

This work attempts to discuss the performance of a mobile robot using the Fuzzy Logic controller that incorporates the gaussian membership for mobile robot decision. Simulation setting in [9] is referred for verification and comparison to validate the performance between triangular and gaussian memberships. Gaussian membership is chosen as it correlates fairly fuzzy set and approximates the human sense.

The remaining of this paper is organized as follows. Section II described the mobile robot kinematics. Next section III, explains the fuzzy controller design which use the gaussian membership to present the fuzzy sets. This is followed by section IV that discusses the simulation results of the fuzzy logic controller for three different cases of gaussian memberships. Finally, section V concludes our paper.

2   Mobile Robot Kinematics

A mobile robot with two wheels is considered in this paper. With reference to the Instantaneous Center of Curvature (ICC), the mobile robot will only moves based on one axis for rotation purposes. Figure 1 is explains the kinematic structure

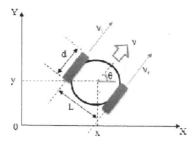

Fig. 1. Mobile robot kinematic

of a mobile robot that consists of the velocity of the mobile robot v; v_l, v_r are for the left wheel and right wheel respectively. The diameter of the mobile robot is d and L is the distance between two wheels. x, y constitutes the x, y positions of the mobile robot respectively. /$theta$ is the mobile robot heading angle.

The mobile robot right and left velocities are provided as follows.

$$v_r = \frac{d}{2}\omega_r, \quad \frac{d}{2}\omega_l \tag{1}$$

$$\omega = \frac{v_r - v_l}{L}, \quad v = \frac{v_r + v_l}{L} \tag{2}$$

where ω_r, ω_l are the right and left wheel angular velocities. From above equations, the following are obtained.

$$\omega = \frac{d}{2L}(\omega_r - \omega_l) \tag{3}$$

$$v = \frac{d}{4}(\omega_r + \omega_l) \tag{4}$$

Using above information and notations, the mobile robot velocity v can be divided to its respective axis of x and y frames i.e v_x and v_y. The angular acceleration ϕ can also be derived from those equations and is shown as follows.

$$v_x = v \cos \theta, \quad v_y = v \sin \theta, \quad \phi = \omega \tag{5}$$

According to the above information, now it is possible to determine the x, y, θ of the mobile robot.

$$x = \int_0^t v(t) \cos \theta(t) dt \tag{6}$$

$$y = \int_0^t v(t) \sin \theta(t) dt \tag{7}$$

$$\theta = \int_0^t \omega(t) dt \tag{8}$$

Alternatively, (6),(7) and (8) can be represented by

$$
\begin{bmatrix} v_x \\ v_y \\ \theta \end{bmatrix} = \begin{bmatrix} \cos\theta & 0 \\ \sin\theta & 0 \\ 0 & 1 \end{bmatrix} \begin{bmatrix} v \\ \omega \end{bmatrix}
$$
$$
= \begin{bmatrix} \frac{(v_r+v_l)\cos\theta}{2} \\ \frac{(v_r+v_l)\cos\theta}{2} \\ \frac{(v_r-v_l)\cos\theta}{2} \end{bmatrix} \tag{9}
$$

Equation (9) described the kinematic model of the mobile robot. The associated noises to the robot motion are also required to be considered as this will be effecting the performance of the mobile robot during position and orientation acquisition.

3   Fuzzy Logic Controller Design

Fuzzy Logic Controller (FLC) is designed to control the nonholonomic mobile robot in providing the suitable velocities on both wheels. Our approach is similar to R.Rashid et al. This is made purposely to ease the comparison between our results and their results. The inputs of the FLC are the angle and distance error between mobile robot and any objects found during mobile robot observations. In this paper, the mobile robot must follow the wall in a pre-determined range as well as to avoid collision. The FLC generates the right and left wheels angular velocity for the output. The heading angle is defined such that if robot turn left, then the heading angle is negative. This definition is used for our evaluation presented in section IV later. The designed Fuzzy Logic is comprises of three general procedures as follows.

1. Fuzzification

   In this step, the inputs are classified to the identified fuzzy sets i.e for the far, medium, near for the distance error fuzzy and negative, zero, positive for the angle. The fuzzy sets values of the fuzzy variables are defined in Table 1.

2. Creating Fuzzy Rules

   This step explains the fuzzy rules design for our system. The fuzzy rules which associated to Table 1 are not included as it defines the same descriptions as presented by Rashid et al.

3. Defuzzification

   This step computes the output (angular velocity) of the fuzzy logic. Mamdani technique is used and the output is calculated through MATLAB Simulink environment. Based on the given output, mobile robot then moves accordingly until it reach its target.

Table 1. Fuzzy Logic : Fuzzy sets Input

Angle Error	Dist. error
Negative	Far
Zero	Medium
Positive	Near

4 Preliminary Results and Discussions

Gaussian membership is proposed in this paper for the mobile robot to make its decision. This method is proposed referring to the claims that the membership can considered as more practical than the triangular membership. To determine and evaluates the results, performance between a model that used the triangular membership and a model which applies the gaussian membership function is presented. The analysis are also considers the effect of increasing number of membership to the mobile robot tracking;3 memberships, 5 memberships and 7 memberships cases. In this simulation, the mobile robot is randomly placed in an unknown environment and assigned to follow a wall until it has reached its target. Remark that, this performance is not considering any sensors failures as such situation may exhibits system error and collisions.

Based on figure 2 for 3 memberships condition, the gaussian membership has exhibits better tracking movements than the triangular membership. A different mobile robot movements case was also examined using the same simulation settings in figure 3. As illustrated in these figures, the results have positively supported our claims. Similar performance have also been identified for the case of 5 and 7 memberships as shown in figure 4 and figure 5 respectively. Again, compared to triangular membership, it is clear that gaussian memberships is able to guarantee better solutions than the triangular membership.

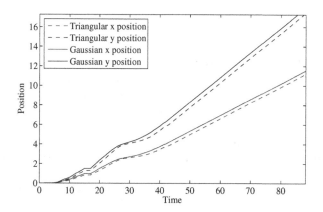

Fig. 2. Comparison between 3 triangular membership function and 3 gaussian memberships function for mobile robot x,y positions

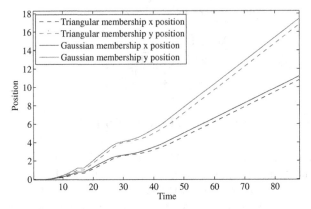

Fig. 3. Comparison between 3 triangular membership function and 3 gaussian memberships function for mobile robot x,y positions with different mobile robot movements

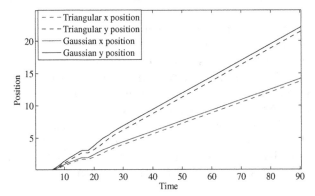

Fig. 4. Comparison between 5 triangular memberships function and 5 gaussian memberships function for mobile robot x,y positions

Through those figures, it can be explained that the gaussian membership could offer a better choice for navigation than the triangular membership. We also noticed that, in the case of gaussian membership, if more membership is being applied to the system, then the mobile robot achieved better tracking result. Interestingly, the performance seems to arrive at its maximum performances when the system has 7 memberships. Even if this is the case, we still perceived the very same results proposed above i.e more membership is preferable for tracking purpose in Gaussian membership case. In fact, the result of using triangular membership also support our claims that if more membership are being assigned, then the mobile robot shows better tracking. Our results also supports what has previous findings in [11] suggested that the gaussian membership is suitable for better tracking performance in comparison to the triangular membership.

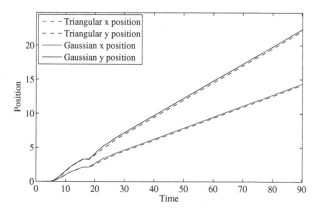

Fig. 5. Comparison between 7 triangular memberships function and 7 gaussian memberships function for mobile robot x,y positions

5 Conclusion

This paper proposed the study of different membership function for FLC in a mobile robot application. The results have shown that, the gaussian membership function can delivers better and good tracking performance for the mobile robot. Besides, we discovered that if more membership is applied in the fuzzy sets, then the mobile robot could perform the best tracking performance. However, based on the analysis, there are not much changes if the membership function has more than 5 memberships.

Acknowledgment. This projects is sponsored by University Malaysia Pahang under RDU110381.

References

1. Ahmad, H., Namerikawa, T.: Robot Localization and Mapping Problem with Unknown Noise Characteristics. In: 2010 IEEE Multi-conference on Systems and Control, Japan, pp. 1275–1280 (2010)
2. Huang, S., Dissayanake, G.: Convergence and consistency Analysis for Extended Kalman Filter Based SLAM. IEEE Transaction on Robotics 23(5), 1036–1049 (2007)
3. Ahmad, H., Namerikawa, T.: Measurement in Robotic Localization and Mapping with Intermittent FIM Statistical Bound. IEEJ Transaction on Electronics, Information and Systems, Section C 131(5) Sec.C, (2011)
4. Xie, T.T., Yu, H., Wilamowski, B.M.: Comparison of Fuzzy and Neural Systems for Implementation of Nonlinear Control Surfaces. Advances in Intelligent and Soft Computing 99, 313–324 (2012)

5. Joshi, P., Valasek, J.: Direct Comparison of Neural Network, Fuzzy Logic and Model Predictive Variable Structure Vortex Flow Controllers. In: AIAA-99-4279-CP, Proceedings of the AIAA Guidance, Navigation and Control Conference, Portland (1999)
6. Majidiana, A., Saidi, M.H.: Comparison of Fuzzy Logic and Neural Network in life prediction of boiler tubes. International Journal of Fatigue 29(3), 489–498 (2007)
7. Kanta, A.-F., Montavon, G., Vardelle, M., Planche, M.-P., Berndt, C.C., Coddet, C.: Artificial Neural Networks vs. FuzzyLogic: Simple Tools to Predict and Control Complex Processes Application to Plasma Spray Processes. Journal of Thermal Spray Technology 17(3), 365–376 (2008)
8. Peri, V., Simon, D.: Fuzzy Logic Control for an Autonomous Mobile Robot. In: North American Fuzzy Information Processing Society Conference, Ann Arbor, MI, pp. 337–342 (2005)
9. Singh, M.K., Parhi, D.R., Bhowmik, S., Kashyap, S.K.: Intelligent Controller for Mobile Robot: Fuzzy Logic Approach. In: 12th International Conference of International Association for Computer Methods and Advances in Geomechanics, IACMAG (2008)
10. Olunloyo, V.O.S., Ajofoyinbo, A.M., Ibidapo-Obe, O.: On Development of Fuzzy Controller: The Case of Gaussian and Triangular Membership Functions. Journal of Signal and Information Processing 2, 257–265 (2011)
11. Green, A., Sasiadek, J.Z.: Heuristic design of a fuzzy controller for a flexible robot. IEEE Transactions on Control Systems Technology 14(2), 293–300 (2006)

A Braitenberg Approach to Mobile Robot Navigation in Unknown Environments

Mohsen Shayestegan and Mohammad Hamiruce Marhaban

Faculty of Engineering, Electrical and Electronic Department,
Universiti Putra Malaysia, 43400 UPM, Serdang, Selangor, Malaysia
mohsen_sh1361@hotmail.com

Abstract. In this paper a new approach is developed for a two-wheeled mobile robot to navigate smoothly in unknown environments. This approach uses the ideas of Braitenberg strategy. The strategy is reactive when it perceives the sensory information and uses online path navigation. Furthermore, an algorithm called switching command strategy (SCS) has been developed in which the navigation method provides simple, efficient and effective motion path. The SCS is applied in order for the robot to skip out from a "dead cycle" problem. The algorithm is constructed for doing two principal tasks. The first task is reaching the goal safely in stationary environment while avoiding the static objects and the second task is to navigate in dynamic and complex environment by mobile robot while avoiding moving objects. During the experiments, a simple obstacle avoidance has been extensively tested with various static and dynamic environments. The results of the study showed the efficiency and enhanced performance of the navigation algorithm.

Keywords: Local navigation, Braitenberg strategy, Static environment, Dynamic environment, Local minimum problem.

1   Introduction

The mobile robot should have an ability to reach a target from its initial position without any collision by sensing its environment for real time navigation [1]. Some of the path-planning approaches include the virtual target method [2], wall following approach [3], fuzzy and neural network [4-7]. The above-mentioned approaches have been designed for static environments and extended to environments with moving objects. However, these methods do not perform well in dynamic environments and have a good performance in static environments [8, 9]. The earliest approaches have been developed to detect collisions and safely navigate in dynamic environments where they consider an obstacle with constant speed that moves at linear direction [10-12]. Recently, various sensor based approaches have been designed for navigation in dynamic environments [13]. Since the introduction of the Braitenberg strategy which is a sensor based approach [14], it has been used for mobile robot navigation in a number of researches including a goal seeking approach using vehicle 3a [15], Fuzzy Braitenberg controller using 2b and 3a [16], wall following and obstacle avoidance using vehicle 3b [17], and navigation and collision avoidance [18].

The above-mentioned methods are limited to static environments and there is no guarantee to work in unknown environments. On the other hand, some of them are

S.G. Ponnambalam et al. (Eds.): IRAM 2012, CCIS 330, pp. 75–93, 2012.

limited to dynamic environments with constant speed and linear motion. In this paper, two main issues are addressed, namely local mobile navigation in static environment even escaping from local minimum avoidance and capability of avoiding dynamic obstacles in an unknown environment. The proposed method in this study can be used in a mobile robot which moves in an unknown environment.

2   Navigation Law and Obstacle Avoidance

2.1   Reactive Obstacle Avoidance

The idea used in this study is taken from Braitenberg's Vehicles 2 and 3 as these two vehicles have two sensors and two motors (see Figures 1 and 2). There are different connections in their sensors and their motors, and the sensor of each of the vehicles (2a and 3a) is connected to the motor on the same side (direct-connection). The sensor connections in the vehicles 2b and 3b are on the opposite side (crossed-connection). Nevertheless, '+' in the diagrams shows the higher the readings of the sensor, the faster the motor runs while '-' shows the higher the readings, the slower the motor runs. Moreover, 'S' illustrates which source can be detected by the sensors. The configuration of Vehicle 2 used the source directly with both vehicles hitting the source and deflecting away. Figures 1 and 2 show that when the source is one sided, the closer sensor to the source becomes excited with the corresponding motor that is running faster, while another motor turns away from the source. The configuration of Vehicle 3 reveals that vehicle 3a which is on an oblique course gets oriented and slows down, gets nearer to the source, produces a turn and comes to rest while facing the source. Though vehicle 3b can rest facing the source, it can equally drift away especially when it is sourced from the original [16]. The Braitenberg's vehicles could be related to the problems in the sense that vehicles 2a and 3b can serve the purpose of obstacle avoidance. However, vehicle 3b can be used for solving the problem of collision avoidance for front and side obstacles. Mobile robot can safely slow down and avoid obstacles with the help of the vehicle 2a. Figures 1 and 2 illustrate the navigation scheme for a differential drive mobile robot with the sensors detecting obstacles in negative crossed-connections. Vehicle 3b is used to reveal that the sensors detect obstacles despite the propinquity of the robot with motor being slower on the opposite side. The vehicle 2a is equally used to reveal that sensors at the back of the robot are in positive direct-connection with the motors, whereas the object which is closer to the robot on the rear makes the motor to be faster. This makes the robot avoid collisions with the rear objects [16]. These strategies will be used in the following equations to detect the obstacles.

The connection between the actuators and sensors has been proven to solve mobile robot behavior to navigate [14]. Based upon the Braitenberg's vehicles theory which is shown in Figures 1 and 2, it can be understood that for the purposes of avoiding collision, the vehicles 3b and 2a are appropriate. Obviously, in vehicle 3b theory, the slower movement toward the obstacles is safer than faster movement toward them. It is also suggested that the front and side sensors should have negative connection with measurement sensors which cause the slower motion on the opposite side. Rear sensors have positive connection with the actuators in vehicle 2a theory. This means that measuring rear sensors causes faster motion on the same side of the robot [16].

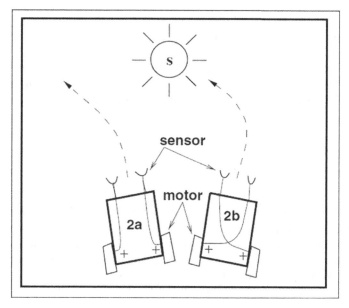

Fig. 1. Two types of Braitenberg's Vehicles 2 near a source [16]

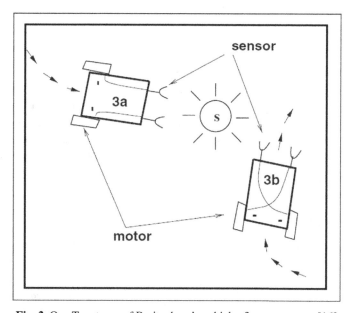

Fig. 2. One Two types of Braitenberg's vehicles 3 near a source [16]

The effect of sensors values on the velocity of each wheel is indicated via the following equation:

$$v_s = f(\sum_{1}^{n} \omega_i \times d_i) \tag{1}$$

Where ω_i, d_i are the weight and sensor values and f is the maximum velocity function of the wheels. Generally, the weight values are unknown and depend on the problem features [18].

The equation below shows the active function of robot sensors. It is a clear front sensor that has a higher active value because of sensors angle (β_i) from robot heading direction. The active function of the robot sensor is shown in:

$$\omega_i = k_1 \times e^{-\frac{d_i}{k_2}} \times e^{-\frac{\beta_i^2}{2 \times \sigma^2}}$$

$$d_i = 1 - \frac{r_i}{r_{max}}$$

(2)

When k_1 is the overall strength, k_2 is the rate of decay, and d_i is normalized distance between the robot and obstacle [15]. The activation sensors values are considered between zero and one to normalize sensors' values. Obviously, when the robot faces an obstacle in front should turn more than the obstacle in its side of the robot. From effect of target angle when the robot faces with an obstacle, it is considering that the activation of this angle to smoother navigation. The overall active function will be as follows:

$$\varphi_s = \sum_{i=1}^{n_l} \omega_{il} \times (\frac{r_i}{r_{max}}) - \sum_{i=1}^{n_r} \omega_{ir} \times (\frac{r_i}{r_{max}})$$

(3)

$$\varphi_{sl} = \sum_{i=1}^{n_l} \omega_{il} \times (\frac{r_i}{r_{max}})$$

(4)

When φ_s is a repulsive force to avoiding obstacles, r_{max} is maximum ranges, and r_i is a measurement range sensor. The φ_{sl} and φ_{sr} depend on eight sensors that are connected to left wheel and right wheel, respectively. If the obstacle be at the right side, in the equation 4, the sensors 1, 2 and 3 have negative values and other sensors have positive values. Otherwise, if the obstacle be at the left side, in the equation 5, the sensors 6, 7 and 8 have negative values and other sensors have positive values. From equation 2, each sensor has a different value depending on the angle and distance of the obstacle from the robot.

2.2   The Target Seeking Control Law

The attractive force to reaching to the goal is defined in the following equation:

$$\gamma_g = (1 - e^{-p}) \times e^{\alpha - 1}$$

(6)

Note that $-1 \leq \alpha \leq 1$, γ_g is normalized and $0 \leq \gamma_g \leq 1$. From Braitenberg strategy, the attractive force value for velocity of robot would be with positive value.

2.3   The Overall Control Algorithm

Figure 3 shows the robot's configuration with eight infrared sensors that can be controlled by left and right linear velocity as the objective in safely navigation is that the robot moves toward reaching the goal. From the potential field method, in the proposed method, the resultant force on the left and right velocity of the robot is defined as follows:

$$F_l = w_1 \times (1 - e^{-p}) \times e^{\alpha - 1} + w_2 \times \varphi_{sl},$$
$$F_r = w_1 \times (1 - e^{-p}) \times e^{-\alpha - 1} + w_2 \times \varphi_{sr} \tag{7}$$

The weighting values w_1 and w_2 indicate the ratio between attractive and repulsive forces. Note that $0 \leq w_1, w2 \leq 1$ and $w_1 + w_2 = 1$. Therefore, the whole control law can be defined as follow:

$$v_l = k \times F_l \times v_{max},$$
$$v_r = k \times F_r \times v_{max} \tag{8}$$

"k" is the gain value of velocity of the robot.

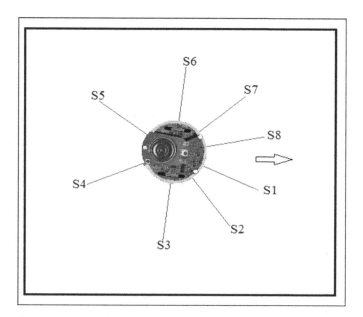

Fig. 3. The e-puck robot with 8 infrared sensors

2.4   Switching Command

Although typical navigator technique may simplify navigation problems, there are situations in local work space where a reactive approach fails in taking appropriate action. Of these troublesome situations, obstacles forming a loop shape also called dead-end traps are the most common. The local minimum situation occurs when a robot navigating past obstacles toward a target with no prior knowledge of the

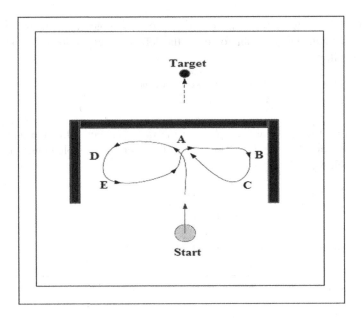

Fig. 4. The local minimum problem

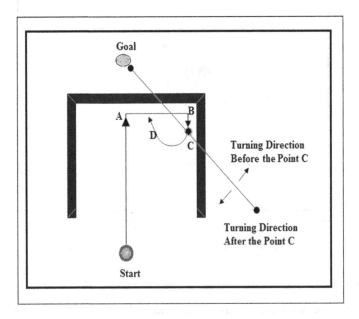

Fig. 5. Robot behavior at the point C

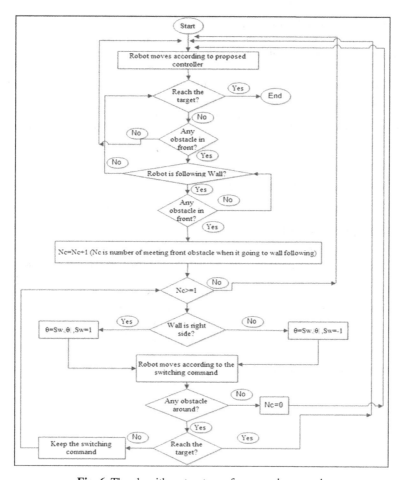

Fig. 6. The algorithm structure of proposed approach

environment gets trapped in a loop. This happens if the environment consists of concave obstacles. Moreover, Figure 4 shows a robot getting trapped in a U-shape dead-end. Here, typical controller that is performed for target attractor and obstacle repulsor modules give output actions that neutralize each other. Therefore, the robot gets into an infinite loop or local minimum. Initially the robot moves directly toward the target due to its target seeking behavior up to the point "A" where the robot detects an obstacle at the direct front. Then it makes a right turn due to obstacle avoidance behavior which results to wall following until the robot reaches the point "C". This is because until this point, both the target and the obstacle are at the left-hand side of the robot. However, as the robot is passing by point "C", the target is going to be at the right-hand side of the robot, while the obstacle is still located at the left-hand side. Therefore, at point "D", the robot goes back toward the target due to both target seeking and obstacle avoidance behaviors. The result of this behavior is that the robot wanders indefinitely in the dead-end trap called the limit cycle problem or local minimum [19].

From Figure 5, it can be found that the point "C" is critical point resulting in the "dead end" path. At this point, if the robot can go straight instead of turning left, the problem may be resolved. Without changing the designed controller, in the second wall, if the robot can assume the sign of the target angle change to opposite sign (in point "C" the target is in positive sign, so the robot considers the negative sign), the robot will go straight and try to pass the obstacles. Based upon this idea, an assistant switching command strategy as is shown in equation 9 is considered for the system. The overall algorithm to robot navigation in an environment is shown in Figure 6.

$$F_l = w_1 \times (1 - e^{-p}) \times e^{Sw \times (|\alpha| - 1)} + w_2 \times \varphi_{sl},$$

$$F_r = w_1 \times (1 - e^{-p}) \times e^{-Sw \times (|\alpha| - 1)} + w_2 \times \varphi_{sr} \tag{9}$$

3   Simulation Result

The performance of the proposed technique was shown using the e-puck at two wheeled mobile robot in Webots software with MATLAB programming. The demonstration in Figure 3 shows that the e-puck is equipped with eight infrared sensors. The difference between robot heading angle, sensor 1 and sensor 8 is 16 degrees, whereas the difference recorded in sensors 2 and 7 is 45 degrees, with sensors 3 and 6 is 90 degrees while sensors 4 and 5 have 150 degrees different angle.

By considering the maximum value $e^{-\frac{\beta_i^2}{2 \times \sigma^2}} = 0.99$ for sensors 1 and 8, the value of σ is given equal to 0.44 because the most dangerous situation is when the obstacle is in front of the robot. By replacing the σ for other sensors, the values of each of them are

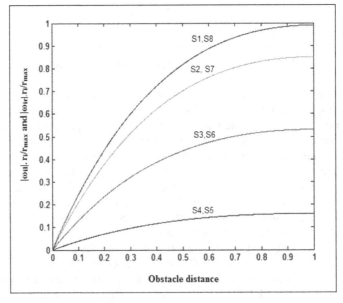

Fig. 7. The relationship between the $\omega_i \times (r_i / r_{max})$ and the obstacle distance

specified in tables below. After numerous tests in simulation to find the values of k_1 and k_2 in equation 2, the value of them is considered 1. The relationship between the $\omega_i \times (r_i / r_{max})$ and the obstacle distance is shown in Figure 7.

Table 1. The sensors value for φ_{sl}

Sensor 1	Sensor 2	Sensor 3	Sensor 4	Sensor 5	Sensor 6	Sensor 7	Sensor 8
- 0.99	-0.85	-0.53	0.16	0.16	0.53	0.85	0.99

Table 2. The sensors value for φ_{sr}

Sensor 1	Sensor 2	Sensor 3	Sensor 4	Sensor 5	Sensor 6	Sensor 7	Sensor 8
0.99	0.85	0.53	0.16	0.16	-0.53	-0.85	-0.99

3.1 Navigation in Static Environment

Different examples have been presented to illustrate the performance of the mobile robot in various unknown environments. The three behaviors of the robot (goal seeking, collision avoidance and wall following) in simulation results show the capability of the controller in safe navigation. One of the simulation results is shown in Figure 8. It shows the successfully navigation in an environment with randomized static obstacles with different shapes. The result also shows that the robot seeks the target in static environment, with the effectiveness of proposed approach, and it was validated with numerous simulation tests.

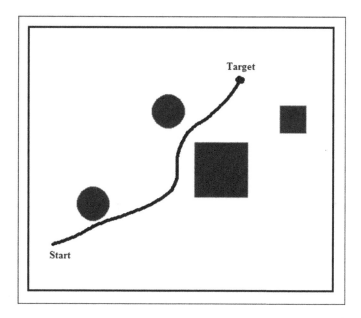

Fig. 8. The path of mobile robot in environment with randomly static obstacle

3.2   Navigation in Static Environment with Dead End Trap

The most famous example is u-shape obstacle that is tested in this study. The case in Figure 9 shows the mobile robot navigation when its trajectory is from position

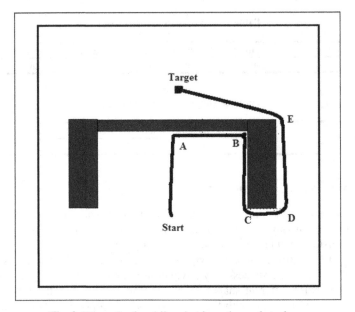

Fig. 9. The path of mobile robot in u-shape obstacle

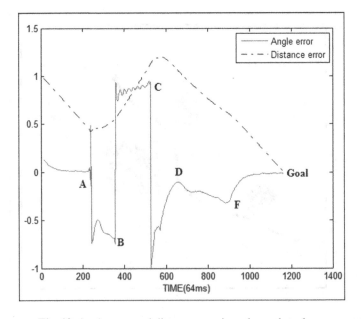

Fig. 10. Angle error and distance error in u-shape obstacle

"start"->A->B->C->D->E to the goal position. Figure 10 shows the angle error and distance error of the robot during its trajectory. Basically, the robot moves toward the

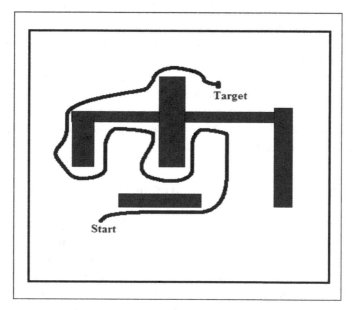

Fig. 11. The path of mobile robot in complex environment

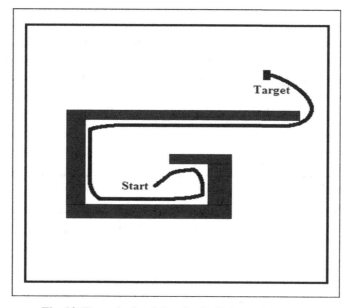

Fig. 12. The path of mobile robot in G-shape obstacle

target and reaches the point "A" with zero angle's error and then turns right to avoid the obstacle and follows the wall to reach the point "B". At this point, the robot turns to the right and follows the wall until reaches the point "C" according to its switching command. At the end of the wall, the robot turns to the left at the angle of 90 degrees and turns again to the left with the new angle of 90 degrees at the point "D", and follows the wall until reaches the point of "F". At this point, the robot turns toward the target and moves with the zero angle error until it reaches the final goal. In other cases (Figures 11 and 12), in different dead cycle obstacles, the robot has the same performance to avoid obstacles and follows the wall until it reaches the goal position. The simulation results show that the robot can reach a goal position from an initial position with different dead cycle obstacles.

4   Navigation in Dynamic Environment

Various simulation examples have been tested for the efficiency of the mobile robot performance in a dynamic environment with moving objects. In the simulation, we assume that the velocity of obstacles is half of the velocity of the robot. The simulation results are shown in figures where the robot avoids moving obstacles and reaches the goal smoothly for all of the situations. Figure 13 shows that an object is coming with linear motion from the right side of the robot to cross the robot trajectory. Obviously, the robot changes its direction and moves faster to over tacking of the moving object. When the robot reaches a safe region, it starts to move toward the goal position. Figure14 illustrates that the robot avoids two obstacles with nonlinear motion by changing its direction to safe region and moving toward the target with no collision. Figure15 demonstrates the high dynamic environment with objects, which are moved with linear and nonlinear motion, where the robot avoids obstacles without collision, and reaches the goal position. All details in these cases are illustrated in Table3. The obtained results present the effectiveness of proposed method.

Table 3.   The results of navigation in dynamic environment

No. obstacle	Tests	Collision	Time (second)	Success Navigation	Reliability
1	20	0	12:432	20	100%
2	20	0	13:311	20	100%
4	20	4	16:678	16	80%
10	20	6	22:292	14	70%

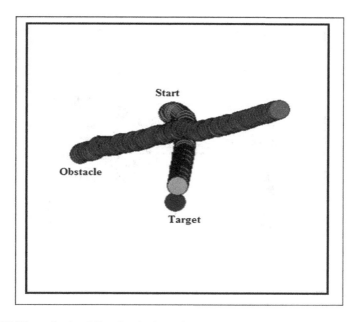

Fig. 13. The path of mobile robot in dynamic environment with one moving object

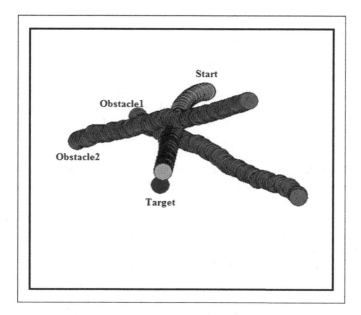

Fig. 14. The path of mobile robot in dynamic environment with two moving objects

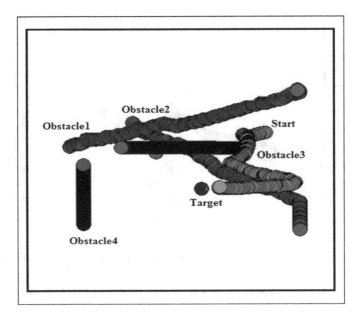

Fig. 15. The path of mobile robot in dynamic environment with four moving obstacles

5   Comparison

5.1   Comparison in Dynamic and Static Environments

The performance of the proposed method was compared to the performance of the Potential Field Method [20]. In Potential Field Method, it is assumed that the mobile robot moves under the effect of two potential field forces. The attractive force generated by the target attracts the robot to the position of the target. The other force is the repulsive force generated by the obstacles that moves the robot away from the obstacles. The mobile robot moves under the sum of these two forces.

As it can be noticed from the Potential Field Method, the repulsive force is greater than or equals to the attractive force where the target and obstacle get closer to the robot, so the robot will take away from the target or stops. Figure 16 shows the robot path whether the robot and the target are on the same line, and two obstacles are between the robot and the target. By using the Potential Field Method, the robot turns around the obstacle and changes its location and gets away from the path to the target (see Figure 16 (a)). On the other hand, the proposed Braitenberg approach does not suffer from such a problem.

As Figure 16 (b) shows, the robot moves in a straight line until it reaches the target. It can be concluded that the robot using the proposed method can deal with this difficult situation and reaches the target through the shortest path. Moreover, the proposed Braitenberg approach is more efficient than the Potential Field Method.

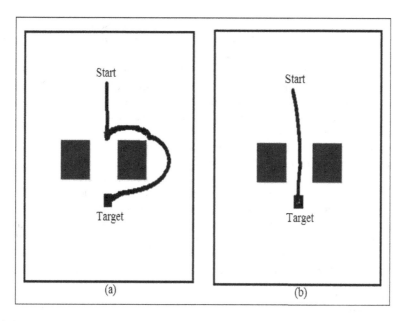

Fig. 16. Comparison of the Potential Field Method (a) and the proposed Braitenberg method (b)

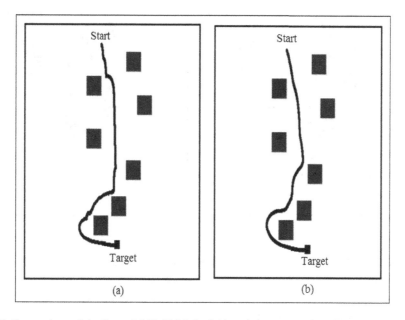

Fig. 17. Comparison of the Potential Field Method (a) and the proposed method (b) in a static environment

Figure 17 shows the result of the robot navigation with only seven static obstacles. As it can be observed in Figure17 (a and b), all seven obstacles were avoided successfully through using the both methods. The methods avoided the obstacles by changing direction as the robot approached the obstacles. As Figure 17 shows, the robot uses safe region in both methods during avoidance of obstacles. The results of path navigation to reach the target are different compared to the results obtained from other methods (see Figure 17 (a and b). The smooth path was obtained with proposed Braitenberg navigation strategy.

As it can be observed in Figure 18, a simulation was used for testing the proposed method and the Potential Field Method in a dynamic environment. The scenario assumes that the robot moves in a dynamic environment where the two obstacles move at linear and nonlinear velocity. Figure 18 (a) shows the robot path by the Potential Field Method. The result shows that the robot collides with obstacle 2 after detecting the obstacle 1 and changing its direction. As Figure 18 (b) shows, the robot reaches the target without any collision and moving through a reasonable path. From the previous discussions, it can be seen that the proposed Braitenberg method is a very efficient method and can accomplish the navigation process for a smooth motion.

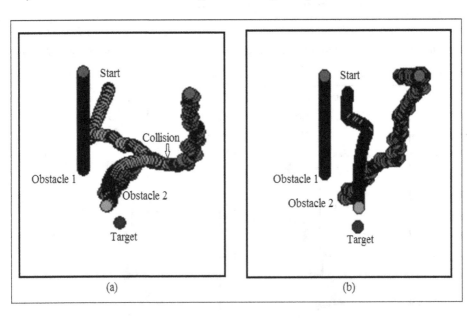

Fig. 18. Comparison of the Potential Field Method (a) and the proposed method (b) in a dynamic environment

5.2   Comparison in Dead Cycle Environment

A new fuzzy controller was developed by Motlagh [19] to overcome multiple dead end problems. It was mainly developed for local navigation when considering the sum of the turning robot angle. The robot goes toward the goal when the sum of the turning angle is near 0 degree while the clockwise motion occurs when the total

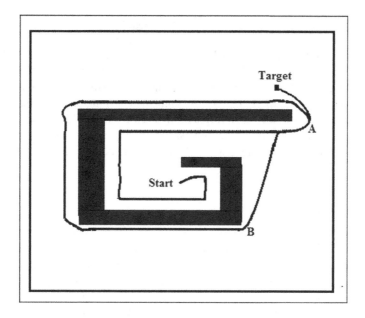

Fig. 19. Local minimum avoidance based upon Motlagh method

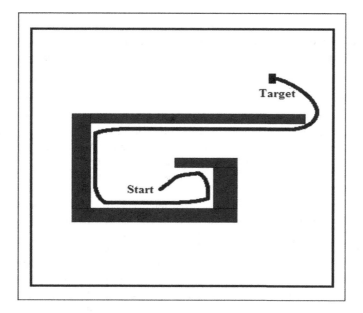

Fig. 20. Local minimum avoidance based upon proposed Braitenberg method

amount of this angle is positive. Therefore, the robot must have a counter clockwise motion whenever it reaches the goal and where there is no obstacle around until the total amount is equal to zero. Additionally, it must have clockwise motion to compensate the turning angle whenever it has negative value. Figure 19 shows the robot trajectory which was developed by Motlagh approach as it appears in G-shape obstacle. The results obtained from the method showed that the robot reached the goal through travelling long path. This is because at point "A" the robot turned counter clockwise to compensate the amount of turning angle. However, it will follow the wall up to the point "B" when the total amount of the turning angle becomes zero and the robot goes toward the goal. Figure 20 shows the results obtained from the proposed Braitenberg method in the same situation. It is understood that the robot has considerable shorter travelling path and time when compared with other related studies [19].

6   Conclusion

The results of this study showed that the new controller can work well with low level sensory information in unknown environments. The performance of the mobile robot was specified by eight infrared sensors, and information to control the left and right mobile robot velocity based upon three actions which are including target seeking, wall following and the obstacle avoidance. Moreover, the performance of the proposed Braitenberg method is tested in Webots simulator software in both dynamic and static environments.

Acknowledgments. The authors would like to thank Mr. Arash Toudeshki for his editorial help in proofreading this manuscript and for his supportive comments.

References

1. Zhu, A., Yang, S.X.: Neuro fuzzy-based approach to mobile robot navigation in unknown environments. IEEE Trans. Systems, Man, Cybernet, part C: Appl. Rev. 37(4) (July 2007)
2. Xu, W.L., Tso, S.K.: Sensor based fuzzy reactive navigation for a mobile robot through local target switching. IEEE Trans. Systems, Man, Cybernet, PartC: Appl. Rev. 29(3), 451–459 (1999)
3. Bemporad, A., Marco, M.D., Tesi, A.: Wall-following controllers for sonar-based mobile robots. In: Proc. 1997. IEEE Int. Conf. Decision and Control, vol. 3, pp. 3063–3068 (1997)
4. Wang, M., Liu, J.N.K.: Fuzzy logic based robot path planning in unknown environments. In: Proc. 2005 Internat. Conf. on Mach. Learn. and Cybernet., vol. 2, pp. 813–818 (2005)
5. Wang, M., Liu, J.N.K.: Fuzzy logic-based real time robot navigation in unknown environment with dead ends. Robot. Auton. Syst. 56, 625–643 (2008)
6. Yang, X., Moallem, M., Patel, R.V.: A layered goal oriented fuzzy motion planning strategy for mobile robot navigation. IEEE Trans. Systems, Man, Cybernet, PartB: Cybernet. 35(6), 1214–1224 (2005)
7. Zhu, A., Yang, S.X.: A fuzzy logic approach to reactive navigation of behavior-based mobile robots. In: Proc. 2004 IEEE Internat. Conf. on Robotics and Automat, vol. 5, pp. 5045–5050 (2004)
8. Ge, S., Cui, Y.: Dynamic motion planning for mobile robots using potential field method. Auton. Robots 13(3), 207–233 (2002)

9. Valavanis, K., Hebert, T., Kolluru, R., Tsourveloudis, N.: Mobile robot navigation in 2-d dynamic environments using an electrostatic potential field. IEEE Trans. Robot. Autom. 30(2), 187–196 (2000)
10. Fujimura, K., Samet, H.: Time minimal paths among moving obstacles. In: Proc. IEEE International Conf. on Robotics and Automation, Arizona, pp. 1110–1115 (1989)
11. Fujimura, K., Samet, H.: Motion planning in dynamic domain. In: Proc. IEEE International Conf. on Robotics and Automation, Ohio, pp. 324–330 (1990)
12. Fujimura, K., Samet, H.: Planning a time minimal motion among moving obstacles. Algorithmica 10, 41–63 (1993)
13. Philippsen, R., Jensen, B., Siegwart, R.: Towards real-time sensor based path planning in highly dynamic environments (Tracts on Advanced Robotics), vol. 35, pp. 135–148. Springer, Berlin (2007)
14. Braitenberg, V.: Vehicles. Experiments in synthetic psychology, The MIT Press (1984)
15. Bicho, E., Schoner, G.: The dynamic approach to autonomous robotics demonstrated on a low-level vehicle platform. Robotics and Autonomous Systems 21, 23–35 (1997)
16. Yang, X., Patel, R.V., Moallem, M.: A Fuzzy-Braitenberg Navigation Strategy for Differential Drive Mobile Robots. Journal of Intelligent Robotic Systems 47, 101–124 (2006)
17. Capozzo, L., Attolico, G., Cicirelli, G.: Building low cost vehicles for simple reactive behaviors. In: Proceedings of the IEEE International Conference on Systems, Man, and Cybernetics, vol. 6, pp. 675–680 (1999)
18. Molina, J.M., Sanchis, A., Berlanga, A., Isasi, P.: Evolving Connection Weight Between Sensors and Actuators in Robots. In: IEEE International Symposium on Industrial Electronics, Gimaraes, Portugal (1997)
19. Motlagh, O.R.E., Hong, T.S., Ismail, N.: Development of a new minimum avoidance system for a behavior based mobile robot. Fuzzy sets syst. 160, 1929–1946 (2009)
20. Ren, J., McIsaac, K.A.: A Hybrid-Systems Approach to Potential Field Navigation for a Multi-Robot Team. In: IEEE Proceedings of 2003, International Conference on Robotics & Automation, Taipei, Taiwan, September 14-19 (2003)

SCARA Robot: Modeled, Simulated, and Virtual-Reality Verified

Yousif I. Al Mashhadany

Electrical Engineering Department, College of Engineering,
University of Anbar, Baghdad, Iraq
Yousif_phd@hotmail.com

Abstract. Articulated-morphology robots, with applications ranging from the basic to the sophisticated, have increased in importance and popularity, especially with decreasing costs of computers and increased studies on feasibility. The development of a complete mathematical model for industrial, selective compliance articulated (SCARA) robot arm including its servomotor dynamics, and simulation of the dynamics, are presented here, as are the analytical inverse kinematic problem (AIKP) and the forward kinematic solution with D-H parameters. The robot arm is built for trajectories in handling, manufacture, assembly, etc. The 3D virtual reality (VR) model realizing it builds and receives commands through a MATLAB/Simulink link, for the design to be simulated on MATLAB Version R2012a. The analytical solution of IKP and modelling under real phasic rule consideration are done here. The integrated approach improves system performance, cost-effectiveness, efficiency, dynamism, and high reality performance. The method's effectiveness is proved, as is the faster response (settling). It is advantageous to industry, and real-time application is possible through interface cards.

Keywords: SCARA robot, mathematical modeling, analytical inverse Kinematic problem (AIKP), DC servomotor, MATLAB/Simulink.

1 Introduction

Robots today feature prominently in human life, ranging from toys to office use and from the industrial to the ultra-sophisticated. The use of robots, its design, modeling, and control form the science of robotics, which feature widely in manufacturing processes. Industrial robots have manipulators whose joints could be rectangular, cylindrical, spherical, revolute, or horizontal. A horizontal revolute robot, the selective compliance articulated robot arm (SCARA), has four degrees of freedom (DOF), with two or three horizontal servo-controlled joints for shoulder, elbow, and wrist. Real robotics is the aim, but simulation prior to investigation with real robots often are useful; simulation is easier to set up, cheaper, faster, and more convenient; new robot models and experiments can be set up quickly. A simulated robotic setup costs less than do real robots and real-world setups, and designs can be better explored. Simulation often is faster than the real movement, and parameters are visible on screen [1-5].

S.G. Ponnambalam et al. (Eds.): IRAM 2012, CCIS 330, pp. 94–102, 2012.

Advanced stages of design demand real-time simulation, to verify the final design before costly and time-consuming prototyping begins. Higher accuracy and more computationally effective manipulator dynamics are being increasingly demanded. Modeling and simulation of potential robots facilitate design, construction, and inspection of real robots. Simulation is important for evaluation and prediction of robot behavior, also to verify and optimize process path planning. Time and money will be saved, and the optimization is necessary consideration in automating manufacturing. Simulation creates options to creative solving of problems. Inexistent objects can be visualized into existence, investigated, designed, and tested [6-8].

The methodology of this work is developing through Virtual Reality Modeling Language (VRML) a 4-axis SCARA robot system for handling small things (see Figure 1). The implement through VR depends upon high accuracy modeling of SCARA robot and simulation this model by preparing suitable commands for certain trajectory. The structure to be built depends on the principles of solid-body modeling with VR technology [9]. Simulation on MATLAB/Simulink software will reinforce the results obtained by SD program. The results of both will be presented and discussed. This work developed with D-H formulation, the kinematic equations of the SCARA robot with robot dynamics and the actuators-dc servomotors for each joint. Actuator characteristics; dc servo motors were studied in detail. The paper is organized as follows: Section 2 introduces robotics and robot kinematics. Section 3 presents the robot's inverse kinematics, section 4 presents the model design in VRML environment, whereas Section 5 presents the simulation and results, and concludes.

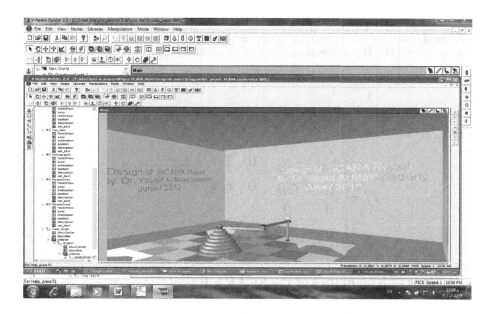

Fig. 1. 3D VR window for the SCARA robot at position zero with orthographic view

2   Robot Kinematics

The Table 1 defines the Denavit-Hartenberg (D-H) parameters specifying the SCARA robot [8,10].

Table 1. D-H parameters of the robot

i	θ_i	d_i	a_i	α_i
1	θ_1	0	L_1	0
2	θ_2	0	L_2	0
3	0	d_3	0	0
4	θ_4	d_4	0	0

By using (D-H) convention [10], the transformation matrices result in:

$$T_1^0 = A_1 = \begin{bmatrix} c_1 & -s_1 & 0 & L_1 c_1 \\ s_1 & c_1 & 0 & L \\ 0 & 0 & 1 & 0 \\ 0 & 0 & 0 & 1 \end{bmatrix}; \quad T_2^1 = A_2 = \begin{bmatrix} c_2 & -s_2 & 0 & L_2 c_2 \\ s_2 & c_2 & 0 & L_2 s_2 \\ 0 & 0 & 1 & 0 \\ 0 & 0 & 0 & 1 \end{bmatrix} \quad (1)$$

$$T_3^2 = A_3 = \begin{bmatrix} 1 & 0 & 0 & 0 \\ 0 & 1 & 0 & 0 \\ 0 & 0 & 1 & -d_3 \\ 0 & 0 & 0 & 1 \end{bmatrix} \quad T_4^3 = A_4 = \begin{bmatrix} c_4 & -s_4 & 0 & 0 \\ s_4 & c_4 & 0 & 0 \\ 0 & 0 & 1 & -d_4 \\ 0 & 0 & 0 & 1 \end{bmatrix} \quad (2)$$

After the multiplication and use of addition matrices, one gets the total transformation matrix:

$$T_4^0 = \begin{bmatrix} c_{124} & -s_{124} & 0 & L_2 c_1 + L_1 c_1 \\ s_{124} & c_{124} & 0 & L_2 s_{12} + L_1 s_1 \\ 0 & 0 & 1 & -d_3 - d_4 \\ 0 & 0 & 0 & 1 \end{bmatrix} \quad (3)$$

3   Inverse Kinematics of the SCARA Robot

Desired location of the SCARA robot [8,11]

$$T_H^R = \begin{bmatrix} n_x & o_x & a_x & p_x \\ n_y & o_y & a_y & p_y \\ n_z & o_z & a_z & p_z \\ 0 & 0 & 0 & 1 \end{bmatrix} \quad (4)$$

The final equation representing the robot is:

$$T_H^R = A_1 A_2 A_3 A_4 = T_4^0 \quad (5)$$

To solve for the angle θ4, both sides of equation (7) are successively pre-multiplied with $A_3^{-1} A_2^{-1} A_1^{-1}$ matrices, such that:

$$A_3^{-1} A_2^{-1} A_1^{-1} T_H^R = A_4 \quad (6)$$

The left side of the equation (6) ($A_3^{-1} A_2^{-1} A_1^{-1} T_H^R$)

$$\begin{bmatrix} 1 & 0 & 0 & 0 \\ 0 & 1 & 0 & 0 \\ 0 & 0 & 1 & -d_3 \\ 0 & 0 & 0 & 1 \end{bmatrix} \times \begin{bmatrix} c_2 & s_2 & 0 & -L_2 \\ -s_2 & c_2 & 0 & 0 \\ 0 & 0 & 1 & 0 \\ 0 & 0 & 0 & 1 \end{bmatrix} \times$$

$$\begin{bmatrix} c_1 & -s_1 & 0 & -L_1 \\ -s_1 & c_1 & 0 & 0 \\ 0 & 0 & 1 & -d_1 \\ 0 & 0 & 0 & 1 \end{bmatrix} \times \begin{bmatrix} n_x & o_x & a_x & p_x \\ n_y & o_y & a_y & p_y \\ n_z & o_z & a_z & p_z \\ 0 & 0 & 0 & 1 \end{bmatrix} =$$

$$\begin{bmatrix} n_x c_{12} + n_y s_{12} & o_x c_{12} + o_y s_{12} & a_x c_{12} + a_y s_{12} & p_x c_{12} + p_y s_{12} - L_1 c_2 - L_2 \\ -n_x s_{12} + n_y c_{12} & o_x s_{12} + o_y c_{12} & -a_x s_{12} + a_y c_{12} & -p_x s_{12} + p_y c_{12} - L_1 s_2 \\ n_z & o_z & a_z & p_z + d_3 \\ 0 & 0 & 0 & 1 \end{bmatrix} \quad (7)$$

From 1 and 2 elements of the equations (3) and (4)

$$p_x = L_1 c_1 + L_2 c_{12} \quad ; p_y = L_1 s_1 + L_2 s_{12} \quad (8)$$

From equation 7 and equation 8,

$$c_2 = \frac{1}{2L_1L_2}\left(p_x^2 + p_y^2 - L_1^2 - L_2^2\right) ; \quad s_2 = \pm\sqrt{1-c_2^2} ; \quad \theta_2 = \tan^{-1}\frac{s_2}{c_2} \tag{9}$$

Rearranging equation (7) and equation (8) yields:

$$p_x = (L_1 + L_2c_2)c_1 - L_2s_2s_1 ; \quad p_y = L_2s_2c_1 + (L_1 + L_2c_2)s_1 \tag{10}$$

Solving equations (10) by kramer's rule:

$$\Delta = \begin{bmatrix} L_1 + L_2c_2 & -L_2s_2 \\ L_2s_2 & L_1 + L_2c_2 \end{bmatrix} = (L_1 + L_2c_2)^2 + (L_2c_2)^2 \tag{11}$$

$$\Delta s_1 = \begin{bmatrix} L_1 + L_2c_2 & -p_x \\ L_2s_2 & -p_y \end{bmatrix} = (L_1 + L_2c_2)p_y - (L_2s_2)p_x \tag{12}$$

$$\Delta c_1 = \begin{bmatrix} p_x & -L_2s_2 \\ p_y & L_1 + L_2c_2 \end{bmatrix} = (L_1 + L_2c_2)p_x + (L_2s_2)p_y \tag{13}$$

$$s_1 = \frac{\Delta s_1}{\Delta} = \frac{(L_1 + L_2c_2)p_y - L_2s_2p_x}{(L_1 + L_2c_2)^2 + (L_2s_2)^2} = \frac{(L_1 + L_2c_2)p_y - L_2s_2p_x}{p_x^2 + p_y^2} \tag{14}$$

$$c_1 = \frac{\Delta c_1}{\Delta} = \frac{(L_1 + L_2c_2)p_x - L_2s_2p_y}{(L_1 + L_2c_2)^2 + (L_2s_2)^2} = \frac{(L_1 + L_2c_2)p_x - L_2s_2p_y}{p_x^2 + p_y^2} \tag{15}$$

$$\theta_1 = \tan^{-1}\frac{s_1}{c_1} = \tan^{-1}\frac{(L_1 + L_2c_2)p_y - L_2s_2p_x}{(L_1 + L_2c_2)p_x - L_2s_2p_y} \tag{16}$$

From 4,4 elements of the equation (5) and (6):

$$d_3 = -p_z - d_4 \quad ; \quad \text{We have} ; \quad \theta_3 = 0 \tag{17}$$

From 1 and 2 elements of the equation (3) and (7):

$$c_4 = n_xc_{12} + n_ys_{12} ; \quad s_4 = -n_xs_{12} + n_yc_{12} \tag{18}$$

$$\theta_4 = \tan^{-1}\frac{-n_x\sin(\theta_1 + \theta_2) + n_y\cos(\theta_1 + \theta_2)}{n_x\cos(\theta_1 + \theta_2) + n_y\sin(\theta_1 + \theta_2)} \tag{19}$$

4   The Model, in Virtual Reality

The requirements for design in VRML are explained in *finite processing allocations, autonomy, consistent self-registration* and *calculability* [13] Design in VRML depends on the designer's information and his imagination of the object. VR design choices are standard configurations (sphere, cone, cylinder, etc.) and free-form (the indexed face set button is selected, to get many configurations with points that can be rearranged) [14]. Fig. 2 is the design, in full VR, of an SCARA robot.

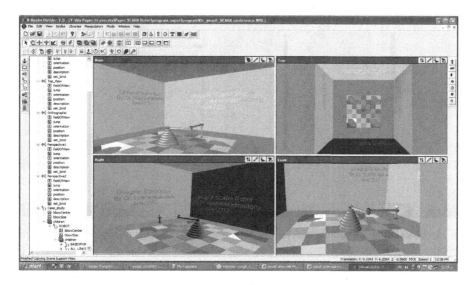

Fig. 2. A SCARA robot left arm, in VR

Every real-form design is considered free-form designing, which starts with building parts one by one and checking the shape against a related, real manipulator part. That manipulator part cannot be simulated in VR when the standard shape from the VR library is used, where they are not uniform shape [14-16]. The design uses the indexed face set in VR. The next design step is connecting all the parts to produce the object and to limit the object's point of origin. This job was made by setting the first shape (e.g. the base) and then connecting the next shape (joint two) in the "children" button; the same procedure is repeated with other parts [17].

5   Simulation Results and Discussions

Fig. 3 is the Simulink model with analytical solution of IKP and calculation of the SCARA robot trajectory, in Matlab R2012a VR model. To start the simulations and representation of real trajectory in VR environment, the command of movement has to be calculating first from the Sinulink window in Matlab. After all the preliminary operations, the simulations begin by calling the VR model through the interface block between Matlab and the VR model. Fig. 4 shows the simulation SCARA robot trajectory as handling robot. The workspace-data variables are loaded onto the firing pulse to be applied to the actuator of each motor joint, through the calculated command value. Post-simulation, the robot's performance is evaluated through its movements, recordable in video or photograph, and observable according to scope.

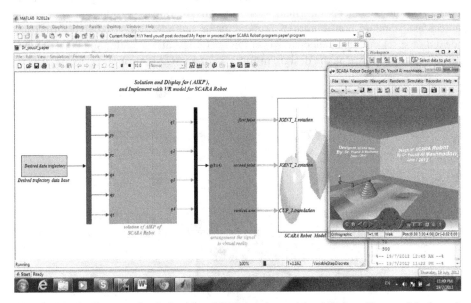

Fig. 3. Block diagram simulation for SCARA robot with virtual reality model through trajectory of handling robot

Fig. 4. Implement of desired trajectory for SCARA robot

6   Conclusion

The results verify complete mathematical modeling of the SCARA robot including its equations of the forward and inverse kinematics, the modeling is very accurate for investigation of the robot's parameters. The robot's Simulink model has been developed, together with analytical solution of IKP. The calculation of trajectory for SCARA robot is calculated with each certain real physics job. The envelop of this robot is calculated and can be implement this envelop as real application. The high accuracy for trajectory implement of handling robot depends upon the accurate analytical solution of IKP and the accurate of representation physics quantity in the mathematical model. The implement of trajectory through VR environment has many advantages with industrial robot, reduce the cost, and reduce the efforts of trail in the design process.

References

[1] Vasconcelo, F., Hernández, G.: Improvement and Extension of Virtual Reality for Flexible Systems of Manufacture. International Journal of Computers, Communications & Control 1(2), 95–101 (2006)

[2] Sharma, R., Gopal, M.: A Markov Game-Adaptive Fuzzy Controller for Robot Manipulators. IEEE Transactions Fuzzy Systems 16(1), 171–186 (2008)

[3] Sesar, V., Bogdan, S., Kovacic, Z.: An Internet-based System for Remote Planning and Execution of SCARA Robot Trajectories. IEEE Industrial Electronics, 3485–3490 (2008)

[4] Lee, S., Jeong, D., Kim, I., Lee, D., Yeon, D., Lee, M.: Control of Robot Manipulator for Storing Cord Blood in Cryogenic Environments. In: ICROS-SICE International Joint Conference, Japan, pp. 4256–4259 (2009)

[5] Spong, M., Hutchinson, S., Vidyasagar, M.: Robot Dynamics and Control, 2nd edn. (January 28, 2004)

[6] Akmeliawati, R., Waladin, S., Safanah, R.: Improving Trajectory Tracking of a Three Axis SCARA Robot Using Neural Networks. In: IEEE Symposium on Industrial Electronics and Applications, Kuala Lumpur, pp. 283–288 (2009)

[7] Khongsomboun, K., Benjanarasuth, T., Komine, N.: IMC-Based PID Controllers Design for a Two-Links SCARA Robot. In: IEEE Region 10 Conference, TENCON, pp. 1030–1034 (2011)

[8] Marghitu, G.: Mechanisms and Robots Analysis with MATLAB. Springer, London (2009) ISBN 978-1-84800-390-3

[9] Aroca, V., Tavares, M., Caurin, G.: Scara Robot Controller Using Real Time Linux. In: IEEE International Conference On Advanced Intelligent Mechatronics, pp. 1–6 (2007)

[10] Al-Kasasbeh, R., Ionescu, F., Alshamasin, M.: Kinematic Modeling and Simulation of a SCARA Robot by Using Solid Dynamics and Verification by MATLAB/Simulink. European Journal of Scientific Research 37(3), 388–405 (2009)

[11] Knani, J.: Dynamic modelling of flexible robotic mechanisms and adaptive robust control of trajectory computer simulation-—Part I. Applied Mathematical Modelling Elsevier Journal 26, 1113–1124 (2002)

[12] Toshiba Machine Manual: The TH series, Flexible and Fast Maneuver of Time-Space SCARA Robot. Catalog TH0026-CJD-01, 1 – 20 (2010)

[13] Paşc, I., Ţarcă, R., Vlădicescu, F.: The VRML Model and VR Simulation for a SCARA Robot. Fascicle of Management and Technological Engineering, 909–914 (2007)

[14] Prempraneerach, P., Kulvani, P.: Implementation of Resolved Motion Rate Controller with 5-Axis Robot Manipulator Arm. In: The First TSME International Conference on Mechanical Engineering, pp. 1–8 (2010)

[15] Şahın, Y., Tinkir, M., Ankarali, A.: Trajectory Planning and Adaptive Neural Network Based Interval Type-2 Fuzzy Logic Controller Design of 3-DOF Robot. In: 2011 IEEE 3rd International Conference on Computer Research and Development, pp. 114–119 (2011)

[16] Arshad, H., Jamal, J., Sahran, S.: Teaching Robot Kinematic in a Virtual Environment. In: Proceedings of the World Congress on Engineering and Computer Science, San Francisco, vol. 1 (2010)

[17] Carey, R., Bell, G., Marrin, C.: ISO/IEC 14772-1:1997 Virtual Reality Modeling Language (VRML97) (2008), http://www.vrml.org

Real Time Mobile Robot Navigation
of Virtually Created Environments

Fawaz Y. Annaz and Ahmed Hikmat Saeed

University of Nottingham (Malaysia Campus),
Department of Electrical & Electronic Engineering,
Faculty of Engineering, Jalan Broga, 43500 Semenyih, Malaysia
Fawaz.Annaz@nottingham.edu.my, ahmedhikmetsaeed@gmail.com

Abstract .esearch in autonomous mobile robots is gaining much more attention in recent years, particularly in coordinating rescue missions and inspections of affected structures within disaster zones. It is the aim of this paper to contribute towards such advancements by introducing mobile robots navigation in virtually generated rescue mission environments. The randomly generated missions are mapped to real environments hosting mobile robots, which can unrestrictedly move in any open surroundings, without the need for the physical obstacles presence. To achieve this, a GUI was developed to randomly create missions of different sizes and complexities. The GUI offers the developer the choice of automatically generating such missions, edit them and/or create them. The robots may be programmed by various solving algorithms to complete the course and find a solution. The advantage of this approach is that it offers environment and robot real-time merging, robot performance tracking and rapid (on-the-fly) algorithms development. In this paper, the rescuing robot will follow an embedded Wall-Following algorithm.

Keywords: mobile robot, maze solving, rescue mission, robot navigation, virtual missions.

1 Introduction

Realistic rescue missions usually start with a search in unknown environments, before reaching regions where trapped victims can be detected. It is also usual for rescuers to discretely report their locations to mission headquarters, as they progress along a certain path, which will (hopefully) lead to the victim's final location, identifying . It is also usual for a rescue team to identify and report deadened paths, to avoid delays in further support of other fellow rescuers.

Traditionally, researchers have to physically develop and build mazes to emulate set-scenarios that reflect a particular mission, with programmed robots navigating their way to the final goal. Such mazes have to be substantially rugged to survive the repeated tests, hence, they are naturally expected to be heavy, difficult to move around, and they usually occupy (even when not used) unnecessary space. In this approach, a new maze has to be reconstructed or modified to meet newly proposed

S.G. Ponnambalam et al. (Eds.): IRAM 2012, CCIS 330, pp. 103–110, 2012.

architecture, which can clearly be very costly and time consuming. Furthermore, it is also possible that in the course of training or testing of new algorithms robots might experience physical damage when erroneously and frequently collide with obstacles or walls.

To eliminate the above disadvantages and to offer higher degree of portability, the virtual maze concept is proposed, where users may create, load and edit virtual mazes that can be mapped on mobile robot. Thus, a virtual maze environment approach is more suitable, as it permits unlimited in-depth algorithm performance assessments and can effectively and efficiently be modified to meet architectures with various degrees of complexity, including those mimicking real rescue missions.

As for the robots used in rescue missions training and evaluations, researchers have designed and built their own robots with specs to help in solving traditional mazes. However, those who are interested in algorithm development used commercially available mobile robots that are suitable for research, such as the Khepera II and III from K-Team, Lego Mind storms from the Lego Company and Create from iRobot, and the open-hardware e-puck educational mobile robot (developed at the École Polytechnique Fédérale de Lausanne, EPFL).

In this research, the Epuck was selected for its small size, reliability, onboard sensors and input output devices. The virtual maze was discretely revealed to the E-puck via the built in Bluetooth, the E-puck is then made discrete decisions in negotiating the revealed maze, and continuously updating its location on the virtual maze as it solved the maze. It is the aim of this paper to present real time navigation of an E-Puck mobile robot in a virtual environment. The robot was programmed with the Left/Right-Wall-Following (LWF or RWF) Algorithm.

2   The e-Puck Mobile Robot

The 2-wheeled e-puck mobile robot (shown in Fig. 1) is only 7cm in diameter, 6cm tall and 660g in weight with a simple and reliable design. Despite its small size the e-puck is rich in sensors and input–output devices, and need little maintenance. In fact, we have been experimenting with a set of 3 E-pucks, which were purchased at the same time, and none of them has failed, yet.

In its basic configuration, the E-Puck is equipped with 8 Infra-Red proximity sensors, 3 microphones, a loudspeaker, an Infra-Red remote control receiver, a ring of LEDs (9 red and 2 green), 1 3D accelerometer, 1 CMOS camera, and a Bluetooth that facilitates wireless programs uploading, general monitoring, debugging, and continuous communication between the virtual maze and the robot. All sensors and motors are processed and controlled with a dsPIC30F6014A microprocessor, which has certain limitations, including the obvious limited on-board memory (8KB RAM and 144 KB of flash memory) and computation 16 MIPS of peak processing power. To overcome such limitations, the E-puck hosts extension sockets for connecting additional extension boards (interfacing via an I2C bus or RS232 serial ports) with slave microprocessor modules to manage own sensors or actuators. Many of such extensions have been developed by different institutions, such as: The Fly-Vision Turret, Ground Sensors, Colour LED Communication Turret, Omni directional vision, ZigBee Communication Turret [1], Range and Bearing Turret [2] and e-puck display module [3].

Fig. 1. The 2-wheeled e-puck mobile robot

This paper reports on results as the e-puck navigated around randomly generated virtual mazes, with its DSPIC processor programmed with the LWF or RWF Algorithm. Bluetooth communication was utilized in revealing to the robot its immediate surroundings (Left, Right and Ahead), and to continuously update the new robot position on the virtual maze.

3   Traditional Versus Virtual Mazes

Autonomous robots are designed to discretely discover and interpret their surroundings and they are expected to orient themselves around obstacles to reach a target from an initial position. This is what is referred to as path planning. In real-time autonomous navigation, path planning becomes more challenging in an unknown-dynamically-changing environment [4] and [5] . The virtual maze environment is specifically developed to handle such dynamically changing environments, thus depicting various rescue mission scenarios.

Many maze solving algorithms can be applied to solve static missions, with various success and efficiency levels, depending on the mission nature, the way maze information is revealed and the goal location. Some of the online approaches in autonomous robots, includes: wall following method [6] ; potential field methods [7] and [8]; virtual target approach [9] and [10]; landmark learning [11] ; edge detection and graph-based methods [12]; vector field histogram methods, dynamic window approaches, neural network based methods, and fuzzy logic methods [13]-[18] and many others. [13] [14] [15] [16] [17] [18]

Regardless of the solving algorithm, traditionally, the common steps have been to physically develop and build the maze, and then robots are programmed or trained to navigate their way to reach the final goal. Such mazes have to be substantially rugged to survive the repeated tests, hence, they are naturally expected to be heavy, difficult to move around, and occupy unnecessary space (when not in use). A further drawback in this approach is that, a maze has to be reconstructed or modified to meet new static architectures, which could be both costly and time consuming. Furthermore, it is also possible that in the course of training or the testing of new algorithms robots might experience physical damage when erroneously and frequently collide with obstacles or walls.

A virtual maze environment approach does not suffer from any of the above disadvantages. It has a high degree of portability and can be implemented in any open space. It permits unlimited in-depth algorithm performance assessment, and can be effectively and efficiently modified to architectures with various degrees of complexity, including those mimicking real rescue missions.

Moreover, our approach offers real-time-merging and robot-performance-tracking, with "on the fly" different algorithms testing in fixed, variable or random dynamic environments.

4   The Virtual Maze Environment

Figure 2 shows a GUI environment that was developed in Visual Basic, allowing users to (manually or randomly) generate mazes with initial robot and final goal locations. Users may create, load and edit mazes (by either modifying the paths or introducing new start and goal locations). Users may also save mazes before and after solution, hence enabling assessment of various algorithms efficiency and robot performance tracking. The GUI was also developed to enable communications with one or more robots to discretely reveal and update current surroundings.

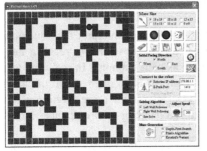   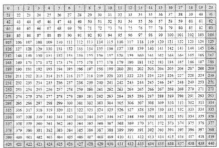

Fig. 2. The Virtual Maze Development GUI   **Fig. 3.** Maze Area coding

The current GUI hosts command buttons, frames, labels and text boxes for different functionalities and to display time and other information. The user can also create mazes of different sizes (a minimum of 9x9), however, here a 21x21 example will be used to explain the development. This maze is made up of 441 cells or arrays of small pictures that are arranged from 0 to 440, as shown in Fig 3.

By default, all cells are initially assumed to be open paths, and are assigned 0, whereas cells that contain objects other than a Path, then appropriate numbers referring to those objects are assigned. Other objects include Walls, Borders, Start-points, and Stop-points, which are given the numerical values 1, 2, 3 and 4, respectively. Therefore, if a cell contains a Wall, then a 1 is assigned to it. This numbering assignment scheme is used during maze construction and editing. It is also used by the robot to learn about its immediate (Left, Front, and Right) surroundings and use this information to navigate its way around the maze. In fact, surroundings will be translated by the robot as passable, impassable or finish-point to solve the virtual maze.

5   The Left/Right-Wall-Following Algorithm

In order to keep track of the e-puck movement and its orientation, the wheels position must be monitored through the encoder device. The e-puck (unlike other robots) does not actually have a physical encoder device that registers the position of the wheels, however, there is a counter that changes its value according to the wheel position. If the wheel moves forward, the counter value will be increased, and if the wheel moves backward then the counter value will be decreased. As mentioned earlier the e-puck possesses two stepper motors, where each of the stepper motors breaks up full rotation into 1000 steps. The encoder resolution of the e-puck is equal to 159.23 which mean that there are 159.23 pulses per radian. This information can be utilized together with the wheel radius (0.0205 m) and the e-puck axle length (0.052 m) to calculate the distance covered by the right and left wheels, as well as to find the orientation of the e-puck. All together if plotted against time a bigger picture on the robot behaviors might be concluded. Following a movement or change in orientation, the e-puck feeds back its encoder values to the computer (via a Bluetooth). The distances covered by the Left and Right wheels, as well as the E-Puck Orientation are given by: Encoder-Right /159.23) x 0.0205; (EncoderLeft /159.23) x 0.0205; and (DRight-Wheel - DLeft-Wheel) x(180/π)/0.052.

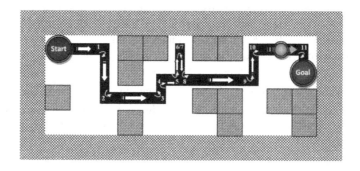

Fig. 4. Left-Wall-Following Algorithm

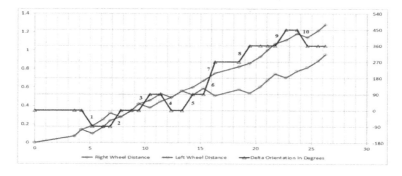

Fig. 5. Distance covered and Orientation with the Left-Wall-Following Algorithm

This data was made available in a Log file that was plotted to trace the robot movement and orientation. As example, Figure 4 and 5 show a basic maze that was solved using the LWF algorithm. And the data-log plot of the Epuck movement and orientation to the solution. It can be seen clearly that the robot changes its orientation 11 times before reaching the final goal. *Abbreviating, Moving Forward by MF, Turning by $90°$ Clockwise by $90°CW$, Turning by $90°$ Counter Clockwise by $90°CCW$*, where $90°CCW|_8$ represents the Eighth-$90°CCW$. Therefore, the robot has made the following movements to reach the final goal: MF; MF; $90°CW|_1$; MF; MF; $90°CCW|_2$; MF; MF; $90°CCW|_3$; MF; $90°CW|_4$; MF; $90°CCW|_5$; MF; $90°CCW|_6$; $90°CCW|_7$; MF; $90°CCW|_8$; MF; MF; MF; $90°CCW|_9$; MF; $90°CW|_{10}$; MF; MF; $90°CW|_{11}$; MF; Goal Reached.

6   Real Time Hardware Robot Coordinates

To navigate the maze, two main processes take place, the first is computer based and the second is mobile robot based. The computer discretely reveals the adjacent Front, Left, and Right (F, L and R) locations to the robot, the robot then decides on the next move (using its own algorithm) and then it updates the computer with its new location. The cycle repeats until the goal is reached. Here, it is important to note that the adjacent grids to the robot (F, L and R) are based on the direction the robot faces, however, the robot is never given position coordinates since it is intended that the robot constructs and memorizes its own coordinate system with respect to the initial deployment position. Here, the robot position is traced on the virtual maze, as the robot transmits information about its position and heading.

The surroundings information is stored continuously. On start up, the robot first receives a 5 integers string (transmitted as $a_1a_2a_3a_4$ & a_5), where a_1 determines the solving algorithm; $a_1a_2a_3a_4$ & a_5 give the surroundings information. The robot reacts according to the information and the onboard algorithm. As it then moves to the next locations, the virtual world is updated and the process keeps on repeating until the maze is solved.

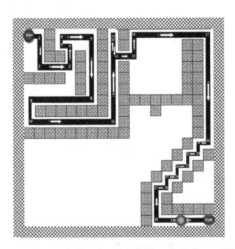

Fig. 6. The Left-Wall-Following Algorithm Solution to 18x18Maze

This can be seen clearly in the example in Figure 6, with the complete discrete steps taken by the E-Puck and its change in Orientation to solve the mission is shown in the graph of Figure 7. Here, the robot makes 28 turns before it finds the final goal.

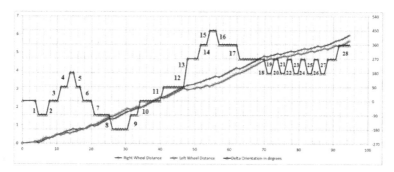

Fig. 7. Distance and Orientation for the rescue mission in Fig 6

7   Conclusion

This paper presented a real-time merging of virtual maze with a mobile robot. The work presented the Left/Right-Wall-Following maze solving algorithm to solve randomly generated rescue missions with a single start and stop points. Environment robot interaction was also described: by addressing the Robot's location and direction indexing strategy; along with how the robot navigated its way in response to the (discretely revealed) immediate surroundings. All data exchange was achieved through discrete communications between the robot and the computer via wireless communication. Real-Time Robot maneuvers were plotted with Left and Right wheels distances and robot orientation plotted against time. The work might easily be extended to utilize other algorithms that guarantee solutions, or provide more efficient solutions.

References

[1] Cianci, C.M., Raemy, X., Pugh, J., Martinoli, A.: Communication in a Swarm of Miniature Robots: The e-Puck as an Educational Tool for Swarm Robotics. In: Şahin, E., Spears, W.M., Winfield, A.F.T. (eds.) SAB 2006 Ws 2007. LNCS, vol. 4433, pp. 103–115. Springer, Heidelberg (2007)

[2] Gutierrez, A.: Open E-puck Range & Bearing miniaturized board for local communication in swarm robotics. In: IEEE International Conference on Robotics and Automation, Madrid, Spain (2009)

[3] Wenguo, L., Winfield, A.F.T.: Open-hardware e-puck Linux extension board for experimental swarm robotics research. Microprocessors & Microsystems 35(1), 60–67 (2011)

[4] Motlagh, O.R.E., Tang, S.H., Napsiah, I.: Development of a new minimum avoidance system for a behavior-based mobile robot. Fuzzy Sets and Systems 160(13), 1929–1946 (2009)

[5] Autonomous, G.K.: mobile robot mechanical design. Verije University, Brussels (2006)
[6] Owen, Y., Andrew, G.: Dynamical wall following for a wheeled robot, University Baltimore (March 2006)
[7] Koren, Y., Borenstein, J.: Potential Field Methods and Their Inherent Limitations for Mobile Robot Navigation. In: Proceedings of the IEEE Conference on Robotics and Automation, Sacramento, California (1991)
[8] Massari, M., Giardini, G., Bernelli-Zazzera, F.: Autonomous Navigation System for Planetary Exploration Rover based on Artificial Potential Fields. In: 6th International Conference on Dynamics and Control of Systems and Structures In Space, Riomaggiore, Italy (2004)
[9] Xu, W., Tso, S., Fung, Y.: Sensor-based reactive navigation of a mobile robot through local target switching. In: 8th International Conference on Advanced Robotics, Univ. of Hong Kong (1997)
[10] Yang, X., Moallem, M., Patel, R.: A layered goal-oriented fuzzy motion planning strategy for mobile robot navigation. IEEE Transactions on Systems, Man, and Cybernetics, Part B (2005)
[11] Madhava, K.K., Prem, K.K.: Perception and remembrance of the environment during real-time navigation of a mobile robot. Robotics and Autonomous Systems 37(1), 25–51 (2001)
[12] Marcel, D.: Graph Algebras and Automata, New York (2003)
[13] Meng, W.: Fuzzy logic based robot path planning in unknown environment. In: International Conference on Machine Learning and Cybernetics, Hung Hom, China (2005)
[14] Anmin, Z., Yang, S.: A fuzzy logic approach to reactive navigation of behavior-based mobile robots. In: IEEE International Conference on Robotics and Automation, Ont, Canada, (2004)
[15] Janet M., S.: Neural networks for decision tree searches. In: Proc. of IEEE/EMBS-9 Conference, Clark Univ., Worcester, MA USA (1987)
[16] Simon, X.Y., Max, M.: An efficient neural network approach to dynamic robot motion planning. Neural Networks 13(2), 143–148 (2000)
[17] Roy, G., Andrzej, K., Stan, C.G.: Neural Network Dynamics for Path Planning and Obstacle Avoidance. Neural Networks 8(1), 125–133 (1995)
[18] Basem, A.: Cellular automata for solving mazes. Dr. Dobb's 18(2), 32–38 (1993)

GUI Teaching Pendant Development
for a 6 Axis Articulated Robot

Malaka Miyuranga Kaluarachchi and Fawaz Yahya Annaz

The University of Nottingham, Malaysia Campus, Faculty of Engineering, School of Electrical
& Electronic Engineering, JalanBroga, 43500 Semenyih, Selangor, Malaysia
kecy1mmk@exmail.nottingham.edu.my,
keczfan@exmail.nottingham.edu.my

Abstract .he main objective of this paper is to replace an Industrial Teach-Pendant with a virtual GUI that contains many of the main traditional functions that are found in pendants designed to drive the Motoman HP3J by Yaskawa. The GUI is made up of separate Tabs for authentication, descriptive help, validations and descriptive error messages, all of which are presented in an aesthetically pleasing appearance with menus and buttons that depict the different functionalities. Some of the main functions include direct and inverse kinematics, as well as path planning. The paper will present a GUI Teaching Pendant interface that employs Linear Interpolation and Joint Interpolation, to navigate to control navigate and plan the robot arm path movement. Furthermore, direct and inverse kinematics, as well as the DH parameters of the HP3J manipulator will be explained along with the special functions that are used to enhance the safety and invalid inputs. The paper will conclude by comparing the GUI Teach Pendant functions to those of the Industrial Teach Pendant, highlighting the advantages of this proposal. The system was tested in the University of Nottingham and has proven to be a good teaching tool to aid students in understanding basic robotics, direct and inverse kinematics, and path planning.

Keywords: Industrial Teach Pendant, Industrial Robot, Manipulator, GUI Teaching Pendant, GTK+.

1   Introduction

An Industrial Teaching Pendant, ITP, is similar to that shown in Fig. 1 is portable equipment that is employed to control a manipulator arm, via navigation buttons for each joint of the arm, thus the user can easily perform the motion of the robot. Apart from controlling the motion of the arm the Pendant can be used to program and edit the provided functions to achieve robot motion. Buttons in the Pendant are clustered according to their operation, for example, numeric keys, motion control keys, program control keys, cursor keys, menu keys and function keys [1].

In industrial Teach Pendants all the functional keys are packed in one limited area, thus descriptive area of functions and other user options are limited. In this designed interface, the design is made simple and the user has access to online support.

S.G. Ponnambalam et al. (Eds.): IRAM 2012, CCIS 330, pp. 111–118, 2012.

1: LCD Display
2:Emergency Stop
3:Multifunctional keys
4:Esc key
5:Decrement key
6:Increment Ke
7:Return Key
8:Dual function key

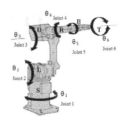

Fig. 1. Industrial Teach Pendant to a 6-axis robot

2   Industrial vs. Virtual Teaching Pendant

Unlike Industrial Teaching Pendants (ITPs) function keys on the Virtual Teaching Pendant (VTPs) need not be limited to one area and have sufficient accompanying descriptions. Furthermore, implementation of new functions in the VTP is much easier and does not require the remanufacturing of a new pendant.

The VTP GUI could be implemented on any computers or other portable devices such as an Ipads, phones, or Laptops, therefore, robot control be achieved with any of these devices. To increase security, user authentication could also be implemented to prevent the unauthorized access to the system [2].

Other additional features, such as the limiting of activation functions, which can be either operation related or user security clearance related. Traditional ITPs do not have this facility and have tangible buttons that users can still pressed, despite the fact that they are not related to the current training operation, and regardless of the user ability and security clearance.

3   Designing the GUI Virtual Teach Pendant on GTK+

GTK+ is a software toolkit, which was used to design the VTP-GUI on the Linux operating system. The software is developed using the C language, however, it supports a range of other languages such as Perl and Python [3]. It contains all the widget required in designing a GUI, such as Buttons, Textboxes, Labels, Tables etc.

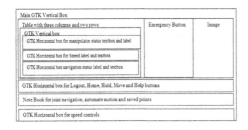

Fig. 2. Functions positioning in GTK+

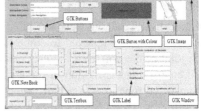

Fig. 3. GTK objects Implementation

Figure 2 shows the VTP-GUI, which was created using GTK+, where the display panel was divided to create a teaching environment where the user could perform both control and analysis, as well as receive help and guidance. The GUI utilizes RTLab API functions to perform joints movements. The display panels are subdivided according to the required functions, which were positioned accordingly in vertical and horizontal boxes. Figure 3 describes the different the type of GTK+ objects used in the screen implementation.

The use of such vertical and horizontal sub panels makes the design more clear. For example, the main window that hosts the "Manipulator Status", "Speed""Navigation Status", "Emergency Button" and "The Robot Arm Image' was designed as follows: The "Manipulator Status", "Speed""Navigation Status" were placed in sub horizontal boxes, that are contained in a vertical box, next to the "Emergency Button" and "Manipulator Image" vertical boxes, as shown in Fig. 2. Below this set of three vertical boxes, three horizontal boxes were marked as follows: The First contains the "Logout, Home, Hold, Move, and Help" buttons; the second contains the "Notebook for the three tabs used to place the controls of Joint Navigation, Automate Motion and Saved Points"; and the last horizontal box is to contain the "speed controls". GTK+ attached options such as "GTK_EXPAND" and "GTK_SHRINK" were placed appropriately to make the "Emergency Button" more visible [3]. The "GTK_EXPAND" and "GTK_SHRINK" function will maintain the defined size and position of the "Emergency Button", whereby changing the size or the position of the GUI screen changes the orientation of the buttons. Here, it is worth mentioning that the "Emergency Button" is an important safety feature, thus it is included in the design. Fig. 3 shows the GUI with all GTK objects been Implemented.

4   The Yaskawa Motoman HP3J Manipulator

Linux was used in implementing this research. Red Hat Linux version 9 was used in the designing of the system, for its compatibility with the RTLinux version 3.2 and the manipulator used, as was recommended by the manipulator provider [4].

This paper considers the Yaskawa Motoman HP3J robot, which is an articulated robot with 6 revolute joints: the first 3 joints (as shown in Fig. 1) are to position the robot; and the remaining three joints are to orient the robot. The manipulator has a payload of 3kg and the power requires is 0.5KVA.The base (named by Yaskawa as "S") of the manipulator that can be revolved from the centre point to right or left. This sweeping motion extends the work area to include the area on either side and behind the arm. This joint allows the robot to spin up to $\theta 1=180o$ from the centre point. The forward and backward reaching that mainly moves the lower arm is referred to as "L" and is performed by joint 2. The robot arms vertical space approach is performed by elevating the up and down of the upper arm (named "U"), allowing a better reach with joint 3. Joints 4 and 5 (named "R" and "B") perform horizontal (left-right) and vertical (up-down) motion of the upper arm, describing a circular motion. These are also referred to as Yaw and Pitch motions, where the pitch movement resembles the lifting up and down a lid of a box. The Yaw motion describes a motion similar to the door swinging motion. The turning motion of the robot arm wrist is performed by joint 6 (called T) allowing circular ($\approx\pm360°$) wrist motion.

5   YaskawaRTLab API

Yaskawa RTLab API functions were used in controlling the manipulator motion and in input/output operations. The functions were provided by the Yaskawa Company, who is the provider of the HP3J robot arm. These functions were combined with C programming to perform the relevant operations. Some of the API functions are listed below, which may be categorized into "System Control" and "Motion Control" API functions, as follows [5]:

System Control API

- RtlOpen(int bid):Open the control module connection
- RtlClose(int mid):End up the connection of the control module
- RtlServoOn(int mid):Turn on the servo power supply
- RtlServoOff(int mid):Turn off the servo power supply

Motion Control API

- RtlSetSpeed(intmid,int rate): Sets the speed of motion of the manipulator
- RtlMoveJoint(intmid,RtlJoint*dst): Starts the motion of the arm according to the values provided in the joint interpolation motion
- RtlMoveLineart(intmid,RtlJoint*dst): Starts the motion of the robot arm according to the values provided in Cartesian straight line motion
- RtlMovePause/RtlMoveRestart: Stops the motion of the robot and can be restarted using the RtlMove Restart API
- RtlMoveCancle (int mid): Stops the motion of the robot completely and cannot be restarted

6   The GUI Teach Pendant

Figure 4 shows the VTP-GUI, which was created using GTK+, to create a teaching environment where users could perform both control and analysis, as well as receive help and guidance.   The GUI utilizes RTLab API functions to perform joints movements. The GUI design and the functions that includes are explained as follows:

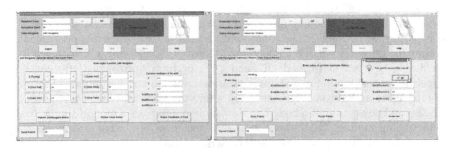

Fig. 4. Teaching Pendant GUI   **Fig. 5.** The Automate Motion Panel GUI

Authenticated access: The application starts by requesting a login authentication, where users are prompted to enter a Username and Password, before getting access to the VTP-GUI, otherwise an error message will be displayed and the user will be denied permission.

Manipulator in Power-on Status: To activate GUI functions, the robot arm must be in "Power-on" status, thus the first function that should be performed is to "switch-on" the robot arm, and otherwise GUI functions will be disabled. Once the manipulator is in the "Power-on" status, the manipulator status textbox changes to "On", the "On" button is disabled, and all the other functions will be enabled.

Failing to initialize the manipulator (remaining in the "Power-off Status"), the Pendant and the robot arm will remain unchanged: the manipulator status textbox will display as "off"; and all other function keys remain disabled.

Operation Mode: Following a successful initialization, users can select an "Operation-Modes", such as, Automatic-Mode, Joint-Navigation-Mode, and View-Saved-Points-Mode. Each mode is activated by selecting a panel, which will display dedicated functional buttons for that particular mode of operation, however, some functions remain common to all modes of operation. The panel approach makes the design simple and reduces the complexity, where it is based on the user choice of joint motion planning. For example, motion is planned by entering 3D-Space-Coordinates or Angles to a fixed reference frame. The next sections will address these modes of operation and their associated functions, before addressing the common functions.

7   Motion and Path Planning Methods

Joint Navigation Panel: The "Joint Navigation" panel (shown in Fig. 4) separately moves specific joints in the manipulator. It includes six buttons for the six different joint, namely: The Base, Lower-Arm, Upper-Arm, Wrist-Roll, Wrist-Pitch, and Wrist-Twist, which are named to match the relevant axis.

Textboxes are attached to each button to display the angles in degrees, which could be entered manually or incremented/decremented through the "+" and "-" buttons, which are useful when minor movements are desired. Once entered, the corresponding joint of the arm will move by that angle amount. All entries are validated to avoid driving a joint into out of range regions that are defined by the manufacture. Wrong entries will result in an "Out of Range Error Message".

If the exact angle of each joint is known, then it is easier to enter these values directly into the corresponding textboxes so that the arm can be moved directly to the desired point by using the "Perform Joint Navigation Motion Function" button, otherwise the arm has to be moved a joint at a time to reach to the desired point. This function performs the motion of the arm in a Joint interpolation method, where the "Linear Navigation Function" is implemented to move the manipulator. The Panel in Fig. 4 also utilises another Yaskawa API function (the "Display Cartesian Coordinates" function) to identify the final Tool coordinates.

Automate Motion Panel: If the user does not have an idea about the angle value of each joint, however, knows the coordinates of the final point that should be reached, then in this mode of operation the End-Effectors desired (x,y,z)coordinates maybe entered. The "Automate Motion Panel" GUI is shown in Fig. 5.

The GUI was designed so that entries are made to move the manipulator to two consecutive points, that is, between P1(x1, y1, z1) and P2(x2, y2, z2) should be entered into the respective textboxes, so that the arm moves from P1 to P2.

If the manipulator were to move to a single point in space only, then the user is required to enter P1(x1, y1, z1)as the single desired point, neglecting the P2(x2, y2, z2)point coordinates. Consecutive twin entries maybe saved with the "Save function" with an assigned job description as shown in Fig. 5. Here, the Yaskawa API "RtlInverseKinematics function" call is made to calculate the Joints angles corresponding to achieving the desired point. These points are saved in to a text file with a job description that will be available for the future use. Therefore, users will be able to know the values of the points needed to perform an operation according to a specific job, without re-entering the points.

View Saved Points Panel: Users may choose to view the saved points in this third (shown in Fig. 6) STP-GUI. Here, users are allowed to save points to a file for future reference, using the "Save Points function" available in the previously described "Automate Motion Panel". This tab can be used to select already saved points to start movement that is described by a set of points in space corresponding to (x, y, z) End-Effector coordinates, which describe a particular job. The selection is achieved through check boxes, thus paths maybe modified too.

In this Tab, there are many dedicated functions (displayed at the bottom of the table in Fig. 6), which may be described as follows:

The "Automate Selected Points Joint Navigation Motion function", which moves the robot arm to the selected points following a set described by a check box selection.

"Joint Interpolation function", which performs the motion of the arm in "Joint Interpolation" method ,where all the joints of the robot start moving simultaneously to reach a desired point in space. Once that point is reached, the motion of all the joints will be halted immediately. This function helps to achieve smooth continuous motion [5] .

"Linear Navigation function": This performs the motion of the manipulator in "Linear Interpolation" method, in which the manipulator tries to follow a linear line path to reach a desired point. The straight line motion is maintained by varying the speed of each joint along the path. "Linear Interpolation" is useful in industrial applications such as drilling, arc welding, loading and many more applications [6].

"Automate Selected Points Linear Motion function": It performs the same previous function, but the manipulator arm performs "Linear Navigation" motion to achieve the desired points.

"Start Loop Joint function": This function repetitively performs the "Joint Interpolation Navigation" method. Here, the manipulator will continue to move to the points assigned continuously, until the "Stop Loop function" is invoked.

"Start Loop Linear function": This function moves the manipulator to the selected points repetitively in a "Linear Interpolation navigation" method. The function is similar to the "Start Loop Joint function", however, the motion method of the manipulator is "Linear Interpolation navigation". The motion of the manipulator can be stopped similarly using the stop loop function.

Both of the above functions ("Start Loop Linear function" and "Start Loop Joint function") continue to perform repetitive manipulator motions until the loop condition is made "false" by the function "Stop Loop". These functions are important when performing industrial functions such as welding, packing, picking objects, etc., where the robot is required to moves to same set of points repeatedly. The "Reset All Saved Points function": This is employed to clear all the saved points available in the file.

8   The Functions Common To All Panels

Home Function: It is implemented to bring the manipulator arm to the "Home" position or to the starting position of the robot. It is in an inactive status at the time of motion of the arm.

Hold Function: Pauses the robot arm operation. When pressed, it deactivates other functional keys except the

"Emergency Stop" and "Move" functions, when the manipulator is in "Hold" status, where manipulator status will be changed to "Hold". This is a useful feature in industrial operation, when (for example) operators need a break, the robot maybe paused without completely switching it off [7]. The operator may resume the operation again using the "Move" function.

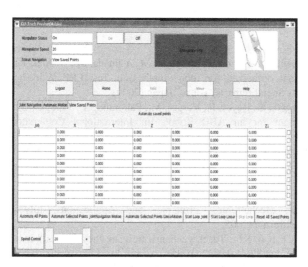

Fig. 6. View Saved Points Panel

Move Function: It reactivates the operation following going into a "Hold" status. When activated, the manipulator status changes to "on" and all buttons will be reactivated. Emergency Stop Function: It is implemented in an emergency situation, triggering the "Emergency Stop function", bringing the robot to a halt regardless promptly, thus, enhancing the safety of the Pendant [8].

a. **Motor On Function:** Checks the conditions and switches the servos on.
b. **Motor off Function:** Switches off the servos once the robot arm is home.
c. **Set Speed Function:** Controls the manipulator speed in the range from 0 to 100.
d. **Logout:** Logs out the user from the GUI application.
e. **Help:** This button provide detailed help of all the VTP-GUI functions.

9   Conclusion

The main objective of this paper was to introduce a Virtual-Teaching-Pendant-GUI to control an industrial robot manipulator in main operation modes, namely: Automatic-Mode, Joint-Navigation-Mode, and View-Saved-Points-Mode. The main aims were to: Duplicate and simplify functionalities found in a standard industrial robot arm; Teach industrial navigation methods such as "Linear Navigation" and "Joint Interpolation Navigation"; Include industrial safety features, such as, User-Authentication, and Emergency Stopping; and Provide online help of functions and operations; and detailed error messages due to invalid system inputs.

The paper briefly also described the GTK+ working environment, where the GUI was developed, and associated API functions which were used to programme the VTP-GUI to the HP3J manipulator. The system was tested in the University of Nottingham and has proven to be a good tool to aid students in understanding basic robotics, direct and inverse kinematics, and path planning.

References

[1] Fukui, H., Yonejima, S., Yamano, M., Dohi, M., Yamada, M., Nishiki, T.: Development of teaching pendant optimized for robot application. In: IEEE Workshop on Advanced Robotics and its Social Impacts, Tokyo, Japan (2009)

[2] Garcia, E., Vergara, S., Reyes, F., Vargas, M., Palomino, A., Villegas, G.: Development of a Teach Pendant for an ABB Robot. In: International Conference on Electrical, Communications, and Computers, Cholula, Puebla (2009)

[3] Andrew, K.: Foundations of GTK+ Development, April 25. Apress, New York (2007)

[4] Robert, J.S.: Fundamentals of Robotics: Analysis and Control, January 12. Prentice Hall, New Delhi (1990)

[5] Yaskawa Electric Cooperation, API for RTLab Instructions (2009)

[6] Onwubolu, G.: Mechatronics: Principles and Applications, July 8. Butterworth-Heinemann, California (2005)

[7] Emma, C.M., Chanan, S.S.: Teach pendants: how are they for you? Industrial Robot: An International Journal 22(4), 18–22 (1995)

[8] American National Standard for Industrial Robots, ANSI/RIA R15.06-1999, Robot Safety Standards, USA (1999)

UTHM HAND: Kinematics behind the Dexterous Anthropomorphic Robotic Hand

Amran Mohd Zaid and M. Atif Yaqub

Faculty of Electrical and Electronics Engineering, University Tun Hussein Onn Malaysia,
86400 Parit Raja, Batu Pahat, Johor, Malaysia
amranz@uthm.edu.my, ge100181@siswa.uthm.edu.my

Abstract. This paper describes a novel wireless robotic hand system. The system is operated under master-slave configuration. A human operator tele-operates the slave robotic hand by wearing a master glove embedded with BendSensors. Bluetooth has been chosen as the communication medium between master and slave. The master glove is designed to acquire the joint angles of the operator's hand and send to slave robotic hand. The slave robotic hand imitates the movement of human operator. The UTHM robotic hand comprises of five fingers (four fingers and one thumb), each having four degrees of freedom (DOF), which can perform flexion, extension, abduction, adduction and also circumduction. For the actuation purpose, pneumatic muscles and springs are used. The paper exemplifies the design for the robotic hand and provides the kinematic analysis of all the joints of the robotic hand. It also discusses different robotic hands that have been developed before date.

Keywords: Robotic hand, Tele-operation, Multi-fingered hand, pneumatic muscles, solenoid valves, kinematics.

1   Introduction

Robots have become an integral part of modern human life. With every passing year the population of robots is being increased. The industry has replaced a large number of human workers with lesser number of robots on the grounds of economy and efficiency. A robot is a modern version of slave, which perform any task in its capacity satisfying the old human instinct to rule. A robot follows the command as ordered by the human master. Therefore the humans can still enjoy mastering a dumb but efficient slave under their supremacy.

The intelligence of humans has been linked to the hands. Aristotle and Anaxagoras had been discussing this association hundreds of years ago [1]. Humans are the only specie that has been gifted with this kind of dexterous hands, where the universe of full of various species. These hands are capable of doing so many tasks in our routine like dexterously handling different things and even sensing. Therefore this has been discussed from long to be one of the reasons that humans are so intelligent.

The human hand consists of fifty four bones whereas the complete body of an adult human contains two hundred and six bones [2], which is around 26% of the total

S.G. Ponnambalam et al. (Eds.): IRAM 2012, CCIS 330, pp. 119–127, 2012.

human bones. When discussing the robotic hands, the segments or parts that join together to build the robotic hand are mostly less than this number. Even after reaching this number, it cannot compete with the human hand in a broad range of tasks. The reason is the structure of human hand and the material used in human hand that cannot be compared by the material available for robotic hands. The toolset and materials of Mother Nature is far advance than any of the latest technology.

A robotic hand system has been developed that is perfectly compliant to the needs of industry and the hand alone can also be used in prosthetics and rehabilitation. The shape, size and weight of the hand is comparable to actual human hand, therefore it is an anthropomorphic hand. The robotic hand is very flexible so that it can attain dexterous manipulation and can pick and place different things of different shapes and sizes like a normal human hand. The complete system should be able to fix the reprogramming issue and reduce the human injuries in extreme environments.

2   Literature Review

The research on robotic hands is being done for a long period of time. Looking back to the history of robotic hands, in 1961 Heinrich Ernst developed for the first time, the MH-1 a computer operated mechanical hand at MIT [4]. Theoretically the least number of DOF to achieve dexterity in a robotic hand with rigid, hard-finger, non-rolling and non-sliding contacts, is nine [5]. The proof for this theory was the development of Stanford/JPL hand.

The development of MIT/UTAH hand [6] was the beginning of more complex robotic hand structures. It was the first robotic hand capable of dexterously manipulating objects. A detailed study on the robotic hands performing dexterous manipulation can be seen in [3].

In order to actuate the finger joints in the robotic hand artificialitists has been using electric motors quite frequently [7], [8]. Electric motors have been proved to be very accurate in position and velocity control and also provide much force for the grasping function required by the robotic hand.

The MIT/UTAH hand had three fingers and one thumb [6]. They removed the little finger to avoid complexity in their dexterous robotic hand NASA's Robonaut Hand had twelve DOF and five fingers like human hand [9]. Brushless DC motors and gear head were used for the finger actuation. The anthropomorphic NTU hand had seventeen DOF with five fingers and was comparable to the size of human hand [10]. Similarly the DIST-Hand was developed with sixteen DOF and high level of dexterity [11]. It had four fingers actuated by tendon drive and DC motors. The DLR-Hand also used dc motors with transmission tooth belt and harmonic drive gears [12]. Compact fluidic hand had been developed and reported with fourteen DOF [13]. The hand is powered by fluidic actuators and a miniaturized hydraulic system was developed to be embedded inside the robot hand. The Keio hand had been developed having twenty DOF almost the same as human hand [14]. This hand has been actuated uniquely using ultra-sonic motors along with elastic elements. Another unique design using spring as actuating element has been reported [15]. The said robot had three fingers and was reported achieve very high acceleration. This robotic hand was reported for capturing purposes.

3   Master Glove

The control of the under discussion robotic hand is done by using tele-operation. For the actuation of anthropomorphic and dexterous robotic hand, all the angles of finger joints of the human operator must be tracked. Tracking of angles is done by a special glove, which is embedded by BendSensors and it is also capable of tracking the sideways movement of the joint that connects the finger to the palm as well i.e. abduction and adduction. The details of calculations, the sensors location in the glove and the modeling for torque produced at all joints can be seen in [16]. The operator wearing the specially designed master glove, by the authors, is shown in Figure 1.

Fig. 1. UTHM hand operator wearing master glove embedded with sensors

In this project, BendSensors are embedded in the glove to track the joint angles. This is a kind of potentiometer strip that changes the value of resistance when it is bent. The change of resistance value is proportional to the angle that the sensor is bent. This sensor has been used in voltage divider configuration. To sense the voltage levels, high speed Analog to Digital Converter (ADC) has been used which is capable of giving throughput of 50 kilo samples per second with each sample of 12 bits. The maximum angle of $120°$ can be observed between the joint joining the proximal and middle segment of the finger. The microcontroller acquires the digital values of the BendSensors. These sensor values are sent to the robot hand so that the robot hand can mimic the movement of the human operator. The robot hand has been setup in the listening mode so that the glove module can send connection request. After the establishment of connection the master glove transmits the angle while the slave robotic hand receives it. This is a one way data transfer, therefore the master acts as a transmitter and slave acts as a receiver.   The transfer rate has been set to 10 packets per second, where each packet contains the angle information of complete hand.

4   Robotic Hand

The theme of UTHM hand is to develop a dexterous and anthropomorphic robotic hand; therefore the inspiration for the look and feel has been taken from human hand. The look and feel as well as the size of all the fingers and palm is very much comparable to human hand. The hand comprises of five fingers including the thumb. The structure for all the fingers including the thumb is same while the difference is size, as the sizes varies among the fingers in normal human hand. The designed hand is capable of twenty DOF which does not include the wrist and arms. Twenty DOF is from the summation of all the fingers as each finger exhibits four DOF. All the joints are pin joints using the dowel pins for connecting the different segments of hand. The details of mechanical design and motion mechanism can be seen in [17].

Jacques Denavit and Richard Hartenberg introduced a convention in order to standardize the coordinate frames for spatial linkages [18], [19]. The Denavit-Hartenberg parameters (also referred as DH parameters) are the four parameters associated with this convention for attaching reference frames to the links of a spatial kinematic chain, or robot manipulator. This convention will be used in this robotic hand as every finger of the robotic hand represents one serial chain. There have been many conventions being developed in the past but the reason to choose this approach is because this approach remains standard for the serial linkages in robot manipulators.

In this convention, coordinate frames are attached to the joints, as shown in Figure 2, between two links such that one transformation is associated with the joint, [Z], and the second is associated with the link [X]. The coordinate transformations along a serial robot consisting of n links form the kinematics equations of the robot;

$$[T]=[Z_1][X_1][Z_2][X_2]...[X_{n-1}][Z_n]$$

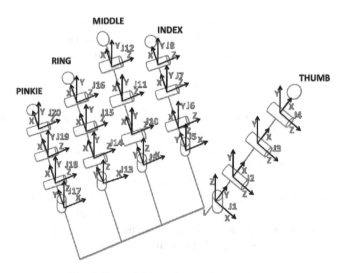

Fig. 2. Denavit-Hartenberg reference frames

This convention allows the definition of the movement of links around a common joint axis S_i by the screw displacement,

$$[Z_i] = \begin{bmatrix} \cos\theta_i & -\sin\theta_i & 0 & 0 \\ \sin\theta_i & \cos\theta_i & 0 & 0 \\ 0 & 0 & 1 & d_i \\ 0 & 0 & 0 & 1 \end{bmatrix}$$

where θ_i is the rotation around and d_i is the slide along the Z axis, either of the parameters can be constants depending on the structure of the robot. Under this convention the dimensions of each link in the serial chain are defined by the screw displacement around the common normal $A_{i,i+1}$ from the joint S_i to S_{i+1}, which is given by

$$[X_i] = \begin{bmatrix} 1 & 1 & 0 & r_{i,i+1} \\ 0 & \cos\alpha_{i,i+1} & -\sin\alpha_{i,i+1} & 0 \\ 0 & \sin\alpha_{i,i+1} & \cos\alpha_{i,i+1} & 0 \\ 0 & 0 & 0 & 1 \end{bmatrix}$$

where $\alpha_{i,i+1}$ and $a_{i,i+1}$ define the physical dimensions of the link in terms of the angle measured around and distance measured along the X axis.

It is common to separate a screw displacement into the product of a pure translation along a line and a pure rotation about the line, such that

$$[Z_i] = Trans_{(Z_i)}(d_i)Rot_{(Z_i)}(\theta_i) \text{ and}$$

$$[X_i] = Trans_{X_i}(r_{i,i+1})Rot_{X_i}(\alpha_{i,i+1})$$

Using this notation, each link can be described by a coordinate transformation from the previous coordinate system to the next coordinate system.

$$^{n-1}T_n = Trans_{Z_{n-1}}(d_n).Rot_{Z_{n-1}}(\theta_n).Trans_{X_n}(r_n).Rot_{X_n}(\alpha_n)$$

Note that this is the product of two screw displacements. The matrices associated with these operations are:

$$Trans_{Z_{n-1}}(d_n) = \begin{bmatrix} 1 & 0 & 0 & 0 \\ 0 & 1 & 0 & 0 \\ 0 & 0 & 1 & d_n \\ 0 & 0 & 0 & 1 \end{bmatrix}$$

$$Rot_{Z_{n-1}}(\theta_n) = \begin{bmatrix} \cos\theta_n & -\sin\theta_n & 0 & 0 \\ \sin\theta_n & \cos\theta_n & 0 & 0 \\ 0 & 0 & 1 & 0 \\ 0 & 0 & 0 & 1 \end{bmatrix}$$

$$Trans_{X_n}(r_n) = \begin{bmatrix} 1 & 0 & 0 & r_n \\ 0 & 1 & 0 & 0 \\ 0 & 0 & 1 & 0 \\ 0 & 0 & 0 & 1 \end{bmatrix}$$

$$\text{Rot}_{X_n}(\alpha_n) = \begin{bmatrix} 1 & 0 & 0 & 0 \\ 0 & \cos\alpha_n & -\sin\alpha_n & 0 \\ 0 & \sin\alpha_n & \cos\alpha_n & 0 \\ 0 & 0 & 0 & 1 \end{bmatrix}$$

Solving for $^{n-1}T_n$

$$^{n-1}T_n = \begin{bmatrix} \cos\theta_n & -\sin\theta_n\cos\alpha_n & \sin\theta_n\sin\alpha_n & r_n\cos\theta_n \\ \sin\theta_n & \cos\theta_n\cos\alpha_n & -\cos\theta_n\sin\alpha_n & r_n\sin\theta_n \\ 0 & \sin\alpha_n & \cos\alpha_n & d_n \\ 0 & 0 & 0 & 1 \end{bmatrix}$$

From the above matrix, rotation (R) and translation (T) can be visualized as;

$$R = \begin{bmatrix} \cos\theta_n & -\sin\theta_n\cos\alpha_n & \sin\theta_n\sin\alpha_n \\ \sin\theta_n & \cos\theta_n\cos\alpha_n & -\cos\theta_n\sin\alpha_n \\ 0 & \sin\alpha_n & \cos\alpha_n \end{bmatrix}, T = \begin{bmatrix} r_n\cos\theta_n \\ r_n\sin\theta_n \\ d_n \end{bmatrix}$$

Then the position and orientation of the end-effector attached to serial chain of n joints with reference to initial frame are given by

$$^0T_n = ^0T_1 ^1T_2 \ldots ^{n-2}T_{n-1} ^nT_n$$

Using the DH transformation matrix from one frame to the other frames, the position of one segment relative to the other segment can be calculated in this robotic hand. The calculated values of DH parameters are as follows;

Table 1. DH parameters for the robotic UTHM Hand

Joint	d(mm)	θ	r(mm)	α
J1- J2	0	90°	6.7	90°
J2- J3	0	0°	33	0°
J3-J4	0	0°	33	0°
J5-J6	0	90°	6.7	90°
J6-J7	0	0°	26.4	0°
J7-J8	0	0°	26.4	0°
J9-J10	0	90°	6.7	90°
J10-J11	0	0°	26.4	0°
J11-J12	0	0°	33	0°
J13-J14	0	90°	6.7	90°
J14-J15	0	0°	26.4	0°
J15-J16	0	0°	26.4	0°
J17-J18	0	90°	6.7	90°
J18-J19	0	0°	26.1	0°
J19-J20	0	0°	19.8	0°

The transformation matrices from base joint to the distal segment of each finger using the values of DH parameters of the UTHM Hand are computed individually. The resultant matrices after solving for the values of DH parameters of each finger are as follows;

$$^{J1}T_{J4} =\, ^{J1}T_{J2}\, ^{J2}T_{J3}\, ^{J3}T_{J4} = \begin{bmatrix} 0 & 0 & 1 & 0 \\ 1 & 0 & 0 & 72.7 \\ 0 & 1 & 0 & 0 \\ 0 & 0 & 0 & 1 \end{bmatrix}$$

$$^{J5}T_{J8} =\, ^{J5}T_{J6}\, ^{J6}T_{J7}\, ^{J7}T_{J8} = \begin{bmatrix} 0 & 0 & 1 & 0 \\ 1 & 0 & 0 & 59.5 \\ 0 & 1 & 0 & 0 \\ 0 & 0 & 0 & 1 \end{bmatrix}$$

$$^{J9}T_{J12} =\, ^{J9}T_{J10}\, ^{J10}T_{J11}\, ^{J11}T_{J12} = \begin{bmatrix} 0 & 0 & 1 & 0 \\ 1 & 0 & 0 & 66.1 \\ 0 & 1 & 0 & 0 \\ 0 & 0 & 0 & 1 \end{bmatrix}$$

$$^{J13}T_{J16} =\, ^{J13}T_{J14}\, ^{J14}T_{J15}\, ^{J15}T_{J16} = \begin{bmatrix} 0 & 0 & 1 & 0 \\ 1 & 0 & 0 & 69.5 \\ 0 & 1 & 0 & 0 \\ 0 & 0 & 0 & 1 \end{bmatrix}$$

$$^{J17}T_{J20} =\, ^{J17}T_{J18}\, ^{J18}T_{J19}\, ^{J19}T_{J20} = \begin{bmatrix} 0 & 0 & 1 & 0 \\ 1 & 0 & 0 & 52.9 \\ 0 & 1 & 0 & 0 \\ 0 & 0 & 0 & 1 \end{bmatrix}$$

This kinematics analysis can be further used for the dynamics of the robotic hand by calculating the force, velocity, contact locations etc. These transformation matrices help in transforming the base axes to the distal segment of the corresponding finger, which is mostly utilized in grasping. Therefore we can know the location of distal segments with respect to the base of the finger. It is pertinent to mention here that, the circular or rotational motion of the finger can be traced as the combination of extension, flexion, adduction and abduction movements of the fingers. The final transformation matrices of the fingers are already shown to be encapsulating the translational and rotational components.

5   Conclusion

The overview of the dexterous anthropomorphic robotic hand system has been elaborated in this paper. The robotic hand system is based on Tele-operation using

Bluetooth as the communication channel between them. The design has been made simpler and its demand for space has been reduced from previous designs of robotic hands by using combination of pneumatic actuator and springs. The state of the art microcontroller has been used as the control and processing unit for both the master glove and robotic hand. This robotic system has many applications for the developments of safe industrial environments, whereas the robotic hand alone can also be used for different applications in industry as well as for rehabilitation. The paper has focused on the kinematic analysis by using the standard DH parameters convention by calculating the reference frames and the parameter values of all the joint of the UTHM Hand.

Acknowledgments. This research work is fully funded by Fundamental Research Grant Scheme (FRGS) (VOT 0715), Ministry of Higher education, Malaysia and Graduate Researcher Incentive Grant (VOT 0868), University Tun Hussein Onn Malaysia (UTHM). We would like to thank the staff of Electrical Instrumentation and Measurement Laboratory of UTHM for the technical support.

References

1. Aristotle, Di partibus animalium: 687a 7, CA. 340 BC
2. Thibodeau, G.A., Patton, K.T.: The Human Body In Health & Disease, 3rd edn. The University of Michigan, Mosby (2002)
3. Bicchi, A.: Hands For Dexterous Manipulation And Robust Grasping: A Difficult Road Toward Simplicity. IEEE Transactions on Robotics and Automation 16(6), 652–662 (2000)
4. Ernst, H.A.: MH-1 A Computer- Operated Mechanical Hand, D.Sc. Thesis, MIT
5. Salisbury, K., Mason, M.: Robot Hands And The Mechanics Of Manipulation. MIT Press, Cambridge (1985)
6. Jacobsen, S., Iversen, E., Knutti, D., Johnson, R., Biggers, K.: Design of the Utah/M.I.T. dexterous Hand. In: 1986 IEEE International Conference on Robotics and Automation, vol. 3, pp. 1520–1532 (April 1986)
7. Lotti, F., Vassura, G.: A Novel Approach To Mechanical Design Of Articulated Fingers For Robotic Hands. In: International Conference on Intelligent Robots and Systems, vol. 2 (2002)
8. Ahmadi, A., Bogosyan, S., Gokasan, M., Abedi, M.: Simulation Studies for Permanent Magnet Synchronous Motors Position Control in Direct Drive Robotic Application. International Review of Automatic Control 2(6), 668–678 (2009)
9. Lovchik, C.S., Diftler, M.A.: The Robonaut Hand: A Dexterous Robot Hand For Space. In: IEEE International Conference on Robotics and Automation, vol. 2, pp. 907–912 (1999)
10. Lin, L.-R., Huang, H.-P.: Mechanism design of a new multifingered robot hand. In: IEEE International Conference on Robotics and Automation, vol. 2 (April 1996)
11. Casalino, G., Giorgi, F., Turetta, A., Caffaz, A.: Embedded Fpga-Based Control Of A Multifingered Robotic Hand. In: IEEE International Conference on Robotics and Automation, ICRA 2003, vol. 2, pp. 2786–2791 (September 2003)
12. Butterfass, J., Grebenstein, M., Liu, H., Hirzinger, G.: DLR-Hand II: Next Generation Of A dexterous Robot Hand. In: IEEE International Conference on Robotics and Automation, ICRA 2001, vol. 1, pp. 109–114 (2001)

13. Tan, L.Q., Xie, S.Q., Lin, I.C., Lin, T.: Development Of A Multifingered Robotic Hand. In: International Conference on Information and Automation, pp. 1541–1545 (June 2009)
14. Yamano, I., Maeno, T.: Five-Fingered Robot Hand Using Ultrasonic Motors And Elastic Elements. In: IEEE International Conference on Robotics and Automation (April 2005)
15. Kaneko, M., Higashimori, M.: Design Of 100G Capturing Robot. In: World Automation Congress, vol. 15, pp. 117–122 (June-July 2004)
16. Zaid, A.M., Atif Yaqub, M.: UTHM Hand: Design of Dexterous Anthropomorphic Hand. International Review of Automatic Control 4, 969–976 (2011)
17. Zaid, A.M., Atif Yaqub, M., Arshad, M.R., Wahab, M.S.: UTHM Hand: Mechanics Behind The Dexterous Anthropomorphic Hand. World Academy Of Science, Engineering And Technology 74, 154–158 (2011)
18. Denavit, J., Hartenberg, R.S.: A kinematic notation for lower-pair mechanisms based on matrices. Trans ASME J. Appl. Mech 23, 215–221 (1955)
19. Hartenberg, R.S., Denavit, J.: Kinematic Synthesis of Linkages. McGraw-Hill, New York (1964)

An Efficient Grid Based Navigation
of Wheeled Mobile Robots Based on Visual Perception

Yap Ping Yean and Kuppan Chetty RM

Monash University Sunway Campus, Bandar Sunway, Selangor, Malaysia
kuppanchetty.ramanathan@monash.edu

Abstract. Navigation is one of the major challenges and a key ability for the mobile robots to accomplish the given task. It is a two point problem where the accurate positioning and path planning is necessary. The efficient path planning and positioning with the use of conventional sensors becomes cumbersome when the robots are resource constrained and uses minimal information of the environment. Therefore, a simple heuristic navigation algorithm based on grids is addressed in this paper. A simple visual perception method with a use of line scan camera is also employed in this work, as an alternative to the existing methods with conventional sensors, towards the identification of grids and lines in the workspace. The efficiency of the proposed technique is investigated experimentally by applying on a miniature wheeled mobile robot "Grid-bot" and the results are discussed. The results reveals that the proposed method be a viable alternative for a resource constrained robot to plan its path and navigate the environment efficiently in indoor applications.

Keywords: Path Planning, Navigation, Visual Perception, Mobile Robots, Sensors.

1   Introduction

Navigation is one of the key ability and major challenge for the Autonomous Mobile Robots to perform in arbitrary indoor complex environments. In such environments, navigation involves accurate positioning and path planning for the robots to reach a specific goal/target from its initial position [1]. Therefore, the robots need to be equipped with sensors to perceive the information of the environment and to have robust control algorithms to act upon the perceived information. In the recent past several intelligent algorithms such as the behavior based [2], topological maps [3], combination of sensor based and topological maps are utilized for these purposes. These methods acts upon the information perceived by sensors such as IR's, sonars and lasers [4, 5], vision [6, 7], Information assisted by RFID and GPS [8] etc. The combination of such sophisticated sensors and algorithms requires extensive computational capability and resources on a robotic platform to have efficient planning and navigation capability. However, it becomes a cumbersome method if the robot platforms are severely resource constrained in power, architecture and computational capability.

S.G. Ponnambalam et al. (Eds.): IRAM 2012, CCIS 330, pp. 128–135, 2012.
© Springer-Verlag Berlin Heidelberg 2012

Grid based navigation method, seems to be a potential alternative to the conventional methods which uses minimal information from the environment. Buschmann et al. [4] developed a navigation method based on grids which uses minimal information from the environment using pairs of light sensors to identify the grids. However, this method lacks accurate estimation of grids and grid crossing events. Similarly Silva et al. [6] addressed the use of vision for the estimation of grid information from the environment. The major drawback in the above methods is either the lack of accurate sensory information in the first case or the need of high computational resources used in the later ones. Further, these methods require high processing capabilities of estimated signals. Therefore it is required to devise a simple robust navigational algorithm which works on minimal information perceived from the environment, less processing capability as well as on a computational platform limited with resources.

Inspired from the literatures, this work focuses on developing a robust navigational algorithm based on heuristic approaches which uses a simple vision sensor perceiving information from the environment. A line scan camera is used as the visual preceptor, which distinguishes the gird lines and background information accurately rather than providing an image of the entire environment for estimation. The resource constrained controller is used as a platform to govern the navigation based on the perceived information. Towards the objective of this work, our contribution is of two folds. Firstly, a simple heuristic navigation technique based on topological grids, to plan the path of the robot is developed and addressed in this work. Secondly, a simple visual perception method based on image threshold is also addressed in this work, in order to identify the lines and grid crossing events efficiently. A line scan camera is used as the visual sensor and integrated with the resource constraint robot for this purpose. The performance of the proposed method is also investigated through real time implementation on a miniature robot (Grid-bot) built in house.

Section 2 details about the method that have been adopted for the identification of lines and grids using visual sensor and the algorithm that have been used for path planning by the robots. Further, it also provides the details of the experimental platform that are used for real time implementations. Section 3 provides the experimental details and the results which are carried out to prove the effectiveness of the proposed algorithm in the laboratory environment. Finally, this paper concludes with the summary and scope of extension of this work in future.

2   Methodology

2.1   Sensing Method

The grid based methodology adopted in this work is illustrated in Fig. 1, where the environment of interest is divided into equal squares in a Cartesian coordinate system. The grids are numbered at the intersection as shown in figure. The robot is made to start from a predefined position called the home position (0, 0) and the orientation. The robot is oriented towards Y-axis initially at /4 rad w.r.t inertial frame and it is the frame of reference for the robot itself. The target positions are defined based on the grid values (for. ex. 3, 2) in the workspace. Robot navigates the environment by identification of grid numbers by the estimation of grid crossing points without

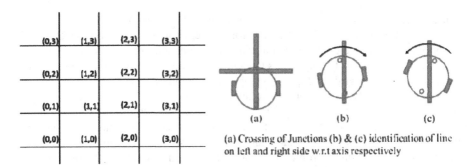

(0,3)	(1,3)	(2,3)	(3,3)
(0,2)	(1,2)	(2,2)	(3,2)
(0,1)	(1,1)	(2,1)	(3,1)
(0,0)	(1,0)	(2,0)	(3,0)

(a)   (b)   (c)

(a) Crossing of Junctions (b) & (c) identification of line on left and right side w.r.t axis respectively

Fig.1. Grid based environment with coordinated points

Fig. 2. Identification of lines and crossing of junctions at grids

having the information on the dimension of the grids. The grid crossing points are estimated by the information perceived by the line scan camera, which is used as the visual preceptor. While heading towards the goal the robot distinguishes the driving directions by means of estimation of turn directions using the kinematic equations of the robot. In this case for simplicity the robot is made to reach the coordinate point in y-axis initially and then in the x-axis to reach the target position. In order to reach the target of 3, 2 in the grid, robot reaches the position 2 in the y-axis initially and then it turns on the suitable direction and reaches the value of 3 in the x-axis, thus reaching the desired target. The grids are made out on a flat surface in the laboratory with black adhesive tapes of about 25.4mm on grey background with the gird size of 300 by 300mm.

As mentioned earlier, Parallax line scan camera is used to perceive the information of the lines and grid crossings from the environment. This visual preceptor perceives the information in form of image values in one dimension with the resolution of 128-pixel per field of view. Here the field of view equals the distance of the object. Even though it provides a linear range of values of the lines of the grid, it is necessary to establish a relationship that distinguishes between the lines and the grid crossings during the fly. Before distinguishing the lines and grid crossings it is also necessary to distinguish between the background (grey) and foreground (black lines) of the grid. The image is converted into a greyscale image with the resolution of 255 per pixel, and a pixel value at the valley point of the histogram is selected as suitable threshold value. In this case the threshold value is identified to be of 150. Therefore any pixel value greater than 150 is identified as white/ grey region and given a value of logic '1'; other than that are identified as black and given logic '0' and it is given as an empirical relationship given by Eqn. 1.

$$P_i = 1; \ g_i > 150 - White$$

$$= 0; \ g_i < 150 - Black \tag{1}$$

Therefore, the background information has the value of '1' and the lines and grids have the values of '0'. During the fly, it is necessary for the robots to distinguish between the lines and the grid crossings and there could be a possibility to encounter three different situations as indicated in Fig. 2. The pixel values are calibrated and the threshold values are obtained for such scenarios as indicated in Fig. 3.

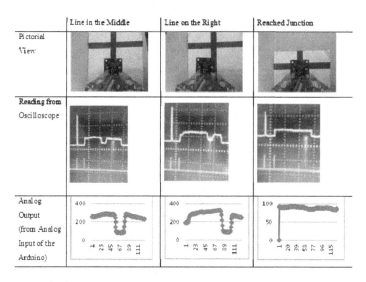

Fig. 3. Estimation of threshold values of lines and junctions

Based on the calibrated values, a simple relationship as given in Eqn. 2 and 3 is derived to solve such problems. In order to identify the pixel values between the positions of the robot w.r.t the lines, the entire 128 pixel is divided into equal half of 64 to represent both sides of the car. The sum of pixel values of the image on both left side and right side is calculated using the relationship as given by Eqn. 2.

$$P_R = \sum_{i=0}^{63} P_i \quad ; P_L = \sum_{i=64}^{123} P_i \tag{2}$$

Where, P_R and P_L are the total pixel values that correspond to the component of black and white region in right and left side of the robot respectively.

Therefore the heuristic decision is made such that when

$P_R = P_L$; it is identified as line sensed and the robot is at the middle

$P_R > P_L$; identified as robot deviates towards the right from the grid with more background region on right

$P_L > P_R$; identified as robot deviates towards the left from the grid with more background region on Left

Once the grids are identified the robots are made to move along the black line i.e. the grid. As mentioned earlier, the next important task is to look for the crossing of the grids at the intersection of grid lines. This is important since the grids are numbered at the intersections and it provides the position of the robot in the Cartesian space. Therefore, the calibrated data suggests that the grid intersections are of black values and the sum of pixels equals zero theoretically. However, in practical situations it is not feasible to achieve the value of 0, due to the fading of paints of the line and the illumination factor that affects the quality of the measurement. In this case, a constant value of 35 is used as the threshold and the grid crossing relationship 'P_g' is given by

$$P_g = \sum_{i=0}^{123} P_i \geq 35$$

(3)

2.2   Algorithm

The devised heuristic algorithm used to drive the robot to the desired destination on the grids is illustrated in Fig. 4. It consists of two major behaviors which makes the robot to reach the desired target by navigating 'Y – axis" and then the "X-axis" in the 2D workspace. These two major behaviors are further discretized as low level behaviors that are responsible for low level control of the robot such as the turn directions, estimation of reaching the junctions etc., as mentioned in the flowchart. These behaviors are encoded using a simple prepositional representation by an if-then-else rule based technique.

In this algorithm the robot is made to reach the target by reaching the grids in y-axis first and then to turn towards reaching the grids in x-axis. It considers the gird crossing to be happen in between during the fly and determines the next location of the grids and the turn directions. Once the path and the turn directions have been derived at the intersections it heads to the next location. Turn directions has to be estimated in advance since it always keeps the heading positioned towards the direction of the next intersection. Once the desired target has been reached, the robot waits for the next target to be returns to the home position similar to the previous one.

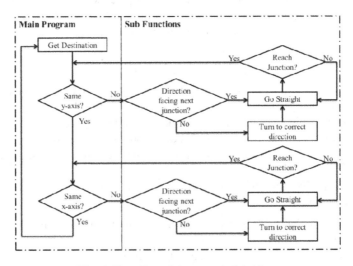

Fig. 4. Flowchart of the control algorithm

2.3   Experimental Setup

Figure 5 shows the hardware block diagram of the differential drive mobile robot called 'Gridbot' built in house. This robot is non-holonomic in nature and is driven with two independent wheels with zero instantaneous center of radius. Two standard analogue servo motors actuated by PWM signals are used as the actuators to govern the motion of the robot in the workspace. As mentioned earlier a Parallax line scan camera is used as the visual preceptor and an Arduino Mega with Atmega 1258 microcontroller is used as the CPU of the system. In addition to the visual sensor, encoder of 4096 count per revolution is used as the dead reckoning sensor to localize the robot in the grid environment. In order to build a complete system, the individual modules are integrated together and implemented as a Grid Bot as shown in Fig. 6. This Gridbot is resource constrained in reality since it has only 128KB of flash memory and a 16MHz operating clock to support the processing of the proposed algorithm and sensing methods. In addition the actuators and sensors are inexpensive and imprecise. Further, the driving capacity of the robot is heavily depend upon the onboard battery, which necessitates a simple navigational algorithm as the proposed ones.

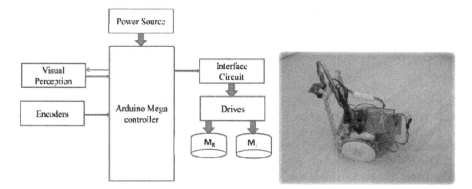

Fig. 5. Block diagram of the robot architecture   **Fig. 6.** Monash Grid Bot with line scan sensor

3   Results and Discussion

Experiments are carried out in a 1500mm by 1500mm flat environment divided into topological grids of size 300mm each. Grid-bot with line scan camera is used as the experimental platform. A total of two different experiments are conducted where, the robot is made to reach the target of grid (3, 2) in the first one and a multi-target of grids (3, 1; 2, 2 and 1, 3) sequentially. In both the experiment the robot starts from the initial position of 0, 0 as the home position and it is also made to return to the home position after reaching the target. The robots are run with the piecewise constant translational velocity of 100mm/s and rotational velocity of /6 rad/s.

Figures 7 and 8 shows the results of the first experiment, where performance of the proposed method could be observed. Figure 7 shows the trajectory of the robots in the grid environment. As mentioned earlier, the robot plan its path by navigating two grids in the y-axis initially by reaching (2, 0) and then it navigates three grids in x-axis to reach the specified target of (3, 2). After reaching the goal it returns to the home position by following the path of (3, 1; 3, 0) in y axis and then (2, 0; 1, 0) and finally (0, 0).

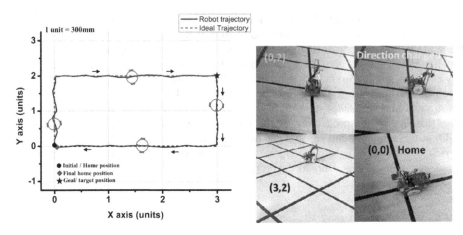

Fig. 7. Trajectory of robots navigating in the grid

Fig. 8. Snapshot of robot in the workspace during fly

Figure 8 shows the snap shot of the robot in the grid environment during fly. Therefore, It could be observed from the above result, that the robot relative trajectory closely matches with the ideal one by reaching the vicinity of target position of (3, 2) with an inaccuracy of less than 3%. Similarly, Fig. 9 shows the trajectory of the robot reaching multiple targets of (3, 1; 2, 2 and 1, 3) in the laboratory environment with grids. It could be observed that the robot reaches the desired target by navigating the grids in y-axis initially and then in the x-axis similar to the previous results.

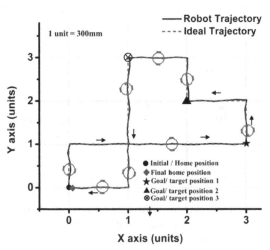

Fig. 9. Trajectory of robots in the grid navigating multipoint goals and back to home position

Moreover, the proposed algorithm positions the robot in the nearby vicinity of target with the error of 3% similar to the previous ones. A zigzag trajectory of the robots is observed in the above results, which is due to the result of the inaccuracy in robot actuators. Further, it could be also due to the skid and tire differences of the robot. In addition, the simple construction of the robot with cost effective resource constrained hardware's and driving and turning speeds constitutes to the path error. However, it shows that the algorithm makes the robot to follow the line of the grid by the estimation of the threshold data from the visual perception of line information. Therefore, the proposed heuristic algorithm provides the necessary corrective actions to the robot control whenever, it deviates from the line and also plans the path of the robot to reach the target position efficiently.

4   Conclusions and Future Scope

In this paper a simple heuristic approach for mobile robot navigation based on topological grid is presented. A visual perception method based on the line scan camera for the identification of lines of the grid and crossing of grids is also presented in this paper. The line scan camera provides minimal data for computation of grids to the robot controller. A cost effective miniature wheeled mobile robot (Gridbot) is also developed in house with the minimal hardware and resource constraint arduino controller. The efficiency of the proposed approach is investigated experimentally and the results provide to be a cost effective viable alternative navigation methods for the mobile robots in indoor environments with path error in the vicinity of target less than 3%. This could be due to the tire differences of the robot, skid and steer errors and selection of threshold for estimation of grids. Apart from navigation of mobile robots addressed in this work, the incorporation of obstacle avoidance strategy could be a possible improvement over this approach. Further, the proposed simplistic algorithm is far from optimum and the use of Neuro fuzzy, GA for effective estimation of grid crossing, position in the grids could be a future research direction.

References

1. Barfoot, T.D., Clark, C.M.: Motion Planning for Formations of Mobile Robots. Robotics and Autonomous systems 46(2), 65–74 (2004)
2. Kuppan Chetty, R.M., Singaperumal, M., Nagarajan, T.: Distributed formation planning and navigation of wheeled mobile robots. Journal of Applied Sciences 9(11), 1501 (2011)
3. Rawlinson, D., Jarvis, R.: Topologically-directed navigation. Robotica 26, 189–203 (2008)
4. Buschmann, C., Müller, F., Fischer, S.: Grid Based Navigation for Autonomous Mobile Robots. In: Proceedings of the Workshop on Positioning, Navigation and Communication (WPNC 2004), pp. 157–162 (2004)
5. Raghavan, V., Jamshidi, M.: Sensor Fusion Based Autonomous Mobile Robot Navigation. In: Proceedings of the IEEE international Conference on System of Systems Engineering, San Antonio, pp. 1–6 (2007)
6. Silva, A., Menezes, P., Dias, J.: Grid Based Navigation for Autonomous robots: An Algorithm Based on the Integration of Vision and Sonar Data. In: Proceedings of the IEEE International Symposium on Industrial Electronics, Portugal, pp. 802–806 (1997)
7. Gopalakrishnan, A., Greene, S., Sekmen, A.: Vision based Mobile Robot Learning and Navigation. In: Proceedings of the IEEE International Workshop on Robots and Human Interactive Systems, Hatfield, UK, pp. 48–53 (2005)
8. Milella, A., Cicirelli, G., Distante, A.: RFID assisted mobile robot system for mapping and surveillance of indoor environments. Industrial Robot: An International Journal 35(2), 143–152 (2008)

Bond Graph Based Unified Modeling Framework
for Aerial Service Robots

Veera Ragavan S.[1,*], Madhavan S.[1], Velappa Ganapathy[3], and Bijan Shirinzadeh[2]

[1] School of Engineering, Monash University, Sunway Campus, Malaysia
[2] Department of Mechanical and Aerospace Engineering,
Monash University, Clayton Campus, Australia
[3] Department of Electrical Engineering, University of Malaya, Kuala Lumpur, Malaysia
{veera.ragavan,madhavan.shanmugavel,
bijan.shirinzadeh}@monash.edu, velappa.ganapathy@um.edu.my

Abstract. This paper presents a novel Unified modeling approach using Bond Graphs (BG) as framework for Unified Modeling and validation of Aerial Service Robots. The proposed framework is generic and supports a concurrent design approach across multiple domains. A general parametric Non Linear Bond Graph Model that can be used for all types of rotorcraft UAVs with 6 DOF has been developed from the first principles using Newton Euler formalism. By employing a judicious mixture of 1-Dimensional, Multi-bonds and Junction structures, an Integral causal structure has been maintained, thus avoiding algebraic loops. This results in a compact computationally efficient model. Using experimental data from system identification, these generic models have been refined to develop accurate dynamic models for a specific Quad rotor and validated using 20-SIM. Simulation results obtained are in general conformity to those reported.

Keywords: Unified Modeling, Bond Graph Modeling framework, Quad rotors, UAVs, Model development, nonlinear dynamic Model, 6 DOF nonlinear models.

1 Introduction

There has been a renewed scientific interest in the development of Aerial Service Robots capable of missions in complex environments. Most Service robotic developments are environment and task specific [1]. A class of Unmanned Aerial Vehicle (UAV), popularly known as Quad rotor has emerged as a popular industrial, academic and research platform. Simple construction, low cost, agility, hovering ability, Vertical Takeoff and landing (VTOL) capabilities, small size and survivability of Quad copters has extended application area to: both indoor and outdoor environments; civilian and military missions, where fixed wing aircrafts cannot be deployed. Application examples [2] include Surveillance and Monitoring (forest fire

---

* Corresponding author.

S.G. Ponnambalam et al. (Eds.): IRAM 2012, CCIS 330, pp. 136–148, 2012.

monitoring, agriculture), Inspection (power lines, bridges, meteorological observation) Search and Rescue, law enforcement (intrusion detection) and military applications (reconnaissance).

Irrespective of the type of Micro Air vehicle (MAV) platform or application, autonomous navigation in general and controller development in particular, face a common set of challenges such as dynamic instability, limited flight envelope, trajectory tracking, nonlinear and coupled dynamics, under-actuated control, robustness to noise and disturbances etc. While *Kinematic* models are sufficient for controller development of most indoor terrestrial robots, modeling of UAVs require accurate *Dynamic* models which include gravity effects, aerodynamics and rigid body dynamics [3]. Earlier attempts to develop controllers were based on linear techniques and for limited flight envelopes[4-6]. Nonlinear controllers on the other hand can improve controller performance and enable tracking aggressive trajectories [4]. Recent trend to use Nonlinear Control laws has resulted in improved controllability and performance. However most of the controllers developed in the past were Aeromechanical platform specific [7]. A survey establishes that no *Unified Frameworks* that are generic are available[1] and Bond graphs in spite of widespread acceptance by automobile community have not been adopted by aerospace community [8]. This paper aims at bridging this gap.

A closer look at the taxonomy of UAVs [9], reveal many similarities which can be gainfully leveraged to device a general modeling strategy which can be abstracted as sub-models and reused. These sub-models when developed in a unified framework can then be hierarchically aggregated to produce accurate and composite models. For example all Rotorcrafts use thrust as the primary force to counter gravity, are under actuated, have coupled translational and rotational dynamics and can be modeled as rigid bodies [5].

We show in this paper that based on these similarities and conceptual requirements, a generic physical model using first principles can be built using *unified frameworks* in a *Top-down* approach. Provisions have been made in these generic models so that it can then be detailed in a *Bottom-up* approach to be iteratively refined to yield accurate models specific to the vehicle by incorporating data from complementary experimental techniques such as system identification, CFD etc. This model when refined further iteratively can be used to benchmark dynamics of UAVs. For this, we propose to use *Bond Graph* (BG) grammar [10] and transformation [11]-[12] to develop a *Unified Framework* where Top-down and Bottom-up approaches can be gainfully utilized to develop accurate models for benchmarking.

Autonomous flight poses unique research (intelligent control, 3D trajectory planning), technical (sensor fusion, path planning, collision avoidance and navigation) and logistics (involving disparate teams working collaboratively and concurrently on a rapidly evolving model) challenges. It is a daunting task to develop generic frameworks that can quantitatively evaluate performance based on all these measures [13]. Using Bond Graph semantics for *Meta-Modeling* in a *Collaborative* and *Concurrent* development framework, we argue it is possible to iteratively develop a generic Model for design, development and benchmarking of Autonomous systems which can be used throughout the product life cycle from *Concept* design to

Commissioning phases without *Architectural* degradation. The IEEE Robotics and Automation Society advocates *integrability, interoperability* and *reusability* of architectural concepts and components in Robotics and Automation technology [14]. *Unifying* frameworks proposed here can be used and this paper is a contribution in this regard.

In Section 2 we provide an introduction to unified methods, state of art and introduction to BG as a *Unified Modeling Framework*. Section 3 discusses the methodology of the proposed general unified framework for design and validation based on Bond Graphs. In section 4, we develop a generic parametric based Non Linear Model that can be used for all UAVs with 6 DOF. This is possible due to the judicious mix of One-dimensional and Multidimensional Bond Graphs and through the use of Junction structures to maintain integral causality thereby avoiding the Algebraic loops inherent in Multidimensional Bond Graphs. In section 5 we present the Simulation results. The generic models have also been enhanced to improve the accuracy of the models in a bottom up fashion through incorporation of iterative experimental data. This is followed by conclusion in Section 6.

2   Unified Modeling Approach

Modeling is an approximate, useful representation of a real system based on physical principles whereas Simulation is realistic imitation of actual behavior using Mathematical Models [15]. It is important to use a systematic framework/methodology to derive highly accurate models of a physical system. A high fidelity model goes through several iterations and the architectural framework of the model has to be preserved.

Unified Variables: They are a set of four variables which can be used across domains to describe analogous system variables, Power and/or Energy interactions in a multi-domain physical system [16] [17]: *Effort (e), Momentum (p), Flow (f) and Displacement (q).*

Unified Methods for modeling physical systems are based on the central premise that energy exchange between systems, components and environment are fundamental processes that determine the dynamic behavior of the system [16]. Through systematic classification of physical components and their energy handling characteristics, a unified method for analysis can be developed.

Unified Framework in this context can be defined as a common, collaborative environment in which modelers from various domains (electrical, mechanical, aerodynamic, electromagnetic etc.) from diverse backgrounds share a common knowledge infrastructure to model, analyze and validate concepts and architectures for complex systems.

3   Unified Framework for Physical Systems

A unified framework that can be used for Conceptual, Detail and Recursive Design Phases is proposed as shown in Fig. 1. It is a systematic iterative process for Physical

Modeling and can be used for validation of all types of UAV Systems. It can also be used as a general purpose modeling framework for multi domain engineering systems.

Word Bond Graph (WBG) is the first step to conceptual modeling phase in a top down approach. Words or alphanumeric symbols are used to denote subsystem and components. The vertices of a Word Bond Graph represent subsystems and components. They clearly represent large models in a hierarchical manner, and also help to visualize the energy exchanges between subsystems and components, even at the conceptual level when subsystems are not completely defined and component specifications are not available.

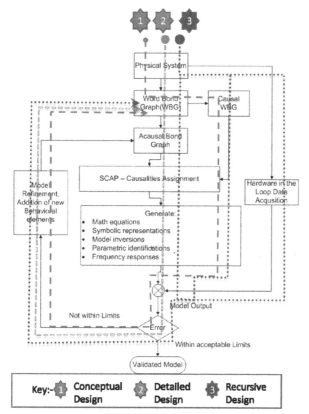

A topological scheme can be used to guide the construction of a WBG model which can be decomposed into sub processes. Word bond graph sufficiently indicates the qualitative behavior of a system or part with respect to the power flow. Fig. 2 shows the topological scheme of the Navigation and control architecture for a general UAV system comprising of the Controller, Flight dynamics, Navigation and Trajectory Generator subsystems. The system composed of WBG subsystems (represented by elliptical boxes) is also shown in Fig. 2. Each of these subsystems can be modeled by domain specialists using BG or other languages in a

Fig. 1. Bond Graph based modeling and validation framework

Unified, Concurrent and *Collaborative* manner in a *Top-down, Bottoms up* or *Iterative* approaches. During Conceptual design, requirements drive the design and analysis from requirements stage. Once the feasibility has been established using preliminary top Down Models, detailed modeling using BG can be done without any architectural discontinuity or degradation. Word bond graph can also be used hierarchically, recursively or in a bottom-up approach. For example the Propulsion Group subsystem shown in Fig 2 is composed of energy source (Power Pack), Motor driver which supplies power required for the motor, and coupled to the rotor through a transmission system.

Aerodynamic forces and torques in the rotor and the control signal input from the controller determine the dynamics of the Propulsion Group. The *Energy flow* and *Information flow* can be also be readily visualized. The Power bonds in red color show the energy exchange and the black arrow shows the signal flow.

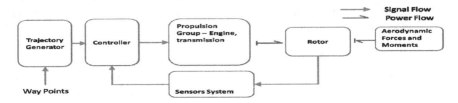

Fig. 2. Topological scheme of a UAV Control and Navigation System as Causelled Word Bond Graph and Activated Bonds (Signal Flow)

Following the system decomposition into WBG, the next process is to augment the WBG's using Causal Marks (Vertical Lines attached to the power bond) using *Sequential Causal Assignment Procedure. Causality or cause and effect relationship on the other hand, allows* power flow modeling even before inputs and outputs are completely fixed. Moreover the assigned *Causality* can be subsequently reassigned manually or using automatic procedures.

Sequential Causal Assignment Procedure (SCAP) are the Rules for systematically assigning Causality [10], which allows large scale systems to be aggregated from component subsystems.

Generating Math Models: Compiling the BG model enables running simulations for analysis and generates Mathematical models required for analysis. The above steps are repeated until the model is validated. Benefits of BG modeling in current context include:

- Ability to predict system response even before physical prototype is assembled.
- Easy linearization of Nonlinear Kinematics allows developing an intuitive feeling which is hard to get from pure computer simulations [10].
- Predicting the system response and stability using computer simulation
- Automated simulation for Nonlinear Systems. Advanced packages that can generate causality and state equations automatically are available today.
- BG is systematic and graphical. No analytical derivation is usually necessary to construct the Bond Graph. It also gives a more graphically and analytically exploitable representation compared to other methods.

The most important advantage of using Bond Graphs based Unified Modeling framework is that the designer need **not** derive complicated mathematical or analytical formulation in the initial or later stages. Automatic generation of state space[18] and other mathematical models using tools is now possible. Visual representation of power flow (Power Bonds) and causal augmentation result in automatic generation of System Equations. Many Software packages such as 20-SIM are available today where automatic causal assignment options are available.

4   Quad Rotor Modeling

Quad rotor is an under actuated, Vertical Take- off and Landing (VTOL) UAV with four input forces due to the thrust provided by four fixed angle rotors and six output coordinates (spatial movements) [4] as shown in Fig. 4. Due to the 4 independent rotors, it has high payload and omnidirectional movements due to independent control of rotors when compared to conventional helicopters. Quad rotors have six degrees of freedom with respect to an earth fixed inertial reference frame as shown in Fig. 6. The general configuration of UAVs as a six dimensional vector is: $\xi = (x \quad y \quad z \quad \phi \quad \theta \quad \psi)^T$. The change in direction of movement is achieved by varying the angular speed of the individual rotors which in turn changes the thrust produced and the counter rotating torques. The variation in thrust and torque combination generates the desired movement (*Altitude, Yaw, Pitch, Roll*). If T_i is the thrust of rotor i, the change in the total thrust U_1 applied to the quad rotor causes change in *altitude* given by

$$U_1 = b\sum_{i=1}^{4} \omega_i^2 \text{ where } T_i = b\omega_i \qquad (1)$$

where ω_i and T_i are the speed and thrust of individual rotor. The four rotors are divided into two pairs: the front and rear rotor forming the 1st pair rotate in one direction (clockwise) and the left and the right which form the 2nd pair rotate in the opposite direction (anticlockwise) thereby cancelling the aerodynamic torques and gyroscopic effects in a perfectly trimmed flight. This paring also helps to represent the quad as a combination of two Planar VTOLS, each one of them with independent torque control [19]. Quad rotors do not require cyclic and collective pitch control as in the case of helicopters.

The difference in angular velocity of the Left and Right Rotors produces **Roll** as given by

$$U_2 = b(-\omega_2^2 + \omega_4^2) \qquad (2)$$

The difference in angular velocity of the Front and Rear Rotors produces **Pitch** as given by

$$U_3 = b(-\omega_3^2 + \omega_1^2) \qquad (3)$$

The change in angular velocity of the Front and Rear Rotor pair produces **Yaw** as given by

$$U_4 = d(-\omega_1^2 + \omega_2^2 - \omega_3^2 + \omega_4^2) \qquad (4)$$

a.   Bond Graph Model of Coordinate Transformation

Modeling Quad rotor kinematics requires the use of many reference frames and coordinate systems to describe the position and orientation. Let I denote the inertial frame and position vector $\xi=(x,y,z)$ denote the origin of the body fixed frame fixed at the Centre of Mass of the Quad rotor.   Bond Graph Modeling for coordinate transformation is shown in Fig 3. The corresponding Rotation matrices and Euler Transformation matrices used for force and velocity transformations are given below:

$$R_\phi = \begin{bmatrix} 1 & 0 & 0 \\ 0 & \cos\phi & -\sin\phi \\ 0 & \sin\phi & \cos\phi \end{bmatrix} ; R_\theta = \begin{bmatrix} \cos\theta & 0 & \sin\theta \\ 0 & 1 & 0 \\ -\sin\theta & 0 & \cos\theta \end{bmatrix} ; R_\psi = \begin{bmatrix} \cos\psi & -\sin\psi & 0 \\ \sin\psi & \cos\psi & 0 \\ 0 & 0 & 1 \end{bmatrix} \quad (5\text{-}7)$$

Using these rotation matrices the velocities and angular velocity transformations are obtained from the *Inertial frame I* to *Body fixed frame B* of the Quad rotor shown in Fig. 6 using the following transformations:

$$\begin{bmatrix} v_X \\ v_Y \\ v_Z \end{bmatrix} = R_\psi R_\theta R_\phi \begin{bmatrix} v_{Xb} \\ v_{Yb} \\ v_{Zb} \end{bmatrix} \quad ; \begin{bmatrix} \omega_X \\ \omega_Y \\ \omega_Z \end{bmatrix} = R_\psi R_\theta R_\phi \begin{bmatrix} \omega_{Xb} \\ \omega_{Yb} \\ \omega_{Zb} \end{bmatrix} \quad (8\text{-}9)$$

Forces and torque transformations are obtained using:

$$\begin{bmatrix} F_X \\ F_Y \\ F_Z \end{bmatrix} = \left(R_\psi R_\theta R_\phi\right)^T \begin{bmatrix} F_{Xb} \\ F_{Yb} \\ F_{Zb} \end{bmatrix} \quad ; \begin{bmatrix} \tau_X \\ \tau_Y \\ \tau_Z \end{bmatrix} = \left(R_\psi R_\theta R_\phi\right)^T \begin{bmatrix} \tau_{Xb} \\ \tau_{Yb} \\ \tau_{Zb} \end{bmatrix} \quad (10\text{-}11)$$

We choose *Multi-bond* representations [20], [21], so that these coordinate transformations are easily represented in three dimensions. A Bond Graph representation of Coordinate Transformation from Inertial Frame to Body Fixed Frame of a UAV is shown in Fig. 3. This representation allows forces such as Gravity effects and (if required) Wind directions to be specified at the inertial frame.

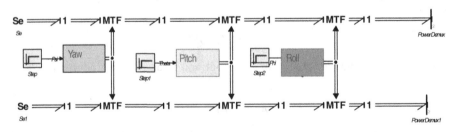

Fig. 3. Multi Bond Graph Model for Coordinate transformation of forces, torques and velocities between Inertial and Body Fixed Frames

b   Bond Graph Model of a Quad Rotor

Using a *Top-down* approach an accurate model of the Quad rotor will be obtained. Very few researchers attempt top down approach. We present the mathematical preliminaries for describing the dynamical behavior of UAV which can be treated as a rigid body with 6 DOF, using a six dimensional position vector $\xi = (x \quad y \quad z \quad \phi \quad \theta \quad \psi)^T$ to describe the general configuration of UAV.

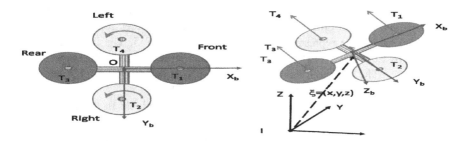

Fig. 4. Forces and Moments acting on a Quad rotor

In research literature, Dynamics of a Quad rotor as a rigid body about its center of mass and subject to external forces and torques have been expressed in various formalisms such as Newton-Euler (NE) [5], Lagrangian [4] and Hamiltonian [7] formalisms. No major attempts to use Bond Graphs have been cited. While all the above methods can be used, we prefer to use the Newton –Euler formalism as it provides a compact representation in 1-D Bond Graphs. This also results in fewer or no algebraic loops prevalent in Multi bond graphs. The Dynamics of the Quad rotor is given by

$$\begin{bmatrix} F \\ \tau \end{bmatrix} = \begin{bmatrix} mI_{3x3} & 0 \\ 0 & J \end{bmatrix}\begin{bmatrix} \dot{V} \\ \omega \end{bmatrix} + \begin{bmatrix} \omega \times mV \\ \omega \times J\omega \end{bmatrix} \tag{12}$$

where $J \in \Re 3$ is the inertia matrix, V and ω are instantaneous linear and angular velocities, F and τ are external forces and torques applied and m is the mass of the system. Equations of Motion in Newton-Euler formalism for a rigid body with 6-DOF is given by [10]:

$$\dot{p}_x = F_x - m\omega_y \frac{p_z}{m} + m\omega_z \frac{p_y}{m} \tag{13}$$

$$\dot{p}_y = F_y - m\omega_z \frac{p_x}{m} + m\omega_x \frac{p_z}{m} \tag{14}$$

$$\dot{p}_x = F_x - m\omega_y \frac{p_z}{m} + m\omega_z \frac{p_y}{m} \tag{15}$$

$$\dot{p}J_x = \tau_x - J_z\omega_z \frac{pJ_y}{J_y} + J_y\omega_y \frac{pJ_z}{J_z} \tag{16}$$

$$\dot{p}J_y = \tau_x - J_x\omega_x \frac{pJ_z}{J_z} + J_z\omega_z \frac{pJ_x}{J_x} \tag{17}$$

$$\dot{p}J_z = \tau_x - J_y \omega_y \frac{pJ_x}{J_x} + J_x \omega_x \frac{pJ_y}{J_y} \qquad (18)$$

where F is the force, τ is the torque, ω the angular velocity, J the Moment of Inertia, p the momentum and m the mass of the UAV and $\omega_x = pJ_x / J_x$; $\omega_y = pJ_y / J_y$; $\omega_z = pJ_z / J_z$. Each of the above six equations can be represented in bond graphs using a special junction structure known as *Euler Junction Structure* (EJS) [10]. Using *1-Junctions* to represent 1-DOF, using Modulated *Gyrators (MGY)* elements to transform forces into displacements (linear Velocity) and *0-Junctions* to sum efforts, the energetic coupling of forces represented by the equations above can be represented in BG as shown in Fig. 5. The linear dynamics represented by Eqs. (13) – (15) appear in a triangular structure (red color) represented by nodes 4-6.   The angular dynamics represented by equations (16) – (18) appear in a triangular structure (blue color) represented by nodes 1-3.

Assuming that the external Forces and Torques are available in the Body Fixed Coordinates, we proceed to create a BG model. If the rigid body is said to have 6 DOF, 3 linear and 3 angular, then using six *1-Junction* elements all the 6 DOF are sufficiently represented. The Rigid Body constraints are introduced between these *1-junctions* through appropriate BG elements such as *Modulated Gyrators (MGY)*. Using a judicious mixture of 1-Dimensional, Multi-bonds and Junction structures, an integral causal structure has been maintained avoiding algebraic loops resulting in a compact computationally efficient model.

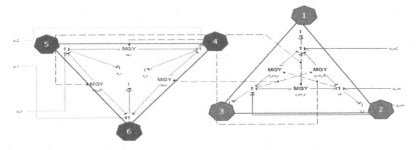

Fig. 5. Bond Graph Model of UAV as a Rigid Body using Newton Euler Formalism

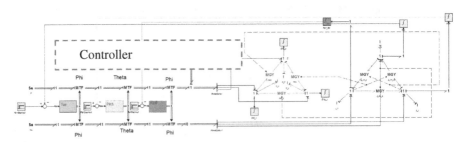

Fig. 6. Bond Graph Model of UAV System

The simple structure of a quad rotor, leads to complex control system design. Even though the cross coupling of Quad rotor dynamics is minimal, the low rate of damping makes the vehicle difficult to control [3]. The difficulty of controlling the vehicle is more as the size of the quad rotor decreases. Moreover existing dynamical models are usually developed on restrictive hypothesis of a single unique rigid body where as a real Quad is composed of 5 Rigid bodies. This makes modeling the behavior of quad rotor like gyroscopic effects difficult. Using the Modules developed earlier; we proceed to assemble the Complete Model of a UAV Control and Navigation system as shown in Fig. 6 . As the Bond graph model shown is parametric and allows recursion, accurate models can be created as required for detailed analysis. This obviates the need to simplify models in the development stages thus preventing misleading interpretations [3]. Models can be extended iteratively, increasing the accuracy of the model. For example the initial parameter estimates have been refined by using the experimental parameters obtained by [6] to obtain a more accurate model and simulation. Controllers typically handle limited error bands (10-15%) and hence with these accurate models better controllers can be designed. Many advantages accrue in designing controllers in the physical domain [22].

5   Simulation Results and Discussion

Using Top-down approach, for the conceptual design and a Bottom-up approach for detailed design, results in a nonlinear parametric Bond Graph Model as shown in Fig. 6 . The BG Model can be solved using tools such as 20-Sim. This resulted in 93 Equations; 144 Variables and 13 Independent states. The magnitude of effort saved in developing Mathematical Models is readily apparent.

Based on the general model obtained in the Section above on Quad rotor , we proceed to refine the model using system data obtained from experimental identification techniques. For the purposes of validation of this model, we use inertial parameters obtained from experiments for a X-4 Quad rotor as reported in [6].

Table 1. Inertial Parameters for Rigid Body dynamics [6]

Parameters	Value	Unit	Remarks
I_{XX}	0.0820	$Kg.m^2$	[6]
I_{YY}	0.0845	$Kg.m^2$	[6]
I_{ZZ}	0.1377	$Kg.m^2$	[6]
Mass	1.318	$Kg.$	[6]
Roll Maximum	-90 - +90	deg	
Yaw Step input	0.3928	Rad/s	

Preliminary results obtained using the modeling framework is provided below and qualitatively matches the results reported in the literatures.   As Quad rotor is a coupled system any movement along one axis will affect the velocities in the other axes. A small pitch rate resulting in a change of pitch and a change in Velocity in Z direction can be observed from Fig. 7 .

Fig. 8 shows the distance traversed due to uniform thrusts and forces along the three axes (X, Y, Z). The angular dynamics create difficulties in controlling the Quad rotor in hover and forward flights as seen from Fig. 7. The same effect can also be seen Fig. 9 and Fig. 10; where angular rate changes result in drifts. A stabilization of the quad rotor at hover will require a controller to compensate for the drift with inverse dynamics.

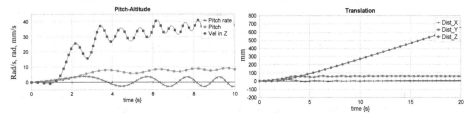

Fig. 7. Coupling of Pitch and climb in a Quad rotor

Fig. 8. Increasing altitude in the Z direction

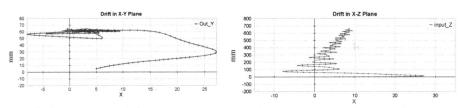

Fig. 9. Drift in the Quad rotor in the X-Y plane

Fig. 10. Drift in the Quad rotor in the X-Z plane

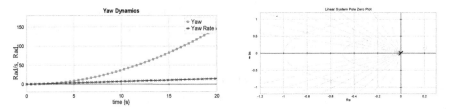

Fig. 11. Yaw rate effect on yaw dynamics

Fig. 12. Pole-Zero Plot

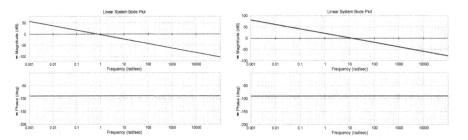

Fig. 13. Open loop response for input F_X

Fig. 14. Open loop response for input τ_X

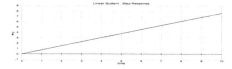

Fig. 15. Step Response – Force -Fx

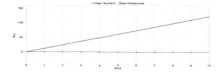

Fig. 16. Step Response - Torque

Similarly the system response due to a uniform input force F_X on the UAV in Open loop configuration is shown in Fig 13. and Fig. 15 . The effects of a constant Torque input along the X axis is shown in Fig 14. and Fig. 16. The open loop transfer Function for Positional Hovering obtained is $0.7587/s2$ and Linear system matrix A = $[0, 0 ; 0.7587,0]^T$. The open Loop Transfer Function for Roll rate is $12.1951/s$. The stability (Pole-Zero Plot in Fig. 12) and the Yaw dynamics as shown in Fig. 11 are as expected for a typical marginally stable quadcopter.

6   Conclusions

In this paper, a novel unified approach for physical modeling of UAVs in general was proposed and adapted for Quad copters. Using Bond Graphs we developed a generic nonlinear dynamic model for Quad rotors in a generic form suitable for developing Navigation and Control Systems. Simulation results were used to validate the model.

Recursive model improvement using actual parameters obtained through system identification and simulation help to develop an accurate dynamic parametric model of Quad rotor. The time savings it provides in model development stage and the immense insight it provides to control designers are obvious. The Developed Model also provides the much needed physical insight for Controller design using Bond Graph and will be discussed in a separate paper.

Developing a generic framework is a nontrivial exercise. We argue that as Bond Graph framework supports collaborative and concurrent development it may be possible to iteratively develop a framework generic enough to design, develop and benchmark intelligent systems. Our hope is that using BG meta-modeling frameworks such a generic unified framework may eventually be possible and will gain widespread acceptance in future among the aerospace community.

References

[1] Ragavan, S.V., Ganapathy, V.: A General Telematics Framework for Autonomous Service Robots. In: IEEE International Conference on Automation Science and Engineering, CASE 2007, pp. 609–614 (2007)

[2] Finn, R.L., Wright, D.: Unmanned aircraft systems: Surveillance, ethics and privacy in civil applications. Computer Law & Security Review 28, 184–194 (2012)

[3] Salih, A.L., Moghavvemi, M., Mohamed, H.A.F., Gaeid, K.S.: Flight PID controller design for a UAV quadrotor. Scientific Research and Essays 5, 3660–3667 (2010)

[4]   Castillo, P., Lozano, R., Dzul, A.: Stabilization of a mini rotorcraft with four rotors. IEEE Control Systems Magazine 25, 45–55 (2005)

[5]   Bouabdallah, S., Siegwart, R.: Full control of a quadrotor, pp. 153–158 (2007)

[6]   Pounds, P., Mahony, R., Corke, P.: Modelling and control of a quad-rotor robot (2006)

[7]   Mersha, A.Y., Carloni, R., Stramigioli, S.: Port-based modeling and control of underactuated aerial vehicles, pp. 14–19 (2011)

[8]   Montgomery, R., Granda, J.: Automated modeling and simulation using the bond graph method for the aerospace industry (2003)

[9]   Tsach, S., Tatievsky, A., London, L.: Unmanned Aerial Vehicles (UAVs). In: Encyclopedia of Aerospace Engineering (2010)

[10] Karnopp, D.C., Margolis, D.L., Rosenberg, R.C.: System Dynamics: Modeling, Simulation, and Control of Mechatronic Systems. Wiley (2012)

[11] Borutzky, W.: Bond Graph Modeling and Simulation of Mechatronic Systems: An Introduction into the Methodology (2006)

[12] Mukherjee, A., Samantaray, A.K.: Bond graph in modeling, simulation and fault identification. CRC Press (2006)

[13] Madhavan, R., Lakaemper, R., Kalmár-Nagy, T.: Benchmarking and standardization of intelligent robotic systems, pp. 1–7 (2009)

[14] Prassler, E., Nilson, K.: 1,001 robot architectures for 1,001 robots [Industrial Activities]. IEEE Robotics & Automation Magazine 16, 113–113 (2009)

[15] Foeken, M.J., van Tooren, M.J.L.: Object-oriented simulation model generation in an automated control software development framework (2009)

[16] Layton, R.A.: Principles of analytical system dynamics. Springer (1998)

[17] Gawthrop, P.J.: Bond graphs: a representation for mechatronic systems. Mechatronics 1, 127–156 (1991)

[18] Rosenberg, R.C.: State-space formulation for bond graph models of multiport systems. Journal of Dynamic Systems, Measurement, and Control 93, 35 (1971)

[19] Garcia Carrillo, L.R., Rondon, E., Sanchez, A., Dzul, A., Lozano, R.: Stabilization and trajectory tracking of a quad-rotor using vision. Journal of Intelligent & Robotic Systems 61, 103–118 (2011)

[20] Tiernego, M.J.L., Bos, A.M.: Modelling the dynamics and kinematics of mechanical systems with multibond graphs. Journal of the Franklin Institute 319, 37–50 (1985)

[21] Filippini, G., Delarmelina, D., Pagano, J., Alianak, J.P., Junco, S., Nigro, N.: Dynamics of multibody systems with bond graphs. Mecnica Computacional 26, 2943–2958 (2004)

[22] Sharon, A., Hogan, N., Hardt, D.E.: Controller design in the physical domain. Journal of the Franklin Institute 328, 697–721 (1991)

Waypoint Navigated Unmanned
Aerial Vehicle Autopilot System

Chamira Sooriyakumara[1], Veera Ragavan S.[2], and Madhavan S.[2]

[1] School of Engineering, Monash University Sunway Campus, Malaysia
[2] School of Engineering, Monash University Sunway Campus, Malaysia

Abstract. This paper describes the design and development of an Unmanned Aerial Vehicle (UAV) and the implementation of a Waypoint Navigation System built using low cost, commercially available components. The scope of development consists of an aerial vehicle platform, communication system and ground control system. The UAV is constructed by using GAUI 330X quad copter platform and combining a custom designed onboard controller which carries out quad copter stabilization and waypoint navigation. The communication system is constructed using XBEE Pro modules. The ground control system carries out path planning and waypoint generation using A-star algorithm, video processing to identify the landing pad and management of communication between UAV and ground control station.

Keywords: Quad-copter, UAV, Waypoint navigation, Image processing.

1 Introduction

Unmanned Aerial Vehicles (UAV), also known as drones are aircrafts without a pilot onboard [1]. These aerial vehicles are capable of operating semi autonomously without operator assistance. The UAVs differ from remote control aircrafts as it has intelligence built on board [2]. The remote controlled aircrafts cannot be controlled further than the line of sight because the operator requires clear vision of the aircraft to be maneuvered properly, the UAV addresses this issue by controlling flight according to the automated guidance system [2]. Even though the UAVs possesses intelligent decision making and self-flight capabilities, an operator is assigned to the UAV to assist it or to be controlled in the time of need. Usually the operator is positioned in a command room and controls the UAV wirelessly [3] [4].

The cost factor of commercially available UAVs prohibit the exploration of uses for UAVs hence the quad copter based low cost UAV system was constructed which can carry out most of the requirements of UAVs. The design and implementation of the UAV system consists of four main components; the *UAV Platform, Onboard Controller, Communications System and Ground Control Station.*

The UAV System was constructed using a commercially available quad copter platform known as GAUI 330X . The quad copter frame was fitted with a custom built on board UAV controller consisting of electronic hardware, Sensor modules and

S.G. Ponnambalam et al. (Eds.): IRAM 2012, CCIS 330, pp. 149–158, 2012.

intelligent software algorithms. The UAV controller carries out quad copter stabilization as well as waypoint navigation of aerial vehicle. The communication system was constructed using two XBEE Pro communication modules. One XBEE Pro module mounted on the UAV controller and the other connected to the ground control station PC via a custom built electronic circuit.

The ground control system was constructed by using a portable PC. MATLAB software is used to create the interface of the UAV ground control system and to implement path planning and waypoint navigation for UAV and also the ground control station software processes the live video stream sent from quad copter for landing pad position identification [5].

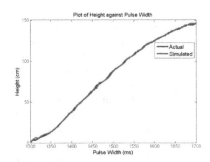

Fig. 1. Quad copter based UAV in flight hovering about a predefined set point

Fig. 2. Altitude response of quad copter for throttle input (blue) and simulated output (red)

2   Design and Implementation

2.1   Quad Copter Modifications

The GAUI 330X quad copter frame was fitted with landing gear and mounting plates on top and bottom sides of the centre frame to mount custom built controller, ultra sound sensor and wireless camera and the bottom plate also holds 2650mAh LiPo battery which powers the quad copter.

2.2   Quad Copter Dynamics Modeling

The quad copter parametric model was created using system identification method [6] [7]. The corresponding angle changes of way, pitch, roll and altitude change for throttle input were recorded and used as inputs for the system identification. The system identification was carried out assuming first order transfer function model. The altitude change for throttle input is shown in figure 2.

The data for system identification was obtained by using the onboard controller during remote controlled flight. The values of throttle and altitude were transmitted in real-time to the PC. The obtained transfer function is shown in Eq1.

$$OLTF = \frac{1.268}{z - 0.0017} ----- Eq\ 1$$

Once the transfer function was obtained, the simulated plot was generated and error between the experimental data and transfer function output was analyzed and the error was found to be 0.24. Hence the first order approximation of transfer function can be used to model altitude control of quad copter.

Similarly the transfer functions for yaw, pitch and roll of the quad copter was also obtained using the system identification method.

2.3   UAV Controller Design

The main controller of UAV carries out quad copter stabilization and waypoint navigation. The controller has a fast running uninterrupted inner loop which carries out computation of PID controller for stabilizing quad copter and slow running outer loop for navigation and communication. The inputs to fast running inner loop controller were obtained from accelerometer, gyro, digital compass and ultra sound sonar sensor. The fast running inner loop also consist of an Inertial Measurement Unit (IMU) which computes angles of yaw, pitch and roll inputs used by PID controller.

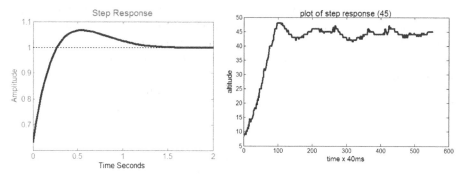

Fig. 3. Step response of UAV for an altitude of 45 height units

Fig. 4. Step response of altitude approximation transfer function

The readings obtained from accelerometer and gyroscope sensor are noisy due to electrical and mechanical noise present in quad copter. The angles from gyroscope was obtained by integrating angular velocity outputs, hence the calculated value of angle drifts over time. The tilt angle calculated from the accelerometer suffers from mechanical vibrations and the reading obtained is accurate for longer periods of time. By combining values from accelerometer and gyroscope sensor an approximately accurate value of tilt angle can be obtained. The method used to combine accelerometer and gyroscope sensor is known as a complementary filter [8]. The complementary filter weighs the accelerometer and gyroscope angle calculations to generate the tilt angle. The structure of complementary filter can be seen in Eq2.

$$\theta_n = (1 - R) \times (\theta_{n-1} + Gyroscope\ reading \times dt) + R \times Accelerometer\ reading ----- (Eq\ 2)$$

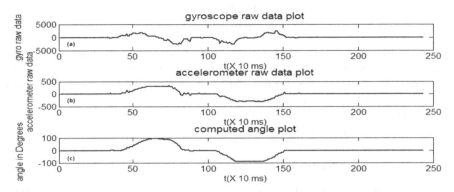

Fig. 5. (a) Gyroscope angular reading, (b) accelerometer angle reading and (c) complementary filter output of angle

The value 'R' is the relationship between the accelerometer and gyroscope angle value calculations. The value of 'R' was found using MATLAB by trial and error from data logged from accelerometer and gyroscope. The output of the complementary filter is shown in figure 5. Once the complementary filters were implemented for yaw, pitch and roll angle outputs, the PID controller parameters had to be found by using Ziegler -Nichols reaction curve method [9]. Firstly the step responses for altitude, yaw pitch and roll were obtained from quad copter during flight and corresponding PID values were calculated. Table 1 represents the PID values calculated.

Despite the higher value of integral component of PID, the response from the simulated controller appears to be reducing the settling time of the system.

Table 1. PID values for yaw, pitch, roll and altitude controller

Controller	P	I	D	E^2 Error from SID
Yaw	3.8	31.7	0.1140	0.108
Pitch	4.93	54.8	0.1110	0.797
Roll	4.35	54	0.0870	0.053
Altitude	13.56	33.9	1.35	0.240

It can be seen from the Figure. 6 and Figure.7 a significant improvement can be seen in settling time once the PID controller is implemented. But the overshoot of 29% is introduced by the PID controller and further tuning had to be done manually to obtain optimal PID values.

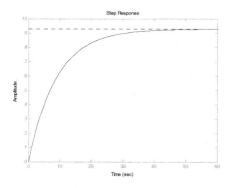

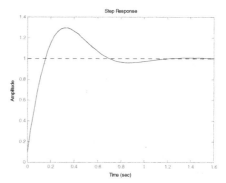

Fig. 6. Step response of transfer function obtained for pitch angle estimation

Fig. 7. Step response of pitch angle with PID controller

The waypoint navigation system is implemented in the slow running outer loop of the control algorithm. Once the waypoints from the ground control station are received, the corresponding 'angle to' and 'angle from' waypoints are calculated by the UAV controller using Eq3.

$$\theta = atan2(sin(lon1 - lon2) \times cos(lat2), cos(lat1) \times sin(lat2) - sin(lat1) \times cos(lat2) \\ \times cos(lon1 - lon2)) \tag{Eq 3}$$

The angle θ represents the angle of next waypoint from current waypoint respective to north. The *Lat* and *Lon* refers to latitude and longitude respectively

Once the angles are pre-computed, the UAV heading direction is set towards the next waypoint by inner loop controller. The controller tries to minimize the heading direction error of UAV. The Figure 14 represents the complete control structure of quad copter controller.

2.4   Development of UAV Controller Hardware

The controller of UAV was designed using an ARM STM 32 processor. The ADXL345 accelerometer, L3G4200 gyroscope, MAG3110 digital compass, FASTRAX UP501 GPS module and XBEE Pro communication module constitute the controller hardware. The components were mounted on a custom built PCB and then mounted on to the quad copter.

The power for the onboard wireless camera was obtained from a separate battery to minimize interference signals to the controller circuitry. The power for the controller was obtained from an isolated power supply which draws power from quad copter battery.

2.5   Fail Safe UAV / RC Mode Switch

The quad copter was fitted with a custom made switch which allows the user to select between the UAV *Autonomous* mode and *Remote Control* mode of operation. The switch between the modes can be activated in flight controller through an auxiliary output of the remote controller. The switch consisted of a 2 to 1 multiplexer and simple logic which is activated by pulse width of auxiliary output of remote controller. Once the threshold limit of activation pulse width is reached, the multiplexer is given an output signal which causes the throttle, rudder, aileron, elevator signals to be switched to RC receiver or UAV controller output.

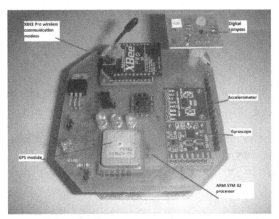

Fig. 8. UAV controller board made for quad copter

Fig. 9. Custom made Fail safe UAV/RC mode switch PCB with components mounted

2.6   Ground Control Station (GCS)

The ground control station consists of a PC running MATLAB software. MATLAB is a powerful software which can be used to create interfaces and has standard libraries which can be used to carry out complex mathematical operations. The main purpose of the ground control station is to carry out computationally intensive tasks such as computing shortest path from initial position to destination using A-star algorithm [10,11] and to generate flyable paths (waypoints). The ground control station software also carries out live video processing to identify the landing pad location from video stream sent from quad copter wireless camera to authorize landing. The GCS software also generates a .KML file of the path computed which can be used to viewed and simulate the path using Google Earth software.

The path planning section of interface obtains current landing pad location of the quad copter by requesting the GPS coordinates. Then the GPS coordinates of current location is set as initial location and the destination is entered. Then the obstacles can be entered using the interactive interface.

Once all the information is entered, the software computes the shortest path by using A-star algorithm. Firstly the 'Degrees Minutes Seconds' latitudes and longitudes are converted in to degrees and the distance between the waypoints are calculated using Haversine [12] formula and x, y plane size is set twice the distance between points. Then the spherical coordinates are converted to Cartesian coordinates and plotted on x, y axis. Then the A-star algorithm is applied to compute the shortest path.

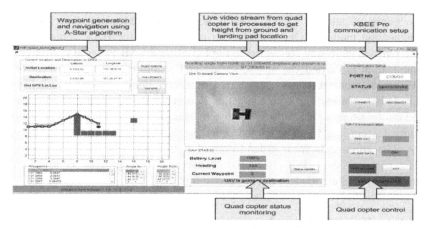

Fig. 10. Interface of UAV system ground control system

The ground station software carries out image processing by using MATLAB image acquisition toolbox. Firstly the frame is captured from streaming video. Then the image is converted in to grayscale and converted into a binary image. The binary image is then analyzed for connected objects and all small connected objects are filtered out and landing pad is extracted. The extracted landing pad location is then analyzed using blob statistics to find its center of gravity. Once the center of gravity is found, the location of COG is given as an x, y location in the frame. This landing pad location information can be used in assisting of landing. The figure 12 shows the steps of video processing.

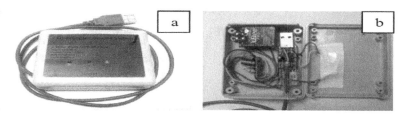

Fig. 11. Ground control station modem constructed using XBEE Pro communication module. (a) Enclosure, (b) cover opened.

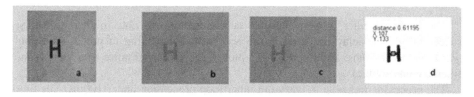

Fig. 12. Steps of image processing used in landing pad identification. (a) live video stream, (b) captured image, (c) grayscale image, (d) processed image with landing pad.

The communication of UAV system was constructed using two XBEE Pro communication modules. One module was connected to the UAV controller board and the other module was connected to the PC using a USB to serial converter. The communication is carried out at 9600 baud and according to the datasheet of the XBEE Pro communication module the, maximum communication distance is listed as 1.6 Km [13] outdoors. The communication between the UAV and ground station is carried out by using a packet based approach. The packets are of variable length and transmitted according to a predefined order between the UAV and ground control station. The commands from ground control station are sent using corresponding 'COM' port of the USB to serial converter. The ground control station communication system modem can be seen in figure 11.

3   Results and Discussion

The system identification models obtained for altitude estimation, yaw, pitch and roll of quad copter was able to predict the response of the system with minimum absolute error. The error calculated can be seen in Table 1.

The step response obtained for the hovering model of the quad copter and actual response obtained from the quad copter altitude sonar sensor expresses similar settling time of about 2 seconds. The hovering controller of UAV was able to obtain hovering at given set points with an accuracy of 10cm. The value of hovering accuracy was obtained by analyzing the response plot of hovering altitude for a given set point.

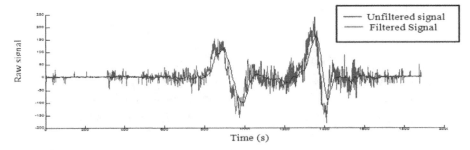

Fig. 15. Plot of accelerometer raw data in red and filtered data in blue, x axis is accelerometer data and y axis is time

The low pass filter implemented for accelerometer was able to filter out noise successfully. The delay observed in the accelerometer reading to processed output was found to be 50ms. The figure 13 is a plot of accelerometer noise data (in red) and filtered data (in blue).

The processor was able to carry out inner loop processing under 100ms. The time delay of 100ms is due to the bottle neck created by I2C reading of accelerometer, gyroscope and digital compass sensor using the same I2C lines.

The communication distance of 700 meters was able to achieve between the UAV and ground station. The results obtained are less than half of the capable of distance of XBEE Pro communication modules. The shorter distance could be due to the external RF interference or power supply noise in the XBEE Pro circuit. But the distance achieved was sufficient for testing of UAV.

The testing of the GPS module in an enclosed area surrounded by buildings obtained an error of 9 meters in latitude difference and error of 58 meters in longitude difference from actual position. However the test carried out in an open ground area obtained results with 11 meters error in longitude and 5 meters error in latitude from actual position.

The ultra sound sonar sensor (Maxbotics EZ1) used in the quad copter UAV had a minimum sensor reading distance of about 20cm. If the sensor was brought too closer (less than 20cm) to a surface the reading value output of the sensor becomes chaotic and it is observed when landing of the UAV was carried out. Once closer to the ground the sonar values tend to be unstable and causes false altitude estimation by the PID controller and the response is reflected in quad copter as sudden variations in altitude.

4   Conclusion and Future Improvements

The UAV system was successfully implemented by using low cost off-the-shelf components. The ground control station was implemented using MATLAB software which carries out image processing, path planning and waypoint generation. The robust communication between aerial vehicle and ground control station was obtained by using XBEE Pro communication modules and the possible distance of communication was found to be around 700m. The UAV was successfully implemented by taking a quad-copter frame and by integrating custom built UAV controller. The UAV was able to takeoff, land and hover at a given set point autonomously. The hovering accuracy was found to be around 10cm.

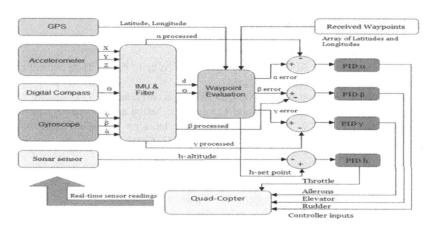

Fig. 16. Control system of the UAV including sensors

The future improvements would include moving MATLAB based ground control station software in to a standalone application using programming language such as Microsoft Visual studio, due to the high latency of MATLAB. The use of a Kalman [14, 15] filter needs to be incorporated in the navigation process when the GPS signal is not present. The analog wireless camera should be replaced with a digital wireless camera to minimize RF noise interference to the XBEE Pro communication modules.

References

[1] Gertler, J.: U.S. Unmanned Aerial Systems: CRS Report for Congress, pp. 1–2, January 3 (2012)

[2] Savla, K.D.: Multi UAV Systems with Motion and Communication Constraints, pp. 1–6 (2007)

[3] Bone, E.: UnmannedAerialVehicles:Background and Issues for Congress. ForeignAffairs, Defense, and Trade Division, p. 1 (2003)

[4] Valavanis, K.: Advances in unmanned aerial vehicles: state of the art and the road to autonomy. Springer (2007)

[5] Lange, S., Sünderhauf, N., Protzel, P.: Autonomous Landing for a Multirotor UAV Using Vision. In: Proceedings of SIMPAR, pp. 482–491 (2008)

[6] Sa, I., Corke, P.: Estimation and Control for an Open-Source Quadcopter. In: Proceedings of the Australasian Conference on Robotics and Automation, p. 4 (2011)

[7] Pounds, P., Mahony, R., Corke, P.: System Identification and Control of an Aerobot Drive System, pp. 154–159. IEEE (2007)

[8] Colton, S.: A Simple Solution for IntegratingAccelerometer and Gyroscope Measurements for a Balancing Platform (2007)

[9] Zhong, J.: PID Controller Tuning: A Short Tutorial. In: Mechanical Engineering, Purdue University, pp. 1–10 (Spring 2006)

[10] Dechter, R., Pearl, J.: Generalized best-first searchstrategies and the optimality of A*. Journal of the ACM (JACM) 32(3), 505–536 (1985)

[11] VeeraRagavan, S., Ganapathy, V., Aiying, C.: Simple LowCost Autopilot System for UAVs. Intelligent Robotics and Applications 1, 324–334 (2011)

[12] Chang, J.-R.: A Novel Approach to Great CircleSailings: The Great Circle Equation. Journal of Navigation 57, 311–320 (2004)

[13] XBee® Multipoint RF Modules, p. 2, http://www.digi.com/pdf/ ds_xbeemultipointmodules.pdf

[14] Veera Ragavan, S., Ganapathy, V., Xian, E.C.M.: A reconfigurable FPGA framework for data fusion in UAV's. In: 2009 World Congress on Nature and Biologically Inspired Computing, NABIC 2009 - Proceedings, Coimbatore, India, pp. 1626–1631 (2009)

[15] Simon, D.: Embedded Systems Programming, pp. 72–79 (2007)

A Study on Vehicle Lateral Motion Control
Using DGPS/RTK

Kwanghee Lee, Jeong-Hyeon Bak, and Chul-Hee Lee[*]

Department of Mechanical Engineering, Inha University, 402751, Incheon, South Korea
chulhee@inha.ac.kr

Abstract. In recent days, most vehicles have become equipped with electric assist systems helping drivers driving safe in roads. Sudden lateral motion of vehicle due to drivers' fatigue, inattention, and drowsiness are major causes of accidents in roads. In order to prevent possible accidents due to such motions of vehicle, lateral motion control system of vehicle is designed and validated in this study. The location of vehicle is obtained by using Differential Global Positioning System/Real Time Kinematic (DGPS/RTK). When vehicles depart from any lanes, vehicle motion control system is activated to put vehicles back to lanes.

Keywords: Vehicle control, DGPS, Lateral motion, Safe driving, Advanced Driver Assist System.

1 Introduction

The major causes of accidents in roads when driving in high speed are due to illness, inattention and drowsiness of drivers. Vehicle defects or external conditions like nasty weather or road conditions are also causes of accidents in roads. Especially driving off a centerline of a lane in roads due to the reasons mentioned above causes serious accidents compared to other types of accidents. In order to prevent accidents, vehicles have been equipped with control systems assisting and helping drivers driving safe, especially in the case of lane departure. Lane departure warning system (LDWS) has become one of necessary equipment for drivers' safety. It provides drivers warnings with sound or vibration when the edge of any front tires cross lane in road to regain drivers' attention. An another advanced technology is Lane Keeping Assistant System (LKAS) that maintains vehicles' path at the centerline of lane even if drivers lose their control of vehicle to prevent accidents caused by lateral collisions [1-5]. Electric assist systems such as LDWS or LKAS use vision sensors (image or video) to detect the lane and the current location of vehicle to control lateral motion of vehicles to prevent lane departure. In this paper, lateral motion control of vehicle using Differential Global Positioning System/Real Time Kinematics (DGPS/RTK) has been designed and validated. The work presented in this paper aims at controlling lateral motion of vehicles to recover its path to the canter line of lane from lane departures.

---

[*] Corresponding author .

S.G. Ponnambalam et al. (Eds.): IRAM 2012, CCIS 330, pp. 159–166, 2012.

2   Main

2.1   Background

The road curvature is neglected and it is assumed that the road is straight that is driving condition addressed in this study. Lateral motions of vehicles in roads are frequently occurred and such motions can be one of main causes of accidents. Most cases of electrical assist system for drivers' safety such as LDWS and LKAS are based on in-built vision camera that can detect lanes and the current location of a vehicle. Those technologies provide drivers safe driving conditions with either giving warnings when vehicles are to drive off the lane and having ability to keep vehicles remain at the center line of lane in road to minimize possible accidents.

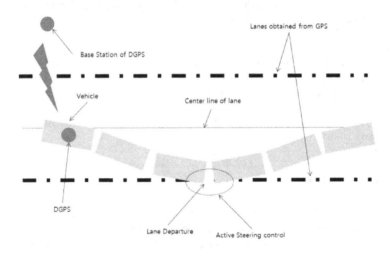

Fig. 1. Lateral motion control process

2.2   Simulation Model

In contrast to those technologies, the work presented here is based on only DGPS/RTK and GIS. It is assumed that all the location data of lanes in road are provided via implemented network. The controlling process is shown in Fig. 1. The purpose of this study is focusing on controlling lateral motion of vehicle to minimize possibilities of accidents from sudden lane departure. The classical bicycle dynamic model is used to control lateral motion of vehicle [6][7]. The vehicle model is given by following (1) ~ (4)

$$\dot{x} = A \cdot x + B \cdot T. \tag{1}$$

$$x = (\beta \quad r \quad \psi \quad y \quad \delta_f \quad \dot{\delta_f})^T. \tag{2}$$

$$A = \begin{pmatrix} a_{11} & a_{12} & 0 & 0 & b_1 & 0 \\ a_{21} & a_{22} & 0 & 0 & b_2 & 0 \\ 0 & 1 & 0 & 0 & 0 & 0 \\ v & l_s & v & 0 & 0 & 0 \\ 0 & 0 & 0 & 0 & 0 & 1 \\ \dfrac{Ts_\beta}{I_sR_s} & \dfrac{Ts_r}{I_sR_s} & 0 & 0 & \dfrac{2K_pC_f\eta_t}{I_sR_s^2} & \dfrac{B_s}{I_s} \end{pmatrix}. \tag{3}$$

$$B = \begin{pmatrix} 0 & 0 & 0 & 0 & 0 & \dfrac{1}{R_sI_s} \end{pmatrix}^T. \tag{4}$$

where

$$a_{11} = -\frac{2(c_r+c_f)}{mv}, \quad a_{12} = -1 + \frac{2(l_r c_r - l_f c_f)}{mv^2}$$

$$a_{21} = \frac{2(l_r c_r - l_f c_f)}{J}, \quad a_{22} = -\frac{2(l_f^2 c_r + l_f^2 c_f)}{Jv}$$

$$c_r = c_{r0}\mu, c_f = c_{f0}\mu$$

$$b_1 = \frac{2c_f}{mv}, \quad b_2 = \frac{2c_f l_f}{J}$$

$$T_{S\beta} = \frac{2K_p c_f \eta_t}{R_s}, \quad T_{Sr} = \frac{2K_p c_f l_f \eta_t}{R_S v}$$

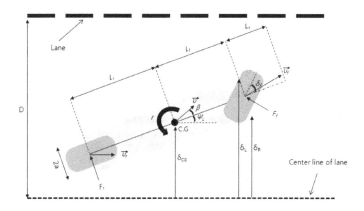

Fig. 2. Classical bicycle model

Here x is a state vector, where β is side slip angle, r is yaw rate, ψ is relative yaw angle, y is distance from the center line, δ_f is steering angle, and $\dot{\delta}_f$ is its derivative. The schematic diagram of a vehicle model is shown in Fig. 2. showing all the parameters.

In order to prevent any possible accidents caused by sudden lateral motion of vehicle, lateral motion control system should be properly activated in time. Activation is followed by warning to drivers when they drive off the lane in road. Warning system offers drivers time to regain the control of vehicle to get back to the centerline of lane. Otherwise, lateral motion control system will be activated then drivers still cannot obtain the control of vehicle. Warning zone and activation zone and line can be obtained by following equations and conditions. Parameters for equations and conditions are explained in Fig. 3.

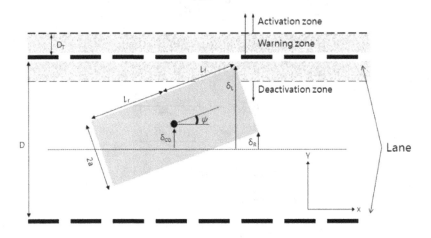

Fig. 3. Activation zones for controlling vehicle

$$\delta_L = L_f \cdot sin\psi + \delta_{CG} + a \cdot cos\psi \qquad (7)$$

The lateral offset of left front tire from center line is given in (7). It is assumed that yaw angle is very small then Eq. (7) can be expressed by Eq. (8)

$$\delta_L = L_f \cdot \psi + \delta_{CG} + a \qquad (8)$$

When the distance of δ_L gets equal to the distance of D/2, the warning system become activated as long as the vehicle remains outside of lanes. The distance from centerline to activation line can be defined as follows.

$$\frac{1}{2}(D + L_f \cdot \psi + a) \qquad (9)$$

There are three zones for active steering control system: warning zone, activation zone, and deactivation zone. The threshold, D_T, between warning and activation line is defined from (8), which is $\frac{1}{2}(L_f \cdot \psi + a)$. Vehicle is controlled to get back to the centerline of lane and it is deactivated since crossing deactivation line. After deactivation, vehicles return the control of vehicle to drivers.

- Activation zone : $\delta_L > \frac{1}{2}(D + L_f \cdot \psi + a)$
- Warning zone : $\frac{D}{2} \leq \delta_L$
- Deactivation zone : $\delta_L < \frac{1}{2}(D - L_f \cdot \psi - a)$

The reason threshold is defined from Eq. (8) is that DGPS has some errors due to lack of visibility of satellites or satellite shading. That threshold area can compensate DGPS error at the point of both warning and activation in this study. The average value of error will not affect the activation of control because it remains in warning region. The defined zones mentioned above are shown in Fig. 3 showing that where activation, warning, and deactivation line is placed. Activation of steering control system is also dependent on using turn signals. Using turn signals are considered that drivers want to keep the control of vehicle even they are fatigued or slightly sleeping during driving.

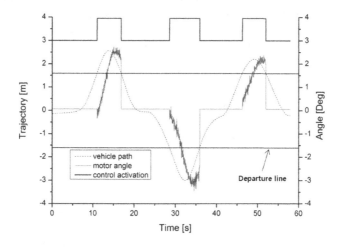

Fig. 4. Test vehicle for lateral motion control

Simulation result is shown in Fig. 4. The result shows that when the vehicle departs from lanes lateral control system is properly activated and deactivated.

2.3   Vehicle Test

DGPS/RTK has been used for controlling lateral motion of vehicle in this study. Actual vehicle test to validate the simulation results has been done. The test vehicle is shown in Fig. 5. Motor Driven Power steering System (MDPS) is used as actuator for this study.

Fig. 5. Test vehicle for lateral motion control

Test results are shown in Fig. 6. The path of vehicle is shown in black dot line and red line shows the controlled angle for lateral motion control of vehicle. The vehicle and road parameter are also shown in Table 1. This research is in early stage that the vehicle speed is fixed to 20km/h which is low speed.

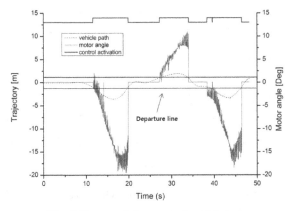

Fig. 6. Test result from actual vehicle tests

Table 1. Vehicle and road parameters

Symbols	Explanation	Value
B_s	steering system damping coefficient	15
c_{f0}	Front cornering stiffness	40,000N/rad
c_{r0}	Rear cornering stiffness	35,000N/rad
I_s	Inertial moment of steering system	0.05kgm^2
J	Vehicle yaw moment of inertia	2454kgm^3
K_p	Manual steering column coefficient	1
l_f	Distance from CG to front axle	1.3m
l_r	Distance from CG to rear axle	1.4m
l_s	Look ahead distance	1m
a	Half of vehicle width	1.4m
m	Total vehicle mass	1500kg
R_s	Steering gear ratio	14
v	Longitudinal velocity	20m/s
η_t	Tire length contact	0.13
$\eta\,\eta$	adhesion	1
$\eta\,\eta$	Lane width	3.5m

3   Conclusion

The purpose of this study is to reduce the possibilities of accidents caused by sudden lateral motion of vehicle in roads. DGPS/RTK is used to obtain the location of vehicle and lanes in road compared to existing technology using vision sensor for same purpose. Lateral motion control system has been validated through simulation and actual vehicle test has also been done to compare the results.

1) Logic for lateral motion control of vehicle has been designed with linear bicycle model

2) DGPS/RTK has been used for obtaining location of vehicle and lanes in roads

3) Simulation results have been validated by doing actual vehicle test

4) Singularity has been observed in the controlling process and control logic should be upgraded for better performance in lateral motion control in the future.

Acknowledgments. This research was supported by the MKE (The Ministry of Knowledge Economy), Korea, under the CITRC (Convergence Information Technology Research Center) support program (NIPA-2012-H0401-12-1007) supervised by the NIPA (National IT Industry Promotion Agency). This research was also supported by a grant from Construction Technology Innovation Program (CTIP) funded by Ministry of Land, Transportation and Maritime Affairs (MLTM) of Korean government.

References

1. Wang, J., Schroedl, S., Mezger, K., Ortloff, R., Joos, A., Passegger, T.: Lane keeping based on location technology. Intelligent Transportation Systems 6(3), 351–356 (2005)
2. Liu, J.-F., Wu, J.-H., Su, Y.-F.: Development of an Interactive Lane Keeping Control System for Vehicle. In: Vehicle Power and Propulsion Conference, pp. 702–706 (2007)
3. Mammar, S., Glaser, S., Netto, M.: Time to line crossing for lane departure avoidance: a theoretical study and an experimental setting. Intelligent Transportation Systems 7(2), 226–241 (2006)
4. Bajikar, S., Gorjestani, A., Simpkins, P., Donath, M.: Evaluation of in-vehicle GPS-based lane position sensing for preventing road departure. Intelligent Transportation System, 397–402 (1997)
5. Yang, J., Chang, T.N., Hou, E.: Lateral control for vehicles' automatic steering with front sensor and GPS. In: Control Automation and Systems (ICCAS), pp. 928–932 (2010)
6. Minoiu Enache, N., Netto, M., Mammar, S., Lusetti, B.: Driver steering assistance for lane departure avoidance. Control Eng. Pract. 17(6), 642–651 (2009)
7. Ackermann, J., Guldner, J., Sienel, W., Steinhauser, R., Utkin, V.I.: Linear and nonlinear controller design for robust automatic steering. Control Systems Technology 3(1), 132–143 (1995)

Van Der Pol Central Pattern Generator (VDP-CPG) Model for Quadruped Robot

Farahiyah Jasni and Amir Akramin Shafie

Mechatronics Department, Kulliyah of Engineering, International Islamic University Malaysia,
P.O. Box 10, 50728 Kuala Lumpur, Malaysia
farahiyahjasni@gmail.com, aashafie@iium.edu.my

Abstract. The Central Pattern Generators (CPGs) are becoming a popular method as the alternative control mechanism replacing the conventional trajectory-based method for designing the locomotion gait of mobile robot nowadays. CPG is described as a set of neural networks that have the ability to produce rhythmic movements, such as walking, swimming and flying without intervention from the sensory inputs and higher level control. This paper aims to highlight the efficiency of the biologically inspired, VDP-CPG based control method in modelling the walking gait for a quadruped robot. A new approach of VDP-CPG based walking gait model is developed in which 3-D foot trajectories are generated by mapping the output from CPG. The simulated foot trajectories of the CPG-based control and conventional trajectory-based method are compared to confirm the performance.

Keywords: quadruped robot, Central Pattern Generator (CPG), Van Der Pol(VDP) Oscillators, locomotion control.

1   Introduction

Legged robots are preferable than wheeled robot is because of its ability to move in rugged terrains. Therefore, an ideal locomotion gait control of a legged robot is the one that can provide effective control while moving in a smooth terrain and can quickly adapt to the changes in the terrain structures. In other words, a legged robot should possess an adaptive locomotion control system that can quickly change the control algorithm to adapt with different environment.

The most common approach to design the locomotion gait control of the legged robot is the pre-designed trajectory based method in which the foot trajectory is designed for each leg and the joint angle parameters are calculated via inverse kinematics accordingly to follow the trajectory that has been designed [1]-[4]. However, the control mechanism has become very complicated and tedious once the number of legs increases as each leg will need separate analysis and calculation. Furthermore, this method is no longer efficient if the ground condition changes. The robot might need to change the step's distance and height, as well as the speed of walking as the ground condition changes to ensure the stability of the robot which eventually will lead to very complex control architecture. Thus, a better approach is needed to tackle the problem of robots' walking in unknown terrains.

S.G. Ponnambalam et al. (Eds.): IRAM 2012, CCIS 330, pp. 167–175, 2012.
© Springer-Verlag Berlin Heidelberg 2012

Referring to animal's biological locomotion system as motivation, the CPG method is proposed to provide the solution of robot's adaptive locomotion problem. Central Pattern Generator (CPG) is described as a set of neural networks that can continuously produce rhythmic patterned signals without input from the rhythmic sensory system or the central control system (i.e. the brain) [5]. Studies in neurobiology found out the CPGs that are located in spinal cord are responsible in generating the basic rhythmic patterns for locomotion; meanwhile the higher level control (i.e. the brain) is responsible in adjusting the patterns according to the environmental conditions [6]. Motivated by these findings, many researchers in robotics area have started to design a locomotion system mimicking the biological CPGs.

Generally, the idea of simulating the biological CPG in robotics locomotion system is by introducing the oscillators that generate rhythmic signal at the joints. The oscillators are coupled and synchronized together. The output of properly coupled oscillators will produce a locomotion gait of the robot [7]-[15].

However, most of the CPG design mentioned earlier are using the CPG to generate the joint parameters of the robot. This method has one deficiency that is, at least one oscillator need to be allocated in each joint as the joint angles are generated via the oscillator. This will results to a complex CPG network and consequently caused a tedious work in coupling the CPGs together. Chengju [16] has proposed a very interesting method that is called a CPG-workspace control method in which the oscillator output will be mapped to a set of mapping functions to generate 3-D workspace trajectories for the robot. Therefore, only one oscillator is assigned for each leg and the CPG network is easier to modulate. This paper is using the same approach of CPG-workspace control method. Nonetheless, this paper is using the VDP-CPG model for the CPG network design. Besides, a new set of mapping functions are introduced for the 3-D workspace trajectories generation.

2   CPG-Based Workspace Trajectories Generation

In this section, the process of 3-D workspace trajectories generation based on VDP-CPG model is explained. Figure 1 shows the flowchart of the process. LF, RF, LR and RR in the figure represent Left front, Right Front, Left Rear and Right Rear leg respectively. Figure 2 shows the desired workspace trajectories to be generated in this paper.

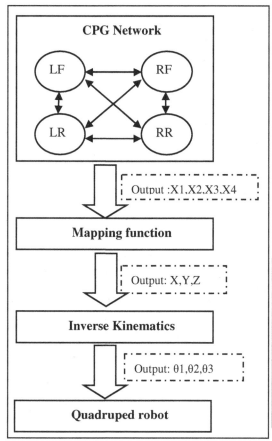

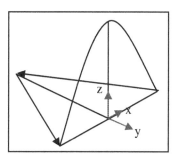

Fig. 2. The 3D workspace trajectories. x, y and z represents the reference axis in this analysis.

Fig. 1. Flowchart of the process

Fig. 3. The Bioloid quadruped robot used in this research work

2.1   Van Der Pol (VDP) Oscillator

Van Der Pol oscillator is commonly used in representing biological modelling for its stable limit cycle quality (shown in Figure 3). In this paper, the VDP oscillator is used to represent the CPG design. (1) is the expressions that represent the relaxation VDP oscillator.

$$\dot{x} = y$$
$$\dot{y} = \mu(p^2 - x^2)\dot{x} + g^2 x \tag{1}$$

x represents the output of the oscillator. μ generally responsibles in shaping the wave, while p^2 is the constant that modulate the amplitude of the wave and finally g^2 is responsible in adjusting the frequency of the wave. However, due to its close relationship, changing one parameter might also affect the other parameters.

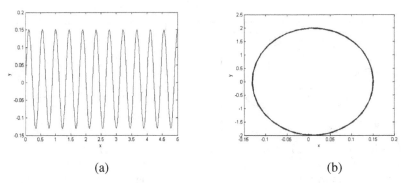

(a)   (b)

Fig. 4. VDP relaxation oscillator's limit cycle behavior Parameters are set to $\mu=1$, $p^2=2$ and g^2 =200.(a) Output 'x' versus time. (b) 'y' versus 'x'

2.2   CPG Network

This paper is focusing on the walking gait for a quadruped, therefore, the quadruped animal walking gait is analyzed. Figure 4 illustrates the walking leg sequence of 4-legged animal and figure 5 is the CPG network design where Left Front (LF) leg is represented byoscillator no 1, right front(RF) leg is represented by oscillator 2 and right rear (RR) and left rear (LR) is represented by oscillator 3 and 4 respectively.

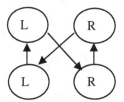

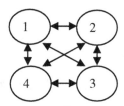

Fig. 5. Walking gait of quadruped animal   **Fig. 6.** CPG network configuration

To produce a gait, the oscillators are coupled together and the relationship parameters are properly configured. By solving equation (1) above for second order differential equation, the expressions that illustrate the coupled non-linear VDP oscillators are described as below:

$$\ddot{x}_i = \mu_i \left(p_i^{\,2} - x_{ai}^{\,2} \right)\dot{x}_i - g_i^{\,2} x_{ai} + q_{ai}$$
$$where \qquad x_{ai} = x_i + \Sigma \lambda_{i,j} x_j \tag{2}$$
$$i = leg \quad index$$
$$j = connecting \qquad leg \quad index$$

The parameter $\lambda_{i,j}$ is the connection weight between the two oscillators.

$$\omega = (\lambda)_{4x4}$$

From the experiments that have been conducted, it is found out that the negative value will cause the output to be out of phase between each other, meanwhile the positive value will cause the output to be in phase between each other.

For this paper, the connection weight matrix that is used to get the walking gait in Figure 4 configuration is:

$$\omega = \begin{bmatrix} 0 & 0 & -0.2 & 0 \\ -0.2 & 0 & 0 & -0.2 \\ 0 & -0.2 & 0 & -0.2 \\ -0.2 & 0 & 0 & 0 \end{bmatrix}$$

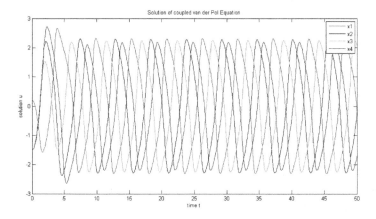

Fig. 7. The VDP-CPG Output for walking gait. LF->RR->RF->LR

2.3   Mapping Function

In this paper, instead of directly extract the joint angle from the output of the oscillator, the foot workspace trajectories was generated via a mapping function. The output from the VDP-CPG is mapped into the mapping functions to generate the desired 3-D workspace trajectory, $x(i)$, $y(i)$, and $z(i)$. The advantage of implementing this is to eliminate the needs to have too many oscillators and to simplify the control architecture. In addition, the mapping function offers an adaptive control system to the robot since the workspace trajectories can be modulated via the CPG parameters (i.e. Parameters in equation (2)). Thus, the robot with this system can adapt better in unknown environment.

Chengju described the set of mapping function in her paper[16]. The mapping functions are cited in this paper but some modifications were made to suit the application for this research work. The trajectories of the robot are categorized into two section; the swinging phase and the stance phase. The swing phase is the trajectories when the leg is lifted to make a step. The set of mapping function for the swinging phase is:

$$x(i) = K_x \cdot (t - \frac{T_{sw}}{2})$$
$$y(i) = 0 \tag{3}$$
$$z(i) = K_z \cdot (X_i(t))$$

Where Kx and Kz are the gain coefficients. t is the time at particular point and Tsw is the total time of swing phase and $X_i(t)$ is the respective output of the CPG for that particular index.

As for the stance phase, it is divided into two parts as well; the front stance phase and the back stance phase.

$$x(i) = K_x S \cdot \left(\frac{1}{2} - \frac{t - T_{sw}}{T_{sp}} \right)$$

$$y(i) = \mp K_y \cdot \left(\frac{2\gamma}{S} \cdot x(i) - \gamma \right) \quad \text{where +ve for left legs and −ve for right legs} \tag{4}$$

$$z(i) = 0$$

And for back stance phase:

$$y(i) = \pm K_y \left(\frac{2\gamma}{S} + \gamma \right) \quad \text{where −ve for left legs and +ve for right legs} \tag{5}$$

S is referring to the total step's distance of the leg. This can be calculated via the difference x(i) during the swing phase. While v is introduced to enhance the stability during the support phase [16].

3   Results and Discussion

In this section, the workspace trajectory that are generated using the mapping function of the oscillator output will be compared to the theoretical workspace trajectories from conventional tajectory-based method. The trajectory-based method utilized for this comparison is based on the composite cycloid function.

It is seen that the results obtained using CPG method is slightly deviate from the curves obtained using composite cycloid function. The main factor of this error is because the analysis done is mainly based on the CPG output. Therefore, the shape and curve of the CPG output plays the great role in determining the data for the mapping functions and the process afterwards. Thus, the deviation in results seen in this paper is because the imprefection of the CPG output obtained. This error can be minimized by properly configuring the CPG parameters to get the most similar curve to the foot trajectory obtained using composite cylcoid function.

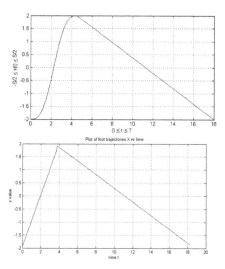

(a)Left: X trajectory based on trajectory-based method. Right : X trajectory based on CPG-based method

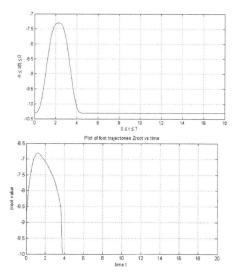

(b)Left: Z trajectory based on trajectory-based method. Right : Z trajectory based on CPG-based method

Fig. 8. The comparison between both methods

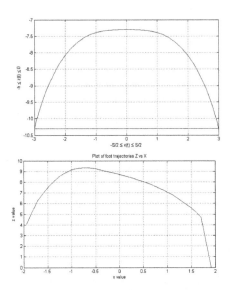

(c)Left:Foot trajectory Z vs X for trajectory-based method. Right: Foot trajectory Z vs X for CPG-based method.

Fig. 8. (*Continued*)

4   Conclusion and Future Work

From the results shown above, the CPG-based method with the utilization of mapping function performs well as the trajectories generated are quite similar to the trajectories derived using typical pre-designed trajectory based method. Therefore, it can be concluded that this biologically inspired method is efficient for designing the locomotion control for quadruped.

Nonetheless, as discussed earlier, CPG model consists of quite a number of parameters. Therefore, to find a better solution for parameters selection task other than trial and error method is the next research scope to be conducted in the future.

References

1. Debao, Z., Low, K.H.: Design of a quadruped walking machine for terrain adaptation. In: First Workshop on Robot Motion and Control, Singapore, pp. 59–64 (1999)
2. Tee, T.W., Low, K.H., Ng, H.Y., Young, F.: Mechatronics Design and Gait Implementation of a Quadruped Legged Robot. In: International Conference on Control, Automation and Vision (ICARCV), Singapore, pp. 826–832 (2002)
3. Shaoping, B., Low, K.H., Zielinska, T.: Quadruped free gait generation combined with body trajectory planning. In: First Workshop on Robot Motion and Control, Singapore, pp. 165–170 (1999)

4. Mitobe, K., Satoh, M., Capi, G.: A ZMP control of a powered passive dynamic walking robot. In: World Automation Congress (WAC). TSI Press, Japan (2010)
5. Marder, E., Bucher, D.: Central pattern generators and the control of rhythmic movements. Elsevier Science Ltd. (11), 986–996 (2001)
6. Ijspeert, A.J.: Central pattern generators for locomotion control in animals and robots: A review. Neural Networks 21(4), 642–653 (2008)
7. Venkataraman, S.T.: A model of legged locomotion gaits. In: 1996 IEEE International Conference on Robotics and Automation, vol. 4, pp. 3545–3550 (1996)
8. Liu, C., Chen, Q., Xu, T.: Locomotion Control of Quadruped Robots Based on Central Pattern Generators. In: 8th World Congress on Intelligent Control and Automation. IEEE Press, Taipei (2011)
9. Ishii, T., Masakado, S., Ishii, K.: Locomotion of a quadruped robot using CPG. In: Proceedings 2004 IEEE International Joint Conference on.Neural Networks, vol. 4, pp. 3179–3184 (2004)
10. Cheng, Z., Zheng, H., Zhang, X., Zhao, L.: The CPG-based bionic quadruped system. In: IEEE International Conference on Systems, Man and Cybernetics, vol. 2, pp. 1828–1833 (2003)
11. Righetti, L., Ijspeert, A.J.: Pattern generators with sensory feedback for the control of quadruped locomotion. In: IEEE International Conference on Robotics and Automation, pp. 819–824 (2008)
12. Fukuoka, Y., Nakamura, H., Kimura, H.: Biologically-inspired adaptive dynamic walking of the quadruped on irregular terrain. In: 1999 IEEE/RSJ International Conference on Intelligent Robots and Systems, vol. 3, pp. 1657–1662 (1999)
13. Maufroy, C., Kimura, H., Takase, K.: Biologically Inspired Neural Controller for Quadruped. In: International Conference on Robotics and Biomimetics, pp. 1212–1216. IEEE Press, Sanya (2007)
14. Zhang, J., Tomizuka, M., Chen, Q., Liu, C.: Dynamic Walking of AIBO with Hopf Oscillators. Chinese Journal of Mechanical Engineering 24, 1–6 (2011)
15. Liu, C., Chen, Q., Zhang, J.: Coupled Van Der Pol oscillators utilised as Central pattern generators for quadruped locomotion. In: Control and Decision Conference, China, pp. 3677–3682 (2009)
16. Liu, C., Chen, Q., Wang, D.: CPG-Inspired Workspace Trajectory Generation and Adaptive Locomotion Control for Quadruped Robots. IEEE Transactions on Systems, Man, and Cybernetics, Part B: Cybernetics 41(3), 867–880 (2011)

Twin-Hull URRG Blimp Control
for Low Altitude Surveillance Application

Guan Yap Tan, Mohd Rizal Arshad, and Herdawatie Abdul Kadir

Underwater Robotics Research Group (URRG), School of Electrical and Electronic Engineering,
Engineering Campus, Universiti Sains Malaysia (USM)
14300 Nibong Tebal, Pulau Pinang, Malaysia
geneyap1189@gmail.com, rizal@eng.usm.edu.my, watie@uthm.edu.my

Abstract. Blimp system with cameras is an appropriate method to conducts environmental surveillance, which offers the ability to hover at low altitude with less noise. However, blimps envelope causes large drag coefficient value compared to other aircrafts. Therefore, the structural design and motion control of the blimp system are very crucial thus contribute to the overall system performances. This paper presents the structural design and motion control method for low altitude surveillance system. The structural design of the Twin-hull blimp system (THCS) is separated into three parts, which are designs of blimp envelope, design of gondola and motion control mechanism. For the motion control, both open-loop and closed-loop control system are implemented into THCS for horizontal and vertical motion control. Several experiments with a real constructed blimp are performed in indoor environment to confirm the design performance and stability of THCS.

Keywords: blimp, aerial vehicles, control, airship, surveillance system.

1 Introduction

Airship is a Lighter-Than-Air (LTA) aircraft that able to float in the air using the buoyancy principle; the total weight is less than buoyancy forces of air that acting on it. The airship can be classified based upon the hull design (1) non-rigid (2) semi-rigid, and (3) rigid, production lifting force and payload ability. Generally, there are two airship types: the conventional type and unconventional type. The conventional airships have a streamline symmetric body with long drag shape, generate aerostatic lift by an envelope, lower payload capability and a power source. All the other types of airship that have different characteristics with conventional airships are classified as unconventional airships [1].

Recently, many researchers have been exploring back the blimp technology. The research fields of the blimp include surveillance or real time monitoring [2], the indoor blimps [3], the outdoor blimps [4] [5], wind hardness control [6], navigation control [7] [8]. A blimp is an ideal stable platform for low-altitude surveillance. It is much more stable than other aircraft such as helicopter and airplane. It takes the best advantage to provide high quality live video streaming. Blimp also able to hover and

S.G. Ponnambalam et al. (Eds.): IRAM 2012, CCIS 330, pp. 176–182, 2012.

stay aloft from hours to day compared to other aerial vehicles. Unlike other aircraft, blimps are sustainable, which used low energy consumption. Blimps use lifting power of helium gas to keep them in the air and not the lifting power from an engine. In this design, electrical energy is used to power up the motors. Moreover, blimps are also generally much quieter than other aircraft hence reduce the sound pollution.

In this work, the blimp was used as a surveillance platform; it enables easier data gathering for an area. It will also capable to observe an area safely and quickly from sky [5]. Furthermore, the surveillance systems will also able produce a map thus contributes the path planning for an area. The blimp design was based on non-rigid airship using unconventional airship design. The non-rigid airships are often called "blimp." Unlike other rigid and semi-rigid airships, a blimp is an airship without an internal framework or keel to support the envelope shape. The hull depends on the helium gas to produce good shape.

This paper proposed a small structural design and motion control method for an indoor blimp. The development and stability performance of the blimp system will be discussed throughout this paper. Fig. 1 shows the blimp platform used in this experiment.

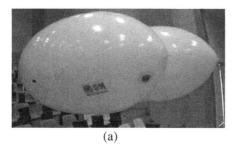
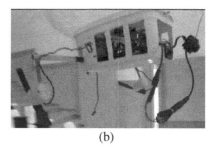

(a)   (b)

Fig. 1. Surveillance system (a) Twin Hull design (b) Gondola

2   Structural Design

In this work, the structural design of a blimp is divided into three main parts, which are blimp envelope, gondola, and motion control mechanism. Blimp envelope design is focused on its size and shape. The size and shape of blimp envelope play the most important role for blimp to be able to float in the air. While the gondola holds and protects all the hardware on the blimp. The design was also equipped with two DC motors mounted on the gondola to control the motion of the blimp. A wireless camera is attached in front of the gondola for surveillance purposed.

The blimp design is based on unconventional airship design, which is used twin hull design as illustrated in Fig. 2(a). For twin hull design, two conventional envelopes with streamlined bodies are joined together without any solid structures. The main advantage in this design is the reduction of overall length for a given volume of gas. This means greater volume of gas can be used for this design to achieve the same overall length as conventional design. With the larger volume of gas, double envelope design leads to increase aerodynamic lift and payload capacity. Lifting force equation (1) is used to calculate the optimum blimp's size and payload capacity.

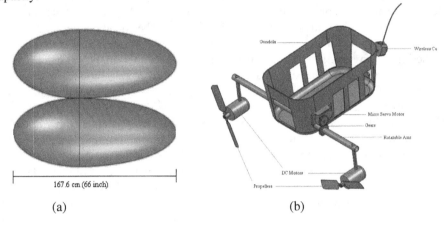

(a)   (b)

Fig. 2. (a) Blimp Envelope (b) Gondola and Motion Control Mechanism

$$F_L = Vg(\rho_{air} - \rho_{he}) - W_o \qquad (1)$$

Gondola of a blimp is used to hold the hardware such as batteries, microcontroller, sensors, servo motor, wireless module and wireless camera. Two dc motors with the propeller are mounted on the gondola, where one motor on the left-hand side and the other one on the right-hand side. The structure of the gondola needs to be light and also strong. In choosing the size of the gondola, there are two considerations need to be consider. First, the space inside the gondola needs to be large enough to enclose all the electronic components and batteries. Second, the width of the gondola needs to be long enough for supporting the rotatable axis and the weight of the DC motors. We introduce open areas on the gondola surface in order to reduce the weight and enhance the performance of wireless communication. The propulsion system were equipped with two DC motors mounted at each side and connected to a rotatable axis to produce vertical take-off and landing (VTOL) capabilities. The angular position of rotatable axis is controlled by a micro servo motor as shown in Fig. 2(b). Two gears are used to join the servo motor and the rotatable axis, which allow the motors to perform precise pitch rotation.

3   Blimp Control System

The control system of the blimp is design for 2 modes which are manual control and automatic control. The manual control is implementing an open-loop control system, which directly controlled by an input signal without any feedback signals. On the contrary, automatic control is a closed-loop control system, which utilized feedback sensors to control the motion of the blimp. It used to control the altitude of the blimp.

As mention in the blimp structural, the blimp has two motors mounted at each side of the gondola. A servo motor is used to control the angular position of rotatable axis. In this case, only two angular positions are used for rotatable axis, which are 0° and 90°. The 90° of angular position used for vertical motion and 0° of angular position used for horizontal motion. Fig. 3 shows the block diagram of a closed-loop control system of altitude control.

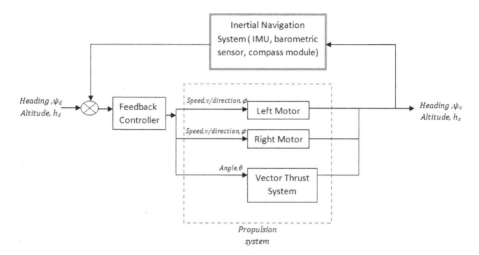

Fig. 3. Closed-loop Control System

The barometric pressure sensor is used as a feedback sensor for altitude control. The altitude's values that provided by this sensor is fed to the controller as the feedback signal. By comparing with the desired altitude that set by the user, the controller will drive the motors to the desired speed and direction, and lift the blimp to the desired altitude. Due to the sensitivity and stability of sensor's output, processing speed and other factors, it is impossible to lift the blimp to the altitude that exactly equals to desired altitude without any error. Therefore, a control limit is chosen for altitude control, which is plus-minus one meter. The permissible error range of altitude control is two meters.

4   Result and Discussion

In order to verify the capability of the developed blimp platform, we have done real time testing in a large indoor environment. In our experiments, the evaluations of system performance were done on altitude control and forward navigation of the blimp. In the altitude analysis, the real time output was recorded every 5 seconds starting from 0 s to 70 s for three different altitudes, which are 3 m, 4 m, and 5 m. Fig.4 shows the real time blimp output, while deviation value from desired altitude was stated in Table 1.

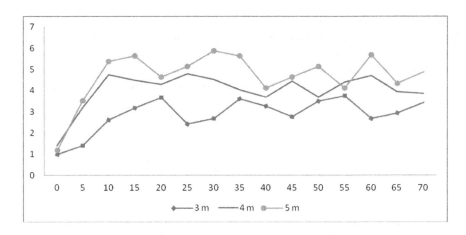

Fig. 4. Real-time output

The results show that altitude response produced an oscillation response to the maximum of 25 % deviation from the desired response. We can observe that this system was very sensitive to the environment due to buoyancy effect produced by the helium gas. However, the responses were able operate within acceptable altitude tolerance value.

Table 1. Altitude performances

Time (s)	3 m		4 m		5 m	
	different	error (%)	different	error (%)	different	error (%)
5	1.6	53	0.8	20	1.48	29.6
10	0.4	13	-0.75	-18.75	-0.38	-7.6
15	-0.17	-6	-0.5	-12.5	-0.63	-12.6
20	-0.67	-22	-0.29	-7.25	0.37	7.4
25	0.58	19	-0.79	-19.75	-0.13	-2.6
30	0.33	11	-0.54	-13.5	-0.88	-17.6
35	-0.6	-20	-0.04	-1	-0.63	-12.6
40	-0.25	-8	0.3	7.5	0.88	17.6
45	0.25	8	-0.45	-11.25	0.37	7.4
50	-0.5	-17	0.3	7.5	-0.13	-2.6
55	-0.76	-25	-0.4	-10	0.88	17.6
60	0.33	11	-0.7	-17.5	-0.67	-13.4
65	0.08	3	0.05	1.25	0.67	13.4
70	-0.42	-14	0.13	3.25	0.13	2.6

In the navigation analysis, the stability testing for forward navigation is performed with initial altitude of 2 meters. The parameters used to analyze the stability performance include heading angle, pitch and roll angle, and altitude. The results are shown in Fig. 5. The pitch angle produces maximum output deviation of 8%, while heading generated only 1.5% yawing error with 0.4 altitude error.

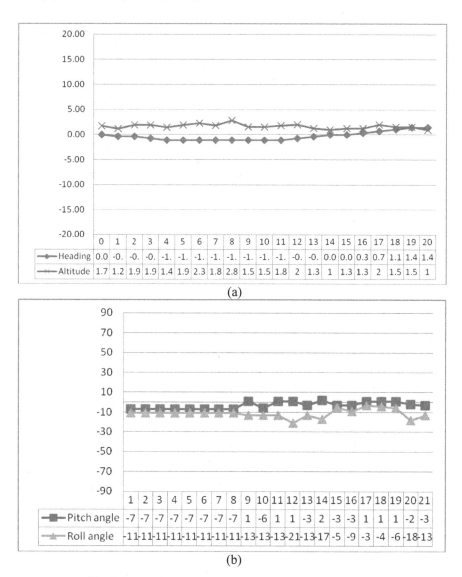

(a)

(b)

Fig. 5. Graph of Effect of Parameters for Forward Navigation

From the overall analysis, we can conclude that the blimp design is able to navigate with acceptable response. Although the system were very sensitive to the real environment, proper design and control method will be able to help to generate good response thus produce good stability response. Thus this design offer more payload and easier to manage due to smaller size.

5   Conclusion

In this paper, we presented structural design and an approach motion control method of a blimp to conduct low altitude surveillance. We performed some experiments with a real constructed surveillance blimp in a large indoor environment. The twin-hull design was able to reduce the overall length of blimp and produced heavier payload capacity. The optimum size and payload capacity was calculated and successfully lift the blimp to desired altitude and compensated the disturbances. The motion control method presented in this paper was successfully controlled the motion of blimp in horizontal and vertical plane, and performed VTOL. Based on the experiment results, our blimp was able to navigate with acceptable response and conducts low altitude surveillance in the indoor environment. In future work, we would like to consider increasing the payload capacity, and making it possible to hover and navigate in outdoor environment.

Acknowledgements. The authors would like to thank Malaysia Ministry of Science, Technology and Innovation (MOSTI), e-Science 305/PELECT/6013410, Ministry of Higher Education (MOHE), Universiti Sains Malaysia and Universiti Tun Hussein Onn Malaysia for supporting the research.

References

1. Lioa, L., Pasternak, I.: A Review of Airship Structural Research and Development. Progress in Aerospace Sciences 45, 83–96 (2009)
2. Fukao, T., Fujitani, K., Kanade, T.: An Autonomous Blimp for a Surveillance System. In: Intelligent Robots and Systems, Las vegas, Nevada (2003)
3. Shimida, A., Furukawa, H., Uchimura, Y.: A Movement Control on Indoor Blimp Robots. In: SICE Annual Conference (2010)
4. Saiki, H., Fukoa, T., Urakubo, T., Kohno, T.: A Path Following Control Method under Wind Disturbances for Outdoor Blimp Robots. In: IEEE/SICE International Symposium on, pp. 978–984 (2011)
5. Saiki, H., Fukoa, T., Urakubo, T., Kohno, T.: Hovering Control of Outdoor Blimp Robots Based on Path Following. In: 2010 IEEE International Conference on Control Applications, pp. 2124–2129 (2010)
6. Shimada, A., Fukurawa, H.: An Approach to Wind Harness Control on Blimp. In: Proceedings of SICE Annual Conference (SICE), pp. 368–369 (2011)
7. Muller, J., Kohler, N., Burgard, W.: Autonomous Miniature Blimp Navigation with Online Motion Planning and Re-planning. In: IEEE/RSJ International Conference on Intelligent Robots and Systems (IROS), pp. 4941–4946 (2011)
8. Yiwei, L., Zengxi, P., David, S., Fazel, N.: Q-Learning for Navigation Control of an Autonomous Blimp. In: Australasian Conference on Robotic and Automation (2009)

Drag Analysis of URRG Vertical Profiler (UVP) Using Integration of Computational Fluid Dynamics (CFD) and Design of Experiments (DOE)

Muzammer Zakaria, Syafizal Ishak, and Mohd Rizal Arshad

Underwater Robotics Research Group (URRG) School of Electrical and Electronic Engineering Universiti Sains Malaysia, Engineering Campus 14300 Nibong Tebal, Penang, Malaysia
muzammer_zakaria@yahoo.com, syafizal3107@gmail.com,
rizal@eng.usm.my

Abstract. Dynamics analysis of a system is important before any controller can be applied on a system, especially for autonomous system. For underwater system, the dynamic analysis is a critical stage since the operator do not have any access on what happen to the system when it have been deploy. This paper suggest on analysis on underwater vertical profiler system using integration of Computational Fluid Dynamics (CFD) and Design of Experiments (DOE). It is to analyze the vertical drag coefficients when the velocity and the depth are varied.

Keywords: Vertical Profiler, CFD, DOE, Factorial Design, Cd.

1   Introduction

Underwater vertical profiler system is an underwater system that used for profiling the water while moving vertically through water column [1]. The system is widely use in oceanographic field. There are two types, one is called mooring which the system is anchored at the bottom of the sea or lake and the other is current drifter which are not attach to anything. The current URRG vertical profiler is the second type which is the current drifter. Usually the second type is more mobile and handy since it not needs any installation.

The vertical profiler system only has one degree of freedom to control, which is the heave movement. Which the hydrodynamics force that acting on the system that will be takes in considers is the forces that act in vertical.

CFD simulation is to analysis the fluid dynamics that act on the system, which is the drag force if the system when it moves up and down. The simulation is to know the change of drag coefficient when the system moves at certain velocity and at certain depth.

While, DOE analysis is used since there are numbers of successful similar application using DOE approach, and for one-factor-at-a-time design and random design were ruled out due to low level of complexity [2]. In DOE, factorial design procedure is used to analyze the effect of each factors and the interaction between them, if any, in statistical way. In this paper integration of CFD and DOE are used to analysis the dynamics of the URRG vertical profiler system.

S.G. Ponnambalam et al. (Eds.): IRAM 2012, CCIS 330, pp. 183–189, 2012.

1.1   Dynamics

The hydrodynamics force acting on the system is as Fig. 1. Since the system movement is vertical through the water column, only forces acting in vertical plane will be considered.

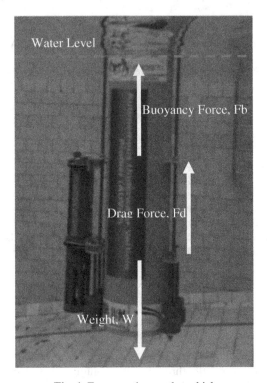

Fig. 1. Forces acting on the vehicle

From the illustration, the forces equation is given by, (1)

$$Fb + Fd = W \tag{1}$$

We know that the gravitation force, buoyancy force and drag force equations are given as follow,

$$W = mg \tag{2}$$

$$Fb = \rho g V \tag{3}$$

$$Fd = 1/2 \ Cd \ A \ \rho \ v^2 \tag{4}$$

where:

m = *Total mass of the vehicle*
g = *gravitational acceleration*

ρ = *density of seawater*
V = *volume of the hull*
A = *projected area of the hull*
v = *velocity*
Cd = *drag coefficient*

Drag coefficient are depend on the shape of the object, Reynolds Number, Compressibility effects, and surface roughness [3].

1.2   Computational Fluid Dynamics, CFD

CFD is the analysis of systems involving fluid flow, heat transfer and associated phenomena such as chemical reactions by means of computer-based simulation. It has been used widely as research and design tool [4].

The advantages of CFD simulation are substantial reduction of lead time, ability to study systems where controlled experiments are difficult to perform and practically unlimited level of detail of results [5].

1.3   Design of Experiments (DOE) Method: Factorial Design

DOE is a methodology to study or analysis the behavior of a system using statistical methods. DOE refers to the process of planning the experiment so that appropriate data can be analyzed by statistical methods will be collected, resulting in valid and objective conclusions [6].

In many study of a process, there will be many factors that give effect to the process. To study the effect of two or more factors, generally factorial design is the most efficient method. For the UVP CFD analysis, the effect of two factors which is velocity and pressure will be analyzed to observe the change in drag coefficient. The factors are chosen since the Cd is proportional to velocity and since the UVP move vertically through water column, so there will be change in the depth or the underwater pressure. The factorial design helps to analysis either there are any interactions or not to avoid misleading conclusions and also allow the effects of a factor to be estimated at several levels of the other factors [6].

2   Simulation

2.1   CFD Simulation

The CFD simulation is to study the effect of velocity-pressure on drag coefficient, Cd for the UVP model characteristic. Geometry meshing was generated using GAMBIT software in order to perform numerical investigation. The mesh file was then imported to FLUENT™ for numerical study. In this simulation, laminar models were chosen to investigate the design influence on the drag coefficient behavior.

The velocity and pressure coupling set up are follows the Factorial Design method , where factor a is in the row which is the velocity and factor b is in the column which is the pressure.

The experimental design are interested in testing hypotheses about the equality of row (factor a) treatment effects

$$H0 : \tau 1 = \tau 2 = \ldots = \tau a = 0$$
$$H1 : \text{at least one } \tau i \neq 0$$

(5)

and the equality of column (factor b) treatment effects

$$H0 : \beta 1 = \beta 2 = \ldots = \beta b = 0$$
$$H1 : \text{at least one } \beta j \neq 0$$

(6)

Determine whether row and column treatments have interaction.

$$H0 : (\tau \beta)ij = 0 \text{ for all } i,j$$
$$H1 : \text{at least one } (\tau \beta)ij \neq 0$$

(7)

These hypotheses are tested using two-factor analysis of variance. The simulation procedures are:

1. Set the pressure act on the system.
2. Define the vertical velocity of the system and doo iteration to get Cd value.
3. Repeat step 2 with different velocity until max velocity and record the Cd value.
4. After finish, change the pressure value and repeat step 2 for every change of pressure value.

The results are then analyzed using Minitab software using two-factorial design method.

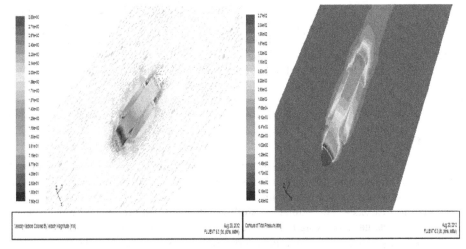

Fig. 2. UVP contour (a) Velocity contour and (b) Pressure contour

3   Results and Discussion

The CFD simulation result as shown as Table 1 shows the Drag coefficient value for each velocity and pressure coupling.

Table 1. Simulation result

Velocity (m/s)	Pressure (atm)			
	1.49602	1.99204	2.48806	2.98407
0.5	1.3675	1.3671	1.3675	1.3663
1.0	1.0895	1.0896	1.0895	1.0894
1.5	0.9824	0.9825	0.9825	0.9825
2.0	0.9296	0.9787	0.9296	0.9296

From Table 1, the results show that there are no changes in Cd value when pressures are varied. The results are then analyzed Minitab software to testing hypotheses (5), (6) and (7). The ANOVA for two-factorial is as shown in Table 2.

Table 2. Analysis of Variance

Source	Degrees of Freedom	Sum of Squares	Mean Square	F	P
Main Effects	2	0.403054	0.201527	45.44	0.0000
Velocity, v	1	0.403054	0.403054	90.87	0.0000
Pressure, atm	1	0.00	0.00	0.00	0.996
2-way interactions					
Velocity, v*	1	0.00	0.00	0.00	0.994
Pressure, atm					
Error	12	0.053224	0.004435		
Total	15	0.456278			

Table 2 shows that the P-value for Velocity is near to zero and can be concluding that the null hypothesis, H_0 (5) can be rejected. Therefore, not all of different levels of Velocity result are in the same response means. From the table, we also can see that the P-value for Pressure factor and for the interactions between the two factors are more than zero which mean the null hypothesis in (6) and (7) are accepted. So from the results it shows that only Velocity factor give the effect on the change of the Cd while the change of Pressure and the interactions of the two factors are not significant on change of the Cd value. Fig. 3, show the main effect plot of Cd value.

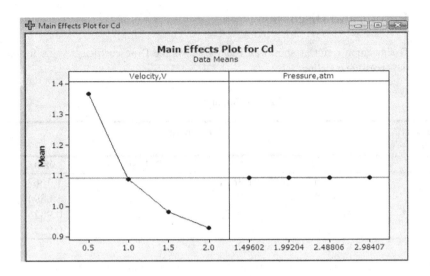

Fig. 3. Main effects plot for Cd value shows that the main effect are from varying the Velocity value

4   Conclusions

This paper shows the Drag coefficient analysis of the UVP in cylindrical shape using CFD method. The CFD simulation is run using the 2 factorial design procedures. By runs the CFD simulation using the DOE method, the effects of two factors effects on the Cd coefficient values can be explains statistically.

From the result of the analysis of the variance, can be concluding that the only factors that give effect on the change of Cd value is the velocity, while pressure and the interaction between the two factors do not give any effect.

As figure of the contour in the simulation in Fig.2, we can observe that most of the drag force or the drag coefficients are created due to rough UVP shape. The drag can be decrease by change the shape of the UVP.

Next for the future works is to apply the relationship equation of the Cd versus velocity into the UVP control system simulation, and do the pool test for the validation.

Acknowledgements. We are very grateful to Ministry of Science, Technology and Innovation (MOSTI) for providing E-Science 305/PELECT/6013410 to pursue our research in underwater system technology. We would also like to thank to Universiti Sains Malaysia (USM) for supporting the research.

References

1. Zakaria, M., Arshad, M.R.: URRG Underwater Vertical Profiler (UVP). In: 2nd Postgraduate Colloquium School of Electric & Electronic USM, EEPC (2009)
2. Jirásek, A.: Example of Integrated CFD and Experimental Studies: Design of Flow Control in the FOI-EIC-OI Inlet. In: 3rd International Symposium on Integrating CFD and Experiments in Aerodynamics (2007)
3. Munson, B.R., Young, D.F., Okiishi, T.H.: Fundamental of Fluid Mechanics. Wiley Asia Student Edition, 5th edn.
4. Anderson Jr., J.D.: Computational Fluid Dynamics – The Basic with Applications. McGraw-Hill, Inc.
5. Versteeg, H.K., Malalasekera, W.: An Introduction to Computational Fluid Dynamics – The Finite Volume Method. Longman Scientific & Technical
6. Montgomery Douglas, C.: Design and Analysis of Experiments, 7th edn. John Wiley & Sons (2009)
7. Anthony, J.: Design of Experiments for Engineers and Scientist. Elsevier Ltd.
8. Sumantr, B., Karsiti, M.N., Agustiawan, H.: Development of Variable Ballast Mechanism for Depth Positioning of Spherical URV. IEEE (2008)
9. Fossen, T.I.: Marine Control System, Guidance, Navigation, and Control of ships, Rigs and Underwater Vehicles. Marine Cybernetics (2002)
10. Minitab user's Guide: Data Analysis and Quality tools. Release 16 UK, Minitab inc (2000)
11. Brown, M., Kelley, M., McGill, P.: MBARI Vertical Profiler. Monterey Bay Aquarium Research Institute. IEEE (2000)

Biologically Inspired Architecture
for Spatiotemporal Learning of Mobile Robots

Ludmilla Kleinmann and Bärbel Mertsching

GET Lab, University of Paderborn, Pohlweg 47-49,
33098 Paderborn, Germany
kleinmann@get.upb.de

Abstract. Biological systems can adapt excellently to the demands of a dynamic world and changing tasks. What kind of information processing and reasoning do they use? There are numerous studies in psychology, cognitive neuroscience and artificial intelligence which complement each other and help in getting a better understanding of this riddle. Our paper presents a biologically inspired architecture for a spatiotemporal learning system. Multiple interconnected memory structures are used to incorporate different learning paradigms. Concurrent inherent learning processes complete the functionality of corresponding memory types. Our architecture has been evaluated in the context of mobile rescue robots: The task consists of searching objects while navigating in an unknown maze.

Keywords: learning, spatiotemporal learning, combination of learning paradigms, reinforcement learning, multiple memory systems, mobile robots, rescue robots.

1 Introduction

Improvements in the hard- and software for mobile robot systems have enabled their application for sophisticated tasks and scenarios, e. g. in the domain of rescue robotics. Today, mainly teleoperated robot systems are used while autonomous systems are still a topic of research. The RoboCup Rescue League offers a testbed for autonomous mobile robots where the tasks for the robots consist of exhaustive exploration of different previously unknown arenas and victim search [1]. Usually heuristic path planning algorithms are applied for the exploration in order to find real-time solutions (see e. g. [2]). However, for real-world applications these methods are not flexible enough: the behavior of a mobile agent has to be adjusted constantly during a rescue mission due to the altering character of a scenario. Learning strategies may dramatically increase the adaptability of rescue systems.

Several approaches exist already for the learning of the navigational behavior of mobile robots [3, 4]. Reinforcement learning (RL) provides some benefits compared to fuzzy systems and most neural network learning algorithms because it does not require expert knowledge or examples of correct actions. The main drawback of RL applications is the high number of necessary trials for learning of a goal-directed

S.G. Ponnambalam et al. (Eds.): IRAM 2012, CCIS 330, pp. 190–197, 2012.

behavior. Biological systems in contrary apply different learning schemes besides using highly parallel processing units. They combine RL with other methods to obtain synergy effects between concurrent learning processes. Combination of feedbacks of the separate processing learning approaches reduces the number of trials before an optimal behavior can be achieved. Our goal has been to use these ideas for developing a flexible architecture which allows real-time behavior of autonomous systems in real-world scenarios.

Our project has an interdisciplinary character. The proposed system architecture is developed on the base of findings in computational neuroscience. It consists of multiple memory structures. The output of two separate learning processes which process concurrently is combined to generate goal-directed behavior of an agent. Besides enabling an autonomous system to learn the current task, the architecture allows furthermore to store salient navigation data in such a way that it can be generalized and used flexibly for other tasks in the explored site.

In this paper we describe first the biological background of our architecture, its structure and realization. In a second step we depict the realized learning approaches and their integration in a memory frame. Finally we show the performance of the presented architecture by placing our agent in a maze unknown to it where it has to find some objects in a prespecified order.

2   Biological Background

Our perception, the rules that we use in our daily life, the way we behave, the things that make us happy or unhappy are shaped by our experience. Each important event, all salient information is registered in our brain. Several neuroscientific studies and experiments reveal that input data are processed in several dissociated interconnected memory systems whose outputs converge to accomplish behaviors (refer to [5] for a survey). Different aspects of the data describing our experiences are stored in corresponding memory structures which are distributed in various cortical and subcortical areas; the data forms the memories and influence the retrieval from them. The *long-term declarative memory* consists of two parts: an *episodic memory* (EM) with time sorted sequences of personally experienced events located in the hippocampus and a *semantic memory* (SM) describing learned facts and objects located in the perirhinal cortex. The *procedural memory* (PM) system located in the striatum stores and provides skills. An *emotional memory* system residing in the amygdala maps the learned emotional significance to diverse objects and events. The data from all memory units is retrieved with respect to the current task and instantaneous environmental situation in order to generate an adaptive behavior which is based on past experiences. The *working memory* (WM) as part of the prefrontal cortex (PFC) merges the feedback from different brain units and holds a limited amount of the most salient information for a short time in conscious state. The signals of all units converge in the PFC to produce the best suitable action and behavior for a current situation.

The most known and successful theory of brain's decision-making in neurophysiological research is *action selection* based on temporal difference learning of dopamine response [5]. The phasic responses of dopamine neurons reinforce successful action in such a way that it will be repeated in the future as a feedback to the encountered conforming stimuli. A variety of studies give evidence that RL describes the seminal aspect of learning in many animal species. This learning approach depicts one of the most common adaptation mechanisms of nature. Generalization of the perceived data and the use of the generalized knowledge for anticipating subsequent situations is the other crucial point in the creation of adaptive behavior [6]. Internal predictive models arise due to lateral learning in hippocampus and bias the current behavioral decision-making due the prediction of future states after executing the chosen action.

3   Related Works

Cognitive Systems: The aim is to create a general architecture which can interpret facts and make decisions in different knowledge domains in a similar way as humans do. The most popular approaches SOAR [8] and ACT-R [9] are built as production systems, representing their knowledge as production rules and using chaining as the main learning method. The progress in this field and, especially to realize acquisition, representation and use of knowledge have generated a foundation for autonomous embodied agents.

Episodic Memory (EM) Projects: A great number of EM models is based on an anatomical prototype of the hippocampus. Different variants of Hebb's learning are used to realize coding, retrieval [10-12] and formation of hierarchies between single entries. The real time models [13-15] realize the EM functionality with data banks.

4   System Configuration and Realization

Our current system configuration (Fig. 1) includes four major forms of memory: The declarative episodic and semantic memories are realized in a simplified way using relational database. Quick one trial learning in the EM acquires time-ordered sequences of single events, each consisting of the simultaneously perceived bits of the current situation. The SM contains detailed information about each already seen object and generalized or cached-value knowledge about related solved tasks. The PM of a rescue agent encompasses skills for moving in the desired direction or to the specified position by avoiding obstacles, rotating, walking left or right or around the object. These operations allow a flexible navigation of the agent in highly cluttered environments. The WM maintains salient information about the current situation and passes it on to other memory units and concurrent learning processes of the agent. Up to now two biologically inspired learning approaches are integrated in the system (model-based RL will follow next). Model-free RL was modified according to the way information is processed in the brain. The *latent* learning uses experience data in the EM to build a spatial model of the explored area which is able to plan the agent's paths to each already seen object in domain. The feedbacks of the learning units describing the next best suitable actions are combined in the WM and finally a chosen action is requested from PM. The distributed system is realized on the base of Robot Operating System (ROS) [16]. Concurrent processing and communicating nodes cooperate to generate the goal-directed vehicle behavior.

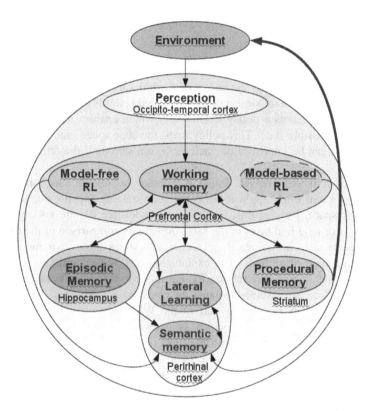

Fig. 1. System structure and communication between concurrently processing ROS-Nodes

4.1 Model-Free Reinforcement Learning

RL [17] is a quickly growing area in neuroscience and machine learning connected to trial and error learning of an agent from the reaction to an initially novel environment. Its goal is the determination of the optimal behavior (strategy) to accomplish a given task. Two units interact during RL: the agent and the surrounding environment. The agent gets information about the state s_t of the environment and chooses an action a_t from a set of available actions. The execution of action a_t changes the state of the environment to s_{t+1}. The agent is then informed about the new state and additionally, about the reward (feedback) r_{t+1} of the environment showing the positive or negative quality of the executed action. The agent learns from the feedback and chooses the next action. This loop continues until the task is solved or a predefined maximum number of learning steps is reached.

The formal modeling of the environment in RL is based on a Markov Decision Process (MDP). This mathematical framework assists in modeling the decision making also by partly random outcomes of actions. The Markov process is completely described by the 4-tuple (S, A, $P_{ss'}^a$, $R_{ss'}^a$) where S is a set of states, A is a set actions available in the whole environment, $P_{ss'}^a$ specifies the probability of transition from state s to state s' after the action a and $R_{ss'}^a$ indicates the reward achieved after the transition ss'. The agent gets the reward R_t during the time segment $[t, T]$

$$R_t = \sum_{k=0}^{T-t-1} \gamma^k r_{k+t+1}. \tag{1}$$

Discount coefficient γ depicts the decay of reward values during future time steps. The goal of an agent is to maximize the accumulated rewards during the processing of the task. The agent learns a policy π (strategy) which enables it to choose the best action for each possible state. This policy maps the state space onto the action space $\pi: S \rightarrow A$ and can be improved on each execution step until the termination of the process.

The use of a model-free RL frame is popular in autonomous robotics. The shortcoming for real world applications is the great training expense due to searching the huge task space. Besides this, results from model-free RL are not applicable to other domains or modified tasks in the same domain. A comparison of the model-free RL for the same tasks in biological and technical systems shows extreme advantages in the learning time of animals. The explanation of this fact is the hypothesis that biological systems do not only rely on RL but make use of other learning paradigms also. Synergy effects are assumed to cause the observed acceleration.

Our RL approach is realized as part of the WM and uses a high-level abstract representation of the task space which is gathered during the navigation. Such processing is strongly associated with the object-oriented situation representation in WM which originates following the object and scene recognition in the V4/IT area of the visual cortex. The set of the previously observed salient objects defines the current space state vector. Our RL realization uses varying number of actions (skills from the PM) depending on the current situation and shows considerable acceleration of learning comparing to conventional RL implementations.

4.2   Latent Spatial Learning

We use Bayesian learning to reproduce latent spatial learning detected in animals [18]. The learned internal representation of the environmental configuration is saved in the SM of the agent. This representation is mapped as a Dynamical Bayesian Network (DBN) [19] model. A DBN is the extension of Bayesian Network (BN) concept [20] used for dynamic processes. The learned environmental DBN model is able to predict the effect of a chosen action and propose (calculate) the path to the target object, if this object was already seen during one of the previous explorations. Utilization of a factored Markov Decision Process (fMDP) [21] is a common way for modeling of decision processes with DBN. The Markov property forms the graphical structure of the model. The seen configurations of objects in the environment of the agent composing an event are used to build the state vector for each step of the fMDP.

The probability propagation on each time step of the DBN conforms to the step of mental simulation of the internal spatial model for current environment. Time-sorted sequence of events in episodic memory describes transitions after the execution of the specified actions. Event data gathered in the EM provides the initial information for the construction of conditional probability tables (CPT) which builds the quantitative background of the DBN model..

The forward instantiation of DBN and propagation of beliefs continues until the probability of the goal state in one time step is more then zero. Placement (assignment) of evidence to the goal state leads to propagation of network beliefs in the backward direction and calculation of the multi-step path to the specified object. Robustness to variations in the surrounding environment is ensured through the online replanning of the prepared multi-step trajectory.

5   System Evaluation

We evaluated the entire architecture in real-time on a virtual robot in our 3D robot simulator. The robot was placed in an initially unknown maze (Fig. 2). Boards with digits (from 0 to 9) were fixed to the walls of the labyrinth. The task consisted of detecting three different digits in a predefined order. The vehicle was equipped with laser scanner and camera for recognition of the gaps (openings in the maze) and the digits. The agent got a negative reward of -5 for each step except for steps when the right digit in the sequence was found. Such successful steps were rewarded with 100.

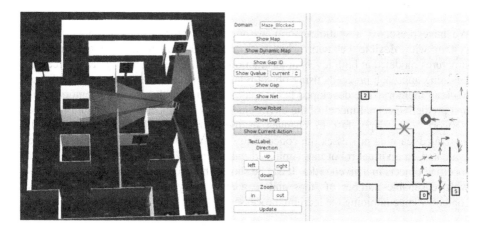

Fig. 2. Left: An autonomous agent navigating in the maze. Right: Internal representation of the perceived world with robot position (green circle) and next chosen gap (brown cross).

Fig. 3 summarizes the results of the evaluation: The first part of experiments was done using only model-free RL. The blue graph in the left image shows the learning results after 20 consecutive episodes: Only few episodes were needed to obtain an acceptable path for task.

In the second part of the experiments we combined RL with latent spatial learning. The red curve demonstrates impressively that the number of navigation steps can be reduced considerably due to planned paths predicted by the DBN based model of the environment. If the agent is given a second task (see right image) the system has to learn from scratch if using only RL (blue curve) while the already learned predictive model provides an optimal path even faster than before.

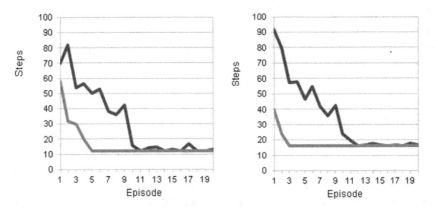

Fig. 3. Evaluation results for task 1 (left) and task 2 (right): Comparison of learning with RL only (blue curve) and its combination with the latent spatial learning (red curve)

6   Conclusions

We have presented a spatiotemporal learning architecture for an autonomous robot system with flexible behavior which is based upon interrelated multiple memory structures modeled at high levels of abstraction. The realized model-free Reinforcement Learning approach proceeds using object-related symbolic state representations from a working memory. The developed latent spatial learning in the episodic memory results in a predictive spatial model of the environment that is mapped to a Dynamic Bayesian Network and adapts fast to changes in the surrounding. These two biologically motivated learning processes run concurrently in one system. The architecture has been evaluated on a virtual robot in a simulated unknown maze which had to search a set of specified objects in a given order. It can be shown that the agent is able to fulfill the task with reasonable number of steps and to adapt rapidly to modifications of the task content when combining the learning processes.

References

1. National Institute of Standards and Technology: Performance Metrics and Test Arenas for Autonomous Mobile Robots, http://www.nist.gov/el/isd/testarenas
2. Pellenz, J., Gossow, D., Paulus, D.: Robbie: A Fully Autonomous Robot for Robo Cup Rescue. Advanced Robotics 23(9), 1159–1177 (2009)

3. Mendonca, M., Ramos de Aruda, L., Neves, F.: Autonomous Navigation System UsingEvent Driven-Fuzzy Cognitive Maps. Appl. Intelligence 37(2), 175–188 (2012)
4. Zou, A., Hou, Z., Fu, S., Tan, M.: Neural Networks for Mobile Robot Navigation: A Survey. In: Wang, J., Yi, Z., Żurada, J.M., Lu, B.-L., Yin, H. (eds.) ISNN 2006. LNCS, vol. 3972, pp. 1218–1226. Springer, Heidelberg (2006)
5. White, N.M.: Multiple memory systems. Scholarpedia 2(7), 2663 (2007)
6. Niv, Y.: Reinforcement Learning in the Brain. J. Math. Psychology 53(3), 139–154 (2009)
7. Butz, M.V., Sigaud, O., Gérard, P.: Internal Models and Anticipations in Adaptive Learning Systems. In: Butz, M.V., Sigaud, O., Gérard, P. (eds.) Anticipatory Behavior in Adaptive Learning Systems. LNCS (LNAI), vol. 2684, pp. 86–109. Springer, Heidelberg (2003)
8. Laird, J.E., Rosenbloom, P.S., Newell, A.: Chunking in SOAR: The Anatomy of a General Learning Mechanism. Machine Learning 1, 11–46 (1986)
9. Anderson, J., Lebiere, C.: The Atomic Components of Thought. Lawrence Erlbaum (1998)
10. Rolls, E.T.: Memory, Attention, and Decision-making: A Unifying Computational Neuroscience Approach. Oxford University Press, Oxford (2008)
11. Hasselmo, M.E.: What is the Function of Hippocampal Theta Rhythm?—Linking Behavioral Data to Phasic Properties of Field. Hippocampus 15(7), 936–949 (2005)
12. Sato, N., Yamaguchi, Y.: Simulation of Human Episodic Memory by Using a Computational Model of the Hippocampus. In: Adv. Artificial Intelligence (2010)
13. Nuxoll, A.M.: Enhancing Intelligent Agents With Episodic Memory. PhD thesis, University of Michigan (2007)
14. Brom, C., Pešková, K., Lukavský, J.: What Does Your Actor Remember? Towards Characters with a Full Episodic Memory. In: Cavazza, M., Donikian, S. (eds.) ICVS-VirtStory 2007. LNCS, vol. 4871, pp. 89–101. Springer, Heidelberg (2007)
15. Tecuci: A Generic Memory Module for Events, PhD thesis, University of Texas in Austin (2007)
16. ROS, http://www.ros.org
17. Sutton, R.S., Barto, A.G.: Reinforcement Learning: An Introduction. MIT Press, Cambridge (1998)
18. Tolman, E.: Cognitive Maps in Rats and Men. Psych. Review 55, 189–208 (1948)
19. Murphy, K.: Dynamic Bayesian Networks: Representation, Inference and Learning. Ph.D. thesis, University of California, Berkeley (2002)
20. Jensen, F.V.: An Introduction To Bayesian Networks. UCL Press (1996)
21. Boutilier, C., Dearden, R., Goldszmidt, M.: Exploiting Structure in Policy Construction. In: Proc. IJCAI, pp. 1104–1111 (1995)

Analysis of Electrocardiogram (ECG) Signals for Human Emotional Stress Classification

Siao Zheng Bong, M. Murugappan, and Sazali Yaacob

School of Mechatronics Engineering, Universiti Malaysia Perlis,
Perlis, Malaysia
wendy880806@gmail.com, murugappan@unimap.edu.my

Abstract. Electrocardiogram (ECG) signal significantly reflects autonomic nervous system (ANS) activities during emotional stress changes. Undeniably, a variety of valuable information can be extracted from a single record of ECG signal. Audio-visual stimuli are selected arbitrarily for the laboratory experiment in order to induce emotional stress on 5 healthy subjects. Time domain features: heart rate (HR), mean R peak amplitude (MRAmp), and mean R-R intervals (MRRI) are extracted from ECG signals and mapped into emotional stress classification using K-nearest neighbor (KNN) and Support Vector Machine (SVM). Classification performance has been investigated on three different sets of training and testing feature vector. The best mean classification accuracy for HR, MRAmp and MRRI in three classes is 66.49%, 56.95% and 61.52%, respectively and two classes are 77.69%, 61.48% and 60.21%, respectively. These results indicate that, the proposed methodology have a higher significance on distinguishing the emotional stress state of the subjects.

Keywords: Emotional stress, Electrocardiogram (ECG), K-Nearest Neighbor (KNN), Support Vector Machine (SVM*).*

1 Introduction

1.1 Importance of ECG Signal Analysis in Human Emotional Stress Assessment

ECG signal provides useful information in recognizing human emotional stress. Studies and innovations on emotional stress have been done since decades ago but mostly in the psychological aspects. Mental diseases such as depression, anxiety disorders and bipolar disorders are mainly due to emotional stress [1]. Emotions are broadly categorized into positive emotions (happy, surprise) and negative emotions (sad, anger, fear, and disgust). The main aim of this work is to investigate the relationship on time domain features of ECG signal to discriminate the emotional stress level of the subjects. Continuous existence of negative emotions will be highly influence human's life and cause major psychological diseases. We believe that human will feel emotional stress after a long and continuous experience of negative

S.G. Ponnambalam et al. (Eds.): IRAM 2012, CCIS 330, pp. 198–205, 2012.

emotions. The changes in emotional states are reflected in human physiological activities such as changes in muscle tension, respiration and heart rate [2]. The autonomic nervous system (ANS) plays as key role on indentifying human physiological characteristics [3]. Since heart rate is greatly affected when emotional changes occur, ECG signal becomes one of human physiological signals that is very crucial to be investigated and explored.

1.2   ECG Signal Analysis Using Different Types of Statistical Features

ECG signal has been used an effective indicator for diagnosing several medical diseases related to heart, emotions, stress, etc. However, most of the researchers have investigated this signal for diagnosing cardiovascular diseases [4]. ECG signals can be easily characterized by using three different approaches for any research investigations such as: time domain, frequency domain and time-frequency domain. Time-domain analysis usually involves heart rate variability (HRV) which portrays features such as heart rate, R-R intervals, R peak value, standard deviation of NN intervals (SDNN) and root mean square for standard deviation (RMSSD) [5, 6]. Frequency domain analysis is performed through spectral analysis such as Power Spectral Density (PSD) [7]. Discrete Wavelet Transform (DWT) and Discrete Wavelet Packet Transform (DWPT) are more popular methods in time-frequency domain analysis to extract the features from low frequency (LF, 0.04-0.15 Hz) components and high frequency (HF, 0.16-0.4 Hz) components of ECG signals. LF and HF represent the parasympathetic nervous function (PNS) and sympathetic nervous function (SNS), respectively [8-9]. Statistical analysis is also very common in HRV analysis. Features such as mean, maximum, minimum, variance, and standard deviation are widely used for ECG signal analysis [10-11].

This paper is organized as below: Section 2 describes about the research methodology. Results and discussion is presented in Section 3. Finally, the conclusion of this work is given in Section 4.

2   Research Methodology

2.1   Emotional Stress Model and Data Acquisition Protocol

Emotions are universally modeled using different approaches. In general, all the six basic emotions (happy, sad, anger, fear, disgust, surprise) are modeled on two dimensional plane (valance – arousal) [12]. Based on the Russell's Circumplex model of emotion, we have proposed a novel emotional stress model for this work in Figure 1. This emotional stress has two important regions such as emotional stress and non-emotional stress. Fear, anger, disgust and sadness are among the emotions that have higher potential to enter into emotional stress region. In this work, emotional stress is induced by using audio-visual stimuli (short videos/ clips) with the time length ranges from a minimum of 30 seconds to maximum of 5 minutes for each stimulus. The complete protocol design and its description have been given in [13].

We have shown 15 video clips on each emotion to the subject. At the end of each set of emotional stimuli, the subjects are asked to rate the emotion they experienced and the intensity of the video clips through self assessment manikin (SAM). Finally, 12 video clips on disgust emotion, 13 video clips on fear emotion and 10 each video clips on sad, anger, surprise, and happy are reported by the subjects as more dynamic video clips on inducing different emotion and stress. The complete protocol on data acquisition protocol takes approximately 2 hours and 30 minutes. The authors hope that, the continuous exposition of negative and positive emotional video clips to the subjects will certainly induces the emotional stress on them. ML818 Powerlab 15T from AD Instrument is used as an ECG data acquisition system for this research work. Three electrodes have chosen for this work and we followed Ethovan triangle method for placing the electrodes. Two active electrodes are placed on the left wrist, right wrist and reference electrode is placed on right leg. All the electrodes are made up of Ag/Ag-Cl and acquired at a constant sampling rate of 1000 Hz.

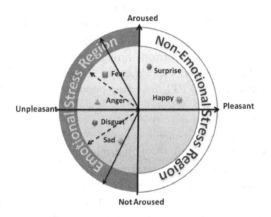

Fig. 1. Proposed Emotional Stress Model

2.2   Preprocessing and Feature Extraction

Raw ECG signals are preprocessed using Elliptic band pass filter and discrete wavelet transform to eliminate motion artifact, 50 Hz power interference and baseline wanders. After preprocessing, ECG signal recorded for each stimulus is fragmented into five equal frames of constant duration. This allows the authors to investigate HR, MRA and MRRI more precisely since the onset of each emotion is different from one individual to the others [14]. Next, QRS detection is computed to acquire time-domain HRV information such as R peak and R-R intervals from the ECG signals [15]. The statistical features such as HR, MRAmp and MRRI are calculated from the ECG signal morphology. HR is computed by multiplying the total number of R peak in a frame with 60 seconds and divided by the total time length of the frame in seconds (Eqn 1). MRA is the mean of the R peak value in one frame while MRRI is the mean value for the interval time between two successive R peaks. Theoretically, R peak is the highest peak value in a complete ECG waveform. R-R intervals represent the time intervals between two successive R peaks where a heartbeat occurs. Hence, mean R-R interval simply means the averaged value from all the R-R intervals detected in a given period of time. Mean R amplitude of the ECG waveform indicates the averaged value of total number of R peaks in a certain period of time. In phase one classification, a total number of 1775 samples for each feature are extracted from five subjects over 10 frames. 1125 features for negative emotions, 500 for positive emotions and 150 for neutral state. In the second phase of classification, a total number of 1125 features are used as input; 550 features for non-emotional stress and 575 features for emotional stress.

$$HR = \frac{60}{t_{frame}} \times R_{peaks\,frame}$$

(1)

2.3   Emotional Stress Classification

These extracted features are given as the input data for the emotional stress classification system. Before classifying the emotional stress states, the input feature vector is classified into three classes: negative emotions, positive emotions and neutral. The negative emotion is then further classified into two classes: emotional stress and non-emotional stress by using the same features (HR, MRAmp and MRRI) as input data. Two classifiers are used in the classification stage: k-nearest neighbor (KNN) and support vector machine (SVM). In KNN, an object is classified by a majority vote of its neighbors and it is assigned to the class most common amongst its k nearest neighbors, while SVM constructs a hyperplane or set of hyperplanes in a high- or infinite-dimensional space. In this work, the value of "k" is arbitrarily chosen from 2 to 10 and the maximum value of classification rate is achieved on k=3. The complete structure of classification system has been shown in Fig 3. In addition to the classification accuracy, sensitivity and specificity are also computed using Eqn 2 and Eqn 3. In addition to classification rate, we also computed the sensitivity and specificity for investigating the potential on classifying the emotions and emotional stress.

Fig. 3. Structure of Emotional Stress Classification

$$Sensitivity = \frac{TN}{TN + FP}$$

(2)

$$Specificity = \frac{TP}{TP + FN}$$

(3)

where, TP: True positive; TN: True negative; FP: False positive; FN: False negative.

3   Result and Discussion

In this work, total number of video clips used for statistical features extraction on each class is: negative – 45 clips, positive – 20 clips and neutral – 6 clips. Table 1 shows the results of three different cases such as Case A (60% training data, 40% testing data), Case B (70% training data, 30% testing data) and Case C (80% training data, 20% testing data) for classifying three classes (positive emotions, negative emotions and neutral. HR stands out as the best feature while mean R amplitude gives poor classification rate on for three-class classification over three cases. Major reason for getting lower classification rate on neutral state is due to its insufficient feature vectors. Since, the features are derived only from 6 clips which are collected after the end of series of each emotional stimulus. However, the value of sensitivity shows the capability of the testing data points in negative emotions hit the training data points while specificity reflects the capability of the classifier to detect the remaining two emotions (positive and neutral emotion). The good performance on classifier is purely decided by the higher value of sensitivity and specificity. From the same table, sensitivity and specificity of HR appears to be the highest among all features in all cases (A, B and C).

Table 1. KNN classification for three emotions (positive, negative and neutral)

	Negative	Positive	Neutral	Acc	Sen	Spe
Case A: 60% Training and 40% Testing						
HR	**84.39**	33.58	**41.92**	**66.49**	**0.71**	**0.59**
MRAmp	78.40	24.36	4.65	56.95	0.65	0.40
MRRI	78.04	**41.86**	3.17	61.52	0.70	0.53
Case B: 70% Training and 30% Testing						
HR	**82.43**	33.07	**55.33**	**66.22**	**0.71**	**0.57**
MRAmp	74.24	27.27	7.33	55.34	0.65	0.41
MRRI	76.85	**42.47**	4.89	61.07	**0.71**	0.53
Case C: 80% Training and 20% Testing						
HR	**85.08**	34.65	**45.57**	**67.54**	**0.71**	**0.61**
MRAmp	79.91	24.74	5.10	58.05	0.65	0.43
MRRI	79.10	**42.91**	2.27	62.41	**0.71**	0.55

Sen: Sensitivity; Spe: Specificity

In emotional stress (two-class) classification, both KNN and SVM classifiers are implemented. Since, implementing SVM for three classes (neutral, positive, and negative) are highly complicated and this classifier is only suitable for two class classification. HR and MRAmp features are giving higher classification rate in KNN and SVM, respectively. The complete results of second phase of KNN classification are shown in Table 2. It shows that, sensitivity of HR feature is the highest through KNN classifier. The specificity turned out to be higher in the remaining features: MRAmp and MRRI. For SVM classifier, the performance rates of all the features are giving approximately similar results in Table 3. The specificity of SVM classifier is much higher than sensitivity and this show on classifying emotional stress than non-emotional stress. The highest averaged accuracy for KNN is 77.69 % (HR) while the highest averaged accuracy for SVM is 66.09 % (MRAmp).

Table 2. Classification of emotional stress and non-emotional stress using KNN

	Non-emo	Emo-stress	Accuracy	Sen	Spe
Case A: 60 % Training and 40 % Testing					
HR	**76.32**	**73.09**	**74.67**	**0.73**	**0.76**
MRAmp	58.91	62.39	60.69	0.60	0.61
MRRI	57.32	62.83	60.13	0.60	0.61
Case B: 70 % Training and 30 % Testing					
HR	**80.30**	**75.17**	**77.69**	**0.76**	**0.80**
MRAmp	59.03	63.84	61.48	0.61	0.62
MRRI	59.27	61.10	60.21	0.59	0.61
Case C: 80 % Training and 20 % Testing					
HR	**81.09**	**73.91**	**77.42**	**0.75**	**0.80**
MRAmp	59.27	66.43	62.93	0.63	0.63
MRRI	60.64	60.70	60.67	0.60	0.62

Non-emo: Non emotional stress; Emo-stress: Emotional stress

Table 3. Classification of emotional stress and non-emotional stress using SVM

	Non-emo	Emo-stress	Accuracy	Sen	Spe
Case A: 60 % Training and 40 % Testing					
HR	42.05	63.65	53.09	0.53	0.53
MRAmp	45.82	**83.30**	**64.98**	**0.73**	**0.62**
MRRI	**48.95**	65.17	57.24	0.57	0.57
Case B: 70 % Training and 30 % Testing					
HR	42.55	65.87	54.45	0.55	0.54
MRAmp	46.61	**83.66**	**65.52**	**0.73**	**0.62**
MRRI	**48.18**	66.10	57.33	0.58	0.57
Case C: 80 % Training and 20 % Testing					
HR	41.91	65.39	53.91	0.54	0.54
MRAmp	**47.36**	**83.91**	**66.04**	**0.74**	**0.63**
MRRI	46.09	65.65	56.09	0.56	0.56

Non-emo: Non emotional stress; Emo-stress: Emotional stress

In [13], we have achieved a maximum classification accuracy of 75% - 80% using 10 fold cross validation method. Indeed, the ECG signals have been segmented into 10 frames. However, the R peak detection error rate of this present work is lower than our earlier work [13]. In this work, we have proposed a new threshold value for efficiently detect the R peaks from the ECG signals. This QRS detection algorithm with new threshold value has been tested with MIT arrhythmia database to confirm its lower error detection rate. The mean error rate for the new threshold value is 0.46 % compared to the old threshold value which is 1.06 %. In [13], the threshold value is determined by multiplying the total number of R peaks in a thread of ECG signals with the mean of R peaks and maximum point among the R peaks [16]. In this work, we modified the equation and considered the threshold value as 1.15 times of original threshold value (Eqn 4). This constant (1.15) value had chosen arbitrarily by testing with several values.

$$threshold_{new} = 1.15 \left(\max_{n=1}^{N}(x[n]) \times \frac{\sum_{n=1}^{N} x[n]}{N} \right) \tag{4}$$

The mean classification accuracy of this present work is decreased due to the insufficient database for emotional stress classification. Hence, the authors have decided to collect more quality data with improved data acquisition protocol for enhancing the classification accuracy in the future. Instead of using ten frames, the authors chosen five frames for the dataset framing. This is due to the fact that, we have ultra short length of six seconds (6000 samples only for each frame) after data framing is performed. This phenomenon is resulted from the shortest video clip (30 seconds only) which is one of the stimuli used in the protocol with minimum duration. The shortest time or the ultra short term is possible for HRV analysis is 10 seconds [17].

4   Conclusion

This present work has discussed the time domain statistical features based emotional stress classification using ECG signals. Proposed QRS detection algorithm gives lower R peak error detection rate compared to our earlier work. Statistical features such as HR and MRA plays a significant role on efficiently classifying the emotional stress using two classifiers (KNN and SVM). We also tested the classifiers using three different ratio's of training and testing data. However, there is not much difference in terms of classification accuracy, sensitivity and specificity among three cases. Hence, the proposed system has an ability to classify the emotional stress even with lower number of testing rate. In addition, the proposed customized protocol has efficiently induces the emotional stress on the subject. In the future, different types of time domain features can be investigated for improving the classification rate of emotional stress states through different types of classifier. Improving the quality of present data base with more number of subjects is also highly inevitable for generalizing the proposed system. Also, investigating different levels of emotional stress state also play a significant role on developing intelligent emotional stress assessment system.

References

3. Zhai, J., Barreto, A.: Stress Detection in Computer Users Based on Digital Signal Processing of Noninvasive Physiological Variables. In: 28th Annual International Conference of the IEEE Engineering in Medicine and Biology Society, EMBS 2006, pp. 1355–1358 (2006)
4. Graff, B.: Entropy Measures of Heart Rate Variability for Short ECG Datasets in Patients with Congestive Heart Failure. Acta Physica Polonica B Proceedings Supplement 5 (2012)
5. Hosseini, S.A., Khalilzadeh, M.A.: Emotional Stress Recognition System Using EEG and Psychophysiological Signals: Using New Labelling Process of EEG Signals in Emotional Stress State. In: 2010 International Conference on Biomedical Engineering and Computer Science (ICBECS), pp. 1–6 (2010)
6. Wu, D., Courtney, C.G., Lance, B.J., Narayanan, S.S., Dawson, M.E., Oie, K.S., Parsons, T.D.: Optimal Arousal Identification and Classification for Affective Computing Using Physiological Signals: Virtual Reality Stroop Task. IEEE Transactions on Affective Computing, 109–118 (2010)
7. Hayashi, T., Mizuno-Matsumoto, Y., Okamoto, E., Ishii, R., Ukai, S., Shinosaki, K.: Anterior Brain Activities Related to Emotional Stress. IEEE (2008)
8. Kim, K.H., Bang, S.W., Kim, S.R.: Emotion Recognition System using Short-term Monitoring of Physiological Signals. Medical & Biological Engineering & Computing 42 (2004)
9. Hao, M., Liu, G.-Y., Ma, C.-W., Cai, J.: An Application of Electrocardiography to Emotion Recognition. In: Fifth International Conference on Natural Computation (2009)
10. Yang, R., Liu, G.: Emotion Feature Selection from Physiological Signal Based on BPSO. In: International Conference on Intelligent Systems and Knowledge Engineering (2007)
11. Bong, S.Z., Murugappan, M., Yaacob, S.: Methods and approaches on inferring human emotional stress changes through physiological signals: A review. In: International Conference on Man Machine Systems (2011) (unpublished)
12. MRC Cognition and Brain Sciences Unit, Facial Expression Perception, http://www.mrc-cbu.cam.ac.uk/research/emotion/san/perception.html
13. Zheng, B.S., Murugappan, M., Yaacob, S.: Human Emotional Stress Assessment Through Heart Rate Detection in a Customized Protocol Experiment. In: 2012 IEEE Symposium on Industrial Electronics and Applications, ISIEA 2012 (accepted on June 21, 2012)
14. Nakasone, A., Prendinger, H., Ishizuka, M.: Emotion recognition from electromyography and skin conductance. In: The Fifth International Workshop on Biosignal Interpretation (BSI 2005), pp. 219–222 (2005)
15. Kathirvel, P., Sabarimalai Manikandan, M., Prasanna, S., Soman, K.: An Efficient R-peak Detection Based on New Nonlinear Transformation and First-Order Gaussian Differentiator. Cardiovascular Engineering and Technology, Biomedical and Life Sciences 2(4), 408–425 (2011)
16. http://farukuysal.net/QRSDetection.aspx (retrieved on February 3, 2012)
17. Li, K., McNames, J., Aboy, M., Goldstein, B.: Accuracy of ultra-short heart rate variability measures. Engineering in Medicine and Biology Society. In: Proceedings of the 25th Annual International Conference of the IEEE, vol. 3, pp. 2424–2427 (2003)

Kinematics and Kinetics Studies on Upper Extremity during Walking Frame Ambulation

Choo Ching Tat, Veronica Lestari Jauw, and S. Parasuraman

School of Engineering, Monash University Sunway Campus, 46150 Bandar Sunway, Malaysia
{veronica.ljauw,s.parasuraman}@monash.edu

Abstract. The studies of upper extremity on bio mechanics during walker assisted gait provides perception into the novel design of the ambulatory device as well as the rehabilitative strategy for those who are in need. Thus far, the knowledge of kinetic, kinematics and functional requirements to efficiently use the walking aid device is still inadequate. Hence, this paper addresses the theoretical analysis through the skeleton model created by Visual 3D. The infrared cameras are used to capture the still position of the individual as well as their moving position. The purpose is to find the position difference aiding in data and gait analysis. Subsequently, other kinetics parameters can be tabulated based on the position difference. Furthermore, the kinematics data which is forces and moments can also be tabulated based on the kinetics data. These simulated data will be compared with the measured data that can be attained through the pressure sensors.

Keywords: Biomechanics, walking aid, gait analysis, ambulatory device.

1 Introduction

Numerous efforts developing ambulatory device have been attempted with the intention to improve the comfort and nurture of the elderly community. Therefore, the existing devices have always taken those aspects into consideration while modeling the ambulatory devices and system. The existing devices have aimed at advanced and intelligent approach such as power assisting [1]; passive omni-directional walker [2] and physical support [3].

Extensive research on the kinematics of individual's walking locomotion and the distribution of forces to the upper extremity is essential. It is to provide comprehensive information modeling an excellent ambulatory device. Bachschmidt et al [4] has developed a 6 DOF strain gauge based system to measure the resultant force of individual's hand. It is concluded that the maximum joint moment is found at the elbow followed by the shoulder and wrist respectively. Further kinematics approach is addressed by J.Crosbie [5, 6] where the dynamic motion of the individual on the sagittal plane is observed. There are several assumptions made to identify the kinematics features of the walking gait. The idea of this approach is to estimate the resultant forces on the hand that may be transferred to the shoulder and elbow.

S.G. Ponnambalam et al. (Eds.): IRAM 2012, CCIS 330, pp. 206–215, 2012.

With the exception of the above, it is also essential to discover distinct techniques to study the stability of the ambulatory device. The preceding works concentrated on the force distribution while A.B.Deathe et al [7] introduced the WTI (Walker Tipping Index). This index is to define and evaluate the stability of the ambulatory device. The aim of this study is to distinguish the appropriate height to be standardized for each individual when modeling the device.

This paper presents the comprehensive kinematics, kinetics and gait analysis of the upper extremity through Visual 3D motion analysis system and flexi force sensor. By doing so, the internal force which acted on the joint along with the moment of the wrist, elbow and shoulder can be attained. These data are to be integrated with the proposed dynamical models and implemented to the proposed novel design of the ambulatory device.

2   Experimental Studies

A total of 7 test subjects took part of this study where two of them are female elder adults; 53 and 80 years old respectively. Five of them are male adult within the age range of 22 to 24 years old. All test subjects are physically fit meaning that they have not undergone lower extremity surgery, musculoskeletal pathology, cardiovascular limitation and stroke. Table 1 describes the physical elements of the individuals.

Table 1. Physical profile of the individual subject

Weight (kg)	Height (cm)	Age (yrs)	BMI (kg/m^2)	Comments
83	176	22	26.8	Overweight
56	170	24	19.1	Normal
54	168	23	19.1	Normal
57	170	23	19.2	Normal
66	175	23	21.6	Normal
53	160	52	20.7	Normal
47	150	80	19.6	Normal

2.1   Methodology

This study employs a similar approach to Bachschmidt [4] where the kinematics data are attained by the constructed skeleton model. Our study utilizes infrared cameras which are able to attain the kinetics data of individual subject. These data's are then incorporated with Visual 3D analysis to construct the model. The kinetics data of individual subject is detected through the reflective markers attached to the subject.

The subject is asked to walk freely on the 5 meters experimental walkway for a minute without the aid of the walking device. This serves as warm up exercise for the subject and also camera testing. Subsequently, the subject is instructed to stand still enabling the recording of the static 3D image of the individual segment. The purpose is to capture the static position of individual segment and construct the 3D model of the subject. The static position is used as reference to obtain the change in position when the subject began to use the walking device and walk on the experimental walkway.

Based on Nabizadeh [8], the height of the walking device has to be altered approximately at the level of the distal ulnar styloid of individual subject. The aim is to let the subject's arm in the relax position when the subject stood next to the walker frame. Once the experimental preparation is done, the subject was instructed to lift the walking device and move it forward approximately 0.15-0.3 meter ahead; in front of their toes. This action is to be repeated until the walkway is completed. The horizontal direction of the movement is not important. Prior to the collection of data, the subject is allowed to practice until the subject is confident to use the standard walking device. A minimum of 7 trials or 5 minutes is conducted for all the subjects.

2.2   Force Measurements

Altogether, there are 3 unknown axial forces to be determined utilizing an instrumented walker. Three flexi sensors are attached on each grip of the standard ambulatory device which is clearly shown in Fig 1(b). Each sensor is placed 2 cm apart allowing maximum area coverage for resultant force measurements. The readings of the sensor have been amplified with a unit gain using amplifier system. Moreover, the readings are also filtered with 15Hz cut off frequency and the sampling rate of 6.25 Hz. The process of attaining the measurements and their signal processing is done at different systems

2.3   Markers and Model Construction

As mentioned earlier, the kinetics data of individual subject is attained through the position of the markers. The markers are placed based on the purpose of the markers; to track the motion or to construct the 3D skeleton model. The tracking markers reveal the kinetics data of individual's movement during the experiment whereas the construction markers provide the kinetics data of individual in the static position. The upper extremity segments to be tracked are the thorax, upper arm, forearm and hand. The placement of the tracking markers followed closely with Bachschmidt [4]. Fig 1(a) and Fig 1(c) illustrate the position of the markers to the individual subject. The clustered markers that can be observed in Fig 1(a) are so-called model construction markers and the individual markers are so-called tracking markers.

The inter-relationship between individual segments is described using Denavit-Hartenberg parameters. While, the rotations of individual upper extremity joints are determined using Euler angle which is relatively similar to the existing work done by Kadaba et.al [9]. Prior to the reflective marker position, the system has to be set up along with the establishment of the global coordinates. Hence, the kinetics data are all referenced to the global coordinates.

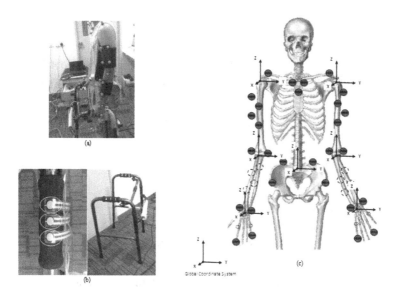

Fig. 1. The position of (a) the tracking markers and model construction markers, (b) the flexi sensors on the standard ambulatory device and (c) markers (tracking and model construction) anatomically

2.4   2D Representation of the Upper Extremity Forearm Flexion Extension

Constructing the 2D representation of the upper extremities allows prediction of the forces and joint moments that has been propagated from the ambulatory device's grip. Nevertheless, the construction is based on several assumptions which are essential to predict the kinetics data of the upper extremity.
The assumptions are listed as below:

a.   The upper arm, forearm and thorax segment is assumed to be the rigid links.
b.   There is no resultant forces acted on z-axis.
c.   The resultant forces propagate immediately to the contact area which is the palm of the individual's hand.

With the available kinetics data (i.e. forces and joint moments), the physical relationship of individual segment is described with Denavit- Hartenberg parameters. The rotations that are originated from the walking movement are determined using Euler angle theory. The local forces and moments that acted on individual segment can be determined using (4) to (9). However, (1) to (3) is essential to attain certain parameters that will be used in the later equation.

$$f_i = R_i^{i+1} f_{i+1} + F_i \tag{1}$$

$$n_i = R_i^{i+1} n_{i+1} + p_i \times \left(R_i^{i+1} f_{i+1} \right) + s_i \times F_i + N_i \tag{2}$$

$$\tau_i = n_i \cdot \left(R_i^{i-1} Z_0 \right) + b_i \dot{\theta}_i \tag{3}$$

The equations onwards are connected to the preceding equations to obtain the forces and moments for each link. Link 1, 2 and 3 denote the forces acted on the shoulder, upper arm and forearm respectively.

$$f_{2x} = \cos(\theta_2) f_x - \sin(\theta_2) f_y \tag{4}$$

$$f_{2y} = \sin(\theta_2) f_x + \cos(\theta_2) f_y \tag{5}$$

$$f_{1x} = \cos(\theta_1 + \theta_2) f_x - \sin(\theta_1 + \theta_2) f_y \tag{6}$$

$$f_{1y} = \cos(\theta_1 + \theta_2) f_y - \sin(\theta_1 + \theta_2) f_x \tag{7}$$

The torque for individual link can be attained through the below equations:

$$\tau_1 = l_2 f_y + l_1 f_x \sin(\theta_2) + l_1 f_y \cos(\theta_2) \tag{8}$$

$$\tau_2 = l_2 f_y \tag{9}$$

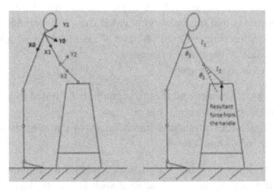

Fig. 2. The outline of the arm representation in 2D. Left side - Force distribution in xy-direction of individual joint. Right side - The joint angle of individual joint and resultant force acted on the palm from the handle.

3   Results and Discussion

The visual3D offers the analysis on the temporal and spatial parameters. The parameters include cadence, velocity, stride length, and stance-to-swing, kinetic (e.g. internal joint forces and moments) and kinematics variables (e.g. joint angular position, velocity and acceleration). These parameters are normalized as percentage of the walker stride cycle. The cycle is defined by the subsequence contact of the walker which is adopted by [4]. It considered as a cycle if these actions are covered in sequence: walker contact, foot off, foot contact, opposite foot contact, walker lift off and walker contact. However, kinetics variables are all normalized with the subject's arm length and body weight. These variables are measured through the flexi sensors and processed through the customized signal processing.

3.1   Kinematics of the Upper Extremity

Fig 3 illustrates the mean and standard deviation of the joint angles of an individual's upper extremity (right side) when using the walking device. In the sagittal plane, the shoulder was observed to stay at the flexion position during initial walker contact. Subsequently, the extension joint angle of the shoulder increased while the subject walked into the walker frame. It is the observed that the shoulder extension angle began to lessen during the lifting and swinging process. There are insignificant changes on the shoulder during 0-50% stride cycle of coronal plane. Nevertheless, the maximum angle of shoulder abduction adduction occurred at 75% of the cycle. The maximum external rotation was observed to occur at the initial lift of the walker.

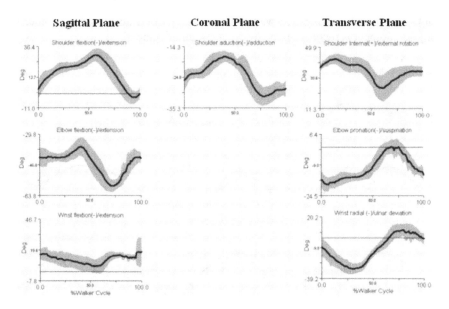

Fig. 3. Mean and standard deviation of joint angles of the upper extremity of a test subject using standard walking device

Further observation on the elbow flexion extension is done where the elbow flexion stays at approximately -290 to -450 during the initial walker contact until the subject is within the walker frame. An increment behavior is observed during the initial swing of the walker which occurred at approximately 75% of the stride cycle but it soon diminished when the subject walked forward. Looking into the elbow rotation, the joint rotation was not defined in the coronal plane. Nevertheless, the maximum and minimum elbow supination is observed in the traverse plane throughout the cycle. The minimum occurred when the subject was walking into the walker frame whereas the maximum occurred at approximately 75% of the cycle. The wrist is maintained at the flex pattern during 0-50% of stride cycle and extended to the maximum during initial swing of the walker. Again, the wrist rotation was not determined in the coronal plane but it decreases in the transverse plane at 0-50% of the stride cycle. An increment behavior of the wrist ulnar is soon to be followed for the subsequent stride cycle.

3.2   Kinetics of the Upper Extremity

Fig 4 depicts the mean and standard deviation of the joint moment acted on the upper extremity (right side) over 7 full stride cycles. These data are also filtered using a 6 Hz dual pass, 2nd order Butterworth filter, infinite impulse response (IIR) algorithm. Moreover, the measured joint moments are normalized to the arm length (meter) and body weight (kg). Through observation, the joint moments of individual segment are found to be greatest at the sagittal plane. In this plane, the maximum moment of the shoulder is obtained during mid-walker stance and ¾ of walker stance. While, the wrist joint moment is recorded to be low in the sagittal plane

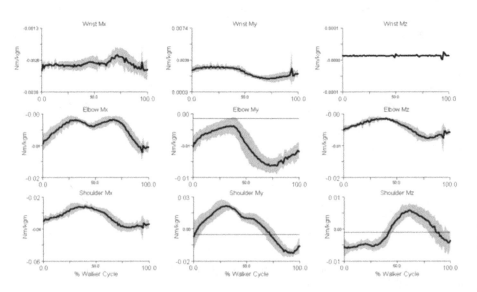

Fig. 4. Mean and standard deviation of the joint moments acted on the upper extremity from a test subject using standard walking gait

3.3   Gait Analysis

Table 2 listed the time and distance parameters that are attained in the full cycle stride experiments. The parameters are velocity, cycle time, stride length and cadence. Subject 7 shows the minimum velocity and stride length which is believed due to the age and height factors. It is clear that elderly tends to walk slowly to maintain their balance and hence the minimum velocity is attained. This can reason the huge amount of cycle time which is 5.2 seconds. The minimum stride length can also be found in subject 7. This is due to the height of the subject which is relatively low to others and therefore the stride length is directly proportional to the height.

Table 2. The kinematics parameters (velocity, cycle time and stride length)

Subject ID	Velocity (m/s)	Cycle time (seconds)	Stride Length (meter)
1	0.092	3.103	0.285
2	0.123	4.065	0.5
3	0.078	3.205	0.25
4	0.084	2.9	0.243
5	0.04	5.75	0.23
6	0.076	4.523	0.343
7	0.033	5.2	0.173

From the table listed below (Table 3), the maximum resultant forces acted on the hand was found at 50% of the walker stride cycle. This is when the subject was walking into the walker frame. The maximum force was concentrated at the end of the palm which. This can be proven where the sensor 3 which is attached at the end of the palm detected the maximum force.

Table 3. The resultant of the axial forces acted on the left and right grip during 50% of the stride cycle

Sensors	Force from left grip (% of body weight)	Force from right grip (% of body weight)
1	2.033	1.656
2	4.134	3.449
3	6.994	7.381

Table 5 shows the propagated force and moments from the grip and walker weight. The utilization of the standard walking device has yielded significant differences in two calculated modes which are the propagated force and moments from grip to lower and upper arm or the propagated force and moments from walker weight to lower and upper arm. Based on the above table, the force and moment that propagated from the grip is found to be greater compare to the walker weight. It is desired to reduce the propagated force and moment to improve the comfort and nurture of the patient. Hence, a crutch type of support system is incorporated with standard walking device as a novel proposed design. This design is anticipated to be one of rehabilitative strategies and to reduce the force acted on the upper extremity.

Table 4. The propagated force and joint moment from the grip

Average	Axis	Forearm	Upper arm
Force propagates from the grip (N)	X	25.94	36.23
	Y	39.66	0
Joint Moment (Nm)	Z	4.3	17.6

Table 5. The propagated force and joint moment from the walker weight

Average	Axis	Forearm	Upper arm
Force propagates from the walker weight (N)	X	4.7	5.17
	Y	13.36	0
Joint Moment (Nm)	Z	2.32	6.97

4   Conclusion

The characteristic of the upper extremity using the standard walking device have been determined. It is noted that the majority of the maximum joint rotation can be found during 50% to 100% of cycle stride. These rotations occurred mainly due to the demands for the motion of lifting and swinging the walking device. Statistically, the highest rotation is found on the shoulder followed by elbow flexion extension and wrist radial and ulnar deviation respectively. The shoulder and elbow is in the flexion mode at the initial walker contact. Nevertheless, it switched into extension mode when the subject was walking into the walker frame. Due to this, the extension movement allows the force to be propagated vertically supporting the upper body.

The rotation of wrist joint expressed in radial and ulnar deviation is essential to allow the subject's hand to keep in contact with the walking device. Looking into the moments, the experiments have verified that the greatest moment is recorded at the shoulder, elbow and wrist in the sagittal plane respectively. The greatest moment at shoulder is occurred when the subject was walking into the walking frame. This may be due to the fact that the subject tried to control the deceleration of the movement. While, the elbow moment reached its greatest at 75% of the stride cycle which mainly due to the demands of the swinging moment during walking. There is little or no moment recorded at the wrist. Through observation, kinetics parameters of the elderly (Subject 7) are found to be the minimum. Subject 7 took the slowest time to complete the experiment which can be caused by the age and height factors. Subject 7 had the shortest height and this explains the lowest stride length. The age factor explains the low velocity and hence high cycle time.

References

1. Yu, H., Spenko, M., Dubowsky, S.: An Adaptive Shared Control System for an Intelligent Mobility Aid for the Elderly. Autonomous Robots 15, 53–66 (2003)
2. Nejatbakhsh, N., Hirata, Y., Kosuge, K.: Passive omnidirectional walker - design and control. In: Proceedings. 12th International Conference on Advanced Robotics, ICAR 2005, pp. 518–523 (2005)
3. MacNamara, S., Lacey, G.: A Smart Walker for the Frail Visually Impaired. In: Proceeding of the 2000 IEEE International Conference on Robotics & Automation, pp. 1354–1359 (2000)
4. Bachschmidt, R.A., Harris, G.F., Simoneau, G.G.: Walker-assisted gait in rehabilitation: a study of biomechanics and instrumentation. IEEE Transactions on Neural Systems and Rehabilitation Engineering 9(1), 96–105 (2001)
5. Crosbie, J.: Kinematics of walking frame ambulation. Clinical Biomechanics 8(1), 31–36 (1993)
6. Crosbie, J.: Comparative kinematics of two walking frame gaits. J. Orthop. Sports Phys. Ther. 20(4), 186–192 (1994)
7. Deathe, A.B., Pardo, R.D., Winter, D.A.: Stability of walking frames. J. Rehab. Res. Dev. 33(1), 30–35 (1996)
8. Nabizadeh, S.A., Hardee, T.B., Towler, M.A., Chen, V.T., Edlich, R.F.: Technical considerations in the selection and performance of walkers. J. Burn Care Rehab. 14(2), 182–188 (1993)
9. Kadaba, M.P., Ramakrishnan, H.K., Wootten, M.E.: Measurement of lower extremity kinematics during level walking. J. Orthop. Res. 8, 383–392 (1990)

Investigation on Upper Limb's Muscle Utilizing EMG Signal

Veronica Lestari Jauw and S. Parasuraman

School of Engineering, Monash University Sunway Campus, 46150 Bandar Sunway, Malaysia
{veronica.ljauw,s.parasuraman}@monash.edu

Abstract. Neurorehabilitation aims to aid the recovery/rehabilitation of neurological patients following strokes, spinal cord injuries, traumatic brain injuries as well as other neurological diseases. The utilization of a rehabilitative robot can offer a repetitive and intensive rehabilitation training which helps improve the recovery rate and introduce a channel for patients to train independently or with minimal supervision. The future system will leverage on the utilization of EMG signal to drive the control system controlling the rehabilitative robot. Hence, it is necessary to investigate the influence of each muscle to the upper extremity's movement. This paper presents the comprehensive observation on how 8 different muscles contribute to the flexion extension and abduction adduction movement of the upper limb. These muscles are biceps, triceps, deltoid, latissimus dorsi, brachioradialis, brachialis, flexor carpi radialis and flexor carpi ulnaris. The impact of each muscle to the upper limb's movement will help in determining the EMG-force/torque relationship.

Keywords: Rehabilitation, EMG system, stroke, muscle.

1   Introduction

The Central Nervous System (CNS) requires a constant blood supply which carries vital oxygen and nutrients. [1]. The lack of the blood flow due to the blockage or leakage of the arteries causes the brain cells to be deprived of oxygen and nutrients resulting in a stroke [2]. A blockage may be caused by blood clots that are formed inside an artery in the brain and a leakage is caused by the ruptured arteries [3]. As a result, that part of the brain starts to die causing the body parts controlled by the damaged cells to be unable to function properly.

Decades of research and development in the pharmacology of CNS recovery has concluded that there are no essential clinical treatments to recover the function of damage cells [4]. However, there are extensive efforts seen to enhance the recovery rate. One of the major efforts that are used of the late is neurorehabilitation. This corresponds to therapy or rehabilitation which are performed mainly to patients with paralysis resulting from lesions in the central nervous system (e.g. after a stroke).

Initially, the rehabilitation is done in a conventional manner where the therapist has to manually attend the patients and assist them throughout the session. The problem encountered with conventional rehabilitation is that a sizeable amount of effort is

S.G. Ponnambalam et al. (Eds.): IRAM 2012, CCIS 330, pp. 216–225, 2012.

required by the therapist to support and assist the patient through the motion. This leads to therapy sessions being shorter, labor intensive, and expensive. Robot assisting physiotherapy can addressed the mentioned problems [5, 6] and has been proven to be more successful [7-9] in rehabilitating patients who lost the neuro-capabilities to control their movement.

Electromyography (EMG) concerns more on the underlying source of the patient's inability to move the arm by looking at the muscle strength. It predicts the intended motion of the patient by detecting the muscle strength. It also provides information of muscle abnormalities, muscle activation and muscle strength which cannot be attained by looking at the kinematics and kinetics data. Hence, EMG is a better approach in the function restoration.

Rigorous research has to be done to utilize EMG signals as the foundation to establish the controller [10,11]. Some of the challenges that are encountered by many researchers is to predict the EMG to force/torque relationship, as EMG reflects the action potential in the underlying muscles [12, 13]. Therefore, it is also dependant on the proportion of slow and fast fibers [14], thickness of fat under the skin [15], placement of electrodes, age [12], and muscle temperature [13]. Even now, there is still a debate on its relationship.

The previous work done [16-18] finds that the relationship is exponential with adjustable parameters using biceps and triceps myoelectric signal. However, upper limb's movement predictions are insufficient by relying just on those muscles. Therefore, this paper investigates the influence of each muscle to the flexion extension and abduction adduction activity of the upper extremity. This is necessary to establish the EMG force/torque relationship.

2 Experimental Results and Observations

The experiment is conducted by placing the electrodes on the area where the muscle of interest lies beneath the skin. The test subjects are then asked to perform flexion extension and shoulder abduction adduction for number of cycles repetitively. **Error! Reference source not found.** describes the upper arm's movement performed by the test subjects.

Anatomically [19], there are 40 different muscles allocated at the upper limb of human body. Each of them has their individual functions contributing to the upper extremity's movement. Hence, it is essential to look into the specific function of the muscles and observe how they affect the movement. This paper investigates the behavior of 8 individual muscles to determine the major role of individual muscle. The performances of each muscle to the upper limb's movement are illustrated as below. Nevertheless, the explanation of individual muscle to the upper limb's movement will be discussed further in the next sub section.

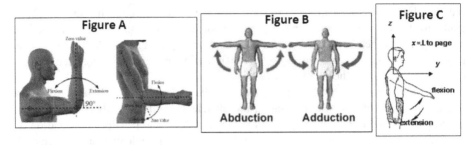

Fig. 1. The general motion of (a) elbow flexion extension, (b) shoulder abduction adduction and (c) forearm flexion extension

2.1 Biceps

2.1.1 Forearm Flexion Extension

Fig 2 shows that the muscle has no response at the origin but gradually increases as the forearm moved towards the final position[1]. Nevertheless, the response starts to subside midway through and ultimately settles down at zero at the final position. This observation signifies that biceps serve as the flexor muscles throughout flexion extension. Furthermore, the identical behavior is also observed when the forearm moved towards the origin[2] from final position. This shows that biceps also have involvement in the flexion of forearm.

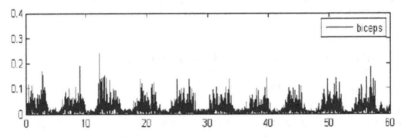

Fig. 2. The muscle strength of biceps during forearm flexion extension

2.1.2 Elbow Flexion Extension

Fig 3 depicts that the response of the muscle reaches its highest peak when the elbow is at the final position[1]. Subsequently it starts to decrease once the elbow is extended towards the origin and settles down at zero gradually upon the arrival at the origin[2]. The increment behavior of the response can be perceived only when the elbow left the origin and moved towards the final position. The observation indicates that the muscle has an increased strength when the muscle is flexed. This is supported by [20] where biceps is selected to be the flexor muscle after several trials of experiment. The results from [20] have shown an increased voltage throughout the flexion activity.

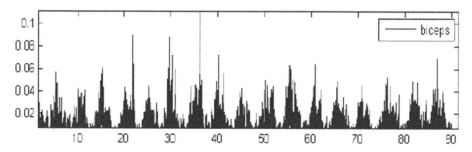

Fig. 3. The muscle strength of biceps during elbow flexion extension

2.1.3 Shoulder Abduction Adduction

The monotonous EMG's behavior of the biceps indicates that biceps has no contribution to shoulder abduction adduction movement. Fig 4 shows that the EMG signal oscillates about zero supporting the preceding statement. Therefore, the noise interference may be the source of the oscillation.

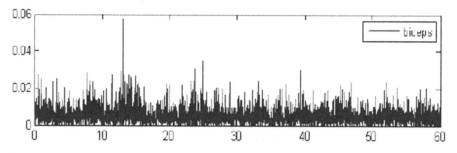

Fig. 4. The muscle strength of biceps during shoulder abduction adduction

2.2   Triceps

2.2.1   Forearm Flexion Extension

In the contrary with biceps, the result shows that the triceps starts off with small responses at origin[2]. It continues to behave indifferently but with insignificant fluctuations when the forearm headed towards the final position[1]. The identical phenomena still can be observed even after the forearm left its final position. Nevertheless, the signal starts to fluctuate excitedly midway towards the origin and subside upon the departure from the origin. This observation signifies that the triceps act as the extensor muscle throughout the flexion and extension. The identical result was obtained by [20] where the triceps act as the extensor muscle.

2.2.2   Elbow Flexion Extension

The rise in the triceps' response is observed in the results. This happens when the elbow moves towards the origin[2] from its final position[1] and reaches its maximum peak after. Then, it gradually decreases once the elbow moved away from the origin heading towards the final position. The lowest peak is found at the final position. This does make perfect sense because the behavior of the triceps is absolutely in contrast with the biceps. It is anatomically known that both muscles are antagonistic muscle [21]. Hence, they must behave in a contrary manner.

2.2.3 Shoulder Abduction Adduction

Insignificant changes in the magnitude are observed in the experimental results. The results display a constant response throughout the cycle and hence, the triceps are concluded to have no contribution in abduction adduction. However, the existence of noise can still be observed.

2.3 Brachioradialis

2.3.1 Forearm Flexion Extension

The EMG results show random fluctuations with insignificant magnitude which is ±0.02 mV. This proves that brachioradialis does not contribute to the forearm flexion extension. Nonetheless, the interference of noise may be the cause of the random fluctuations. However, [22] affirmed that the brachioradialis acts as flexor muscle throughout the flexion extension. These contradictory experimental results encourage the need to start the experiment again. Even so, the results turn out to be identical with the previous results. This is most likely due to the noise that just happens to overpower the actual readings and hence, the actual measurement is concealed.

2.3.2 Elbow Flexion Extension

Random signals with no repetitive unique pattern are observed and hence, brachioradialis has no contribution to the flexion extension. Nevertheless, this observation does not make sense as brachioradialis serves as flexor muscle in flexion extension. Further experiments are done to justify the incongruity of the results and identical results are obtained. The same reasoning applied where the randomness of the noise hid the real characteristics of the muscle and hence, false analysis.

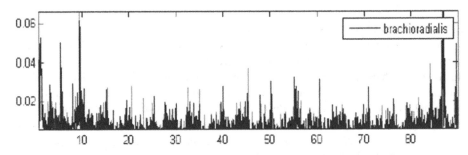

Fig. 5. The muscle strength of brachioradialis in elbow flexion extension

2.3.3 Shoulder Abduction Adduction

The results clearly exemplify the response to be random noise with low magnitude. This shows that brachioradialis has no contribution to the abduction adduction. It is an expected result because brachioradialis serves as flexor muscle.

2.4   Brachialis

2.4.1   Forearm Flexion Extension

The results present rapid responses that are observed continuously throughout the entire cycle. These rapid responses always occur only when the forearm moves towards the origin[2]. Hence, it is concluded that this muscle serves as a brake to the forearm's extension activity.

2.4.2   Elbow Flexion Extension

The results show an increased magnitude when the elbow leaves the origin[2] and moves towards the final position[1]. The signal reaches its highest peak right before reaching the final position and stays constant until the final position is reached. Subsequently, the signal starts to decrease when the elbow left its final position; moving towards the origin. However, the signal settles down at zero midway through and stays constant until the elbow reaches its origin. Hence, this muscle contributes in elbow flexion.

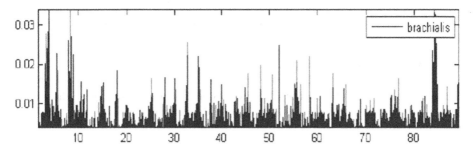

Fig. 6. The muscle strength of brachialis in flexion extension

2.4.3   Shoulder Abduction Adduction

The results shows responses when abduction adduction is performed despite the fact that brachialis is a flexor muscle. An increased magnitude is illustrated when the elbow leaves the origin[2] and moves towards the final position[1]. The signal reaches its highest peak right before reaching the final position and stays constant until the final position is reached. Subsequently, the signal starts to decrease when the elbow leaves its final position; moving towards the origin. However, the signal settles down at zero midway through and stays constant until the elbow reaches its origin.

2.5   Deltoid

2.5.1   Forearm Flexion Extension

The results show that EMG signal starts off with no response at the origin[2]. It increases when the forearm moves towards the final position[1] and reaches its maximum potential at the final position. The muscle will be contracted when the forearm is brought up to the final position (shoulder level). The muscle's strength will increase by nature to encounter the gravity force that rises as the forearm is further away from the origin. Hence, the increment in muscle's strength can be validated. Nevertheless, it starts to decline when the forearm left the final position and gradually settles down at zero before reaching the origin. This stays constant until the forearm arrived at the origin. The gravity force is declining as the forearm is brought to the origin where it is closer to the ground. Therefore, the observation is valid as the strength that is used to bring the forearm to the final position will be reduced to adapt the declined gravity force.

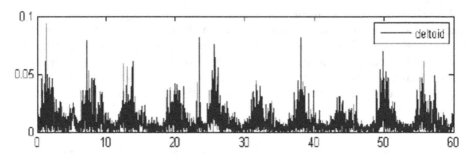

Fig. 7. The muscle strength of deltoid in forearm flexion extension

2.5.2 Elbow Flexion Extension

The results exhibit the constant behavior of the deltoid where the rapid rise in the response is observed. This verifies that the deltoid has no contribution to the elbow flexion extension. Nevertheless, the origin of the rapid rise could be from the noise interference.

2.5.3 Shoulder Abduction Adduction

By looking at Fig 8, no response is observed at the origin[3] but it starts to increase once the forearm moves towards the final position[4]. The greatest magnitude is measured when the final position is reached. Nevertheless, it starts to decline immediately when the forearm left the final position heading towards the origin. Upon the arrival at the origin, the response settles down at zero. This complies with [22] where deltoid plays significant role in abduction adduction.

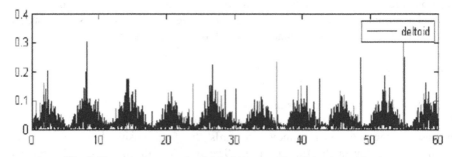

Fig. 8. The muscle strength of deltoid in shoulder abduction adduction

2.6   Latissimus Dorsi (Antagonist Muscle)

2.6.1 Forearm Flexion Extension
The results reveal that the latissimus dorsi is involved in driving the flexion and extension movement. The EMG signal starts off with zero implying that this muscle has no response at the origin[2] and only starts to increase when the forearm leaves the origin and moves towards the final position[1]. Its highest action potential is reached upon the arrival to the final position and instantaneously decreases afterwards. It continues to decrease even after the forearm left the final position and moved towards the origin. The action potential exhibits zero voltage when the origin is reached.

2.6.2 Elbow Flexion Extension
The substantial amount of spikes is perceived continuously as shown in Fig 9 suggesting that the latissimus dorsi only contributes to the certain degree of the flexion extension activity. To be specific, the spikes only occurred at the following event: 35^0 and 62^0 away from the origin[2], 20^0 and 62^0 away from the final position[1] and the arrival of the elbow at the origin and final position.

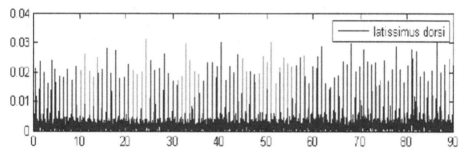

Fig. 9. The muscle strength of latissimus dorsi in elbow flexion extension

2.6.3 Shoulder Abduction Adduction
From Fig 10, the EMG signal is found to be zero at the origin[3]and gradually increases when the forearm moves towards the final position[4] as obtained in the results. The signal reaches its highest peak at the final position. Then, it starts to decline when the forearm moved towards the origin. However, the signal settles down at zero midway through and stays constant until the origin is reached. The observation proves that

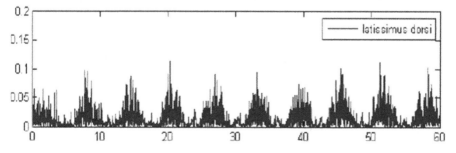

Fig. 10. The muscle strength of latissimus dorsi in shoulder abduction adduction

3   Conclusion

The investigation confirms that each of the muscle has their individual function to the upper limb's movement. Each of the muscle may share the force load required by a specific activity or they may have no contribution at all. From the results' analysis, both biceps and triceps play major roles in driving the flexion and extension of both forearm and elbow. Nevertheless, it is evident that they have no contribution in shoulder abduction adduction. On the other hand, deltoid and lattisimus dorsi have proven that they both are antagonist muscle based on the results. The results show that deltoid is the abductor muscle while latisimus dorsi is the adductor muscle. However these muscles have minor contribution to the forearm flexion extension but not to the elbow flexion extension. This may be due to the location of the muscle which is very near to the shoulder.

The experiment also shows the variance of the theoretical and experimental result. Brachialioradialis is known to be the flexor muscle in flexion extension activity. However, the results have shown that this muscle offers no contribution to the activity and only noise signals are detected. This incongruity may happen due to the high frequency noise that overshadows the actual readings.

Looking through the brachialis behavior, it assists the elbow flexion extension reducing the load force of biceps. Theoretically, brachialis is the flexor muscle at the elbow and hence, the experimental results abide the theoretical analysis. However, the results also show the existence of EMG signal in shoulder abduction adduction. This error may be due to the small displacement of EMG sensor. The displacement causes the merge readings of two muscles and hence, error occurs.

The contribution of this study is to offer comprehensive information on the influence of each muscle to the upper limb's movement. These pieces of information serve as a study platform to investigate the EMG-force/torque relationship.

References

1. Hademenos, G.J., Massoud, T.F.: Biophysical Mechanism of Stroke. American Heart Association, 2067–2077 (1997)
2. Hademenos, G.J., Massoud, T.F.: The Physics of Cerebrovascular Diseases: Biophysical Mechanism of Development, Diagnosis and Therapy (1997)
3. Grad, Y., Sievert, H., Nishri, B., Stone, G.W., Katzen, B.T., Yodfat, O., Higashida, R., Harris, D., Wakhloo, A.K., Assaf, Y., Norbash, A., Bushi, D., Lieber, B.B.: A Novel Endovascular Device for Emboli Rerouting: Part I: Evaluation in a Swine Model. Journal of the American Heart Association 2860–2866 (2008)
4. Stein, G.D., Hoffman, S.W.: Concepts of CNS plasticity in the context of brain damage and repair. The Journal of Head Trauma Rehabilitation 18, 317–341 (2003)
5. Kexin, X., Jian, H., Qi, X., Yongji, W.: Design of a wearable rehabilitation robotic hand actuated by pneumatic artificial muscles. In: Asian Control Conference, ASCC 2009, pp. 740–744 (2009)
6. Sucar, L.E., Leder, R., Hernandez, J., Sanchez, I., Azcarate, G.: Clinical evaluation of a low-cost alternative for stroke rehabilitation. In: IEEE International Conference on Rehabilitation Robotics, ICORR 2009, pp. 863–866 (2009)

7. Turolla, A., Tonin, P., Zucconi, C., Agostini, M., Piccione, M., Piron, L.: Reinforcement Feedback in Virtual Environment vs. Conventional Physical Therapy for arm motor deficit after Stroke. In: Virtual Rehabilitation, pp. 49–52 (2007)
8. Piron, L., Tombolini, A., Turolla, C., Agostini, M., Dam, M., Santarello, G., Piccione, F., Tonin, P.: Reinforced Feedback in Virtual Environment Facilitates the Arm Motor Recovery in Patients after a Recent Stroke. In: Virtual Rehabilitation, pp. 121–123 (2007)
9. Rosati, G., Gallina, P., Masiero, S.: Design, Implementation and Clinical Tests of a Wire-Based Robot for Neurorehabilitation. IEEE Transaction on Neural Systems and Rehabilitation Engineering 15, 560–569 (2007)
10. Dapeng, Y., Jingdong, Z., Yikun, G., Li, J., Hong, L.: EMG pattern recognition and grasping force estimation: Improvement to the myocontrol of multi-DOF prosthetic hands. In: IEEE/RSJ International Conference on Intelligent Robots and Systems, IROS 2009, pp. 516–521 (2009)
11. Siegler, S., Hillstrom, H.J., Freedman, W., Moskowitz, G.: Effect of myoelectric signal processing on relationship between muscle force and processed EMG. Arm. J. Phys. Med., 130–149 (1985)
12. Merletti, R., Sabbahi, M.A., De Luca, C.J.: Median frequency of the myoelectric signal: Effects of muscle ischemia and cooling. Eur. J. Appl. Physiol. Occup. Pysiol., 258–265 (1984)
13. Petrofsky, J., Laymon, M.: The relationship between muscle temperature, MUPA conduction velocity and the amplitude and frequency components of the surface EMG during isometric contractions. Basic Appl. Myol., 61–74 (2005)
14. Broman, H., Bilotto, G., De Luca, C.J.: Myoelectric signal conduction velocity and spectral parameters influence of force and time. J. Appl. Physiol., 1428–1437 (1985)
15. Bilodeau, M., Arsenault, A.B., Gravel, D., Bourbonnais, D.: The influence of an increase in the level of force on the EMG power spectrum of elbow extensors. Eur. J. Appl. Physiol. Occup. Pysiol., 461–466 (1990)
16. Oyong, A.W., Parasuraman, S., Jauw, V.L.: Estimation of Muscle Forces and Joint Torque from EMG using SA Process. In: IEEE EMBS Conference on Biomedical Engineering and Sciences (IECBES 2010), Kuala Lumpur, Malaysia (2010)
17. Parasuraman, S., Arif, W.O., Veronica, L.J.: AI Technique to estimate muscle force and joint torque upper extremity. Key Engineering Material 467-469, 788–793 (2011)
18. Oyong, A.W., Parasuraman, S., Jauw, V.L.: Robot Assisted Stroke Rehabilitation: Estimation of Muscle Force/Joint Torque from EMG using GA. In: IEEE EMBS Conference on Biomedical Engineering & Sciences (IECBES 2010), Kuala Lumpur, Malaysia (2010)
19. Patton, K.T., Thibodeau, G.A.: Anthony's Textbook of Anatomy & Physiology. In: Wilhelm, T. (ed.), 19th edn. (2010)
20. Jacob, R., Moshe, B., Moshe, B.F., Mircea, A.: A Myosignal based powered exoskeleton system. IEEE Transactions on System, Man and Cybernetics 31(3) (2001)
21. Rhoades, R.A., Bell, D.R.: Medical Physiology: Principal for Clinical Medical, 3rd edn. Lippincott Williams & Wilkins
22. Kenneth, S.S.: Anatomy&Physiology: The Unity of Form and Function, 4th edn.

---

[1] Final – the position of the forearm/ elbow is parallel to the transverse plane but perpendicular to coronal plane.

[2] Origin – the position of the forearm/ elbow is parallel to the coronal plane of human body.

[3] Origin (shoulder) – the position of the forearm is parallel to the sagittal (vertical) plane of human body.

[4] Final (shoulder) – the position of the forearm is parallel to transverse plane but perpendicular to sagittal plane of human body.

Genetic Algorithm and Bayesian Linear Discriminant Analysis Based Channel Selection Method for P300 BCI

Chea Yau Kee, R.M. Kuppan Chetty[*], Boon How Khoo, and S.G. Ponnambalam

School of Engineering, Monash University Sunway Campus, Jalan Lagoon Selatan,
Bandar Sunway 46150, Selangor, Malaysia
{kee.chea.yau,kuppanchetty.ramanathan,khoo.boon.how,
sgponnambalam}@monash.edu

Abstract. Most electroencephalography (EEG) based brain-computer interface (BCI) systems perform brain signal recording using all possible electrodes. Recent studies have shown that the performance of a BCI system can be enhanced by removing noisy or task-irrelevant electrodes. This paper presents an automated channel selection algorithm using genetic algorithms (GA) and Bayesian linear discriminant analysis (BLDA) for a P300 based BCI. The proposed method was implemented on data set II obtained from the third BCI competition (2005). It was found that the proposed algorithm outperforms other existing channel selection method in terms of character recognition rate. The character recognition rate is maintained at approximately 90% when the number of channels used is reduced from 64 to 8. This confirms the validity of stochastic based GA as an alternative channel selection method. The selected channels indicate that the task-relevant features are concentrated mainly on the parietal and occipital lobe which agrees well with previous findings.

Keywords: Brain-computer interface, P300, Genetic algorithm, EEG channel selection, Bayesian linear discriminant analysis.

1 Introduction

Brain-computer interfaces (BCIs) are systems that convert electrophysiological input from the brain into output commands for external devices [1]. These systems provide direct communication pathway from brain to device bypassing conventional neuromuscular channel. Owing to the rapid advancement in technology, BCI are now implemented in a widespread of clinical applications [2] to restore lost abilities of individual suffering from motor impairment, thus improving their quality of life.

Electroencephalography (EEG) is by far the most widely used neuro-imaging modality due to its high temporal resolution, affordability, portability, and most importantly, there is no known risk to the user [3]. Compared to other EEG-based neuro-meachanism [4], P300 event-related potentials (ERP) remained a popular choice because they are the natural responses of brain when subjected to specific

---

[*] Corresponding author.

S.G. Ponnambalam et al. (Eds.): IRAM 2012, CCIS 330, pp. 226–235, 2012.

external stimuli. This ERP is usually elicited through oddball paradigm where infrequent auditory, visual and somatosensory stimuli will cause a positive deflection (peak at 300ms) in EEG signal when interspersed with routine stimuli. The practical usage of BCI systems based on existence or absence of P300 speller was apparent when Farwell and Donchin introduced the P300-based BCI speller in 1988. In [5], minor modifications were made to the basic speller to accommodate additional function for internet browsing which is demonstrated to be a useful even for individuals suffering from advanced amyotrophic lateral sclerosis (ALS).

EEG-recordings for P300-based BCI are usually carried out using all accessible electrodes because identifying the exact electrode positions that would result in ideal performance remains a major challenge and it falls under the broader field of feature selection. From previous studies [6-8], it was revealed that the number of channels used can be significantly reduced without compromising the classification accuracy. In addition, the dimensionality reduction of input features can greatly lower the computational cost and complexity of training a classifier.

For practical BCI systems, fully automated channel selection methods are preferred because selecting channels manually based on neurophysiological knowledge does not necessarily yield optimum results [6]. In addition, the positions of EEG electrodes that give optimum classification accuracy are subject-dependent [12]. More importantly, an automated channel selection algorithm allows relevant recording positions to be found without requiring any prior knowledge about the paradigm and mental task used. Among various channel selection techniques proposed in the literature, methods based on common spatial pattern (CSP), support vector machine (SVM) and mutual information (MI) are commonly used.

In literature [9-10], recursive feature elimination (RFE) based on SVM was implemented for channel selection. Qi et al. [9] first ranked each features using RFE and margin variance minimization strategy; and later mapped the previously obtained feature ranking into channel ranking. Rakotomanmonj et al. [10] devised a much comprehensive approach whereby, arbitrarily selected channels are temporarily removed and the performance of trained classifier is re-evaluated. The channels are permanently eliminated if their removal enhances the classifier performance. It is questionable that the combination of top ranked channels obtained through RFE is able to produce good results since combinations of individually good features does not necessarily leads to the good classification performance [14].

Mutual information based channel selection is a method which iteratively selects new channels that have the largest dependency on the target class and minimal redundancy among the selected channels [8]. In some variants MI, channels are ranked individually without considering the joint effect of feature on the target class. Although mainly used as feature extractor, the CSP algorithm has also demonstrated its effectiveness in channel selection [6]. The CSP algorithm discriminates two classes of EEG data by maximizing the variance of one class while minimizing the variance of the other class.

In this paper, a new method using combination of genetic algorithm (GA) and Bayesian linear discriminant analysis (BLDA) for channel selection is proposed. As genetic algorithm is computationally expensive, it is reasonable to convolve it with a robust yet less demanding classifier, BLDA [7]. In BCI systems, stochastic methods outperform many deterministic optimization techniques in high dimensional space, especially when the underlying physical relationships are not fully understood [15]. Moreover, genetic algorithm exhibits great potential to study the correlation and the joint effect of various channel combination as the fitness value is not biased to the performance of individual channel. The proposed method is carried out on data set II obtained from the third BCI competition (2005) and the character recognition rate with and without channel selection is compared. This is to study the effect of channel reduction on the character recognition rate. Other than that, the character recognition rate of the devised algorithm is compared with other existing channel selection method to verify the performance of GA for channel selection.

2   Methodology

2.1   Data Set

Data set II from the third BCI competition consists of a complete record of P300 evoked potential recorded from two different subjects and the detailed description of the experiment is found in [17]. The resulting data for both subjects was divided into two parts, the first 85 characters is to be used as training samples while the remaining 100 characters are used to evaluate the robustness of BCI system constructed.

2.2   Data Pre-processing and Feature Extraction

It is well established that P300 ERP corresponds to a positive deflection in EEG voltage at latency of about 300 ms after the stimulus. Therefore, only data samples between time windows of 0 to 700 ms posterior to each row or column intensifications are extracted. The extracted signals are bandpass filtered between cut-off frequencies of 0.1 to 20 Hz as suggested in [10, 13] to reduce noise from irrelevant frequencies. Subsequently, the filtered signals are downsampled from 240Hz to 20Hz (high cut-off frequency) which reduces the feature vector from 168 data points to 14 data points. By reducing the feature dimension, the complexity of classifier is reduced thus lowering the computational time. In succession, the samples from each channel are normalized using zero-score normalization to regularize the contribution of each channel in classification stage. Lastly, the data samples from each channel are concatenated into a feature vector to be used for classification.

2.3   P300 Detection and Post-processing

This section describes the transformation of two-class classification problem into a decision for 36-class problem. First, Bayesian linear discriminant analysis (BLDA) is employed for the detection of P300. As the presence or absence of P300 component in a signal is a binary-class problem, the class label y consists of 1 and -1. Assuming that the target y and the feature vector X are linearly related with additive white Gaussian noise b, the linear classifier is represented by the following form,

$$y = w^T X + b \tag{1}$$

In BLDA, the weight vector w and bias term b are obtained by solving the parameter selection problem using maximum-likelihood estimates. The detailed description of methods employed in BLDA to obtain a linear decision boundary could be found in [16]. The output of the classifier is perceived as the confidence level of P300 detection.

In a P300 speller, post-processing algorithm converts the presence or absence of P300 ERP in each intensified row or column into a predicted character. There are 12 intensifications for each repetition since the display matrix consists of 6 rows and 6 columns. For each repetition, each row and column is assigned a score and the character is predicted using the intersection of row and column with the highest score. The cumulated score of row and column is computed to minimize the effect of random noise in EEG data so that the later repetitions have higher recognition rate. The vector S, containing the cumulative score of each row and column is computed as follow,

$$S_n = \sum_{r=1}^{r=n}(w.x_r + b) \quad 1 \le n \le 15. \tag{2}$$

where x_r is a feature matrix, r is the repetition index, n is the number of repetition, w and b are the feature weights and bias term obtained previously. After each repetition, the predicted row and column are identified as follow,

$$predicted\ column = \underset{1 \le i \le 6}{\operatorname{argmax}}\ S(i). \tag{3}$$

$$predicted\ row = \underset{7 \le i \le 12}{\operatorname{argmax}}\ S(i). \tag{4}$$

3   Channel Selection Using Genetic Algorithm

The previous section mentions that the signals are collected from 64 ear-referenced channels. However, it is possible to lower the computational cost while maintaining the character recognition rate by selecting only task-relevant channels. As exhaustive search for good channel combination is impractical, adaptive heuristic search algorithm such as genetic algorithm (GA) could greatly enhanced the speed of optimization process while arriving at satisfactory solution. The purpose of GA in this study is to optimize the channel subsets using only the training samples. The testing samples are then used to evaluate the selected channel combination through character recognition rate. Although the proposed algorithm is able to handle any number of channels, the number of channels is reduced from 64 to 8 for fair comparison with other channel selection methods in the literatures [8-10, 13].

3.1   Design of Chromosome and Population Size

One of the major aspects in genetic algorithm is the design of chromosome. Each gene in a chromosome holds an integer value which corresponds to the electrode number. There are two major constraints that a chromosome has to follow throughout the evolution process. First, a gene must only contain a value ranging from 1 to 64 and second; there must be no repetition of same value in a chromosome. The size of chromosome depends on the number of channels, j to be used for character recognition as shown in Fig. 1. As mentioned previously, 8 channels are to be selected; hence each chromosome consists of 8 different integers which represent the combination of channels. The initial population consists of 200 individual chromosomes and the population size remains the same throughout the whole algorithm. In addition, the individual chromosomes generated for the initial population are completely random, abiding the two constraints stated previously.

Fig. 1. Chromosome representation of selected channels

3.2   Fitness Function and Selection Operator

Since each chromosome described previously represents a potential solution, it is very crucial to design a fitness function that can appositely map a chromosome representation into a scalar value, which quantifies the quality of a chromosome. Therefore, the fitness function is selected as follow,

$$\mathcal{F}_{EA} = \sum_{r=1}^{n}(w_r A_r) \, . \tag{5}$$

where $\mathcal{F}_{EA}$ is the fitness value of each chromosome and A_r is the number of character that are recognized correctly the in r repetition. In equation (5), the corresponding weight w_r is added alongside A_r so that the user is able to manually adjust the weights to change the nature of the search. For instance, weights from repetition 11 to 15 are set higher if the objective is to achieve maximum accuracies for the later repetitions. To achieve a more practical BCI system, it is always preferable to achieve high recognition rate with the least number of repetition. In such cases, it is advisable to have higher weights for the lower repetitions. However, unity weights are used to provide equal fairness for all repetitions and equation (5) is simplified as follow,

$$\mathcal{F}_{EA} = \sum_{r=1}^{n} A_r \tag{6}$$

In each generation, individuals from the current generation are selected to produce a new generation of individuals through cross-over, mutation and elitism. As this new generation represents a new set of potential solution, it would be desirable for the 'superior' individuals to reproduce and propagate their 'superior' genetic material. In this case, the chance of an individual being selected is proportional to the fitness value and the probability distribution with respect to the fitness value which as follow,

$$Prob(\vec{C}_r) = \frac{\mathcal{F}_{EA}(\vec{C}_r)}{\sum_{r=1}^{n} \mathcal{F}_{EA}(\vec{C}_r)} \tag{7}$$

where $Prob(\vec{C}_r)$ is the probability of individual chromosome $\vec{C}_r$ being select, given that $\mathcal{F}_{EA}(\vec{C}_r)$ is the fitness value of that individual. This fitness proportionate selection mechanism is also known as the roulette wheel selection where 'superior' individuals are more likely to be selected as they claim a bigger slice of the wheel.

3.3   Elitism, Crossover and Mutation

Elitism is used in the proposed algorithm to retain the top five percent of the fittest individuals from the current generation to survive to the next generation, without any alteration in genetic materials. This is done to ensure that the maximum fitness value does not decrease over a generation. However, these individuals are not removed from the roulette wheel as it would be disadvantageous if these superior individuals are refrained from passing down their genetic materials through crossover operation.

Fig. 2. Visualization of Crossover and Mutation Operation

After a pair of chromosomes is selected, a random point is generated where these two parent chromosomes exchange genetic materials to produce two offspring chromosomes as shown in Fig. 2. The crossover probability is set to be 1.0 due to the implementation of elitism. Hence, there is no reason to avert crossover since every possible chromosome variants are encouraged to increase the learning rate. However, the offspring has to abide one constraint where every gene must contain a different number. Repetition of the same number could occur during crossover when two parts of chromosome received from both parents contains the same channel. This issue is addressed by randomly changing one of the repeated numbers until no repetition is observed.

The main purpose of mutation is to prevent genetic algorithms from reaching local optimum by adding diversity to the genetic characteristics of a population. In [15], it was stated that large mutation are preferred for search space exploration in early generation and small mutation steps are desirable in the later generation to fine-tune suboptimal chromosomes. For this case, it is the exact opposite as low mutation rate are required to prevent significant distortion of good solutions in early generations while higher mutation rate is encouraged to prevent the dominance of suboptimal solution in later generations. In this study, the mutation rate which is the probability of one gene mutating is kept low at a constant value of 0.15. Having the same constraints as previously discussed, the value of mutated gene is repeatedly randomized if repetition of electrode number occurs.

3.4   Stopping Criterion

The genetic algorithm is devised to terminate when either one of the three stopping criterion is met. The first stopping criterion could be met by achieving perfect character recognition rate in the training samples. As satisfying the first criterion is improbable, a second stopping criterion which emerges when the maximum fitness value remains stagnant for 15 consecutive generations is introduced. If neither of the above criteria is met, the third criterion is satisfied upon reaching the 75th generations and the chromosome with the highest fitness value represents the solution for best channels combination.

4   Results and Discussion

The proposed channel selection method using combination of GA and BLDA is used to select eight channels that would give a good character recognition rate. As GA utilizes a stochastic optimization approach, it is expected to have different combination of channels selected for each and every GA run which results in the difference in character recognition rate. Thus, the result from one GA run is insufficient to summarize the performance of the proposed algorithm. In this work, 30 GA runs was carried out for each subject and the character recognition rate was averaged as presented in Table 1. It is evident that the recognition rate for subject A decreases more as compared to subject B when less channels are used. The same pattern could also be observed for convolutional neural network (CNN-2b) based channel selection algorithm [13]. From this observation, it is concluded that for subject A, the task-relevant information on P300 is spread over more electrodes than for subject B. From Table1, it is observed that the devised algorithm performs slightly better than CNN-2b for almost every repetition. On the 15th repetition, this algorithm performs 4% (on average) more accurate when compared to the CNN-2b. One possible reason is that the CNN-2b ranked the electrodes based on their discriminant power. Although task-relevant channels usually have high discriminant power, combination of individually good channels might not provide the best outcome. On the contrary, the proposed algorithm heuristically searches for the optimum channel combination without considering the individual strength of each channel. Another reason might be the effectiveness of BLDA as a classifier for P300 detection.

Table 1. Character recognition rate without channel selection, with 8 selected channels (mean results of 30 GA trials) and CNN-2b adopted from [13] for comparison

Methods	Subject	Repetitions/Epochs								
		1	5	9	10	11	12	13	14	15
GA_BLDA	A	18	71	86	88	93	96	97	97	99
64 Channels	B	38	79	91	93	95	96	96	96	97
	Mean	28.0	75.0	88.5	90.5	94.0	96.0	96.5	96.5	98.0
GA_BLDA	A	13.3	47.1	73.0	77.0	78.4	81.1	84.0	87.3	88.9
8 Channels	B	35.3	71.7	88.4	89.8	90.3	90.3	89.7	90.8	93.4
	Mean	24.3	59.4	80.7	83.4	84.3	85.7	86.9	89.1	91.2
CNN-2b [13]	A	12	48	67	67	69	74	75	83	87
8Channels	B	32	72	82	82	82	86	87	87	87
	Mean	22.0	60.0	74.5	74.5	75.5	80.0	81.0	85.0	87.0

Table 2. A comparison of character recognition rate (15th repetition) obtain using channels selected by the proposed algorithm and algorithms from literatures [8, 9, 10, 13], manual channel selection are marked with * while the others are fully automated

	Methods	Channels								Character Recognition (%)
Subject A	GA_BLDA	Varies for every GA trial								88.9 (Average)
	MICS [8]	FC_1	PO_7	CP_z	P_7	C_1	PO_z	C_z	CP_5	83.0
	CNN-2a *[13]	F_z	C_z	P_z	P_3	P_4	PO_7	PO_8	C_z	84.0
	CNN-2b [13]	P_z	PO_7	C_1	PO_z	C_5	CP_z	PO_8	C_z	87.0
	E-SVM *[10]	F_z	C_z	P_z	C_3	C_4	P_3	P_4	O_z	80.0
	RFE-SWM [9]	O_1	P_z	P_7	P_8	C_z	F_4	F_7	O_z	~87
		P_3	FP_z			(10 channels)				
Subject B	GA_BLDA	Varies for every GA trial								93.4 (Average)
	MICS [8]	PO_8	PO_7	P_z	P_2	CP_z	O_2	O_z	P_1	89.0
	CNN-2a *[13]	F_z	C_z	P_z	P_3	P_4	PO_7	PO_8	O_z	91.0
	CNN-2b [13]	PO_8	O_1	PO_7	C_z	PO_3	P_z	CP_z	PO_4	87.0
	E-SVM *[10]	F_z	C_z	P_z	C_3	C_4	P_3	P_4	O_z	80.0
	RFE-SWM [9]	P_4	P_z	O_1	O_2	C_z	C_3	F_7	P_7	~87
		P_3	FP_z	T_7	T_8	FP_2	(13 channels)			

Table 2 summarizes the channels selected by various channel selection methods and the corresponding character recognition rate (15th repetition). Some of these methods use predefined channels which are suggested in previous studies while other methods involve fully automated channel selection algorithm. Instead of limiting it to only 8 channels, RFE-SVM [9] finds the optimal channel set which is 10 channels for subject A and 13 channels for subject B. Through comparison of character recognition rate, it was found that the proposed channel selection method slightly outperforms the other methods for both subjects. Unlike the other algorithms, the proposed algorithm performs stochastic optimization instead of deterministic approach. In general, stochastic approach is comparatively more useful in cases where the underlying physical relationship between channel combinations and recognition rate is still uncertain.

For the proposed algorithm, P_z, PO_8, PO_7, O_1 and P_5 are dominant electrode for subject A while I_z, PO_8, PO_7 and O_1 are dominant electrode for subject B as these electrodes as selected more than 70% of the time (>21/30 GA Trials). In this case, PO_8, PO_7 and O_1 are the common dominant channels shared by both subject A and subject B. Krusienski et al. [11] performed principle component analysis on Oddball data and demonstrated that a component extending from C_z to O_z and P_7 to P_8 accounted for the largest portion of variance. This coincides with the channels selected by the proposed algorithm as P_z, PO_8, PO_7 and O_1 lies between the regions described earlier. In addition, PO_8 and PO_7 were also selected by other fully automated channel selection method such as MICS and CNN-2b. This further proves the relevance of posterior electrodes in P300 related mental task.

This experiment further elucidates the importance of automated channel selection due the subject dependency of optimum channel set. Furthermore, an automated channel selection algorithm is especially useful in locating task-relevant region when prior knowledge is limited. In this dataset, it is obvious that selecting a predefined number of task-relevant channels causes minor degradation in BCI performance. Hence, it is necessary to consider the worth of reducing computational complexity at the expense of classification accuracy.

5   Conclusions

The proposed channel selection algorithm using combination of BLDA and GA is evaluated using data set II of the third BCI competition and the averaged character recognition rate is found to be slightly above 90%. Moreover, the result shows that the proposed algorithm outperforms other channel selections by at least 3% in character recognition rate. This confirms the feasibility of stochastic based GA as an alternative for channel selection and the proposed fitness function is suitable for this BCI application. The results also indicate that the task-relevant electrodes are subject-dependent, hence automated channel selection methods are important to locate the optimal channel subset for character recognition.

In short, fully automated channel selection method can broaden the usability of current BCI due to the reduction in electrode usage. Despite having good accuracy, the proposed algorithm is currently confined to off-line analysis as GA is computationally demanding. Therefore, the enhancement of speed and robustness of the proposed algorithm by compromising between the accuracy of the algorithm and the number of selected electrodes is to be investigated.

References

1. Wolpaw, J.R., Birbaumer, N., Heetderks, W.J., McFarland, D.J., Peckham, P.H., Schalk, G.S., Donchin, E., Quotrano, L.A., Robinson, C.J., Vaughan, T.M.: Brain-Computer Interface Technology: A Review of the First International Meeting. IEEE Trans. Neural Syst. Rehabil. Eng. 8(2), 164–173 (2000)
2. Mak, J.N., Wolpaw, J.R.: Clinical Applications of Brain-Computer Interfaces: Current State and Future Prospect. IEEE Reviews in Biomed. Eng. 2, 187–199 (2009)
3. Nicolas-Alonso, L.F., Gomez-Gil, J.: Brain Computer Interfaces, a Review. Sensors 12, 1211–1279 (2012)
4. Bashashati, A., Fatourechi, M., Ward, R.K., Birch, G.E.: A survey of signal processing algorithms in brain-computer interfaces based on electrical brain signals. J. Neural Eng. 4, 32–57 (2007)
5. Mugler, E.M., Ruf, C.A., Halder, S., Bensch, M., Kubler, A.: Design and Implementation of a P300-Based Brain-Computer Interface for Controlling an Internet Browser. IEEE Trans. Neural Syst. Rehab. Eng. 15(6), 599–609 (2010)
6. Arvaneh, M., Guan, C., Ang, K.K., Quek, C.: Optimizing the Channel Selection and Classification Accuracy in EEG-Based BCI. IEEE Trans. Biomed. Eng. 58(6), 1865–1873 (2011)
7. Hoffmann, U., Yazdani, A., Vesin, J.M., Ebrahim, T.: Bayesian Feature Selection Applied in a P300 Brain-Computer Interface. In: Proc 16th European Signal Processing Conf. (2008)

8. Shahriari, Y., Erfanian, A.: A Mutual Information Based Channel Selection Scheme for P300-Based Brain Computer Interface. In: Proc. 5th Int. IEEE EMBS Conf. on Neural Eng., pp. 434–437 (2011)

9. Qi, H., Xu, M., Li, W., Yuan, D., Zhu, W., An, X., Ming, D., Wan, B., Wang, W.: Feature Selection Study of P300 Speller Using Support Vector Machine. In: Proc. IEEE Int. Conf. Robotics and Biomimetics, pp. 1331–1334 (2010)

10. Rakotomamonjy, A., Guigue, V.: BCI competition III: Dataset II- Ensemble of SVMs for BCI P300 Speller. IEEE Trans. Biomed. Eng. 55, 1147–1154 (2008)

11. Krusienski, D.J., Sellers, E.W., McFarland, D.J., Vaughan, T.M., Wolpaw, J.R.: Toward enhanced P300 speller performance. J. Neurosci. Methods 167(1), 15–21 (2007)

12. Blankertz, B., Losch, F., Krauledat, M., Dornhege, G., Curio, G., Muller, K.R.: The Berlin brain-computer interface, Accurate performance from first session in BCI-naïve subjects. IEEE Trans. Biomed. Eng. 55(20), 2452–2462 (2008)

13. Cecotti, H., Graser, A.: Convolutional Neural Networks for P300 Detection with Application to Brain-Computer Interface. IEEE Transactions on Pattern Analysis and Machine Intelligence 33, 433–444 (2011)

14. Peng, H., Long, F., Ding, C.: Feature Selection Based on Mutual Information: Criteria of Max-Dependency, Max-Relevance, and Min-Redundancy. IEEE Transactions on Pattern Analysis and Machine Intelligence 27(8), 1226–1238 (2005)

15. Yang, J., Singh, H., Hines, E.L., Schaghecken, F., Iliescu, D.D., Leeson, M.M., Stocks, N.G.: Channel Selection and Classification of electroencephalogram signals: An artificial neural network and genetic algorithm-based approach. Art. Intell. Med. (2012)

16. Hoffmann, U., Vesin, J.M., Ebrahim, T., Diserens, K.: An efficient P300-based brain-computer interface for disabled subjects. J. Neurosci. Methods 167(1), 115–125 (2008)

17. Blankertz, B., Muller, K.R., Krusienski, D.J., Schalk, G., Wolpaw, J.R., Schlogl, A., Pfurtscheller, G., Millan, J.R., Schroder, M., Birbaumer, N.: The BCI competition III: Validating alternative approaches to actual BCI problems. IEEE Trans. Neural Syst. Rehabil. Eng. 14(2), 153–159 (2006)

EMG Signal Based Human Stress Level Classification Using Wavelet Packet Transform

P. Karthikeyan, M. Murugappan, and Sazali Yaacob

School of Mechatronics Engineering, Universiti Malaysia Perlis (UniMAP)
Ulau Pauh, 02600, Arau, Perlis, Malaysia
karthi_209170@yahoo.com

Abstract. Recent days, Electromyogram (EMG) signal acquired from muscles can be useful to measure the human stress levels. The aim of this present work to investigate the relationship between the changes in human stress levels to muscular tensions through Electromyography (EMG) in a stimulated stress-inducement environment. The stroop colour word test protocol is used to induce the stress and EMG signal is acquired from left trapezius muscle of 10 female subjects using three surface electrodes. The acquired signals were preprocessed through wavelet denoising method and statistical features were extracted using Wavelet Packet Transform (WPT). EMG signals are decomposed to four levels using db5 mother wavelet function. Frequency band information's of third and fourth levels are considered for descriptive analysis. Totally, seven statistical features were computed and analyzed to find the appropriate frequency band and feature for stress level assessment. A simple non-linear classifier (K Nearest Neighbor (KNN)) is used for classifying the stress levels. Statistical features derived from the frequency range of (0-31.5) Hz gives a maximum average classification accuracy of 90.70% on distinguishing the stress levels in minimum feature.

Keywords: Stress, EMG, stroop colour word test, wavelet packet transform, KNN classifier.

1 Introduction

Stress is one of the major factors that affect the life style of most adults in developed and developing countries. Especially in US, 90% diseases and disorders is related to stress [1]. Stress levels can be computed using a scientific stress level measurement tool and to relive the stress by suggesting suitable relaxation methods. In this view, several researches have investigated different methods to compute stress level using biochemical or physiological signals [2, 3]. Physiological signal based approach is more futuristic than biochemical methods due to its unobtrusive and simple measurement. However, physiological signal based approach has several issues in data acquisition and processing. Solving of these issues will greatly enhance the results of stress assessment experiment. Researchers have investigated different types of physiological signals such as Electrocardiogram (ECG), EMG, Galvanic Skin

S.G. Ponnambalam et al. (Eds.): IRAM 2012, CCIS 330, pp. 236–243, 2012.

Response (GSR), Electroencephalogram (EEG), and Skin Temperature (ST) for stress assessment [4-10]. Compared to other physiological signals, ECG discussed in several stress assessment studies [11]. We have already carried out a series of analysis on ECG signals to assess the stress level of the subjects using different stress inducement protocol [7]. This present study is focusing on investigating the EMG signal from trapezius muscle for stress assessment. Human muscles consist of voluntary and involuntary contractions. Voluntary muscle is to move the body that could be easily controllable by brain through Autonomic Nervous System (ANS). Similarly, involuntary muscles are not easily controllable through brain such as cardiac muscles, blood vessels, muscles in digestive and reproductive systems. This involuntary muscle also generates action potential during the stress state. This action potential is reflected on facial and trapezius muscles [12]. Researchers have found that, trapezius muscle is an ideal location to identify involuntary muscles activity of cardiac regions. Previously, Healey and Lundeberg et al. studied the characteristic changes on EMG signal in trapezius locations and confirmed the measurable changes on the signal stress [6, 13]. However, Very few literatures only reported on EMG signals based stress assessment. Indeed, the discussion on the effects of different frequency bands, more feasible signal processing methodology for non-linear signals for assessing stress level changes is also limited. This present study is concentrated to solve the above issues using suitable signal processing methodology to identify the optimum frequency bands and features after applying the involved in preprocessing, feature extraction, and classification.

2   Methods and Materials

2.1   Research Methodology

This present work mainly aim to investigate the characteristics of EMG signals on assessing the stress level changes of the subjects. Fig 1 shows the research methodology of this work. Initially, stroop colour word test based stressor was used to induce the stress and EMG signals are simultaneously acquired from left trapezius muscle, which is an indicator of soft muscle activity. The acquired EMG signals are preprocessed using wavelet denoising method [14] and wavelet packet transform (WPT) is used for extracting the statistical features. These features were normalized and finally these statistical features are mapped into four different stress levels namely; relax, low, medium and high using a simple non-linear (KNN) classifier. Three EMG electrodes made up of Ag/Ag-Cl are placed on the trapezius muscle of the subjects and signal was obtained with sampling frequency range of 500 Hz. Acquired EMG signals are preprocessed using DWT based denoising method for removing the noises (power line, external interferences) and artifacts (respiration). The complete stress inducement protocol and data acquisition information is explained our previous work [7].

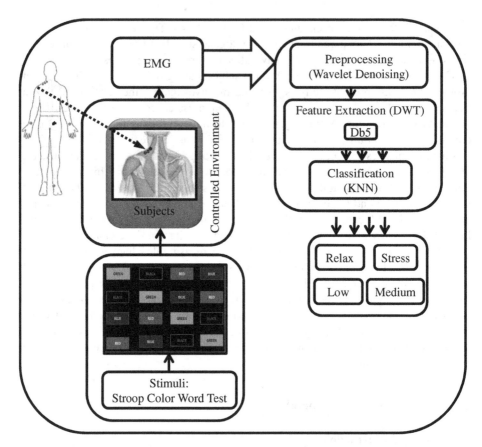

Fig. 1. Research methodology for stress assessment using EMG signals

2.2   Wavelet Packet Transform

The Discrete Wavelet Transform (DWT) has been widely applied on several applications. Indeed, this transform is an efficient technique to analyze the input signal both in time and frequency domain. DWT has the filter bank structures for decomposing the input signal. However, DWT only decomposes low frequency components into further levels. Wavelet Packet Transform (WPT) is used for analyzing the input signal in both low and high frequency information's of the input signals. Fig 2 shows the operation of filter bank implementation of WPT. Hence, WPT is considered to localize the frequency bands in large frequency range signals like EMG signal (0-2000) Hz, which is usually in the applications of gait analysis, and muscle rehabilitation studies. Similarly, Fig.3 illustrates the original sub signal in vector subspace (round shapes), which indicates the uniform frequency division with equal frequency resolution. X[n] is the representation of raw signal, H1[n], H2[n],.... Hn[n] and G[n], G2[n],.... Gn[n] is the approximation and detailed coefficient of wavelet packet transform. Which is also called the low pass and high filters coefficient of WPT. Similarly, W_{00}, W_{10},.....W_{nm} indicates wavelet coefficients in the nth level of mth frequency band.

According the Nyquist criteria, in this research an acquired EMG signal can be analyzed up to 250 Hz. Table 1 presents the details about the frequency ranges respective decomposition levels. In this work, WPT coefficients in third and fourth levels are considered for analyzing the input signal ranging from (0 – 250) Hz.

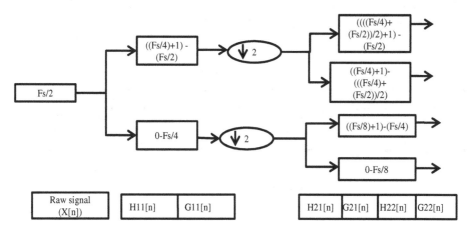

Fig. 2. Filter structure and cutoff frequency WPT in each level

Totally, 24-frequency bands (8 bands in level 3, 16 bands in level 4) have been derived from the input EMG signal for classifying the stress levels of the humans.

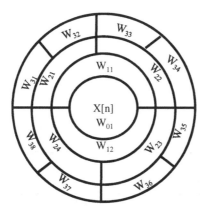

Fig. 3. WPT in each level Equal frequency band of represented in vector sub space

2.3   Feature Extraction and Normalization

Selection of most appropriate frequency band information from the input signal is highly useful for minimize the computation complexity, computation time, and to increase the classification rate. Previously, The EMG signal frequency from (0– 16) Hz is analyzed for estimating the stress levels in car drivers [6]. In addition, another studied are sampled the signal at 10 KHz [13]. In this work, signal was sampled at 500 Hz for detail investigation and to localize frequency bands. Seven basic statistical features such as minimum maximum, mean, standard deviation, power, energy and entropy of wavelet packet transform coefficients are derived from each frequency band in level 3 and level 4. 180 sec relax data were windowed into 5.625 sec of 32 epochs for trail and obtained the total of 640 feature vector of 2 trails over the 10 subjects. Similarly, Table 2 shows the remaining level time and feature information's.

Table 1. Frequency band information on each level of 500Hz sampled signals

Raw Signal		Level 1		Level 2		Level 3		Level 4	
Frequency range	Label of the band	Frequency range	Label of the band	Frequency range	Label of the band	Frequency range	Label of the band	Frequency range	Label of the band
						$0-31.5$	W_{31}	$0-15.63$	W_{41}
								$15.625-31.25$	W_{42}
				$0-62.5$	W_{21}	$31.5-62.5$	W_{32}	$31.25-46.88$	W_{43}
								$46.875-62.5$	W_{44}
		$0-125$	W_{11}			$62.5-93.75$	W_{33}	$62.5-78.13$	W_{45}
				$62.5-125$	W_{22}			$78.125-93.75$	W_{46}
						$93.75-125$	W_{34}	$93.75-09.4$	W_{47}
								$109.375-125$	W_{48}
$0-250$	W_{01}					$125-156.25$	W_{35}	$125-40.6$	W_{49}
								$140.625-156.3$	W_{410}
				$125-187.5$	W_{23}	$156.25-187.5$	W_{36}	$156.25-171.9$	W_{411}
								$171.875-187.5$	W_{412}
		$125-250$	W_{12}			$187.5-218.75$	W_{37}	$187.5-203.1$	W_{413}
								$203.125-218.8$	W_{414}
				$187.5-250$	W_{24}	$218.75-250$	W_{38}	$218.75-234.4$	W_{415}
								$234.375-250$	W_{416}

Table 2. Statistical feature computation from EMG signals over four different stress levels

States	Duration	Duration of epochs	Total number of epochs in each state	Total number of features in two trails	Total number of features in each class
Relax	180 sec	5.625 sec	32	64	640
Low	128 sec	4sec	32	64	640
Medium	64sec	2sec	32	64	640
High	32 sec	1sec	32	64	640

2.4   K Nearest Neighbor Classifier

KNN is well known discriminator for classifying different features. This classifier works based on the distance between the query scenario (features) and set of scenario in the data set (class) [7]. In this work, seven statistical features calculated over the 24 frequency bands in level 3 and level 4. The 430080 (24 features*7 features * 640 vectors in each class*4 class) feature vectors of all the subjects including all the classes were computed. Each feature consists of 2560 vectors and in Training phase 60% (1536) data were given to KNN and 40% (1024) data were tested. This method does not require building up any model and it completely works on local information (nearest training points). This method is also called as "instance-based learning". The minimum K value indicates the features are exactly fitted with class. In this work, K value is tested from 1 to 10 and best value of K and its relevant classification accuracy is reported in section 3.

3   Results and Discussion

3.1   Recognition of Stress Levels

Recent way to analyze nonlinear EMG signal have demonstrated in human stress research. Measurement of involuntary muscle activity in cardiac region explored using advanced signal processing techniques. Total of 24 different frequency band with 7 simple features of EMG signals were analyzed. Result indicates that one frequency band is produced the maximum classification accuracy up to 90.7%. This highest accuracy is obtained in minimum features whilst k is 5 in the frequency range of (0– 31.5) Hz in level 3 (W_{30}) which is shown in Table 3. This identifies WPT is an effective for investigating the performance of large frequency ranges of EMG signals in other application like gait analysis, rehabilitation etc.

In order to discuss more detail, Results of two frequency bands related to (0 – 31.5) Hz are analyzed and such frequency bands are adjacent and two equal half of frequency range (0– 31.5) Hz. The results of those frequency bands are (W_{31}), (W_{40}) and (W_{41}) ((31.6 – 73) Hz, (0 – 15.8) Hz and (15.8 – 31.6) Hz) are also included in Table 3.

Table 3. Result of various frequency bands using KNN classifier

Frequency bands	Feature	K Value	Relax	Stress			Average accuracy
				Low	Medium	High	
(0-15.8) Hz	Minimum	10	98.49	84.27	61.25	84.32	82.08
(15.8-31.6) Hz	Minimum	10	43.44	31.25	45.57	74.43	48.67
(0-31.6) Hz	Minimum	5	93.49	86.93	92.50	89.90	90.70
(31.6-73) Hz	Mean	9	51.82	65.63	73.54	91.30	70.57

The result shows the significant reduction in the frequency band (31.6 – 73) Hz of level 3. In this frequency range, the mean features only produced the maximum accuracy 70.57% rather than minimum feature. It desires the obtained recognition rate is inadequate to measure the stress.

Similarly, the first two frequency band in level 4 are (0 – 15.8) Hz and (15.8 – 31.6) Hz) produced the maximum classification rate of 82.08 % and 48.87% respectively. (0 – 15.8) Hz is produced maximum rate than (0 – 15.8) Hz which is the first and second of second half (0 – 31.5) Hz, and first (W_{40}) and (W_{41}) second frequency band of level 4.

3.2 Analysis of Minimum Feature

In this present work, a simple statistical feature called "minimum value" of WPT coefficients on various stress levels with relaxation state gives the maximum accuracy in stress assessment. Fig 4 describes the average minimum value of all subjects in each class. Minimum value is gradually reduced from 0.0403 to -626.33 of relax and high stress levels. However, the individual variations between the subjects are the reason for reduction of classification accuracy.

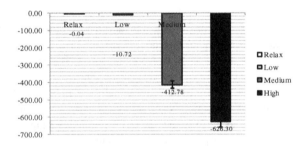

Fig. 4. Overall response of Minimum feature in (0 -31.5) Hz

4   Conclusion

This present work concludes the different levels of the using EMG signals. Initially, the stroop colour word test based stress inducement was done in a controlled environment with minimal surrounding disturbances. Wavelet Packet Transform is used for extracting the features over the 24 different frequency bands of preprocessed EMG signals. Among the different frequency bands, the frequency band information from (0– 31.5) Hz gives a maximum average stress level classification rate of 90.70% compared to other frequency bands. It implies that, the muscle activity under lower frequency range is highly useful for investigating the autonomic nervous system activities, specifically on stress assessment. In this work, we have only investigated seven simple features of WPT coefficients. Perhaps, the statistical features related to EMG signal characteristics such as mean absolute value, Wilson amplitude, kurtosis might be improve the average classification rate on stress level classification.

In future work, we will focus on investigating the EMG signals using different mother wavelet functions, statistical features, and classifier for enhancing the this research. In addition, so far we tested only with 10 subjects. In future, this population size will be increased to improve and validate our research methodology using some other advanced features.

Acknowledgments. This project work is financially supported by Ministry of Higher Education (MOHE), Malaysia through Fundamental Research Grant Scheme (FRGS). Grant Code: 9003-00341.

References

1. Frey, R.J.: Stress (2012), `http://www.minddisorders.com/Py-Z/Stress.html#b` (cited June 2 2012)
2. Tulen, H.M., et al.: Characterization of Stress Reactions to the Stroop Color Word Test. Pharmacology Biochemistry & Behavior 32(1), 9–15 (1989)
3. Ushiyama, K., et al.: Mental Physiologic Neuroendocrine Arousal by Mental Arithmetic Stress Test in Healthy Subjects. The American Journal of Cardiology 67, 101–103 (1991)
4. Knowledge Weavers Project -ECG, `http://library.med.utah.edu/kw/ecg/ecg_outline/Lesson1/lead_dia.html`
5. Hassellund, S.S., et al.: Long term stability of cardiovascular and catecholamine responses to sress tests an 18- year follow - up study. Journal of American Heart Association 55, 131–136 (2010)
6. Healey, J.A., Picard, R.W.: Detecting stress during real-world driving tasks using physiological sensors. IEEE Transactions on Intelligent Transportation Systems 6(2), 156–166 (2005)
7. Karthikeyan, P., Murugappan, M., Yaacob, S.: ECG signals based mental stress assessment using wavelet transform. In: 2011 IEEE International Conference on Control System Computing and Engineering, ICCSCE (2011)
8. Lundberg, U., Melin, B.: Psychophysiological stress and emg activity of the trapezius muscle. International Journal of Behavioral Medicine 1(4), 354–370 (1994)
9. Pehlivanoglu, B., Durmazlar, N., Balkanci, D.: Computer Adapted Stroop Colour-Word Conflict Test as a Laboratory Stress Model. Erciyes Medical Journal 27(2), 58–63 (2005)
10. Zhai, J., Barreto, A.: Stress Detection in Computer Users Based on Digital Signal Processing of Noninvasive Physiological Variables. In: 28th Annual International Conference of the IEEE Engineering in Medicine and Biology Society, EMBS 2006 (2006)
11. Karthikeyan, P., Murugappan, M., Yaacob, S.: A review on stress inducement stimuli for assessing human stress using physiological signals. In: 2011 IEEE 7th International Colloquium on Signal Processing and its Applications, CSPA (2011)
12. Waested, M.: Attention Related Muscle Activity. National Institute of Occupational Health, Oslo (1997)
13. Lundberg, U., et al.: Effect of experimentally induceed stress on motor unit recruitment in the trapezius muscle. Work and Stress 16(2), 166–178 (2002)
14. Karthikeyan, P., Murugappan, M., Yaacob, S.: ECG Signal Denoising Using Wavelet Thresholding Technique in Human Stress Assessment. International Journal on Electrical Engineering and Informatics 4(2) (2012)

Controlling of a Biped System
Using SSC Visual Sequencer

Sew Ming Low

School of Engineering, Monash University Sunway Campus,
Jalan Lagoon Selatan, Bandar Sunway, 46150 Selangor, Malaysia
low.sew.ming@monash.edu

Abstract. The humanoid robot has attracted much interest of many researchers all over the world over the last three decades because of its high possibility to replace human in more difficult and dangerous tasks besides as a household helper and entertainer. However, there was not much activities reported in this area in Malaysia. In this paper, the author reports the initial attempt made in his research work in a biped robot. The biped system was a home-made aluminium structure resembling the 2 human legs. It was installed with 6 DC servo motors allowing for 6 degrees of freedom and the movement of the biped robot was controlled by using a SSC-32 servo controller and SSC Visual Sequencer. Although crude in design, the author has made the biped robot to walk, slowly though.

Keywords: Biped, humanoid robot, SSC visual sequencer.

1 Introduction

Over the last 30 years, humanoid robot has attracted the attention of many engineers and scientists all over the world. The motivation of research in humanoid robot is greatly due to the desire that the robot could be used to perform tasks that are either too difficult or dangerous for humans, such as, just to name a few possible applications, rescue operation in a fire breakout or a mine disaster, nuclear power plant inspection, space exploration. Recently we also observed the intended use of humanoid robots in domestic household such as assisting the elderly or disabled people or attending to one who falls sick and has nobody in the house to look after.

Tracking the development of humanoid robot, Leonardo da Vinci is considered as the first to design a humanoid robot in 1495. However, the robot is only able to wave arms, move head while opening and closing its jaw. It was not until last century that the development of humanoid robot picked up its momentum. In 1973, the first computer controlled humanoid robot, Wabot-1, was designed and built at Waseda University. Honda introduced their first humanoid robot, named E0, in 1986, and in year 2000 announced the well-known humanoid robot, ASIMO. ASIMO is able to walk dynamically and naturally, up and down a staircase, running and other features.. In 2003, Sorry announced the QRIO which is able to walk and dance and also has sound and face recognition abilities. Inspired by Honda's success, many organizations

S.G. Ponnambalam et al. (Eds.): IRAM 2012, CCIS 330, pp. 244–251, 2012.

around the world introduced their own robot [1]. The development of humanoid robot has sped up even more than before over the last few years. This includes HOAP by Fujitsu (2001-2005), Actroid by Osaka University (2003), Wakamaru by Mitsubishi (2005), Nexi, by MIT (2008), SURALP by Sabanci University (2009), Robonaut 2 by NASA & GM (2010), just to name a few.

Despite the rapid development of the humanoid robot worldwide, there was not much progress reported in Malaysia.

This paper reports the initial attempt made by the author in the research of humanoid robot. The current work concerned the investigation of the walking ability of a biped system using a SSC-32 Servomotor Controller and SSC Visual Sequencer.

2   The Biped System

Humanoid robots are robotic systems which are created to imitate human capabilities. A humanoid robot which uses 2 legs for movement is called biped robot. The biped system used in this work, as shown in Fig. 1, was a "2-legged" structure made from aluminium and has three degrees of freedom (DOF) per leg: one at hip, one at knee and one at ankle. The actuators for the robot are DC servo motors. The movement of the biped robot is made possible using microcontroller to control the servo motors.

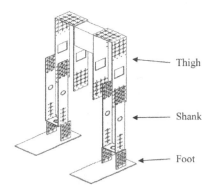

Fig. 1. The biped system structure used for this work

There are many microcontrollers available in the market. In order to choose the right microcontroller, there are many aspects that need to be considered such as: price, capability, efficiency, user-friendliness, etc. Two of these microcontrollers were considered for this work. One is the PIC microcontroller and the other the SSC-32 servo controller. PIC microcontroller is very popular among developers and hobbyist due to low cost and large user base. It uses Harvard architecture and has features such as digital I/O ports, analog input, analog comparator, on-chip timer, power-on-reset, watchdog timer, RAM memory, Flash or EPROM memory and internal oscillator. The accompanying software for PIC microcontroller is MPLAB IDE (Integrated Development Environment) which runs on Windows Operating System PC and can be programmed using C language. The number of servomotors controllable by PIC microcontroller depends on the number of I/O ports of the particular microcontroller. The latter also partly determined the type of PIC microcontroller to be used.

SSC-32 servo controller is a small preassembled servo controller capable of controlling up to 32 servos. This controller is also a popular microcontroller for biped robot because of its easy to use features. It has high resolution (1µS) for accurate positioning, and extremely smooth moves. The time range is 0.5mS to 2.5mS for an angle range of about 180°. The motion control can have immediate response, speed controlled, or time controlled. A unique "Group Move" provides any combination of servos to commence and end motion at the same time, even if the servos have to move different distances. This is a very powerful feature for creating complex walking gaits for multi servo walking robots. The servo's position or movement can be requested to provide feedback to the host computer. There are 4 digital inputs that are static or latched, that can also be used as analog inputs. There are also three terminal blocks for powering options. The DB9 input installed in the controller supports RS-232 communication with a PC. The accompanying software for SSC-32 servomotor controller is SSC Visual Sequencer which also runs on Windows Operating System PC [2].

After much consideration, SSC-32 servomotor controller and SSC visual sequencer was chosen instead of the PIC microcontroller because of (1) it has more features which is likely to provide easier and better approach to control the 6 servomotors, and (2) more user-friendly which enables the user to visualise and to control the combinations of the angular movements of the robot from the main screen of the visual sequencer [3]

Fig. 2. SSC-32 Servomotor controller [2]

The servo controller (Fig. 2) was installed in the biped robot and was connected to a computer through DB9 RS-232 cable. Thus, the servo's position and reading from the accelerometers can be queried to provide feedback to the computer through the controller. From the SSC visual sequencer it is then possible to visualise and control the position of the servo motors in the biped robot. The main screen (Fig. 3) allows the user to add servo control boxes, and position them on a grid. This visual representation of the robot makes it easier to position the servos for each sequence of movement.

The 6 DC servo motors and the SSC-32 servo motor controller are powered by 4 pieces of Energizer 2450 mAh 1.5 V NiMH rechargeable batteries.

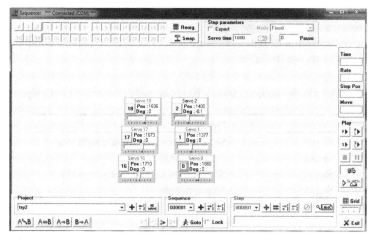

Fig. 3. Main screen window of SSC Visual Sequencer

Servomotor is a DC motor equipped with electronic circuit for controlling the motor rotation direction and position. The commercially available servomotors can rotate to 90^0, 180^0, and even 360^0. Each servomotor has 3 wires, usually coloured as red, black and yellow, allowing connections be made to 4.8V – 6V DC source, ground, and to the signal generator respectively. The servomotor uses Pulse Width Modulation (PWM) signal for controlling the motor direction and position. It works well on 50 Hz PWM frequency, which mean that the signal has 20ms period. The servomotor's electronic circuit interprets the pulses sent by the signal generator and rotates its shaft either clockwise or counter clockwise, depending on the pulse width. The pulse width ranges from 1ms to 2ms. A pulse width of 1.5ms will typically set the servomotor to its neutral position (center), while 0.7ms to 1ms pulse width will turn it clockwise and 1.7ms to 2ms pulse width will turn it counter clockwise [4].

3   Results and Discussions

A non-trivial problem in biped robot is the instability produced during the transition in the walking process [5]. It is very challenging because of the many degrees of freedom involved and the non-linear and hard to stabilize system dynamics. As a result, many control algorithms for biped robot have been developed. These include the use of zero momentum point (ZMP) criterion [6], central pattern generator (CPG) [7], pulsed-CPG [8], experience-based learning neural controller [9] and many more. Due to page limitation, the details and analysis of the stability of the biped robot will not be discussed here.

In short, to make the biped robot walk, the first thing to do is to determine the suitable walking gait for the biped robot, that is, the steps needed to make a complete cycle of walking. This is to ensure that the robot has a stable walking style. After finding the suitable steps, the angle combination for the servomotors are entered into the SSC visual sequencer.

The experiment showed that there were 4 steps needed to make a complete cycle of walking robot as shown in Table 1.

Table 1. The 4 steps needed to make a complete cycle of walking for the biped robot

	Description
Step 1	Shift weight to the robot's right side
Step 2	Step forward
Step 3	Shift weight to the robot's left side
Step 4	Step forward

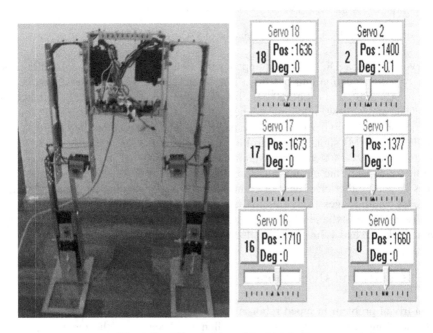

Fig. 4. Standing position of the biped robot

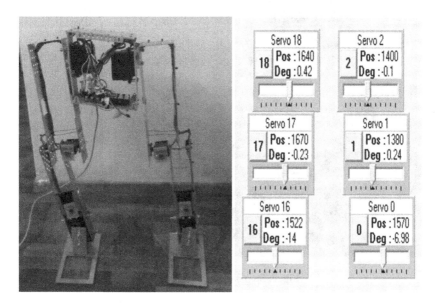

Fig. 5. Step 1 of the biped robot

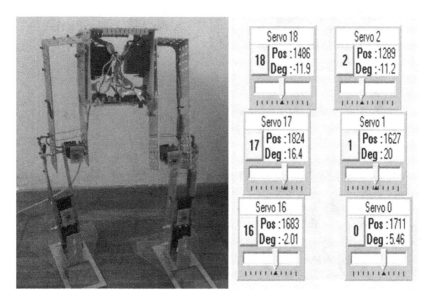

Fig. 6. Step 2 of the biped robot

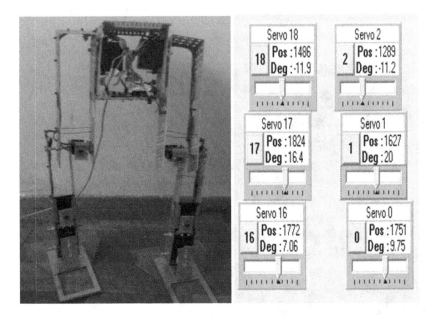

Fig. 7. Step 3 of the biped robot

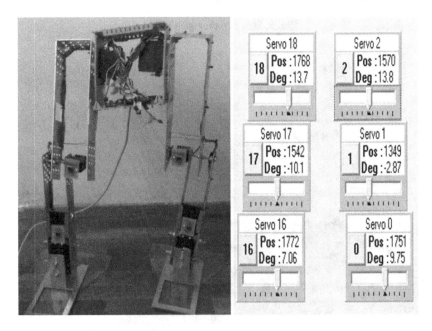

Fig. 8. Step 4 of the biped robot

The reason to shift the weight to the right side is to enable the movement of the left leg forward. Similarly the same reason for shifting the weight to the left side during the walking cycle. Figure 4 shows the result of the standing position. Figure 5 to Figure 8 show the results of the 4 walking steps.

It is obvious that the walking gait and angle combination for the servomotors depend on the structure of the biped robot. Experimentally this can be determined through trial and error even a different structure is used. Further work was planned to further perfect the walking of this biped system.

4   Conclusion

A biped system was constructed using aluminium and 6 servo motors in combination with a SSC-32 servo controller and SSC Visual Sequencer. The walking gait of this system was found to comprise 4 steps. The steps and angle combinations to complete the walking cycle was determined, and the biped robot was made to walk. Further work to make a good walking biped robot was planned.

Acknowledgement. The author wished to thank Mr. Johanes Cendana for his assistance in implementing the SSC-32 servo controller and the SSC Visual.

References

1. Akhtaruzzaman, M., Shafie, A.A.: Evolution of Humanoid Robot and Contribution of Various Countries in Advancing the Research and Development of the Platform. In: International Conference on Control Automation and Systems (ICCAS) (October 2010)
2. Lynxmotion, SSC-32 Servo Controller, http://www.lynxmotion.com/p-395-ssc-32-servo-controller.aspx (accessed June 2011)
3. Lynxmotion, SSC-32 Sequencer, http://www.lynxmotion.com/p-443-ssc-32-sequencer.aspx (accessed June 2011)
4. Ermicro, Basic Servo Motor Controlling with Microchip PIC Microcontroller, http://www.emicro.com/blog/zp=771 (accessed May 2011)
5. Cuevas, E.V., Zaldivar, D., Rojas, R.: Walking Trajectories Control of A Biped Robot. Freie Universitat Berlin and Universidad de Guadalajara, Technical Report B-04-18 (2004)
6. Huang, Q., et al.: A High Stability, Smooth Walking Pattern for a Biped Robot. In: Proceedings of IEEE International Conference on Robotics and Automation, vol. 1, pp. 65–71 (May1999)
7. Habib, M.K., Watanabe, K., Izumi, K.: Biped locomotion using CPG with Sensory Interaction. In: IEEE International Symposium on Industrial Electronics (July 2009)
8. Owaki, D., Matsuno, Y., Ishiguro, A.: Efficient and Adaptive Control of Walking Biped by Exploiting a Pulsed-CPG. In: IEEE/ICME International Conference on Complex Medical Engineering (May 2007)
9. Nassour, J., Henaff, P., Ben Ouezdou, F., Cheng, G.: Experience-based Learning Mechanism for Neural Controller Adaptation: Application to Walking Biped Robots. In: IEEE/RSJ International Conference on Intelligent Robots and Systems (October 2009)

Cordless Cart Follower for Wheelchair User

Noridayu Abdullah Sani, Syed Sahal Nazli Alhady bin Syed Hassan,
W.A.F.W. Othman, and Suardi bin Kaharuddin

School of Electrical & Electronic Engineering, Engineering Campus,
Universiti Sains Malaysia, 14300, Nibong Tebal, Pulau Pinang, Malaysia
noridayu.as@gmail.com, {sahal,eeamirfuad,suardi}@eng.usm.my

Abstract. A wheelchair bound person requires the freedom of upper limb body movement to move around. Any attachment to the wheelchair in the form of luggage will restrict the performance of such person to navigate the wheelchair. Poor navigation of a wheelchair might, in the worst case scenario, lead to an accident that would cause injury to the person. In addition, the durability of the wheelchair might also be affected if the weight put onto it is increase. In this project, a cart follower is introduced to overcome the above mentioned problems faced by wheelchair bound person who need to carry around their luggage. The cart follower has been specifically designed for wheelchair bound persons to help them carry around their luggage. It will automatically track and follow the wheelchair without any attachment or cord between the wheelchair and the cart. Microcontroller, sensors, motors, and servo are used in order to achieve the objective. A CMUCam3 camera with vision sensors is used to track an object, which is in this case, a predefined color from an image pattern. The cart will only move when the configured color is detected and stops when there is no configured color detected. The cart will move backward in decreasing speed from 100 to 70 percent duty cycle if the infrared distance sensor detects an obstacle or if the wheelchair is in the range of 10-28cm a head and then maintains a distance of 28cm as the wheelchair is moving backward. Pulse Width Modulation (PWM) is applied to control the speed and a servo motor is used to control the angle rotation of the cart.

Keywords: Cordless cart follower, CMUCam3 camera, distance sensor.

1   Introduction

Theoretically, the cordless cart follower might seem like a normal and typical bulky luggage commonly found in the market. But the intelligent capability applied onto the cart sets it as different from the others. This cart follower is specifically designed for the wheelchair bound to help them carry around their luggage. It will automatically track and follow the wheelchair without any attachment or wire between the wheelchair and the luggage. In order to archive the objective, the project required development in electronic and mechanical area.

The cart consists of microcontrollers, several sensors, motors, and actuators to make the cart follow the wheelchair without losing the track. One of the sensors used

S.G. Ponnambalam et al. (Eds.): IRAM 2012, CCIS 330, pp. 252–262, 2012.
© Springer-Verlag Berlin Heidelberg 2012

is a camera, which is a CMUcam3 with a vision sensor. Color tracking function of the camera is used to do the task of following. Following robot has been developed using various methods including using the same camera CMUcam but such development is for a different application [1]. There is a similar application involving person following robot but a different type of camera was used [2]. Apart from color tracking, line tracking was also developed by using the same camera [3].

When the object moves to a particular degree on the same axis, the camera will track it and notifies the microcontroller. Based on the information provided by the camera, the microcontroller will process the information and will instruct the driver motor and servo motor on the further actions to be taken. The servo motor will act accordingly. Therefore the movement of the cart is in line with the wheelchair. Furthermore, a distance sensor is used to measure the distance between the cart and the wheelchair. The measured distance will then be fed to the microcontroller which in turn will cause the motor to move the cart. As a result, the distance between the wheelchair and the luggage is fixed over time. The cart also can perform navigation task such as going through the door, moving up and down ramps and turning at sharp corners. The end product is an intelligent autonomous luggage which is able to follow the wheelchair and can navigate safely through the surroundings without requiring the control from a human being.

2   Methodology

2.1   Cordless Cart Follower Specification

A similar application of an electronic Luggage follower but applied to normal user was developed using aluminum alloy and plastic ABS material with different sensor and microcontroller [10]. Our cordless cart follower was designed to carry heavy things. The design kept on changing from time to time according to the current suitable new discoveries. Fig. 1 (a) shows the first rough design according to perfectly needed specification. Fig. 1 (b) shows the fabricated design with certain parts being cut off or added according to the cost budget and the complication of the design. Fig. 1 (c) shows the modified design for the purpose of the separation of the controller part, sensory part and the luggage part. Figure 1 (d) shows the latest design of fabrication developed. The plywood used as the cast to cover the battery compartment and the controller compartment. The sensory part was mounted in front of the cart and level with the wanted color image mounted at the back of the wheelchair. The latest cart is approximately 500mm in length, 450mm in width, 300mm in height, and 10kg in weight. It has one driven wheel at the back and two castor wheels in front. The castor wheel is connected to a parallel linkage and attached to the servo horn. The cart gets the image to follow a specific configured color by received T packet color from CMUCam3 to the microcontroller. The camera position angle is adjustable according to the mounted color level on the wheelchair. The cart is powered by lead acid battery and can operate for approximately 4 hours straight. The PIC Microcontroller is the main controller which controls the whole system. It contains tasks such as the interfacing with the vision camera sensor, motors, and distance sensor for obstacle detection for the purpose of avoiding obstacles.

(a)   (b)   (c)   (d)

Fig. 1. (a) First Design. (b) After Fabricated. (c) Modification after fabricated. (d) Final cordless follower.

2.2   Function

Cordless cart follower will be able to trace the configured color and follow the direction of the source color. In our case we attach the color at the back of the wheelchair and level it with the available angle of the camera or can be seen by the camera. The algorithm was developed to differentiate and detect specific color for the task of following.

(a) Following
Mobile robot requires a really good navigation system such as the vision system. The vision meant in here is the optical sensor used in the camera. One of the tasks is color tracking. The further section will discuss about the well known vision sensor camera CMUcam and the color tracking that is related to the embedded system.

(b) Moving forward and backward
The cart will move only when the camera detects the matching color. In our case we use red light LED form the one that is mounted on warning light of a bicycle. The light was mounted at the back of a wheelchair and at the same height level of the camera on the cart to make it easier for the camera's angle detection coverage. When the camera detects the red LED light in front of it, the cart will move forward in different speed according to the distance of the cart and the wheelchair. If the distance between them is large, the speed of cart is increased to catch up the wheelchair. If the distance between them is small, the speed of the cart is decreased. The backward movement is applied for the purpose of avoiding obstacles. This function is also applied when the wheelchair moves backward and so do the cart and the cart will keep a distance between them.

(c) Obstacle avoidance
As what has been mentioned about the moving backward function in the above section, infrared distance sensor is actually the thing that makes the auto detection of obstacle working. This sensor is a distance measuring sensor with integrated signal processing and analog voltage output [4]. The effectiveness of this version sensor is from the distance of 3cm to 30cm. The microcontroller is programmed if the obstacle detected in the range of 10cm to 28cm the cart will move backward. But if the distance is 10cm and shorter the cart will stop moving.

(d) Turning left and right
The moving direction of turning left and right of the cart is controlled by the servo motor. The servo motor angle rotation is programmed to keep on changing according to the camera on which direction of the color is detected.

2.3   Microcontroller and Other Hardware

Fig. 2 shows the block diagram of the whole system and the control flow of the input and output. The cart is controlled by the main controller PIC18F4550. As illustrated in Fig. 2, PIC18F4550 is the brain or the main controller and run with 20 MHz clock crystal oscillator. The voltage from a lead acid battery are regulated using switching regulator LM2672 to +5V before connected to the whole circuit since this type of regulator easily powering the heavy load system of the cart. The linear voltage regulator LM7806 for the CMUcam3 camera is separated as the working voltage range of the camera is from 6V to 15V [5].

The ICSP circuit was built to enable download the program. CMUcam3 is considered as input and output as the two way communication between camera and PIC is occurred while PIC transmit the color information to the camera and receive back the information of the color position and confidence value from the camera.

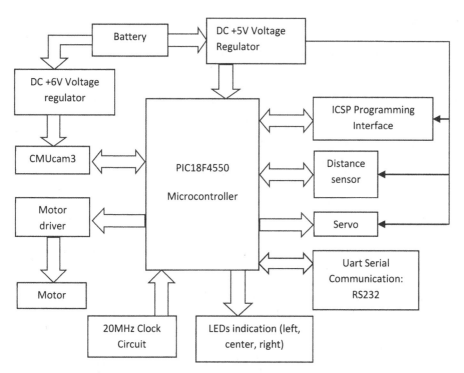

Fig. 2. Block Diagram for the cordless cart follower system

The process flow in Fig. 2 shows the PIC controls the movement of the motor driver. Motor driver MD30B from Cytron is used to drive the motor of the cart and the motor itself directly operated by the battery of 12V. The operating voltage for the driver board is +5V and supplied via I/O pin of PIC itself since PIC are programmed to enable the power for driver motor when needed in order to get minimum current drawn from the circuit [7]. The distance sensor is considered as input and output as the transmitted infrared is as an output and the output voltage is as an input to the microcontroller. Infrared sensor will send data to the PIC in real time. The PIC will process the raw analog input data and transfers it into the digital form by using internal analog digital converter (ADC). Then the PIC will give an order to the motor driver to move the motor to a direction according to the data from the distance sensor. The data from distance sensor will decide whether the cart will move forward and backward direction.

All the data received from the camera and the distance sensor is viewed via hyperterminal of the PC for experimental purpose. No external IC like MAX232 used as TTL logic converter as the invert function is used in the programmed code to make it compatible to transmit the data.

2.4   Color Tracking Using CMUcam3 Vision Camera

CMUcam3 is used for the following purpose. CMUcam is a low cost vision camera which has vision potential in embedded system to form an intelligent vision sensor [8]. The upgraded version of CMUcam is CMUcam3 is programmable and processed in real time [9]. For tracking color CMUcam shows its performance when there are high contrast and intense color viewed [5]. Color tracking is the ability to take an image then isolate a particular color and give the location of the area of that particular color [5].

The allowable range of maximum and minimum of three RGB (Red Green Blue) is needed to set a color to be tracked. The light and color of an object is not perfectly uniform in different environment so that these maximum and minimum ranges are needed. In other words there are six values needed for the tree color channel to create the boundaries. The camera later on will process the image and only will track the color within the boundaries. However, the light source in different environment will affect the brightness and the contrast of an object. Therefore the RGB ranges of that particular object are changing from what we set for the first place for the vision camera CMUcam3 to detect. A bright LED needed as the tracked color or object as its contrast is less changing in most of the environments that tested.

The camera needs to be operated in standalone mode for the first time to configure the RGB boundaries. Standalone mode result is discussed in result and discussion subtopic. The camera will later on connected to a microprocessor for more complicated system. The communication between both is transmitted in fixed command from the camera containing the information of the RGB boundaries that we find in standalone mode. The camera will respond in T packet data type.

The CMUcam communicate with the main processor PIC via serial communication rs232. Transmit and receive from the camera connected to rx and tx pin of PIC pin B0 and B1 that is configured as receive and transmit in the program code. By writing the main program to detect the color or the maximum and minimum boundaries of RGB that determined with the GUI is enough to track the color. The command applied is TC R_{max} R_{min} G_{max} G_{min} B_{max} B_{min}. A few commands lines we must take note to do the color tracking. They are TC, TI, TW, NF, LM, GT, and ST [5]. All commands are sent using visible ASCII characters. The successful transmission command will return the ACK string or which mean acknowledge and NCK returned when unsuccessful transmission occurs. TC command meant to be tracking the color. The input values to be keyed are the minimum and maximum RGB (YCbCr) and gives the output of T packet type. TW command also gives the output of T packet type.

2.5   The Cart Movement According to Color Detection

After configured color detected and if the confidence value that mention is above 180 the cart will move forward. This means that the cart will only move if it detects the wanted color. After that color detected the cart will move forward following the direction of the wheelchair. The movement to the left and right later on will be decided according to the *mx* position send by the camera and actuated by servo motor.

While moving the speed of the cart also changing based on the distance of the cart and the wheelchair. If the wheelchair if too far the cart will move faster and vice versa, but only when configured color detected. Motor library file coded for controlling the speed of the motor using PWM function of the PIC. The speed of the cart will decrease to 70 percent of the duty cycle when moving backward. The motor driver MD30B is used for controlling the direction and speed of the motor. The cart will stop when configured color not detected.

2.6   Angle Rotation of the Servo According to the Color Detection

The servo is programmed to rotate slowly according to the value of middle mass of x axis, *mx* of the color blob which is discussed in result and discussion section. This slowly rotating result is occurs by manipulating a set of array to change pulse width according to the *mx* value. In our program an equation is evaluated so that the pulse width is varied from 1100 to 1709ms with the change of the middle mass x value from 0 to 87.

Three LEDs are used as indicators of the position of the wheelchair since the detected red LED is mounted at the back of the wheelchair. The result of LEDs indicator is discussed in result and discussion section.

2.7   Obstacle Avoidance Using Analog Infrared Distance Sensor (GPD120)

Besides just following the cart also need to overcome the obstacle that occur while moving. This cart will not complete without the important intelligent feature like obstacle avoidance. A lot of studies have been developed to do obstacle avoidance. Various type of different device or sensor used to complete the task like GPS and sound sensor [6]. In this research we used infrared analog distance sensor.

The GP2D120 module can do the distance measuring and obstacle detection using infrared light feature to this mobile robot. The mobile robot can avoid obstacle without having to make any physical contact. The GP2D120 used infrared light reflection to measure range [4]. It can measure a range from 3 to 30cm [4]. The GP2D120 infrared distance measuring sensor module has 3 terminals: Power input (Vcc), Ground (GND), and Voltage (Vout). The output voltage of this sensor will change according to the distance detected. Internal ADC with 10-bit resolution of PIC18F4550 is used to convert the raw data to the digital form. The Vout pin connected to analog input pin of PIC Microcontroller.

3   Results and Discussion

3.1   Overview

The end result shows the design is working as a whole unit as the cart able to follow a wheelchair that is mounted with light up red LED without any attachment between the cart and the wheelchair. This project has been awarded bronze medal on a recent competition of ITEX2012. The working result can be viewed in the video link http://www.youtube.com/watch?v=DqSkTDa6sas. The result for the vision sensor and the distance sensor is discussed in the next section.

3.2   CMUcam3

Standalone mode is the mode of camera operating by itself and directly connected to the PC via serial communication to transmit command and receive data. CMUcam2 Graphical User Interface (CMUcam2GUI) a java program provided by developer is used in order to make it easy to find the RGB boundaries. This program also provides other useful function to visualize and interface the user and the camera.

In order to set the selected color, the red LED light chosen as the color of a light is less changing the every situation depends on the contrast with thing in the background. The LED light hovered in front of the camera in order to grab a frame from the GUI as shown in Fig. 3 (a). In the Grabbed frame, the wanted color is selected by clicking the color image of LED light. The blue range is occurred as the uniform color selected an shown in Fig 3 (b). The color tab option chosen to track the selected color and the track color button is clicked. Once again the LED light hovered in front of the camera and a blob or a rectangular blue form is appeared in the GUI window with pink dot in the middle which represents the centroid of the tracked color as shown in Fig. 3 (c). This blob keeps moving according to where we moved the LED. In this color tab also we can find the RGB boundaries automatically determined at the bottom GUI window. With this range already determined in the GUI it makes us easier to plan the range of RGB in any application involving color tracking in the future.

After RGB range configured during standalone mode, the camera is connected to the main microcontroller and data received is display on the PC. Fig. 4 shows an example the data received viewed on the hyper terminal. The VOLT value is taken from the voltage ranging of the distance sensor based on 10-bit ADC value. The distance value is viewed in centimeter and in two decimal places. The next line is the middle mass of x value (mx), the confidence value and the last one is the ranging value of servo position starting form a constant and yet to be converted to the general angle degree value.

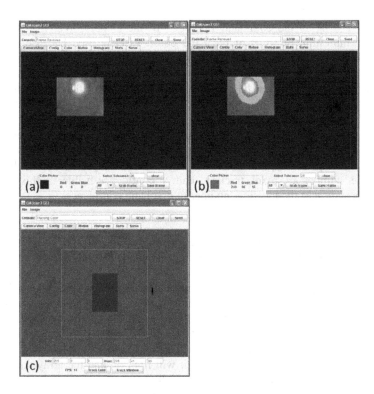

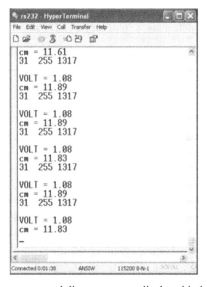

Fig. 3. (a) Grabbed image of LED light. (b) Grabbed image with blue region appear after a color selected. (c) Image of a blue rectangle blob appear and moved according to where we move the LED light.

Fig. 4. Data from camera and distance sensor displayed in hyperterminal

TC 215 25 0 41 0 41 is the command line send to the camera. Which is the maximum and the minimum of RGB of red LED color. LED is used because the uniform of the color in various situation depend on the brightness of an object. For example in a square orange paper is detected by the camera while running the experiment in a room with florescent lamp light up the room, but while running the camera to detect that orange paper in outside the room with bright sun rays will cause no detection at all from the camera. That is because the color of that orange paper is already out of the boundaries that set on the first place. But light up LED color have high contrast and close to uniform in every environment that tested in room or outside the room. By default, T packet type return the middle mass x and y coordinates, the bounding box, the number of pixel tracked, and a confidence value. This is containing the information of the location, number of pixel and confidence.

$$T\ mx\ my\ x1\ y1\ x2\ y2\ pixels\ confidence$$

mx and my are middle mass of x and y value accordingly. The $x1$ and $y1$ are the value of the left most corner's of x and y axis. The $x2$ and $y2$ are the value of the right most corner's of x and y axis.

This reading returned by the camera to microcontroller and the microcontroller will determine the next step to be taken based on the information given. The information received is enough to know the position of the tracked color and the confidence value of the color. From the value given, microcontroller will arrange the position of the servo based on the location of the middle mass of the color. Table 1 shows the data of middle mass x value, which LED position indicator will light on and the array value range based on the location of middle mass x. The middle mass of x value of the color then noted ranging from 0-87. X1 is an array data start with constant value of 1100, and keep ranging to 1709. This array range was manipulated in program code to give different pulse width to servo motor at a time in order to make the servo position keep changing according to color position based on x-axis.

Table 1. Data of middle mass, x value range, LED indicator and X1 array range

Middle mass x	Led Indicator	X1
0<mx<30	right	1100-1310
60<mx<87	left	1520-1709
30<mx<60	center	1310-1520

3.3   Infrared Distance Sensor

The output voltage and digital value of the distance sensor are tabulated according to the actual distance. Based on the result collected, the graph of GP2D120 output voltage Vo (V) against distance (cm) is shown below in Fig.5.

The plotted graph in Fig. 5 shows the smooth curve and the effective range detection for the sensor is between 3 and 30 cm. The output voltage of the sensor is approximately inversely proportional to the distance measured from object.

The ranges from 0 to 3 cm are assumed not effective for the sensor to detect the presence of the object within that range.

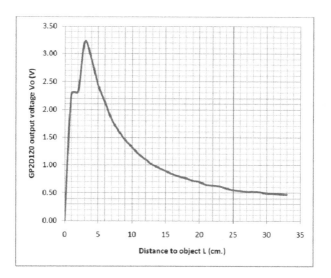

Fig. 5. The graph of GP2D120 output voltage Vo (V) versus distance (cm)

The program then coded if it detect the configured color and detect an object in range of 10 to 28cm cart will move to opposite direction. But if sensor detect the object in less that 10cm distance it will stop. There is also no movement of the cart if configured color not detected. The distance and output voltage of the sensor are then displayed via serial communication on the HyperTerminal as shown in Fig. 3 for experimental purpose. This sensor is mounted in front of the cart parallel with the CMUcam3 camera.

4   Conclusion

In this paper, we discussed mostly the technical and hardware part of the cordless cart follower. The cart was developed from scratch until it complete with controller and sensory part in affordable budget. This cordless cart follower has a bright future as it has its own commercialize value and it is an invention that will aid for the wheelchair users. The wheelchair user will easily carry their luggage using the cart without having difficulties.

References

1. Bikman, J.D., Meiswinkel, T.W., Conrad, J.M.: Vehicle Implementation Of A Color Following System Using The Cmucam3. In: Proceeding IEEE International Conference (March 2009)

2. Yoshimi, T., Nishiyama, M., Sonoura, T., Nakamoto, H., Tokura, S., Sato, H., Ozaki, F., Matsuhira, N., Mizoguchi, H.: Development of a Person Following Robot with Vision Based Target Detection. In: 2006 IEEE/RSJ International Conference on Intelligent Robots and Systems, October 9-15, pp. 5286–5291 (2006)
3. Girbes, V., Armesto, L., Tornero, J.: PISALA project. Intelligent Sensorization for Line tracking with Artificial Vision. In: Robotics (ISR), 2010 41st International Symposium on and 2010 6th German Conference on Robotics (ROBOTIK), June 7-9, pp. 1–6.
4. Sharp, GP2D120 datasheet, Sharp (2010),
   http://www.technologicalarts.com/myfiles/data/gp2d120.pdf
5. Carnegie Mellon University, CMUcam2 User Guide, Version 1.06 (2003),
   http://www.cmucam.org/wiki/Documentation
6. Gonzales, R.A., Gaona, F.A., Peralta, R.R.: An autonomous robot based on a Wheelchair. In: 2012 22nd International Conference on Electrical Communications and Computers (CONIELECOMP), February 27-29, pp. 283–287 (2012)
7. Tips 'n Tricks Power Managed PIC® MCU,
   http://ww1.microchip.com/downloads/en/DeviceDoc/41200c.pdf
8. CMUcam Website, http://www.cmucam.org
9. Rowe, A., Goode, A.G., Goel, D., Nourbakhsh, I.: CMUcam3: An Open Programmable Embedded Vision Sensor. Tech. report CMU-RI-TR-07-13, Robotics Institute, Carnegie Mellon University (May 2007)
10. César, N., Alberto, G., Raimundo, O., Daniel, A., Sabri, T.: Electronic Luggage Follower. In: Florida Conference on Recent Advances in Robotics, FCRAR 2010, Jacksonville, Florida, May 20-21 (2010)

A Brief Introduction to Intrusion Detection System

Ashara Banu Mohamed, Norbik Bashah Idris, and Bharanidharan Shanmugum

Universiti Teknologi Malaysia, UTM, Kuala Lumpur
asharabanumohamed@yahoo.com, {norbik,bharani}@ic.utm.my

Abstract. Intrusion Detection System (IDS) is a security system that acts as a protection layer to the infrastructure. Throughout the years, the IDS technology has grown enormously to keep up with the advancement of computer crime. Since the beginning of the technology in mid 80's, researches have been conducted to enhance the capability of detecting attacks without jeopardizing the network performance. In this paper we hope to provide a critical review of the IDS technology, issues that transpire during its implementation and the limitation in the IDS research endeavors. Lastly we will proposed future work while exploring maturity of the topic, the extent of discussion, the value and contribution of each research to the domain discussed. At the end of this paper, readers would be able to clearly distinguish the gap between each sub-area of research and they would appreciate the importance of these research areas to the industry.

Keywords: IDS, machine learning, forecasting, prediction, correlation.

1 Introduction

We are now living in a borderless world where nothing is beyond reach. The profound and rapid technology growth has given rise to new vulnerabilities and threats to the computerization era. In addition, the dependency on network and internet amenities to support the growing need for online services has definitely increases the cyber crime rate. In the late 70's and early 80's, monitoring user activities for any malicious or unusual behaviors were done manually using the printed audit logs, however this has evolved significantly [1]. Threats and attacks are becoming more frequent and has to be handled in a more efficient and effective way. Nowadays we see new attack technique in a daily basis, therefore, there must be a mechanism to monitor and control these activities. There is a definite need for new type of protection against this new hazard.

There will never be enough or too much security implemented, especially with all the online services made available through internet; however the security implemented should be reliable and at the same time will not jeopardize the performance of a network or system. IDS provide a second layer of defense prior to conventional security technique such as authentication and access control [2]. Because of the importance of maintaining confidentiality, availability and the integrity of our most valuable assets which is the information, IDS has become a necessity. Nevertheless before investing in an IDS, it is important to understand the

S.G. Ponnambalam et al. (Eds.): IRAM 2012, CCIS 330, pp. 263–271, 2012.

current infrastructure and the actual needs of the proprietor. There are many types of IDS with its own set of classification out there in the market; host or network based, signature or anomaly based, active or passive monitoring, real-time or interval processing and finally will the implementation be centralized or distributed. All the above classifications have their own advantages and disadvantages. Moreover, many researches have been carried out in the attempt to understand the subject better and in the long run to produce a more effective and efficient IDS.

The purpose of this paper is to give a brief overview on the development of IDS technology throughout the years. Since early 1990's, most studies on IDS have been focusing on data reduction and classification. However this paper attempt to bring out different areas of research on IDS technologies, which is presented in Section 2. Section 3 will highlight issues raised by the authors concerning their research. In Section 4 we will discuss the result of the review by stating the limitation of the research mentioned in the paper and also provide some future research direction. Lastly section 5 will conclude the paper.

2   Intrusion Detection System (IDS)

The concept of monitoring user activity through logs and computer records was first introduced in 1980 by Jim Anderson. It was to protect information from being accessed by unauthorized external or internal users and also to protect information from 'misfeasors', users that misused their privilege [3]. It was the initial beginning of host-based IDS [4] [4]. Since then, the idea has been researched and developed to keep up with the growing public usage of internet with its share of vulnerabilities. The first real-time intrusion detection system is called Intrusion Detection Expert System (IDES); a product of a research conducted in the Computer Science Laboratory at SRI International.   IDES is an independent real-time intrusion detection system that combines both anomaly and rule based detection; anomaly-based detection uses statistical algorithms meanwhile expert system was used to build the rule-based components[5]. It is said to be independent because it is not tied to any particular system, environment, vulnerability or type of intrusion. The IDES model launched in 1986 was for a general-purpose and the framework could be used as foundation to develop a much more robust and powerful IDS[6].   IDS technology has become a very popular and well researched field, due to its demand in the industry.   The unrelenting interest in this technology has continuously enhanced IDS performance and accuracy.

Since the formation of IDES, there are many more intrusion detection products in the market for users to choose and implement. In 1999, Kevin Richards did a review on five different IDS product to evaluate their performance in a production environment [7].   In his review he highlighted the importance of the packet processing engine in IDS. If the engine is not effective and efficient, the sensor or IDS will start to drop packets and this will reduce the ability to detect attacks, especially if it involves an attack with multiple packets which needs to be assembled before an attack could be determined. Each of the five IDS was subjected to a number of qualitative and quantitative tests; qualitative focus on the usability of the product meanwhile quantitative test looks into the functional and performance area of the IDS. The quantitative aspect of the IDS can be categorized as the detection and processing mechanism.

2.1   Detection Method

The IDS technology has two major approaches that differentiate between one model to another which is the anomaly-based IDS and misuse or signature-based IDS. Though the main objective of both approaches is the same which is to detect intrusion however the mechanism of detecting is different [8]. Anomaly-based IDS allows transactions or activities that are considered as normal behavior. These normal behaviors of users were predefined and modeled into the system, and any abnormal activities will be blocked immediately. In the case of misuse or signature-base IDS, the sensor will allow all activities except activities that are predefined as attacks. All known attacks are stored in the sensor in the form of rules; these rules will be used to match against all incoming and outgoing traffic. The differences between these two approaches were compared and according to Biermann et al., both approaches have their own limitation in detecting all types of intrusion [9]. Due to these limitations, most researches opt to use the combination of both anomaly and misuse detection in order to get a better result [10]; which is also known as a hybrid.

A machine learning-based IDS, a new named coined to describe the characteristic of the system, for it is able to function as an anomaly and misuse detection system [11]. Machine learning (ML) techniques have become one of the most popular choices among researches in the IDS domain. ML has been used as a technique in the Artificial Intelligence discipline since mid 1950's. It is a well researched area and has become very popular among other researcher from different disciplines. ML is sought after because of its ability to learn, which is a sign of intelligence and the making of high performance system[12].   In 2009, Chih-Fong Tsai et al. did a review on intrusion detection that uses ML technology and according to the authors many different ML techniques were used in developing anomaly detection system [13]. Due to its learning capabilities, robustness and adaptability to change [14], it is the most appropriate technique to train IDS to identify or learn new type of attacks[15]. Meanwhile, in the case of signature-based IDS, ML technique was used to improve the matching mechanism [16] to produce better result and   lessen the false alarm rate. To further increase an IDS performance in terms of maximizing the accuracy of detection and minimizing the computational complexity, hybrid intelligent systems are used in the IDS model; for example the hybrid models which combines decision tree (DT) with support vector machine (SVM) and an ensemble approach that combines the base classifiers [2].

Another interesting development in the IDS technology is the attempt to predict user's actions. IDS was first developed to monitor users activities and to detect cyber attacks detection. But as technology progresses vulnerabilities become bigger and greater. There is a need for a much better and sophisticated security system. Detecting alone is no longer sufficient. An intrusion detection system should be able to predict users' behavior, forecast future attack and stop an attack from commencing. Because of these new demands, there has been a continuous stream of research carried out. Pikoulas, J. (2001) introduced a distributed approach to network security with Bayesian forecasting technique to predict users' actions; this IDS maintain two functionality, the detection module uses a hybrid technique where invalid behavior is determine by comparing it with the users' current and typical behavior together with a set of rules which reflect legal activities that is determine by the administrator meanwhile the second function is the prediction module that implement the Dynamic Liner Model (DLM), in this module the system will monitor a user's behavior for about 15 times, than after evaluating itself for 5 times the system is ready to make a prediction [17].   The next intrusion forecasting system employs a Weather Forecasting Model, which also implement statistical model with a dynamic linear model (DLM). Besides predicting intrusion; this forecasting model is able to estimate potential damage caused from an intrusion and identify counter-measures to minimize damages [18]. In this instance the IDS model is also an incident handling tool.

2.2   Alert Processing

Alerts are the product of the detection mechanism. The accuracy of the alerts largely depends on the detection criteria. IDS generate a very large amount of alerts. However most of these alerts are false positive, legal human activity that is regarded as an intrusion by the IDS[9]. Many new methods have been research with the objective of reducing the amount of alerts generated and at the same time making it possible to process these alerts in a more effective manner , which in the long run it will enhance the alerts processing technique. In 2007, Safaa, O.Al-Mamory et al. did a survey on IDS processing techniques. In this survey the author grouped the alert processing techniques into two categories; Alert Pre-Processing that operates at the network meanwhile Alert Correlation   handles attacks at the application layer. There have been many developments under Alert Correlation compared to Pre-Processing category. The function of a network layer alert processing is to reduce or mitigate the false positive for a more accurate analysis. The objective is to remove noise from a stream of alerts to make it more significant. Meanwhile under the Alert Correlation category, which is defined as 'a conceptual interpretation of multiple alerts that new meaning is assign to it' [19]; this task is performed after most redundant alerts have been filtered at the network layer. The revised taxonomy of alert processing at the application layer is discussed in detail in [20]; this new taxonomy highlighted the importance of data reduction technique at the application layer. Furthermore, from previous researches it is clear that both techniques are being implemented by researchers in the process of developing the ultimate solution.

3   Highlighted Issues

IDS technology has evolved significantly due to the growing dependencies on computer technologies, internet and mostly online services. Even though it has been a continuous effort in trying make a robust and refined intrusion detection system, however it is still a long way from being full proof. From the literature review above there are many issues highlighted by the authors in regards to the research they conducted, which is categorized as pre issues in Table 1 and post issues in Table 2.

Table 1. Types of IDS and Limitation – Pre Issues

Type	Highlighted Issue	Limitation	Proposed Solution
Anomaly Detection	• In anomaly detection approach, everything that is not modeled or predefined in advanced as normal activity is considered as an intrusion. Using this approached users have limited access to the network or host, a price to pay for security [8]. • Another main drawback in the anomaly-based detection is the huge amount of false positive alert generated by the system [4] [10] [14, 17] [21]. Because of the nature of the detection mechanism, even though the activities are legitimate, because it is not predefined therefore it will trigger an alert[9]. • Due to the huge amount of false positive alert the speed and accuracy of detection decreases.	• User activities are restricted to a specified routine and menial task. • The huge amount of data reduces the processing accuracy and performance, due to the low classification ability.	• Predefined activities have to be updated frequently by an administrator. • Introduced Machine Learning technique. This technique is able learn users new behavior and store it the database to be used as a new detection criteria.
Misuse Detection	• Misuse or signature based detection approach is the most common IDS in the industry[14] [21]. This is because it generate less false positive alert compared to the previous approach, however the main setback in this approach is that misuse-based IDS is not able to detect new or unknown attacks [9] [10] [17] [14] [21]. • Signature of new attacks need to be updated into the system manually and has to be customized to prevent from positive alert.	• The biggest disadvantage is the inability of the detection approach to detect unknown attacks. It is insufficient to detect all types of attack [14] • The pattern matching technique usually used by the characteristic consumes lots of processing time and disk space [22].	• Uses Artificial Intelligent technique such as Expert System and Fuzzy to enhance the IDS performance [5] [6] [21] [22]. • Anomaly based IDS which uses Machine Learning technique that implement Learning Behavior model [14].

Table 1. (*Continued*)

Machine Learning Detection	• Some machine learning has a certain presumption that has to be followed, for example in the case of Bayesian technique the data is assumed to be linear because it is not able to operate efficiently in a non-linearity data set [23]. To ignore this would decrease the accuracy of detection [8]. • The biggest problem faced by unsupervised classification method is the 'curse of dimensionality' due to the large number of input features. ML technique such as Artificial Neural Network (ANN) is use to solve the problem, but because of the complexity of the system and the number of input features the task of clustering of events is time consuming and computationally expensive. Trying to reduce the input features would reduce the detection accuracy [8]. • When there is an imbalance in the distribution of different types of attack, it will render ML technique incapable of learning the new pattern. This will lower the detection precision; this is so, especially when the attack seldom submerge [3].	• Processing time for detection is one of the most crucial element in IDS, most ML technique consume too much time for the computational activities [8].	• The computational problem could be addressed using Embedded Programming IDS and Agent Based IDS [8] • Used a Hybrid intelligent system that incorporate both anomaly and misuse detection approach/charact eristic using Machine Learning and data mining techniques [3] [4, 11]

Table 2. Implementation Issues – Post Issues

Issues	Solution - technique	Description
Amount of alert generated	• Classification • Data reduction • Correlation	Due to the amount of alert generated which is mostly false positive, studies are conducted to find the best method in reducing the amount of alert generated by IDS and at the same time managing the alerts. This way the processing activity will be more accurate and time effective. [22] [4]
Accuracy of detection	• Hybrid method • Machine learning • Data Mining	Traditional approach that is the Anomaly-Based and Misuse-based has limitation, hence the increase in false positive. New hybrid IDS with the used of ML technique and data mining method has been developed and research on in the attempt to increase the accuracy of detection. [6]

Table 2. (*Continued*)

Performance- Time Factor	• Hybrid method • Machine Learning • Data mining • Correlation	Because of amount of alerts generated daily, more time is needed in the processing and analyzing activity. To further increase an IDS performance in terms of maximizing the accuracy of detection and minimizing the computational complexity, hybrid intelligent systems are used in the IDS model. Data mining is also used to enhance the performance. [4]
Future Attacks	• Machine Learning • Artificial Intelligent • Data mining	Because of the overwhelming increase of computer abuse, detecting attack is no longer sufficient. Human actions are predicted and learned in the attempt of stopping future attack. [17-18] [23]
Human Intervention	• Data mining • Machine learning • Artificial intelligence	Experts are needed to manually process alerts and writing the rules. Research in reducing the dependency.[21]

4   Result

Based on the literature review conducted, listed below are some of the findings on the limitation of previous researches and also proposed direction for future research.

4.1   Research Limitation

- The human roles in the IDS operations have not been given a lot of thought; administrator, security expert and security analyst. For example a lot of configuration on a daily basis for the administrator (update new rules), security expert need to monitor new attack technique and write new rules, finally the security analyst is responsible in processing a huge number of alert manually on a daily basis.
- Since in the early 1990's the focus of research has always been on data reduction and classification, it is high time the research is diversified into new fields such as analyzing trend of attacks and making use of the payload captured by the IDS.

4.2   Future Research

- Develop IDS that could stop intrusion from happening.
- A method to estimate the cost of an attack or incident to an organization.
- Investigate the survival time of an infrastructure after being hit by a certain attack detected by the IDS

- Create an Intelligent IDS that is able to investigate the root cause of an incident from previous or historic events which lead to the incident.
- Reduce human's intervention in the day to day operations of the IDS; a fully automated IDS.

5   Conclusion

IDS technology has progress significantly since it first started in the 80's. Because of the ongoing cyber threats and crime, the development of the technology will never rest. From the review we did, it is obvious that every research conducted is to solve a limitation that exists in the system, to make it more resilient to combat all the attacks and misuse. However, there is still room for improvement. Mostly the improvement made today is because of the intrusion of yesterday. We are always being reactive, instead of proactive, which is why the technology will never be ahead of the attacks. The review has clearly exemplifies the progress made in the IDS technology throughout the years. The mechanism and tools of detecting attacks are abundantly available in the market. Nevertheless, the effectiveness and efficiency in processing the detected attacks in the process of providing the best solution in preventing incidents still remains to be desired. The question put forth by Denning in 1986 ' The important question is not whether we can detect a particular low-level action that exploit the system flaw, but whether intrusion that are manifest by activity that can be monitored, be detected' , is still remained unanswered and unsolved. Through this review we have outlined many upcoming research possibilities. However, for our future research we would be concentrating on the alert processing technique. The main aim is to further enhance the approach for a better and richer processed alert quality which would greatly benefit the incident handling.

References

1. Kemmerer, D., Vigna, G.: Intrusion detection: A brief history and overview. Computer 35(4), 27–30 (2002)
2. Peddabachigari, S., Abraham, A., Grosan, C., Thomas, J.: Modeling intrusion detection system using hybrid intelligent systems. Journal of Network and Computer Applications 30(1), 114–132 (2007)
3. Lunt, T.F.: Automated audit trail analysis and intrusion detection: A survey. In: 11th National Computer Security Conference (1988)
4. Dewan, M.F., Mohammad, Z.R.: Anomaly Network Intrusion Detection Based on Improved Self Adaptive Bayesian Algorithm. Journal of Computers 5(1) (2010)
5. Lunt, T.F., Tamaru, A., Gilham, F., Jagannathan, R., Jalali, C., Neumann, P.G., Javitz, H.S., Valdes, A., Garvey, T.D.: A Real-Time Intrusion-Detection Expert System (IDES). Final Technical Report, SRI International (1992)
6. Denning, D.E.: An Intrusion-Detection Model. IEEE Transactions on Software Engineering, 222–232 (1987), ANSI Std Z39-18
7. Richadson, K.: Network Based Intrusion Detection: A Review of Tecnologies (1999)

8. Kabiri, P., Ghorbani, A.A.: Research on intrusion Detection and Response: A Survey. International Journal of Network Security 1(2), 84–102 (2005)
9. Biermanm, E., Cloete, E., Venter, L.M.: A comparison of Intrusion Detection systems (2001)
10. Verwoerd, T., Hunt, R.: Intrusion detection techniques and approaches. Computer Communications 25(15), 1356–1365 (2002)
11. Mahmud, W.M., Agiza, H.N., Radwan, E.: Intrusion Detection Using Rough Set Parallel Genetic Programming Based Hybrid Model. International Journal of Computer Science and Network Security 9(10), 23–33 (2009)
12. Quinlan, J.R.: Induction of Decision Trees. Kluwer Academic Publishers, Boston (1986)
13. Tsai, C.F., Hsu, Y.F., Lin, C.Y., Lin, W.Y.: Intrusion Detection by machine learning: A review. Expert System with Application 36, 11994–12000 (2009)
14. Balajinath, B., Raghavan, S.V.: Intrusion detection through learning behavior model. Computer Communications 24(12), 1202–1212 (2001)
15. Zhang, Q., Hu, G., Feng, W.: Design and Performance Evaluation of a Machine Learning-Based Method for Intrusion Detection. In: Lee, R., Ma, J., Bacon, L., Du, W., Petridis, M. (eds.) SNPD 2010. SCI, vol. 295, pp. 69–83. Springer, Heidelberg (2010)
16. Kruegel, C., Tóth, T.: Using Decision Trees to Improve Signature-Based Intrusion Detection. In: Vigna, G., Kruegel, C., Jonsson, E. (eds.) RAID 2003. LNCS, vol. 2820, pp. 173–191. Springer, Heidelberg (2003)
17. Pikoulas, J., Buchan, W.J., Mannon, M., Triantafyllopoulos, K.: An Agent-based Bayesian Forecasting Model for Enhanced Network Security. In: Proceedings of the International Symposium and Workshop on Engineering of Computer Based Systems, pp. 247–254 (2001)
18. Chung, Y.-J., Kim, I.J., Lee, C.S., Im, E.-G., Won, D.H.: Design of an On-Line Intrusion Forecast System with a Weather Forecasting Model. In: Gavrilova, M.L., Gervasi, O., Kumar, V., Tan, C.J.K., Taniar, D., Laganá, A., Mun, Y., Choo, H. (eds.) ICCSA 2006. LNCS, vol. 3983, pp. 777–786. Springer, Heidelberg (2006)
19. Al-Mamory, S.O., Zhang, H.L.: A survey on IDS alerts processing techniques. In: Proceedings of the 6th Wseas International Conference on Information Security and Privacy (Isp 2007), pp. 69–78 (2007)
20. Mohamed, A.B., Norbik, B.I., Shanmugum, B.: Alert correlation using a novel clustering approach. In: 2012 International Conference on Communication Systems and Network Technologies (CSNT), Rajkot, India, pp. 720–725 (2012)
21. Shanmugam, B., Idris, N.B.: Improved Intrusion Detection System using Fuzzy Logic for Detecting Anamoly and Misuse type of Attacks. In: International Conference of Soft Computing and Pattern Recognition, pp. 212–217 (2009)
22. Nehinbe, J.O.: Automated Method for Reducing False Positives. In: Intelligent Systems, Modelling and Simulation (ISMS), Liverpool, pp. 54–59 (2010)
23. Sindhu, S.S.S., Geetha, S., Sivanath, S.S., Kannan, A.: A neuro-genetic ensemble short term forecasting framework for anomaly intrusion prediction. In: International Conference on Advanced Computing and Communications, pp. 181–184 (2007)

Experimental Investigations on Piezoelectric Based Prototype Actuator

Muralidhara, Rithesh Baliga B., Gokul R.,
Gregory Prashanth D'Souza, and Gireesh Madev Moger

Department of Mechanical Engineering, NMAM Institute of Technology, Karnataka, India
mr_kallya@yahoo.com

Abstract. Present positioning applications demand macro positioning range with micro/nano positioning accuracy. This paper describes the development of a new prototype actuator with piezoelectric stack actuator as a primary actuation system for micro/macro positioning applications. The displacement of the primary actuator is amplified by a hydraulic displacement amplification mechanism. A displacement amplification factor of 72.2 is observed at an actuation frequency of 1Hz which is in good agreement with the theoretically estimated value. The behavior of the prototype actuator is studied at different loads and frequencies.

Keywords: Piezoelectric stack actuator, hydraulic displacement amplification, actuator displacement.

1 Introduction

Piezo-actuators are widely used in different engineering applications because of their high dynamic response, high stiffness, high resolution and compact design. But they have limited displacement range i.e. Up to 0.1 %(1μm/mm) elongation of piezo-actuator [1], [2]. Though piezo-actuators have smaller displacement range they can generate large forces and have higher positioning accuracy in the order of micrometers and nanometers which make them suitable for micro and nano postioning applications [3]. Present positioning applications demand for macro positioning range with micro/nano positioning accuracy. Hence there is a need for amplification of displacement of piezo-actuators to make them suitable for macro/micro range positioning applications.

In recent years, researchers have developed different techniques to utilize the stack actuators in macro/micro positioning applications. Flexural displacement amplification system, hydraulic displacement amplification system and mechanism based amplification system (e.g. inchworm actuators) are used to amplify the displacement of a stack actuator. In flexural displacement amplification system, piezoelectric stacks are pre-stressed inside an elliptical metallic frame which produces larger displacement range i.e. up to 1% (10μm/mm) elongation of piezo-actuator and generates relatively smaller force [4]. Inchworm actuators make use sequence of clamping and releasing mechanism by using a piezoelectric material subjected to

S.G. Ponnambalam et al. (Eds.): IRAM 2012, CCIS 330, pp. 272–279, 2012.

electric field. Inchworm actuator produces a larger output force and smaller step displacement [5]. By providing the large number of repeated stepped motions larger displacements can be obtained.

In addition these two mechanisms, numerous fluidic mechanism having hydraulic amplification units were also developed to amplify the displacement of the piezoactutor [6-11]. Hydraulic displacement amplification technique is used in piezoelectric micro valves in Hydraulic Micro pumping Systems and Micro jet Flow Control device because power can be easily transmitted through hydraulic lines. Moreover, the Piezoelectric Hydraulic Pump which can easily work in conjunction with hydraulic motion control device have been extensively used since it helps in elimination of centralized pump of conventional system and thereby avoiding the losses in hydraulic line.

In this paper, a novel piezoelectric based prototype Actuator with hydraulic amplification mechanism is developed and experimentally investigated for its static and dynamic characteristics.

2   Piezoelectric Based Prototype Actuator

Figure 1 shows a piezoelectric based prototype actuator with piezoelectric stack actuator as a primary actuator with a hydraulic amplification unit which is used to amplify displacement. There are two sections, one with the larger cross sectional area with diameter of 50 mm i.e. oil reservoir and the other with smaller cross sectional area with diameter of 5.8mm i.e. inner cylinder. One end of oil reservoir is attached to diaphragm which is intern attached to the circular disc. The displacement of piezoactuator results in the movement of the oil from oil reservoir to the inner cylinder which moves the piston and hence there will be amplification of displacement. Work table is provided for the application of the load.

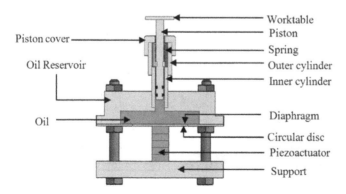

Fig. 1. Piezoelectric based prototype actuator

If V_1 is the volume of oil displaced by the plastic diaphragm from oil reservoir to the inner cylinder and V_2 the volume of the oil moved in to the inner cylinder. Then

$$V_1 = V_2 \tag{1}$$

$$A_1 L_1 = A_2 L_2 \tag{2}$$

where A_1 and A_2 are the cross sectional areas of oil reservoir and inner cylinder respectively and L_1 and L_2 are the stack and piston displacements respectively. The ratio of the piston displacement to the stack displacement which is defined as amplification ratio can be obtained as:

$$\frac{L_2}{L_1} = \frac{A_1}{A_2} \tag{3}$$

The theoretical amplification factor of the piezoelectric based prototype actuator AF_{th} is given as:

$$AF_{th} = \frac{D_1^2}{D_2^2} \tag{4}$$

where D_1 and D_2 are the diameters of oil reservoir and inner cylinder respectively. For the developed piezoelectric based prototype actuator, the theoretical amplification factor is found to be 74.32.

3   Experimental Setup

Figure 2 shows experimental setup for measuring the displacement characteristics of the prototype actuator which includes a signal generator, laser displacement sensor Opto-NCDT 1402, data acquisition system NI USB 6251, Voltage amplifier,

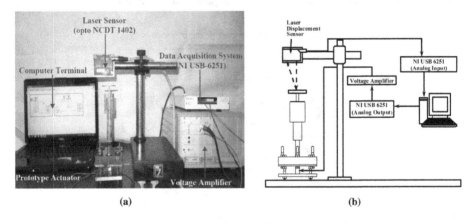

(a)   (b)

Fig. 2. Experimental Setup (a) Photograph of experimental setup (b) Block diagram of experimental setup

prototype actuator and a computer installed with LabVIEW software. Using LabVIEW software, a triangular signal is generated and fed to the voltage amplifier through NI USB 6251 data acquisition system. The amplitude of the signal is 7.5 Volts. A voltage amplifier amplifies the triangular voltage signal by a factor of 20. The amplified voltage signal is supplied to the prototype actuator. The laser sensor senses the displacement which is recorded on the computer through NI USB 6251 data acquisition system.

4   Results and Discussions

4.1   Displacement Characteristics of Stack Actuator (No Load) for 1Hz

Figure 3 shows the displacement characteristics of the piezoelectric stack actuator for a triangular input signal of amplitude 150V at a frequency of 1Hz. As the Voltage increases from zero, the stack actuator starts reacting to the applied voltage. The maximum displacement that was achieved is 11.5 μm as shown in Fig. 3(a).

Figure 3(b) shows the variations in the stack displacement with the voltage applied at a frequency of 1Hz. When the voltage is increased from 0 V to 150V, the displacement also picks up and reaches a maximum of 11.5 μm. In the second half of the cycle as the voltage reaches to 0V amplitude, a remnant displacement of approximately 2.9 μm was observed. This is due to the hysteresis behavior of the piezoactuator between the applied voltage and the resulting displacement. Also a time delay of 35ms is observed between the voltage input and the resulting displacement.

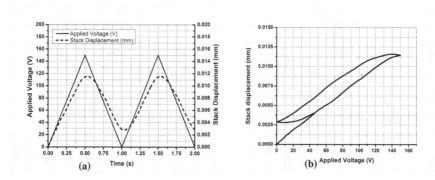

Fig. 3. Displacement characteristics of the Stack Actuator at frequency 1 Hz and no load condition (a) Voltage and Displacement variation with time (b) variation of displacement with applied voltage

4.2   Displacement Characteristics of Prototype Actuator

Figure 4(a) shows the displacement characteristics of the prototype actuator when a triangular voltage signal of 150V amplitude is supplied to the stack actuator at a frequency of 1Hz. The hydraulic displacement amplification system amplifies the stack displacement and is measured using the laser displacement sensor. As the voltage increases from 0V, the actuator system starts reacting to the applied voltage after a time lag of 0.08s. The maximum displacement achieved is 0.83 mm.

Figure 4(b) shows the variations in the amplified displacement with the applied Voltage for a frequency of 1Hz. In the second half of the cycle as the voltage decreases to 0V, the remnant displacement of 0.155mm is observed due to the hysteresis behavior of the stack actuator. Experimental amplification factor which is defined as ratio of displacement of prototype actuator to the displacement of the stack actuator is found to be 72.2. From Fig. 4(a) and (b), it is clear that up to a time of 0.1 s, which is corresponding to a input voltage signal of 30V, no considerable displacement is observed in the prototype actuator even though a displacement of 2.5 micrometer is observed in the stack actuator. This may be due to the expansion of the diaphragm and losses inside the hydraulic medium during the initial stage of stack displacement.

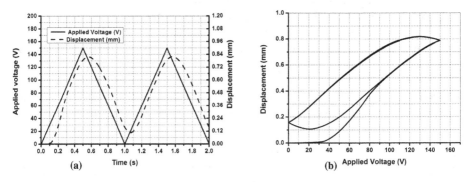

Fig. 4. Displacement characteristics of the prototype actuator at frequency 1 Hz and no load condition (a) Voltage and Displacement variation with time (b) variation of displacement with applied voltage

4.3   Displacement Characteristics at a Load of 0.1 kgf

A load of 0.1 kgf is applied to the prototype actuator and Fig. 5 shows the displacement characteristics of the prototype actuator when a triangular voltage signal of 150V amplitude is applied to the stack actuator at a frequency of 1Hz. A maximum displacement of 780 µm is observed as shown in the Fig. 5(a). When an external load is applied to the prototype actuator, the load acting on the stack actuator increases by a factor equivalent to the displacement amplification factor. Hence, when a load of 0.1kgf is applied to the prototype actuator, stack actuator would be experiencing a load of 7.22kgf. At this loading condition, the displacement of the stack actuator will reduce and hence resulted in reduction of the displacement of the prototype actuator from 830 µm to 780 µm. From the Fig. 5(a) and (b) it can also be observed that there is no considerable displacement of the prototype actuator till an input of 40V.

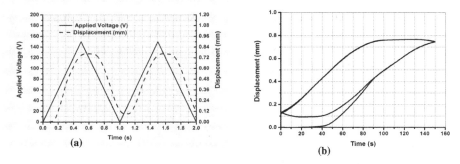

Fig. 5. Displacement characteristics of the prototype actuator at frequency 1 Hz and 1N load (a) variation of Voltage and Displacement with time (b) variation of displacement with applied voltage

4.4   Effect of External Load and Actuation Frequency on the Prototype Actuator

The developed prototype actuator is checked for various loads varying from no-load to 0.2kgf and the maximum displacement achieved for various loads is plotted as shown in Fig. 6(a). The maximum displacement observed to be decreasing with increasing load. This is mainly due to the increase in amplified load that is acting on the stack actuator which is expected to result in reduced stack actuator displacement. Furthermore, the prototype actuator is subjected to different actuation frequencies ranging from 0.5 Hz to 15 Hz without loading. The corresponding displacements are acquired using the laser displacement sensor and the amplification factors are estimated and are plotted as shown in Fig. 6(b). At 0.5 Hz, an amplification factor of 74 is obtained which is very close to the theoretical value. The amplification factor is found to be decreasing with increase in frequency as shown Fig. 6(b).

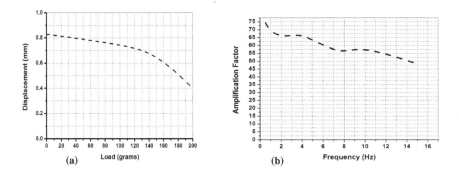

Fig. 6. (a)Variation of maximum displacement for varying load at 1 Hz (b)Variation of amplification factor at different frequency at no-load condition

4.5   Step Response

A step signal of 100V is applied to the stack actuator and the corresponding displacement of the prototype actuator is plotted as shown in the Fig. 7. The output of the actuator reached to a displacement value of 0.55mm after a delay of 375milliseconds as shown in the Fig. 7.

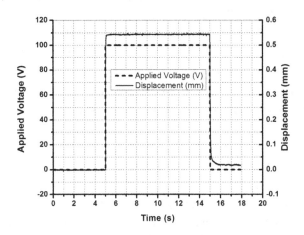

Fig. 7. Variation of maximum displacement for varying load

5   Conclusions

In this research work, a piezoelectric based prototype actuator was developed with hydraulic amplification mechanism to amplify displacement of stack actuator. Experiments are carried out to measure the displacement of the stack actuator and the amplified displacement of the prototype actuator to estimate the displacement amplification factor. A displacement amplification factor of 72.2 is obtained at an actuation frequency of 1Hz which is in close agreement with the theoretically estimated value. Experiments are also carried out at varying frequencies and 3dB bandwidth of the actuator is found to be 13Hz. Experiments are carried out at varying loads to investigate the load carrying capacity of the prototype actuator and the amplitude of the displacement found to be decreasing mainly due to increase in amplified load that is acting on the stack actuator. This novel design of prototype actuator can be used in low frequency positioning applications such as tool and workpiece positioning in micromachining and sample positioning in a precision microscope which demands for macro positioning range and micro positioning accuracy.

References

1. Hubbard, N.B., Culpepper, M.L., Howell, L.L.: Actuators for Micropositioners and Nanopositioners. Trans. of the ASME 59, 324–334 (2006)
2. Pozzi, M., King, T.: Piezoelectric actuators in micro positioning. J. Engineering Science and Education, 31–36 (2001)
3. Goldfarb, M., Celanovic, N.: Modeling Piezoelectric Stack Actuators for Control of Micromanipulation. J. IEEE Control Systems, 69–79 (1997)
4. Petitniot, J.L., Des Rochettes, H.M., Leconte, P.: Experimental Assessment and Further Development of Amplified Piezo Actuators for Active Flap Devices. In: 8th: International Conference on New Actuators, Bremen, pp. 181–184 (2002)
5. Li, J., Sedaghati, R., Dargahi, J., Waechter, D.: Design and development of a new piezoelectric linear Inchworm actuator. J. Mechatronics, 651–681 (2005)
6. Liu, F., Oates, W.S.: Piezohydraulic Actuation for Next Generation Microjet Flow Control. In: Proceedings of the ASME Conference on Smart Materials, Adaptive Structures and Intelligent Systems, pp. 1–10 (2008)
7. Roberts, D.C., Li, H., Steyn, J.L., Yaglioglu, O., Spearing, S.M., Schmidt, M.A., Hagood, N.W.: A Piezoelectric Microvalve for Compact High-Frequency, High-Differential Pressure Hydraulic Micropumping Systems. J. Microelectromechanical Systems 12, 81–92 (2003)
8. Chaudhuri, A., Wereley, N.: Compact hybrid electrohydraulic actuators using smart materials: A review. J. Intelligent Material Systems and Structures 23, 597–634 (2011)
9. Lynch, C.S., Mauck, L.D.: Piezoelectric Hydraulic Pump Development. J. Intelligent Material Systems and Structures 11, 758–764 (2000)
10. Lynch, C.S., Oates, W.S.: Piezoelectric Hydraulic Pump System Dynamic Model. J. Intelligent Material Systems and Structures 12, 737–744 (2001)
11. Yoon, H.S., Washington, G.: A Millimeter-Stroke Piezoelectric Hybrid Actuator using Hydraulic Displacement Amplification Mechanism. In: IEEE International Symposium of Industrial Economics, pp. 2809–2813 (2006)

Development of Mechanical Actuator
for Deep-Hole Measurement System

Md. Hazrat Ali[1,*], Akio Katsuki[2], Takao Sajima[2,]
Hiroshi Murakami[3], and Syuhei Kurokawa[2]

[1] Graduate School of Engineering, Kyushu University, 744 Motooka, Nishi-ku,
Fukuoka 812-8581, Japan
[2] Kyushu University, Fukuoka, Japan
[3] Kyushu Sangyo University, Fukuoka, Japan
hazratalidu07@yahoo.com

Abstract. This paper presents a new type of mechanical actuator which is used to help in measuring deep holes that carry up to a load of 26kg during measurement. Often the measurement probe`s attitude is misaligned due to acting force on it. Actuator prevents or controls the misalignment of such probe during measurement. In this research, the complete measurement system consists of a servo motor, a laser diode, a laser interferometer, an optical system as well as the integrated computer system. The main purpose of this research is to develop the new type of actuator which can control the attitude (position and inclination) of a measurement probe. The experimental results show that it is possible to carry mechanically the loads up to 26kg of the measurement probe during measurement of deep-holes. In this paper, the developed actuator's mechanical function and its performance have been discussed with the experimental results.

Keywords: Actuator, Accuracy, Deep-hole, Laser Interferometer, Measurement.

1 Introduction

Mechanical Actuators are used as a mechanism to translate mechanical motion (often rotary) into linear motion or with the help of gearing into rotary motion at a different speed. These actuators are typically part of a larger system which includes a power drive, mechanical interconnects, and feedback devices to control the motion of multiple devices.

In mechanical systems measurement is very important in order to observe the efficiency of the machines, tools etc. Previous works cannot carry a load up to 26kg [2-6]. Measurement of a deep hole's accuracy is very difficult. Mechanical actuator can help to ease this problem [2]. Previous studies that have been used the piezoelectric actuators of attitude control system, generates several problems such as the allowable load is small, the stroke of the supporting pad is small, creates

---

* Corresponding author.

S.G. Ponnambalam et al. (Eds.): IRAM 2012, CCIS 330, pp. 280–287, 2012.

hysteresis loop, and it is expensive [6].The measurement of deep hole also possible to compare with the data acquired by electric micrometer and roundness tester [3]. Deep-hole with 3m-length and 63mm-diameter was measured by the measurement unit with the cylindrical long measurement bar [5]. In our past study [4], measurement unit which can measure holes with a diameter of 70 to 168 mm was developed and discussed. In the piezoelectric actuator stroke is 0.35mm, allowable load is 16kg [4]. Response speed is also very fast.

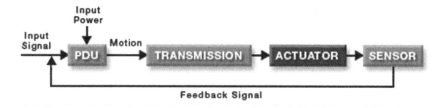

Fig. 1. Functional diagram of a Mechanical Actuator [1]

2   Experimental Apparatus

2.1   Mechanical Actuator

Figures 2, 3 and 4 show the experimental apparatus of a mechanical actuator system that was used earlier for other measurement purpose. Figure 1 has the piezoelectric actuators whereas fig.3 does not have piezoelectric actuators. In fig. 3, the stepping motor is connected to the actuator in order to push and pull it upwards as well as downwards respectively. Worm and worm wheel transfer the rotational speed to the supporting shaft through belt and pulley system. The supporting shaft's movement is controlled via servo motor controller. This experiment was examined in relation to the load and speed of the supporting shaft.

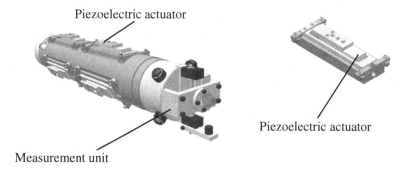

Piezoelectric actuator

Piezoelectric actuator

Measurement unit

Fig. 2. Measurement system

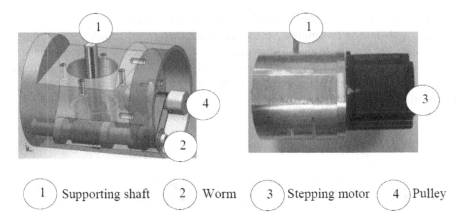

(1) Supporting shaft   (2) Worm   (3) Stepping motor   (4) Pulley

Fig. 3. Mechanical actuator

The worm and worm wheel system integrated with pulley and belt is essential in order to transform the rotational motion into linear motion. It was done by calculating the appropriate gear ratio.

Fig. 4. Lifting shaft connected with pulley

2.2   Combined Actuator

Figure.5 (a), (b), and (c) show the possible controlling method of the developed actuators instead of using six piezoelectric actuators. Combined actuators can be controlled in the ways showed in fig.5 (a), (b), and (c).The alignment or arrangement of the actuators in (a) are based on 90^0 inclination angle. It refers that each actuator is positioned 45 degree angular inclined ways with respect to each other. Similarly, in (b), and (c) are 60^0, and 120^0 respectively. The alignments can be controlled using servo motors and controllers separately. Equation (1) is to control the angle of the actuator and the shaft speed. Where v represent the shaft speed mm/s and θ represent the angle of the actuator with respect to each other. Figure 5 (c) is the most effective control strategy for this case where a measurement unit attached to the front side of the combined actuators. The length of each actuator is 110mm and diameter is 70mm. The combined actuators total length is 660mm.

$$v = 0.8928 sinh\theta. \tag{1}$$

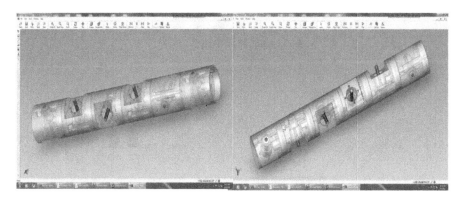

(a) 0,90,180,270,360,0   (b) 0, 60,120,180,240,300

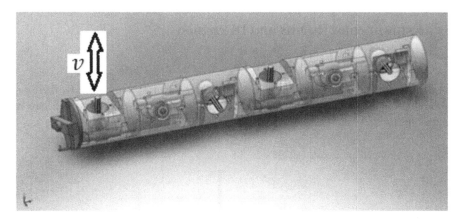

(c) 180, 60, 240, 180, 60, 240

Fig. 5. Combined six actuators and its controlling methods (a), (b), and (c)

3   Experimental Methods

The load was set on the supporting shaft, and subsequently actuated the stepping motor while observing the operating conditions. The data for shaft movements were recorded using a laser length measuring interferometer. The load on the supporting shaft was set while the stepper motor run 25s. Once the motor totally stopped then the data was measured using a scale while observing the operating conditions. The optimum load was between 1.5kg ~ 26kg. The measurement was observed under the following conditions. 1) Shaft speed 0.64 mm/s at 0.9° per pulse, 2) Shaft speed 0.32 mm / s at 0.45° per pulse , 3) Shaft speed 0.16mm / s at 0.225 ° per pulse. Figure 6 shows the basic experimental apparatus of the system. The laser interferometer on the top is to record the lifting displacement in mm. Finally the data was calibrated to its actual value by considering the experimental conditions.

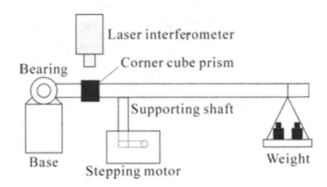

Fig. 6. Experimental apparatus

4   Experimental Results and Discussion

4.1   Determination of Optimum Speed

Based on several experimental data it was observed that at some speeds, there are some remarkable changes in the rise and fall and at some other speeds there are no changes in rise and fall.

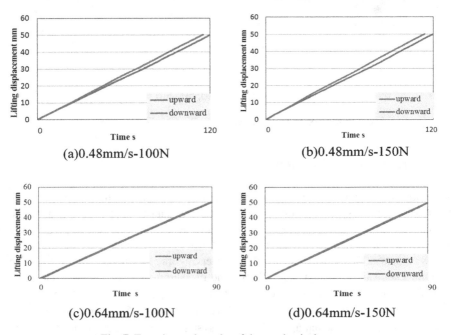

Fig. 7. Experimental results of the mechanical actuator

Low speeds sometimes give better result but it takes longer time so the optimum speed is necessary to complete the tests. In figs.7 (c), (d) and 8(a), compared to that of the piezoelectric actuator (fig.3), hysteresis was not found. Sometimes, the speed becomes unstable, and it causes due to slip of the supporting shaft via belt and changes in torque of the stepping motor by pulse frequency through driver and controller.

4.2   Determination of Allowable Load

Speed controller was set to VR800 and VR600 as stable condition for the experiments. During our investigation in each load we found the responses shown in fig.7 and fig.8. The important factor is that the instability of the shaft increases with the increment of the speed.

4.3   Mechanical Actuator (0.64 mm /s-100N)

Figure 6(c, d) show that the shaft speed 0.64mm/s is appropriate for the load of 150N.It refers that this actuator can support a load of 150N during the experiment with an optimum shaft speed of 0.64mm/s.

4.4   Mechanical Actuator (0.48 mm / s-200N)

Figure 8 shows that stability of the supporting shaft due to loads was observed when the shaft speed is 0.48mm / s. At this speed an optimum load of 200N can easily be carried during the measurement experiments.

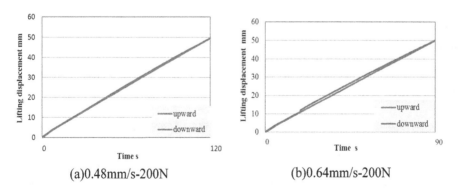

(a)0.48mm/s-200N   (b)0.64mm/s-200N

Fig. 8. Result of speed experiment

Compare to the piezoelectric actuator in fig.9 we can observe that the lifting stroke is 0.35mm in piezoelectric actuator whereas in the developed system the stroke is 50mm. In the developed system the hysteresis error does not exist. Measurement error is not likely to occur even if the load varies during the measurement.

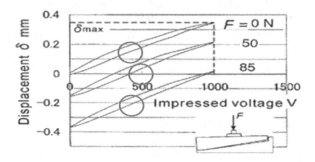

Fig. 9. Hysteresis of piezoelectric actuator

5   Conclusion

The new type actuators advantages over piezoelectric actuator can be summarized as below.

    1) The developed actuator's stroke is larger.

    2) Its allowable load is greater than the piezoelectric actuator which is improved from 160N to 200N.

    3) There is no hysteresis error in the mechanical actuator.

    4) Inexpensive

    5) Attitude control of the probe is easier.

On the other hand, the advantage of the piezoelectric actuator is its response speed which is very fast. If we need high response actuator then piezoelectric has better performance.

References

1. Precision motion control products and systems, http://www.moog.com
2. Katsuki, A., et al.: Development of a Laser-Guided Deep-Hole Measurement System: Automatically Adjustable probe to variable hole diameter, Kanazawa, Japan (2011)
3. Katsuki, A., Onikura, H., Sajima, T., Murakami, H., Sato, T., Nishi, H., Pietri, V., Ali, M.H.: Development of a Laser-Guided Deep-Hole Measurement System with Lower Production Cost. In: 25th Annual Meeting of the American Society for Precision Engineering Atlanta, USA (2010)
4. Katsuki, A., Onikura, H., Sajima, T., Murakami, H., Doi, T., Sato, T., Ali, M.H., Berjaud, A.: Development of a Laser-guided Deep-hole Measurement System with High-performance Mechanical Actuators. In: The 26th ASPE Annual Meeting, Denver, USA, November 13-18 (2011)

5. Katsuki, A., Ali, M.H., Sajima, T., Murakami, H., Onikura, H.: Development of a Laser-guided Deep-hole Measurement System: Usage of Long Measurement Bar. In: Mechanical Engineering Conference, Chittagong, Bangladesh (December 2011)
6. Katsuki, A., Onikura, H., Sajima, T., Mohri, A., Moriyama, T., Hamano, Y., Murakami, H.: Precision Engineering 35, 221–227 (2011); Development of a Practical Laser Guided Deep Hole Boring Tool: Improvement in Guiding Strategy

PD-Fuzzy Logic Controller Design for Position Control of Intelligent Pneumatic Actuator System

Ahmad 'Athif Mohd Faudzi Faudzi[1,*], M. Asyraf Azman[1], Khairuddin bin Osman[2], Nu'man Din Mustafa[1], and Koichi Suzumori[3]

[1] Department of Mechatronics and Robotics Engineering, Faculty of Electrical Engineering, Universiti Teknologi Malaysia, 81310 Skudai, Malaysia
[2] Department of Industrial Electronics, Faculty of Electrical and Electronics, Universiti Teknikal Malaysia Melaka, Hang Tuah Jaya, 76100 Durian Tunggal, Melaka, Malaysia
[3] Graduate School of Natural Science and Technology, Okayama University, Okayama, Japan
athif@fke.utm.my

Abstract. Intelligent Pneumatic Actuator is a system that has been developed for application that requires better control and accuracy. The purpose of this paper is to present a controller design for position control of an Intelligent Pneumatic Actuator (IPA) system using Proportional-Derivative Fuzzy Logic Controller (PDFLC) and PID Controller. The controller is designed based on 3rd order transfer function of the system. The performance of the designed PDFLC controller is tested to the actuator position control in MATLAB environment and the results show fast response and good stability. The simulation result is compared and analyzed with PID Controller to illustrate the performance of the proposed controller. The result obtain in this paper are useful towards a proposed Pneumatic Actuated Ball Beam System (PABBS).

Keywords: Intelligent Pneumatic Actuator (IPA), Proportional-Derivative Fuzzy Logic Controller (PDFLC), PID controller.

1 Introduction

Pneumatic actuator is a device that converts energy in the form of compressed air into motion. Pneumatic actuators are widely used in industrial robotics and automation, such as drilling, gripping, spraying, packaging and other applications [1]. However, the non-linearity characteristic of a pneumatic actuators causes difficulties in controlling the system. This non-linerity characteristic is occured due to the valve dead zone problems, mass flow rate parameters and compliance variation [2].

Many previous works try to solve problems of the controller design for position control. One of the well known intelligent controller such as fuzzy logic was proposed to control the pneumatic systems [3]. Fuzzy Logic Control (FLC) method approach is introduced by Mamdani based on Lotfi Zadeh's earlier development of linguistic approach and system analysis on fuzzy sets [3,4]. Fuzzy Logic Controller shows a

---

* Corresponding author.

S.G. Ponnambalam et al. (Eds.): IRAM 2012, CCIS 330, pp. 288–295, 2012.
© Springer-Verlag Berlin Heidelberg 2012

good performance as a controller design in giving a desirable performance which give the smallest possible value for the rise time, overshoot and the settling time [5].

This paper presents combination of Proportional-Derivative (PD) and Fuzzy Logic Controller (FLC) as a proposed Proportional-Derivative Fuzzy Logic Controller (PDFLC) in MATLAB-Simulink platform. The algorithm is applied to an intelligent pneumatic actuator (IPA) system which integrates pneumatic cylinder with sensors and valves in a single system. PID controller is used as a reference for validation of PDFLC because of its simplicity, easy to use and do not required the plant model to perform the controller [6-7]. With PDFLC, the overshoot for close loop response will be minimized and yield a good accuracy for position control. The flow of the paper starts with the introduction, Intelligent Pneumatic Actuators plant, controller design, results and discussion and finally the conclusion section.

2   Intelligent Pneumatic Actuators Plant

The Intelligent Pneumatic Actuator (IPA) plant as shown in Fig. 1 which was develop by A. A. M. Faudzi *et al.* [8-11]. The IPA has five extensive elements which are optical encoder, laser stripe code, Programmable System on a Chip (PSoC) board, pressure sensor (KOGANEI: PSU-EM-S) and valves (KOGANEI: EB10ES1-PS-6W). The optical encoder is used to read the laser stripe code for position reading and pressure sensor is used to verify the chamber pressure to perform control action of the cylinder. The cylinder applies two on/off valves (two ports two positions) for driving the cylinder. A miniature valve is attached at the end of the cylinder and a microcontroller board which consists of PSoC as the central processing unit that is fixed at the top of the actuator. The body part of the actuator is a linear double acting cylinder (KOGANEI – HA Twinport Cylinders) with two air inlets and one exhaust outlet. The actuator has 200mm stroke and force up to 100N. The 0.169mm laser stripe pitch can give high accuracy for position control.

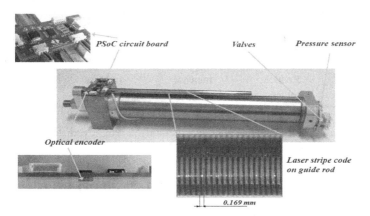

Fig. 1. Intelligent Pneumatic Actuator Plant

3   Controller Design

Pneumatic position control research is rapidly increased since 1990s [12]. Many approaches have been investigated and developed in attempt to overcome difficulties in pneumatic actuators. This research will discuss two controllers design strategy. The first design is the classical control of Proportional-Integral-Derivative (PID) Controller [3, 13-14] and the second controller design is the Fuzzy Logic Controller; where Proportional-Derivative Fuzzy Logic Controller (PDFLC) is developed. PDFLC is implemented for position tracking control of IPA system and will be validated with the PID Controller.

3.1   PID Controller

The mathematical description of a general PID Controller is given by equation (1).

$$U(t) = K_p \left(e(t) + \frac{1}{T_i} \int_0^t e(\tau) d\tau + T_d \frac{d}{dt} e(t) \right) \tag{1}$$

where, $U(t)$ is a control signal applied to plant K_p, K_i and K_d are the proportional, integral and derivative gains, respectively. The selection of these K_p, K_i and K_d values will cause variations in the observed response with the respect to the desired response. In general, the dependency is presented in Table.1. From the table, it is observed that PI-Controller reduces steady state error, PD-Controller causes steady state conditions to respond faster, and PID-Controller attains all the advantages of individual control actions. Therefore, in order to achieve the desired characteristic, the selection of controller's combinations and the algorithm for tuning the controller gains must be appropriate.

Table 1. Kp, K_i and K_d Characteristic

CL Response	Rise Time, Tr	%OS	Settling Time, Ts	Steady-state error, ess
K_p	Reduce	Increase	Small change	Reduce
K_i	Reduce	Increase	Increase	Eliminate
K_d	Small change	Reduce	Reduce	Small change

In this research, the Ziegler–Nichols method is employed to tune the PID parameters and manual adjustment using MATLAB.

3.2   Proportional-Derivative Fuzzy Logic Controller (PDFLC)

The Proportional-Derivative Fuzzy Logic Controller (PDFLC) Simulink Model design is shown in Fig. 2. The model consists of the Fuzzy Logic Controller block and IPA block which is represented by the transfer function (TF) of the system. The TF was previously obtained using System Identification method. The Fuzzy Logic Controller box contains references to a fuzzy logic inference system. The inference system has three linguistic variables which are the two inputs (error and rate of change of error) and the output (control signal). The fuzzy logic inference system for the PDFLC contains a set of fuzzy logic rules that define the behavior of the system in relation between the error signal, rate of change of error signal and the control signal of the controller [15]. The tuning of the Fuzzy Logic Controller can be achieved by either adjusting the range of the universe of discourse for the linguistic variables, adjusting the input and output scaling gains of the controller or adjusting the number, type and positions of the membership functions used.

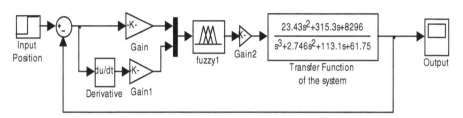

Fig. 2. Simulink Model for PD-Fuzzy Logic Controller

The PDFLC membership function for the output of the Fuzzy Logic Controller block is shown in Fig. 3. Table 2 shows the relationship between the input and output (fuzzy logic rules) in tabular linguistic format. The input consist of five fuzzy set where BN = Big Negative, SN = Small Negative, Z = Zero, SP = Small Positive and BP = Big Positive. The output consist of three fuzzy sets where V2 = Valve 2, Off = off and V1 = Valve 1. The output is either 1 or -1 similar to concept of on/off valve which activates or deactivates the valve.

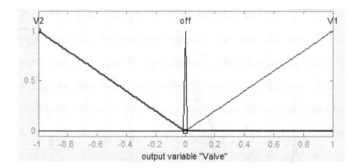

Fig. 3. Membership Function plot for output of Fuzzy Logic Controller block (control action)

Table 2. Proportional-Derivative Fuzzy Logic Rules

Error rate \ Error	BN	SN	Off	SP	BP
BN	V2	V2	V2	V2	-
SN	V2	V2	V2	-	V1
Off	V2	V2	Off	V1	V1
SP	V2	-	V1	V1	V1
BP	-	V1	V1	V1	V1

4   Results and Discussion

The result of PID Controller design using square wave input is shown in Fig. 4(a). From the result, PID Controller gives good response but the time response is slow and has a small overshoot. This is possibly due to the inability of on/off valve to open and close at its capable rate [16]. In addition, the starting result of step response has a small friction and small overshoot.

To overcome this problem, Proportional-Derivative Fuzszy Logic Controller (PDFLC) is designed with tuned K_p and K_d. Figure 4(b) shows the result of PDFLC for step input signal. The comparison of PID Controller and PDFL Controller with square wave input is shown in Fig. 5. The PDFL Controller shows better performance of faster response and better stability compared to PID Controller. Table 3 shows the comparison for step response position tracking between PID Controller and PDFL Controller analysis.

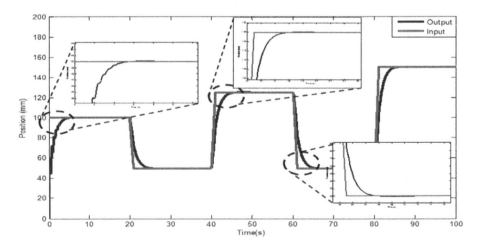

Fig. 4(a). PID Controller result

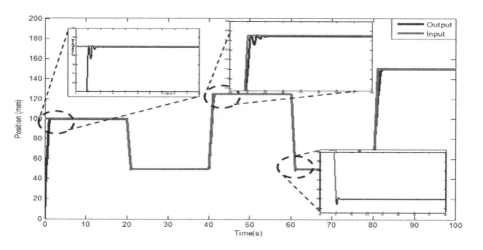

Fig. 4(b). Proportional-Derivative Fuzzy Logic Controller (PDFLC) result

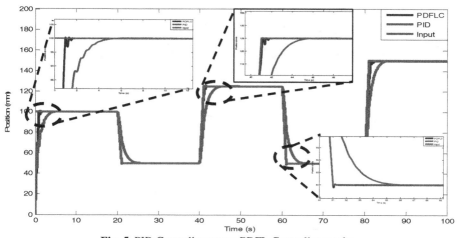

Fig. 5. PID Controller versus PDFL Controller results

Table 3. Comparison for step responses position tracking between PID Controller and PDFL Controller analysis results

Analysis	PID Controller	PDFL Controller
Percent Overshoot (%OS)	0.2%	0.1%
Peak Time (Tp)	6.86s	1.33s
Settling Time (Ts)	3.69s	1.27s
Rise Time (Tr)	2.18s	0.76s
Percent Steady State Error (%ess)	0.001%	0.08%

5   Conclusion

In this paper, controller design using PID Controller and Proportional-Derivative Fuzzy Logic Controller (PDFLC) has been analyzed. The PID Controller is used to validate the PDFL Controller performance. To perform comparison between both controllers, the criterion for measuring the response is identified. The most common criterion of comparison are the percentage of overshoot (%OS), peak time (TP), settling time (TS), rise time (TR) and percent steady state error (%ess), PDFL Controller is more stable and give faster response than PID Controller for the IPA position control. Both of these characteristics, stability and fast response are important in developing an application of Pneumatic Actuated Ball Beam System (PABBS) as shown in Fig. 6.

Ball beam system is a basic stabilizing system that has been used widely using DC motor. In this paper, the ball beam system will apply the IPA instead of DC motor as it actuator. By using PDFLC, it is hoped that this application will have fast response and stable in controlling the ball movement.

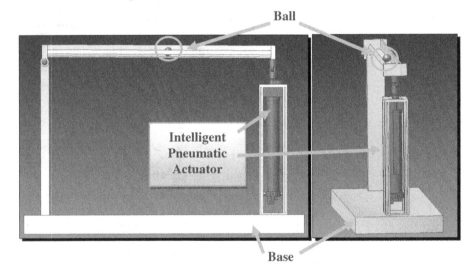

Fig. 6. Proposed Stabilizing System (Ball Beam)

Acknowledgements. The authors would like to thank Universiti Teknologi Malaysia (UTM) by UTM-NAS Grant No R.J130000.7723.4P008, Ministry of Higher Education (MOHE) Malaysia and Okayama University for their support.

References

1. Rahmat, M.F., Salim, S.N., Faudzi, A.M., Ismail, Z.H., Samsudin, S.I., Sunar, N.H., Jusoff, K.: Non-linear Modeling and Cascade Control of an Industrial Pneumatic Actuator System (2011)

2. Priyandoko, G., Mailah, M., Jamaluddin, H.: Vehicle Active Suspension System Using Skyhook Adaptive Neuro Active Force Control. Mechanical Systems and Signal Processing 23(3), 855–868 (2009)
3. Narayana, E.V., Bonu, V.S., Mallikarjuna Rao, G.: PID Versus Fuzzy Logic Based Intelligent Controller Design for a Non Linear Satellite's Attitude Control: Performance Analysis using MATLAB/Simulink. International Journal Of Advanced Engineering Sciences And Technologies 11(1), 190–195 (2011)
4. Franklin, G.F., David Powell, J., Emami-Naeini, A.: Feedback Control of Dynamic System. Pearson Education Ltd. (2006)
5. Nagi, F., Perumal, L.: Optimization of fuzzy controller for minimum time response. Mechatronics 19(3), 325–333 (2009)
6. Kiam Heong, A., Chong, G., Yun, L.: PID control system analysis, design, and technology. IEEE Transactions on Control Systems Technology 13(4), 559–576 (2005)
7. Silva, G.J., Datta, A., Bhattacharyya, S.P.: New results on the synthesis of PID controllers. IEEE Transactions on Automatic Control 47(2), 241–252 (2002)
8. Faudzi, A.A.M., Suzumori, K., Wakimoto, S.: Distributed Physical Human Machine Interaction Using Intelligent Pneumatic Cylinders. In: International Symposium on Micro-NanoMechatronics and Human Science (MHS 2008), pp. 249–254 (2008)
9. Faudzi, A.A.M., Suzumori, K., Wakimoto, S.: Design and Control of New Intelligent Pneumatic Cylinder for Intelligent Chair Tool Application. In: IEEE/ASME International Conference on Advanced Intelligent Mechatronics (AIM 2009), pp. 1909–1914 (2009)
10. Faudzi, A.A.M., Suzumori, K., Wakimoto, S.: Development of Pneumatic Actuated Seating System to aid Chair Design. In: IEEE/ASME International Conference on Advanced Intelligent Mechatronics (AIM 2010), pp. 1035–1040 (2010)
11. Faudzi, A.A.M.: Development of Intelligent Pneumatic Actuators and Their Applications to Physical Human-Mechine Interaction System., Ph.D. thesis, The Graduate School of Natural Science and Technology, Okayama University, Japan (2010)
12. Rahmat, M.F., Sunar, N.H., Salim, S.N.S., Abidin, M.S.Z., Fauzi, A.A.M., Ismail, Z.H.: Review On Modeling And Controller Desig. In: Pneumatic Actuator Control System. International Journal On Smart Sensing And Intelligent Systems 4(4) (December 2011)
13. Van Varseveld, R.B., Bone, G.M.: Accurate position control of a pneumatic actuator using on/off solenoid valves. IEEE/ASME Transactions on Mechatronics 2, 195–204 (1997)
14. Fok, S., Ong, E.: Position control and repeatability of a pneumatic rodless cylinder system for continuous positioning. Robotics and Computer-Integrated Manufacturing 15, 365–371 (1999)
15. Khan, S., Abdulazeez, S.F., et al.: Design and implementation of an optimal fuzzy logic controller using genetic algorithm. Journal of Computer Science 4(10), 799–806 (2008)
16. Adnan, R., Rahiman, M.H.F., Samad, A.M.: Model identification and controller design for real-time control of hydraulic cylinder. In: 2010 6th International Colloquium Signal Processing and Its Applications (CSPA), pp. 1–4 (2010)

Design of an Acceleration Sensor Embedded RFID (SE-RFID) Tag for Highway Guardrail Monitoring

Muhammad S. Khan, Ardhendu Saha, and Hai Deng

Department of Electrical and Computer Engineering
Florida International University, Miami, FL, USA
{mkhan055,asaha007,hai.deng}@fiu.edu

Abstract. An acceleration sensor embedded semi-passive RFID tag has been successfully designed and prototyped for highway guardrail monitoring. The tag can sense acceleration of the tagged guardrail in 3 directions (X, Y & Z) and successfully communicate with a nearby reader based on the *EPC* Generation 2 protocol. A complete frame structure has also been defined to fit the dynamic data within the standardized framework. The sensor tag data can be further relayed to a remote data processing center via WLAN and the Internet.

Keywords: Wireless sensor, radio frequency identification, RFID tags, guardrail monitoring.

1 Introduction

It has been estimated that about one third of highway collisions are the ones between vehicle and guardrail [1]. A study conducted by Fatality Analysis Reporting System (FARS) revealed that about 46% of highway accidents in US between 2000-2005 involved cars crashing into the guardrail [2]. Therefore, it is critical for highway management and law enforcement to have an effective and practical way of monitoring highway guardrail in real time and being able to locate the collision spot immediately once such collisions occur. There are possible ways to monitor highway safety and collisions including using video image monitoring [3], [4]. However, highways in rural areas are generally not well lit and motion-based acceleration sensing is argued to be more effective in monitoring and locating possible 24-hour highway vehicle-guardrail collision incidents [1]. Hence, in this work we are set to design an acceleration-based sensing approach for monitoring highway guardrail in real time.

An acceleration sensor based wireless network solution was reported in [1] for highway guardrail monitoring. During a collision between running vehicle and guardrails, whenever the acceleration impact level recorded by the wireless sensor units attached to the guardrails crosses a preset value, the collision information is transmitted to the remote data processing center via using *ZigBee* technology, i.e. IEEE 802.15.4 short distance communication protocol. However, in the reported approach, the large power consumption by the wireless sensors and their high production and maintenance costs make their widespread adoption impractical.

S.G. Ponnambalam et al. (Eds.): IRAM 2012, CCIS 330, pp. 296–302, 2012.

Therefore, alternative more power efficient and cost-effective wireless sensors are needed for highway guardrail monitoring.

Recently RFID technology has been applied to many different technological fields including wireless sensing, system automation, security monitoring, robotic sensing, and etc. [5- 8]. Integration of RFID into the wireless sensor networks has enabled the concept of ubiquitous sensing and computing feasible and practical [5], [9]. The most intriguing part of expanding RFID functions is the inclusion of sensing capability in RFID tags. The distinguish feature of RFID sensing tags are energy-efficient and cost-effective. In [10], Deng et al., proposed two kinds of possible architectures for sensor-embedded RFID (SE-RFID) tag network, which has been used in sensor RFID tag design. Passive RFID tags embedded with different sensors such as corrosion, humidity, pressure, or temperature sensor haven been reported [5], [11-13]. Since passive tags operate through the energy absorbed from the electromagnetic wave radiated by the reader, they are normally compact, durable and inexpensive. However, the shortcoming of passive sensing RFID tags is that they cannot acquire the sensing data if not in the reader's integration range. In this work, an acceleration sensor RFID tag with semi-passive structure is designed for guardrail monitoring to improve the sensing capability and energy-efficiency of the system. The low-power and semi-passive acceleration sensing RFID tag uses an internal tiny power source to power the sensor to implement the functions of monitoring, processing and triggering data transmission. But the power for providing the energy for the other parts of the part is still from the reader radiation.

2   Sensor-Embedded RFID

Though a RFID tag is well known for its ability of identifying the tagged object based on the information stored inside it, it is hardly a sensor itself. Normally it cannot acquire real-time data from the outer world without having a sensor integrated in it. SE-RFID, a newer generation of the conventional RFID tag, can sense and acquire information from the varying environments, and further communicate with the reader using the RFID communication protocol [8], [9], [14].

Based on the power management, SE-RFID tag can be classified into three major types [15], [16]: i) passive tags which perform the sensing operation only when they are within the interrogation zone of the reader; ii) semi-passive tags with an internal power source powering sensing and data processing operations and data transmission is completely performed via the reader's radiated energy [17] and iii) active tags with data acquiring, processing and transmission powered by the internal power source of the tag. Figure 1 shows the block diagram of an acceleration sensor embedded semi-passive RFID tag structure used in this design.

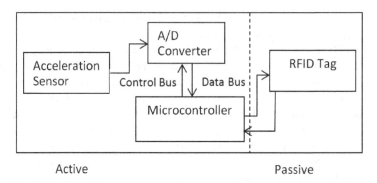

Active   Passive

Fig. 1. Semi-passive SE-RFID tag structure

3   SE-RFID Tag Design

With an aim to achieve a very low power and affordable design goal, the acceleration
sensor embedded tag has been designed with the commercially available low power
and low cost components. The schematic diagram of the design is shown in Figure 2.
In the design, we have chosen an acceleration sensor IC, ADXL330 from Analog
Devices which can sense the vibration of the guardrail by generating an acceleration
data in real time. The sensitivity of this sensor: input range of this sensor is ±3.3g and
the output is typically 300mV/g along the X, Y & Z axis. The sensor is connected to an
AT Mega48v which is a low power 8 bit microcontroller. The microcontroller
monitors the output pin of the sensor IC periodically and compares it with a preset
threshold value. Whenever acceleration level crosses the threshold value, the
microcontroller outputs an ID frame according to the EPC Generation 2 protocol and
a part of the serial number field is modified based the sensor data. In this design, the
serial number field is consisted of two sub fields: a constant field corresponding to the
reduced, unique ID of the tag and a variable field carrying the information acquired
from the sensor—magnitude and direction (X, Y & Z) of acceleration. This system
also monitors the voltage level of the source (V_{cc}) through the R_1 and R_2 resistors and
sends feedback to the base station or the monitoring center.

3.1   Frame Generation

According to the EPC Gen2 framework, due to the presence of the assisting battery
the tag belongs to the class 3 (semi-passive) category [15]. However, to generate the
ID frame Class 0 type II (SGTIN-64) protocol has been followed [18] because any
definite protocol for Class 3 frame structure has not yet been defined. Table 1 shows
the complete frame structure for the Serialized Global Trade Item Number-64
(SGTIN-64).

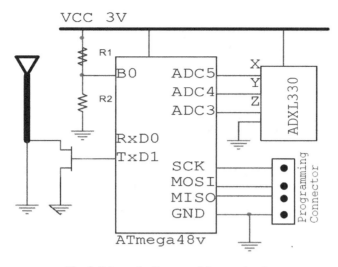

Fig. 2. Schematic diagram of the tag circuitry

To fit the sensor data within this framework, only the serial number field has been taken into consideration. As shown in Table 2, the whole 25-bit long serial number field is now divided into three sub fields: 13-bit long reduced unique ID field, 3-bit direction field and 9 bit magnitude field. This 3-bit direction field represents the 3 directions (X, Y & Z) of acceleration along with their axis directions (+Ve or -Ve). At any particular position, within this direction field, the bit '0' indicates the acceleration along the positive axis and '1' indicates the acceleration along the negative axis. Even if, at any particular direction, any acceleration is not sensed, the position bit of the respective field will remain to be '0'. For representation of the magnitude of the sensed acceleration in each direction, this system uses 3-bit data representing 8 different levels of acceleration in any certain axis (+Ve or -Ve) thereby with totally 16 different magnitude levels in any direction.

Table 1. Typical SGTIN-64 frame structure

Field Name	Number of bits
Header	02
Filter value	03
Company prefix	14
Item reference	20
Serial no	25

Table 2. Rearranged serial number field

Field type	Field Name	Number of bits
Constant field	Unique ID	13
Variable field	Direction	03
Variable field	Magnitude	09

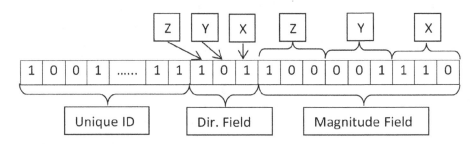

Fig. 3. Schematic frame diagram for the serial number field

4   Testing Results

The designed sensor tag was tested to establish a communication with the guardrail monitor center via an UHF RFID reader. A RFID reader from Alien technology was used in the test to read the tag sensing information. In our experimental setup, the reader was connected to the monitoring center's PC using the serial port RS232, but it can also be connected to the remote monitoring center via IEEE 802.11 (WIFI) protocol. Application software using .NET framework was developed to interface and interpret the data acquired from the tag for the test. The test setup is shown in Figure 4.

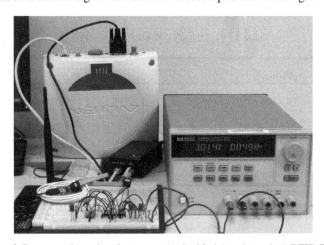

Fig. 4. Prototyped acceleration sensor embedded (semi-passive) RFID Tag

5   Conclusion

A semi-passive acceleration sensor- embedded RFID tag has been successfully designed and tested for highway guardrail monitoring. This tag is capable of sensing the acceleration in three directions and communicating with a nearby UHF reader based on EPC Gen 2 protocol. The sensitivity of the acceleration sensor is ±*3.3g* in any direction (X, Y & Z). To accommodate the dynamic sensor data within a standard ID frame, a complete frame structure has also been developed based on the EPC Gen2, Class 0 framework. According to this framework this tag uses 3 bits of resolution in each direction to indicate the quantized levels of acceleration with an additional one bit representing the axis (+*Ve* or -*Ve*) direction.

References

1. Jiao, W., Wang, X., Zhao, L.: Monitoring system of car-guardrail accident based on wireless sensor networks. In: 8th International Conference on ITS Telecommunications, pp. 146–149 (2008)
2. Hampton, C., Gabler, D., Gabauer, J.: Opportunities for Reduction of Fatalities in Vehicle-Guardrail Collisions. In: Annual Proceedings, Association for the Advancement of Automotive Medicine, vol. 51, pp. 31–48 (2007)
3. Highway Performance Monitoring System (HPMS), Federal Highway Administration, US Department of Transportation, http://www.fhwa.dot.gov/policyinformation/hpms/volumeroutes/ch4.cfm
4. Zhu, K., Li, S.: Risk Management and Assessment of Upgrading and Standardizing Guardrail. Joint Transportation Research Program Technical Report Series, Purdue University Purdue e-Pubs (2009)
5. Want, R.: "Enabling ubiquitous sensing with RFID. Computer, 84–86 (2004)
6. Cicirelli, G., Milella, A., Paola, D.: Supervised learning of RFID sensor model using a mobile robot. In: IEEE International Conference on RFID-Technologies and Applications (RFID-TA), pp. 32–36 (2011)
7. Mitsugi, J., et al.: Architecture Development for Sensor Integration in the EPCglobal Network. Auto-ID Labs White Paper, Software & Network, WP-SWNET-018 (2007)
8. EPC™ Radio-Frequency Identity Protocols Class-1 Generation-2 UHF RFID Protocol for Communications at 860MHz – 960MHz Version 1.0.9. Specification for RFID Air Interface, EPCglobal Inc™ (2005)
9. Englund, C., Wallin, H.: RFID in Wireless Sensor Network. Technical. Report, Dept. of Signals and Systems, Chalmers Univ. Technol., Sweden (2004)
10. Deng, H., et al.: Design of Sensor-Embedded Radio Frequency Identification (SE-RFID) Systems. In: IEEE International Conference on Mechatronics and Automation (2006)
11. Leon-Salas, W., Kanneganti, S., Halmen, C.: Development of a smart RFID-based corrosion sensor. In: 2011 IEEE Sensors, pp. 534–537 (2011)
12. Jia, Y., Heiss, M., Qiuyun, F., Gay, N.A.: A Prototype RFID Humidity Sensor for Built Environment Monitoring. In: International Workshop on ETT and GRS 2008, vol. 2, pp. 496–499 (2008)

13. Shrestha, S., et al.: A Chipless RFID Sensor System for Cyber Centric Monitoring Applications. IEEE Transactions on Microwave Theory and Techniques 57(5), 1303–1309 (2009)
14. Liu, H., Bolic, M., Nayak, A., Stojmenovic, I.: Taxonomy and challenges of the integration of RFID and wireless sensor networks. IEEE Network 22(6), 26–35 (2008)
15. Draft protocol specification for a 900 MHz Class 0 Radio Frequency Identification Tag. MIT Auto ID Center (2003)
16. RFIDLabeling.Com, http://www.rfidlabeling.com/tag_types.html
17. Feldhofer, M., Aigner, M., Baier, T., Hutter, M., Plos, T., Wenger, E.: Semi-passive RFID development platform for implementing and attacking security tags. In: International Conference for Internet Technology and Secured Transactions, ICITST (2010)
18. EPCTM Generation 1 Tag Data Standards Version 10 1.1 Rev.1.27. Standard Specification, EPCglobal Inc^{TM} (2005)

From Cloud Computing
to Cloud Manufacturing Excution Assembly System

M. Giriraj[1] and S. Muthu[2]

[1] Research Scholar, Anna University, Chennai
[2] M.P. Nachimuthu M. Jaganathan Engineering College, Erode
girirajmannayee@gmail.com

Abstract. In this paper we investigate guaranteeing assembly process information flow in real time, enterprise wide, from assembly station sensors directly to the industry policy making offices, is the true solution for improving productivity competence, reducing loses and greater than ever profits. In fact, the ideal production lies on the real machine or assembly capabilities of working non-stop at maximum speed, lacking downtimes or inactivity and assembled goods reject threats. Assembly lines will be prone to standstills and will produce defective pieces if the machines are unable to working to their full capability or demands made of them. This is often the case of misinformed factory management on real time factory floor performances. Even though equipped with original equipment manufacturer indicator knowledge about their systems, they still ca n' t get t hat efficiency so needed to improve yield. Transformation is necessary to ride the expected tide of change in the today's manufacturing environment, particularly in the information technology and automation landscape. A multinational company strives to reduce computing costs, to improve plant floor visibility and to achieve more efficient energy and surroundings use of their IT hardware and software investments. Cloud computing infrastructure accelerates and promotes these objectives by providing unparalleled flexible and dynamic IT resource collection, virtualization, floor visibility and high accessibility. This paper establish the value of realize cloud connect and usage state of affairs in cloud manufacturing environment, especially in automotive assembly stations which typically have large numbers of mixed applications, various hardware and huge data amount generated from sensors and devices in real-time and event-based exploration and assembly operations. The purpose of this paper is to behavior an Information Technology automotive assembly environment Systems analysis in the case of MNC's . To validate this objective, the article has been divided into two parts: monitoring vision and control and case study with the help of manufacturing execution assembly system. The purpose of the theory part of the study is to first introduce the concept of Cloud connect in the respective field of manufacturing execution assembly system, and then chat about the substance of Service management in information technology.

Keywords: Cloud computing, Cloud manufacturing execution system, monitoring vision and control, Shop floor data collection, Programmable logic controller.

S.G. Ponnambalam et al. (Eds.): IRAM 2012, CCIS 330, pp. 303–312, 2012.
© Springer-Verlag Berlin Heidelberg 2012

1   Introduction

In this paper, we investigate feasibility of the state-of-the-art of cloud computing and its usage of manufacturing execution system with the aim of providing a clear understanding of the opportunities present in cloud connect and upcoming scenario, along with knowledge about the boundaries and face up to in designing systems for cloud and manufacturing execution assembly environments.[1] [2] We squabble that this familiarity is essential for prospective adopters, yet is not readily available due to the confusion currently surrounding cloud connect and manufacturing execution assembly system environment. Cloud computing and manufacturing execution system is the notion of abstracting and out sourcing hardware or software resources over the web word and sophistication,[7][8] often to a third party on a pay-as-you-Go basis.[3][5] This up-and-coming concept is sometimes claimed to represent a completely new paradigm with cloud manufacturing execution system, with disruptive effects on our means of viewing and accessing multiplication resources.[4][6]. Our findings reveal that confront connected with hosting and server systems in cloud environments include increased latency due to longer network distances between third party client and server systems, limited bandwidth since packets must cross the web world to reach the cloud computing and manufacturing execution assembly system, as well as reduced portability because cloud environments are currently lacking data security and standardization. [11][12] Furthermore, systems must be designed in a loosely coupled and fault-tolerant way to fully exploit the energetic features of cloud computing, implication that existing relevance might require considerable modification before being able to fully utilize a cloud computing and manufacturing execution system environment. These faces up to also restrict some systems from being suitable for running in the cloud connect. Furthermore, we have implemented a prototype in cloud manufacturing assembly test bench to investigate the feasibility of moving an enterprise search service to a cloud environment. We base the feasibility of our approach on measurements of response time, band width and scalability. We conclude that our cloud-based search service is feasible due to its opportunities for implementing dynamic scaling and reducing local infrastructure in a novel fashion.

2   Manufacturing Execution Assembly Systems of Cloud Connect

On top to web-based email, some online services have started expanding their offerings by providing document processing and other office applications online. Google Docs is one example, all we need is access to the Internet, and we can generate and store manufacturing execution assembly system files in these Cloud-connect based applications. Intermediate documents can be uploaded from our hard drive and stored on the cloud connect, allowing us to freedom to access them from any computer, and collaborate with other users, without having multiple copies of the document spread around different computers. In Cloud-based computing, there's no software to download, and we can even store our documents online or cloud environment. Everything happens in the Cloud, via our web browser. We may already be using Cloud connect, and not know it. We are storing our cloud manufacturing execution assembly systems data in the Cloud. Other software companies are already working on the idea of Cloud computing, as an alternative to the traditional method of downloading or installing software on a hard drive. We simply enter a user name and password in order to get access to our accounting cloud connects files.

2.1   Manufacturing Execution System

A manufacturing execution system is a "manufacturing oriented system that interacts and shares information with other manufacturing applications. These are the information systems that reside on a plant-floor between the planning systems in offices and direct industrial controls at the processes itself. " The integration of manufacturing execution system, as middle layer of manufacturing planning and control system, with the other levels provides real time information and helps managers to make decision based on facts. Although specific functions are assigned to each level, there are no clear boundaries between these levels and the functions included in each level can be moved with respect to each company's circumstances. The term manufacturing execution system is examined from two aspects, first functions covered by the software and then the nonfunctional requirements that should be considered for implementing and operating manufacturing execution system solutions. Machine monitoring sensors and shop floor data collection; terminals transmit production data from the factory floor to manufacturing execution system software. Manufacturing execution system software that includes supervisory control and data acquisition features can collect data from machine-mounted sensors. This information is then transmitted to a central computer for processing. In turn, software-based algorithms send real-time instructions to devices such as programmable logic controllers. Some manufacturing execution system software is designed for use with manual shop floor data collection sensors.

3   Experimental Setup

Figure1 shows the experimental manufacturing system. Its represents a component product sorting, and assembly processes that can be controlled by programmable logic controller. The upper conveyor and the lower conveyor are driven by the rotary actuator 1 and the lower conveyor rotary actuator 2 respectively. A random selection of metallic pegs and plastic rings are placed on the upper conveyor. The rings and pegs need to be identified and separated.

Fig. 1. Manufacturing Execution system setup

This is done by two sensors, a proximity sensor1 and an infra-red reflective sensor2. By using these two sensors a distinction can be made between the peg and the ring. By means of the sort linear actuator 3, plastic rings can be ejected down the assembly chute, which can have up to plastic rings. Metallic fasteners, meanwhile, continue on the upper conveyor and are defected down the feeder chute. The feeder chute automatically feeds fasteners onto the lower conveyor. An infra-red sensor is used to determine whether or not the assembly area is empty. If it is, the assembly solenoid base rotary actuator is used to dispense a ring from the assembly channel into the assembly area. The assembly area is positioned just above the lower conveyor and, when a metallic fasteners passes, the fastener engages with the hole in the ring and the two components are assembled. The lower conveyor is used to carry completed components into the collection tray. Printing module interfaced with the programmable logic controller, retrieves data from the system and print over the component with relevant parameters, like manufacturer, license no, batch no, mfg. date, expiry date etc... In this work, a Siemens S7-30 0 programmable logic controller is used to control the process and software called "Simatic Manager" is used to program the programmable logic controller. Programmable logic controller inputs and outputs are given in tables 1 and table 2, respectively.

Table 1.		Table 2.	
IINPUT MODULE		OUTPUT MODULE	
SYMBOL	ADDRESS	SYMBOL	ADDRESS
LIN_IND_DN	I0.0	ROT_PIL_PL_INDEX_SI DE	
LINEAR_IND_UP	I0.1	LINEAR_UP_DN	Q0.0
LIN_IND_EXTE	I0.2	LINEAR_IND_EXT_RET R	Q0.1
LIN_IND_RETR	I0.3	DISPENCER	Q0.2
DISP_RETR	I0.4	PUSHER_EXT_RETR	Q0.3
DIS_EXET	I0.5	ASS_LIN_EXT	Q0.4
NON_METAL	I0.6	ASS_LIN_RETR	Q0.5
METAL	I0.7	ASS_PUNC_RETR	Q0.6

ASS_LIN_EXT_SEN	I1.1	ASS_PUNC_EXTE	Q0.7
ASS_LIN_RETR_SEN	I1.0	ROT_PI_PL_LINEAR_SI	Q1.0
PUNC_RETR	I1.2	DE	Q1.1
ROT_P_P_LIN_SIDE	I1.4	LIN_GRI_OPEN	Q1.4
ROT_PI_PL_INDEX_SID E_SE	I1.5	LIN_GRI_CLOSE	Q1.5
ROT_PI_PL_UP_SEN	I1.6	ROT_GRIP_CLOSE	Q1.6
ROT_PI_PL_DN_SEN	I1.7	SCREW_MOTOR	Q1.7
PUSH_EXTE	I2.1	LIN_PI_PL_RETR	Q2.0
PUSH_RETR	I2.0	LIN_PI_PL_EXTE	Q2.1
SCREW_CYL_UP	I2.2	PRINT_UP_DN	Q2.2
PRINT_EXTE	I2.5	SCREW_MOD_UP_DN	Q2.3
PRINT_RETR	I2.4	LIN_PI_PL_UP_DN	Q2.4
SCRE_MOD_CYL_DN	I2.3	ROT_GRIP_OPEN	Q2.5
LIN_PI_PL_UP_SEN	I2.6	BELT_CONVEYOR	Q2.6
LIN_PI_PL_DN_SEN	I2.7	INEX_MOTOR	Q2.7
LIN_PI_PL_EXT_SEN	I3.0		
LIN_PI_PL_RETR_SEN	I3.1		
INDEX_SEN	I3.2		
OBJECT_PRES	I3.3		
INDEX_OBJECT_SEN	I3.4		
START	I3.5		
E_STOP	I3.7		

3.1 Manufacturing Execution System Data Captivating and Visualization

The mission to visualize the assembly process is paramount to any supervision of manufacturing execution system. The more translucent process visualization means more efficient floor management. Users now explicitly demand that their plant floor and progression be represented as near to reality as possible. The instant look, feel and touch experience allow to run free extra sensory sensitivity. The being there but not being there, virtual reality is the key factor and this is where graphics play a foremost role. Most project development time is spent in creating the real thing on screen and online monitoring vision and control is supreme in this meadow. By using the gigantic range of the most powerful online monitoring vision and control graphics ever, won't take we long at all to achieve the real thing on screen.

3.2 Open Database Connectivity

The monitoring vision and control mission is to consent data aggregation in the simplest way possible and allow recording and file management modalities to be defined and setup in the most appropriate way well-matched. This important job is thoroughly done by monitoring vision and control based on the concepts of simplicity, reliability and openness. Monitoring vision and control has three recording engines, based on an Open database Connectivity. Monitoring vision and control supports all relational data base via Open database Connectivity but will automatically uses the Structured Query Language Server for default, if not specified otherwise. One recording engine has been designated the task of recording process data using the data logger resource, another engine has been designated to the event log and the last one designated to the powerful and sophisticated variable tracing management. As an alternative to using the Open database Connectivity recording engines, monitoring vision and control also provide the immigration database manager, which permits you to record data on simple text format files which then can be encrypted to allow recorded data to be only viewed exclusively through the monitoring vision and control controlled access modalities.

3.3   Connectivity with Manufacturing Execution Assembly System

Communicating in the fast lane safely at top speed is necessary for manufacturing execution assembly system. The supervision systems are meeting points of all process data. The crossroads of non-stop production (sensor) information flow of execution enterprise resource planning systems. The communication's strategic role is deeply rooted in monitoring vision and control, Monitoring vision and control provides with a rich library of Input and output drivers, integrated and included free in the product. Communication with control systems (manufacturing execution assembly system) has never been so quick to configure and never been so quick performing. It is very helpful wizards are at hand to automatically import and configure project variables directly from the Programmable logic controller, helping we beat configuring times and reduce the risk of making errors. The Input and output driver library supports all programmable logic controllers and systems found on the market today, and can be added to by third parties using an appropriate software development kit. The monitoring vision and control applications guarantee maximum security and reliability. The end user and password management, complete and robust, has been explicitly designed to guarantee that projects are realized. Monitoring vision and control ensures maximum data and system access protection. Manufacturing execution assembly system end users can be shared with the domain, allowing the option to integrate and centralize user profiles. All the security criteria have been fully integrated and can be configured with the electronic Signature management system, unauthorized persons access attempts control, password expiries, automatic log-off and the audit Trail management. Monitoring vision and control also lets you define protection levels and traceability directly in each single Tag, independently from the commands they have been associated with. Moreover, Monitoring vision and control supports the windows services and consents total or partial access block to the Windows desktop. Data is recorded on safe relational database system.

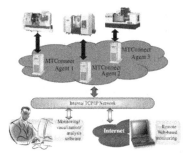

Fig. 2. Connectivity with manufacturing execution system

3.4   Real Time Database from Manufacturing Execution Assembly System

Figure 3 shows real time database guarantees top level managers all the information they need for analyzing ways to improve identify and isolate anomalous behavior of the execution system. The manufacturing execution assembly system job is to consent data aggregation, define and set data recording and archive management modes in the plant floor visibility.

 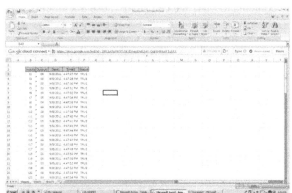

Fig. 3. Real time data base

Monitoring vision and control provides all the tools we will ever need to accomplish plant floor data. Monitoring vision and control provides three recording servers, based on an open database connectivity top level manager replica to guarantee maximum performance in data. Monitoring vision and control supports all relational data base management system by proposing an automatic selection between structured query languages, Ms Access via open database connectivity. Monitoring vision and control uses the Microsoft Structured Query Language server for default, If not specified otherwise. Each of the three engines has different tasks. One records process data using the data logger resource, other logs events while the remaining one is assigned the powerful and sophisticated. Windows as the main tool, the data loggers permit simple and robust process data acquiring. Data base table records can be executed on preset time domain frequencies, event or variations. Data recorded on data base is then automatically available in the manufacturing execution assembly system through deliberately designed graphical objects, which includes database table display windows, grids, trends, reports. Monitoring vision and control has supreme improved report management. This feature now has an additional and authoritative built-in report generator based on the .Net technology, which consents influential reports to be generated visually with statistical and graphical chart and graph functions to further simplify report generating within the manufacturing execution assembly system. The Monitoring vision and control report designer is one of the most influential reporting tools to have in any supervisory system. The great simplicity of the textual reports allows we create reports on RTF or HTML files also for simple compact systems.

3.5   Manufacturing Execution System-Reports Uploading-to Cloud Connect

Figure 4 shows MES reports uploading to cloud connect, Cloud Connect helps we to bring manufacturing execution assembly system files to cloud as cloud connect docs or cloud computing documents. Cloud connect integration was never so easy. This is a very useful add-in for those who use cloud connect docs like cloud computing doc's spread sheets an d manufacturing execution assembly system documents on a daily or shift basis. We need to upload the files or create a new file in cloud connect docs and add contents to that. We can share those documents with whomever we want. We can

Fig. 4. MES reports uploading to cloud connect

directly save and share documents directly from cloud connect. This add-in helps us to share, backup, and simultaneously edit manufacturing execution system documents with coworkers. We need to authorize Google Cloud Connect to connect to our cloud computing account. Also we can select cloud connect document sync options as manual and automatic.

3.6   Reports View or Download from Cloud Connect

Fig. 5 shows the cloud connects manufacturing assembly execution system's real time report. It is downloaded from cloud connect and it can be used to work together on a document. If what we all like best is to work on our document in Office on our own computer, this could be the solution for us. Each person can download and edit the document, according to ERP requirement and then sync it to the cloud. If you're all working g on it at the same time, we might get messages. Fig shows cloud connect document.

Fig. 5. Reports download to cloud connect

4   Conclusion

Cloud connect is shifting the way cloud manufacturing automation industries and enterprises do their dealing. With wider cloud adoption, access to dealing -significant data and analytics will not just help visibility of plant floor operation. Stay ahead; it will also be crucial to their existence. There are three architectural features of cloud computing in terms of the execution system end-users, enterprises that use the cloud connect as a platform, and cloud providers themselves. These architectural features play a major role in the adoption of the cloud connect exemplar as mainstream goods in the plant floor inspection world. Cloud connect is emerging as one of the major enablers for the manufacturing industry, transforming manufacturing execution assembly system its production information, helping it align product innovation with business policy. Type of cloud connect adoptions in the manufacturing sector have been suggested, manufacturing with direct adoption of cloud connect technologies and cloud manufacturing the manufacturing version of cloud computing. In terms of direct adoption of cloud computing in the manufacturing sector, the key areas are around IT and new models.

References

[1] Dikaiakos, M.D., Katsaros, D., Mehra, P., Pallis, G., Vakali, A.: Cloud computing: distributed internet computing for IT and scientific research. IEEE Internet Computing 13(5), 10–13 (2009)

[2] Campos, J.G., Miguez, L.R.: Manufacturing traceability data management in the supply chain. International Journal of Information Technology and Management 8(3), 321–339 (2009)

[3] Tao, F., Hu, Y., Zhou, Z.: Application and modeling of resource service trust-QoS evaluation in manufacturing grid system. International Journal of Production Research 47(6), 1521–1550 (2009)

[4] Foster, I., Zhao, Y., Raicu, I., Lu, S.: Cloud computing cloud computing and grid computing 360 degree compared. In: Grid Computing Environments Workshop (2008)

[5] Guo, H., Zhang, L., Tao, F., Ren, L., Luo, Y.L.: Research on the measurement method of flexibility of resource service composition in cloud manufacturing. In: Proceedings of the International Conference on Manufacturing Engineering and Automation ICMEA, December 10-12 (2010)

[6] Mokhtar, A., Houshmand, M.: Introducing a roadmap to implement the universal manufacturing platform using axiomatic design theory. International Journal of Manufacturing Research 5, 252–269 (2010)

[7] Pallis, G.: Cloud computing: the new frontier of internet computing. IEEE Internet Computing, [14:5: 5562494:7073] (2010)

[8] Kunio, T.: NEC cloud computing system. NEC Technical Journal 5(2), 10–15 (2010)

[9] Suh, S.H., Shin, S.J., Yoon, J.S., Um, J.U.: A new paradigm for product design and manufacturing via ubiquitous computing technology. International Journal of Computer Integrated Manufacturing 21(5), 540–549 (2008)

[10] Lee, B.E., Suh, S.-H.: An architecture for ubiquitous product life cycle support system and its extension to machine tools with product data model. International Journal of Advanced Manufacturing Technology 42, 606–620 (2009)

[11] Above the Clouds: A Berkeley View of Cloud Computing. Technica Report No.UCB/EECS-2009-28

[12] Atluru, S., Deshpande, A., Huang, S., Snyder, J.P.: Smart Machine Supervisory System: Concept, Definition and Application. In: Society for Machinery Failure Prevention Technology 62nd Meeting Conference, Virginia Beach, VA, May 6-8 (2008)

Transient Analysis of Structronics Shell

Hussain H. Al-Kayiem and Thar M. Badri

Mechanical Engineering Department, Universiti Teknologi PETRONAS,
Bandar Seri Iskandar, 31750 Tronoh, Perak, Malaysia
t.albarody@ymail.com

Abstract. Based on the first-order shear deformation shell theory involving Co-dazzi-Gauss geometrical discretion, Hamilton's principle and Gibbs free energy function, this paper presents the analytical solution for magneto-thermo-electro-elastic structronics shell. In which the fundamental equations and its boundary conditions were solved using the generic forced-solution procedure, and its frequency parameters were evaluated in the simply supported boundary condition. Then, the transient solution is obtained by Newmark's method to evaluate the influence of magnetic and electric parameters on the structure response. Results have been shown that the effect of the transverse shear is greater on the dynamic response than the static response. However, it is also observed that the ratio of transient to static deflection takes less with increasing of side to thickness ratio of the shell. The present results may serve as a reference in developing the structronics shell theories and to improve the benchmark solutions for judging the existence of imprecise theories and other numerical approaches.

Keywords: Magneto-thermo-electro-elastic control, Nerves structure, Adaptive sensors/actuators, Piezo-laminated shell, Structural health monitoring.

1 Introduction

Structronics is concept of "Structures + Electronics", which are synergistic integration of adaptive or functional materials (e.g., piezoelectric, piezomagnetic, electrostrictive, magnetostrictive, and the alike materials). Furthermore, structronics had the capability of simultaneously sensing/ actuating; mechanical, electrical, magnetic and even thermal effects, as well as simultaneously generating response to eliminate or enhance the desirable effects. Whereas, structronics are largely improves the working performance and lifetime of devices that construct from it [1-4]. Several accurate solutions of structronics shell have been proved for special cases of Pan's analysis for multi-layered piezoelectric-magnetic [5]. Pan and Heyliger [6] demonstrated the free vibration analysis of the simply supported and multilayered magneto-electro-elastic (MEE) plates under cylindrical bending. The open literature relevant to a transient analysis of structronics shell elements is rather scanty and directed, in general, toward specified structronics problems. Ootao *et al.* [7] obtained the exact solution for the simply supported and multilayered magneto-thermo-electro-elastic (MTEE) strip under a plane strain state to simulate the temperature change, stress, displacement, electric

S.G. Ponnambalam et al. (Eds.): IRAM 2012, CCIS 330, pp. 313–321, 2012.

potential, and magnetic potential distributions in a transient state. Dai et al. [8] presented an analytical solution for the MTEE problems of a piezoelectric hollow cylinder placed in an axial magnetic field subjected to arbitrary thermal shock, mechanical load, and transient electric excitation. In this article, exact model for structronics shell based on the first-order transversely shear deformation (FOSD) theory will be developed. Meanwhile, new issues elicited by structronics parameters, such as the transient behavior of the structure due to material properties and shell dimension are addressed.

2   Kinematic Equation

According to the FOSD, the following representation for MEE fields is postulated:

$$u(\alpha_1, \alpha_2, \zeta) = u_o(\alpha_1, \alpha_2) + \zeta\psi_\alpha(\alpha_1, \alpha_2), v(\alpha_1, \alpha_2, \zeta) = v_o(\alpha_1, \alpha_2) + \zeta\psi_\beta(\alpha_1, \alpha_2),$$
$$w(\alpha_1, \alpha_2, \zeta) = w_o(\alpha_1, \alpha_2), \tag{1}$$
$$\varphi(\alpha_1, \alpha_2, \zeta) = -\varphi_o(\alpha_1, \alpha_2) - \zeta\varphi_1(\alpha_1, \alpha_2), \quad \vartheta(\alpha_1, \alpha_2, \zeta) = -\vartheta_o(\alpha_1, \alpha_2) - \zeta\vartheta_1(\alpha_1, \alpha_2),$$

where, u_o, v_o and w_o are referred to as the midsurface displacements and ψ_α and ψ_β are midsurface rotations of the shell, φ_o is the electric potential, and ϑ_o is the magnetic potential. The strains at any point in the shells can be written as: [9]

$$\varepsilon_{ii} = \frac{1}{\gamma_i}\frac{\partial u_i}{\partial \alpha_i} + \frac{1}{\gamma_i\gamma_j}\frac{\partial \gamma_i}{\partial \alpha_j}u_j + \frac{1}{\gamma_i\gamma_3}\frac{\partial \gamma_i}{\partial \zeta}u_3, \qquad \varepsilon_{ij} = \frac{\gamma_i}{\gamma_j}\frac{\partial}{\partial \alpha_j}\left(\frac{u_i}{\gamma_i}\right) + \frac{\gamma_j}{\gamma_i}\frac{\partial}{\partial \alpha_i}\left(\frac{u_j}{\gamma_j}\right),$$

$$\varepsilon_{33} = \frac{1}{\gamma_3}\frac{\partial u_3}{\partial \zeta} + \frac{1}{\gamma_3\gamma_1}\frac{\partial \gamma_3}{\partial \alpha_1}u_1 + \frac{1}{\gamma_2\gamma_3}\frac{\partial \gamma_3}{\partial \alpha_2}u_2, \quad \varepsilon_{ij} = \frac{\gamma_3}{\gamma_i}\frac{\partial}{\partial \alpha_i}\left(\frac{u_3}{\gamma_3}\right) + \frac{\gamma_i}{\gamma_3}\frac{\partial}{\partial \zeta}\left(\frac{u_i}{\gamma_i}\right),$$

$$\xi_{o\alpha} = -\frac{1}{A_1}\frac{\partial \varphi_o}{\partial \alpha}, \quad \xi_{1\alpha} = -\frac{1}{A_1}\frac{\partial \varphi_1}{\partial \alpha}, \quad \xi_{o\beta} = -\frac{1}{A_2}\frac{\partial \varphi_o}{\partial \beta}, \quad \xi_{1\beta} = -\frac{1}{A_2}\frac{\partial \varphi_1}{\partial \beta}, \tag{2}$$

$$\chi_{o\alpha} = -\frac{1}{A_1}\frac{\partial \varphi_o}{\partial \alpha}, \quad \chi_{1\alpha} = -\frac{1}{A_1}\frac{\partial \varphi_1}{\partial \alpha}, \quad \chi_{o\beta} = -\frac{1}{A_2}\frac{\partial \varphi_o}{\partial \beta}, \quad \chi_{1\beta} = -\frac{1}{A_2}\frac{\partial \varphi_1}{\partial \beta},$$

where $u_i = u_i(\alpha_1, \alpha_2, \zeta)$, $u_3 = u_3(\alpha_1, \alpha_2, \zeta)$, $\gamma_i = A_i(1 + \zeta/R_i)$, and $\gamma_3 = 1$.

3   Energy Variational Principle

The energy functional are important for deriving a consistent set of equations of motion that coupled with free charge equilibrium equations and equipping its boundary conditions [10-12]. In summary, the total energy of a shell element is defined as:

$$\delta \int_{t_o}^{t_1} [\mathcal{K} - \mathcal{P}]\, dt = 0, \tag{3}$$

where $\mathcal{P}$ is total potential energy;-

$$\mathcal{P} = \iiint_V \left[\varrho(s_i, \varepsilon_j, \mathcal{G}_l, \mathcal{T}) + (\mathcal{T}\tau) \right] dV - \iint_{\Omega_o} \left(t(s_i, \varepsilon_j, \mathcal{G}_l) + \mathcal{W}(s_i, \varepsilon_j, \mathcal{G}_l) \right), \tag{4}$$

$Q(S_i, \mathcal{E}_j, \mathcal{G}_l, \mathcal{T})$, $t(S_i, \mathcal{E}_j, \mathcal{G}_l)$ and $\mathcal{W}(S_i, \mathcal{E}_j, \mathcal{G}_l)$ are the thermodynamic potential "Gibbs free energy", tractions and the work done by body force, electrical and magnetic charge, respectively. Moreover, the kinetic energy is

$$\mathcal{K} = \frac{1}{2} \iiint_{\mathcal{V}} [\dot{u}^2 + \dot{v}^2 + \dot{w}^2] \, d\mathcal{V}. \tag{5}$$

Substituting Equations (2) and (3) into Equation (1) yields

$$\int_{t_o}^{t_1} \frac{1}{2} \iiint_{\mathcal{V}} [\dot{u}^2 + \dot{v}^2 + \dot{w}^2] \, d\mathcal{V} \, dt - \left\{ \int_{t_o}^{t_1} \iiint_{\mathcal{V}} [\delta Q(S_i, \mathcal{E}_j, \mathcal{G}_l, \mathcal{T}) + (\mathcal{T}\delta\tau)] d\mathcal{V} dt \right.$$
$$\left. - \int_{t_o}^{t_1} \iint_{\Omega_o} \left(\delta t(S_i, \mathcal{E}_j, \mathcal{G}_l) + \delta\mathcal{W}(S_i, \mathcal{E}_j, \mathcal{G}_l) \right) dA dt \right\} = 0. \tag{6}$$

The kinetic energy of the shell can be expressed as

$$\mathcal{K} = \frac{1}{2} \iint_{\Omega_o} \int_{-h/2}^{h/2} \left(\begin{array}{c} [\dot{u}_o^2 + \dot{v}_o^2 + \dot{w}_o^2] \\ +\zeta^2 [\dot{\psi}_\alpha^2 + \dot{\psi}_\beta^2] \\ +2\zeta [\dot{u}_o^2 \dot{\psi}_\alpha^2 + \dot{v}_o^2 \dot{\psi}_\beta^2] \end{array} \right) \times \left(1 + \frac{\zeta}{R_\alpha} \right) \left(1 + \frac{\zeta}{R_\beta} \right) AB d\zeta dA. \tag{7}$$

Based on the conservation laws of electro-magnetic field, the linear thermodynamic potential energy Q for quasi-static infinitesimal reversible system, subject to mechanical, electric, magnetic, and thermal influences from its surroundings, can be approximated by

$$Q(S_i, \mathcal{E}_j, \mathcal{G}_l, \mathcal{T}) \cong \frac{1}{2} (S_{ij} \, \varepsilon_{kl} - \mathcal{E}_n \, \xi_n - \mathcal{G}_q \, \chi_q - \mathcal{T}\tau), \tag{8}$$

means that S_{ij}, $\mathcal{E}_k$, $\mathcal{G}_l$, and $\mathcal{T}$ are the dependent variables of Q, while ε_{ij}, ξ_k, χ_l, and τ are the natural independent variables. In order to obtain the thermodynamic potential for which these variables are natural, is performed [13], that is

$$2Q = \varsigma_{ijkl}^{\mathcal{E},\mathcal{G},\mathcal{T}} \varepsilon_{ij}\varepsilon_{kl} - \epsilon_{mn}^{S,\mathcal{G},\mathcal{T}} \xi_m\xi_n - \mu_{pq}^{S,\mathcal{E},\mathcal{T}} \chi_p\chi_q - \theta^{S,\mathcal{E},\mathcal{G}}\tau^2 - 2\varrho_{mkl}^{\mathcal{G},\mathcal{T}}\varepsilon_{kl}\xi_m - 2\kappa_{pkl}^{\mathcal{E},\mathcal{T}}\varepsilon_{kl}\chi_p$$
$$- 2\lambda_{kl}^{\mathcal{E},\mathcal{G}}\varepsilon_{kl}\tau - 2\eta_{pn}^{S,\mathcal{T}}\xi_n\chi_p - 2\rho_n^{S,\mathcal{G}}\xi_n\,\tau - 2\gamma_q^{S,\mathcal{E}}\chi_q\,\tau, \tag{9}$$

where Q is commonly known as Gibbs free energy, the superscripts indicate that the magnitudes must be kept constant when measuring them in the laboratory frame. The constitutive relations can be expressed formally by differentiation of Q corresponding to each dependent variable as

$$S_{ij} = \left(\frac{\partial Q}{\partial \varepsilon_{kl}} \right) = \varsigma_{ijkl}^{\mathcal{E},\mathcal{G},\mathcal{T}} \varepsilon_{ij} - \varrho_{mkl}^{\mathcal{G},\mathcal{T}}\xi_m - \kappa_{pkl}^{\mathcal{E},\mathcal{T}}\chi_p - \lambda_{kl}^{\mathcal{E},\mathcal{G}}\tau,$$

$$\mathcal{E}_k = \left(\frac{-\partial Q}{\partial \xi_n} \right) = \varrho_{ijn}^{\mathcal{G},\mathcal{T}} \varepsilon_{ij} + \epsilon_{mn}^{S,\mathcal{G},\mathcal{T}}\xi_m + \eta_{pn}^{S,\mathcal{T}}\chi_p + \rho_n^{S,\mathcal{G}}\tau, \tag{10}$$

$$\mathcal{G}_l = \left(\frac{-\partial \mathcal{Q}}{\partial \chi_q}\right) = \kappa_{ijq}^{\mathcal{E},\mathcal{T}} \varepsilon_{ij} + \eta_{mq}^{\mathcal{S},\mathcal{T}} \xi_m + \mu_{pq}^{\mathcal{S},\mathcal{E},\mathcal{T}} \chi_p + \gamma_q^{\mathcal{S},\mathcal{E}} \tau,$$

$$\mathcal{T} = \left(\frac{-\partial \mathcal{Q}}{\partial \tau}\right) = \lambda_{ij}^{\mathcal{E},\mathcal{G}} \varepsilon_{ij} + \rho_m^{\mathcal{S},\mathcal{G}} \xi_m + \gamma_p^{\mathcal{S},\mathcal{E}} \chi_p + \theta^{\mathcal{S},\mathcal{E},\mathcal{G}} \tau,$$

(11)

Moreover, the external work is

$$\mathcal{W}(\mathcal{S}_i, \mathcal{E}_j, \mathcal{G}_l) = \begin{pmatrix} \mathcal{F}_\alpha^{\mathcal{S}} u_0 + \mathcal{F}_\beta^{\mathcal{S}} v_0 + \mathcal{F}_n^{\mathcal{S}} w_0 + \mathcal{C}_\alpha^{\mathcal{S}} \psi_\alpha + \mathcal{C}_\beta^{\mathcal{S}} \psi_\beta \\ -\mathcal{F}^{\mathcal{E}} \varphi_0 + \mathcal{C}^{\mathcal{E}} \varphi_1 - \mathcal{F}^{\mathcal{G}} \vartheta_0 + \mathcal{C}^{\mathcal{G}} \vartheta_1 \end{pmatrix},$$

(12)

where $\mathcal{F}_\alpha^{\mathcal{S}}$, $\mathcal{F}_\beta^{\mathcal{S}}$, and $\mathcal{F}_n^{\mathcal{S}}$ are the distributed forces in α, β and ζ directions, respectively, and $\mathcal{C}_\alpha^{\mathcal{S}}$, and $\mathcal{C}_\beta^{\mathcal{S}}$ are the distributed couples about the middle surface of the shell. In addition $\mathcal{F}^{\mathcal{E}}$, $\mathcal{C}^{\mathcal{E}}$, $\mathcal{F}^{\mathcal{G}}$ and $\mathcal{C}^{\mathcal{G}}$ are the distributed forces and couples due to electrical and magnetic charge. Substituting Equations (10), (11) and (12) in Equation (4) and equating the resulted equation with Equation (7), yields the equations of motion of structronics shell as shown in Equation (13) below:

$$\int_{t_0}^{t_1} \iint_{\Omega_0} \delta \begin{pmatrix} \frac{\bar{I}_1}{2}[\dot{u}_0^2 + \dot{v}_0^2 + \dot{w}_0^2] \\ \frac{\bar{I}_3}{2}[\dot{\psi}_\alpha^2 + \dot{\psi}_\beta^2] \\ \bar{I}_2[\dot{u}_0^2 \dot{\psi}_\alpha^2 + \dot{v}_0^2 \dot{\psi}_\beta^2] \end{pmatrix} ABdAdt - \left\{ \int_{t_0}^{t_1} \iiint_V \begin{pmatrix} (\varsigma_{ij}\varepsilon - \varrho_{ij}\xi - \kappa_{ij}\chi - \lambda_i\tau)\delta\varepsilon \\ -(\varrho_{ij}\varepsilon + \epsilon_{ij}\xi + \eta_{ij}\chi + \rho_i\tau)\delta\xi \\ -(\kappa_{ij}\varepsilon + \eta_{ij}\xi + \mu_{ij}\chi + \gamma_i\tau)\delta\chi \\ -(\lambda_i\varepsilon + \rho_i\xi + \gamma_i\chi + \theta\tau)\delta\tau \\ +(\lambda_i\varepsilon + \rho_i\xi + \gamma_i\chi + \theta\tau)\delta\tau \end{pmatrix} dVdt \right.$$

$$- \int_{t_0}^{t_1} \iint_{\Omega_0} \begin{pmatrix} (\mathcal{F}_\alpha^{\mathcal{S}} u_0 + \mathcal{F}_\beta^{\mathcal{S}} v_0 + \mathcal{F}_n^{\mathcal{S}} w_0 + \mathcal{C}_\alpha^{\mathcal{S}} \psi_\alpha + \mathcal{C}_\beta^{\mathcal{S}} \psi_\beta) \\ -(\mathcal{F}^{\mathcal{E}} \varphi_0 + \mathcal{C}^{\mathcal{E}} \varphi_1) - (\mathcal{F}^{\mathcal{G}} \vartheta_0 + \mathcal{C}^{\mathcal{G}} \vartheta_1) \end{pmatrix} ABdAdt \left. \right\} = 0. \quad (13)$$

Note that, the kinetic relations (i.e., the force and moment resultants per unit length at the boundary Ω) are obtained by integrating the stresses over the shell thickness as in Equation (14).

$$\begin{Bmatrix} N_x^{\mathcal{S}}, & M_x^{\mathcal{S}} \\ N_x^{\mathcal{E}}, & M_x^{\mathcal{E}} \\ N_x^{\mathcal{G}}, & M_x^{\mathcal{G}} \end{Bmatrix} = \int_{-h/2}^{h/2} (1, \zeta) \begin{pmatrix} \varsigma_{ijkl}^{\mathcal{E},\mathcal{G},\mathcal{T}} \varepsilon_{ij} - \varrho_{mkl}^{\mathcal{G},\mathcal{T}} \xi_m - \kappa_{pkl}^{\mathcal{E},\mathcal{T}} \chi_p - \lambda_{kl}^{\mathcal{E},\mathcal{G}} \tau \\ \varrho_{ijn}^{\mathcal{G},\mathcal{T}} \varepsilon_{ij} + \epsilon_{mn}^{\mathcal{S},\mathcal{G},\mathcal{T}} \xi_m + \eta_{pn}^{\mathcal{S},\mathcal{T}} \chi_p + \rho_n^{\mathcal{S},\mathcal{G}} \tau \\ \kappa_{ijq}^{\mathcal{E},\mathcal{T}} \varepsilon_{ij} + \eta_{mq}^{\mathcal{S},\mathcal{T}} \xi_m + \mu_{pq}^{\mathcal{S},\mathcal{E},\mathcal{T}} \chi_p + \gamma_q^{\mathcal{S},\mathcal{E}} \tau \end{pmatrix} \left(1 + \frac{\zeta}{R_y}\right) d\zeta \quad (14)$$

where the subscripts x and y denote either of α_1, or α_2 in which $x \neq y$, h is the shell thickness. By recasting Equation (13) to put in the familiar form, the governing equations of motion and the charge equilibrium equations could be derived based on the fundamental Lemma of calculus of variations. E.g., by integrating the field gradients by parts to relieve the virtual fields and setting its coefficients to zero individually.

4   Analytical Solution

Here, we introduce the following assumptions to cast the equation of motion in thick (or shear deformation) shell theories. Deepness (or shallowness) of the shell, is also one criterion used in developing shell equations. Thus, shell is referred to as a plate, when it has zero curvature or infinity radius of curvature (i.e., the term $(1 + \zeta/R_i) = 1$: where R_i is either of the curvature parameter $R_{\alpha_1}, R_{\alpha_2}, or\ R_{\alpha_1\alpha_2}$ [14]. If it is represented by the plane coordinate systems for the case of rectangular orthotropy, this leads to constant Lame´ parameters (i.e., $A_i = 1$). In additional, the radii of curvature are assumed very large compared to the in-plane displacements. (i.e., $u_i/R_i = 0, where\ i = \alpha_1, \alpha_2\ \&\ \alpha_1\alpha_2, u_i = u_o$, or v_o).
Appling the above assumptions yield;

$$\frac{\partial}{\partial\alpha}N_\alpha^S + \frac{\partial}{\partial\beta}N_{\beta\alpha}^S + \mathcal{F}_\alpha^S = \left(\bar{I}_1\frac{\partial^2 u_o}{\partial t^2} + \bar{I}_2\frac{\partial^2\psi_\alpha}{\partial t^2}\right) \qquad : \delta u_o$$

$$\frac{\partial}{\partial\beta}N_\beta^S + \frac{\partial}{\partial\alpha}N_{\alpha\beta}^S + \mathcal{F}_\beta^S = \left(\bar{I}_1\frac{\partial^2 v_o}{\partial t^2} + \bar{I}_2\frac{\partial^2\psi_\beta}{\partial t^2}\right) \qquad : \delta v_o$$

$$-\left(\frac{N_\alpha^S}{R_\alpha} + \frac{N_\beta^S}{R_\beta} + \frac{N_{\alpha\beta}^S + N_{\beta\alpha}^S}{R_{\alpha\beta}}\right) + \frac{\partial}{\partial\alpha}Q_\alpha^S + \frac{\partial}{\partial\beta}Q_\beta^S + \mathcal{F}_n^S = \left(\bar{I}_1\frac{\partial^2 w_o}{\partial t^2}\right) \qquad : \delta w_o$$

$$\frac{\partial}{\partial\alpha}M_\alpha^S + \frac{\partial}{\partial\beta}M_{\beta\alpha}^S - Q_\alpha^S + \mathcal{C}_\alpha^S = \left(\bar{I}_2\frac{\partial^2 u_o}{\partial t^2} + \bar{I}_3\frac{\partial^2\psi_\alpha}{\partial t^2}\right) \qquad : \delta\psi_\alpha$$

$$\frac{\partial}{\partial\beta}M_\beta^S + \frac{\partial}{\partial\alpha}M_{\alpha\beta}^S - Q_\beta^S + \mathcal{C}_\beta^S = \left(\bar{I}_2\frac{\partial^2 u_o}{\partial t^2} + \bar{I}_3\frac{\partial^2\psi_\beta}{\partial t^2}\right) \qquad : \delta\psi_\beta$$

$$\frac{\partial}{\partial\alpha}N_\alpha^\mathcal{E} + \frac{\partial}{\partial\beta}N_\beta^\mathcal{E} - \mathcal{F}^\mathcal{E} = 0 \quad : \delta\varphi_o, \qquad\qquad \frac{\partial}{\partial\alpha}M_\alpha^\mathcal{E} + \frac{\partial}{\partial\beta}M_\beta^\mathcal{E} - \mathcal{C}^\mathcal{E} = 0 \quad : \delta\varphi_o$$

$$\frac{\partial}{\partial\alpha}N_\alpha^\mathcal{G} + \frac{\partial}{\partial\beta}N_\beta^\mathcal{G} - \mathcal{F}^\mathcal{G} = 0 \quad : \delta\vartheta_o, \qquad\qquad \frac{\partial}{\partial\alpha}M_\alpha^\mathcal{G} + \frac{\partial}{\partial\beta}M_\beta^\mathcal{G} - \mathcal{C}^\mathcal{G} = 0 \quad : \delta\vartheta_o$$

Hence, the procedure outlined above, is valid irrespective of using the Navier solution. The Navier-type solution can be applied to obtain exact solution as $\left(\mathcal{K}_{ij} + \lambda^2\mathcal{M}_{ij}\right)\{\Delta\} = \{\mathcal{F}\}$, which is an eigenvalue problem. For nontrivial solution, the determinant of the matrix in the parenthesis is set to zero. Then the configuration of $\mathcal{K}_{ij}$ terms for SS-1, cross-ply and rectangular plane form is listed in the Appendix.

In the other hand, the transient response is solved by Newmark's integration method that receipts advantage of the static solution form for spatial variation, and uses the numerical method to solve the resulting differential equations in time. The constant-average acceleration scheme is used for linear transient problems due to the well-known stability in such problems [15].

5   Illustrated Example

In the present examine, laminated composite square shell $(a/b = 1)$ is considered here made of BaTiO$_3$ and CoFe$_2$O$_4$ materials that are given in [1], but in (cm) scale. The shell is assumed of $(R_\alpha, R_\beta, R_{\alpha\beta} = \infty)$ and the shear correction factor used in FSDT is $(K^2 = 5/6)$. Since, no estimate on the time-step for the stable analysis is obtainable, therefore, a normative study is performed to select the appropriate time-step that yields a stable, accurate solution and preserves the computational time. In fact, $\delta t = 50\,\mu s$ is investigated and selected for the present transient analysis.

Therefore, the effect of the in-plane stresses is depicted. Figure 1 shows the effect of the side to thickness ratio for a shell of two layers subjected to sinusoidal load. The maximum transverse deflection versus the fleeting time is also investigated and tabulated in Table 1 for each plate and shallow shell.

It is interesting to note, that the ratio of transient to static deflection is defined as $\bar{w}_D/\bar{w}_S$, where max $\bar{w}_D$ is the maximum dynamic displacement and $\bar{w}_S$ is the static converged displacement value. It is also observed that the ratio of $\bar{w}_D/\bar{w}_S = 1.06294$ for plate, whereas it is 1.19668 for shallow and it is found that takes less with increasing of side to thickness ratio in both of plate and shallow case. One may conclude that the effect of the transverse shear is greater on the dynamic response than the static response. Having contemplated the enter deflection behavior, it is found that the magnetostrictive materials also exhibit faster responses than the piezoelectric material. It is concluded that this is because $CoFe_2O_4$ is considered as a stiffer material than $BaTiO_3$

Table 1. Maximum values of the shell[1] deflections $\bar{w} = 10^2 \times w_0 E_2 h^3 / P_0^S \alpha^4$ for node at a crucial position (x = 0.75a, y = 0.25b)

a/R	a/h	Time (μs)								
		100	200	300	400	500	600	700	800	900
(0.0)	1.0	0.212	0.799	1.621	2.482	3.176	3.538	3.481	3.020	2.264
	1.5	0.132	0.465	0.832	1.052	1.015	0.741	0.364	0.072	0.010
	2.0	0.091	0.293	0.444	0.424	0.249	0.058	0.004	0.129	0.334
	2.5	0.066	0.192	0.238	0.153	0.031	0.008	0.108	0.222	0.223
(0.5)	1.0	0.224	0.835	1.686	2.549	3.228	3.512	3.401	2.790	2.082
	1.5	0.139	0.481	0.851	1.048	0.982	0.663	0.304	0.008	0.087
	2.0	0.095	0.300	0.446	0.405	0.221	0.031	0.026	0.151	0.411
	2.5	0.069	0.195	0.234	0.137	0.023	0.012	0.140	0.215	0.232

1 The properties are taken for shell of (P/M, N = 2, δt = 50 μs, a/b = 1, K2 = 5/6, P = BaTiO$_3$, and M = CoFe$_2$O$_4$).

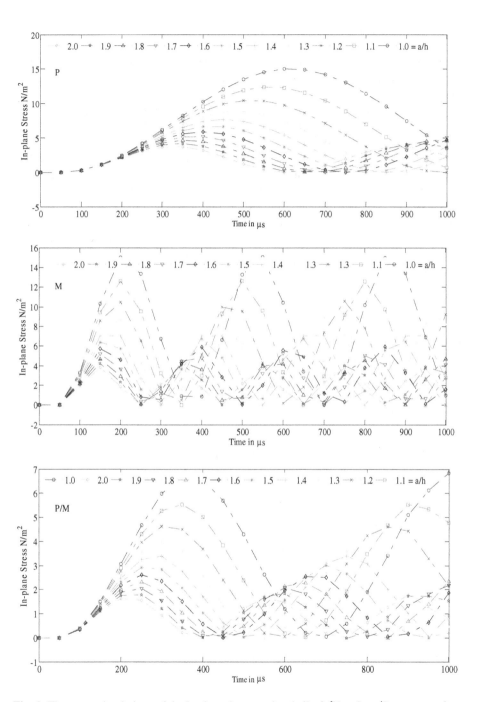

Fig. 1. The stress simulations of the laminated composite shell of $(N = 2,\ a/R = \infty,\ a = b = 25\text{cm},\ m = n = 1$, where $P = BaTiO_3$ and $M = CoFe_2O_4)$

6   Conclusion

In this paper model that governing the magneto-electro-elastic shell and incorporating thermal field is derived based on FSDT involving Codazzi-Gauss geometrical discretion. The generic forced-solution procedures for the response were derived, and its frequency parameters were evaluated in simply supported boundary condition. Then, the transient solution is obtained by Newmark's method to evaluate the influence of magnetic and electric parameters on the structure response. Results have been shown that the effect of the transverse shear is greater on the dynamic response than the static response. However, it is also observed that the ratio of transient to static deflection takes less with increasing of side to thickness ratio in both of plate and shallow case. One may conclude also that structronics are capable to simultaneously sensing; mechanical, electrical, and magnetic fields, as well as simultaneously generating control forces to eliminate the adverse effects or to enhance the vibrations attenuation. Finally, the present results may serve as a reference in developing the structronics shell theories and to improve the benchmark solutions for judging the existence of imprecise theories and other numerical approaches.

Acknowledgments. The authors would like to acknowledge Universiti Teknologi PETRONAS for sponsoring the research work under the GA scheme.

Appendix

$$\mathcal{K}_{11} = -\bar\varsigma_{11}^1\alpha_m^2 - \tilde\varsigma_{66}^1\beta_n^2, \ \ \mathcal{K}_{12} = -(\varsigma_{12}^1 + \varsigma_{66}^1)\alpha_m\beta_n \ , \ \ \mathcal{K}_{22} = -\tilde\varsigma_{22}^1\beta_n^2 - \bar\varsigma_{66}^1\alpha_m^2,$$

$$\mathcal{K}_{13} = \left(\frac{\bar\varsigma_{11}^1}{R_\alpha} + \frac{\varsigma_{12}^1}{R_\beta}\right)\alpha_m, \ \ \mathcal{K}_{23} = \left(\frac{\varsigma_{12}^1}{R_\alpha} + \frac{\tilde\varsigma_{22}^1}{R_\beta}\right)\beta_n \ , \ \ \mathcal{K}_{35} = \left(-\tilde\varsigma_{44}^1 + \frac{\varsigma_{12}^2}{R_\alpha} + \frac{\tilde\varsigma_{22}^2}{R_\beta}\right)\beta_n \ ,$$

$$\mathcal{K}_{33} = -\tilde\varsigma_{44}^1\beta_n^2 - \bar\varsigma_{55}^1\alpha_m^2 - \left(\frac{\bar\varsigma_{11}^1}{R_\alpha^2} + \frac{2\varsigma_{12}^1}{R_\alpha R_\beta} + \frac{\tilde\varsigma_{22}^1}{R_\beta^2}\right), \mathcal{K}_{14} = -\bar\varsigma_{11}^2\alpha_m^2 - \bar\varsigma_{66}^2\beta_n^2,$$

$$\mathcal{K}_{24} = -(\varsigma_{12}^2 + \varsigma_{66}^2)\alpha_m\beta_n \ , \ \ \mathcal{K}_{34} = \left(-\bar\varsigma_{55}^1 + \frac{\bar\varsigma_{11}^2}{R_\alpha} + \frac{\varsigma_{12}^2}{R_\beta}\right)\alpha_m \ , \ \ \mathcal{K}_{44} = -\bar\varsigma_{55}^1 - \bar\varsigma_{11}^3\alpha_m^2 - \tilde\varsigma_{66}^3\beta_n^2$$

$$\mathcal{K}_{15} = -(\varsigma_{12}^2 + \varsigma_{66}^2)\alpha_m\beta_n \ , \ \ \ \ \mathcal{K}_{25} = -\tilde\varsigma_{22}^2\beta_n^2 - \bar\varsigma_{66}^2\alpha_m^2, \ \ \mathcal{K}_{55} = -\tilde\varsigma_{44}^1 - \bar\varsigma_{66}^3\alpha_m^2 - \tilde\varsigma_{22}^3\beta_n^2,$$

$$\mathcal{K}_{45} = -(\varsigma_{12}^3 + \varsigma_{66}^3)\alpha_m\beta_n \ , \ \ \mathcal{K}_{16} = \left(\frac{\varrho_{14}^1}{R_{\alpha\beta}} + \frac{\bar\varrho_{15}^1}{R_\alpha}\right)\alpha_m \ , \ \ \mathcal{K}_{26} = \left(\frac{\tilde\varrho_{24}^1}{R_\beta} + \frac{\varrho_{25}^1}{R_{\alpha\beta}}\right)\beta_n$$

$$\mathcal{K}_{36} = -(\bar\varrho_{15}^1\alpha_m^2 + \tilde\varrho_{24}^1\beta_n^2), \ \ \mathcal{K}_{66} = -(\bar\epsilon_{11}^1\alpha_m^2 + \tilde\epsilon_{22}^1\beta_n^2),$$

$$\mathcal{K}_{46} = \left(-\bar\varrho_{15}^1 + \frac{\bar\varrho_{15}^2}{R_\alpha}\right)\alpha_m, \ \ \mathcal{K}_{56} = \left(-\tilde\varrho_{24}^1 + \frac{\tilde\varrho_{24}^2}{R_\beta}\right)\beta_n \ , \ \ \mathcal{K}_{17} = \left(\frac{\varrho_{14}^2}{R_{\alpha\beta}} + \frac{\bar\varrho_{15}^2}{R_\alpha}\right)\alpha_m,$$

$$\mathcal{K}_{27} = \left(\frac{\tilde\varrho_{24}^2}{R_\beta} + \frac{\varrho_{25}^2}{R_{\alpha\beta}}\right)\beta_n \ , \ \ \mathcal{K}_{37} = -(\bar\varrho_{15}^2\alpha_m^2 + \tilde\varrho_{24}^2\beta_n^2), \ \ \mathcal{K}_{47} = \left(-\bar\varrho_{15}^2 + \frac{\bar\varrho_{15}^3}{R_\alpha}\right)\alpha_m$$

$$\mathcal{K}_{67} = -(\bar\epsilon_{11}^2\alpha_m^2 + \tilde\epsilon_{22}^2\beta_n^2), \ \ \mathcal{K}_{77} = -(\bar\epsilon_{11}^3\alpha_m^2 + \tilde\epsilon_{22}^3\beta_n^2),$$

$$\mathcal{K}_{18} = \left(\frac{\kappa_{14}^1}{R_{\alpha\beta}} + \frac{\bar\kappa_{15}^1}{R_\alpha}\right)\alpha_m, \ \ \mathcal{K}_{28} = \left(\frac{\tilde\kappa_{24}^1}{R_\beta} + \frac{\kappa_{25}^1}{R_{\alpha\beta}}\right)\beta_n \ , \ \ \ \ \ \mathcal{K}_{38} = -(\bar\kappa_{15}^1\alpha_m^2 + \tilde\kappa_{24}^1\beta_n^2),$$

$$\mathcal{K}_{48} = \left(-\bar{\kappa}_{15}^1 + \frac{\bar{\kappa}_{15}^2}{R_\alpha}\right)\alpha_m, \quad \mathcal{K}_{57} = \left(-\tilde{\varrho}_{24}^2 + \frac{\tilde{\varrho}_{24}^3}{R_\beta}\right)\beta_n, \quad \mathcal{K}_{58} = \left(-\bar{\kappa}_{24}^1 + \frac{\bar{\kappa}_{24}^2}{R_\beta}\right)\beta_n$$

$$\mathcal{K}_{68} = -(\bar{\eta}_{11}^1\alpha_m^2 + \bar{\eta}_{22}^1\beta_n^2), \quad \mathcal{K}_{78} = -(\bar{\eta}_{11}^2\alpha_m^2 + \bar{\eta}_{22}^2\beta_n^2), \quad \mathcal{K}_{88} = -(\bar{\mu}_{11}^1\alpha_m^2 + \tilde{\mu}_{22}^1\beta_n^2),$$

$$\mathcal{K}_{19} = \left(\frac{\kappa_{14}^2}{R_{\alpha\beta}} + \frac{\bar{\kappa}_{15}^2}{R_\alpha}\right)\alpha_m, \quad \mathcal{K}_{29} = \left(\frac{\tilde{\kappa}_{24}^2}{R_\beta} + \frac{\kappa_{25}^2}{R_{\alpha\beta}}\right)\beta_n, \quad \mathcal{K}_{39} = -(\bar{\kappa}_{15}^2\alpha_m^2 + \bar{\kappa}_{24}^2\beta_n^2),$$

$$\mathcal{K}_{49} = \left(-\bar{\kappa}_{15}^2 + \frac{\bar{\kappa}_{15}^3}{R_\alpha}\right)\alpha_m, \quad \mathcal{K}_{59} = \left(-\bar{\kappa}_{24}^2 + \frac{\bar{\kappa}_{24}^3}{R_\beta}\right)\beta_n, \quad \mathcal{K}_{69} = -(\bar{\eta}_{11}^2\alpha_m^2 + \bar{\eta}_{22}^2\beta_n^2),$$

$$\mathcal{K}_{79} = -(\bar{\eta}_{11}^3\alpha_m^2 + \bar{\eta}_{22}^3\beta_n^2), \quad \mathcal{K}_{89} = -(\bar{\mu}_{11}^2\alpha_m^2 + \tilde{\mu}_{22}^2\beta_n^2), \quad \mathcal{K}_{99} = -(\bar{\mu}_{11}^3\alpha_m^2 + \tilde{\mu}_{22}^3\beta_n^2).$$

References

1. Badri, T.M., Al-Kayiem, H.H.: Analysis Of Electro/Mgneto-Mechanical Coupling Factor: In Laminated Composite Plate Construct From Rotated Y-Cut Crystals. In: National Postgraduate Conferencec (NPC). IEEE, Malaysia (2011)
2. Badri, T.M., Al-Kayiem, H.H.: Reducing The Magneto-Electro-Elastic Effective Properties For 2-D Analysis. In: Colloquium On Humanities, Science And Engineering Research (CHUSER 2011). IEEE, Malaysia (2011)
3. Badri, T.M., Al-Kayiem, H.H.: Free Vibration Analysis Of Piezo-Laminated Shell Structure. In: The World Engineering, Science And Technology Congress, ESTCON 2012, Malaysia (2012)
4. Badri, T.M., Al-Kayiem, H.H.: A Static Analysis Of Piezo-Laminated Shell Structure. In: The World Engineering, Science And Technology Congress (ESTCON 2012), Malaysia (2012)
5. Pan, E.: Exact Solution For Simply Supported And Multilayered Magneto-Electro-Elastic Plates. Asme Transactions of the Asme 68, 608 (2001)
6. Heyliger, P.R., Pan, E.: Static Fields In Magnetoelectroelastic Laminates. Aiaa Journal 42, 1435–1443 (2004)
7. Yoshihiro Ootao, Y.T.: Transient Analysis Of Multilayered Magneto-Electro-Thermoelastic Strip Due To Nonuniform Heat Supply. Composite Structures 68, 471–480 (2005)
8. Dai, H.L., Wang, X.: Magneto-Thermo-Electro-Elastic Transient Response In A Piezoelectric Hollow Cylinder Subjected To Complex Loadings. International Journal Of Solids And Structures 43, 5628–5646 (2006)
9. Nellya, N.R.: The Theory Of Piezoelectric Shells And Plates. CRC Press, Moscow (1993)
10. Reddy, J.N.: Energy And Variational Methods In Applied Mechanics. John Wiley & Sons, Ltd., New York (1984)
11. Bao, Y.: Static And Dynamic Analysis Of Piezothermoelastic Laminated Shell Composites With Distributed Sensors And Actuators. In: Mechanical Engineering. University Of Kentucky, Lexington (1996)
12. Tzou, H.S., Lee, H.-J., Arnold, S.M.: Smart Materials, Precision Sensors/ Actuators, Smart Structures, And Structronic Systems. Mechanics of Advanced Materials And Structures 11, 367–393 (2004)
13. Pérez-Fernández, L.D., Bravo-Castillerob, J., Rodríguez-Ramosb, R., Sabinad, F.J.: On The Constitutive Relations And Energy Potentials Of Linear Thermo-Magneto-Electro-Elasticity. Mechanics Research Communications 36, 343–350 (2009)
14. Qatu, M.S.: Vibration Of Laminated Shells And Plates. Elsevier, London (2004)
15. Reddy, J.N.: Mechanics of Laminated Composite Plates and Shells. CRC Press, New York (2004)

Free Vibration Analysis of Structronics Shell

Thar M. Badri and Hussain H. Al-Kayiem

Mechanical Engineering Department, Universiti Teknologi PETRONAS,
Bandar Seri Iskandar, 31750 Tronoh, Perak, Malaysia
t.albarody@ymail.com

Abstract. An exact analysis for magneto-thermo-electro-elastic structronics shell is presented in this paper. The model was derived based on the first-order shear deformation shell theory involving Codazzi-Gauss geometrical discretion. The fundamental equation and its boundary conditions were derived using variational energy method. The generic forced-solution procedure for the response was derived, and its frequency parameters were evaluated in the simply supported boundary condition. Then, solution is obtained to evaluate the influence of magnetic and electric parameters on the structure frequencies. Whereas, result have shown a close agreement with alternative models that reported in literature. The present results may serve as a reference in developing of various sensors/actuators that formed from magneto-electro-elastic materials. Accordingly, the present results could improve the benchmark solutions for judging the existence of imprecise theories and other numerical approaches.

Keywords: Magneto-thermo-electro-elastic control, Nerves structure, Adaptive sensors/actuators, Piezo-laminated shell, Structural health monitoring.

1   Introduction

Structronics is concept of "Structures + Electronics", which are synergistic integration of adaptive or functional materials (e.g., piezoelectric, piezomagnetic, electrostrictive, magnetostrictive, and the alike materials). Furthermore, structronics had the capability of simultaneously sensing/ actuating; mechanical, electrical, magnetic and even thermal effects, as well as simultaneously generating response to eliminate or enhance the desirable effects. Whereas, structronics are largely improves the working performance and lifetime of devices that construct from it [1-4]. Several accurate solutions of structronics shell have been proved for special cases of Pan's analysis for multi-layered piezoelectric-magnetic. Pan and Heyliger [5] demonstrated the free vibration analysis of the simply supported and multilayered magneto-electro-elastic (MEE) plates under cylindrical bending. Following up the previous Stroh formulation, Pan and Han [6] presented the 3-D solutions of multilayered functionally graded (FG) and MEE plates. By an asymptotic approach, Chih Ping Wu and Yi Hwa Tsai [7] studied 3-D static and dynamic behavior of doubly curved FG-MEE shells under the mechanical load, electric displacement, and magnetic flux by considered the edge boundary conditions as full simple supports. In comparison with the recently development of smart composite, the literature dealing with theoretical work in structronics shell

S.G. Ponnambalam et al. (Eds.): IRAM 2012, CCIS 330, pp. 322–330, 2012.
© Springer-Verlag Berlin Heidelberg 2012

concerning coupled field phenomena magneto-thermo-electro-elastic (MTEE) field, is rather scarce. In this article, a model for structronics shell based on the first-order transversely shear deformation (FOSD) theory will be developed. In additional, new issues elicited by structronics parameters, such as the difference in the classes of vibration due to material properties are addressed. The results supplied herein are expected to provide a foundation for the investigation of the interactive effects among the thermal, magnetic, electric and elastic fields in thin-walled nerves structures.

2 Kinematic Equation

According to the FOSD, the following representation for MEE fields is postulated:

$$u(\alpha_1,\alpha_2,\zeta) = u_o(\alpha_1,\alpha_2) + \zeta\psi_\alpha(\alpha_1,\alpha_2), v(\alpha_1,\alpha_2,\zeta) = v_o(\alpha_1,\alpha_2) + \zeta\psi_\beta(\alpha_1,\alpha_2),$$
$$w(\alpha_1,\alpha_2,\zeta) = w_o(\alpha_1,\alpha_2), \tag{1}$$
$$\varphi(\alpha_1,\alpha_2,\zeta) = -\varphi_o(\alpha_1,\alpha_2)-\zeta\varphi_1(\alpha_1,\alpha_2), \quad \vartheta(\alpha_1,\alpha_2,\zeta) = -\vartheta_o(\alpha_1,\alpha_2)-\zeta\vartheta_1(\alpha_1,\alpha_2),$$

where, u_o, v_o and w_o are referred to as the midsurface displacements and ψ_α and ψ_β are midsurface rotations of the shell, φ_o is the electric potential, and ϑ_o is the magnetic potential. The strains at any point in the shells can be written as: [8]

$$\varepsilon_{ii} = \frac{1}{\gamma_i}\frac{\partial u_i}{\partial \alpha_i} + \frac{1}{\gamma_i\gamma_j}\frac{\partial \gamma_i}{\partial \alpha_j}u_j + \frac{1}{\gamma_i\gamma_3}\frac{\partial \gamma_i}{\partial \zeta}u_3, \quad \varepsilon_{ij} = \frac{\gamma_i}{\gamma_j}\frac{\partial}{\partial \alpha_j}\left(\frac{u_i}{\gamma_i}\right) + \frac{\gamma_j}{\gamma_i}\frac{\partial}{\partial \alpha_i}\left(\frac{u_j}{\gamma_j}\right),$$

$$\varepsilon_{33} = \frac{1}{\gamma_3}\frac{\partial u_3}{\partial \zeta} + \frac{1}{\gamma_3\gamma_1}\frac{\partial \gamma_3}{\partial \alpha_1}u_1 + \frac{1}{\gamma_2\gamma_3}\frac{\partial \gamma_3}{\partial \alpha_2}u_2, \quad \varepsilon_{ij} = \frac{\gamma_3}{\gamma_i}\frac{\partial}{\partial \alpha_i}\left(\frac{u_3}{\gamma_3}\right) + \frac{\gamma_i}{\gamma_3}\frac{\partial}{\partial \zeta}\left(\frac{u_i}{\gamma_i}\right),$$

$$\xi_{o\alpha} = -\frac{1}{A_1}\frac{\partial \varphi_o}{\partial \alpha}, \quad \xi_{1\alpha} = -\frac{1}{A_1}\frac{\partial \varphi_1}{\partial \alpha}, \quad \xi_{o\beta} = -\frac{1}{A_2}\frac{\partial \varphi_o}{\partial \beta}, \quad \xi_{1\beta} = -\frac{1}{A_2}\frac{\partial \varphi_1}{\partial \beta}, \tag{2}$$

$$\chi_{o\alpha} = -\frac{1}{A_1}\frac{\partial \varphi_o}{\partial \alpha}, \quad \chi_{1\alpha} = -\frac{1}{A_1}\frac{\partial \varphi_1}{\partial \alpha}, \quad \chi_{o\beta} = -\frac{1}{A_2}\frac{\partial \varphi_o}{\partial \beta}, \quad \chi_{1\beta} = -\frac{1}{A_2}\frac{\partial \varphi_1}{\partial \beta},$$

where $u_i = u_i(\alpha_1,\alpha_2,\zeta)$, $u_3 = u_3(\alpha_1,\alpha_2,\zeta)$, $\gamma_i = A_i(1 + \zeta/R_i)$, and $\gamma_3 = 1$.

3 Energy Variational Principle

The energy functional is important for deriving a consistent set of equations of motion that coupled with free charge equilibrium equations and equipping its boundary conditions [9-11]. In summary, the total energy of a shell element is defined as:

$$\delta \int_{t_o}^{t_1}[\mathcal{K} - \mathcal{P}]\,dt = 0, \tag{3}$$

where $\mathcal{P}$ is total potential energy;-

$$\mathcal{P} = \iiint_V [\mathcal{Q}(\mathcal{S}_i,\mathcal{E}_j,\mathcal{G}_{l,}\mathcal{T}) + (\mathcal{T}\tau)]dV - \iint_{\Omega_o}\left(t(\mathcal{S}_i,\mathcal{E}_j,\mathcal{G}_{l,}) + \mathcal{W}(\mathcal{S}_i,\mathcal{E}_j,\mathcal{G}_{l,})\right), \tag{4}$$

$Q(S_i, \mathcal{E}_j, G_l, \mathcal{T}\ )$, $t(S_i, \mathcal{E}_j, G_{l,})$, and $W(S_i, \mathcal{E}_j, G_l)$ are the thermodynamic potential "Gibbs free energy", tractions and the work done by body force, electrical and magnetic charge, respectively. Moreover, the kinetic energy is

$$\mathcal{K} = \frac{I}{2} \iiint_V [\dot{u}^2 + \dot{v}^2 + \dot{w}^2]\, dV. \tag{5}$$

Substituting Equations (2) and (3) into Equation (1) yields

$$\int_{t_0}^{t_1} \frac{I}{2} \iiint_V [\dot{u}^2 + \dot{v}^2 + \dot{w}^2]\, dV\, dt - \left\{ \int_{t_0}^{t_1} \iiint_V [\delta Q(S_i, \mathcal{E}_j, G_l, \mathcal{T}) + (\mathcal{T}\delta\tau)]\, dV dt \right.$$
$$\left. - \int_{t_0}^{t_1} \iint_{\Omega_0} \left(\delta t(S_i, \mathcal{E}_j, G_{l,}) + \delta W(S_i, \mathcal{E}_j, G_l) \right) dA dt \right\} = 0. \tag{6}$$

The kinetic energy of the shell can be expressed as

$$\mathcal{K} = \frac{I}{2} \iint_{\Omega_0} \int_{-h/2}^{h/2} \begin{pmatrix} [\dot{u}_o^2 + \dot{v}_o^2 + \dot{w}_o^2] \\ +\zeta^2[\dot{\psi}_\alpha^2 + \dot{\psi}_\beta^2] \\ +2\zeta[\dot{u}_o^2\dot{\psi}_\alpha^2 + \dot{v}_o^2\dot{\psi}_\beta^2] \end{pmatrix} \times \left(1 + \frac{\zeta}{R_\alpha}\right)\left(1 + \frac{\zeta}{R_\beta}\right) AB\, d\zeta\, dA. \tag{7}$$

Based on the conservation laws of electro-magnetic field, the linear thermodynamic potential energy Q for quasi-static infinitesimal reversible system, subject to mechanical, electric, magnetic, and thermal influences from its surroundings, can be approximated by

$$Q(S_i, \mathcal{E}_j, G_l, \mathcal{T}\ ) \cong \frac{1}{2}(S_{ij}\, \varepsilon_{kl} - \mathcal{E}_n\, \xi_n - G_q\, \chi_q - \mathcal{T}\tau), \tag{8}$$

means that S_{ij}, $\mathcal{E}_k$, G_l, and $\mathcal{T}$ are the dependent variables of Q, while ε_{ij}, ξ_k, χ_l, and τ are the natural independent variables. In order to obtain the thermodynamic potential for which these variables are natural, is performed [12], that is

$$2Q = \varsigma_{ijkl}^{\mathcal{E},G,\mathcal{T}} \varepsilon_{ij}\varepsilon_{kl} - \epsilon_{mn}^{S,G,\mathcal{T}} \xi_m\xi_n - \mu_{pq}^{S,\mathcal{E},\mathcal{T}} \chi_p\chi_q - \theta^{S,\mathcal{E},G}\tau^2 - 2\varrho_{mkl}^{G,\mathcal{T}}\varepsilon_{kl}\xi_m - 2\kappa_{pkl}^{\mathcal{E},\mathcal{T}}\varepsilon_{kl}\chi_p$$
$$- 2\lambda_{kl}^{\mathcal{E},G}\varepsilon_{kl}\tau - 2\eta_{pn}^{S,\mathcal{T}}\xi_n\chi_p - 2\rho_n^{S,G}\xi_n\,\tau - 2\gamma_q^{S,\mathcal{E}}\chi_q\,\tau, \tag{9}$$

where Q is commonly known as Gibbs free energy, the superscripts indicate that the magnitudes must be kept constant when measuring them in the laboratory frame. The constitutive relations can be expressed formally by differentiation of Q corresponding to each dependent variable as

$$S_{ij} = \left(\frac{\partial Q}{\partial \varepsilon_{kl}}\right) = \varsigma_{ijkl}^{\mathcal{E},G,\mathcal{T}} \varepsilon_{ij} - \varrho_{mkl}^{G,\mathcal{T}}\xi_m - \kappa_{pkl}^{\mathcal{E},\mathcal{T}}\chi_p - \lambda_{kl}^{\mathcal{E},G}\tau,$$
$$\mathcal{E}_k = \left(\frac{-\partial Q}{\partial \xi_n}\right) = \varrho_{ijn}^{G,\mathcal{T}} \varepsilon_{ij} + \epsilon_{mn}^{S,G,\mathcal{T}}\xi_m + \eta_{pn}^{S,\mathcal{T}}\chi_p + \rho_n^{S,G}\tau, \tag{10}$$

$$
\mathcal{G}_l = \left(\frac{-\partial Q}{\partial \chi_q}\right) = \kappa_{ijq}^{\mathcal{E},\mathcal{T}}\varepsilon_{ij} + \eta_{mq}^{S,\mathcal{T}}\xi_m + \mu_{pq}^{S,\mathcal{E},\mathcal{T}}\chi_p + \gamma_q^{S,\mathcal{E}}\tau,
$$

$$
\mathcal{T} = \left(\frac{-\partial Q}{\partial \tau}\right) = \lambda_{ij}^{\mathcal{E},\mathcal{G}}\varepsilon_{ij} + \rho_m^{S,\mathcal{G}}\xi_m + \gamma_p^{S,\mathcal{E}}\chi_p + \theta^{S,\mathcal{E},\mathcal{G}}\tau,
\tag{11}
$$

Moreover, the external work is

$$
\mathcal{W}(S_i,\mathcal{E}_j,\mathcal{G}_l) = \begin{pmatrix} \mathcal{F}_\alpha^S u_o + \mathcal{F}_\beta^S v_o + \mathcal{F}_n^S w_o + \mathcal{C}_\alpha^S\psi_\alpha + \mathcal{C}_\beta^S\psi_\beta \\ -\mathcal{F}^{\mathcal{E}}\varphi_o + \mathcal{C}^{\mathcal{E}}\varphi_1 - \mathcal{F}^{\mathcal{G}}\vartheta_o + \mathcal{C}^{\mathcal{G}}\vartheta_1 \end{pmatrix},
\tag{12}
$$

where $\mathcal{F}_\alpha^S$, $\mathcal{F}_\beta^S$, and $\mathcal{F}_n^S$ are the distributed forces in α, β and ζ directions, respectively, and $\mathcal{C}_\alpha^S$, and $\mathcal{C}_\beta^S$ are the distributed couples about the middle surface of the shell. In addition $\mathcal{F}^{\mathcal{E}}$, $\mathcal{C}^{\mathcal{E}}$, $\mathcal{F}^{\mathcal{G}}$ and $\mathcal{C}^{\mathcal{G}}$ are the distributed forces and couples due to electrical and magnetic charge. Substituting Equations (10), (11) and (12) in Equation (4) and equating the resulted equation with Equation (7), yields the equations of motion of structronics shell as shown in Equation (13) below:

$$
\int_{t_o}^{t_1}\iint_{\Omega_o}\delta\begin{pmatrix} \frac{\bar{I}_1}{2}[\dot{u}_o^2+\dot{v}_o^2+\dot{w}_o^2] \\ \frac{\bar{I}_3}{2}[\dot{\psi}_\alpha^2+\dot{\psi}_\beta^2] \\ \bar{I}_2[\dot{u}_o^2\dot{\psi}_\alpha^2+\dot{v}_o^2\dot{\psi}_\beta^2] \end{pmatrix}ABdAdt - \left\{\int_{t_o}^{t_1}\iiint_V\begin{pmatrix} (\varsigma_{ij}\varepsilon-\varrho_{ij}\xi-\kappa_{ij}\chi-\lambda_i\tau)\delta\varepsilon \\ -(\varrho_{ij}\varepsilon+\epsilon_{ij}\xi+\eta_{ij}\chi+\rho_i\tau)\delta\xi \\ -(\kappa_{ij}\varepsilon+\eta_{ij}\xi+\mu_{ij}\chi+\gamma_i\tau)\delta\chi \\ -(\lambda_i\varepsilon+\rho_i\xi+\gamma_i\chi+\theta\tau)\delta\tau \\ +(\lambda_i\varepsilon+\rho_i\xi+\gamma_i\chi+\theta\tau)\delta\tau \end{pmatrix}dVdt\right.
$$

$$
\left. -\int_{t_o}^{t_1}\iint_{\Omega_o}\begin{pmatrix} (\mathcal{F}_\alpha^S u_o+\mathcal{F}_\beta^S v_o+\mathcal{F}_n^S w_o+\mathcal{C}_\alpha^S\psi_\alpha+\mathcal{C}_\beta^S\psi_\beta) \\ -(\mathcal{F}^{\mathcal{E}}\varphi_o+\mathcal{C}^{\mathcal{E}}\varphi_1)-(\mathcal{F}^{\mathcal{G}}\vartheta_o+\mathcal{C}^{\mathcal{G}}\vartheta_1) \end{pmatrix}ABdAdt\right\} = 0. \tag{13}
$$

Note that, the kinetic relations (i.e., the force and moment resultants per unit length at the boundary Ω) are obtained by integrating the stresses over the shell thickness as in Equation (14).

$$
\begin{Bmatrix} N_x^S, & M_x^S \\ N_x^{\mathcal{E}}, & M_x^{\mathcal{E}} \\ N_x^{\mathcal{G}}, & M_x^{\mathcal{G}} \end{Bmatrix} = \int_{-h/2}^{h/2}(1,\zeta)\begin{pmatrix} \varsigma_{ijkl}^{\mathcal{E},\mathcal{G},\mathcal{T}}\varepsilon_{ij} - \varrho_{mkl}^{\mathcal{G},\mathcal{T}}\xi_m - \kappa_{pkl}^{\mathcal{E},\mathcal{T}}\chi_p - \lambda_{kl}^{\mathcal{E},\mathcal{G}}\tau \\ \varrho_{ijn}^{\mathcal{G},\mathcal{T}}\varepsilon_{ij} + \epsilon_{mn}^{S,\mathcal{G},\mathcal{T}}\xi_m + \eta_{pn}^{S,\mathcal{T}}\chi_p + \rho_n^{S,\mathcal{G}}\tau \\ \kappa_{ijq}^{\mathcal{E},\mathcal{T}}\varepsilon_{ij} + \eta_{mq}^{S,\mathcal{T}}\xi_m + \mu_{pq}^{S,\mathcal{E},\mathcal{T}}\chi_p + \gamma_q^{S,\mathcal{E}}\tau \end{pmatrix}\left(1+\frac{\zeta}{R_y}\right)d\zeta \tag{14}
$$

where the subscripts x and y denote either of α_1, or α_2 in which $x \neq y$, h is the shell thickness. By recasting Equation (13) to put in the familiar form, the governing equations of motion and the charge equilibrium equations could be derived based on the fundamental Lemma of calculus of variations. E.g., by integrating the field gradients by parts to relieve the virtual fields and setting its coefficients to zero individually.

4   Analytical Solution

Here, we introduce the following assumptions to cast the equation of motion in thick (or shear deformation) shell theories. Deepness (or shallowness) of the shell, is also one criterion used in developing shell equations. Thus, shell is referred to as a plate, when it has zero curvature or infinity radius of curvature (i.e., the term $(1 + \zeta/R_i) = 1$: where R_i is either of the curvature parameter $R_{\alpha_1}, R_{\alpha_2}, or\ R_{\alpha_1\alpha_2}$ [13]. If it is represented by the plane coordinate systems for the case of rectangular orthotropy, this leads to constant Lame´ parameters (i.e., $A_i = 1$). In additional, the radii of curvature are assumed very large compared to the in-plane displacements. (i.e., $u_i/R_i = 0, where\ i = \alpha_1, \alpha_2\ \&\ \alpha_1\alpha_2, u_i = u_o\,, or\ v_o$). Appling the above assumptions yield;

$$\frac{\partial}{\partial\alpha}N_\alpha^S + \frac{\partial}{\partial\beta}N_{\beta\alpha}^S + \mathcal{F}_\alpha^S = \left(\bar{I}_1\frac{\partial^2 u_o}{\partial t^2} + \bar{I}_2\frac{\partial^2\psi_\alpha}{\partial t^2}\right) \qquad : \delta u_o$$

$$\frac{\partial}{\partial\beta}N_\beta^S + \frac{\partial}{\partial\alpha}N_{\alpha\beta}^S + \mathcal{F}_\beta^S = \left(\bar{I}_1\frac{\partial^2 v_o}{\partial t^2} + \bar{I}_2\frac{\partial^2\psi_\beta}{\partial t^2}\right) \qquad : \delta v_o$$

$$-\left(\frac{N_\alpha^S}{R_\alpha} + \frac{N_\beta^S}{R_\beta} + \frac{N_{\alpha\beta}^S + N_{\beta\alpha}^S}{R_{\alpha\beta}}\right) + \frac{\partial}{\partial\alpha}Q_\alpha^S + \frac{\partial}{\partial\beta}Q_\beta^S + \mathcal{F}_n^S = \left(\bar{I}_1\frac{\partial^2 w_o}{\partial t^2}\right) \qquad : \delta w_o$$

$$\frac{\partial}{\partial\alpha}M_\alpha^S + \frac{\partial}{\partial\beta}M_{\beta\alpha}^S - Q_\alpha^S + \mathcal{C}_\alpha^S = \left(\bar{I}_2\frac{\partial^2 u_o}{\partial t^2} + \bar{I}_3\frac{\partial^2\psi_\alpha}{\partial t^2}\right) \qquad : \delta\psi_\alpha$$

$$\frac{\partial}{\partial\beta}M_\beta^S + \frac{\partial}{\partial\alpha}M_{\alpha\beta}^S - Q_\beta^S + \mathcal{C}_\beta^S = \left(\bar{I}_2\frac{\partial^2 u_o}{\partial t^2} + \bar{I}_3\frac{\partial^2\psi_\beta}{\partial t^2}\right) \qquad : \delta\psi_\beta$$

$$\frac{\partial}{\partial\alpha}N_\alpha^\mathcal{E} + \frac{\partial}{\partial\beta}N_\beta^\mathcal{E} - \mathcal{F}^\mathcal{E} = 0 \quad : \delta\varphi_o, \qquad\qquad \frac{\partial}{\partial\alpha}M_\alpha^\mathcal{E} + \frac{\partial}{\partial\beta}M_\beta^\mathcal{E} - \mathcal{C}^\mathcal{E} = 0 \quad : \delta\varphi_o$$

$$\frac{\partial}{\partial\alpha}N_\alpha^\mathcal{G} + \frac{\partial}{\partial\beta}N_\beta^\mathcal{G} - \mathcal{F}^\mathcal{G} = 0 \quad : \delta\vartheta_o, \qquad\qquad \frac{\partial}{\partial\alpha}M_\alpha^\mathcal{G} + \frac{\partial}{\partial\beta}M_\beta^\mathcal{G} - \mathcal{C}^\mathcal{G} = 0 \quad : \delta\vartheta_o$$

Hence, the procedure outlined above, is valid irrespective of using the Navier solution, i.e., the generalized fields $u_o, v_o, w_o, \psi_\alpha, \psi_\beta, \varphi_\alpha, \varphi_\beta, \vartheta_\alpha$, and ϑ_β are expanded in a double trigonometric (Fourier) series in terms of unknown parameters. By the aid of forced solution the fields expansions can be applied to obtain exact solution as $(\mathcal{K}_{ij} + \lambda^2\mathcal{M}_{ij})\{\Delta\} = \{0\}$, which is an eigenvalue problem. For nontrivial solution, the determinant of the matrix in the parenthesis is set to zero. Then the configuration of $\mathcal{K}_{ij}$ terms for SS-1, cross-ply and rectangular plane form is listed in the Appendix.

5   Illustrated Example

In the present examine, laminated composite square shell $(a/b = 1)$ is considered here made of $BaTiO_3$ and $CoFe_2O_4$ materials, which its properties are given in [2]. Table 1 gives the lowest five frequency parameters $\Omega = \omega a^2\sqrt{\rho_{max}/\varsigma_{max}h^2}$ of the fundamental vibrational mode ($m = n = 1$), ς_{max} being the maximum of the ς_{ij} in the whole sandwich plate and $\rho_{max} = 1$. In Table 1, it clearly seen that present model is in close agreement with those obtained by Chen, et al. [14] using alternative state space formulations. In additional, Pan and Heyliger [15] results have been successfully reproduced, and discrepancy around 5% is observed. It should be mentioned here that present model has been verified for results available in literature for pure elastic shell by letting ϱ_{ij} and/or κ_{ij} equal to zero and rigorous agreement was found.

Table 1. The lowest 5 frequency parameters $\Omega = \omega a^2 \sqrt{\rho_{max}/\varsigma_{max}h^2}$ of the sandwich plate that studied by E. Pan and Heyliger [15]

Mode	P only [15]	Present[1]	M only [15]	Pesent	P/M/P[2] [15]	Present	M/P/M [15]	Present
1	2.3003	2.3003	1.9747	1.9747	1.8264	1.8366	1.8986	1.7474
2	2.8014	3.3011	2.3372	2.7774	2.1556	2.8999	2.3155	2.7622
3	3.9392	4.2475	3.1863	3.5198	3.0765	4.0917	3.1155	3.9047
4	5.3198	4.9574	4.2389	4.0664	4.1147	5.3178	4.1767	5.0882
5	6.7968	5.5112	5.3769	4.5048	5.2465	6.5492	5.3070	6.2878

1. Note that the present results are for shell of ($R_\alpha, R_\beta, R_{\alpha\beta} = \infty$) and the shear correction factor used in FSDT is ($K^2 = 5/6$).
2. (P, M, P) is denoted Piezoelectric [inner]/ Magnetostrictive [middle]/ Piezoelectric [outer].

While the bonded error for plate results were predicted and explained as due to the assumption of specialization of shell theory to plate by letting $R_\alpha = R_\beta = R_{\alpha\beta} = \infty$. In essence the plate can be regarded as a special case of the present analysis, but in fact it has a purpose of verification with literature only.

As mentioned in [15], two classes of vibration are brought out, one associated to elastic properties of the structure only, and the second is considering the elastic, electric, and magnetic properties together. A normative paradigm is carried out to study the influence of elastic, electric, and magnetic parameters on the non-dimensional frequency for two classes of vibrations. Figs. 1 and 2 displays the frequency deviation for the two classes of vibrations, via increasing the elastic-stiffing modulus ($\varsigma_{11}/\varsigma_{33}$) for different piezo-electric and -magnetic modulus. On the other hand, the effect of the piezoelectric modulus ($\varrho_{11}/\varrho_{33}$) on the frequency parameter for different dielectric ratio are also investigated and presented in Fig. 3. As well, the effect of permeability modulus on the frequency parameter is shown in Figure 4. From Fig. 1 to 4,

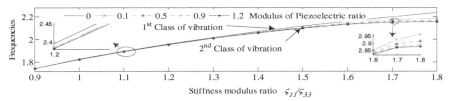

Fig. 1. The frequencies of shell of ($\varsigma_{12}/\varsigma_{33} = \varsigma_{13}/\varsigma_{33} = 0.5$, $\varsigma_{44}/\varsigma_{33} = \varsigma_{66}/\varsigma_{33} = 0.2$, $\varrho_{13}/\varrho_{33} = 0.3$, $\epsilon_{11}/\epsilon_{33} = 1.1$, $\mu_{11}/\mu_{33} = 0.5$, where $\varsigma_{33} = 10^{11}$, $\varrho_{33} = 10$, $\epsilon_{33} = 10^{-9}$, $\mu_{33} = 10^{-6}$and $\kappa_{ij} \approx 0$), and the piezoelectric modulus ratios are; ——, $\varrho_{15}/\varrho_{33} = 0.0$; − × −, $\varrho_{15}/\varrho_{33} = 0.1$; − * −, $\varrho_{15}/\varrho_{33} = 0.5$; − + −, $\varrho_{15}/\varrho_{33} = 0.9$; −• − , $\varrho_{15}/\varrho_{33} = 1.2$.

it has been observed that the lowest frequency parameter usually belongs to the second class of vibrations. Where it is clearly seen that the piezoelectric/magnetic modulus ratios have the tendency to increase the gap between the classes of vibrations, at which the dielectric and permeability have converse effects.

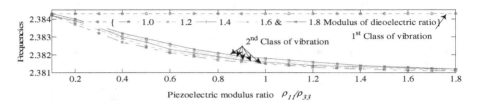

Fig. 2. The frequencies of shell of $(\varsigma_{11}/\varsigma_{33} = 1.2, \varsigma_{12}/\varsigma_{33} = \varsigma_{13}/\varsigma_{33} = 0.5, \varsigma_{44}/\varsigma_{33} = \varsigma_{66}/\varsigma_{33} = 0.2$, $\varrho_{13}/\varrho_{33} = 0.3$, $\mu_{11}/\mu_{33} = 0.5$, where $\varsigma_{33} = 10^{11}$, $\varrho_{33} = 10$, $\epsilon_{33} = 10^{-9}$, $\mu_{33} = 10^{-6}$, and $\kappa_{ij} \approx 0$), and the dielectric modulus ratios are; $-\diamond - \epsilon_{11}/\epsilon_{33} = 1.0$; $-*-$, $\epsilon_{11}/\epsilon_{33} = 1.2$; $-+-$, $\epsilon_{11}/\epsilon_{33} = 1.4$; $-\bullet -$, $\epsilon_{11}/\epsilon_{33} = 1.6$; $-\times -$, $\epsilon_{11}/\epsilon_{33} = 1.8$.

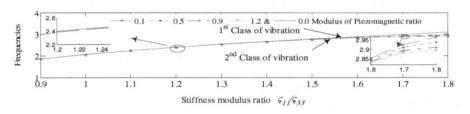

Fig. 3. $(\varsigma_{12}/\varsigma_{33} = \varsigma_{13}/\varsigma_{33} = 0.5, \varsigma_{44}/\varsigma_{33} = \varsigma_{66}/\varsigma_{33} = 0.2, \kappa_{13}/\kappa_{33} = 0.9, \epsilon_{11}/\epsilon_{33} = 0.9, \mu_{11}/\mu_{33} = 3$, where $\varsigma_{33} = 10^{11}$, $\kappa_{33} = 10^3$, $\epsilon_{33} = 10^{-11}$, $\mu_{33} = 10^{-4}$and $\varrho_{ij} \approx 0$), and the piezomagnetic modulus ratios are; ——, $\kappa_{11}/\kappa_{33} = 0.0$; $-\times -$, $\kappa_{11}/\kappa_{33} = 0.1$; $-*-$, $\kappa_{11}/\kappa_{33} = 0.5$; $-+-$, $\kappa_{11}/\kappa_{33} = 0.9$; $-\bullet -$, $\kappa_{11}/\kappa_{33} = 1.2$.

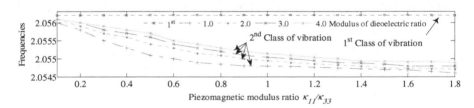

Fig. 4. The frequencies of shell of $(\varsigma_{11}/\varsigma_{33} = 1.0, \varsigma_{12}/\varsigma_{33} = \varsigma_{13}/\varsigma_{33} = 0.5, \varsigma_{44}/\varsigma_{33} = \varsigma_{66}/\varsigma_{33} = 0.2$, $\kappa_{13}/\kappa_{33} = 0.9$, $\epsilon_{11}/\epsilon_{33} = 0.9$, where $\varsigma_{33} = 10^{11}$, $\kappa_{33} = 10$, $\epsilon_{33} = 10^{-9}$, $\mu_{33} = 10^{-6}$, and $\varrho_{ij} \approx 0$), and the permeability modulus ratios are;$-\diamond - \epsilon_{11}/\epsilon_{33} = 0.0$; $-+-$, $\epsilon_{11}/\epsilon_{33} = 1.0$; $-\bullet -$, $\epsilon_{11}/\epsilon_{33} = 2.0$; $-\times -$, $\epsilon_{11}/\epsilon_{33} = 3.0$; $-*-$, $\epsilon_{11}/\epsilon_{33} = 4.0$.

6   Conclusion

In this paper model that governing the MEE shell and incorporating thermal field is derived based on FSDT involving Codazzi-Gauss geometrical discretion.

The formulations are casted in version of shell of rectangular plane-form (for purpose of validation and verification only). At which the generic forced-solution procedures for the response were derived, and its frequency parameters were evaluated in simply supported boundary condition. Results have been shown a close agreement with those obtained by [15]. However, when set the problem to pure elastic by letting ϱ_{ij} and/or κ_{ij} equal to zero a rigorous agreement with literature was also found. The present results may serve as a reference in developing the structronics shell theories and to improve the benchmark solutions for judging the existence of imprecise theories and other numerical approaches.

Acknowledgments. The authors would like to acknowledge Universiti Teknologi PETRONAS for sponsoring the research work under the GA scheme.

Appendix

$$\mathcal{K}_{11} = -\bar{\varsigma}_{11}^1 \alpha_m^2 - \tilde{\varsigma}_{66}^1 \beta_n^2, \;\; \mathcal{K}_{12} = -(\varsigma_{12}^1 + \varsigma_{66}^1)\alpha_m \beta_n, \;\; \mathcal{K}_{22} = -\tilde{\varsigma}_{22}^1 \beta_n^2 - \bar{\varsigma}_{66}^1 \alpha_m^2,$$

$$\mathcal{K}_{13} = \left(\frac{\bar{\varsigma}_{11}^1}{R_\alpha} + \frac{\varsigma_{12}^1}{R_\beta}\right)\alpha_m, \;\; \mathcal{K}_{23} = \left(\frac{\varsigma_{12}^1}{R_\alpha} + \frac{\tilde{\varsigma}_{22}^1}{R_\beta}\right)\beta_n, \;\; \mathcal{K}_{35} = \left(-\tilde{\varsigma}_{44}^2 + \frac{\varsigma_{12}^2}{R_\alpha} + \frac{\tilde{\varsigma}_{22}^2}{R_\beta}\right)\beta_n,$$

$$\mathcal{K}_{33} = -\tilde{\varsigma}_{44}^1 \beta_n^2 - \bar{\varsigma}_{55}^1 \alpha_m^2 - \left(\frac{\bar{\varsigma}_{11}^1}{R_\alpha^2} + \frac{2\varsigma_{12}^1}{R_\alpha R_\beta} + \frac{\tilde{\varsigma}_{22}^1}{R_\beta^2}\right), \mathcal{K}_{14} = -\bar{\varsigma}_{11}^2 \alpha_m^2 - \tilde{\varsigma}_{66}^2 \beta_n^2,$$

$$\mathcal{K}_{24} = -(\varsigma_{12}^2 + \varsigma_{66}^2)\alpha_m \beta_n, \;\; \mathcal{K}_{34} = \left(-\bar{\varsigma}_{55}^1 + \frac{\bar{\varsigma}_{11}^2}{R_\alpha} + \frac{\varsigma_{12}^2}{R_\beta}\right)\alpha_m, \;\; \mathcal{K}_{44} = -\bar{\varsigma}_{55}^1 - \bar{\varsigma}_{11}^3 \alpha_m^2 - \tilde{\varsigma}_{66}^3 \beta_n^2$$

$$\mathcal{K}_{15} = -(\varsigma_{12}^2 + \varsigma_{66}^2)\alpha_m \beta_n, \;\; \mathcal{K}_{25} = -\tilde{\varsigma}_{22}^2 \beta_n^2 - \bar{\varsigma}_{66}^2 \alpha_m^2, \;\; \mathcal{K}_{55} = -\tilde{\varsigma}_{44}^1 - \bar{\varsigma}_{66}^3 \alpha_m^2 - \tilde{\varsigma}_{22}^3 \beta_n^2,$$

$$\mathcal{K}_{45} = -(\varsigma_{12}^3 + \varsigma_{66}^3)\alpha_m \beta_n, \;\; \mathcal{K}_{16} = \left(\frac{\varrho_{14}^1}{R_{\alpha\beta}} + \frac{\bar{\varrho}_{15}^1}{R_\alpha}\right)\alpha_m, \;\; \mathcal{K}_{26} = \left(\frac{\tilde{\varrho}_{24}^2}{R_\beta} + \frac{\varrho_{25}^1}{R_{\alpha\beta}}\right)\beta_n$$

$$\mathcal{K}_{36} = -(\bar{\varrho}_{15}^1 \alpha_m^2 + \tilde{\varrho}_{24}^1 \beta_n^2), \;\; \mathcal{K}_{66} = -(\bar{\epsilon}_{11}^1 \alpha_m^2 + \tilde{\epsilon}_{22}^1 \beta_n^2),$$

$$\mathcal{K}_{46} = \left(-\bar{\varrho}_{15}^1 + \frac{\bar{\varrho}_{15}^2}{R_\alpha}\right)\alpha_m, \;\; \mathcal{K}_{56} = \left(-\tilde{\varrho}_{24}^1 + \frac{\tilde{\varrho}_{24}^2}{R_\beta}\right)\beta_n, \;\; \mathcal{K}_{17} = \left(\frac{\varrho_{14}^2}{R_{\alpha\beta}} + \frac{\bar{\varrho}_{15}^2}{R_\alpha}\right)\alpha_m,$$

$$\mathcal{K}_{27} = \left(\frac{\tilde{\varrho}_{24}^2}{R_\beta} + \frac{\varrho_{25}^2}{R_{\alpha\beta}}\right)\beta_n, \;\; \mathcal{K}_{37} = -(\bar{\varrho}_{15}^2 \alpha_m^2 + \tilde{\varrho}_{24}^2 \beta_n^2), \;\; \mathcal{K}_{47} = \left(-\bar{\varrho}_{15}^2 + \frac{\bar{\varrho}_{15}^3}{R_\alpha}\right)\alpha_m$$

$$\mathcal{K}_{67} = -(\bar{\epsilon}_{11}^2 \alpha_m^2 + \tilde{\epsilon}_{22}^2 \beta_n^2), \;\; \mathcal{K}_{77} = -(\bar{\epsilon}_{11}^3 \alpha_m^2 + \tilde{\epsilon}_{22}^3 \beta_n^2),$$

$$\mathcal{K}_{18} = \left(\frac{\kappa_{14}^1}{R_{\alpha\beta}} + \frac{\bar{\kappa}_{15}^1}{R_\alpha}\right)\alpha_m, \;\; \mathcal{K}_{28} = \left(\frac{\tilde{\kappa}_{24}^1}{R_\beta} + \frac{\kappa_{25}^1}{R_{\alpha\beta}}\right)\beta_n, \;\; \mathcal{K}_{38} = -(\bar{\kappa}_{15}^2 \alpha_m^2 + \tilde{\kappa}_{24}^1 \beta_n^2),$$

$$\mathcal{K}_{48} = \left(-\bar{\kappa}_{15}^1 + \frac{\bar{\kappa}_{15}^2}{R_\alpha}\right)\alpha_m, \;\; \mathcal{K}_{57} = \left(-\tilde{\varrho}_{24}^2 + \frac{\tilde{\varrho}_{24}^2}{R_\beta}\right)\beta_n, \;\; \mathcal{K}_{58} = \left(-\tilde{\kappa}_{24}^1 + \frac{\tilde{\kappa}_{24}^2}{R_\beta}\right)\beta_n$$

$$\mathcal{K}_{68} = -(\bar{\eta}_{11}^1 \alpha_m^2 + \tilde{\eta}_{22}^1 \beta_n^2), \;\; \mathcal{K}_{78} = -(\bar{\eta}_{11}^2 \alpha_m^2 + \tilde{\eta}_{22}^2 \beta_n^2), \;\; \mathcal{K}_{88} = -(\bar{\mu}_{11}^1 \alpha_m^2 + \tilde{\mu}_{22}^1 \beta_n^2),$$

$$\mathcal{K}_{19} = \left(\frac{\kappa_{14}^2}{R_{\alpha\beta}} + \frac{\bar{\kappa}_{15}^2}{R_\alpha}\right)\alpha_m, \quad \mathcal{K}_{29} = \left(\frac{\bar{\kappa}_{24}^2}{R_\beta} + \frac{\kappa_{25}^2}{R_{\alpha\beta}}\right)\beta_n \ , \quad \mathcal{K}_{39} = -(\bar{\kappa}_{15}^2\alpha_m^2 + \bar{\kappa}_{24}^2\beta_n^2),$$

$$\mathcal{K}_{49} = \left(-\bar{\kappa}_{15}^2 + \frac{\bar{\kappa}_{15}^3}{R_\alpha}\right)\alpha_m, \quad \mathcal{K}_{59} = \left(-\bar{\kappa}_{24}^2 + \frac{\bar{\kappa}_{24}^3}{R_\beta}\right)\beta_n \ , \quad \mathcal{K}_{69} = -(\bar{\eta}_{11}^2\alpha_m^2 + \bar{\eta}_{22}^2\beta_n^2),$$

$$\mathcal{K}_{79} = -(\bar{\eta}_{11}^3\alpha_m^2 + \bar{\eta}_{22}^3\beta_n^2), \quad \mathcal{K}_{89} = -(\bar{\mu}_{11}^2\alpha_m^2 + \bar{\mu}_{22}^2\beta_n^2), \quad \mathcal{K}_{99} = -(\bar{\mu}_{11}^3\alpha_m^2 + \bar{\mu}_{22}^3\beta_n^2).$$

References

1. Badri, T.M., Al-Kayiem, H.H.: Reducing The Magneto-Electro-Elastic Effective Properties For 2-D Analysis. In: Colloquium On Humanities, Science And Engineering Research (CHUSER 2011). IEEE, Malaysia (2011)
2. Badri, T.M., Al-Kayiem, H.H.: Analysis Of Electro/Mgneto-Mechanical Coupling Factor: In Laminated Composite Plate Construct From Rotated Y-Cut Crystals. In: National Postgraduate Conferencec (NPC). IEEE, Malaysia (2011)
3. Badri, T.M., Al-Kayiem, H.H.: Free Vibration Analysis Of Piezo-Laminated Shell Structures. In: The World Engineering, Science And Technology Congress (ESTCON 2012), Malaysia (2012)
4. Badri, T.M., Al-Kayiem, H.H.: A Static Analysis Of Piezo-Laminated Shell Structures. In: The World Engineering, Science And Technology Congress (ESTCON 2012), Malaysia (2012)
5. Heyliger, P.R., Pan, E.: Static Field. Magnetoelectroelastic Laminates. Aiaa Journal 42, 1435–1443 (2004)
6. Pan, E., Han, F.: Exact Solution For Functionally Graded And Layered Magneto-Electro-Elastic Plates. International Journal Of Engineering Science 43, 321–339 (2005)
7. Tsai, Y.-H., Wu, C.-P., Syu, Y.-S.: Three-Dimensional Analysis Of Doubly Curved Functionally Graded Magneto-Electro-Elastic Shells. European Journal Of Mechanics A/Solids 27, 79–105 (2008)
8. Nellya, N.R.: The Theory Of Piezoelectric Shells And Plates. CRC Press, Moscow (1993)
9. Reddy, J.N.: Energy And Variational Method. In: Applied Mechanics. John Wiley & Sons, Ltd., New York (1984)
10. Bao, Y.: Static And Dynamic Analysis Of Piezothermoelastic Laminated Shell Composites With Distributed Sensors And Actuators. In: Mechanical Engineering. University of Kentucky, Lexington (1996)
11. Tzou, H.S., Lee, H.-J., Arnold, S.M.: Smart Materials, Precision Sensors/ Actuators, Smart Structures, And Structronic Systems. Mechanics of Advanced Materials and Structures 11, 367–393 (2004)
12. Pérez-Fernándeza, L.D., Bravo-Castillerob, J., Rodríguez-Ramosb, R., Sabinad, F.J.: On The Constitutive Relations And Energy Potentials Of Linear Thermo-Magneto-Electro-Elasticity. Mechanics Research Communications 36, 343–350 (2009)
13. Qatu, M.S.: Vibration Of Laminated Shells And Plates. Elsevier, London (2004)
14. Chen, W.Q., Lee, K.Y., Dinga, H.J.: On Free Vibration Of Non-Homogeneous Transversely Isotropic Magneto-Electro-Elastic Plates. Journal Of Sound And Vibration 279, 237–251 (2005)
15. Pan, E., Heyliger, P.R.: Free Vibrations of Simply Supported and Multilayered Magneto-Electro-Elastic Plates. Journal of Sound and Vibration 252(3), 429–442 (2002)

Improvement of Actuation Speed of Hydraulic Cylinders: Using Novel Flow Control Valve System

Mohd Osman Abdalla, Thirumalaiswamy Nagarajan, and Fakhruldin Mohd Hashim

Mech. Eng. Dept., Universiti Teknologi PETRONAS,
32610 Seri Iskandar, perak, Malaysia
mohamed.osman1@yahoo.com,
{nagarajan_t,fakhruldin_mhashim}@petronas.com.my

Abstract. The aim of the study is to identify the major source of power losses in linear hydraulic actuators and to find suitable solutions. A new energy efficient hydraulic system is proposed. The concept of the proposed system is based on overcoming the back pressure in piston front chamber generated by flow restriction of outlet port. This is achieved by increasing the discharged flow rate of oil by adding two new outlet ports to the conventional hydraulic cylinder. Flow through the new outlet ports is controlled by a novel pressure actuated flow control valve. The discharge oil through the new ports is forwarded directly to the oil tank without passing through the directional control valve that controls the flow to the actuator. The conventional and the proposed hydraulic cylinders are simulated in FLUENT. Results show that the proposed four-port actuators give better performance regarding hydraulic resistance, piston speed and energy savings.

Keywords: Energy Saving in Hydraulic, Hydraulic Actuators, Hydraulic Control, Hydraulic system, Hydraulic Valve.

1 Introduction

Energy efficiency of hydraulic power systems has been particularly important in construction and industrial applications. Hydraulic power technologies have been used in all kinds of mobile machineries such as in construction, agricultural and forestry machines. Hydraulics are used in many other applications such as medical chairs and tables, grounds care equipment, trash compactors and recycling bins, Arial lifts, off-highway trucks and mining machineries. A common hydraulic machinery, i.e. Backhoe Loader, is shown in Fig. 1. The common thing to all these hydraulic applications is that high power is always required to perform the desired job, such as material handling and harvesting. Industrial hydraulic systems often work continuously around the clock, handling large amounts of power. Even little improvements in efficiency therefore will have a significant economic impact on the overall Lifecycle cost of the power hydraulic systems. In the last few years increased fuel prices and stricter environmental regulations regarding engine emissions, are pushing forward the improvement of energy efficient solutions in the field of power

S.G. Ponnambalam et al. (Eds.): IRAM 2012, CCIS 330, pp. 331–339, 2012.

hydraulics [1], [2] and [3]. The prime power sources for such hydraulic systems are usually an internal combustion engine. Energy loss at different components of the hydraulic system is one of the problems encountered in power hydraulics. Linear hydraulic cylinder actuators are classified as one of the power hydraulic components that cause a lot of energy losses.

(http://snowpars.com)

http://www.wordsun.com/

Fig. 1. Backhoe Loader   **Fig. 2.** Double acting hydraulic cylinder

The hydraulic cylinder is a positive displacement reciprocating hydraulic motor, which converts fluid (or hydraulic) energy into useful kinetic energy of the moving piston rods [4]. The hydraulic cylinder is frequently referred to as linear actuator and it consists of two fluid chambers and piston with rod. Hydraulic cylinder has two small ports work alternating as an oil inlet and outlet; one port in the piston chamber and the other in the rod chamber as shown in Fig. 2. When pressurized oil is forced into the piston side chamber the cylinder will take an outward power stroke; and the oil in the rod chamber is pushed out to a reservoir. When oil flow is reversed and the pressurized oil from the pump inters into rod chamber, the cylinder will then take an inward power stroke in a reverse direction; and the oil in the piston chamber is pushed out to a reservoir. The oil flow to the double acting cylinder is usually controlled by reversible pump or by a directional control valve. One of the limitations of cylinder actuators is that they offer a fixed length of straight-line motion.

When the cylinder is actuated the piston is forced to move in the flow direction. The discharge oil from the hydraulic cylinder is highly restricted by the small area of the outlet port. Piston motion, therefore, is greatly resisted and energy is lost. The energy lost in this operation is converted to heat within the cylinder and overloads the pump. An unnecessary additional work of the pump is required to overcome this hydraulic resistance every stroke during its operation. Energy saving possibilities of the existing hydraulic cylinder are investigated and analyzed in this study.

Muvengei et al. (2009) studied and simulate conventional double acting hydraulic cylinders. Some results of their study showed the open loop state response of the cylinder in extension modes as in Fig. 3. Though the piston side chamber of the cylinder is directly connected to the high pressure line of the pump, the pressure in the rod side chamber that connected to the sink records higher values; even higher than the source pressure values. But the force on the piston side, having larger face, is still greater than the force on the rod side face of the piston; hence, the piston will keep moving from the low pressure side to the high pressure side in extension direction [5].

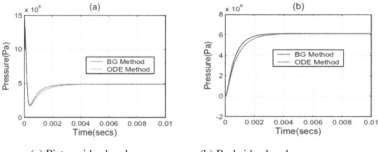

(a) Piston side chamber pressure   (b) Rod side chamber pressure

Fig. 3. Simulated open loop responses of the cylinder in extension mode

The hydraulic cylinder in the contraction mode was also simulated and the pressure response in the piston side chamber was plotted as in Fig. 4. The pressure in the rod side chamber, which is connected to supply pressure in the contraction cycle, is observed to be higher than the pressure on the piston side, or the tank side, chamber.

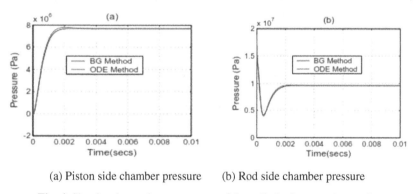

(a) Piston side chamber pressure   (b) Rod side chamber pressure

Fig. 4. Simulated open loop responses of the cylinder in retraction mode

It had been illustrated above that in both motion directions of the conventional hydraulic cylinder the piston always suffers very high hydraulic resistance that oppose and retard its motion. This hydraulic resistance is an inherent characteristic of conventional hydraulic actuators. Eriksson (2007) uses in his study asymmetrical cylinders as a discrete transformer to control loads in order to minimize the losses. He presents a solution enabling lower losses in hydraulic actuator systems. His proposed controller is capable of recuperating energy by letting the overrunning actuator provide any simultaneously operated actuator with flow and pressure [6]. D. B. Stephenson et al., (2008) presented a research study titled "Energy recovery and reuse techniques for a hydraulic system". A hydraulic system having two cylinders connected mechanically in parallel to a machine component was studied [7]. Many other studies have been carried out to improve the performance and the energy efficiency of hydraulic system, such as: Krus (1988) [8], Raymond and Chenoweth (1993) [9], Habibi and Goldenberg (1999) [10], S. R. Habibi and G. Singh (2000) [11]. M. Osman et al., (2010, 2012) [12], [13] and [14]. All these studies showed some contributions regarding the energy saving.

2   Equilibrium of Cylinder Actuator

Hydraulic cylinders are usually subjected to many internal and external forces. A simple conventional hydraulic actuator driving a load, F_L , as in Fig. 5.

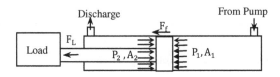

Fig. 5. Forces acting on cylinder actuator

The cylinder shown above is supplied with pump pressure, P_1, in extension mode. The frictional force F_f is always very small compared to pressure forces and can be neglected. Solving for equilibrium of the cylinder, the unknown pressure, P_2, on the tank side can be given by Equation (1):

$$P_2 = (P_1A_1 - F_f - F_L)/A_2 \qquad (1)$$

A_1 and A_2 are piston and rod side areas and are constant for any known cylinder. The frictional force F_f is always very small compared to pressure forces and the load, therefore, it can be neglected. For a given supply pressure (driving pressure) P_1 the load F_L will determine the resisting pressure P_2 for the specific cylinder. In the extension stroke of the cylinder there are three possible cases:

Case 1: $P_2 < P_1$ if $F_L > P_1(A_1 - A_2)$,
Case 2: $P_2 = P_1$ if $F_L = P_1(A_1 - A_2)$,
Case 3: $P_2 > P_1$ if $F_L < P_1(A_1 - A_2)$.

Muvengei et al. (2009) had shown that the pressure value in the rod side chamber is higher than the pump pressure as in Fig. 1. This result agreed with case 3, $(P_2 > P_1)$, which mean that their study was carried on low load conditions. Case 3 shows the possibility of the regeneration in extension mode of the hydraulic cylinder. The hydraulic cylinder in this case can be considered as a pressure amplifier. Another thing of great importance related with case 3 is that: although the pressure in tank side is greater than that in pump side chamber, but still the force on the pump side chamber always greater than the force on the tank side chamber. This fact keeps the piston to continue its motion from low pressure to high pressure side in extension direction. Since the hydraulic oil is incompressible the speed and acceleration of the cylinder actuator is directly related to the flow rates allowed by the ports. The oil zone at the tank side of the cylinder actuator was simulated in Fluent and Equation (1) was used to determine the inlet pressure to this fluid-zone of the actuator.

2.1   CFD Modeling

In this study Fluent/Gambit software was used to simulate the hydraulic cylinder. A steady state 3D model was defined as a solver in Fluent. The fluid used in the simulation was standard hydraulic oil having a density of 870 kg/m^3 and viscosity of 46 cSt. at 40°. Hydraulic cylinders were simulated so as to compute and study the flow variables such as pressures, mass flow rate, and piston velocity. This input pressure corresponds to "P_2" of Equation (1). The outlet ports are open through connector pipes and valves into reservoir of atmospheric pressure. Each model used in the simulation contains two symmetrical outlet ports; the lower ports are assigned as walls (closed) in the Fluent boundary conditions panel when the conventional cylinder with single outlet port is the case; and assigned as flow outlet (open) when the flow is needed through double outlet ports as in the proposed four port cylinder.

3   Simulation of the Conventional Cylinders

The conventional single outlet cylinders with various outlet diameters are simulated under the same inlet pressures; mass flow rates and piston speeds are computed. Contours of static pressure for a 7mm port cylinder is shown in Fig. (6). The pressure gradient is noticed to be very high at the entrance of the exit port. Pressure and energy losses are high at this location. The oil in main chamber in front of the piston is highly pressurized which means that the piston motion suffered high hydraulic resistance. The contour of velocity magnitude for the same 7mm port cylinder is shown in Fig. (7). The velocity in cylinder main chamber is noticed to have low value while the velocity at outlet port is high and turbulent.

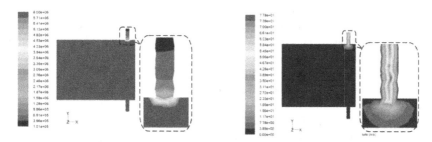

Fig. 6. Static pressure contours for 7mm port   **Fig. 7.** Velocity contours for 7mm port

Mass flow rates under pressure of 100bar at the inlet for the various simulated cylinders are recorded. Mass flow rate vs. port diameters are plotted as in Fig. 8. The results show that the mass flow rate increases rapidly as the outlet diameter increases, provided that the pump supply is sufficient enough. In other words; if other things remain the same, the mass flow rate, and hence, the speed of the actuator are proportional to outlet diameter.

Conventional cylinder having a single outlet port of 7mm diameters is simulated under varied load conditions. The pressure in the tank-side zone was varied from

10bar (highly loaded cylinder) to 100bar (unloaded cylinder). The mass flow rate was computed and plotted in Fig. 9. The mass flow rate increases as the load decreases and the relation is excellently described by the power law as in (2):

$$m = a\,p^{\alpha} \tag{2}$$

Where a and α are constants depend, among other factors on port diameter; and P is the resisting pressure 'P_2'. In the simulated case shown in in Fig. 9, $a = 0.2863$ and $\alpha = 0.5389$

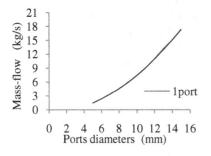

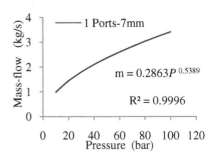

Fig. 8. Mass rate vs. port diameters   **Fig. 9.** Mass rate vs. load pressure

4   The Proposed Cylinder Actuator

Hydraulic cylinder with four ports is proposed in order to improve energy efficiency. The proposed cylinder presented in this study is based on adding two new ports to the conventional linear hydraulic cylinder as shown in Fig. 10. The new ports work as outlet ports only; they function alternately; and the flow through them is directed to the tank. These new ports are never be connected to the directional valve that controls the cylinder; otherwise, the system will become the same as that of the conventional cylinder. Flow through these new ports is controlled by a separate novel flow control valve. The schematic view of this flow control valve is shown in Fig. 11. This flow control valve permits the discharge flow from the tank side of the cylinder and blocks the flow from the pump side of the cylinder. This flow control valve makes the proposed four ports cylinder to operate as a three ports cylinder, i.e. only one inlet port and two outlet ports function at a time. The proposed flow control valve is a spool valve consists of a spool and ports arrangement. The valve arrangement is set in such a way that it operates automatically without the need for operator intervention. It operates due the pressure difference in the piston sides of the hydraulic cylinders. The inlet flow to the cylinder in the proposed system remains as it's in the conventional cylinder.

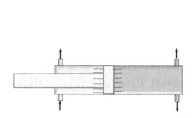

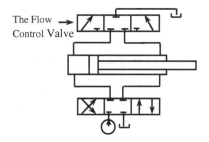

Fig. 10. The proposed hydraulic cylinder   **Fig. 11.** The proposed hydraulic circuit

4.1   Simulation of the Proposed Cylinder

Double outlet ports cylinders with various outlet diameters are simulated under 100bar. The mass flow rate is recorded and plotted in Fig. 12. Recalling the results in Fig. 8 it has been shown that adding additional ports of the same size of the existing one to the conventional cylinder actuator almost doubles the flow rate and the cylinder speed for all port sizes. On the other hand a cylinder with double outlet, 7mm diameter each, was simulated against varied load conditions. The pressure was varied from 10bar to 100bar and the mass flow rate was computed and plotted as in Fig. 13.

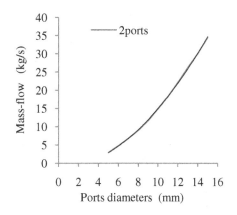

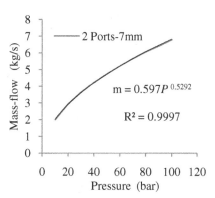

Fig. 12. Mass rate vs. port diameters   **Fig. 13.** Mass rate vs. outlet port size

The pressure-mass rate relationship is found to follow a power law as in (3):

$$m = 0.597 \, P^{\,0.5292} \tag{3}$$

Compared to results in Fig. 9 of the conventional cylinder, it is clear that mass flow rates are doubled as the outlet ports are doubled. Hence, the cylinder speed is also doubled. The increased speed of the proposed cylinder leads to energy saving since the assigned job is completed in a shorter time.

5   Conclusion

The traditional single inlet single outlet hydraulic cylinders were simulated in Fluent for the purpose of speed optimization. Four port cylinder actuator was proposed with a novel flow control valve system. The proposed cylinder is simulated as well. Ports sizes and pressures were varied during simulation of both the traditional and the proposed actuators. The mass flow rates are computed. Results reveal that the outlet ports are the source of energy losses due to throttling effect. The proposed four-port actuators give better performance regarding the piston speed.

Acknowledgement. We would like to express our appreciation to all those who gave us the possibility to complete this study. We would like to thank the Department of Mechanical Engineering at Universiti Teknologi PETRONAS (UTP) for giving permission to commence this study. We have also to thank the Center for Graduate Studies at UTP for sponsoring the study.

References

1. Dallmann, T.R., Harley, R.A.: Evaluation of mobile source emission trends in the United States. Journal of Geophysical Research 115, D14305
2. Facanha, C., Horvath, A.: Evaluation of life-cycle air emission factors of freight transportation. Environmental Science & Technology 41, 7138–7144 (2007)
3. Ravindra, K., Sokhi, R., Van Grieken, R.: Atmospheric polycyclic aromatic hydrocarbons: Source attribution, emission factors and regulation. Atmospheric Environment 42, 2895–2921 (2008)
4. Mobley, R. K.: Fluid power dynamics. Butterworth-Heinemann (1999)
5. Muvengei, M., Kihiu, J.: Bond Graph Modeling of Inter-Actuator Interactions in a Multi-Cylinder Hydraulic System. International Journal of Mechanical, Industrial and Aerospace Engineering 4, 1–10 (2009)
6. Eriksson, B.: Control Strategy for Energy Efficient Fluid Power Actuators: Utilizing Individual Metering, SE-581 83 Linköping. Linköping University, Sweden (2007)
7. Stephenson, D.B., Hamkins, E.P., Pfaff, J.L., Tabor, K.A.: Energy recovery and reuse techniques for a hydraulic system. US Patent 20,080,110,166 (2008)
8. Krus, P.: On Load Sensing Fluid Power Systems. Division of Fluid Power Control Department of Mechanical Engineering, Linkoping University, Sweden (1988)
9. Raymond, E.T., Chenoweth, C.C.: Aircraft flight control actuation system design. Society of Automotive Engineers, Warrendale (1993)
10. Habibi, S., Goldenberg, A.: Design of a new high performance electrohydraulic actuator. In: Proceedings of The International Conference on Advanced Intelligent Mechatronics, IEEE/ASME, pp. 227–232 (1999)
11. Habibi, S.R., Singh, G.: Derivation of design requirements for optimization of a high performance hydrostatic actuation system. International Journal of Fluid Power 1, 11–27 (2000)

12. Osman, M., Nagarajan, T., Fakhruldin, M.H.: Numerical Investigation of Pressure Drop in Hydraulic Spool Valve. In: Proceedings of ICSSST 2010, 3rd International Conference on Solid State Science and Technology, Kuching, Sarawak, Malaysia (2010)
13. Osman, M., Nagarajan, T., Fakhruldin, M.H.: Numerical Investigation of Pressure Drop in Hydraulic Spool Valve, ISSN. Journal of Solid State Science and Technology 19, 48–60 (2011)
14. Osman, M., Nagarajan, T., Fakhruldin, M.H.: Numerical study of flow field and energy loss in hydraulic proportional control valve. In: National Postgraduate Conference NPC 2011. UTP, Seri Iskandar (2011)

Optimum Speed Using Evolutionary Algorithms for Induction Motor Drive

Moulay Rachid Douiri and Mohamed Cherkaoui

Department of Electrical Engineering, Mohammadia School of Engineers,
Rabat, Morocco
douirirachid@hotmail.com

Abstract. This paper proposes a new systematic procedure to design an adaptive proportional-integral (PI) controller using genetic algorithms. The optimization process reduces the effort of tuning the parameters of a learning and adaptive PI controller and ensures global optimization of these parameters. The simulation results of the newly developed control algorithms applied to induction motor control system. The results show enhanced control performance with high adaptation and learning capabilities.

Keywords: genetic algorithm, PI controller, indirect field oriented control, induction motor.

1 Introduction

The concept of field orientation was first proposed by Hasse [1] and Blaschke [2]. In both cases, the flux vector used for field orientation is the flux vector. Hasse suggests a field orientation scheme in which the rotor flux vector is acquired indirectly from measured rotor speed and calculated slip speed. In contrast, in Blaschke's implementation, the flux vector is directly measured using Hall probes, search coils, or other measurement techniques. It is necessary to control the speed of the AC motor to meet desired specifications in various industrial applications [3], [4], [5]. Classical control techniques such as proportional-integral-derivative (PID), proportional-integral (PI), and various adaptive controllers have been used for a long time to control the speed of the AC motor. The disadvantages of using conventional controllers are that they are sensitive to variation in the motor parameters and load disturbance. In addition, it is difficult to tune PI gains to eliminate and reduce the overshoot and load disturbance. Then design of classical linear controller is generally based on linearized model around a steady state point. Hence the PI controller cannot successfully control highly nonlinear plants [6]. For the last two decades researchers have been working to apply artificial intelligent controller for AC motor speed control due to its advantages as compared to the conventional PI controllers. The advantages are that these controllers can deal with the nonlinearity of arbitrary complexity, and their performances are robust. This paper proposes a new systematic procedure to design an adaptive proportional-integral (PI) controller using genetic algorithms. A genetic algorithm is a type

S.G. Ponnambalam et al. (Eds.): IRAM 2012, CCIS 330, pp. 340–348, 2012.

of evolutionary computing that solves problems by probabilistically searching the solution space [7]. In contrast to most algorithms which work by successively improving a single estimate of the desired optimum via iterations, GA's work with several estimates at once, which together form a population. Given an initial population of individuals representing possible solutions to the problem, genetic algorithms simulate evolution by allowing the most fit individuals to reproduce to form subsequent generations. After several generations, convergence to an optimal solution is often accomplished. Determining the fitness of an individual is problem dependent and the fitness function usually incorporates a priori knowledge of the desired optimum. The basic genetic algorithm is improved by using problem specific knowledge in specifying the various operations required to direct the evolution [7], [8], [9].

This paper is organized as follows: The principle of indirect field oriented control is presented in the second part, the optimization PI speed controller based on genetic algorithm in section three, the fourth part is devoted to illustrate the simulation performance of this control strategy, a conclusion and reference list at the end.

2   Indirect Field Oriented Control

In rotor flux orientation the rotor flux vector is aligned with d-axis of synchronously rotating reference frame d-q. Therefore, ω_e is the synchronous speed of rotor flux space vector. The q axis rotor flux Ψ_{rd} is zero, and:

$$\Psi_r = \Psi_{rd} \tag{1}$$

The rotor dynamics are given by the following equations:

$$\frac{d\Psi_r}{dt} = \frac{L_m}{\tau_r} i_{sd} - \frac{1}{\tau_r} \Psi_r \tag{2}$$

$$\frac{d\omega_r}{dt} = \frac{3p^2 L_m}{2JL_r}(\Psi_r i_{sq}) - \frac{F}{J}\omega_r - \frac{p}{J}\Gamma_l \tag{3}$$

$$\Gamma_{em} = \frac{3pL_m \Psi_r}{2L_r} i_{sq} \tag{4}$$

$$\rho = \int \omega_e dt = \int \left(\omega_r + \frac{R_r L_m i_{sq}}{L_r \Psi_r} \right) dt \tag{5}$$

The rotor flux magnitude is related to the direct axis stator current by a first order differential equation so it can be controlled by controlling the direct axis stator current. Under steady state operation rotor flux is constant, so (2) becomes:

$$\Psi_r = L_m i_{sd} \tag{6}$$

Indirect vector control can be implemented using the following equations:

$$i_{sd}^* = \frac{\Psi_r^*}{L_m} \tag{7}$$

$$i_{sq}^* = \frac{1}{p} \frac{L_r}{L_m} \frac{\Gamma_{em}^*}{\Psi_r^*} \tag{8}$$

$$\omega_{sl}^* = \frac{R_r L_m i_{sq}^*}{L_r \Psi_r^*} \tag{9}$$

$$\rho^* = \int \omega_e^* dt = \int (\omega_r + \omega_{sl}^*) dt \tag{10}$$

The speed controller determines the torque reference, in order to maintain the corresponding speed can be controlled using a PI controller whose parameters can be calculated from Fig. 1.

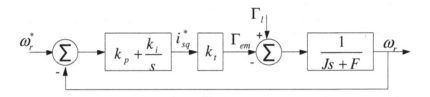

Fig. 1. Block diagram of speed control loop

From Fig. 1

$$\Gamma_{em} = K_T i_{sq}^* \tag{11}$$

$$i_{sq}^* = \frac{2L_r \Gamma_{em}}{3pL_m \Psi_r^*} \tag{12}$$

$$\Psi_r^* = L_m i_{sd}^* \tag{13}$$

K_T is given by

$$K_T = \left(\frac{3pL_m^2}{2L_r} \right) i_{sd}^* \tag{14}$$

The transfer function of closed loop system is given by:

$$\frac{\omega_r}{\omega_r^*} = \frac{K_i K_T}{Js^2 + (F + K_p K_T)s + K_i K_T} = \frac{\omega_n^2}{s^2 + 2\xi\omega_n s + \omega_n^2} \tag{15}$$

where $\xi = \dfrac{F + K_p K_T}{2\sqrt{JK_i K_T}}$ and $\omega_n = \sqrt{\dfrac{K_i K_T}{J}}$

Then, for a unit step input the response is

$$\omega_r = \omega_r^* \frac{\omega_n^2}{s^2 + 2\xi\omega_n s + \omega_n^2} = \frac{1}{s}\frac{\omega_n^2}{s^2 + 2\xi\omega_n s + \omega_n^2} = \frac{1}{s}\frac{\omega_n^2}{s(s + p_1)(s + p_2)} \tag{16}$$

In order to obtain a fast response without overshoot, the system should be critically damped, i.e. $\zeta = 1$ and $p_1 = p_2 = -\omega_n$; then, the above equation becomes

$$\omega_r = \frac{1}{s}\frac{\omega_n^2}{(s + \omega_n)^2} = \frac{1}{s} - \frac{\omega_n}{(s + \omega_n)^2} - \frac{1}{(s + \omega_n)} \tag{17}$$

The transient response of the system is given by

$$\omega_r(t) = 1 - \omega_n t e^{-\omega_n t} - e^{-\omega_n t} \tag{18}$$

The response time of the system is when the controlled variable attains 90 % of the set value

$$0.9 = 1 - \omega_n t e^{-\omega_n t} - e^{-\omega_n t} \tag{19}$$

From the solution of the above nonlinear equation we obtain the value of proper frequency using which parameters of the controller can be computed from the equation given below:

$$\begin{cases} 1 = \dfrac{F + K_p K_T}{2\sqrt{JK_i K_T}} \\ \omega_n = \sqrt{\dfrac{K_i K_T}{J}} \end{cases} \tag{20}$$

3   Genetic Algorithms PI Controller

3.1   Principles of Genetic Algorithms

Genetic algorithms (GA) introduced by John Holland [10] (1975) and his students at the University of Michigan are based on the theory of species survival by

Charles Darwin. As in nature things which breed in the model genetic algorithms, the specimens are also repeated, especially those deemed the strongest breed on a faster pace [9]. Genetic operators are applied to candidates hoping to generate new candidates and more efficient.

In biology, we manipulate genes and chromosomes, it is the same in the model AG, problems and solutions will be encoded. The encoding often takes the form of a bits string. These bit strings are comparable to the chromosomes of biological systems, while bits or characters that make up these chains are comparable to the genes. All these channels form a population, whereas in biology is called genotype [7], [9].

In the search for solutions to a problem, the AG uses a large element of chance. Indeed, candidates are selected for reproduction probabilistically, the population chromosomes are crossed at random in the offspring, and the chromosome genes are mutated in a certain probability [8]. Applying from generation to generation the genetic operators of judged performance of the candidates is seeking an offspring more powerful than the previous generation, making it possible to approach and an optimal solution [7], [11].

3.2   Genetic Algorithms PI Controller

Genetic algorithms are used to tune the proportional (k_p) and integral (k_i) gains of PI controller to ensure optimum performance using the principles of evolution and genetics to select and adapt the controller parameters [12], [13], [14]. k_i and k_p are coded by decimal numbers in chromosome. The members of the population are represented by the candidate controller's genetic PI controller. The algorithm tries to eliminate the bad traits of individuals and develop them on how well it minimizes the time absolute speed error (Fig. 3). The block diagram of the control system is shown in Fig. 2.

The ($\varepsilon_{\omega r}$) is calculated at time t as follows:

$$\varepsilon_{\omega_r} = \omega_r^*(t) - \hat{\omega}_r(t-1) \tag{21}$$

The control signal corresponding to the torque component of stator current Γ_{em}^* (t) is obtained after integrating the output:

$$\Gamma_{em}^*(t) = \Gamma_{em}^*(t-1) + \Delta\Gamma_{em}^*(t) \tag{22}$$

Our objective is to optimize the response time of speed that is to say to minimize the error between the rotational speed and its reference. For this we define the objective function as follows:

$$f_{obj} = \underbrace{\int_0^t |e|\,dt}_{(1)} + \underbrace{6\int_0^t \delta(\frac{dz}{dt}).|z^* - z(t)|\,dt}_{(2)} + \underbrace{\int_0^t |e|t\,dt}_{(3)} \tag{23}$$

with:

(1) Measure of a fast dynamic response;

(2) The penalty on the multiple overshoot of the response, where $\delta(dz/dt)$ detects the instances that overshoots (or undershoots) occur:

$$\int_{0^-}^{0^+} \delta(\frac{dz}{dt}) = \begin{cases} 1 & if & \dfrac{dz}{dt} = 0 \\ 0 & if & \dfrac{dz}{dt} \neq 0 \end{cases} \tag{24}$$

and $|z^*\text{-}z(t)|$ determines the response deviation from the desired value;
(3) Measure the steady state error.
The equations of the new populations generated from crossover are:

$$\begin{cases} c_{01} = (1-\alpha)c_{p1} + \alpha c_{p2} \\ c_{02} = (1-\alpha)c_{p2} + \alpha c_{p1} \end{cases} \tag{25}$$

where c_{p1} and c_{p2} are the old chromosomes, α is the random from 0 to 1, c_{01} and c_{02} are the new chromosomes.

The genetic algorithm with the free parameters shown in Table 1 was able to find the near-optimum solution with a population of 12 individuals, in almost 169 generations Fig. 3. This is due to the large number of design parameters involved in concurrent optimization.

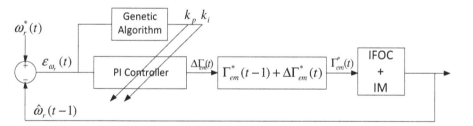

Fig. 2. Genetic algorithms PI controller structure

Table 1. Genetic Algorithm Parameters

GA Property	Value	GA Property	Value/ Method
Number of generations	169	Selection method	Roulette wheel
No of chromosomes in each generation	12	Crossover method	Double-point
No of genes in each chromosome	2	Crossover probability	0.8
Chromosome length	40 bit	Mutation rate	0.05

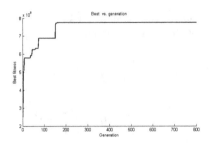

Fig. 3. Speed of convergence

4   Simulation Results

Induction motor parameters:

P_n=3Kw, V_n=230V, R_s=2.89Ω, R_r=2.39Ω, L_s=0.225H, L_r=0.220H, L_m=0.214H, J=0.2Kg.m², p=2.

The optimization algorithm and the motor drive response are then verified under loading and unloading conditions. The unloaded drive is started at 0.15 s and full load is applied at 0.5 s; then load is completely removed at 1 s. Later, after speed reversal, full load is applied at 2 s and the load is fully removed at 2.5 s. The machine is brought to rest at 2.9 s. Fig. 4 shows the speed optimization result and response of the drive system.

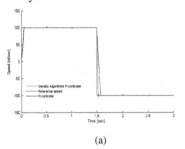

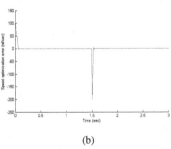

(a)	(b)

Fig. 4. Application and removal of load; (a) Reference, PI controller and genetic PI controller; (b) Speed optimization error

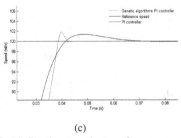

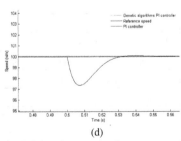

(c)	(d)

Fig. 5. (c) Starting transient performance and overshoot, (d) Disturbance rejection property for PI-GA and PI conventional

The starting transient performance and disturbance rejection property of the induction motor under the different control strategies is shown in Fig. 5. Table 2 show the performance of genetic PI controller compared to PI conventional controller (Fig. 5).

Table 2. Summary of Results

	Rise time (s)	Overshoot (%)	Settling time (%)	Steady state error (%)
PI	0.026	2.78	0.06	0.5
PI-GA	0.024	0.06	0.0012	0.9

5   Conclusion

This work uses the genetic algorithm based PI controller as the speed controller of the indirect field oriented controlled induction motor drives. By comparison with PI controller, it testifies that this method is not only robust, but also can improve dynamic performance of the system. The results simulation results show the performance of genetic PI controller compared to PI conventional controller such as (Table 2):

-Good pursuit of reference speed;
-Starting without overshoot;
-Rapid rejection of disturbances, with a low dropout speed;
-Good support for changes in engine parameters.

References

1. Hasse, K.: On the Dynamics of Speed Control of a Static ac Drive with a Squirrel-Cage Induction Machine. PhD Dissertation, Tech. Hochsch. Darmstadt (1969)
2. Blaschke, F.: The Principle of Field Orientation as Applied to the New Transvector Closed-Loop Control System for Rotating Field Machines. Siemens Review 34(5), 217–219 (1972)
3. Vas, P.: Sensorless Vector and Direct Torque Control. University Press, London (1998)
4. Abbondante, A., Brennen, M.B.: Variable Speed Induction Motor Drives use Electronic Slip Calculator Based on Motor Voltages and Currents. IEEE Trans. Ind. Appl. 1A-11(5), 483–488 (1975)
5. Takahashi, I., Noguchi, T.: A New Quick-Response and High-Efficiency Control Strategy of an Induction Mîtor. IEEE Transactions on Industry Applications IA-22(5) (1986)
6. Shin, E.C., Park, T.S., Oh, W.H., Yoo, J.Y.: A Design Method of PI Controller for an Induction Motor with Parameter Variation. In: The 29th Annual Conference of the IEEE Industrial Electronics Society, IECON 2003, Roanoke, VA, USA, pp. 408–413 (2003)
7. Beasley, D., Bull, D. R., Martin, R. R.: An Overview of Genetic Algorithms. Part 1, Hindamentals. Technical report, Inter-University Commitee on Computing (1993)
8. Back, T.: Evolutronary Algorithm in Tleory and Practice. Oxford University Press, New York (1996)
9. Davis, L.: Handbook of Genetic Algorithms. Van Nostrand Reinhold, New York (1991)
10. Holland, J.: Adaptation in Natural and Artificial Systems: An Introductory Analysis With Applications to Biology, Control, and Artificial Intelligence. University of Michigan Press, Ann Arbor (1975)

11. Goldberg, D. E.: Genetic Algorithms in Search, Optimization and Motor Learning. Reissue. Addison-Wesley Publishing Company (1989)
12. Wang, J., Zhao, Y.: The Optimization of PI Controller Parameters using Genetic Algorithm in the DC Speed Control System. In: Proceedings of the 3rd World Congress on Intelligent Control and Automation, pp. 545–548 (2000)
13. Vlachos, C., Williams, D., Gomm, J.B.: Genetic Approach to Decentralized PI Controller Tuning for Multivariable Processes. IEE Proceedings Control Theory and Applications 146(1), 58–64 (1999)
14. Silva, W.G., Acamley, P.P., Finch, J.W.: Application of Genetic Algorithm to the Online Tuning of Electric Drive Speed Controllers. Trans. Ind. Electron of IEEE 47(1), 217–219 (2000)

Nomenclature

d,q	Direct and quadrature components
R_s , R_r	Stator and rotor resistance [Ω]
i_{sd} , i_{sq}	Stator current dq –axis [A]
v_{sd} , v_{sq}	Stator voltage dq-axis [V]
L_s , L_r, L_m	Stator, rotor and mutual inductance [H]
Ψ_{sd}, Ψ_{sq}	dq stator fluxes [Wb]
Ψ_{rd}, Ψ_{rq}	dq rotor fluxes [Wb]
Γ_{em}	Electromagnetic torque [N.m]
Γ_l	Load torque [N.m]
ω_r	Rotor speed [rad/s]
ω_e, ω_{sl}	Synchronous and slip frequency [rad/s]
J	Inertia moment [Kg.m^2]
p	Motor pole number
σ	Leakage coefficient

DICOM Image Authentication and Encryption Based on RSA and AES Algorithms

A. Kannammal and S. Subha Rani

Department of Electronics and Communication Engineering, PSG College of Technology,
Coimbatore, Tamilnadu, India
{aks,ssr}@ece.psgtech.ac.in

Abstract. Significant advancements in information and communication technologies have made remarkable developments in many fields including healthcare delivery and medical data management. Digital watermarking and encryption techniques have been used to increase medical image security, confidentiality and integrity in addition to conventional network security protection.the work mainly focuses on the DICOM images, DICOM has been an Universal Standard for secured communication of Medical Images over networks. The Digital Envelope method is used to assure data integrity and security.the DE, including the digital signature of the image as well as encrypted patient information from the DICOM image header, can be embedded in the background area of the image as an invisible permanent watermark The watermarked image is then encrypted using AES and RSA algorithms.the encrypted images are then tested with common attacks and the quality measures such as PSNR, correlation coefficient and TAF are calculated to evaluate the behaviour of the algorithms.

Keywords: DICOM, Digital Envelope, Encryption, correlation co efficient.

1 Introduction

Significant advancements in information and communication technologies have made remarkable developments in many fields including healthcare delivery and medical data management. Complementary solutions are needed to meet the new challenges regarding security of the widely distributed sensitive medical information. Digital watermarking and encryption techniques have been used to increase medical image security, confidentiality and integrity in addition to conventional network security protection. The work mainly focuses on the DICOM images, since DICOM has been an Universal Standard for secured communication of Medical Images over public networks. The Digital Envelope (DE) method is used to assure data integrity [1] and security.the DE, including the digital signature (DS) of the image as well as encrypted patient information from the DICOM image header, can be embedded in the background area of the image as an invisible permanent watermark. The Digital Signature is generated by encrypting the hash value of the image. The watermarked image is then encrypted[2] using AES and RSA algorithms to enhance the security

S.G. Ponnambalam et al. (Eds.): IRAM 2012, CCIS 330, pp. 349–360, 2012.

during transmission.The encrypted images are then tested with common attacks and the quality measures such as PSNR and TAF are calculated to evaluate the behaviour of the algorithms..

The performance of AES and RSA algorithms are analysed based on the histograms, correlation coefficients and key strength. On comparison AES proves to be the best. At the receiver side, the encrypted image is decrypted and the Digital Envelope is extracted from the decrypted image. From DE, Digital Signature and the patient information are retrieved. The comparison of the original signature with the extracted signature and the patient information with image header verifies the authenticity of the image. The proposed algorithm offers solution for certain issues associated with medical data management and distribution [3]. The experimental results on different encryption techniques demonstrate the efficiency and transparency of algorithms.

2   Proposed Methodology

2.1   Watermark Embedding

The concept of DE is that someone can 'seal' a message (DS plus patient information) in such a way that no one other than the intended recipient can 'open' the sealed message. The DE method can be revamped as a general method to assure data security for communication of medical images over public networks. This part includes five major steps as follows in Fig 1.

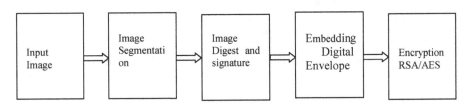

Fig. 1. Black Diagram of Proposed Methodology

2.1.1 Image Segmentation
Image pre-processing consists of background removal and segmentation. The image is first segmented with background removed or cropped by finding the minimum rectangle that covers the image object. In this step, the idea is to segment only the content within the image required for Digital Signature. This is also done in order to speed up the image digest process and to allow a region outside of the image object for data embedding. In background removal, foreign objects that do not belong to the images will be automatically removed.

2.1.2 Image Digest and Signature
Digital signature identifies the signer and ensures the integrity of the signed data. It is a bit stream, generated by a mathematical algorithm and is a unique representation of

the data. If one were to change just one bit in the data stream, the corresponding signature would be different. To create a DS for the image, the sender first computes a condensed representation of the image known as an image hash value (or image digest). The digest is then encrypted using the sender's private key to create the DS. It should be noted that only the digest instead of the image itself is encrypted. This makes sense because the actual image can be very large and public key operations can be extremely slow.

Steps to generate image digest,

➢   Step 1: Resize the segmented image to 8X8 block.

➢   Step 2: Find the mean value of all 64 pixels.

➢   Step 3: Each pixel is converted to a bit on comparison with mean value. i.e. if pixel value is less than   mean value, replace it by a bit 0 else by bit 1.

➢   Step 4: Convert these 64 bits to an equivalent hexadecimal value.

➢   Step 5: This hexadecimal value consisting of 16 bytes represents the image digest.

2.1.3 Digital Envelope

Digital Envelope is the wrapped (sealed) bulk data. This DE method is used to assure data integrity and security. The DE, including the digital signature (DS) [4, 5] of the image as well as encrypted patient information from the DICOM image header, can be embedded in the background area of the image as an invisible permanent watermark. The DE generated in this way ensures not only the privacy of data, but also the image authenticity and the integrity that are the features passed on from the image signature wrapped with it The DE with the image signature and patient data wrapped with it provides an effective tool to ensure image security in a PACS environment.

2.1.4 Data Embedding

Data embedding is a form of steganography that conceal the DE [5] in the image so that the visual quality of the image is not perceptually affected. The obtained DE is converted to a bit data stream. Then the data bit stream is embedded in the background outside the minimum rectangle that encloses the image. In this work, the rows with odd numbers contain the DE values from corresponding odd numbered positions. Similarly, the rows with even numbers contain the DE values from corresponding even numbered positions. This embedded DE acts as a permanent invisible watermark [6, 7]. This provides the image integrity since the watermark does not affect the original part which contains the required information.

2.2   Encryption

The embedded image is encrypted [8] before sending via the public networks to enhance the security. The encryption techniques used here are RSA and AES algorithms, out of which the former belongs to the asymmetric cryptography and the latter to the symmetric cryptography. In RSA algorithm, the image is encrypted using the receiver's public key and then sent to the network. In AES algorithm, the image is divided into blocks and each block is passed through certain number of rounds (depends on the key size) after which the encrypted values of block are obtained. The performance comparison between the two algorithms is done based on various issues.

2.2.1 RSA Algorithm

RSA algorithm involves 1.Key generation 2.Encryption 3.Decryption

---

Key generation : In a nutshell key generation is given as,
- Select random prime numbers p and q, and check that p != q
- Compute modulus n = pq Compute Φ(n)= (p - 1)(q - 1)
- Select public exponent e, $1 < e < \Phi(n)$ such that $gcd\ (e,\ \Phi(n)) = 1$
- Compute private exponent d = phi*k+1 $mod\ e$
- Public key is {n, e}, private key is d.

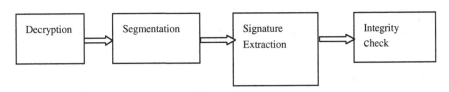

Fig. 2. Integrity check

Encryption

RSA [9] Encryption is done always with public key. The message to be encrypted is represented as number m, $0 < m < n - 1$. If the message is longer it needs to be spitted into smaller blocks. Then compute c,

$$c = \quad mod\ n \tag{1}$$

Where e and n are the public key, m is the message block, c is the encrypted message.

Decryption

The private key d is used to decrypt messages. Compute

$$m = \quad mod\ n \tag{2}$$

Where n is the modulus (from public key) and d is the private key.

2.2.2 AES Algorithm

The Advanced Encryption Standard (AES)[10] specifies a FIPS (Federal Information Processing Standard) approved cryptographic algorithm that can be used to protect electronic data. AES algorithm is a symmetric block cipher that can encrypt (encipher) and decrypt (decipher) information. Encryption converts data to an unintelligible form called cipher text, decrypting the cipher text converts the data back into its original form, called plaintext. This algorithm is capable of using cryptographic keys of 128, 192, and 256 bits to encrypt and decrypt data in blocks of 128 bits

2.3   Image Decryption and Authentication

During reception, the image received is needed to be verified for integrity and authenticity since the diagnosis entirely depends on the received image. This is done by the following procedures are shown in Fig 2.

2.3.1 Decryption

Decryption involves the reverse process of encryption. In case of RSA algorithm, the image is decrypted using receiver's private key. This key is secret and only the person with this key can unwrap it. In case of AES, the received image is divided into 4X4 blocks and passed through certain number of rounds as in the case of encryption. The resultant value forms the decrypted image

2.3.2 Segmentation

The decrypted image is then segmented into two parts, the background of the image which contains scrambled DE and the image object which contains the exact original information. The minimum rectangle containing the original image is formed to do this segmentation process

2.3.3 Signature Extraction

From the background, (i.e outside the rectangle) the scrambled DE is obtained. The Digital Envelope is then used to extract the digital signature and patient information. The signature is then decrypted using sender's public key to obtain the hash value computed by the sender. Also the hash value for the received image inside the rectangle is computed with the same algorithm.

2.3.4 Integrity Check

The two hash values thus obtained are compared to verify the integrity. This is due to the fact that the mechanism of obtaining the hash is designed in such a way that even a single data bit change in the input string would cause the hash value to change drastically. If the two hash values are the same, the receiver (or any other party) has the confidence that the image had been signed off by the owner of the private key and that the image had not been altered after it was signed off. Thus, it assures the image integrity. Also the patient information extracted[11] from DE can be compared with image header to verify authenticity.

2.4   Quality Measure of Proposed Algorithm

Any algorithm should be evaluated on basis of certain quality measures. In this method two quality measures are used for DE embedded image ,they are Peak Signal to Noise Ratio (PSNR) and Tamper Assessment Factor (TAF).Another two messages were used for encryption algorithms, they are histogram analysis and correlation coefficient

2.4.1 Peak Signal to Noise Ratio (PSNR)

PSNR is the ratio between the maximum possible power of a signal and the power of corrupting noise that affects the fidelity of its representation. It is most easily defined via the mean squared error (MSE) for which two $M{\times}N$ images f and z where one of the images is considered a noisy approximation of the other is defined as

$$MSE = \frac{1}{M \times N} \sum_{x=0}^{M-1}\sum_{y=0}^{N-1}\left(f(x,y)-z(x,y)\right)^2 \tag{3}$$

The PSNR is defined as:

$$PSNR = 10 \times \log_{10}\frac{MaxBits^2}{MSE}\,dB \tag{4}$$

Here, *MaxBits* is the maximum possible pixel value of the image. When samples are represented using B bits per sample, *MaxBits* is 2*B*-1.

2.4.2 Tamper Assessment Factor(TAF)

It gives the difference between the actual embedded watermark and the reconstructed watermark. It is given by the expression

$$TAF\left(w,\tilde{w}\right) = \frac{1}{M \times N} \sum_{x=0}^{M-1}\sum_{y=0}^{N-1} w(x,y)\oplus \tilde{w}(x,y) \tag{5}$$

where M,N- dimensions of the image, w - embedded watermark, $\tilde{w}$ - reconstructed watermark

The value of TAF ranges between zero and one.

2.4.3 Histogram Analysis

A histogram is a function that counts the number of observations that fall into each of the disjoint categories. In performance analysis, the histogram of original image and encrypted image are taken and compared. The one with the most variation in histogram proves to be the best.

2.4.4 Correlation Coefficient

Correlation between two images refers to the similarity in them. The similarity aspect is often expressed mathematically in terms of correlation coefficient. In this work the similarity between original image and encrypted image is measured and the one with less correlation coefficient proves to be the best since the chance of resemblance is less

$$r = \frac{\sum_i (Xi - Xm)(Yi - Ym)}{\sqrt{\sum_i (Xi - Xm)^2}\sqrt{\sum_i (Yi - Ym)^2}} \qquad (6)$$

Where Xi is the intensity of a pixel in an image 1, Yi is the intensity of a pixel in an image 2Xm is the mean intensity of image 1,Ym is the mean intensity of image 2.

2.5   Testing for Various Attacks

The water marking procedure was done for two radiological images with different anatomy. The effect of various commonly occurring attacks like Modification, Rotation and cropping, Brightness and Contrast adjustment, noises, was observed. The various attacks for which the authentication effects were observed are listed below.

Table 1.

	Image I	Image 2
Hash values used for segmented image	3 12 7 14 7 15 7 14 7 14 7 12 0 0 0 0	0 0 3 14 7 14 7 14 7 14 3 12 0 0 0 0
Key values used for generating DS:	Sender's private key: 7	Sender's private key: 7
	Sender's public key: 23	Sender's public key: 23
Digital Signature obtained by encrypting hash value using sender's private key:	130 177 182 108 182 108 182 108 182 108 130 177 0 0 0 0	0 0 130 108 182 108 182 108 182 108 182 108 130 177 0 0
Patient Id from header:	1 2 3 5 6 5	1 2 3 8 6 7
Digital Envelope:	130 177 182 108 182 93 182 108 182 108 182 177 0 0 0 0 1 2 3 5 6 5	0 0 130 108 182 108 182 108 182 108 182 108 130 177 0 0 1 2 3 5 6 5
Key values used for RSA Algorithm	Receiver's private key: 3,Receiver's public key: 587,n=943 p=23 q=41	Receiver's private key: 3Receiver's public key: 587n=943 p=23 q=41
Cipher key used for AES algorithm	60 3D EB 10 15 CA 71 BE 2B 73 AE F0 85 7D 77 81 1F 35 2C 07 3B 61 08 D7 2D 98 10 A3 09 14 DF F4	60 3D EB 10 15 CA 71 BE 2B 73 AE F0 85 7D 77 81 1F 35 2C 07 3B 61 08 D7 2D 98 10 A3 09 14 DF F4

3   Results and Discussion

The Digital envelope are generated from the images and encrypted and embedded in the images and then they encrypted by RSA or AES algorithms .he values which are used for this algorithms are tabulated in table 1The results were obtained for two image and they are tabulated in Table 2.Fig3.shows the Histogram of the original image, RSA encrypted image, AES encrypted image Using this histogram plot and correlation coefficient values   the two encryption algorithms were compared and tabulated in Table.3.

Table 2. Output Images

Sl. no		Image 1	Image 2
1	Original Image		
2	Cropped Image		
3	DE embedded Image		

Table 2. (*Continued*)

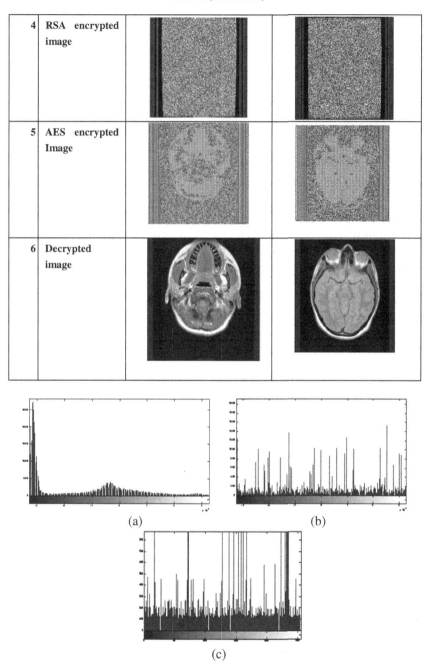

4	RSA encrypted image		
5	AES encrypted Image		
6	Decrypted image		

(a)   (b)

(c)

Fig. 3. Histogram of the (a) original Image, (b) RSA encrypted and (c) AES encrypted

Table 3. Comparison of RSA and AES Algorithms

Parameter	RSA Algorithm	AES Algorithm
Nature of encryption	Asymmetric	Symmetric . Key exchange problem occurs.
Key	Fragile	Strong
Security	Less secure. Brute force attack is possible.	More secure.
Correlation coefficient	0.2246	**0.1590** Highly uncorrelated.

From the correlation coefficient, it is clear that AES encrypted image differs a lot from the original image compared to RSA encrypted image since the value is less for AES. From the histogram, it is understood that AES encrypted image histogram shows large variations from the original histogram compared to RSA. Though AES undergoes key exchange problem, this algorithm proves to be the best. But the safe transmission of cipher key is required. Then the encrypted images were analyzed with different attacks. After decrypted image shows the different attacks which is made on the encrypted image and then their PSNR and TAF values are calculated and tabulated in table.4.

Table 4. Different attacks and its PSNR and TAF values

Attack/Modification	Type	IMAGE 1		IMAGE 2	
		PSNR (decibel)	TAF	PSNR (decibel)	TAF
Flipping	Horizontal	18.2459	2.5406 e-006	19.5924	2.3418e-006
	Vertical	17.5648	2.4429 e-006	16.8924	2.4545e-006
Average Filtering		22.9454	2.0736 e-006	23.6168	2.2149e-006
Gaussian Filtering		28.0362	5.4135 e-006	29.0594	5.5928e-006
Salt and pepper noise	Density= 10%	44.7370	7.5856 e-007	44.9570	7.5786e-007
	Density=25%	36.2580	1.9250 e-006	36.9509	1.8964e-006
	Density=50%	30.4454	3.7858 e-006	31.0193	3.8124e-006

Table 4. (*continued*)

Rotation for whole image	Angle=45°	26.2196	3.3269 e-006	28.0539	3.4003e-006
	Angle=90°	4.1840	4.4974 e-006	36.9331	4.4364e-006
	Angle=180°	42.5587	4.8894 e-007	58.0401	3.7672e-007
	Angle=270°	46.3432	4.4974 e-006	37.4214	4.4364e006
Rotation	Part of image	77.5498	9.3132 e-010	90.3707	9.3132e-010
Contrast adjustment	Top left	48.2854	6.1467e-008	47.2693	1.2293e-007
	Top right	46.2341	5.9614e-008	48.2934	1.2852e-007
	Bottom left	45.3743	5.9139e-008	44.7324	6.6357e-008
	Bottom right	49.8594	6.2674e-008	54.6143	6.8685e-008

4   Conculsion

The scheme proposed here is encryption and authentication of dicom images based on RSA and AES algorithms. The image based Digital Envelope concept provided image security. Encryption after watermarking enhanced the security before transmission. It is very difficult for hackers to retrieve patient information from the encrypted image while transmitting over public networks. The patient information is retrieved from the image during reception. The image cannot be decrypted if it is subjected to attacks such as average filtering, Gaussian filtering and rotation about 45 degrees and can be decrypted for other attacks. The PSNR and TAF values are calculated for all attacks. These quality measures evaluate the security of algorithms. The digital signature verification helps out in finding the tampered image since the signature obtained during reception is not same as the originally generated signature if tampered. The histogram analysis of the both the RSA and AES encrypted dicom image with the original dicom image shows that the image encrypted using AES algorithm is highly uncorrelated with the original image. The Key used in AES algorithm is stronger than the key used in RSA algorithm. Conclusions were drawn from the above analysis that AES algorithm provides more security than RSA algorithm but AES requires safe transmission of cipher key.

References

1. Kobayashi, L.O.M., Furuie, S.S., Barreto, P.S.M.: Providing Integrity and Authenticity in DICOM Images: A Novel Approach. IEEE Transactions on Information Technology in Biomedicine 13(4) (July 2009)

360   A. Kannammal and S. Subha Rani

2. Sreerama Murty, M., Veeraiah, D., Srinivas Rao, A.: Digital Signature and Watermark Methods For Image Authentication using Cryptography Analysis. Signal & Image Processing: An International Journal (SIPIJ) 2(2) (June 2011)
3. Puech, W., Rodrigue, J.M.: A New Crypto-Watermarking Method For Medical Images Safe Transfer. International Journal of Medical Informatics 64, 429–438 (2001)
4. Piao, C.-R., Woo, D.-M., Park, D.-C., Han, S.-S.: Medical Image Authentication Using Hash Function and Integer Wavelet Transform. In: 2008 Congress on Image and Signal Processing (2008)
5. AI-Gindy, A.: A Fragile Invertible Watermarking Technique for the Authentication of Medical Images, pp. 191–195. IEEE (2011)
6. Giakoumaki, Pavlopoulos, S., Koutsouris, D.: Secure efficient health data management through multiple watermarking on medical images. Med. Biol. Eng. Comput. 44, 619–631 (2006)
7. Coatrieux, G., Montagner, J., Huang, H., Roux, C.: Mixed reversible and RONI watermarking for medical image reliability protection. In: IEEE Int. Conf. Eng. Med. Biol. Soc (EMBS), pp. 5653–5656 (2007)
8. Cao, F., Huang, H.K., Zhou, X.Q.: Medical image security in HIPAA mandated PACS environment. Computerized Medical Imaging and Graphics 27, 185–196 (2003)
9. Zhou, X.: Research and Implementation of RSA algorithm for encryption and decryption. In: 2011 6th International Forum Strategic Technology (IFOST), August 22 (2011)
10. Karthigai Kumar, P., Rasheed, S.: Simulation of Image Encryption using AES encryption. In: IJCA Special Issue on Computational Science-New Dimensions and Perspectives NCCSE (2011)
11. Acharya, U.R., Bhat, P.S., Kumar, S., Min, L.C.: Transmission and storage of medical images with patient information. Compt. Biol. Med. 33, 303–310 (2003)

Rain Removal in Image Sequence Using Sparse Coding

C. Ramya and S. Subha Rani

Department of Electronics and Communication Engineering, PSG College of Technology,
Coimbatore, Tamil Nadu, India
ramyamaharajan@yahoo.in

Abstract. One of the major applications of image processing is robot vision. In this paper a rain degraded image enhancement algorithm is proposed, which is one of the applications of robot vision. The objective of the proposed method is to enhance the image sequences degraded by rain using sparse coding. Most of the other methods that deal with rain removal from image sequences are carried out only on continuous frames where temporal correlations among successive images are exploited. In sparse representation, with only a few dictionary elements, compared to the ambient signal dimension, can be used to well-approximate the signals. The proposed method makes use of Enhanced K-SVD (EK-SVD) for dictionary learning and orthogonal matching pursuit (OMP) for sparse coding to retrieve the rain degraded image. This dictionary selection will provide an increased convergence speed and performance to the proposed method by ensuring minimum error as well as sparsity of representation. In this paper the proposed method is also examined with other well known dictionary learning techniques. Simulation results show that the proposed method provides improved performance in visual quality and also provides less computation time.

Keywords: video, dictionary learning, sparse, rain removal.

1 Introduction

Generally in robot vision, autonomous robot navigation, inspection and assembly need the enhancement of the edges of an object to facilitate guidance to robotic gripper. Besides this other enhancement applications are outdoor surveillance, automatic incident detection, vision based driver assistance systems. But these systems can be adversely affected by bad weather conditions. Although most of the algorithms used in outdoor vision systems assume that the image intensities are proportional to scene brightness. However, dynamic weather conditions like rain and snow will violate this basic assumption by introducing sharp intensity fluctuations in images and videos [1-5]. Thus it will degrade the performance of the outdoor vision systems.

Nowadays most of the works were on the removal of rain streaks in videos. A physics-based motion blur model for the detection and removal of rain from videos is presented in [2]. It also provides comprehensive analysis of the visual effects of rain on an imaging system. Some authors [3], utilizes camera parameters such as exposure time and depth of field to mitigate the rain effects.

S.G. Ponnambalam et al. (Eds.): IRAM 2012, CCIS 330, pp. 361–370, 2012.

In paper [4], a photometric model was developed to describe the intensities of individual rain streaks and it also captures the spatio-temporal properties of rain. By incorporating both temporal and chromatic properties of rain, an improved rain streaks removal algorithm was presented in [6]. A survey is presented in [7] based on the outdoor environmental factors, such as static shadows, snow, rain, and glare, to enhance the accuracy of video based automatic incident detection.

The paper [8] presents an improved approach for vision-based driver assistance systems using radio metrically uncalibrated gray value cameras and GPS information. However some works related to vision based driver assistance systems are interested in the detection of rain drops instead of rain streaks, by utilizing photometric raindrop model [9-10]. In paper [11], a single image based rain removal is addressed as an image decomposition problem based on morphological component analysis.

The proposed rain removal frame work focuses on the optimized dictionary selection. Thus it maximizes variance reduction over the set of signals by constraining the size of the dictionary as well as the number of dictionary columns that can be used to represent each signal. Thus it leads to a better convergence speed and also produces improved video quality. The rest of the paper is organized as follows: Section 2 suggests the optimized dictionary design. Section 3 discusses proposed rain streaks removal frame work. Simulation results are reported in section 4 and section 5 concludes the paper.

2   Optimized Dictionary Selections

Sparse signal representations are used in a variety of fields such as image denoising, compression, pattern recognition, image and video coding [12]. Given an over complete set of basis signals, as the dictionary. The dictionary members are the sparse linear combination of the input signals. Here the problem is the selection of optimal size dictionary. A bigger dictionary may give more variety of shapes but has more redundant elements. Excluding such elements can improve the approximation speed but it limits the approximation accuracy. Hence, the dictionary size always has a tradeoff between approximation speed and accuracy.

Recently, there are many dictionary learning algorithms are available to mitigate this problem.

These dictionary learning algorithms are developed to learn a sparsifying dictionary directly from data using techniques such as optimization, clustering, and nonparametric Bayesian inference. The objective of these optimization based approaches is to minimize the data error by $\ell1$ norm to enforce sparsity in the dictionary representation [13]. The most well known dictionary learning algorithm is KSVD, which generalizes the K-means clustering algorithm.

Given, $X = \{x_i\}_{i=1}^{N}$, $x_i \in R^n$ it uses one cluster to represent each x_i. These cluster centers are treated as dictionary elements a_j and the coefficient ω_{ij} as membership of signal x_i into cluster a_j. The minimization function of KSVD is following:

$$\min_{\Phi,W}\left\{\| X - \Phi W \|_F^2\right\} \ subject\,to\ \| \omega_i \|_0 \leq T_0,\ for\,i \in \{1,...,N\} \qquad (1)$$

Let $X \in R^{n \times N}$ is a column matrix of all signals x_i as $X = [x_1 \mid .... \mid x_N]$. $\Phi \in R^{n \times M}$ is a column matrix of all dictionary elements as $\Phi = [a_1 \mid ... \mid a_M]$. $W \in R^{M \times N}$ is a matrix of all coefficients corresponding to dictionary elements a_j and w_i. $\| . \|_0$ is called the ℓ_0 norm. It counts the number of non zero elements in a vector.

KSVD is a two phase approach. In the first phase, it updates the dictionary coefficients by using Matching pursuits (MP). In the second phase, Φ and W are assumed to be fixed and only one column a_k of Φ is updated at a time. By iterating through the two phases, it produces dictionary that approximates given x_i sparsely and accurately. However selection of optimized dictionary is vital to improve the approximation speed and accuracy. Many optimized dictionary learning methods are available.

One such approach is [13] Enhanced K-SVD, which discovers an optimized number of dictionary elements by reducing redundancies in the learned dictionary. The draw back of KSVD is due to manual selection of the elements K. It is rectified by EK-SVD by automatically discovering the value of K during the dictionary learning process. For this it utilizes the CA (Competitive Agglomeration) algorithm to update the dictionary coefficients. CA is a clustering algorithm will provides optimal number of clusters for a given dataset. Thus this approach is utilized in the proposed method.

In this paper image decomposition is done by sparse coding. Many greedy algorithms have been proposed to obtain fast approximate solutions [12]. These algorithms employ sequential selection of basis vectors from an over complete dictionary. Some algorithms are matching pursuit (MP), orthogonal matching pursuit (OMP), and order recursive matching pursuit (ORMP). In that OMP algorithm provides good approximation of signal. Also OMP is easy to implement and provides a satisfactory stable result than other basic methods.

3   Rain Streaks Removal Using EKSVD

Usually the rain removal techniques take various factors like dynamics of rain, photometry of rain, camera parameters such as exposure time, depth of field, temporal, chromatic properties and shape characteristics of rain into consideration. But the proposed method does not consider any of these factors but leads to a more efficient restoration algorithm using sparse coding.

In the proposed method, the input rain degraded image is decomposed into low-frequency and high-frequency parts [11]. Hence, most of the image information will be retained in the low frequency part. The high frequency part contains rain streaks, sharp details like edges and texture information. Then the geometric component of high frequency part is obtained using image decomposition algorithm. Finally, the rain removed image is obtained by integrating the geometric component of high frequency and low frequency part of the rain degraded image. The processing flow of the algorithm is shown in Fig.1.

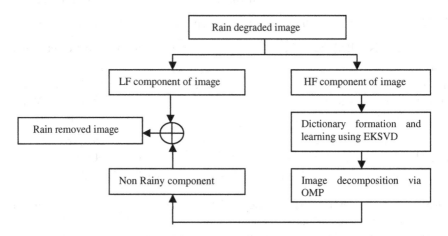

Fig. 1. The processing flow of the algorithm

The proposed method adapts EK-SVD for dictionary learning. In EK-SVD, instead of using MP to update coefficients a_k, it uses the CA algorithm. The dictionary elements a_i as cluster centers. The signal b_i in the cluster a_i has memberships u_{ij} are derived from the coefficient α_{ij}. The objective function of the optimal dictionary design algorithm is as follows:

$$f(\Phi,U,B) = \sum_{j=1}^{M}\sum_{i=1}^{N} u_{ij}^2 d^2(b_i,a_j) - \eta\sum_{j=1}^{P}\left[\sum_{i=1}^{N} u_{ij}\right]^2$$

$$subject\ to \sum_{j=1}^{P} u_{ij} = 1 - \hat{\gamma}_{b_i}, for\ i \in \{1,........,N\}$$

(2)

Initially, the input rainy image B is roughly decomposed into low frequency (B_{LF}) and high frequency components (B_{HF}). In this the high frequency part contains both rain components as well as sharp details of the image. So the extraction of sharp detail will yield better result. For that the proposed method learns dictionary φ_{HF} using EKSVD from B_{HF}. Φ_{HF} is further divided into geometric and rain components of B_{HF} respectively. The problem of rain streak removal for an image is formulated as a sparse decomposition problem as follows:

$$\min_{\Phi_{HF}, U^k} \| y_{HF}^k - \Phi_{HF} U_{HF}^k \|_2^2 \quad subject \ to \ \| U_{HF}^k \|_0 \leq T \tag{3}$$

where $y_{HF} \in R^n$ represents the k- patch extracted from B_{HF}, k=1,2,...,p. $U_{HF}^k \in R^m$ sparse coefficients of y_{HF}^k with respect to $\Phi_{HF} \in R^{nxm}$, n≤m. T denotes the sparsity of U_{HF}^k. For dictionary learning a set of overlapping patches are extracted from the B_{HF} for learning dictionary Φ_{HF}. The dictionary learning problem is formulated as

$$\min_{\Phi_{HF}, U^k} = \sum_{j=1}^{M} \sum_{i=1}^{N} u_{ij}^2 d^2 (b_i, a_j) - \eta \sum_{j=1}^{P} \left[\sum_{i=1}^{N} u_{ij} \right]^2$$

$$subject \ to \ \sum_{j=1}^{P} u_{ij} = 1 - \hat{\gamma}_{b_i}, for \ i \in \{1,......., N\} \tag{4}$$

The atoms in the dictionary Φ_{HF} is roughly divided into geometric and rain components of B_{HF} [11]. Based on the geometric dictionary apply the OMP algorithm for each patch y_{HF}^k extracted from B_{HF}. Each reconstructed patch y_{HF}^k can be used to recover the geometric component B_{HF}^G. Finally, the rain removed image B is obtained by merging both B_{LF} & B_{HF}.

4   Simulation Results

To evaluate the performance of the proposed method different rain degraded images were taken. The original rain degraded image is shown in fig.2 (a), 3(a), 4(a).The results of approximated singular value decomposition (ASVD) is shown in fig.2(b),3(b),4(b). The results of KSVD are shown in fig fig.2(c), 3(c), 4(c). The results of proposed method (PM) are shown in fig.2 (d), 3(d), 4(d). The performance of the proposed method is also evaluated using metrics such as Structural Similarity (SSIM) Index, Tenengrad criteria (TEN), Virtual Image Fidelity (VIF).

4.1   Structural Similarity (SSIM) Index

The structural similarity (SSIM) index is a recent popular image quality assessment algorithm. The SSIM index is a full reference metrics. It is designed to improve on traditional methods like peak signal-to-noise ratio and mean squared error, which have proved to be inconsistent with human eye perception. The SSIM index expresses quality by comparing local correlations in luminance, contrast, and structure between reference and distorted images. The results of SSIM calculation is reported in Table1.

$$SSIM(x, y) = \frac{(2\mu_x\mu_y + C_1)(2\sigma_{xy} + C_2)}{(\mu_x^2 + \mu_y^2 + C_1)(\sigma_x^2 + \sigma_y^2 + C_2)}$$

(5)

$$MSSIM(X, Y) = \frac{1}{M}\sum_{j=1}^{M} SSIM(x_j, y_j)$$

μ_x and μ_y are the average of x and y; σ_x^2 and σ_y^2 are the variance of x and y; σ_{xy} the covariance of x and y; $C_1 = (k_1 L)^2$, $C_2 = (k_2 L)^2$ are constant: L dynamic range of pixel values.

Table 1. Comparison of SSIM values of the proposed method with other dictionary learning techniques

Test Sequence	Asvd	Ksvd	Proposed Method
Man	0.6661	0.6844	0.6901
Umbrella	0.5247	0.5425	0.6444
Frame 80	0.6231	0.6588	0.7553

4.2   Tenengrad Criteria (TEN)

A Tenengrad criterion (TEN) is used to evaluate the sharpness measure [14]. The Tenengrad is based on the gradient $\nabla I(u, v)$ at each pixel (u, v), were the partial derivatives are obtained by high-pass filter, e.g., the sobel operator, with the convolution kernels i_u and i_v. The gradient magnitude is given by:

$$S(u, v) = \sqrt{(i_u * I(u, v))^2 \mid (i_v * I(u, v))^2}$$

(6)

The Tenengrad criteria is formulated as

$$TEN = \sum_u \sum_v S(u, v)^2, for \ S(u, v) > T)$$

(7)

where T is the threshold. When the Tenengrad value is larger than the image quality is considered higher. The results of Tenengrad criteria calculation is reported in Table 2.

Table 2. Comparison of TEN values of the proposed method with other dictionary learning techniques

Test Sequence	Asvd	Ksvd	Proposed Method
Man	14707	15402	19781
Umbrella	16788	12565	16204
Frame 80	49564	48854	51726

4.3   Virtual Image Fidelity (VIF)

VIF was developed for image and video quality measurement based on natural scene statistics (NSS). Image quality assessment is done based on information fidelity. The results of VIF calculation is reported in Table 3.

$$VIF = Distorted\ Image\ Information\ /\ Reference\ Image\ Information \qquad (8)$$

Table 3. Comparison of VIF values of the proposed method with other dictionary learning techniques

Test Sequence	Asvd	Ksvd	Proposed Method
Man	0.1978	0.2014	0.2197
Umbrella	0.2205	0.2305	0.2936
Frame 80	0.1119	0.1325	0.2745

(a) Man image   (b) Output using ASVD

Fig. 2.

(c) Output using KSVD   (d)   Output using PM

Fig. 2. (*continued*)

(a) UMBRELLA image   (b) Output using ASVD

(c) Output using KSVD   (d)   Output using PM

Fig. 3.

(a) Frame 80   (b) Output using ASVD

(c) Output using KSVD   (d)   Output using PM

Fig. 4.

5   Conclusion

In this paper, a single image based rain streak removal is proposed using sparse coding. The proposed method adapt on EKSVD and OMP algorithm to retrieve the degraded high frequency components of the image. However compared to other dictionary learning techniques, EKSVD can improve the convergence speed and performance of the proposed method. Simulation results show that the proposed method provides improved performance in visual quality than other traditional dictionary learning techniques. This is also analyzed using metrics such as Structural Similarity Index, Tenengrad criteria, Virtual Image Fidelity.

References

1. Barnum, P.C., Narasimhan, S., Kanade, T.: Analysis of rain and snow in frequency space. Int. J. Comput. Vis. 86, 256–274 (2010)
2. Garg, K., Nayar, S.K.: Detection and removal of rain from videos. In: IEEE Conf. Comput. Vis. Pattern Recognit., vol. 1, pp. 528–535 (2004)
3. Garg, K., Nayar, S.K.: When does a camera see rain? In: IEEE Int. Conf. Comput. Vis., vol. 2, pp. 1067–1074 (2005)
4. Garg, K., Nayar, S.K.: Vision and rain. Int. J. Comput. Vis. 75(1), 3–27 (2007)
5. Garg, K., Nayar, S.K.: Photorealistic rendering of rain streaks. ACM Trans. on Graphics 25(3), 996–1002 (2006)

6. Brewer, N., Liu, N.: Using the Shape Characteristics of Rain to Identify and Remove Rain from Video. In: da Vitoria Lobo, N., Kasparis, T., Roli, F., Kwok, J.T., Georgiopoulos, M., Anagnostopoulos, G.C., Loog, M. (eds.) S+SSPR 2008. LNCS, vol. 5342, pp. 451–458. Springer, Heidelberg (2008)
7. Shehata, M.S., Cai, J., Badawy, W.M., Burr, T.W., Pervez, M.S., Johannesson, R.J., Radmanesh, A.: Video-based automatic incident detection for smart roads: the outdoor environmental challenges regarding false alarms. IEEE Trans. Intell. Transportation Syst. 9(2), 349–360 (2008)
8. Buciu, I., Gacsádi, A., Grava, C.: Vision based Approaches for Driver Assistance Systems. In: 11th WSEAS international conference on Automation & information, pp. 92–97 (2010)
9. Roser, M., Geiger, A.: Video-based raindrop detection for improved image registration. In: IEEE Int. Conf. Comput. Vis. Workshops, Kyoto, pp. 570–577 (2009)
10. Halimeh, J.C., Roser, M.: Raindrop detection on car windshields using geometric-photometric environment construction and intensity-based correlation. In: IEEE Intell. Vehicles Symp., Xi'an, China, pp. 610–615 (2009)
11. Kang, L.-W., Lin, C.-W., Fu, Y.-H.: Automatic Single-Image-Based Rain Streaks Removal via Image Decomposition. IEEE Transactions on Image Processing 21(4), 1742–1755 (2012)
12. Chaterjee, P., Milanfar, P.: K-SVD Algorithm for Denoising of Gray-Scale Images (Spring 2007)
13. Mazhar, Gader, P.D.: EK-SVD: Optimized Dictionary Design for Sparse Representations. In: 19th International Conference on Pattern Recognition, Raazia (2008)
14. Zuiderveld, K.: Contrast Limited adaptive histogram equalization. In: Heckbert, P. (ed.) Graphics Gems IV, ch. VIII.5, pp. 474–485. Academic, New York (1994)

A Decentralized Resource Monitoring System
Using Structural, Context and Process Information

Lisa Abele[1], Lisa Ollinger[2], Ines Heck[2], and Martin Kleinsteuber[3]

[1] Siemens AG, Otto-Hahn-Ring, München, Germany
[2] DFKI Gmbh, Trippstadter Straße 122, Kaiserslautern, Germany
[3] Department of Electrical Engineering, Technische Universität München

Abstract. Over the past century there has been a dramatic increase in the consumption of resources such as energy, raw materials, water, etc. in the manufacturing domain. An intelligent resource monitoring system that uses structural, context and process information of the plant can deliver more accurate monitoring results that can be used to detect excessive resource consumption. Recent monitoring systems usually run on a central unit. However, modern plants require a higher degree of reusability and adaptability which can be achieved by several monitoring units running on decentralized autonomous devices that allow the components to monitor themselves.

To integrate structural, context and process information on such autonomous devices for resource monitoring, semantic models and rules are appropriate. This paper will present an architecture of a decentralized, intelligent resource monitoring system which uses structural, context and process knowledge to compute the state of the individual components by means of models and rules. This architecture might also be used for other manufacturing systems such as diagnostic or prognostic systems.

1 Introduction

An efficient use of resources in industrial plants is becoming increasingly important. Plant engineers have to be aware of the resource consumption -- e.g. energy, raw materials, water, compressed air, etc. -- of their plants on the level of the incorporated devices so that they are able to optimize the plants' structure and processes accordingly. A resource monitoring system (RMS) is needed to use resources efficiently. Nowadays, monitoring systems run on a central unit that collects all sensor data of the plant to compute the monitoring states of the different components. But modern plants require a higher degree of reusability and adaptability and thus a decentralized monitoring system where components are able to monitor themselves by means of intelligent autonomous devices such as active digital product memories (ADPMs). The advantage of such a decentralized system with ADPMs are manifold: (1) the manufacturer can produce intelligent components that can monitor themselves, using his extensive knowledge about his products, (2) the components can also execute additional monitoring rules defined by the plant engineer, (3) an exchange of

S.G. Ponnambalam et al. (Eds.): IRAM 2012, CCIS 330, pp. 371–378, 2012.

single components does not require modification of the entire system and downtime, (4) failure of one unit of the RMS will not affect the operation of the entire RMS.

A RMS is more advanced as usual Condition Monitoring Systems and requires not only measurement of sensor data, but also an awareness of the components' environment and situation. This additional information is stored in models which explicitly store knowledge about the plant structure, the process steps and the plant context. Thus, it gets possible to reuse this information and new monitoring systems can be defined with lower effort.

The objective of this paper is to describe the architecture of a monitoring system implemented on ADPMs that combines structural, process and context information to allow a manual optimization of the control system of the plant. Especially, research to build a monitoring system with explicit knowledge-based models and logical rules [1] is derived from the experiences gained during design of an application scenario of an industrial plant within the RES-COM project [2]. This research project aims to automatically conserve resources in industrial plants through ADPMs and context-aware embedded sensor-actuator systems.

In this paper we introduce the system architecture of the monitoring system. Then, a detailed description of the structure, process and context information is given. Finally, we show first results with an application scenario addressing issues that can be solved by our system.

2   Related Work

The technologies that are relevant to our research fall in three categories: knowledge-based monitoring systems, industrial applications with DPMs (active and passive digital product memories) and automation systems using structural, context or process knowledge.

Typical knowledge-based monitoring solutions focus either on specific application areas (e.g. electro hydraulic linear drives [3]) or on the deployment of certain tools or methods (e.g. computational intelligence methods [4]). Our goal of research is to develop a generic, tool- and facility-independent RMS. The authors in [5] describe how a generic data exchange format can be used for an automatic configuration of a production monitoring and control system. But the usage of a data exchange format such as CAEX requires tool support. Currently, no wide-spread commercial tool supports CAEX directly or via converters. Some dedicated tools, e.g. the AutomationML Editor of Zühlke Engineering AG [6], offer currently only basic features.

Several industrial applications use DPMs to attach relevant information to plant products or components. In [7] the authors describe how to attach life cycle information to an industrial product to allow an information handover via several stages of the value chain with potentially different stakeholders. One of the stakeholders is the plant engineer. Based on this approach, he can extract the monitoring characteristics of an industrial product out of the life cycle information stored on the component. The authors in [8] present a flexible approach for product-driven manufacturing using a digital product memory. This flexible approach describes a scenario in which the DPM is attached to the product to control the environment and influence the entire production process. The main ideas of the existing approaches based on DPMs were continued and enhanced to define the architecture of the RMS.

A considerable amount of literature has been published on automation systems that use either structural, context or process knowledge or even a combination of them. A plant-wide diagnosis systems is presented in [9] using process knowledge in addition to structural knowledge. An infrastructure which describes context modeling concepts for pervasive computing systems was proposed by [10]. We discovered that much of the work in the field of context awareness [11] is concerned with providing either a framework to support the abstraction of context information from the field level of the plant or high-level models of context information to provide context services. Our approach combines these two levels to provide more accurate context information to the monitoring system. All the studies reviewed so far, however, are not combining all knowledge about the plant to efficiently use them for monitoring.

3   System Architecture

Monitoring of resources in a production plant requires sufficient information granularity and clearly structured data to compute reliable monitoring states of components. One of the main advantage of our architecture compared to the current state-of-the-art is its decentralized character. This means that the manufacturers of components produce intelligent components that can monitor themselves. The main modules of the RMS as shown in Fig. 1 are:

1. Every component in the plant is equipped with an ADPM including a monitoring unit (MU). An ADPM consists of a knowledge base that contains knowledge about the plant in a machine processable way, including a rule base. For our monitoring purpose, we distinguish between three kinds of input, 1) structural information about the plant, e.g. motor is monitored by a temperature sensor and a smart meter, 2) current process step, e.g. conveyor that is driven by the motor is executing process "transport at maximum speed", 3) context information of the plant, e.g. plant is producing at half load. This input and the knowledge-based models and rules are then used by an inference engine in the monitoring unit which computes the component state.

2. Collections of components are combined to groups. Every group has its own decentralized MU which takes the individual component states as input to compute a composite state of the group.

3. The heart of the system is the monitoring unit of the industrial plant. It gets component and group states as input to compute the state of the entire plant. A knowledge base editor assists here in the addition of new knowledge from the plant engineers and performs consistency checks on the updated knowledge base.

4. The plant monitoring state computed by the MU of the plant is provided to the plant engineer. Based on the resulting states provided by the monitoring system the plant engineers react to optimize the resource efficiency of the entire plant. Thus, the control system of the plant has to be adapted in order to optimize the

parameterization of the components and the control procedures. The control procedure in form of a service orchestration (section 3.2) provides a high degree of adaptability so that adaptations can be realized with low effort [12].

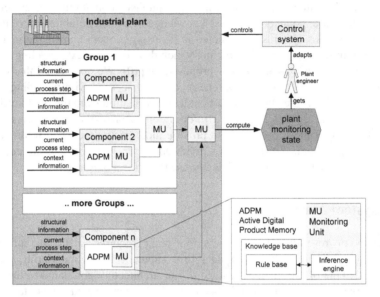

Fig. 1. Architecture of the monitoring system

3.1   Structural Information

To allow reusability and extensibility the structure model of an industrial plant has to be able to include all knowledge of previous knowledge-bases such as wide-spread modeling tools (e.g. Siemens COMOS) and additional knowledge.

The structure model defines two kinds of fundamental information: (1) the *taxonomy* identifies and names element classes and arranges them into a classification hierarchy and (2) the *plant topology* describes the *containment hierarchy* of plant components as defined by the *part of* relation and other functional relations between components as *connected to* or *energy flow*.

The component models also contain individual characteristics of the components including default parameters, e.g. nominal energy, monitoring thresholds and configuration parameters. The default parameters and default monitoring thresholds are stored by the manufacturer of the components on their ADPMs. During plant design, the plant engineer configures the individual components according to the plant environment and stores the configuration parameters on their ADPMs.

3.2   Process Information

To determine the monitoring state of components, the current process of the component or remote components has to be considered. The required process information can be divided in two parts: a model of the production process and the dynamic information about the current process state. Today, this information is contained implicitly in the control procedures of the process control devices like programmable logic controllers (PLCs). Since the control procedures of these controllers are generated on a low implementation level, where the individual binary in- and outputs are processed, the code is complex and monolithic. Due to this the control procedure lacks of clarity, comprehensibility and adaptability. Therefore, this procedure should be developed on a higher abstraction level such as service orchestration [13].

This means that functions of the hardware components are regarded as services that represent the building blocks for the execution of the production process. To get an executable control procedure the services have to be arranged within a process logic in a formal representation The process logic contains states and state transitions with links to the respective services. Thus, the model of the production process stored in the knowledge base can be derived directly from this process logic. During run-time, the control system has to indicate the current active process step and provide process values and dynamic information to the monitoring unit.

3.3   Context Information

To monitor the resource consumption of a production plant or its components, it is not enough to observe just the actual consumption values. An assessment whether the measured values are within acceptable range often depends on the context, for example what kind of product the machine is currently producing or what the average energy consumption was for the last products. To determine the current resource situation of the plant, this additional information has to be evaluated continuously and has to be represented in the underlying monitoring rules.

According to [14], context "is any information that can be used to characterize the situation of an entity. An entity is a person, place or object that is considered relevant to the interaction between a user and an application.". A monitoring system can make more intelligent decisions and determine more accurately the situation of the monitored item if additional information (=Context) is provided about all entities that are in some way relevant to the current monitoring task.

In our RMS, the plant components and their monitoring units are supplied with context information from a central server, the *context broker*, that collects the context information from all participating sources in the plant. The context broker supports several protocols (e.g. OPC UA, Web services, REST) to call the technical interface of the ADPM, read the enabled variables and store the values in its internal database. The individual MUs can request and register all context information that is relevant to their specific monitoring task according to their underlying context and situation model. This context information is used by the MUs to compute the individual monitoring state of a component or a group of components.

3.4   Decision Support System

The monitoring units of the components contain a knowledge base with a rule base and an inference engine. Together they form a decentralized decision support system (DSS). The MU uses the structure, process and context models to annotate sensor data semantically and computes the state of the component. For example, take a group $g1$

that contains a smart meter sm1 that measures the energy consumption of a motor *m1* and reports a value of 50. Then MU of *g1* annotates this as "motor m1 has an energy consumption of 50kW that is within acceptable range".

We distinguish between two kinds of rules: (a) rules that infer the states of single components, (b) composite rules that infer the states of groups including context and process information. The simplest case of (a) is to use thresholds stored by the manufacturer of the components on the ADPMs to compute the current state.

For composite components or groups, the system computes composite rules, a simple example for case (b) is *if one of the motors in the motor group G has the state "error" then the state of G is "error"*. Then the DSS provides the states of the groups and the annotated data to other composite monitoring units and finally it computes the state of the entire plant.

4   Application Scenario

In the context of the RES-COM project, we will implement the RMS on an intelligent plant which produces smart key finders as shown in fig 2. We build a simulation tool based on this application scenario. Let us consider a concrete simulation of the monitoring approach, using the transportation block as example. The transportation block of the plant is used to transport the smart key finder on two conveyors *cv1* and *cv2* which are both running with the same constant speed. The two conveyors are driven by the engines *m1* and *m2* respectively. The entire transportation unit is grouped in the functional drive group *g*.

Fig. 2. Smart key finder production plant

In our simulation tool, a plant engineer can enter monitoring rules in a user interface as shown in Fig 3. Parameters of the plant components, e.g. the resistance of the motor m1 can be addressed with "m1.R". The plant engineer can insert equations.

Simple rules monitor thresholds of components which are stored by the manufacturer on the ADPMs, e.g. the maximum input power of the motor m1 is 500W. Additionally, the process information is considered. The drive group *g* can execute three different processes: a) drive forward, b) drive backward, c) stop. In this application scenario, we can use the process information to compute the standby voltage *Vs* of the group *g*. When the motor is in process "stop" a small standby voltage is acceptable.

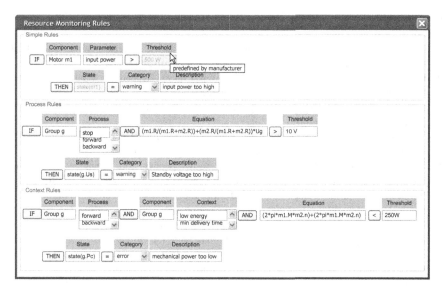

Fig. 3. Resource monitoring rule interface (R = resistance, Ug = measured voltage, Us = standby voltage, pi = π, M = torque, n = rotational speed)

A special feature of the plant is that the operator of the plant can choose between two production contexts: a) produce with lowest energy consumption, b) produce with minimum delivery time. If the operator chooses the first option (*low energy*), the engines' rotational speed is adapted to reach the maximum energy efficiency and the two conveyors run at a lower speed. If the operator chooses the second option (*min delivery time*), the engines' rotational speed is adapted to its maximum.

The knowledge-based models were stored in OWL axioms which allows inference mechanisms. We used *Prolog* as inference engine which stands for *programming in logic*. The rules are processed by the inference engine and finally, the resource monitoring system presents the resulting monitoring states to the plant engineer.

5   Conclusion

In this paper, we have presented a decentralized architecture of a resource monitoring system. In our research, the aim was to describe how structural, process and context models and monitoring rules on ADPMs can be used to provide a high degree of adaptability and reusability. As a result, we implemented the resource monitoring system for a smart key finder production plant based on the proposed architecture.

Acknowledgment. This research was funded in part by the German Federal Ministry of Education and Research under grant number 01IA11001. The responsibility for this publication lies with the authors.

References

1. Brachman, R., Levesque, H.: Knowledge Representation and Reasoning. The Morgan Kaufmann Series in Artificial Intelligence. Morgan Kaufmann (2004)
2. RES-COM - Resource Conservation through Context-dependent Machine-to-Machine Communication, http://www.res-com-project.org
3. Stammen, C.: Condition-Monitoring für intelligente hydraulische Linearantriebe. PhD thesis, RWTH Aachen (2005)
4. Vilakazi, C., Marwala, T., Mautla, P., Moloto, E.: On-Line Condition Monitoring using Computational Intelligence, ArXiv e-prints (2007)
5. Schleipen, M., Drath, R., Sauer, O.: The system-independent data exchange format CAEX for supporting an automatic configuration of a production monitoring and control system, In: IEEE International Symposium on Industrial Electronics, pp. 1786–1798 (2008)
6. Drath, R.: Datenaustausch in der Anlagenplanung mit AutomationML - Integration von CAEX, PLCopen XML und COLLADA. Springer (2010)
7. Stephan, P., Meixner, G., Kößling, H., Flörchinger, F., Ollinger, L.: Product-mediated communication through digital object memories in heterogeneous value chains. In: IEEE International Conference on Pervasive Computing and Communications (2010)
8. Seitz, C., Legat, C., Liu, Z.: Flexible Manufacturing Control with Autonomous Product Memories. In: IEEE Conference on Emerging Technologies and Factory Automation (2010)
9. Christiansen, L., Fay, A., Opgenoorth, B., Neidig, J.: Improved Diagnosis by Combining Structural and Process Knowledge. In: IEEE Conference on Emerging Technologies and Factory Automation (2011)
10. Henricksen, K., Indulska, J., Rakotonirainy, A.: Modeling Context Information in Pervasive Computing Systems. In: Mattern, F., Naghshineh, M. (eds.) PERVASIVE 2002. LNCS, vol. 2414, pp. 167–180. Springer, Heidelberg (2002)
11. Baldauf, M., Dustdar, S., Rosenberg, F.: A survey on context-aware systems. Information Systems 2(4) (2007)
12. Ollinger, L., Schlick, J., Hodek, S.: Leveraging the agility of manufacturing chains by combining Process-Oriented production planning and Service-Oriented manufacturing, In: Proceedings of the 18th IFAC World Congress (2011)
13. Theorin, A., Ollinger, L., Johnsson, C.: Service-oriented process control with grafchart and the devices profile for web services. In: Proceedings of the IFAC Symposium on Information Control Problems in Maufacturing, INCOM 2012 (2012)
14. Dey, K.: Understanding and using context. Personal Ubiquitous Computing 5(1), 4–7 (2001)

Influence of Substrate Temperature, Pressure and Grit Size on Synthesis of SiC Thin Film by Pulsed Laser Deposition Technique

Venkataramesh Bhimasingu[1,*], Nilesh J. Vasa[1], and I.A. Palani[2]

[1] Department of Engineering Design, IIT Madras, Chennai-600036, India
[2] Department of Mechanical Engineering, IIT Indore, Indore-453441, India

Abstract. Pulsed laser deposition (PLD) technique for depositing SiC on Si(100) substrates using Nd^{3+}: YAG laser at 355 nm is studied. Influence of substrate temperature, ambient pressure and SiC powder grit size on both structure and morphology of SiC thin film is investigated. Experimental studies show that multicrystalline SiC film can be obtained with temperature ranging from 600 °C to 700 °C and at an ambient pressure of about 5.5×10^{-3} Pa. Although, alkali free glass show Microcracks on as deposited films, crystalline Si substrate did not show such micro cracks. Further, droplet formation on the deposited film was reduced significantly by selecting the grit size of SiC powder around 120. The X-ray diffraction (XRD) studies on deposited films clearly show multicrystalline (combined 3C-SiC and 4H-SiC) nature of SiC films. Based on the nano-indentation test, elastic modulus and hardness values of thin film were estimated as 300 GPa and 45 GPa.

Keywords: silicon carbide, pulsed laser deposition, thin films, grit size, photovoltaics.

1 Introduction

Silicon carbide (SiC), similar to diamond and other ceramic materials, is a material with excellent physical, chemical and mechanical properties. SiC possesses high hardness, wear resistance, resistance to thermal shock, high thermal conductivity (3.2 - 4.9 W/cm °C), resistance to chemical and radiation exposure, low thermal coefficient of expansion, wide band gap (2.4 to 3.3 eV), high breakdown field (2.1 - 2.5 MV/cm) and high electron mobility. As a results, SiC film is considered as a protective coating for metallic components, abrasion tooling and micro electro-mechanical systems. Crystalline SiC is also used in electronic components, photovoltaic cells, image sensors [1-3]. The growth of bulk single crystals of SiC is difficult, since SiC single crystals can exist in numerous prototypes and SiC cannot be grown from stoichiometric melt. Several important polytypes of SiC are hexagonal (4H- and 6H-SiC) (α-SiC) and cubic (3C-SiC or β-SiC) polytypes. 3C-SiC possesses a cubic structure, and isotropic electron

---

* Corresponding author.

S.G. Ponnambalam et al. (Eds.): IRAM 2012, CCIS 330, pp. 379–388, 2012.
© Springer-Verlag Berlin Heidelberg 2012

mobility of 1000 cm^2/V s. Hence 3C-SiC films on a n-type Si substrates are useful for solar cell applications [4]. On the other hand, 4H-SiC possesses smaller anisotropy and a higher bulk mobility and used for high-voltage applications [5].

Several techniques, such as chemical vapor deposition (CVD), electron beam CVD (EB-CVD), pulsed laser deposition, are used to produce SiC thin films for various functional applications. CVD technique is commonly used for SiC thin film synthesis, which forms epitaxial SiC layers . However the process temperature is above 1400°C. Further mixture of silane and hydrocarbons or various organo silicon compounds are used in hydrogen flow for an epitaxial growth of the film. The hydrogenated a-SiC: H films deposited by various CVD techniques results in reduction of the Si-C bond density, and lowering the mechanical properties such as hardness and Young modulus of the thin film [6-9].

On the other hand,The main advantage of PLD technique over other techniques include: stoichiometric film deposition, wide deposition parameter control, such as temperature, ambient pressure; multiple layer deposition with different target material is possible. These advantages are useful for SiC thin film deposition on different substrates at lower temperatures than the CVD technique. Although, the vaporization temperatures of Si and C are quite different, the PLD technique allows stoichiometric deposition of thin films matching with the target. Further, no hazardous gases are necessary for the stoichiometric film formation as it is the case in the CVD process. Various research groups are working on the PLD of SiC films [10-15]. PLD studies for SiC thin film deposition show that the pulse energy and substrate temperature are the main parameters which influence the deposition process [16,17]. Typically high substrate temperature (>600 °C) is required to produce crystalline SiC thin films. Different types of pulsed lasers, such as excimer lasers (XeCl 308 nm, KrF 248 nm, ArF 193 nm), Nd^{3+}: YAG laser with different output wavelength via harmonic conversion (1064 nm, 532 nm, 355 nm), have been used. In addition, it has been observed that the SiC film also consist of many agglomeration of particles or droplets which is also not desirable for various applications. Different approaches have been studied to avoid droplet formation during the PLD technique. An orthogonal arrangement of the target and substrate surface along with a screen between them have been used to minimize droplets formation during the laser ablation of Si target [18]. A high speed rotating target and filters have been used in PLD process to reduce the droplet formation [19-21]. On the other hand, no studies have been reported on an influence of the grit size of SiC powder used during pelletizing on the droplet formation during the PLD of thin films.

In this paper, grit size of SiC particles influences the compactness of the target used during the PLD technique. Smaller grit size is expected to result in less dense target and hence during the laser ablation process, the loose particles may result in the droplet formation. On the other hand. Large grit size is expected to result in a compact target. As a result particles might not get separated easily and chances of droplet formation are expected to reduce. The aim of the present work is to study the influence of the grit size on SiC thin film formation during the PLD process and also the effect of substrate temperature, pressure and grit size of the particle has been studied. In Sec. 2 experimental details are discussed. In Sec. 3 different characterization techniques for crystalline structure, surface morphology, elemental composition, elastic modulus (GPa), hardness (GPa), thickness etc were investigated by standard techniques like XRDA, SEM, EDS, Nano Indentation and optical surface profilometer measurement techniques are described.

2 Experimental Procedure

SiC pellets used in the PLD were prepared by compacting SiC powder (Carborundum Universal, Different Grit Size) using a hydraulic press (25 Tonnes, SAS Chennai) with a binder. Subsequently pellets (30 mm diameter x 5 mm thickness) with different grit sizes were sintered to attain required handling strength and remove the binder, which might interfere with the PLD process. The process of preparing pallet is as shown in Fig. 1.

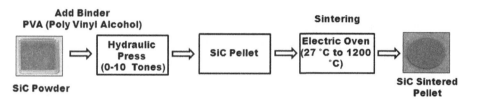

Fig. 1. Process of Pellet Preparation

Pulsed Nd^{3+}: YAG laser with a repetition rate of 10 Hz and pulse width of 8 ns was used. The output wavelength and the energy were 355 nm and around 54 mJ, respectively. As shown in Fig. 2, Nd^{3+}: YAG laser was focused on a SiC target, using a plano convex lens with a focal length of 300 mm, in a vacuum chamber. The laser fluence was estimated to be 1.7 J/cm^2, considering a laser focused spot size of 1 mm.

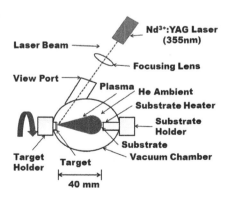

Fig. 2. Experimental Setup of Pulsed Laser Deposition (PLD)

Table 1 shows experimental parameters used for the PLD of SiC thin films on different substrates. Influence of substrate temperature, ambient pressure, substrates (glass or Si) and grit size were studied on characteristics of deposited SiC thin film.

Table 1. Parameters used for PLD of SiC thin films

Parameter	Specification
Laser	Nd^{3+}: YAG (λ=355 nm)
Pulse Duration	8 ns
Pulse Frequency	10 Hz
Pulse Energy (Fluence)	54 mJ (1.7 J/cm^2)
SiC Pellet Size	30 mm diameter and 5 mm thickness
SiC Grit Size	36, 60, 120, 400, 500
Base Pressure	9.9×10^{-3} Pa
Chamber Pressure	5.5×10^{-3} Pa, 2×10^{-2} Pa
Substrates	AFG, c-Si wafer, Size: 10 mm $\times$ 10 mm
Inert Atmosphere	He
Target and Substrate distance	40 mm
Substrate Temperature	400 °C to 800 °C
Duration of Deposition	30 minutes, 1 hour

3   Results and Discussion

3.1   Film-Thickness Measurements

Figure 3 shows Surface profiles of as deposited SiC thin film along with substrate edge were measured by using an optical surface profilometer (Veeco, NT1100) which is a non-contact type profilometer.

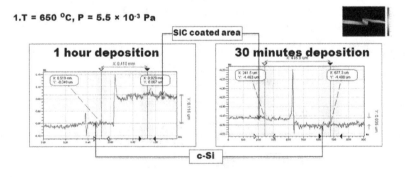

Fig. 3. Surface Profile of SiC deposited on c-Si

Based on Fig. 3, an average thickness of SiC thin film were estimated to be 35 nm and 110 nm for the deposition time of 30 minutes and 60 minutes, respectively, at the substrate temperature of 650 °C and the pressure of 5.5×10^{-3} Pa. The film deposition rate was approximately 2 nm/minute. Almost similar film deposition rate has been reported elsewhere [22].

3.2 X-Ray Diffraction Analysis

XRD studies were performed using (Bruker equipment, Germany) with CuK_{α} line emission mode. Influence of pressure on the crystalline structure of SiC thin films was studied at with c-Si substrates at different temperatures from 600 to 700 °C for 30 minutes and one hour deposited samples. Influence of pressure on the crystalline structure of SiC thin films was studied at with c-Si substrates at different temperatures from 600 to 700 °C. The chamber pressure was varied from 2×10^{-2} Pa to 2 Pa. Figure 4 shows the XRD analysis results at different pressure and deposition duration with the substrate temperatures of 600 °C to 700 °C. SiC (100) peak was observed at $2\theta = 33.46°$ which corresponds to SiC (100) is as shown in Fig. 4. Based on the analysis, the films consisted of polycrystal 4H-SiC structure.

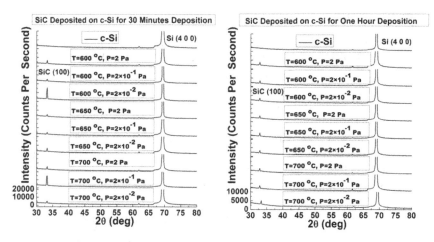

Fig. 4. X-ray diffraction pattern of SiC thin film obtained with different substrate temperatures and different pressures at 30 minutes and one hour deposition

Influence of particle grit size (36 to 500) on the crystallinity structure of SiC thin film was studied at with c-Si (n-type) substrate at different substrate temperature from 600 to 700 °C. The chamber pressure was maintained at 2 Pa. Figure 5 shows the XRD analysis results at different grit size and substrate temperatures of 600 °C to 700 °C. Diffraction peak of SiC(111) having cubic structure is observed at 35.5°. Based on the analysis, the SiC film deposited on Si(100) was polycrystalline in nature.

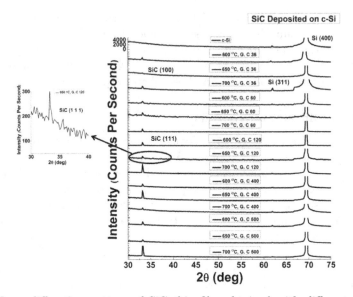

Fig. 5. X-ray diffraction pattern of SiC thin film obtained with different substrate temperatures and different grit size at one hour deposition on Si substrate

3.3   SEM Analysis

The SEM (Quanta FEG 200, FEI) micro-photograph of film at different c-Si substrate temperatures, ranging from 400 °C to 800 °C with the laser irradiation fluence of 1.7 J/cm² was performed. The formation of micro droplets are observed when SiC deposited on c-Si at 400 °C. The size distribution of SiC particles was estimated to be around 100 nm to 900 nm based on the SEM analysis. However, with increase in the substrate temperature, the carbon percentage was decreased. This observation was in accordance with the X-ray diffraction analysis. Gusev et al. have reported that the formation of microdroplets is considered likely to be to splashes of molten layer on the target surface during its boiling and the spattering of liquid phase by pressure shock waves [23].

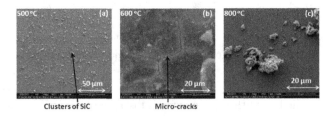

Fig. 6. SEM images of SiC deposited on AFG substrate at different deposition temperatures from 400° C to 800° C

SEM analysis of SiC thin films deposited on AFG substrates at different substrate temperatures the clusters of SiC were observed at lower substrate temperature values which is as shown in Fig. 6. When the temperature was increased micro-cracks were also observed on the thin-film surface. This might be due to amorphous nature of the AFG substrates and different expansion coefficient of the substrate and the thin film. Figure 7 shows the typical SEM micro-photograph of SiC deposited on c-Si for one hour deposition at different pressures ranging from 2×10^{-2} Pa to 2 Pa at the temperature 650 °C. All samples show spherical particles (laser droplets) that were in-homogeneously dispersed on the surface of the thin film. The ambient pressure was decreased from 2 Pa to 2×10^{-2} Pa, the particle density also decreased. The same observation made at the substrate temperature ranging from 600 °C to 700 °C when SiC deposited on c-Si for 30 minutes deposition at different pressures ranging from 2×10^{-2} Pa to 2 Pa. When the pressure is at 2 Pa the plasma expansion is highly directional and with in the smaller area particle density is more due to the agglomeration of the particles. As the pressure starts decrease from 2 Pa to 2×10^{-2} Pa, the plasma expands more so the distribution of the particle is more with in 1 cm × 1 cm area. The particle density decreases when pressure decreases as shown in Fig. 7.

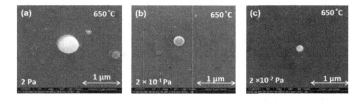

Fig. 7. SEM images of SiC deposited on Si substrate at different deposition temperatures, pressure for one hour deposition

Some studies like Raman Spectroscopy and I-V characteristics of p-n diode were performed on SiC deposited on c-Si (n-type). These studies were performed on thin films synthesized with one hour deposition at different grit sizes (36, 60, 120, 400 and 500) at the substrate temperature ranging from 600 C to 700 C. The influence of the SiC grit size was observed to reduce the droplet formation. When the grit designation increased gradually the particle density and particle diameter were decreased at constant temperature (600 °C) and pressure (2 Pa). Same observation was made for the substrate temperature ranging from 600 °C to 700 °C at constant pressure (2 Pa). Based on the experimental study, it was observed that by varying the grit number from 36 to 500, the droplet size was reduced. However, at a grit number higher than 120, the pellet wear during the laser ablation process was estimated to be higher.

3.4   Nano Indentation

The mechanical properties, such as Young's modulus and hardness of SiC thin films were estimated using the nano-indentation technique. The experimental study was performed using a nano-indentation equipment (TI950, Hysitron). To reduce the influence of substrate, the modulus and the hardness measurements were performed at 30-50% of the film thickness. The peak load was chosen as 10 mN and the pattern of loading was chosen to be trapezoidal.

The average elastic modulus and average Hardness of the thin films deposited on the substrate c-Si wafer are found to be 300 GPa and 45 GPa. The experiment was conducted at constant pressure of 2×10^{-2} Pa for one hour deposition time and different substrate temperature 600 °C, 650 °C and 700°C. The mechanical characteristics of the SiC films were indicative of low porosity structure. The elastic modulus values was lower than the typical value of around 400 GPa. This might be due to the influence of the substrate stiffness. Experimental results in terms of the film hardness were in good agreement with typical values reported in the literature [24].

4   Conclusion

Pulsed Nd^{3+}: YAG (355 nm) laser assisted pulsed laser deposition technique was used for SiC thin film deposition. In PLD of SiC thin film formation, substrate temperature was found to be a critical parameter for crystalline film formation. Experimental studies show that multicrystalline SiC film can be obtained at a temperature ranging from 600 to 700 °C and at a pressure of about 5.5×10^{-3} Pa. Micro-cracks on as deposited films were observed when an alkali free glass was used as a substrate. On the other hand, SiC film deposited on c-Si did not show such an adverse effect. Further, droplet formation was reduced by appropriately selecting the grit size of SiC powder around 120. XRD studies on deposited films clearly show multicrystalline (combined 3C-SiC and 4H-SiC) nature of SiC film. In order to use films for photovoltaic applications, it is necessary to apply laser assisted annealing combined with the PLD technique.

Acknowledgements. Authors are grateful to Mr. Xavier (Universal Carborandum) for providing SiC powder of different grit sizes. Pellet preparation and surface characterization studies were performed at MSRC. Authors also thankful to Mr. Hari Krishna from MEMS lab and Mr. Siva Rama Krishna from SAIF.

References

1. Muller, G., Krotz, G.: SiC for sensors and high-temperature electronics. Sensors and Actuators A 43, 259–268 (1994)
2. Palmour, J.W., Edmond, J.A., Kong, H.S., Carter Jr., C.H.: 6H-silicon carbide devices and applications. Physics B 185, 461–465 (1993)
3. Slusark Jr., W., Lalevic, B., Taylor, G.: Hard Transparent Dielectric Coatings. Thin Solid Films 39, 155–163 (1976)
4. Banerjee, C., Narayanan, K.L., Haga, K., Sritharathikhun, J., Miyajima, S., Yamada, A., Kongai, M.: Fabrication of microcrystalline cubic silicon carbide / crystalline silicon heterojunction solar cell by hot wire chemical vapour deposition. Japanese Journal of Applied Physics 46, 1–6 (2007)

5. Negoro, Y., Kimoto, T., Matsunami, H.: Stability of deep centers in 4H-SiC epitaxial layers during thermal annealing. Applied Physics Letters 85, 1716–1718 (2004)
6. Matsunami, H., Nishino, S., Ono, H.: Hetero-epitaxial growth of cubic siliconcarbide on foreign substrates. IEEE Transactions on Electron Devices 28, 1235–1236 (1981)
7. Tabata, A., Komura, Y., Narita, T., Kondo, A.: Growth of silicon carbide thin films by hot-wire chemical vapor deposition from SiH4/CH4/H2. Thin Solid Films 517, 3516–3519 (2009)
8. Yunaz, I.A., Hashizume, K., Miyajima, S., Yamada, A., Konagai, M.: Fabrication of amorphous silicon carbide films using VHF-PECVD fortriple-junction thin fillm solar cell applications. Solar Energy Materials and Solar Cells 93, 1056–1061 (2009)
9. Golecki, I., Reidinger, F., Marti, J.: Single-crystalline, epitaxial cubic SiC films grown on (100) Si at 750°C by chemical vapour deposition. Applied Physics Letters 60, 1703–1705 (1992)
10. ElGazzar, H., Rahaman, E.A., Salem, H.G., Nassar, F.: Preparation and characterization of amorphous nanostructured SiC thin films by low energy pulsed laser deposition. Applied Surface Science 256, 2056–2060 (2010)
11. Katharria, Y.S., Kumar, S., Choudhary, R.J., Prakash, R., Singh, F., Lalla, N.P., Phase, D.M., Kanjilal, D.: Pulsed laser deposition of SiC thin films at medium substrate temperatures. Thin Solid Films 516, 6083–6087 (2008)
12. Hanyecz, I., Budai, J., Oszko, A., Szilagyi, E., Toth, Z.: Room-temperature pulsed laser deposition of SiC thin films in different compositions. Applied Physics A 100, 1115–1121 (2010)
13. Tang, Y.H., Sham, T.K., Yang, D., Xue, L.: Preparation and characterization of pulsed laser deposition (PLD) SiC films. Applied Surface Science 252, 3386–3389 (2006)
14. Kasumori, T., Muto, H., Brito, M.E.: Control of polytype formation in silicon carbide heteroepitaxial films by pulsed-laser deposition. Applied Physics Letters 84, 1272–1274 (2004)
15. Wang, Y., Wen, J., Guo, Z., Tang, Y., Tang, H., Wu, J.: The preparation of singlecrystal 4H-SiC film by pulsed XeCl laser deposition. Thin Solid Films 338, 93–99 (1999)
16. Pelt, J.S., Ramsey, M.E., Durbin, S.M.: Characterization of crystalline SiC films grown by pulsed laser deposition. Thin Solid Films 371, 72–79 (2000)
17. Tabbal, M., Said, A., Hannoun, E., Christidis, T.: Amorphous to crystalline phase transition in pulsedlaser deposited silicon carbide. Applied Surface Science 253, 7050–7059 (2007)
18. Lackner, J.M., Waldhauser, W., Ebner, R., Fian, A., Jakopic, G., Leising, G., Schoberl, T.: Pulsed laser deposition of silicon containing carbon thin films. Surface and Coatings Technology 177-178, 360–364 (2004)
19. Uetsuhara, H., Goto, S., Nakata, Y., Vasa, N., Okada, T., Maeda, M.: Fabrication of a Ti:sapphire planar waveguide by pulsed laser deposition. Appl. Phys. A 69, 719–722 (1999)
20. Yoshitakea, T., Shiraishi, G., Nagayamab, K.: Elimination of droplets using a vane velocity filter for pulsed laser ablation of FeSi2. Applied Surface Science 197-198, 379–383 (2002)
21. Yoshitakea, T., Nagayama, K.: The velocity distribution of droplets ejected from Fe and Si targets by pulsed laser ablation in a vacuum and their elimination using a vane-type velocity filter. Vacuum 74, 515–520 (2004)

22. Monaco, G., Garoli, D., Natali, M., Pelizzo, M.G., Nicolosi, P.: Synthesis of heteroepytaxial 3C-SiC by means of PLD. Applied Physics A 105, 225–231 (2011)
23. Guseva, A.S., Ryndyaa, S.M., Karginb, N.I., Bondarenkoa, E.A.: Low Temperature Synthesis of SiC Films by Vacuum Laser Ablation and Their Characterization. Journal of Surface Investigation 4, 374–378 (2010)
24. Burton, J.C., Sun, L., Pophristic, M., Lukacs, S.J., Longa, F.H.: Spatial characterization of doped SiC wafers by Raman spectroscopy. Journal of Applied Physics 84, 6268–6273 (1998)

Influence of Sb Coated Substrates in Development of Vertical and Random Oriented ZnO Nanostructures for UV LED Application Using Nano Particle Assisted Pulsed Laser Deposition

I.A. Palani[1,2], D. Nakamura[2], K. Okazaki[2],
T. Shimogaki[2], M. Highasiata[2], and T. Okada[2]

[1] Mechancial Engineering Discipline, Indian Institute of Technology, Indore (IIT Indore), India
[2] Graduate School of Information Science and Electrical Engineering, Kyushu Univeristy, Japan

Abstract. This research highly focuses towards influence of different paprmaters in development of Sb doped ZnO nanostructures using Nano Particle Assisted Pulsed Laser Deposition by using Sb coated substrate.different types of nanostructures were synthesized with vartion in growth temperature. Nano wires generated from Sb coated silicon substrate posses a sharp UV emission from room temperature PL. vertically aligned ZnO nanowires were grown on different ZnO buffer layer thickness ranging from 100 to 1600 nm. With increase in buffer layer thickness a strong UV emission with improved structural properties are observed, which are highly suitable for optoelectronic device application.

Keywords: Laser, Nano-particle Nano-wires, ZnO, Sb, PL emission, UV-LED.

1 Introduction

Quasi-one-dimensional ZnO nano materials such as nanowires, nanorods and nanobelts have attracted much attention due to their remarkable morphology dependent properties and their potential applications in nano-optoelectronic devices. They posses wide band gap (3.37 eV) and large exciton binding energy (60 meV) at room temperature, This makes ZnO an ideal material for studying the transport processes in one dimensionally confined object, which are important for the development of high performance nano devices. Doping of the ZnO nanostructures can be tailored for specific desired applications, and p-type doping of ZnO is of particular interest [1].

To tailor the properties of the 1-D ZnO nanostructures, several doping elements have been used and reported in the literature such as Ga, In, P, Sn and etc. In particular for the p-type doping in ZnO. Among them there are few reports in the literature which demonstrating the growth of Sb-doped ZnO nanowires, due to the high affinity of metallic Sb to get diffused in ZnO lattice. These ZnO nanowires were synthesized by Molecular Beam Epitaxy (MBE), Nano-particle Assisted Pulsed Laser

S.G. Ponnambalam et al. (Eds.): IRAM 2012, CCIS 330, pp. 389–397, 2012.
© Springer-Verlag Berlin Heidelberg 2012

deposition (NAPLD) and carbothermal evaporation methods [2]. Demonstrating the growth of Sb doped ZnO nano wires for realization of p-type is highly attracted as compared to the other materials to efficiently utilize the electro-optical property of ZnO. Basically Sb doped nanowires by carbothermal evaporation were grown by introducing Sb as a precursor [3], but during growth at high temperature the Sb particles may get evaporated, Instead Sb dopant powders coated on the substrate can also act as a dopant source to synthesize Sb doped nanostructures These catalysts commonly induce extra defects in the product, which confirms that the catalyst used can occupy a space in lattice [4]. In this paper an attempt has been made for the first time by synthesizing doped ZnO nanowires from Sb coated substrate.

Different parameters have their own influence in the development of nano structures. Since the nucleation start from the substrate, the substrate have their own influence in the growth of nanostructures. In addition, the different growth parameters such as growth pressure and growth temperature have their own influence. Hence this paper highly focus towards investigation on the influence of substrate (Silicon Vs Sapphire), Growth pressure, Growth temperature and effect of buffer layer in the growth of ZnO nanostructures has been investigated.

The treated samples were analyzed through SEM, to investigate the structural morphological analysis, XRD, TEM and Raman spectroscopic analysis to investigate the structural properties. The optical properties of the samples were investigated through Room temperature PL.

2   Experimental Specifications

Fig.1 shows the schematic layout of NAPLD experimental setup. In these experiments, a sintered intrinsic ZnO target with 99.99% in purity was used as source material to synthesis nanostructures. Intrinsic Si wafer (~15 mm ×15 mm) coated with Sb to a thickness of 100-200 nm using thermal evaporation method was used as a substrate. The substrate was mounted on a layer of SiC and inserted into the horizontal quartz tube chamber. The target to substrate distance was 15 mm. For one growth run 36000 KrF excimer laser pulses with 20 Hz repetition frequency were applied. The laser energy density on the target was about 3 J/cm^2 in the presence of

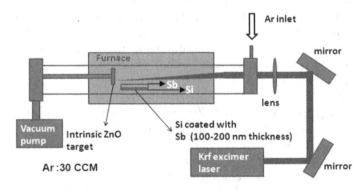

Fig. 1. Nano Particle Assisted Pulsed Laser Deposition experimental setup

argon gas at a pressure of 100 Torr and a constant flow rate of 27.5 sccm. The catalyst Sb coated on the silicon forms a droplet during processing and starts to initiate the growth process by the Vapour-Liquid-Solid (VLS) mechanism. Figure 2 shows the mechanism of growth initiation of the nanostructures. The experiments were performed at different temperature conditions ranging from 700 to 900 °C which is slightly higher than the melting point of Sb, resulting in droplet formation of Sb on the surface of Si. When the samples are kept at a growth temperature of 700°C. This droplet acts as a seed to initiate the growth of nanowires. When the growth temperature was increased to 800 °C, random oriented nanostructures would be synthesized.

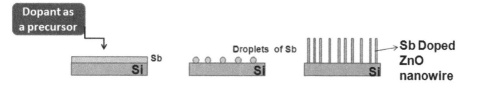

Fig. 2. Mechanism on synthesize of ZnO nanostructures from the Sb coated substrate

The surface characteristics of the synthesized nanostructures were investigated though SEM analysis. The structural characteristics of the samples were investigated through XRD. Raman spectroscopy and TEM analysis. The optical characteristics of the different nanostructures were investigated through room temperature photo-luminescence (PL) spectroscopic studies to analyze the influence of Sb on growth of ZnO nanostructures.

2.1   Influence of Pressure

To investigate the influence of pressure Si samples were coated with Sb and the growth temperature was fixed as 750 °C. The experiments were performed at different pressure condition ranging from 300 to 100 Torr. Figure 2(a) shows the samples developed at the pressure condition of 300 Torr, where cluster of ZnO particles combined with formation of mild nucleation where observed. At 200 Torr, the growths of nanowires have been initiated from the Sb droplets with island like formation was observed. At 100 Torr growth of nanowires were considerably uniform.

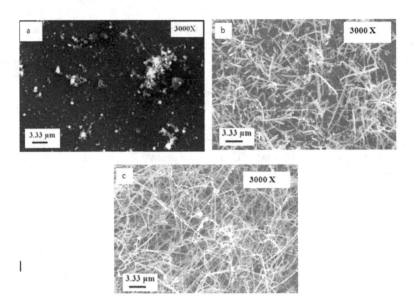

Fig. 3. Influence of pressures at a) 300 Torr b) 200 Torr c) 100 Torr in the development of ZnO nanostructures

2.2   Influence of Temperature

To investigate the effect of temperature in the development of nanostructures. Two different conditions were considered 1) constant temperature condition 2) varying temperature condition.   The nanowires as shown in fig 4(a) were synthesis at a varying the temperature from 680-850 °C. With the fixed growth temperature of 700 °C, with growth duration for period of 20 minutes nanosheets were observed as shown in fig 4(b). Fig. 4 (c and d) shows the Raman spectroscopic analysis of the nanowires and nanosheets. From fig. 4(c), in the case of nanowires, dominant peaks were at 101 cm^{-1}, 439 cm^{-1} and 522cm^{-1}. The 522 cm^{-1} corresponds to the crystalline silicon substrate peak. The first peak 101cm^{-1} is related to the E$_2$(low) phonon frequency and 439 cm^{-1} corresponds to the E$_2$(High) mode of non polar optical phonon. These two peaks from Raman spectroscopy indicate that the ZnO nanostructures are crystals with hexagonal wurzite structures. A small peak suppressed at 556 cm^{-1} attributes to the E$_1$(LO) modes which are associated with the structural defects related to oxygen vacancies. Similar standard peaks at 101 cm^{-1} and 439 cm^{-1} were also observed in nanosheets as shown in Fig. 4(d) In addition to the standard peaks some other peaks were observed at 310 cm^{-1}, 615 cm^{-1}, 665 cm^{-1} and 812 cm^{-1}. The 310 cm^{-1} peak corresponds to the lattice deformation induced by the presence of Sb in the ZnO lattice. The peaks at 615 cm^{-1}, 665 cm^{-1} and 812 cm^{-1} represents the classical second order Raman modes of ZnO TA+TO, TA+LO, LA+LO. Generally this second order Raman modes are not very obvious and not observed even in standard ZnO structures.

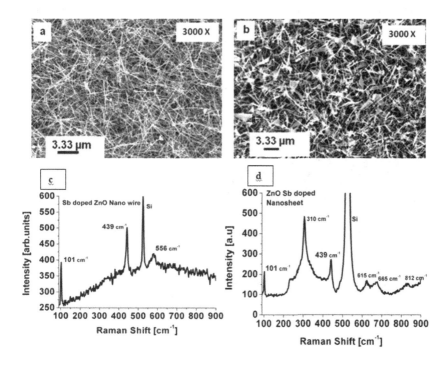

Fig. 4. a) SEM analysis of nanowires grown at varying temperature condition b) SEM analysis of nanosheets grown at constant temperature condition c) Raman Spectroscopic analysis of nanowires grown at varying temperature condition d) Raman Spectroscopic analysis of nanosheets grown at varying temperature condition

2.3   Influence of Substrate (Silicon vs Sapphire)

Substrates have their own effect in the growth of ZnO nano structures. The substrates which are widely used for growth of ZnO are silicon and sapphire substrates. Both theses substrates are coated with Sb and experiments were synthesis at a varying the temperature from 680-850 °C and at a constant pressure condition of 100 Torr. With Sb coated silicon as the substrate a random oriented ZnO nanowires were observed as shown in Fig.5 (a). With Sb coated sapphire as the substrate, ZnO nanodots were observed as shown n fig.5 (b). To have a clear picture on the structure, a roo temperature PL spectroscopic analysis were performed on the samples. In the case of nanodots, as shown in Fig. 5(d), a near band edge (NBE) emission at 380 nm and sharp deep level emission at 490 nm were observed. The deep level emission (DLE) peak is dominant than the near band edge emission. In the case of nanowires, however, as shown in Fig. 5 (c) the PL spectrum of the samples exhibits a dominant peak at 390 nm and a weak DLE with a broad peak located between 450 and 700 nm. From the PL spectrum, the origin of DLE that is the green emission appeared due to the radial recombination of a photogenerated hole with electron of the ionized oxygen vacancies in the surface lattice of the ZnO. The nanodots formed on the sapphire substrate has the radiative transitions between shallow donors (related to oxygen vacancies) and deep acceptor (zinc vacancies), resulting in defect in the luminescence spectra. Thus the PL green emission peak at 520 nm originates from the single ionized oxygen vacancies [5]. This is due to the increase of layer defect during nucleation processes. Whereas in the case of nanowires, a sharp UV emission is observed and no visible luminescence was observed.

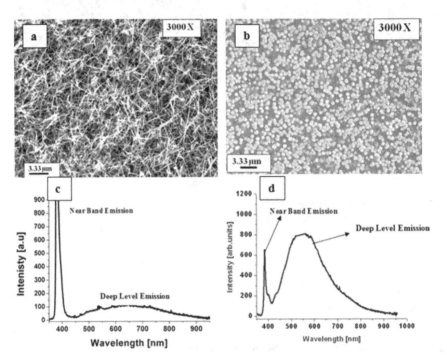

Fig. 5. (a) Nanowires grown on the Silicon substrate (b) Nano dots on the sapphire substrate (c) Room temperature PL of the nanowires grown the silicon substrate (d) Room temperature PL grown of the nanodots grown on the sapphire substrate.

2.4   Influence of Pure ZnO Buffer Layer

A ZnO buffer layer was deposited on the sapphire substrate at a background oxygen pressure of 3.3 Pa with a substrate temperature of 650°C for 1.5 minute for the growth of 100nm, 10 minutes for 800nm thick and 20 minutes for 1600 nm thick. The Si deposited ZnO buffer layer was coated with Sb to a thickness of 80-100 nm using thermal evaporation method. The ZnO nanowires were continuously grown on the Sb coated ZnO buffer layer at 40 kPa with a substrate temperature of 750°C for 30 min.

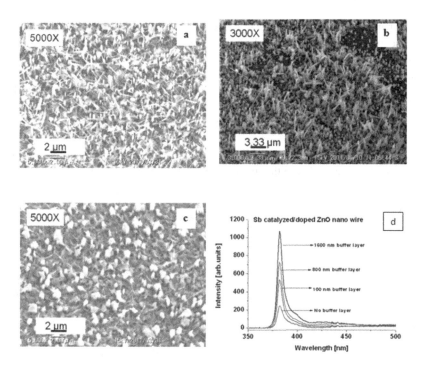

Fig. 6. Surface morphology of ZnO nano structures synthesized at different buffer layer with a thickness of   a) 100nm b) 800 nm c) 1600 d) Room temperature PL spectroscopic measurements

Fig 6. Shows the influence of ZnO buffer layer at varying thickness in generation of Sb doped ZnO nanowires. Horizontally grown nanowires combined with vertically aligned nanowires were observed from the samples grown on the ZnO buffer layer. To investigate the morphology of the vertically aligned nanowires, SEM micrographs are taken at a tilted angle as shown in figure. Figure 6(a) shows the Sb catalyzed doped nanowires synthesized on a buffer layer of 100 nm thickness. The vertically aligned ZnO nanowires with a length of 200nm and a core diameter of around 100 nm were observed. With increase in buffer layer to 800 nm thickness, the nanowires with slight increase in length and diameter of 0.5 μm and 400 nm respectively as shown in fig 6(b). With further increase in buffer layer to thickness of 1600 nm and increase in core diameter of the nanowires of around 800 nm was observed in fig 6(c). fig 6(d) shows the room temperature PL of the samples grown at different buffer layer thickness where with respect to increase in buffer layer the a shrp increase in UV emission is observed and the flanges of visible emission is considerably reduced.

3   Structural Analysis

The phases of the as-grown nanowires were identified by XRD. The XRD results of the pure ZnO and Sb-doped ZnO are shown in Fig.7(a) for comparison. The XRD pattern of the Sb-doped ZnO indicates that the nanowires have the wurzite structure and no secondary phase was found as compared to the XRD spectrum of pure ZnO. The Sb doping in ZnO causes significant change in the lattice constants, resulting in measurable lower angle shift of about 0.06° in the (100) and (101) peak as compared to the pure ZnO nano wires Fig. 7 (b) shows low and high magnification TEM images of the Sb-doped ZnO nanowire and the corresponding fast Fourier transform (FFT) patterns as in the insets. It was observed that the nanowires are structurally uniform with a lattice fringe spacing of 0.54 nm, which confirms that the grown nano-structure are preferentially oriented in the [0001](c-axis) direction. The wider lattice fringe spacing is due to the incorporation of Sb in ZnO lattice.

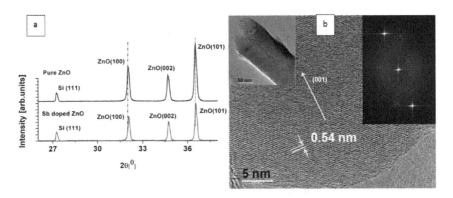

Fig. 7. (a) XRD analysis of pure and Sb doped ZnO (b) TEM analysis

4   Conclusions

This paper highly focuses towards development of ZnO nanostructures using Nano Particle Assisted Pulsed Laser Deposition from Sb (dopant) coated substrate . The influence of different process parameters and different substrate has been investigated. The growths of the nanostructures were performed at different parametric conditions. The experiments were performed at different pressure condition ranging from 300 to 100 Torr. At 100 Torr growth of nanowires were considerably uniform. With variation in growth temperature from 650-850°C random oriented nanowires were observed. With a constant temperature of 700°C nano sheets combined with nanowires were observed. Nano wires generated from Sb coated silicon substrate posses a sharp UV emission from room temperature PL. vertically aligned ZnO nanowires were grown on different ZnO buffer layer thickness ranging from 100 to 1600 nm. The Sb doping in ZnO causes significant change in the lattice constants, resulting in measurable lower angle shift of about 0.06° in the (100) and (101) peak from XRD and wider lattice fringe from TEM confirming the significant change in structural properties. Thus with increase in buffer layer thickness a strong UV emission with improved structural properties are observed which are highly suitable for optoelectronic device application.

References

1. Cao, L., Li, M.K., et al.: The fabrication and electrical characteristics of ZnO twinned nanowires. Mater. Sci. Semicon. Proc. 11, 25–29 (2008)
2. Palani, I.A., Nakamura, D., et al.: Structural and optical properties of Sb Al co-doped ZnO nanowires synthesized using Nanoparticle Assisted Pulsed Laser Deposition (NAPLD) with Sb as catalyst. Journal of Alloys and Compounds 527, 112–116 (2012)
3. Vijaya Prakash, G., Pradeesh, K., et al.: Fabrication and optoelectronics characterization of ZnO photonic structure. Mater. Lett. 62, 1183–1186 (2008)
4. Palani, I.A., Okazaki, K., et al.: Influence of Sb in synthesize of ZnO nanowire using sandwich type substrate in carbothermal evaporation method. Applied Surface Science 258, 3611–3616 (2012)
5. Palani, I.A., Nakamura, D., et al.: Influence of Sb as a catalyst in the growth of ZnO nano wires and nano sheets using Nanoparticle Assisted Pulsed Laser Deposition (NAPLD). Materials Science and Engineering: B 176, 1526–1530 (2011)

Intelligent Design of a Flexible Cell Layout with Maximum Stability in a Stochastic Dynamic Situation

T.S. Lee[*] and Ghorbanali Moslemipour

Faculty of Engineering and Technology, Multimedia University, 75450 Malacca, Malaysia
tslee@mmu.edu.my, ghmoslemipour@yahoo.com

Abstract. Facility layout problem is a critical issue in the early stages of designing a manufacturing system because it affects the total manufacturing cost significantly. This paper proposes a new mathematical model for designing a machine layout having maximum stability for the whole time planning horizon of the stochastic dynamic facility layout problem by using quadratic assignment formulation. This layout has the maximum ability to display a small sensitivity to demand changeability. In this investigation, the product demands are assumed to be independent Poisson distributed random variables with known probability density function in each period. In order to validate the proposed model, a randomly generated test problem is solved by using simulated annealing algorithm. Finally, the computational results are evaluated statistically.

Keywords: Stable layout, Dynamic uncertain environment, Manufacturing system, Simulated annealing.

1 Introduction

Facility layout problem (FLP) is an important subject in the design of manufacturing systems because it has a significant impact on the total manufacturing cost. Material handling cost (MHC) is one of the most appropriate measures to evaluate the efficiency of a facility layout. The MHC forms from 20-50% of the total manufacturing costs and it can be decreased by at least 10-30% by an efficient layout design [1]. Different types of the FLPs are as follows: (i) static (single period) FLP (SFLP) where the flow of materials is deterministic and constant over the entire time planning horizon; (ii) dynamic (multi-period) FLP (DFLP) in which the flow of materials is deterministic and constant for each period, but it changes from period to period; (iii) stochastic static FLP (SSFLP), which is a single period problem with stochastic product demand; (iv) stochastic dynamic FLP (SDFLP) having the stochastic product demand with different parameters in each period.

This paper considers the SDFLP where product demands are assumed to be independent Poisson distributed random variables with known probability density function that change from period to period at random. The Poisson distribution of demands is also considered in the book written by [2]. This distribution can be approximated to a

---

[*] Corresponding author.

S.G. Ponnambalam et al. (Eds.): IRAM 2012, CCIS 330, pp. 398–405, 2012.

normal distribution under particular conditions such as having a large number of parts or time periods. It is also assumed that the parts are moved in batches. The batch production issue is discussed in the following papers [3-5]. The goal of this study is to design a machine layout with maximum stability for the entire multi-period time planning horizon. A brief review of the stochastic FLP is as follows: Gupta [6] solved the layout problem with square-shaped and equal-sized facilities by using the Monte Carlo simulation approach. Rosenblatt and Kropp [7] designed the SSFLP with multiple demand scenarios assigned to randomly generated probability of happenings. Benjaafar and Sheikhzadeh [8] proposed a robust layout by duplicating the same facilities in the FLP to deal with uncertainties in product demands. Braglia et al. [9] designed the most robust layout for a single row FLP by assuming the product demands as normally distributed random variables. Kulturel-Konak et al. [10] considered the most robust layout with minimum region under the total MHC curve over a pre-determined range of uncertainty. Braglia et al. [11] defined the stability of a layout as the ability of a layout to display a small sensitivity to demand changeability. Enea et al. [12] proposed a fuzzy model to design a robust layout for the stochastic FLP with multiple product demand scenarios. Norman and Smith [13] proposed a mathematical model to design the most robust layout by considering a large number of independent product demands as random variables with known expected value and variance. Tavakkoli-Moghaddam et al. [14] proposed a new mathematical model to concurrent design of the optimal machine and cell layouts in for the SSFLP of a cellular manufacturing system. Moslemipour and Lee [15] developed a novel quadratic assignment-based mathematical model to design an optimal layout for each period of the SDFLP by considering independent normally distributed product demands.

2   Quadratic Assignment Problem

Quadratic assignment problem (QAP) is a nonlinear combinatorial optimization problem (COP). The QAP aims to find the optimum assignment of a number of objects to the same number of known positions so that a quadratic objective function is minimized. In general, the FLP having discrete representation and equal-sized facilities assigned to the same number of known locations is usually formulated as the QAP model. In discrete representation, the shop floor is divided into a number of equal-sized facility locations. The first mathematical model of the QAP for the FLP was introduced by Koopmans and Beckman [16] as follows:

$$Minimize \sum_{i=1}^{M}\sum_{j=1}^{M}\sum_{l=1}^{M}\sum_{q=1}^{M} f_{ij}d_{lq}x_{il}x_{jq} \tag{1}$$

Subject to:

$$\sum_{i=1}^{M}x_{il} = 1, \forall l; \ \sum_{l=1}^{M}x_{il} = 1, \forall i; \ x_{il} = \begin{cases} 1 & \text{if machine } i \text{ is assigned to location } l \\ 0 & \text{otherwise} \end{cases} \tag{2}$$

The QAP mathematical model includes three components, *decision variables, objective function*, and *constraints*. The objective function (1) is a second-degree (quadratic) function of the decision variables. In this equation, f_{ij} denotes the flow of materials between facilities i and j. The distance between locations l and q is denoted by d_{lq}. In fact, the objective function represents the total material handling cost (MHC), which is calculated as the summation of the product of materials flow between facilities and distance between the locations of these facilities. The constraint (2) ensures that each facility must be assigned to exactly one location and each location must have only one facility, and the 0-1 integer decision variables x_{il} are the solution of the problem so that they determine the location of each facility.

References [17,18] have shown that the QAP is an NP-complete (Nondeterministic Polynomial) problem and the computational time for solving the QAP is exponentially proportional to the size of the problem. Therefore, it is very difficult to solve the large size QAP by the exact solution approaches. SA is one of the promising tools for solving the COPs [19]. In this paper, due to the above-mentioned reasons and the complexity of the proposed models, the SA meta-heuristic is used in this study.

2.1   Simulated Annealing

Simulated annealing (SA) algorithm is a simulation of physical annealing process of solids in statistical mechanics. In the physical annealing process in thermodynamics, the perfect structure of crystals can be obtained by melting a solid and then reducing the temperature very slowly so that the crystal can reach its minimum energy level named ground state. Consider the COP (S, f), where S is the solution space, including all of the possible solutions and f is the objective (cost) function. The SA algorithm finds the best solution $s = s^* \in S$ such that $f(s^*)$ is the minimum value of the objective function f. A general SA algorithm is illustrated in Figure 1.

3   Problem Formulation

In this section, to design a layout having maximum stability for the whole time planning horizon of the SDFLP, a new mathematical model is proposed by considering the following additional assumptions: (i) The same number of equal-sized machines are assigned to the same number of known locations. (ii) The data on machine sequence, part movement cost, batch size, and distance between locations are known. (iii) Machines can be laid out in any configuration with no constraint for dimensions and shapes of the shop floor.

3.1   Proposed Models

Due to the assumption of using the same number of equal-sized machines and known candidate locations, the QAP model is used for formulating the proposed models. The

data on machine sequence, transfer batch size, part movement cost, Poisson distributed product demands with known PDF for each period, and distance between machine locations are the *inputs* of the models. The *output* of the model is the most stable layout for the entire time planning horizon. The stable layout for this multi-period
machine layout problem is designed in such a way that the average demand of each
part in different periods is considered as the part demand for the entire time planning
horizon. The average demand D_k for part k is calculated by the first term of Eq. (3).
Since D_{tk} is a random variable with the variance Var (D_{tk}), D_k is also a random variable with the variance given in the last term of Eq. (3).

$$D_k = \frac{\sum\limits_{t=1}^{T} D_{tk}}{T}; \ \ Var\left(D_k\right) = Var\left(\frac{\sum\limits_{t=1}^{T} D_{tk}}{T}\right) = \frac{\sum\limits_{t=1}^{T} Var\left(D_{tk}\right)}{T^2} \tag{3}$$

Procedure *Simulated Annealing*

    A known or randomly generated initial solution s^0, $s = s^0$, initial value for
temperature $T_0, el = 0$

    while outer-loop criterion not satisfied (i.e. $el \leq el_{max}$)

        while inner-loop criterion not satisfied (i.e. $il \leq il_{max}$)

            Generate the solution s' in the neighbouring area of s at random

        if $f\left(s\right) \leq f\left(s'\right)$

        $s = s'$

        end

    if $f\left(s\right) > f\left(s'\right)$

        if randomly generated $x \in \left(0,1\right) \leq \exp\left(\dfrac{\left(f\left(s\right) - f\left(s'\right)\right)}{T_{el}}\right)$

        $s = s'$

        end

      end

    $il = il + 1$

    end

    $T_{el} = T_0 \alpha^{el}$ % (Update Temp T_{el} , cooling ratio $\alpha \in \left(0.80, 0.99\right)$

    $el = el + 1$

end   *Simulated Annealing*

Fig. 1. A general simulated annealing algorithm

The flow of materials between machines i and j for part k (*i.e.* f_{ijk}) is calculated by the first term of Eq. (4) where, the condition $|N_{ki} - N_{kj}| = 1$ refers to two consecutive operations done on part k by machines i and j. Since D_k is a random variable, according to the first term of Eq. (4), f_{ijk} is also a random variable with the variance as given in the last term of Eq. (4).

$$f_{ijk} = \begin{cases} \dfrac{D_k}{B_k} C_k & \text{if } |N_{ki} - N_{kj}| = 1 \\ 0 & \text{otherwise} \end{cases} \quad ; \quad Var\left(f_{ijk}\right) = \begin{cases} \dfrac{Var(D_k)}{B_k^{\,2}} C_k^{\,2} & \text{if } |N_{ki} - N_{kj}| = 1 \\ 0 & \text{otherwise} \end{cases} \quad (4)$$

The total flow between machines i and j resulting from all parts (*i.e.* f_{ij}) can be written as given in the first term of Eq. (5). Using Eqs. (3) and (4), the variance of f_{ij}, $Var\left(f_{ij}\right)$, is calculated as given in the second term of Eq. (5).

$$f_{ij} = \sum_{k=1}^{K} f_{ijk}; \quad Var\left(f_{ij}\right) = \begin{cases} \displaystyle\sum_{k=1}^{K}\left(\dfrac{C_k}{T.B_k}\right)^2 \sum_{t=1}^{T} Var(D_{tk}) & \text{if } |N_{ki} - N_{kj}| = 1 \\ 0 & \text{otherwise} \end{cases} \quad (5)$$

According to the Eq. (1), the total MHC of the layout π ($C(\pi)$) is written as Eq. (6). Since f_{ij} is a random variable, due to Eq. (6), $C(\pi)$ is also a random variable. The variance of $C\left(\pi\right)$ is obtained as in Eq. (7) by combining Eq. (5) with Eq. (6):

$$C\left(\pi\right) = \sum_{i=1}^{M}\sum_{j=1}^{M}\sum_{l=1}^{M}\sum_{q=1}^{M} f_{ij} d_{lq} x_{il} x_{jq} \quad (6)$$

$$Var\left(C\left(\pi\right)\right) = \sum_{i=1}^{M}\sum_{j=1}^{M}\sum_{k=1}^{K}\left(\dfrac{C_k}{T.B_k}\right)^2 \sum_{t=1}^{T} Var\left(D_{tk}\right)\left(\sum_{l=1}^{M}\sum_{q=1}^{M} d_{lq} x_{il} x_{jq}\right)^2 \quad (7)$$

The stability of a layout is defined as the ability of a layout to display a small sensitivity to demand changeability [20]. In other words, a layout with minimum variance of product demands has the maximum stability. Demand variability leads to variations in the materials flow between facilities, which in turn causes variations in the total cost. Therefore, the layout with maximum stability is obtained by minimizing the variance of the total cost, Eq. (7), and subject to Eq. (2).

4   Computational Results and Discussion

To validate the proposed model, a randomly generated test problem and a problem from literature (Tavakkoli-Moghaddam et al.) [14] are applied to the model. The test problem includes ten parts, twelve machines, and five time periods. According to size of the problem, it is solved by using SA approach rather that exact methods like dynamic programming. This algorithm is coded in Matlab and run using a personal computer with an Intel 2.10 GHZ CPU and 3 GB RAM. The input data, including the data on machine sequence, batch size, part movement cost, and the variance of part demands for each period are given in Table A.1 in the appendix. In this table, for example the machine sequence for part 3 is $1 \rightarrow 12 \rightarrow 8$. It means that the first, second, and third operations on part 3 are done by machines 1, 12, and 8 respectively. Therefore, the parameter N_{ki}, N_{31}, $N_{3(12)}$, and N_{38} are equal to 1, 2, and 3 respectively. Table A.2 displays the data on distance between machine locations. Table 1 displays the results including the machine layout having maximum stability, the optimal value of the objective function (i.e. the minimum value of the stability measure), and the statistical evaluation of the results obtained by running the SA algorithm ten times. The obtained configuration has the maximum ability to have a small sensitivity to demand variability. In addition, the computational time and the standard deviation value emphasize the capability of the SA algorithm for solving the FLP in a reasonable computational time.

Table 1. The most stable layout along with the statistical evaluation

Location Number	1	2	3	4	5	6	7	8	9	10	11	12
Stable Layout	12	1	8	5	3	10	11	9	4	2	7	6
Objective Function Value (OFV)= 108045						Elapsed time = 0.839047 (seconds)						
Worst = 110301			Mean = 109416			Best OFV= 108045			Std. Dev.=7931.06			

The data of the problem taken from [14] are given in Table A.3. This problem is a single time period problem and it includes seven machines grouped into three cells. We only considered the layout of machines inside the first cell, which consists of machines 1, 5, 7. We calculated the stability of the optimal layout obtained by [14] (i.e. [1 7 5]), which is equal to 5034200. Applying this data to our proposed model leads to design another layout as [1 5 7] that has the stability value equals to 4631460. On comparison, the stability measure is improved by eight percent.

5   Conclusion

This paper proposed a new nonlinear QAP-based mathematical model for design of a machine layout with maximum stability for the entire multi-period time planning horizon in a stochastic situation where the independent product demands are Poisson distributed random variables with known variance changing from period to period. This layout is a powerful configuration to display a small sensitivity to demand changeability. According to size of the randomly generated test problem, which includes ten parts, twelve machines, and five time periods, it was solved by using SA metaheuristic approach in a reasonable computational time. In addition, solving another problem from literature indicated that the proposed model leads to improve in the stability measure and in turn results in a layout with better operational performance.

Acknowledgement. This work was supported by the Ministry of Higher Education of Malaysia through the Fundametal Research Grant Scheme no FRGS/1/2012/TK01/MMU/02/2. The funding is gratefully acknowledged.

References

1. Tompkins, J.A., White, J.A., Bozer, Y.A., Tanchoco, J.M.A.: Facilities planning. Wiley, NwYork (2003)
2. Heragu, S.S.: Facilities Design, 1st edn. PWS Publishing Company, Boston (1997)
3. Groover, M.P.: Automation, production systems, and computer-Integrated manufacturing. Pearson Education Inc., New Jersey (2008)
4. Andre, L., Diane, R., Kathryn, E.S.: Transfer Batch Sizing in Flexible Manufacturing Systems. Journal of Manufacturing Systems 18(2), 140–151 (1999)
5. Das, S.R., Canel, C.: An algorithm for scheduling batches of parts in a multi-cell flexible manufacturing system. Int. J. Production Economics 97, 247–262 (2005)
6. Gupta, R.M.: Flexibility in layouts: A simulation approach. Material Flow 3, 243–250 (1986)
7. Rosenblatt, M.J., Kropp, D.H.: The single period stochastic plant layout problem. IIE Transactions 24(2), 169–176 (1992)
8. Benjaafar, S., Sheikhzadeh, M.: Design of flexible layouts. IIE Transactions 32, 309–322 (2000)
9. Braglia, M., Simone, Z., Zavanella, L.: Layout design in dynamic environments: Strategies and quantitative indices. Int. J. of Production Research 41(5), 995–1016 (2003)
10. Kulturel-Konak, S., Smith, A.E., Norman, B.A.: Layout optimization considering production uncertainty and routing flexibility. Int. J. of Prod. Res. 42(21), 4475–4493 (2004)
11. Braglia, M., Simone, Z., Zavanella, L.: Layout design in dynamic environments: Analytical issues. International Transactions in Operational Research 12, 1–19 (2005)
12. Enea, M., Galante, G., Panascia, E.: The facility layout problem approached using a fuzzy model and a genetic search. Journal of Intelligent Manufacturing 16, 303–316 (2005)
13. Norman, B.A., Smith, A.E.: A continuous approach to considering uncertainty in facility design. Computers and Operations Research 33, 1760–1775 (2006)
14. Tavakkoli-Moghaddam, R., Javadian, N., Javadi, B., Safaei, N.: Design of a facility layout problem in cellular manufacturing systems with stochastic demands. Applied Mathematics and Computation 184, 721–728 (2007)
15. Moslemipour, G., Lee, T.S.: Intelligent design of a dynamic machine layout in uncertain environment of flexible manufacturing systems. J. Intell. Manuf. (2011), doi:10.1007/s10845-010-0499-8
16. Koopmans, T.C., Beckman, M.: Assignment problems and the location of economic activities. Econometric 25, 53–76 (1957)
17. Sahni, S., Gonzalez, T.: P-complete approximation problem. Journal of ACM 23(3), 555–565 (1976)
18. Foulds, L.R.: Techniques for Facilities Layout: Deciding which Pairs of Activities should be Adjacent. Management Science 29(12), 1414–1426 (1983)
19. Alvarenga, A.G., Gomes, N.J., Mestria, M.: Metaheuristic methods for a class of the facility layout problems. Journal of Intelligent Manufacturing 11, 421–430 (2000)
20. Braglia, M., Zanoni, S., Zavanella, L.: Robust versus stable layout design in stochastic environments. Production Planning & Control 16(1), 71–80 (2005)

Table A.1. Input Data

Parts	Machine sequence	Batch size	C_k	The variance of part demands from period 1 to period 5				
				1	2	3	4	5
1	5→3→10→9→11	50	5	1073	1118	2584	2629	1553
2	11→10→3→9→5	50	5	2824	2442	1609	1344	2940
3	1→12→8	50	5	1893	2318	1372	1668	1388
4	12→8→1	50	5	1573	2578	2986	2262	1812
5	8→1→12	50	5	1283	2251	1909	1898	1663
6	7→2→6	50	5	2892	1190	1045	1417	2998
7	2→4→7→6	50	5	1373	2493	2062	2499	1856
8	6→7→4→2	50	5	1030	2751	1195	1052	2355
9	2→6	50	5	1641	2087	1854	1384	2676
10	5→10→3	50	5	2316	1447	1177	2648	1236

Table A.2. Distance between machine locations

To From	1	2	3	4	5	6	7	8	9	10	11	12
1	0	10	20	30	40	50	70	60	50	40	30	20
2	10	0	10	20	30	40	60	50	40	30	20	30
3	20	10	0	10	20	30	50	40	30	20	30	40
4	30	20	10	0	10	20	40	30	20	30	40	50
5	40	30	20	10	0	10	30	20	30	40	50	60
6	50	40	30	20	10	0	20	30	40	50	60	70
7	70	60	50	40	30	20	0	10	20	30	40	50
8	60	50	40	30	20	30	10	0	10	20	30	40
9	50	40	30	20	30	40	20	10	0	10	20	30
10	40	30	20	30	40	50	30	20	10	0	10	20
11	30	20	30	40	50	60	40	30	20	10	0	10
12	20	30	40	50	60	70	50	40	30	20	10	0

Table A.3. Input Data for problem [14]

Parts	Machine sequence	Batch size	C_k	Variance of part demands
1	2→4	100	10	1000
2	1→7	100	10	1000
3	1→5→7	100	10	2000
4	3→6	100	10	1000
5	1→7→5	100	10	2000
6	2→4	100	10	1000
7	3	100	10	3000
8	5→7	100	10	1000

A Web-Based Manufacturing Execution System for Industry Services and Supply Chain Management: Application to Real-Time Process Virtual Monitoring

M. Giriraj[1], S. Muthu[2], and S.A. Pasupathy[3]

[1] Research Scholar, Anna University, Chennai
[2] M.P. Nachimuthu M. Jaganathan Engineering College, Erode
[3] Kumaraguru College of Technology, Coimbatore
girirajmannayee@gmail.com

Abstract. As tier1 and tier 2 manufactures seek solutions to bridge the gap between supply chain management (SCM) and the critical plant floor operations. The classical manufactures are looking for customized solutions to bridge the gap between SCM and plant floor operations. In industries, shop floor and SCM remains a blockade to improve visibility. In floor manipulates more data and gain better control of processes, solutions proliferate, adding new challenges to gaining full visibility and integrating floor and SCM. In order to increase the visibility of plant floor activities, Manufacturing Execution Systems (MES) are often used in conjunction with SCM systems to simplify and enable actual manufacturing processes. This paper proposes a solution to the integration of MES and supply chain management.

Keywords: Manufacturing execution system, Programmable logic controller, Supply chain management.

1 Introduction

Manufacturing Execution Systems (MES) offer a top level visibility of production, but these systems were often inflexible in order to customization and data pumping from plant floor and SCM to operate successfully. The supply chain management systems (SCM) have become the financial backbone of many industries. However, the existing systems do not have the provision to include the dynamics of the shop floor conditions such as unpredictable machine utilization, machine downtime, variability and reliability of tier 2 level of customer [1][8]. The crucial link between MES and SCM systems is weakened by the lack of visibility of data coming from the control systems located in the shop floor. An innovative prototype to integrate the web-enabled intelligence for MES will provide a competent solution and a new standard for manufacturing industries. Manufacturing business enterprise can be classified in to supply chain management system and plant floor system [2] [7]. The supply chain management systems in general include planning, scheduling, routing, controlling,

S.G. Ponnambalam et al. (Eds.): IRAM 2012, CCIS 330, pp. 406–411, 2012.

supply chain activities, sales, and logistics management applications. However, the plant floor systems would include applications directly fasten with machinery details, and target manufacturing operations and activities, such as engineering, manufacturing execution system, and plant floor controls [3] [6]. Gigantic business environments, like automotive manufacturers, could not find a fast solution for the dynamic changes occurring in customer demands and production operations. Integration of MES and SCM will enable the tier1 and tier 2 units of automotive industries to ensure the informed decisions are operational. Material flow management is an essential component and plays a significant role in manufacturing execution system [4] [5]. This paper proposes a solution of customization for reconfigurable and distributed manufacturing execution system. And moreover communication between plant floor systems and SCM was achieved by using autonomous programmable logic controller agents. The management of material movements from stage to stage in the plant floor using MES will also be discussed. MES can be developed by integrating the concept of virtual production lines in the production control. A manufacturing execution system can be formulated as a distributed system through decomposition and coordination, which will result in improved production performance, visibility of plant floor operations, robustness, flexibility, and interoperability for the overall shop floor information systems.

2   Manufacturing Execution System Architecture

Fig.1 shows the manufacturing execution system architecture, it is a system with many layers that fits between the big business environment and the plant floor environment (Fig. 1). This MES is anticipated to bridge the gap between the business planning done in the supply chain management software and the plant floor processing. The MES exchanges the production information to SCM. The interfacing control steps will achieve the desired task in a sequential manner which was scheduled to the manufacturing execution system. The MES uploads process stages information. The foremost function of the middleware is to provide an interface between the supply chain management system and the manufacturing execution system.

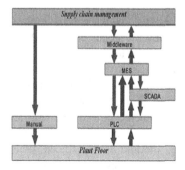

Fig. 1. Manufacturing execution system architecture

3   The Manufacturing Execution System to Programmable Logic Controller Interface

The plant floor control system directly controls the production or assembly line(s). The MES is offered with array of sensory devices for passing the required information to the programmable logic controllers. The manufacturing execution system checks for the critical events online to identify the occurrences of predetermined events. After identification of stages, the manufacturing execution systems right of entry to the database variables for retrieving the information.

4   Experimental Setup

Fig. 2 shows the prototype of a manufacturing execution system. These systems consist of various stages, like component product sorting and assembly processes that can be controlled by programmable logic controller. The upper conveyor and the lower conveyor are driven by the rotary actuator 1 and 2 respectively.

Fig. 2. Manufacturing Execution System setup

A random selection of metallic pegs and plastic rings are placed on the upper conveyor and they need to be identified and separated. The two different components are identified by a proximity sensor and an infra-red reflective sensor, provided with the MES. Based on the data from these sensors, the sort linear actuator 3 ejects the plastic rings to the assembly chute, which can have plastic rings. Metallic fasteners will continuously carry away by the upper conveyor to the feeder chute. This chute automatically feeds fasteners on the lower conveyor. An infra- red sensor checks for the emptiness of the assembly area. If it is empty, the assembly solenoid base rotary actuator will dispense a ring from the assembly channel into the assembly area. The assembly area is positioned just above the lower conveyor, when a metallic fasteners passes, the fastener engages with the hole in the ring and the two components are assembled. The lower conveyor is used to carry the assembled components into the collection tray. A printing module is interfaced with the programmable logic controller, retrieves data from the MES and print over the component with relevant parameters, like manufacturer, license no, batch no., mfg. date, expiry date etc. In this work, a Siemens S7-300 programmable logic controller was used to control the process and software called "middle ware" was used to program the programmable logic controller.

4.1   Implemented Solution

The implemented interface result was split into two modules - one installed in middleware, the other on the plant - floor system. The middleware interface was written in middleware's application programming code and the plant floor system interface written in VB coding. In addition to plant –floor master data, the middleware interface is also responsible for exporting the production plan to the plant floor system, and for posting production data received from the plant -floor system, such as quantities of finished goods produced. The plant -floor system interface exports information's about information's about the status of the production. This will also report the production line run- time. This information will be stored in the plant -floor system database, populated with data from the plant –floor equipments.

4.2   Testing of Simulation and Validation

Fig. 3 shows the simulation, testing and validation of the assembly process, which are crucial to any supervision of manufacturing execution system. The more translucent process simulation, testing and validation mean more efficient floor management. The end users now explicitly demand that their plant floor and progression to be represented as close to reality. The instant look, feel and touch experience allow to run free extra array of sensory sensitivity. "The being there but not being there" [5], the virtual reality is the key factor and this is where graphics play a foremost role. In a project development, much time is spent on creating the real thing on screen for real time shop floor transaction. With help of middleware and software tools, the gigantic range of most powerful shop floor visibility will increased.

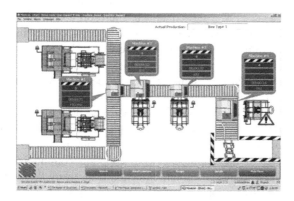

Fig. 3. Manufacturing Execution System Simulation

4.3   Manufacturing Execution System Data

Manufacturing execution system, plant floor automation programs in this level are developed based on middleware principle. The plant floor system may extract programmable logic controller data (through interactive PPI communication Level), Plant-floor production can be tracked with the aid of sensory systems and middleware. Manufacturing data from one assembly process can be viewed in other process. However, all the data can be saved into a database in plant floor system, such as Oracle or Microsoft access. Screenshot shows (Fig. 4) MS access of manufacturing execution system data base. This data base posted to ERP software.

Fig. 4. Screen Shot: Manufacturing Execution System Data (Microsoft access)

5   From Manufacturing Execution System Intermediate Document to Supply Chain Management System

Intermediate document is a well defined standard data structure for electronic data interchange between application programs written for the popular supply chain management system or between an ERP application and an external program. Intermediate document are used for asynchronous transactions: each Intermediate document generated exists as a self-contained Microsoft access file or Excel that can then be transmitted to the requesting system without connecting to the central database. A large multinational company's networked computing environment is likely to connect many geographically (Tier 1 and Tier 2 etc.) distributed computers to the central database. These systems are to be expected to use dissimilar hardware and/or software platforms. In this work, an intermediate document was put in a nutshell data so that it can be swapped over between different systems without the adaptation of format change. After an end user performs a supply chain management transaction, one or more intermediate documents are produced in the transport database and passed to the application link enabling communication layer. This communication layer executes a Remote Function Call, using the port definition and remote function call destination specified by the end user replica. The intermediate document (user Ms Access document) is export to the import, which may be an external server system.

6   Conclusion

This paper discussed Plant floor and SCM integration to improve efficiency of supply chain and increase visibility of floor operations to decision makers. In order to fruitfully implement this integration MES and SCM, the followings things are needed to be implemented: (a) sensory intelligence, (b) customization scenario (c) scalable platform, (d) Information highway between end devices and business scenario mapping, (e) data-to-information-to-knowledge transformation middleware, (f) Harmonization systems for vibrant decision-making, (g) free communication systems to achieve flexible and low-cost automation installation of remote, online monitoring, managers and policy makers who are capable of pacing with the speed of information flow and accepting the overall structure and (h) enterprise culture that has the flexibility of local vibrant decision-making and strength of worldwide competition.

References

1. Rockwell automation e-manufacturing industry road map,
   http://www.rockwellautomation.com
2. Koc, M., Ni, J., Lee, J.: Introduction of e-manufacturing. In: Proceeding of the International Conference on Frontiers on Design and Manufacturing, Dalian, China (July 2002)
3. Morel, G., Panetto, H., Zaremba, M., Mayer, F.: Manufacturing enterprise control and management system engineering: Paradigms and open issues. Annual Reviews in Control 27, 199–209 (2003)
4. Babiceanu, R.F., Chen, F.F., Sturges, R.H.: Framework for control of automated material-handling systems using holonic manufacturing approach. International Journal of Production Research 42(17), 3551–3564 (2004)
5. Barata, J.: Coalition Based Approach for Shop Floor Agility. Orion (ed.), Amadora, Lisbon (2005)
6. Blanc, P., Demongodin, I., Castagna, P.: A holonic approach for manufacturing control: an industrial application. In: Proceedings of the 12th IFAC Symposium on Information Control Problems in Manufacturing (2006)
7. Baina, S., Morel, G.: Product centric holons for synchronisation and interoperability in manufacturing environments. In: Proceedings of the 12th IFAC Symposium on Information Control Problems in Manufacturing, INCOM 2006, St. Etienne, France, May 17-19 (2006)
8. Iwamura, K., Nakano, A., Tanimizu, Y., Sugimura, N.: A Study on Real-Time Scheduling for Holonic Manufacturing Systems – Simulation for Estimation of Future Status by Individual Holons. In: Mařík, V., Vyatkin, V., Colombo, A.W. (eds.) HoloMAS 2007. LNCS (LNAI), vol. 4659, pp. 205–214. Springer, Heidelberg (2007)

Implementation of Multi Objective Fuzzy Integer Programming Technique by Using Suppy Chain Management

C. Kavitha[1] and C. Vijayalakshmi[2]

[1] Department of Mathematics, Sathyabama University, Chennai
ceekavi@gmail.com
[2] Department of Mathematics(SAS),VIT Chennai Campus, Chennai
vijusesha2002@yahoo.co.in

Abstract. Supply chain management plays an important role in firms and organization. Supplier selection and allocating orders to supplier is a complex multi objective problem which includes both quantitative and qualitative factors. In order to achieve an efficient solution in the quantitative factors, a Fuzzy Multi Objective Integer Programming [FMOIP] model with α-cut is formulated to help the management to allocate the optimum order quantities, in which the three objectives are to optimize purchasing cost, quality, and service and satisfy constraints like supplier's capacity, supply chain demand etc are considered. The model has been applied to supplier selection of a high technology company named Multi-Flex Lami-Print Ltd which manufactures Flexible Packaging materials. The result shows that the model is effective and applicable to industries.

Keywords: Supplier selection, Fuzzy multi objective integer programming, α-cut method.

1 Introduction

Supplier selection plays a key role in an organization because order allocation to the suppliers and purchasing cost of a product plays a vital role in supply chain. In addition to cost, the emphasis on quality and timely delivery in today's competitive market place also adds complexities to supplier selection decisions. To have an efficient and effective organization purchasing department plays a key role because it has direct effect on cost reduction, profitability and flexibility of a company. Moreover purchasing department has a key role in cost reduction and supplier selection is one of the most important functions of purchasing management [5]. Supplier selection decision is often made in an uncertain environment filled with multiple objectives and incomplete information. Deterministic model cannot take this vagueness into account. In this case fuzzy set is one of the best tools for dealing with uncertainty. Fuzzy set theories are used because of the presence of vagueness and imprecision of information in the supplier selection problem. A fuzzy programming model for decision –making in fuzzy environment was suggested by [2].In this paper a fuzzy multi objective with fuzzy constraint and

S.G. Ponnambalam et al. (Eds.): IRAM 2012, CCIS 330, pp. 412–425, 2012.

deterministic constraint model has been developed to allocate order to the suppliers in which different weights can be considered for various objectives such as cost, quality, service and constraint such as demand.

2   Literature Review

Multi-objective linear programming for supplier selection, to systematically analyze the trade-off between conflicting factors [16]. Mixed integer programming model to solve the supplier selection with bundling, in which a buyer needs to buy various items from several suppliers whose capacity, quality and deliveries are limited and who offer bundled products at discounted prices [13]. They used single objective programming and considered price, quality, delivery and suppliers' capacity as criteria in their model. Twenty three criteria for supplier selection based on the extensive survey, the result shows that quality is the most important parameter followed by delivery and performance history [3]. A number of quantitative techniques have been used to supplier selection problem such as weighing method, statistical methods, Analytic Hierarchy Process (AHP), Data Envelopment Analysis etc. A multi-objective linear programming model for the special issues of purchasing these raw materials of a large-scale steel plant, and indicates selecting items, selecting suppliers and deciding order quantity as the key issue in optimizing purchasing policies [4]. Fuzzy multi-objective model with capacity, demand and budget constraint for supplier selection problem was used by [6]. They used two models to solve the problem. First Zimmerman's approach of symmetric model is used followed by [15] weighted additive model as asymmetric model. Fuzzy multi-objective mathematical programming for supplier selection with three goals: cost minimization, quality maximization and on-time delivery maximization with constraints as demand, capacity, and quota flexibility [8]. Fuzzy multi-objective linear programming was developed by [1]. Weighted linear programming was developed by [12]. Uncertainty is one of the most challenging but important problems in SCM [11] .A supply network consisting of a manufacturer and its suppliers [7]. They formulated a nonlinear programming model and determined how much of each raw material and component part to order from which supplier according to the capacity of suppliers and manufacturer. It is assumed that demand is stochastic. However, they only determined the order quantity and they did not select the suppliers. A multi-objective supplier selection model under stochastic demand conditions was proposed by [10]. Stochastic supplier selection has been determined with simultaneous consideration of the cost, quality, delivery and flexibility according to the limitations of capacity. Fuzzy multi-objective programming model to take suppliers' risk factors into account was proposed by [17]. In this paper, Fuzzy multi objective model and its crisp formulation for the supplier selection problem is presented in which the objectives are not equally important and have different weights.

3   Multi Objective Linear Programming

A general multi objective model for the supplier selection problem can be stated as follows:

$$\min z_1.z_2,\ldots\ldots\ldots z_k,$$

$$\max z_{k+1}, z_{k+2},\ldots\ldots z_p$$

$$such \ that \ x \in X_d, X_d = \{x / g(x) \le b_r, r = 1,2,\ldots\ldots\ldots m\}$$

Where $z_1,z_2,\ldots\ldots\ldots\ldots\ldots z_k$ are the negative objectives and $z_{k+1},z_{k+2},\ldots\ldots\ldots z_p$ are the positive objectives and X_d is the set of feasible solutions which satisfy the constraints.

3.1   Fuzzy Multi Objective Linear Programming [FMOLP]

A general linear multi objective model can be presented as:

Find a vector x written in the transformed form $x^T = [x_1,x_2,\ldots\ldots\ldots x_n]$ which minimizes objective function z_k and maximizes objective function z_l with

$$z_k = \sum_{i=1}^{n} c_{ki} x_i, \ k = 1,2\ldots\ldots p,$$

$$z_l = \sum_{i=1}^{n} c_{li} x_i, l = p+1, p+2\ldots\ldots q \ \text{and constraints} :$$

$$x \in x_d, x_d = \left\{ x / g(x) = \sum_{i=1}^{n} a_{ri} x_i \le b_r, r = 1,2\ldots\ldots\ldots m, x \ge 0 \right\}$$

where c_{ki}, c_{li}, a_{ri} and b_r are crisp or fuzzy values.

3.2   Zimmermann FMOLP

He formulated the fuzzy linear program by separating every objective function Z_j into its maximum Z_j^+ and minimum Z_j^- value by solving:

$$Z_k^+ = \max Z_k, x \in X_a, \qquad Z_k^- = \min Z_k, x \in X_d, \qquad (1)$$

$$Z_l^+ = \max Z_l, x \in X_d, \qquad Z_l^- = \min Z_l, x \in X_a, \qquad (2)$$

Z_k^-, Z_l^+ are obtained through solving the multi objective problem as a single objective using each time only one objective and $x \in X_d$ means that solutions must satisfy constraints while X_a is the set of all optimal solutions through solving as single objective.

Since for every objective function Z_j, its value changes linearly from Z_j^- to Z_j^+, it may be considered as a fuzzy number with the linear membership function $\mu_{Zj}(x)$ as shown in fig1.

Linear programming problem with fuzzy goal and fuzzy constraints may be presented as follows:

Find a vector x to satisfy:

$$\tilde{Z}_k = \sum_{i=1}^{n} c_{ki} x_i \leq \sim Z_k^0, \text{k} = 1,2\ldots\ldots\ldots\text{p} \tag{3}$$

$$\tilde{Z}_l = \sum_{i=1}^{n} c_{li} x_i \geq \sim Z_l^0, \text{l} = p+1, p+2\ldots\ldots\ldots\text{q} \tag{4}$$

Such that $\tilde{g}_i(x) = \sum_{i=1}^{n} a_{ri} x_i \leq \tilde{b}_r$, r = 1,2........h (for fuzzy constraints)   (5)

$$g_p(x) = \sum_{i=1}^{n} a_{pi} x_i \leq b_p, \text{p} = h+1, h+2\ldots\ldots, \text{m}$$

(For deterministic constraints)   (6)

$x_i \geq 0$, i=1,2...........n

In this model the sign ~ indicates the fuzzy environment. The symbol $\leq \sim$ in the constraints set denotes the fuzzified version of $\leq$ and has linguistic interpretation "essentially smaller than or equal to" and the symbol $\geq \sim$ has linguistic interpretation "essentially greater than or equal to" .Z_k^0 and Z_l^0 are the aspiration levels that the decision-maker wants to reach.

3.3   Membership Functions

Assuming that membership functions, based on preference or satisfaction are linear the linear membership for minimization goals (Z_k) and maximization goals (Z_l) are given as follows:

$$\mu_{Z_k}(x) = \begin{cases} 1 & \text{for } Z_k \leq Z_k^-, \\ \dfrac{(Z_k^+ - Z_k(x))}{(Z_k^* - Z_k^-)} & \text{for } Z_k^- \leq Z_k(x) \leq Z_k^+, \text{k} = 1,2\ldots\ldots\ldots\text{p}, \\ 0 & \text{for } Z_k \geq Z_k^+ \end{cases} \tag{7}$$

$$\mu_{Z_l}(x) = \begin{cases} 1 & \text{for } Z_l \geq Z_l^+, \\ \dfrac{(Z_l(x) - Z_l^-)}{(Z_k^* - Z_k^-)} & \text{for } Z_l^- \leq Z_l(x) \leq Z_l^+, \text{l} = p+1, p+2\ldots\ldots\ldots\text{q}, \\ 0 & \text{for } Z_l \leq Z_l^- \end{cases} \tag{8}$$

The linear membership function for the fuzzy constraints is given as

$$\mu_{g_r}(x) = \begin{cases} 1 & \text{for } g_r(x) \leq b_r, \\ 1 - \dfrac{(g_r(x) - b_r)}{d_r} & \text{for } b_r \leq g_r(x) \leq b_r + d_r, \text{r} = 1,2\ldots\ldots\ldots\text{h}, \\ 0 & \text{for } g_r(x) \geq b_r + d_r \end{cases} \tag{9}$$

d_r is the subjectively chosen constants expressing the limit of the admissible violation of the rth inequalities constraints (tolerance interval). Membership functions for objective function are represented in Fig 1.

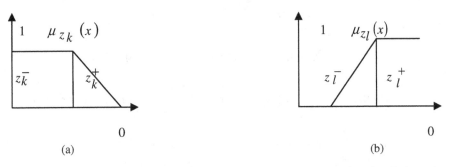

Fig. 1. Objective function as fuzzy number (a) For minimizing objective function Z_k (negative objective) and (b) For maximizing objective function Z_l (positive objective)

3.4   Decision Making Operators

In fuzzy programming modeling, using Zimmermann's approach a fuzzy solution is given by the intersection of all the fuzzy sets representing either fuzzy objective or fuzzy constraints. The fuzzy solution for all fuzzy objectives and h fuzzy constraints may be given as

$$\mu_D(x) = \left\{ \left[\bigcap_{j=1}^{q} \mu_{z_j}(x) \right] \cap \left[\bigcap_{r=1}^{h} \mu_{g_r}(x) \right] \right\} \tag{10}$$

The optimal solution (x^*) is given by

$$\mu_D\left(x^*\right) = \max_{x \varepsilon X_d} \mu_D(x) = \max_{x \in X_d} \min\left[\min_{j=1,2\ldots\ldots q} \mu_{z_j}(x), \min_{r=1,2\ldots\ldots h} \mu_{g_r}(x) \right] \tag{11}$$

In order to find optimal solution (x^*) in the above fuzzy model, it is equivalent to solving the following crisp model (Zimmermann 1978):
    Maximize λ

$$\tag{12}$$

    Such that
    $\lambda \le \mu_{z_j}(x), j = 1, 2\ldots\ldots\ldots q$ (for all objective functions),

$$\tag{13}$$

$\lambda \le \mu_{g_r}(x), r = 1,2\ldots\ldots\ldots\ldots h$ (for fuzzy constraints)

$$\tag{14}$$

$g_p(x) \le b_p$,$p = h+1,\ldots\ldots\ldots\ldots\ldots m$ (for deterministic constraints)

$$\tag{15}$$

$x_i \ge 0$, $i=1,2\ldots\ldots n$ and $\lambda \varepsilon [0,1]$ and $x_i \varepsilon$ integer

$$\tag{16}$$

where $\mu_D(x)$, $\mu_{z_j}(x)$ and $\mu_{g_r}(x)$ represent the membership functions of solution, objective functions and constraints.

In this solution the relationship between constraints and objective functions in a fuzzy environment is fully symmetric [18]. (i.e) there is no difference between the fuzzy goals and fuzzy constraints. But in Supplier selection problem fuzzy goals and fuzzy constraints have unequal importance to DM and other patterns, as the confluence of objectives and constraints should be considered. In this case weighted additive model is used which is described as follows:

The weighted additive model is widely used in vector-objective optimization problems; the basic concept is to use a single utility function to express the overall preference of DM to draw out the relative importance of criteria [9]. In this case, multiplying each membership function of fuzzy goals by their corresponding weights and then adding the results together obtain a linear weighted utility function.

The convex fuzzy model proposed by [2], [14] and the weighted additive model [15] is

$$\mu_D(x) = \sum_{j=1}^{q} w_j \mu_{z_j}(x) + \sum_{r=1}^{h} \beta_r \mu_{g_r}(x) \tag{17}$$

$$\sum_{j=1}^{q} w_j + \sum_{r=1}^{h} \beta_r \gamma_r \tag{18}$$

where w_j and β_i are the weighting coefficients that present the relative importance among the fuzzy goals and fuzzy constraints. The following crisp single objective programming by [1] is equivalent to the above fuzzy model:

$$\text{Max} \sum_{j=1}^{q} w_j \lambda_j + \sum_{r=1}^{h} \beta_r \gamma_r \tag{19}$$

$$\text{Such that } \lambda_j \le \mu_{z_j}(x), \text{j} = 1, 2\ldots\ldots\ldots\ldots\text{q} \tag{20}$$

$$\gamma_r \le \mu_{g_r}(x), \text{r} = 1, 2\ldots\ldots\ldots\ldots\ldots\text{h} \tag{21}$$

$$g_p(x) \le b_p \quad \text{,p} = \text{h+1},\ldots\ldots\ldots\ldots\ldots\text{m} \tag{22}$$

$$\lambda_j, \gamma_r \in [0,1], \text{j} = 1, 2\ldots\ldots\text{q and r} = 1, 2\ldots\ldots\ldots\text{h} \tag{23}$$

$$\sum_{j=1}^{q} w_j + \sum_{r=1}^{h} \beta_r = 1, \text{ w}_j, \beta_r \ge 0 \tag{24}$$

$$x_i \ge 0, \text{i=1, 2}\ldots\ldots\ldots\ldots\text{n and} \quad x_i \, \varepsilon \text{ integer} \tag{25}$$

3.5   FMOLP [Proposed Method]

Find a vector x to satisfy:

$$\tilde{Z}_k = \sum_{i=1}^{n} c_{ki}[(1-\alpha)\bar{x}_i + \alpha\underline{x}_i] \leq \sim Z_k^0, k=1,2\ldots\ldots\ldots p$$

$$\tilde{Z}_l = \sum_{i=1}^{n} c_{li}[(1-\alpha)\bar{x}_i + \alpha\underline{x}_i] \geq \sim Z_l^0, l = p+1, p+2\ldots\ldots\ldots q \qquad \text{Suchthat}$$

$$\tilde{g}_i(x) = \sum_{i=1}^{n} a_{ri}[(1-\alpha)\bar{x}_i + \alpha\underline{x}_i] \leq (\geq, =)[(1-\alpha)\bar{b}_r + \alpha\tilde{b}_r], r=1,2\ldots\ldots h$$

(For fuzzy constraints)

$$g_p(x) = \sum_{i=1}^{n} a_{pi} x_i \leq b_p , p = h+1, h+2\ldots\ldots, m$$

(For deterministic constraints)

$x_i \geq 0$, $i=1,2\ldots\ldots\ldots n$

Here we assume the variable set $X = (x_1, x_2\ldots\ldots\ldots x_n)^T$ and the right hand side vector b_r of constraints are in fuzzy domain. Let x_i's and b_r's be fuzzy triangular numbers and the matrix A is in crisp form whose elements are real numbers.

Define   the   membership   function   corresponding   to   X   as

$$\mu_{x_i}(x) = \begin{cases} 0 \text{ if } x_i < \underline{x}_i \\ \dfrac{x_i - \underline{x}_i}{\bar{x}_i - \underline{x}_i} \text{ if } \underline{x}_i < x_i < \bar{x}_i \\ 1 \text{ if } x_i > \bar{x}_i \end{cases}$$

Fuzzy Multi Objective Linear Programming from [12-16]. FMOLP Optimal will be obtained by the average of the lower and upper bound of the solution then the crisp single objective programming equivalent to above fuzzy model [19-25] is used to find the optimal solution of FMOLP.

4   Mathematical Model for Supplier Selection

4.1   Notations

i-   index for suppliers, i= 1,2……m
j-   index for periods, j= 1,2………n
k-   index for products, k= 1,2……..p
x_{ijk} -   Order quantity of kth product from ith supplier in jth period.
q_{ijk} -   quality level of kth product purchased from ith supplier in jth period.

t_{ijk} -   on-time delivery rate of kth product purchased from ith supplier in jth period.

D_k -   fuzzy demand quantity of kth product.

P_{ijk} –   Unit price of the kth product from the ith supplier in jth period.

B_{kj} –   purchasing budget of the kth product in jth period.

MC_{ijk} –   Maximum supply capacity of the kth product from the ith supplier in jth period.

Q_{kmax} –   buyer's maximum acceptable defective rate of kth product.

T_{kmin} –   buyer's minimum acceptable on time delivery rate on kth product.

4.2   Model Formulation

To allocate the optimum order quantities to the suppliers, we use a MOLP model with three objectives to optimize total purchasing costs, quality and and service. Consider purchasing budget, production demand, suppliers' capacity, and quality control and delivery reliability control constraints. The objective functions are as follows:

Purchasing Cost: To minimize the total purchasing cost. Purchasing cost includes the price, transportation cost and ordering cost.

$$Min\, Z_1 = \sum_{i=1}^{m} \sum_{j=1}^{n} \sum_{k=1}^{p} c_{ijk} x_{ijk} \leq\sim Z_1^0$$

Quality: To maximize the number of non defective items for improving product quality.

$$Max\, Z_2 = \sum_{i=1}^{m} \sum_{j=1}^{n} \sum_{k=1}^{p} q_{ijk} x_{ijk} \leq\sim Z_2^0$$

Service: To maximize the number of items delivered on time.

$$Max\, Z_3 = \sum_{i=1}^{m} \sum_{j=1}^{n} \sum_{k=1}^{p} t_{ijk} x_{ijk} \leq\sim Z_3^0$$

Constraints Are as Follows

Purchasing Budget Constraints: Total purchasing payment for each product cannot exceed the budget of each product in that period.

$$\sum_{i=1}^{m} \sum_{k=1}^{p} p_{ijk} x_{ijk} \leq B_{kj},\, j = 1,2...n$$

Demand Constraints: The assigned order quantity of each product from all suppliers must meet the demand quantity of each product in the total period.

$$\sum_{i=1}^{m} \sum_{j=1}^{n} \sum_{k=1}^{p} x_{ijk} \geq \tilde{D}_k$$

Capacity Constraints: The order quantity of the kth product from the ith supplier cannot exceed each supplier's capacity.

$$x_{ijk} \leq MC_{ijk} \,, i = 1,2\ldots\ldots m, j = 1,2,\ldots\ldots\ldots n, k = 1,2\ldots\ldots\ldots p$$

Quality Control Constraints: The total defect quantity of each product cannot exceed maximum acceptable defective quantity of each product

$$\sum_{i=1}^{m} \sum_{j=1}^{n} q_{ijk} \, x_{ijk} \leq Q_{kmax} D_k \,, k = 1,2\ldots\ldots\ldots p$$

Delivery Constraint: The total late delivery on each product cannot exceed minimum acceptable late delivery.

$$\sum_{i=1}^{m} \sum_{j=1}^{n} t_{ijk} \, x_{ijk} \leq T_{k\,min} D_k \,, k = 1,2\ldots\ldots p$$

Variable Non-negativity Constraints: Non-negativity restrictions on the decision variables is

$$x_{ijk} \geq 0 \,, i = 1,2\ldots\ldots\ldots m, j = 1,2\ldots\ldots\ldots n, k = 1,2\ldots\ldots\ldots p \text{ and } x_{ijk} \text{ } \varepsilon \text{ integer}$$

The above multi objective supplier selection problem is solved as a single objective supplier selection problem using each time only one objective. This value is the best value for this objective as other objectives are absent. After obtaining the results determine the corresponding values for every objective at each solution derived. Then for each objective function find a lower bound and an upper bound corresponding to the set of solutions for each objective. Membership function values are calculated for the objective functions and fuzzy constraints. Using membership function and DM's preferences, based on fuzzy convex decision-making formulate the equivalent crisp model of the fuzzy optimization problem. Find the optimal solution vector x*, where x* is the efficient solution of the original multi objective supplier selection problem with the DM's preferences.

4.3   Numerical Calculations and Graphical Representation

Fuzzy multi objective integer programming model has applied to a professionally managed company namely Multi-Flex Lami-Print Ltd., who manufactures Quality Flexible Packaging Materials against specific orders from their customers like Hindustan Unilever Ltd., ITC Ltd., Tata Tea Ltd., Cavinkare Pvt Ltd..... will produce important raw materials like Polyester film, Bi-axially oriented Poly Propylene film, Polyethylene film and also Printing inks, Lamination adhesives, Diluting Solvents.........from the best suitable supplier's for various production processes such as Printing-Lamination-Slitting-Finishing.

Before selecting / finalizing a best suitable, ideal, reliable supplier from many of them in that category, Multi-Flex will carefully analyse important factors/ parameters in many of their suppliers suiting to their requirements. Finally suppliers meeting / fulfilling all their requirements in terms of most important basic criteria like Cost-Quality-Service will be selected from many of the suppliers in that category.

Basic process of manufacturing Polyester film is Polyester chips will be coextruded to bi-axially oriented thin film in the range of 10m to 200m for the various applications. From these range only 10micron and 12micron thickness of polyester film only are used in packaging industry.

Suppliers of Polyester film are Garware Polyesters Ltd, U Flex Films Ltd, Jindal Films Ltd, Polyplex Ltd, MTZ Polyester Ltd, Venlon Polyester Ltd etc.

Cost, Quality, on time delivery, Capacity, Demand, Budget are said to be the criteria's and the de-fuzzified data's corresponding to each criteria given in Table 1. The demand is a fuzzy number and is predicted to be about 490000,495000,500000 as shown in Table 2. Maximum total damaging rate which can be accepted is 0.05. Minimum acceptable late delivery is 0.15.

The multi objective integer formulation is presented as min Z_1, max Z_2, Z_3.Then the linear membership function is used for fuzzifing the objective functions and demand constraint. The data set for the values of the lower bounds and upper bounds of the objective functions and a fuzzy number for the demand are given in Table 2.

Table 1. Supplier's quantitative information

Su ppl ier	Purchasin g cost		Defects(rate)		On time delivery(rate)		Capacity		Price	
	j=1	j=2	j=1	j=2	j=1	j=2	j=1	j=2	j=1	j=2
1	65	64	0.03	0.05	0.15	0.18	90000	40000	4	2
2	45	48	0.04	0.01	0.09	0.06	85000	95000	2	4
3	50	56	0.03	0.02	0.17	0.07	65000	45000	4	4
4	54	60	0.04	0.02	0.15	0.1	50000	35000	5	5

Table 2. Data set for membership functions

	μ=0	μ=1	μ=0
Purchasing cost	-	26397500	27185000
Quality	13850	14562.5	-
Service	56550	59025	-
Demand	490000	495000	500000

Based on the convex fuzzy decision-making and the weights which are given by DM, the crisp single objective formulation by [1] is

Max $0.17\lambda_1 + 0.37 \lambda_2 + 0.27 \lambda_3 + 0.19\gamma_1$

Subject to

$\lambda_1 \leq (27185000\text{-}(65x_{111} + 45x_{211} + 50x_{311} + 54x_{411} + 64x_{121} + 48x_{221} + 56x_{321} + 60x_{421})) / 787500$

$\lambda_2 \leq ((0.03x_{111} + 0.04x_{211} + 0.03x_{311} + 0.04x_{411} + 0.05x_{121} + 0.01x_{221} + 0.02x_{321} + 0.02x_{421}) \text{-}13850) / 712.5$

$\lambda_3 \leq ((0.15x_{111} + 0.09x_{211} + 0.17x_{311} + 0.15x_{411} + 0.18x_{121} + 0.06x_{221} + 0.07x_{321} + 0.1x_{421}) \text{-}56550) / 2475$

$\gamma_1 \leq (500000 - (x_{111} + x_{211} + x_{311} + x_{411} + x_{121} + x_{221} + x_{321} + x_{421})) / 10000$

$\gamma_1 \leq ((x_{111} + x_{211} + x_{311} + x_{411} + x_{121} + x_{221} + x_{321} + x_{421}) - 485000) / 5000$

$0.03x_{111} + 0.04x_{211} + 0.03x_{311} + 0.04x_{411} + 0.05x_{121} + 0.01x_{221} + 0.02x_{321} + 0.02x_{421} \leq 25000$

$0.15x_{111} + 0.09x_{211} + 0.17x_{311} + 0.15x_{411} + 0.18x_{121} + 0.06x_{221} + 0.07x_{321} + 0.1x_{421} \leq 75000$

$4x_{111} + 2x_{211} + 4x_{311} + 5x_{411} \leq 1200000$

$2x_{121} + 4x_{221} + 4x_{321} + 5x_{421} \leq 800000$

$x_{111} \leq 90000$

$x_{211} \leq 85000$

$x_{311} \leq 65000$

$x_{411} \leq 50000$

$x_{121} \leq 40000$

$x_{221} \leq 95000$

$x_{321} \leq 45000$

$x_{421} \leq 35000$

$x_{ijk} \geq 0$, x_{ijk} ε integer

The optimal solution of FMOLP is x_{111}=90000, x_{211}=85000, x_{311}=65000, x_{411}=50000, x_{121}=40000, x_{221}=89705.5, x_{321}=45000, x_{421}=35000, Z_1= 27110864, Z_2=14547.055, Z_3=58932.33.The membership values are obtained as follows: $\mu_{z_1}(x) = \lambda_1 = 0.3250165$,$\mu_{z_2}(x) = \lambda_2 = 0.9416475$, $\mu_{z_3}(x) = \lambda_3 = 0.8957545$, $\gamma_1 = 0.48535$ .These values represent that the achievement level of quality and service is more than cost. It means that the achievement level of the objective functions is consistent with the DM's preferences. In this solution maximum items are assigned to be purchased from supplier 2 because of the highest quality level on the quality criterion, remaining items are split between the other suppliers. By taking the average of the point we get the point where optimal solution will exist. Values of different approach are seen in Table 3.

According to DM's preference, quality and service is the most important criterion. In Zimmermann's approach there is no possibility to emphasize on objectives with heavy weights but the weighted additive model takes into account the objective's weights. Due to the weighted additive model, the cost performance is improved from 27046190 to 27110864, similarly quality performance is improved from 14493.73 to 14547.06 and service performance is improved from 58718.65 to 58932.33 in comparison with the weightless solution. α-cut approach ensure that the achievement level of objective function should not be less than a minimum level.

Table 3. Solutions by different approaches

	Weighted additive	Zimmermann(weightl ess)
X_{111}	90000	90000
X_{211}	85000	85000
X_{311}	65000	65000
X_{411}	50000	50000
X_{121}	40000	40000
X_{221}	89705.5	95000
X_{321}	45000	45000
X_{421}	35000	29686.5
Z_1	27110864	27046190
Z_2	14547.055	14493.73
Z_3	58932.33	58718.65

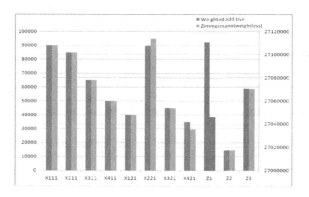

Fig. 2. Graphical Representation of two approaches

5   Conclusion

To allocate order quantity among the selected suppliers is one of the major areas in supply chain. Supply chain includes tangible and intangible factors which should be determined based on organization requirements. In real case, many input data are not known precisely for decision making. In this paper FMOIP model with three objectives and constraints are formulated to handle the vagueness and imprecision of input data and the varying importance of criteria in supply chain problem. The model has applied to professionally well managed company and the results were found out consistent and reliable.

By changing the weights of objectives it help the DM to find out the appropriate order for the suppliers and allows purchasing manager to manage the performance on the objectives in supply chain model. Complexity due to vagueness in allocating the order quantity to the supplier is easily handled by fuzzy multi objective linear program. Fuzzy multi objective supplier selection problem transforms into a convex (weighted additive) fuzzy programming model and its equivalent crisp single objective integer programming. This transformation reduces the dimension of the system giving less computational complexity and makes the application of fuzzy methodology more understandable. α-cut method and fuzzy triangular numbers for the constraint helps to find an solution in an interval on the real line .Based on this method exact fuzzy optimal solutions can be obtained in this method. Management feels that the method adopted is more realistic and promising as it involves the uncertainty in technological coefficients and it is comfortable to find an optimal solution in an interval. Managers are able to calculate the order quantity assigned to each supplier.

References

1. Amid, A., Ghodsypour, S.H., O'Brien, C.: Fuzzy Multi-Objective Linear Model for Supplier Selection in a Supply Chain. International Journal of Production Economics 104(2), 394–407 (2006)
2. Bellman, R.G., Zadeh, L.A.: Decision making a fuzzy environment. Management Sciences 17, B141–B164 (1970)
3. Dickson, G.W.: An analysis of vendor selection systems and decisions. J. Purch. 2(1), 5–17 (1996)
4. Gao, Z., Tang, L.: A Multi-objective Model for Purchasing of Bulk Raw Materials of A Largescale Integrated Steel Plant. International Journal of Production Economics 83, 325–334 (2003)
5. Ghodsypour, S.H., O'Brien, C.: A Decision Support System for Supplier Selection Using An Integrated Analytical Hierarchy Process and Linear Programming. International Journal of Production Economics 56-57, 199–212 (1998)
6. Kagnicioglu, C., Hakan: A Fuzzy Multiobjective Programming Approach for Supplier Selection in a Supply Chain. The Business Review 6(1), 107–115 (2006)
7. Kim, B., Leung, J.M.Y., Taepark, K., Zhang, G., Lee, S.: Configuring a manufacturing firm's supply network with multiple suppliers. IIE Transactions 34(8), 663–677 (2002)
8. Kumar, M., Vrat, P., Shankar, R.: A fuzzy programming approach for vendor selection in a supply chain. Int. J. Prod. Eco. 101(2), 273–285 (2006)
9. Lai, Y.J., Hawang, C.L.: Fuzzy Multiple Objective Decision Making Methods and Applications. Springer, Berlin (1994)
10. Liao, Z., Rittscher, J.: A multi-objective supplier selection model under stochastic demand conditions. International Journal of Production Economics 105(1), 150–159 (2007)
11. Melo, M.T., Nickel, S., Saldanha-da-Gama, F.: Facility location and supply chain management – A review. European Journal of Operational Research 196(2), 401–412 (2009)
12. Ng, W.L.: An Efficient and Simple Model for Multiple Criteria Supplier Selection Problem. European Journal of Operational Research 186(3), 1059–1067 (2008)
13. Rosenthal, E.C., Zydiak, J.L., Chaudhry, S.S.: Vendor Selection with Bundling. Decision Sciences 26, 35–48 (1995)
14. Sakawa, M.: Fuzzy Sets and Interactive Multiobjective Optimization. Plenum Press, Newyork (1993)

15. Tiwari, R.N., Dharmahr, S., Rao, J.R.: Fuzzy goal programming an additive model. Fuzzy Sets and Systems 24, 27–34 (1987)
16. Weber, C.A., Current, J.R.: A Multi-objective Approach to Vendor Selection. European Journal of Operational Research 68, 173–184 (1993)
17. Wua, D., Zhang, Y., Wud, D., Olson, D.: Fuzzy Multi-Objective Programming for Supplier Selection and Risk Modeling:A Possibility Approach. European Journal of Operational Research 200, 774–787 (2010)
18. Zimmermann, H.J.: Fuzzy Programming and linear programming with several objective functions. Fuzzy Sets and Systems 1, 45–55 (1978)

Integrated Layout Design Approach
for Cellular Manufacturing System

I. Jerin Leno[1], S. Saravana Sankar[2], and S.G. Ponnambalam[3]

[1] Sardar Raja College of Engineering, Alangulam, Tamil Nadu, India
[2] Kalasalingam University, Krishanankoil, Tamil Nadu, India
[3] School of Engineering, Monash University, Petaling Jaya, Malaysia
{lenojerin,ssaravanasankar}@yahoo.co.in,
sgponnambalam@monash.edu

Abstract. In traditional layout design approach, inter-cell layout and flow path layout of the Material Handling System (*MHS*) of any manufacturing system is being carried out in step by step manner. This leads to sub-optimal solutions for facility layout problems (FLP). In this work an attempt is made to concurrently design the Inter-cell layout and the *MHS* using GA based meta heuristic using simulated annealing as local search tool (GASAA) for a Cellular Manufacturing System (*CMS*) environment under open field configuration. The proposed algorithm is employed to optimize one of the classical objective namely, Total material handling cost (TMHC). The algorithm is tested on two different bench mark problem instances and with different initial problem data sets. It is found that the proposed algorithm is able to produce good solutions in reasonable computational effort.

Keywords: Integrated Layout Design, Genetic Algorithm, Simulated Annealing, Elitist Strategy, Sequence Pair.

1 Introduction

Facility layout design is an important issue for any industry, as a poor layout may degrade overall efficiency of the production system. The full layout design for a CMS requires four major steps [1]: (1) Cell formation, i.e., to group parts into part families and machines to machine cells; (2) Cell layout (intra-cell layout), i.e., to assign machines or work stations within each cell; (3) Cell system layout (inter-cell layout), i.e., to arrange cells within floor; (4) material handling system (MHS) , i.e., to design material flow paths between the input/output (I/O) stations.

Traditionally, the layout design is being carried out in a sequential manner involving two major steps [2,3], namely (1) Inter-cell Layout design wherein the exact location, orientation, position of input/output stations of each department is determined, (2) Material Handling System (MHS) design wherein the flow path of the materials between input and output stations of different department is determined. The arrangement of manufacturing cells in a two dimensional shop floor so as to minimize the total material handling cost is called inter-cell layout design problem. Similar to VLSI problem, the inter-cell layout design in CMS has department (cell) of

S.G. Ponnambalam et al. (Eds.): IRAM 2012, CCIS 330, pp. 426–435, 2012.

fixed dimension which are to be placed in two-dimensional facility (shop floor) with fixed dimension. From now onwards 'cell' is termed as 'department' throughout this paper. On the other hand the automated material handling equipments such as AGVs, conveyers etc..are needing good flow path layout for transporting materials from input station of one department to output station of another department , as a poor flow path layout degrades the quality and efficiency of material handling system. This is termed as flow path layout (material handling system) design problem. The material moves from the input/output (I/O) point of a department to the I/O point of the next department on the routing specification. Generally, the routings for each product or batch will be different, and each product may only visit a subset of the departments or work stations within a facility.

Traditionally, these two design phases are performed sequentially and separately in a step by step manner, the design procedure invariably leads to solution that can be far from the total optimum [4, 5]. Owing to computational complexity very little work has been done to solve inter-cell and *MHS* design problem simultaneously. In the recent years researchers have focused on concurrent design of both inter-cell and *MHS* design by adopting integrated approach [6-9]. In this work an attempt has been made to develop a methodology to solve an integrated layout design problem. The proposed algorithm is experimented with two test problem instances of different sizes and found consistent in producing good solutions within acceptable computational time.

2   Problem Description

There are N number of departments which are to be placed in a production floor layout of width W and height H. The departments are considered to be rectangular blocks with known dimension. Given the width and height of the individual department (determined by size and shape of the facilities), the predefined Input and Output stations at the boundary of the department, quantum and frequency of material flow between the departments, the aim is to find the exact location (x and y coordinates), the orientation of the individual departments, and to decide the aisle distance between the departments (along the department perimeter) with the objective of minimizing the total material handling cost (TMHC).
The notations used in the model are:

N	the total number of departments in the layout
W	the width of the floor space
H	the height of the floor space
i,j	indices to denote departments
f_{ij}	the directed flow density from department i to department j
w_i	width of department i in the initial orientation
h_i	height of department i in the initial orientation
(I_i^x, I_i^y), (x_i^I, y_i^I)	local coordinates, spatial coordinates of the input station of department i
(O_i^x, O_i^y), (x_i^O, y_i^O)	local coordinates, spatial coordinates of the output station of department i

(x_i, y_i), (x_i', y_i') spatial coordinates of the lower-left corner, the upper- right corner of department i

l_{ij} equals 1 if department i is placed to the left of department j ; (that is $x_i' \le x_j$) and 0 otherwise

b_{ij} equals 1 if department i is placed below department j ; (that is $y_i' \le y_j$) and 0 otherwise

d_{ij} shortest contour distance from the output station of department i to the input station of department j

$$(u_i, v_i) = \begin{cases} (0,0) & \text{cell } i \text{ in its original orientation} \\ (1,0) & \text{cell } i \text{ is rotated } 90^\circ \text{ clockwise from its original orientation} \\ (0,1) & \text{cell } i \text{ is rotated } 180^\circ \text{ clockwise from its original orientation} \\ (1,1) & \text{cell } i \text{ is rotated } 270^\circ \text{ clockwise from its original orientation} \end{cases}$$

c_{ij} the cost of travel of unit material for unit distance between department i and j, $c_{ij} = 1$ $\forall i, j$

The mixed integer programming (MIP) based mathematical model for the integrated layout design problem is formulated based on [6], and shown below:

$$\text{Minimize TMHC} = \sum_{i=1}^{N} \sum_{j=1}^{N} c_{ij} f_{ij} d_{ij} + P \tag{1}$$

Subject to:

$$x_i' = x_i + (1 - u_i)w_i + u_i h_i \qquad \forall i \tag{2}$$

$$y_i' = y_i + (1 - u_i)h_i + u_i w_i \qquad \forall i \tag{3}$$

$$x_i^{I(O)} = x_i + (1 - u_i)(1 - v_i)I(O_i^x) + I(O_i^y)u_i(1 - v_i) + (w_i - I(O_i^x))(1 - u_i)v_i \\ + (h_i - I(O_i^y))u_i v_i \qquad \forall i \tag{4}$$

$$y_i^{I(O)} = y_i + (1 - u_i)(1 - v_i)I(O_i^y) + (w_i - I(O_i^x))u_i(1 - v_i) \\ + (h_i - I(O_i^y))(1 - u_i)v_i + I(O_i^x)u_i v_i \qquad \forall i \tag{5}$$

$$l_{ij} + l_{ji} + b_{ij} + b_{ji} \ge 1 \qquad \forall i \tag{6}$$

$$x_i' \le l_{ij} x_j + W(1 - l_{ij}) \qquad \forall i < j \tag{7}$$

$$y_i' \le b_{ij} y_j + H(1 - b_{ij}) \qquad \forall i < j \qquad (8)$$

$$x_i', y_i', x_i^{I(O)}, y_i^{I(O)} \ge 0 \qquad \forall i \qquad (9)$$

$$u_i, v_i \in \{0,1\} \qquad \forall i \qquad (10)$$

$$l_{ij}, b_{ij} \in \{0,1\} \qquad \forall i,j \qquad (11)$$

Where, $P = \alpha(P_w + P_h)$ is a penalty term the guarantee that the layout solution satisfies the following floor boundary condition

$$x_i' \le w \ \forall i, \ y_i' \le H \ \forall i, \ P_w = \max\left\{0, \max_i \left\{x_i'\right\} - W\right\}, P_h = \max\left\{0, \max_i \left\{y_i'\right\} - H\right\}, \text{ and } \alpha =$$

the weight of penalty and was set to be algebraic sum of flow interaction between each pair of departments.

Constraints (2) and (3) define the x-coordinate of the right boundary and the y-coordinate of the upper boundary of each department. Constraints (4) and (5) are used to specify the x and y coordinates of I/O stations for each department. These coordinates are expressed in generalized terms with respect to the lower-left corner point of the department under the horizontal configuration that is before considering rotation.

Constraints (6) (7) and (8) are to ensure that there is no overlap between any pair of departments by letting each pair of departments be separated in the x or y direction. Constraints (9) (10) and (11) specify the bounds for each variable.

3   Proposed Methodology

The flowchart shown in Fig. 1 is showing the search process of the proposed GA based meta heuristic using simulated annealing as local search tool (GASAA).

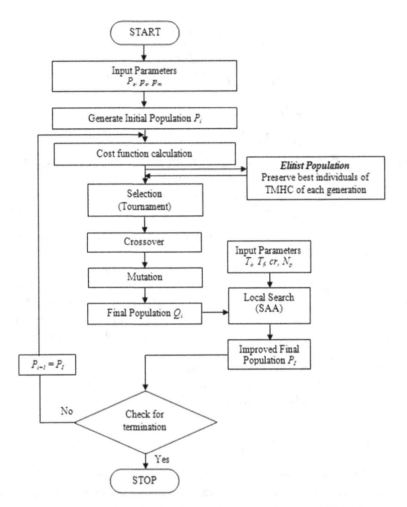

Fig. 1. The flowchart showing the search process of proposed GASAA

3.1   Solution Representation

In a GA approach feasible solutions to the problem are encoded into a string of decision choices that resemble chromosomes. The chromosome that represents a feasible solution is shown in Fig 2.

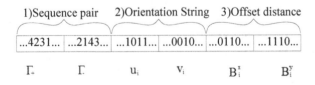

Fig. 2. Chromosome Structure

The chromosome string consists of three parts. For a layout problem of N departments, the first part is first and second sequence (Γ_+ and Γ_-) of sequence pair, the second part is binary code of $2N$ bits that represents u_i and v_i of each department, and the last part is $2N$ bytes which helps to define the offset distances in the x direction and y direction for each department.

3.1.1   Sequence Pair Representation

A cell system layout (CSL) can be represented by a unique sequence pair [10] describing the topology of the department placement. A layout consisting of departments (a,b,c). The dimensions for every departments are: $a(10 \times 5)$, $b(5\times5)$, $c(4\times8)$ and it's corresponding CSL is shown in Fig. 3 which can be represented by a $SP = (bac ; abc)$.

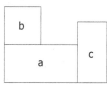

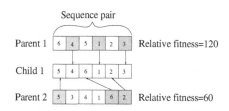

Fig. 3. CSL for $SP = (bac; abc)$

Fig. 4. Crossover operation on the first part $SP = (\Gamma_+, \Gamma_-)$

3.2   Fitness Evaluation

The decoding of a chromosome and finding the objective function value for a feasible solution is done in four steps.

Step 1: Finding the spatial coordinates of the each department
Using first and second part of the chromosome, and the sequence pair evaluation algorithm Algorthim1 found in the literature [11] the spatial coordinates of the lowest left corner of each department in a 2-D planar shop floor region is computed.

Step 2: Finding the spatial coordinates I/O stations
Once the spatial coordinates of each department is obtained, the algorithm is able to generate any CSL that has the topology defined by the corresponding sequence-pair. Then the spatial coordinates of I/O stations can be determined using constraints 4 and 5.

Step 3: Computing the optimal travel distance between the departments (d_{ij})
At first the grid graph [6] is constructed and then through repeated applications of Dijkstra's algorithm [12] the shortest path distance along the department perimeter is determined. The obtained shortest path distance d_{ij} along the department perimeter is unique for corresponding CSL.

Step 4: Objective function value calculation
TMHC is calculated based on the equation (1).

3.3   GASAA Operators

3.3.1   Selection

our initial pilot study reveals that tournament selection performs better than roulette wheel selection [13] approach. In tournament selection a number *Tour* of individuals is chosen randomly from the population and the best individual from this group is selected as parent. This process is repeated as often as individuals must be chosen. The parameter for tournament selection is the tournament size *Tour*. *Tour* =2 for this research work.

The Fitness value for this work is (F) = e $^{(-0.001*TMHC)}$ for 6 and 12 department problem and F = e $^{(-0.000001*TMHC)}$ for 7 and 20 department problem.

3.3.2   Crossover

For the first part, a crossover operator similar to [14] was implemented for first and second sequence of the sequence pair independently. The first child is constructed by randomly picking a gene from the first parent and placed it in a child string at the same location as its position in the parent sequence. This process is continued for *k* departments where *k* is proportional to the relative fitness of the first parent. The missing integers in the first child are filled in the same order as they appear in the second parent. Similarly the second child string is created by reversing the selection order of two strings. For the last two parts of a chromosome, a heterosexual one-point crossover [15] was adopted. An example of this crossover operator is shown in Fig. 4 and Fig. 5

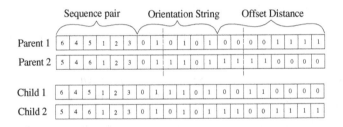

Fig. 5. Crossover operation on the second and third part

3.3.3   Mutation

For first and second sequence of the first part of the chromosome the mutation operator involves a random selection and swapping of two integers. For the second part, the mutation operator involves randomly altering one symbol to another. For the last part, the mutation operation involves replacing a randomly chosen byte with a new value generated at random with range of [0, 255]. An example of the three types of mutation operators is shown in Fig. 6

3.3.4   Neighborhood Generation

The neighborhood solution in the vicinity of current solution is generated by the mutation operation discussed in section 3.3.3.

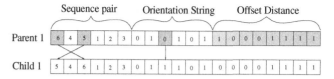

Fig. 6. Mutation operation on the first, second and third part of the chromosome

3.4 Control Parameters

The control parameter values for GASAA was determined based on pilot study which produces satisfactory output are summarized as below. For GA, Population size (P_s) = 5 ×N, Cross over probability (p_c) = 0.6, Mutation probability (p_m) = 0.20 was set as parameter values. For SAA, Initial Temperature (T_i) =3, Final Temperature (T_f) =0, Cooling Rate (cr)=0.85, Number of perturbation at each temperature drop (N_p)=10, and Number solution fed for local search=5% × P_s .was taken as initial parameters. Further to speed up the convergence process of proposed algorithm we incorporate an elitist strategy and its parameters are, Number of elitist preserved populations =1 (one for preserving best solutions of TMHC), Elitism Rate (R_e) = 20 percent of P_s (0.20 × P_s) and Exchange of information with the current generation = every 20 generations. Finally, Termination = stop after 100 generations.

4   Results and Discussion

The proposed genetic algorithm based procedure was coded in MATLAB and implemented in Dual core processor with 2GB RAM. Experiments were conducted using the bench mark problems found in the literature [9] and [16]. For each bench mark problem 10 different initial population set, each population set having 20 different initial solutions were generated at random. The final layout obtained by GASAA is reported in Fig 7. The total material handling cost (TMHC) obtained by GASAA is shown in Table 1. The average computational time taken by the algorithm to reach the optimal solution is given in Table 2.

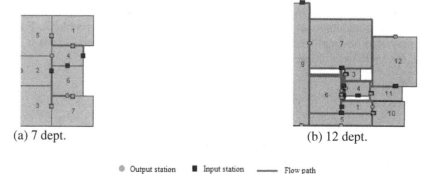

(a) 7 dept.   (b) 12 dept.

◉ Output station   ■ Input station   —— Flow path

Fig. 7. The final layouts obtained by GASAA

Table 1. TMHC obtained by GASAA

Test Problems	Measure Type	7 departments		12 departments	
		Upper Diagonal Flow matrix	Both the diagonal Flow matrix	Upper Diagonal Flow matrix	Both the diagonal Flow matrix
Welgama and Gibson [16]	CDM	-	-	-	5,903
Wu and Appleton [9]	PDM	-	1,30,000	-	-
Hu et al. [6]	PDM	-	1,22,598	5514	-
Proposed GASAA	PDM	-	1,15,331	-	5,983
Percentage improvement over [6]	-	-	5.93	-	-

Table 2. Average Computational time (s)

No of departments	7	12
Proposed GASAA	1750	17460

From the above tables it is evident that the proposed GASAA is performing well even for small to larger size problems reported in the literature.

5   Conclusion and Scope for Future Research

To overcome the limitations out of sequential design procedure in the Layout design process, in this research work an integrated design of inter-cell layout and flow path layout of MHS was adopted. Again, to optimize total material handling cost, a Genetic Algorithm based procedure is proposed in this work. The proposed algorithm was tested with two different problems of different problem sizes. It is found that the proposed algorithm is able to produce satisfactory solutions within an acceptable computational time limit.

A parallel population GA heuristic approach may be adopted for this problem to minimize the computational load involving in solving bigger size problems. Further study may also be employed to minimize the number bends (corners) exists in flow path of the MHS to facilitate smooth material transport.

References

1. Jajodia, S., Minis, I., Harhalakis, G., Proth, J.: CLASS: Computerized layout solution using simulated annealing. Int. J. Prod. Res. 30, 95–108 (1992)
2. Montreuil, B.: Integrated design of cell layout, input/output station configuration, and flow network of manufacturing systems. Research Memorandum No. 87± 9, School of Industrial Engineering, Purdue University (1987)

3. Montreuil, B., Ratliff, H.D.: Optimizing the location of input/output stations within facilities layout. Engineering Cost and Production Economics 14, 177–187 (1988)
4. Kim, J.G., Kim, Y.D.: A space partitioning method for facility layout problems with shape constraints. IIE Trans. 30, 947–957 (1998)
5. Norman, B.A., Arapoglu, R.A., Smith, A.E.: Integrated facilities design using a contour distance metric. IIE Trans. 33, 337–344 (2001)
6. Hu, G.H., Chen, Y.P., Zhou, Z.D., Fang, H.C.: A genetic algorithm for the inter-cell layout and material handling system design. Int. J. Adv. Manuf. Technol. 34, 1153–1163 (2007)
7. Aiello, G., Enea, M., Galante, G.: An integrated approach to the facilities and material handling system design. Int. J. Prod. Res. 40, 4007–4017 (2002)
8. Ho, Y.C., Moodie, C.L.: A hybrid approach for concurrent layout design of cells and their flow paths in a tree configuration. Int. J. Prod. Res. 38, 895–928 (2000)
9. Wu, Y., Appleton, E.: The optimization of block layout and aisle structure by a genetic algorithm. Comput. Indust. Eng. 41, 371–387 (2002)
10. Murata, H., Fujiyoshi, K., Kajitani, Y.: VLSI module placement based on rectangle-packing by the sequence-pair. IEEE Trans. CAD Integ. Circ. Syst. 15, 1518–1524 (1996)
11. Tang, X., Wong, D.F., Tian, R.: Fast Evaluation of Sequence Pair in Block Placement by Longest Common Subsequence Computation. In: Design, Automation and Test in Europe, p. 106 (2000)
12. Cormen, T.H., Leiserson, C.E., Rivest, R.L.: Introduction to algorithms. McGraw-Hill and MIT Press, New York (1990)
13. Goldberg, D.E.: Genetic algorithms in search, optimization, and machine learning. Addison-Wesley, USA (1989)
14. Kochhar, J.S., Foster, B.T., Heragu, S.S.: HOPE: A genetic algorithm for the unequal area facility layout problem. Comput. Oper. Res. 25, 583–594 (1998)
15. Poli, R., Langdon, W.B.: Genetic programming with one-point crossover. In: Second On-line World Conference on Soft Computing in Engineering Design and Manufacturing, pp. 23–27. Springer, London (1997)
16. Welgama, P.S., Gibson, P.R.: A construction algorithm for the machine layout problem with fixed pick-up and drop-off points. Int. J. Prod. Res. 11, 2575–2590 (1993)

Hot Corrosion Studies on Gas Tungsten Arc Welded AISI 304 and AISI 4140 Dissimilar Joints

Arivazhagan N.[1,*], Devendranath Ramkumar K.[1], Karthikeyan S.[2],
Manikandan M.[1], Narayanan S.[1], and Surendra S.[3]

[1] School of Mechanical and Building Sciences, VIT University, India 632 014
[2] CNBT, VIT University, India 632 014
[3] Department of Metallurgical and Materials Engineering,
Indian Institute of Technology Roorkee, India
narivazhagan@vit.ac.in

Abstract. Hot corrosion of Gas Tungsten Arc Welded (GTAW) AISI 304 and
AISI 4140 dissimilar weldment exposed in air as well as molten salt
environment of Na_2SO_4-60%V_2O_5 and K_2SO_4-60% NaCl are discussed. Weight
gain studies were done for composite specimens containing both weld metal
and heat-affected zone. The results indicated that the specimens were more
corroded in molten salt environment as compared to air oxidation. Also weld
interface of the samples showed more attack than base metals.

Keywords: Welding, Corrosion, Scanning electron microscopy microscopy.

1   Introduction

Dissimilar metals are widely used in critical high service temperature applications.
Hence studies on their weldments have gained importance in recent past. Generally,
combination of low alloy steel and austenitic stainless steel weldments are extensively
used for boiler tubing application at elevated temperatures because of its relatively
low cost, good weldability and creep resistance [1, 2]. In power plant engineering
applications it is necessary to join low alloyed ferritic steels to austenitic chromium-
nickel-molybdenum stainless steels. Primary boilers and heat exchangers operate at
high temperatures with corrosive environmental conditions that make low-alloy steels
and austenitic stainless steels the best choice [3].Primary boilers and heat exchangers
operate at high temperatures with corrosive environmental conditions that make low-
alloy steels and austenitic stainless steels the best choice [4]. The role played by
chlorides [5], which enter through ingressed air in marine atmospheres, is also
important in deciding the degree of corrosion. The role of NaCl in hot corrosion by
Na_2SO_4 has been discussed in detail [6, 7]. In this article, the effect of air as well as
mixture of Na_2SO_4-60%V_2O_5 and K_2SO_4-60% NaCl on hot corrosion behaviour of
GTA welded AISI 304 and AISI 4140 specimens are studied. Studies by the authors

---

[*] Corresponding author.

S.G. Ponnambalam et al. (Eds.): IRAM 2012, CCIS 330, pp. 436–441, 2012.

involving detailed metallurgical and mechanical properties of GTA welded samples are published elsewhere [4].

2 Experimental Procedure

To facilitate the hot corrosion tests, the samples are cut into rectangular pieces (20 × 15 × 5 mm with weld zone in the middle of the specimens and mirror polished. Immediately, a coating of uniform thickness with 3–5 mg/cm^2 of salt mixture was applied on the preheated sample (250 °C). On these specimens, cyclic studies were performed in the air as well as molten salt (Na_2SO_4-60%V_2O_5 and K_2SO_4-60% NaCl) for exactly 50 cycles and the duration of each cycle is for 1 h 20 mins in which heating is for one hour at 650 °C in a silicon carbide tube furnace followed by 20 mins of cooling at room temperature. During the corrosion tests, the weight change measurements were taken at the end of each cycle. The spalled scale was also retained during the measurement of the weight change to determine the total rate of corrosion. The samples after corrosion tests are subjected to characterization studies using SEM/EDAX, XRD and EPMA for surface and cross-sectional analysis of the scale.

3 Results and Discussion

Metals and alloys undergo oxidation when exposed at elevated temperatures in air which may be may be protective or non-protective. Whereas the metals exposed in molten salt environment could accelerate the corrosion rate due to combined form of oxidation chloridation and sulphidation. The macrographs for hot corroded samples dictate that the weld interface is more prone to hot corrosion (Fig 1.). Fig 2 shows the plot of weight gain per unit area vs. function of time (number of cycles). These figures indicate that the weight gain kinetics under air oxidation shows a steady-state parabolic rate law, whereas the molten salt environment is a multi stage weight-gain growth rate.

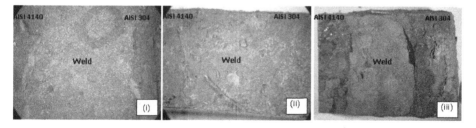

Fig. 1. Macrographs dissimilar TIG Welded AISI 4140 and AISI 304 subjected to cyclic hot corrosion at 650 °C. (i) Air oxidation, (ii) Na_2SO_4 + V_2O_5 (60%) and (iii) K_2SO_4-60% NaCl after 50 cycles.

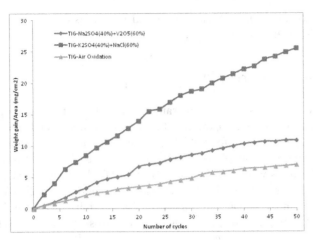

Fig. 2. Plots of cumulative weight gain (mg/cm2) as a function of time (number of cycles)

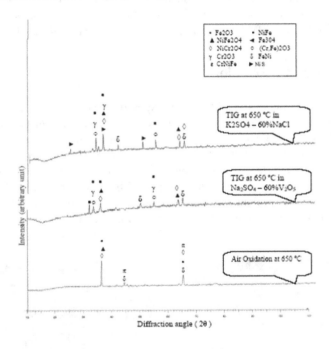

Fig. 3. X-Ray diffraction patterns for hot corroded dissimilar TIG weldment of AISI 4140 and AISI 304 exposed in air, $Na_2SO_4 + V_2O_5$ (60%) and K2SO4 + NaCl (60%) at 650 °C for 50 cycles.

The parabolic rate constants Kp for wledment after exposed in air oxidation, Na2SO4-60% V2O5 and K2SO4-60% NaCl were 2.96, 7.72 and 37.85 ×10 -6 (g^2 cm$^-$ ^{4} s $^{-1}$) respectively (Fig 3). It is noted that, the hot corrosion in molten salt environment was observed to be more extensive. Moreover, higher corrosion rate is observed during initial hours of study and is mainly attributed to the rapid oxygen pick up by diffusion of oxygen through the molten salt layer and is found to be identical to the results reported by Sidhu and Prakash [8], Tiwari and Prakash [9] during their hot corrosion studies. As revealed by XRD, different phases of various reaction products were formed on the weldments after corrosion cycles. Air oxidation at 650 °C, Fe_2O_3 has been predominated with small amount of $NiCr_2O_4$, NiO and FeNi. Hot corrosion under molten salt environment at 650 °C shows that Fe_2O_3 and Cr_2O_3 as the predominant phases and $NiCr_2O_4$, $(Cr, Fe)_2O_3$, FeNi and FeS are observed with low intensity. Many researchers have pointed out that the formation of sodium chromate (Na_2CrO_4) could result from oxy-chloridation even the temperature is lower than the melting point of salt deposits [10-12]. As Na_2CrO_4 is formed, the salt will wet the specimen surface which eventually leads to a mechanism of hot corrosion dominated by molten salt and is further validated by XRD analysis (Fig 3). The analysis of the scale shows predominant Fe_2O_3 with low intensities of Cr_2O_3, Na_2CrO_4, SO_3 and MoO_3. This is in confirmation with past studies on the hot corrosion studies in molten salt environment on boiler tube steel [13].

SEM/EDAX analysis of the corroded sample shows, Fe_2O_3 in the scales of weldment after the corrosion cycles signifies non-protective conditions in Na_2SO_4-60%V_2O_5 and K_2SO_4-60% NaCl at 650 °C (Fig 4-6). Corrosion morphology of the weldment exposed in K2SO4-60% NaCl shows that the weld interface is more prone to formation of fragile scale than base metals. This implies that NaCl plays a vital role in hot corrosion [14-16]. It is observed that, the corrosion rate in K_2SO_4-60% NaCl environment is higher in magnitude as compared to Na_2SO_4-60%V_2O_5 and air oxidation environments.

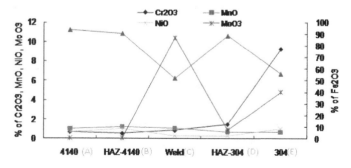

Fig. 4. SEM/EDAX shows the GTAW weldment of AISI 4140 and AISI 304 exposed in $Na_2SO_4 + V_2O_5$ (60%) at 650 °C after 50 cycles

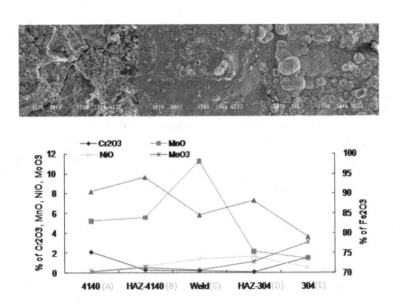

Fig. 5. SEM/EDAX shows the GTAW weldment of AISI 4140 and AISI 304 exposed in K_2SO_4 + NaCl (60%) at 650 °C after 50 cycles

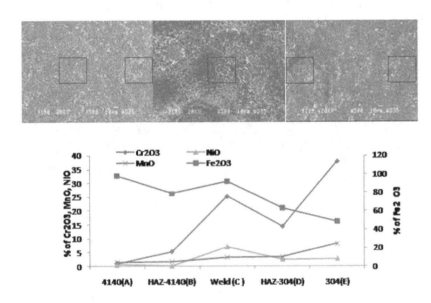

Fig. 6. SEM/EDAX shows the GTAW weldment of AISI 4140 and AISI 304 exposed in air at 650 °C after 50 cycles

4   Conclusion

The corrosion rates for the investigated electron beam welded dissimilar metals based on the overall weight gains after 50 cycles in all the environments could be arranged in the following order: K_2SO_4-60% NaCl > Na_2SO_4-60%V_2O_5 > Air.

Dissimilar weldment suffered accelerated hot corrosion in the chloride mixed molten salt environment in the form of intense spalling and sputtering of its scale.

References

1. Hasçalik, A., Ünal, E., Özdemir, N.: Fatigue behaviour of AISI 304 steel to AISI 4340 steel welded by friction welding. Journal of Materials Science 41, 3233–3239 (2006)
2. Wyatt, L.M.: Materials of construction for steam power plants, London, vol. 182, p. 5 ISBN 085334 661
3. Taktak, S.: Some mechanical properties of borided AISI H13 and 304 steels. Materials & Design 28(6), 1836–1843 (2007)
4. Arivazhagan, N., Singh, S., Prakash, S., Reddy, G.M.: Investigation on AISI 304 Austenitic Stainless Steel to AISI 4140 Low Alloy Steel Dissimilar Joints by Gas Tungsten Arc, Electron Beam and Friction Welding. Materials and Design 32, 3036–3050 (2011)
5. Ahila, S., Ramaktishna Iyer, S., Radlmkrishnan, V.M., Prasad, P.B.S.N.V.: A comparative study of hot corrosion of welded and unwelded 2.25 Cr- 1 MO steel. Mater & Letters 16, 130–133 (1993)
6. Arivazhagan, N., Narayanan, S., Singh, S., Prakash, S., Reddy, G.M.: High temperature corrosion studies on friction welded low alloy steel and stainless steel in air and molten salt environment at 650°C. Materials and Design 34, 459–468 (2012)
7. Arivazhagan, N., Singh, S., Prakash, S., Reddy, G.M.: Hot Corrosion Studies on Dissimilar Friction Welded Low Alloy Steel and Austenitic Stainless Steel under Chlorine-Containing Salt Deposits under Cyclic Conditions. Corrosion Engineering Science and Technology 44 (2009)
8. Sidhu, B.S., Prakash, S.: Evaluation of the corrosion behaviour of plasma-sprayed Ni3Al coatings on steel in oxidation and molten salt environments at 900 °C. Surface and Coating Technology 166, 89 (2003)
9. Tiwari, S.N., Prakash, S.: Symposium on localised corrosion and environmental cracking, Kalpakkam (India), p. 33 (1997)
10. Wang, C.J., He, T.T.: Morphological development of subscale formation in Fe–Cr–(Ni) alloys with chloride and sulfates coating. Oxidation of Metals 58, 415 (2002)
11. Hossain, M.K., Saunders, S.R.J.: A microstructural study of the influence of NaCl vapor on the oxidation of a Ni-Cr-Al alloy at 850°C. Oxidation of Metals 12, 1 (1978)
12. Hiramatsu, N., Uematsu, Y., Tanaka, T., Kinugasa, M.: Effects of alloying elements on NaCl-induced hot corrosion of stainless steels. Materials Science and Engineering A 120, 319 (1989)
13. Uusitalo, M.A., Vuoristo, P.M.J., Maantyla, T.A.: High temperature corrosion of coatings and boiler steels below chlorine-containing salt deposits. Corrosion Science 46, 1311–1331 (2004)
14. Seybolt, A.U.: Oxidation of Ni-20 Cr alloy and stainless steels in the presence of chlorides. Oxidation of Metals 2, 119 (1970)
15. Seybolt, A.U.: Internal oxidation in heat-resisting stainless steels caused by presence of halides. Oxidation of Metals 2, 161 (1970)
16. Shinata, Y., Fujio, T., Kokichi, H.: NaCl-induced hot corrosion of stainless steels. Materials Science and Engineering 87, 399–405 (1987)

A Comparative Study of Oxidation and Hot Corrosion of Electron Beam Welded Low Alloy Steel and Stainless Steel in Different Corrosive Environments

Arivazhagan N.[1,*], Devendranath Ramkumar K.[1], Karthikeyan S.[2], Manikandan M[1], Narayanan S.[1], and Surendra S.[3]

[1] School of Mechanical and Building Sciences, VIT University, India 632 014
[2] CNBT, VIT University, India 632 014
[3] Department of Metallurgical and Materials Engineering,
Indian Institute of Technology Roorkee, India
narivazhagan@vit.ac.in

Abstract. This paper reports on the performance of Electron Beam Welded (EBW) low alloy steel AISI 4140 and stainless steel AISI 304 in air as well as molten salt environments of Na_2SO_4-60%V_2O_5 and K_2SO_4-60% NaCl at 650°C. The corrosion kinetics has been established by thermo-gravimetric technique during the initial stages. In this work, X-ray diffraction, scanning electron microscopy/energy-dispersive analysis and electron probe micro analysis techniques were used to analyze the corrosion products. It is well observed from the experimental results that the weldments suffered accelerated corrosion in K_2SO_4-NaCl environment and showed spalling/sputtering of the oxide scale. Furthermore, corrosion resistance of weld interface was found to be lower than that of parent metals in molten salt environment. It is also inferred from the results that NaCl is the one of the main corrosive species in hot corrosion, involving mixtures of K_2SO_4-NaCl and which is responsible for internal corrosion attack.

Keywords: Electron beam Welding, Hot corrosion, Scanning electron microscopy.

1   Introduction

This Dissimilar metals are widely used in critical high service temperature applications. Hence the studies on their weldments have gained importance in recent past. Generally, the combination of low alloy steel and austenitic stainless steel weldments are extensively used for boiler tubing application at elevated temperatures because of its relatively low cost, good weldability and creep resistance [1]. In power plant engineering applications, it is necessary to join low alloyed ferritic steels to austenitic chromium-nickel-molybdenum stainless steels. Primary boilers and heat exchangers operate at high temperatures with corrosive environmental conditions that

---

[*] Corresponding author.

S.G. Ponnambalam et al. (Eds.): IRAM 2012, CCIS 330, pp. 442–449, 2012.

make low-alloy steels, austenitic stainless steels and their combinations the best choice [2]. Since these steels exhibit vastly different physical, thermal, mechanical and metallurgical characteristics, they are prone to defects during welding as well as in service environment [3]. Ferritic and austenitic stainless steel transition joint failure is a perennial problem in fossil-fired steam plants [4]. Particularly, the failure of dissimilar weldments involving low-alloy steel with austenitic stainless steel has been studied by a number of investigators and factors that contribute to failure have been seldom taken up for research. Advanced welding process like electron beam welding can offer a solution to the problem of sensitization, dilution and cracking of elements in conventional welding. Even though electron beam welding is a comparable alternative, the problem of carbide formation is not yet completely eliminated for the joints when they are exposed to cyclic high temperature service conditions.

Usually, low-grade fuels with high concentrations of sulfur, vanadium and sodium are used in oil- and coal fired power generation. During combustion, alkali metal sulfates and V_2O_5 vapors combine with other ash constituents that deposit onto the component surfaces. The boilers exposed in off-shore industrial rigs undergo hot corrosion when the sodium chloride from the ocean breeze mixes with Na_2SO_4 from the fuel and deposits on the hot-section of the components. This results in severe corrosion attack by oxidation, sulfidation, chloridation and even hot corrosion [5].

It is to be noted that hot corrosion is the serious problem for the weldments exposed to environment containing mixture of the salt K_2SO_4 -NaCl and Na_2SO_4-V_2O_5. The existence of such corrosive condensation layer on the surface leads to hot corrosion which can considerably reduce the service life of high temperature components [6]. Hot corrosion induced by mixtures of $NaCl/K_2SO_4$ has been generally focused on Ni and Co base super alloys and Ni–Cr alloys which are used in turbine engines. It has been reported that severe hot corrosion attack is observed with mixtures of NaCl and K_2SO_4 [7].

The steel's performance in oxidizing environments is well established, but weldment behavior in corrosive environments, particularly those containing sulfidizing and chlorides have not been studied extensively. The eutectic mixture of Na_2SO_4-60% V_2O_5 and K_2SO_4-60% NaCl with a low melting point of 550 °C and 507 °C respectively provides a very aggressive environment for hot corrosion [8]. A cyclic regime of 50 cycles (cycle of 1 h heating and 20 min cooling) is considered adequate for steady-state oxidation studies involving steel [9] as it provides the severe conditions for testing. These conditions correspond to the actual industrial environment where breakdown/shutdown occurs frequently.

In the present investigation, an attempt has been made to evaluate the hot corrosion behavior of electron beam welded AISI 304 and AISI 4140 metals exposed in air as well as molten salt environment consisting of eutectic mixture of Na_2SO_4-60% V_2O_5 and K_2SO_4-60% NaCl at 650 °C under cyclic conditions. Thermogravimetric technique was used to establish the kinetics of corrosion. The products of hot corrosion studies have been analyzed using X-Ray Diffraction (XRD), Scanning Electron Microscope (SEM), Energy Dispersive X-Ray studies (EDAX) and Electron Probe Micro Analyzer (EPMA) techniques.

2   Experimental Procedure

2.1   Electron Beam Welding

In this study, experiments were carried out on a Low KV electron beam welding machine. The chemical compositions of parent metals employed in this study are presented in Table 1 and the welded specimen and its cross sectional macro structure are depicted in Fig 1. Studies by the authors involving detailed metallurgical and mechanical properties of electron beam welded samples are published elsewhere [18].

Table 1. Chemical composition of AISI 304 and AISI 4140

Parent Metal	C	Cr	Mn	Ni	Si	Mo	Fe
AISI 304	0.06	18.4	1.38	8.17	0.32	----	Balance
AISI 4140	0.40	1.1	0.75	----	0.31	0.28	Balance

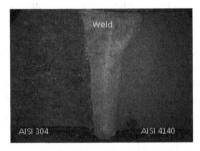

Fig. 1. Macro structure of electron beam welded AISI 4140 and AISI 304 dissimilar metals

2.2   Hot Corrosion Test

Specimens for hot corrosion tests are fabricated using electron beam welding machine. These specimens are initially having the dimensions of 100×50×6 mm. To facilitate the hot corrosion tests, the samples are cut into rectangular pieces (20 × 15 × 6 mm) with weld zone in the middle of the specimens. Mirror polishing down to 1 μm by alumina on a cloth polishing wheel is carried out before the corrosion run. Immediately, a coating of uniform thickness with 3–5 mg/cm^2 of salt mixture was applied with a camel hair brush on the preheated sample (250 °C). Cyclic hot corrosion studies were performed on these specimens by subjecting in the air as well as molten salt (Na_2SO_4-60% V_2O_5 and K_2SO_4-60% NaCl) environments for exactly 50 cycles and the duration of each cycle is for 1 h 20 mins in which heating is for one hour at 650 °C in a silicon carbide tube furnace followed by 20 mins of cooling at room temperature. During the corrosion tests, the weight change measurements were taken at the end of each cycle. The samples after corrosion tests are subjected to characterization studies using SEM/EDAX and XRD analysis.

3   Results

The corrosion kinetics of specimens with and without molten salt deposits is depicted in Fig 2 as a plot of weight gain per unit area vs. function of time (number of cycles). These figures indicate that the weight gain kinetics under air oxidation shows a steady-state parabolic rate law, whereas the molten salt environment is a multi stage weight-gain growth rate. The weight gain square (mg^2/cm^4) vs time (number of cycles) plots are shown in Fig 3 to establish the rate law for the hot corrosion. It is observed from the graph that all the specimens follow nearly parabolic rate law. The parabolic rate constant, K_p, was calculated by a linear least-square algorithm to a function in the form of $(W/A)^2 = K_p t$, where W/A is the weight gain per unit surface area (mg/cm^2) and t indicates the number of cycles representing the time of exposure. XRD analysis has been performed on the weldments before as well as after corrosion run and is shown in Fig 3. Investigations showed that the phases such as FeNi and

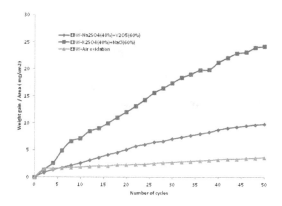

Fig. 2. Plots of cumulative weight gain (mg/cm2) as a function of time (number of cycles)

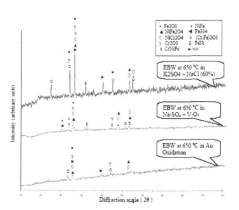

Fig. 3. X-Ray diffraction patterns for hot corroded dissimilar EBW weldment of AISI 4140 and AISI 304 exposed at 650 °C

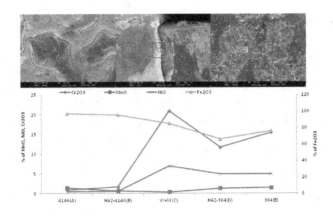

Fig. 4. SEM/EDAX graph shows the EBW weldment of AISI 4140 and AISI 304 exposed at 650 °C in air oxidation after 50 cycles

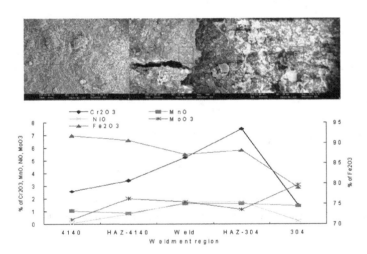

Fig. 5. SEM/EDAX graph shows the EBW weldment of AISI 4140 and AISI 304 exposed at 650 °C under K2SO4 + NaCl (60%) after 50 cycles

Ni_3C, Cr-NiMo, CrNiFe, Ni_3C, and Cr-Si-C are observed in the as-welded samples. Fe_2O_3 has been predominated with lower intensities of $NiCr_2O_4$, NiO and FeNi in the air oxidation samples at 650°C. Whereas Fe_2O_3 and Cr_2O_3 dominate with greater peak intensities with a lesser intensities of $(Cr, Fe)_2O_3$, FeNi and FeS on the hot corroded samples under molten salt environment at 650°C. SEM Surface morphology of dissimilar weldment after hot corrosion treatment by keeping 650°C is shown in Fig 4-6. EDAX analysis for the weldment after air oxidation as well as molten salt environment [Na_2SO_4-60% V_2O_5 and K_2SO_4-60% NaCl] shows Fe_2O_3 to be the predominant phase in the entire region. However Cr_2O_3 content is higher in the scale of heat affected zone of AISI 304. Moreover some minor constituents of MoO_3, MnO and NiO were observed on the weldment as seen in Fig 4-6.

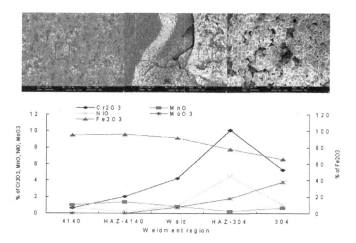

Fig. 6. SEM/EDAX graph shows the EBW weldment of AISI 4140 and AISI 304 exposed at 650 °C under $Na_2SO_4 + V_2O_5$ (60%) after 50 cycles

4   Discussions

The results obtained in air oxidation at 650°C show a better corrosion resistance as compared to molten salt environment. The authors reported the detailed study of the mechanical properties of AISI 4140 and AISI 304 dissimilar metals made by electron beam welding process in their earlier publication [10].

Thermo-gravimetric curve of molten salt environment studies shows the tendency of multi stage weight-gain growth rate (Fig. 2). It could be due to changes in reaction rate which are associated with the formation of a laminated inner-oxide layer made up of fine and coarse grain spinel oxide as suggested by Hurdus et al [11]. The kinetics of hot corrosion with K_2SO_4-NaCl mixtures shows rapid weight gain compared to Na_2SO_4-V_2O_5 as well as air oxidation. In a molten salt environment, sulfur was incorporated into scale and leads to a sulfide formation in the alloy substrate. Therefore, as the formation of protective oxide scale was inhibited by the presence of NaCl, chlorides and sulfides tend to form in the alloy substrate as indicated leading to the propagation of hot corrosion as suggested by Charng et al., [12]. The parabolic rate constants K_p for weldment after exposed in air oxidation, Na_2SO_4-60% V_2O_5 and K_2SO_4-60% NaCl were 0.652, 5.917 and 35.511 ×10^{-6} (g^2 $cm^{-4}s^{-1}$) respectively (Fig 3).

SEM/EDAX analysis of the corroded sample shows, Fe_2O_3 in the scales of weldment after the corrosion cycles signifies non-protective conditions in Na_2SO_4-60% V_2O_5 and K_2SO_4-60% NaCl at 650 °C (Fig 4-6). The formation of Fe_2O_3 in the spalled scale has also been reported to be non-protective during their hot corrosion study on Fe_3Al-based iron aluminides in Na_2SO_4 atmosphere [13, 14]. The corrosion rate of the weldment in Na_2SO_4-60% V_2O_5 is higher as compared to air oxidation at 650 C° due to the formation $NaVO_3$ as proposed by Kolta et al., [15]. As $NaVO_3$ acts like a catalyst and also serves as an oxygen carrier to the base alloy, it tends to oxidize the basic elements rapidly. Furthermore, the increase in magnitude of weight gain is due to the accelerated corrosion in K_2SO_4-60% NaCl environment which also opined by Kofstad [16]. It is widely agreed that the corrosion rate will be more severe when the temperature is higher than the melting point of salt deposits. It is observed that the corrosion rate in K_2SO_4-60% NaCl environment is higher in magnitude as compared to Na_2SO_4-60% V_2O_5 and air oxidation environments.

It is observed that the thickness of scale is more on 4140 side than 304 side after exposed in Na_2SO_4-60% V_2O_5 environment. After the hot corrosion treatment, it is observed that the effect of hot corrosion is more on 4140 side as evident from the degree of scaling and spalling of scale. It is observed that the scales get detached by means of the formation of new scale within already growing scale. This is usually attributed to the two-way flow of the reactants [17].

At the end of corrosion tests, it is noticed that the weld interface of the dissimilar weldment is more degraded as compared to base metals (Fig 4-6). Corrosion morphology of the weldment exposed in K_2SO_4-60% NaCl shows that the weld interface is more prone to formation of fragile scale than base metals. This implies that NaCl plays a vital role in hot corrosion [18]. Moreover the melting of K_2SO_4-60% NaCl mixture at 650 °C makes the weldments susceptible to accelerated oxidation due to acidic and basic-fluxing mechanism. Many researchers have pointed out that the formation of sodium chromate (Na_2CrO_4) could result from oxy-chloridation even the temperature is lower than the melting point of salt deposits [19]. As Na_2CrO_4 is formed, the salt will wet the specimen surface which eventually leads to a mechanism of hot corrosion dominated by molten salt and is further validated by XRD analysis (Fig 3). The analysis of the scale shows predominant Fe_2O_3 with low intensities of Cr_2O_3, Na_2CrO_4, SO_3 and MoO_3. This is in confirmation with past studies on the hot corrosion studies in molten salt environment on boiler tube steel [19].

5   Conclusion

From the experimental studies, some of the important conclusions obtained are as follows.

a) The weight gain of salt coated welded specimen follows a parabolic rate law during hot corrosion. Rate of oxidation was observed to be higher in the earlier cycles of the study in all the aforementioned environments, which may be attributed to the fact that during transient period of oxidation, the scales formed may be providing protection to the underneath metals.

b) In case of salt coated specimens, the surface scale is more porous and spalled out, thereby providing an easy diffusion path for the corrodents. The scale formed due to hot corrosion mainly contains Fe_2O_3 and Cr_2O_3, $NiCr_2O_4$ and $NiFe_2O_4$.

c) The corrosion rates for the investigated electron beam welded dissimilar metals based on the overall weight gains after 50 cycles in all the environments could be arranged in the following order: K_2SO_4-60% NaCl > Na_2SO_4-60% V_2O_5 > Air

d) The cracking of oxide scale might be attributed to different composition of base metals, weldments and oxide formed. Their thermal expansion coefficients are not exactly equal, which inevitably results in thermal-stresses.

References

1. Hasçalik, A., Ünal, E., Özdemir, N.: Fatigue behaviour of AISI 304 steel to AISI 4340 steel welded by friction welding. Journal of Materials Science 41, 3233–3239 (2006)
2. Taktak, S.: Some mechanical properties of borided AISI H13 and 304 steels. Materials & Design 28(6), 1836–1843 (2007)
3. Celik, S., Ersozlu, I.: Investigation of the mechanical properties and microstructure of friction welded joints between AISI 4140 and AISI 1050 steels. Materials & Design 30(4), 970–976 (2009)
4. Singh Raman, R.K., Muddle, B.C.: High temperature oxidation in the context of life assessment and microstructural degradation of weldments of 2.25Cr–1Mo steel. International Journal of Pressure Vessels and Piping 79, 585–590 (2002)
5. Lai, G.Y.: High-temperature corrosion of engineering alloys. American Society for Metals, Metals Park 154 (1990)
6. Zheng, L., Maicang, Z., Jianxin, D.: Hot corrosion behavior of powder metallurgy Rene95 nickel-based superalloy in molten $NaCl–Na_2SO_4$ salts. Materials & Design 32(4), 1981–1989 (2011)
7. Johnson, D.M., Whittle, D.P., Stringer, J.: Mechanisms of Na_2SO_4-induced accelerated oxidation. Corrosion Science 15, 649 (1975)
8. Tiwari, S.N.: Investigations on Hot Corrosion of Some Fe-, Ni- and Co-base Superalloy in Na_2SO_4 -V_2O_5 Environment under cyclic conditions. PhD Thesis, Met. & Mat. Engg. Deptt, UOR, Roorkee, India (1997)
9. Wood, G.C., Hodgkiss, T.: Mechanism of oxidation of dilute nickel-chromium alloys. Nature 211, 1358–1361 (1996)
10. Arivazhagan, N., Surendra, S., Prakash, S., Reddy, G.M.: Investigation on AISI 304 austenitic stainless steel to AISI 4140 low alloy steel dissimilar joints by gas tungsten arc, electron beam and friction welding. Materials & Design 32, 3036–3050 (2011)
11. Hurdus, M.H., Tomlinson, L., Tichmarsh, J.M.: Observation of oscillating reaction rates during the isothermal oxidation of ferritic steels. Oxidation of Metals 34, 5 (1990)
12. Tsaur, C.-C., Rock, J.C., Wang, C.-J., Su, Y.-H.: The hot corrosion of 310 stainless steel with pre-coated $NaCl/Na_2SO_4$ mixtures at 750°C. Materials Chemistry and Physics 89, 445–453 (2005)
13. Das, D., Balasubramaniam, R., Mungole, M.N.: Hot corrosion of carbon-alloyed Fe3Al-based iron aluminides. Material Science and Engineering A 338, 24 (2002)
14. Sidhu, B.S., Prakash, S.: Evaluation of the corrosion behaviour of plasma-sprayed Ni3Al coatings on steel in oxidation and molten salt environments at 900 °C. Surface and Coating Technology 166, 89 (2003)
15. Kolta, G.A., Hewaidy, L.F., Felix, N.S.: Reactions between sodium sulphate and vanadium pentoxide. Thermochimica Acta 4, 151–164 (1972)
16. Kofstad, P.: High temperature corrosion, p. 425. Elsevier Applied Science, London (1988)
17. Atkinson, A.: Conditions for the formation of new oxide within oxide films growing on metals. Corrosion Science 22, 347 (1982)
18. Seybolt, A.U.: Oxidation of Ni-20 Cr alloy and stainless steels in the presence of chlorides. Oxidation of Metals 2, 119 (1970)
19. Wang, C.J., He, T.T.: Morphological development of subscale formation in Fe–Cr–(Ni) alloys with chloride and sulfates coating. Oxidation of Metals 58, 415 (2002)

Hot Corrosion Behavior of Dissimilar GTA Welded Monel 400 and AISI 304

K. Devendranath Ramkumar[*], N. Arivazhagan, S. Narayanan, and S. Karthikeyan

School of Mechanical & Building Sciences, VIT University, Vellore - 632014
deva@vit.ac.in

Abstract. This research work reports on the weldability, microstructure, mechanical and hot corrosion properties of manual Gas Tungsten Arc Welded (GTAW) dissimilar combinations of Monel 400 and AISI 304 stainless steel using ENiCrFe-3 filler metal. Bimetallic combinations of Monel 400 and AISI 304 have been characterized by microstructure examination. Mechanical properties include hardness and tensile strength of the weldment has been estimated for the aforementioned filler wire. Further hot corrosion studies have been carried out on the various zones of the weldment by subjecting to cyclic air oxidation and K_2SO_4 + NaCl (60%) molten salt environment at 600 °C. The corrosion products are systematically characterized using surface analytical techniques. It is a clear indication from the results that the weld region is susceptible to more corrosion in air as well as in the molten salt environment as compared to other regions of the weldment.

Keywords: Monel 400, AISI 304, Gas Tungsten Arc Welding, ENiCrFe-3, Hot Corrosion.

1   Introduction

Welding of dissimilar metals is really cumbersome and challenging task because of the differences existing in the coefficient of thermal expansion, thermal conductivity and the chemical composition existing between two metals. It is also difficult to examine the microstructure of dissimilar weldment as the preparation itself is tedious. The foremost problems encountering during dissimilar welding include elemental migration, micro-segregation, secondary phase formation and the occurrence of hot cracks [1-5]. So it is mandatory to select a suitable filler material to overcome or minimize these problems; however it is also difficult that no single filler metal would be suitable to solve all the problems. Bimetallic combinations of Monel 400 and AISI 304 are used widely in the heat exchangers, super heaters employed in the oil gasification plants and chemical processing equipments. These combinations are usually prone to hot corrosion as these plants are operated at high temperatures.

The typical applications of the bimetallic welding of Monel - Stainless steel and Monel - low carbon steel have been reported by the researchers [2, 3]. Sadek et al. [3]

---

[*] Corresponding author.

S.G. Ponnambalam et al. (Eds.): IRAM 2012, CCIS 330, pp. 450–457, 2012.

reported that the combination of Monel 400 and low carbon steel are employed in the oil gasification plants where they are exposed under corrosive medium of H_2S, SO_2 and SO_3. Also it was reported that the sound weld can be obtained using ENiCrFe-3 for welding Monel 400 and low carbon steel and the problem of sensitization could be minimized on using ENiCrFe-3 filler wire. Hence the choice of filler materials for dissimilar welding of the samples was based on the properties of toughness, thermal fatigue resistance and resistance to hot cracking tendency.

Low-grade fuels with high concentrations of sulphur, potassium and sodium are used in oil and coal fired power generation. During combustion, alkali metal sulphate vapors combine with other ash constituents that deposit onto the component surfaces. Similarly, the boilers exposed in off-shore industrial rigs undergo hot corrosion when the sodium chloride from the ocean breeze mixes with K_2SO_4 from the fuel. This forms the molten deposits on the hot-section of the metal surface through condensation due to volatile compounds present in the gas stream. These deposits produce aggressive conditions leading to rigorous corrosion of the weldment due to oxidation, sulfidation, chloridation [4, 6]. The influence of individual KCl, NaCl and their mixtures with heavy metal chlorides or sulfates on the corrosion behaviour of a series of alloy systems has been studied in detail by Li et al. [7]. However limited work has been reported in the joining of dissimilar combinations of Monel 400 and AISI 304 hitherto. The present study investigates the weldability, micro-structure, mechanical and hot corrosion properties of GTA welded samples. In order to access the corrosion behaviour, these weldments are subjected to air oxidation and molten salt environment of K_2SO_4 + NaCl (60%) at 600 °C. The corrosion products were revealed using the combined techniques of optical microscopy, X-ray Diffraction (XRD), Scanning Electron Microscopy/Energy Dispersive X-ray Analysis (SEM/EDAX).

2   Experimental

2.1   Base Metals and Welding Procedure

The base metals were sliced using Electric Discharge Machining (EDM) - wire cut process to have the dimensions of 100 x 50 x 6 mm. The chemical composition of the base metals and the filler wire employed is given in Table 1. A standard Butt configuration with V-groove is employed for welding of these samples using Manual Gas Tungsten Arc Welding process (GTAW). Three passes of welding has been carried out and the weld parameters such as 10 V and 130 A with the argon pressure of 10-13 psi.

Table 1. Chemical Composition of the base and filler metals

Base / Filler Metal	Composition, Wt%									
	Ni	Cu	C	Si	Mn	Fe	S	P	Cr	Others
Monel 400	65.38	Bal	0.10	0.40	1.07	2.11	Nil	Nil	Nil	Nil
AISI 304	8.13	Nil	0.045	0.39	1.64	Bal	0.006	0.022	18.01	Nil
ENiCrFe-3	61.2	0.5	0.05	0.8	5.5	10.5	0.015	0.03	Bal	0.8 (Al)
										1.5 (Nb)
										0.68 (Mo)

2.2   Weldment Characterization

The welded samples were tested for any surface defects using X-Ray radiography methods. Macro and Microstructure examination was carried out on the various zones of the weldment. Standard metallographic procedures have been adopted for carrying out the microstructure investigation. Micro-structure of parent metal, heat affected zone (HAZ) of Monel 400 side and the weld region is examined using Marble's reagent, on the other hand, electrolytic etching (10% Oxalic Acid – 6 V DC supply; Current density of 1 A/cm^2) is being carried out to reveal the microstructure on the parent, heat affected zone of AISI 304 side. Micro-hardness test has been conducted on the composite region [Parent metal + HAZ + weld] using Vicker's micro-hardness tester keeping weld as the center. Three trials of tensile studies were carried out on the weldments prepared as per the ASTM E8 standards using Electronic tensometer to estimate the strength of the dissimilar weldment.

2.3   Cyclic Hot Corrosion

Dissimilar welded sample is sized to coupons of different dimensions to conduct hot corrosion studies. These corrosion studies were performed on the different regions of dissimilar welded samples of Monel 400 and AISI 304 each measuring 20 x 5 x 6 mm; also on the composite region [Base Metal + HAZ + Weld] measuring 20 x 15 x 6 mm to estimate the corrosion behaviour for 50 cycles (each cycle consists of 1 hour heating followed by 20 minutes of cooling to room temperature) at 600°C. Before corrosion, these samples were polished down to 1 μm finish. Cyclic hot corrosion studies were performed on the different zones of the welded samples exposed under air oxidation and molten salt environment of K_2SO_4 + NaCl (60%) mixture at 600°C. A coating of uniform thickness with 3 to 5 mg/cm^2 of K_2SO_4 + NaCl (60%) was applied using a fine camel hair-brush on the samples. The salt coated samples were first heated and dried at 200 °C in the oven and continued the corrosion run for 50 cycles. The weight changes have been measured for all regions for each cycle using electronic weighing balance with a sensitivity of 1 mg. Weight gain or loss of the spalled scale is also included at the time of measurement to determine the rate of corrosion.

3   Results

3.1   Macro and Micro-structure of the Weldment

Macrographs for longitudinal cut sections for the welds are presented in Fig. 1. Macro-photograph of the dissimilar GTA weldment of Monel 400 and AISI 304 exemplified that

Fig. 1. Macrograph of GTA welded dissimilar Monel 400 and AISI 304

the filler wire ENiCrFe-3 confirm superior fusion to the base metals and the width of the fusion is narrower. On examining the micro-structure of the weldment, it is observed that the formation of secondary phases in the HAZ of AISI 304. Whereas long dendrites are observed in the weld region and coarse grains of Ni-Cu is observed on the HAZ of Monel 400 shown in Fig. 2. This coarseness in grain structure could be due to the heat generated during GTA welding.

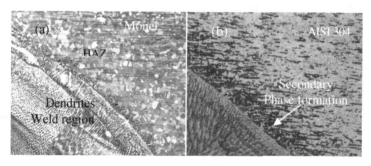

Fig. 2. Microstructure of GTA welded dissimilar weldments (a) Monel 400 side (b) AISI 304 side

3.2   Mechanical Properties of the Weldment

Micro-hardness measurements are carried out on the dissimilar weldments by keeping the weld as a centre is depicted in Fig. 3. It is clear from the hardness profile that the HAZ side of AISI 304 is found to possess higher hardness value as compared to HAZ of Monel 400 for ENiCrFe-3.

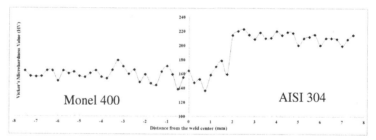

Fig. 3. Hardness profile of GTA welded dissimilar Monel400 and AISI 304 using ENiCrFe-3

Tensile test results showed in Fig. 4 that the fracture has occurred on the parent metal side of AISI 304 for all the trials and the tensile strength is found to be 645 MPa. SEM fractographs confirm the contribution of micro-voids and

Fig. 4. Fractured tensile specimen of GTA welded dissimilar Monel 400 and AISI 304

dimples in a fibrous network and in turn coalesce to undergo ductile fracture in case of dissimilar weldment of Monel 400 and AISI 304 employing ENiCrFe-3 filler wire.

3.3   Cyclic Hot Corrosion Test

3.3.1 Visual Observations and Thermo-Gravimetric Analysis

The macrographs of the hot corroded samples representing various zones of the dissimilar weldment of Monel 400 and AISI 304 at the end of 50th cycle is shown in Fig. 5(a) and 5(b). Changes in the color and texture were noted at the end of each cycle. Thermo gravimetric graphs shown in Fig. 6(a) and 6(b) for

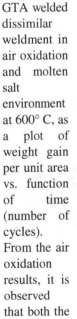
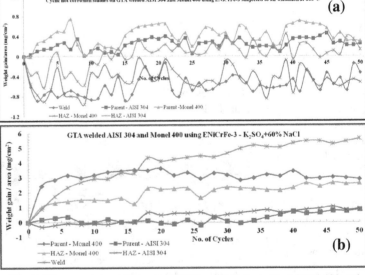

Fig. 5. Macro-photographs of the hot corroded zones of GTA welded dissimilar Monel 400 and AISI 304 (i) Parent Metal - AISI 304 (ii) HAZ - AISI 304 (iii) Weld (iv) HAZ - Monel 400 (v) Parent Metal - Monel 400 subjected to (a) Air oxidation (b) Molten salt environment at 600° C.

GTA welded dissimilar weldment in air oxidation and molten salt environment at 600° C, as a plot of weight gain per unit area vs. function of time (number of cycles). From the air oxidation results, it is observed that both the

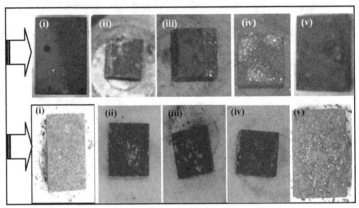

Fig. 6. Thermogravimetric graph of GTA welded dissimilar Monel 400 and AISI 304 using ENiCrFe-3 filler wire subjected to (a) air oxidation (b) Molten salt environment at 600°C

parent metals AISI 304 and Monel 400 acquire weight gain; whereas negligible amount of weight loss is observed in all other zones of weldment. Furthermore, it is observed that the weight changes are fluctuating and hence doesn't obey the parabolic law. Thermogravimetric analysis of the molten salt environment showed that the weld region of ENiCrFe-3 filler metal undergo more corrosion as indicated, in terms of more weight gain.

3.3.2 X-Ray Diffraction Analysis

X-Ray diffraction studies (Fig. 7) were carried out to analyze the various phases formed on the composite region of the weldment after 50 corrosion cycles. Hot corroded GTA weldments employing ENiCrFe-3 filler wire showed the peak intensities as NiO, Cu_2O, $NiCu_2O_3$ and the minor intensities of Cr_2O_3, FeO in both the corrosion environments.

3.3.3 SEM/EDAX Analysis

SEM micrographs of the GTAW specimens exposed in air and at the molten salt environment showing surface morphology after cyclic hot corrosion for 50 cycles at 600 °C are shown in Fig. 8. The air oxidized HAZ of Monel 400 showed the formation of Cu_2O and NiO; the weld region of ENiCrFe-3 possesses FeO, Cr_2O_3, NiO and the spinels of $FeCr_2O_4$, $NiFe_2O_4$. The formation of FeO, Cr_2O_3, NiO, Cu_2O and the spinels of $NiFe_2O_4$, $FeCr_2O_4$ is witnessed at the HAZ of AISI 304. SEM micrographs of ENiCrFe-3 weldments subjected to molten salt

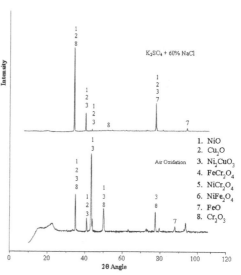

Fig. 7. XRD analysis of the hot corroded composite region of welded Monel 400 and AISI 304

environment of K_2SO_4+ 60% NaCl showed a mushy appearance of white sticky splats in the HAZ of Monel 400; whereas the weld region has large sized splats and the HAZ of AISI 304 has adherent cohesive splats of oxides are observed. Further the EDAX analysis of the scale for the weldment indicate the formation of FeO as the predominant phase formed is FeO for all the regions and with the smaller amounts of NiO, Cu_2O. The scale formed on these regions is found to be adhesive and cohesive in nature.

4   Discussions

Satisfactory and successful dissimilar joints of Monel 400 and AISI 304 could be obtained using manual GTA welding technique employing ENiCrFe-3 filler wire. X-Ray radiography NDT also concluded that there were no surface defects present in these dissimilar joints. The room temperature mechanical properties and high temperature corrosion properties of these weldments are also found to be good. In the microstructure examination, there exists unmixed zone which is found to be

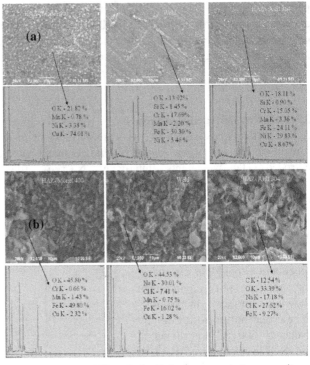

Fig. 8. SEM/EDAX analysis of the hot corroded composite region of welded Monel 400 and AISI 304

available only in fewer regions for ENiCrFe-3. This is attributed to the improper dilution of the filler metal. The welding filler wires of ENiCrFe-3 could readily take into the solution of nickel, copper, chromium and iron to the level likely to be encountered in practice by dilution from parent metals. The weld region, therefore, will have the normal dendritic structure of single phase material, for both filler materials [2]. Also, the presence of Nb content in ENiCrFe-3 would contribute for the better hot cracking resistance Also the inclusions of Al, Mn, Nb, and Mo in the filler metal imparting additional strength and also exhibit reasonable elevated temperature strength up to 650 °C. The degree of ductility and strength is found to be more for the weldments utilizing ENiCrFe-3 filler wire. SEM/EDAX analysis of the hot corroded, air oxidized weld zone employing ENiCrFe-3 filler wire indicate the formation of Cr_2O_3 and NiO in the scales which signifies protective conditions. It is also supported by other researchers who reported the development of oxidation resistance in high temperature environment by the additions of Cr, Ni and Al. GTA weldments employing ENiCrFe-3 has shown spallation in the weld zone till 10th cycle followed by the weight gain. However the weight changes are negligible in the weld zone. In the XRD analysis, the presence of sodium chloride or as chlorides of iron, chromium, molybdenum was not observed on the surface [Fig. 7]. It is well known that chlorides of iron, chromium etc., are volatile. So they might have escaped from the surface or subsurface leaving behind voids, pits, etc. The XRD results described above imply clearly that a high Ni content in the weld zone is very effective in improving the corrosion resistance against K_2SO_4 + NaCl (60%) molten salt environment. In molten salt environments, especially in the chromium depletion region, the corrosion morphologies show large amounts of subscale attack. It is reported that chromium chloride ($CrCl_3$) converts into oxide at very low oxygen pressure, iron chloride at significantly higher oxygen pressure and a much higher oxygen partial pressure is needed to convert nickel chloride into NiO, especially at low temperatures. This means that evaporating chromium chlorides are oxidized closer to the metal surface than iron and nickel chlorides. Severe corrosion is also observed in the weld region of the ENiCrFe-3 weldments. It is evident from the SEM/EDAX analysis that the content of Fe is higher in the weld region. This would probably form the metallic chlorides of Fe which can cause the corrosion attack.

Conclusions

[1]   Sound dissimilar welds of Monel 400 and AISI 304 could be obtained by GTAW process using ENiCrFe-3 filler wire
[2]   The mechanical and hot corrosion properties of these dissimilar joints are found to be good
[3]   Corrosion rate is more in all the zones of the weldment when exposed to the molten salt environment as compared to air oxidation at 600 °C

References

[1] Kim, Y.H., Frankel, G.S., Lippold, J.C., Guaytima, G.: Development of a Chromium-Free Consumable for Austenitic Stainless Steels—Part 1: Monel (Alloy 400) Filler Metal. Corrosion 62(1) (2006)
[2] Figert, J., Rybicki, D.: Developing a Welding Procedure for joining Monel 400 to 316L Stainless Steel. NASA M&P Update (NMPU), NASA M&P Update Newsletter 2(1) (1998)
[3] Alber Sadek, A., Abass, M., Zaghloul, B., Elrefaey, A., Ushio, M.: Investigation of dissimilar Joints between Low Carbon steel and Monel 400. Trans. JWRI 29(1), 21–28 (2000)
[4] Arivazhagan, N., Narayanan, S., Singh, S., Prakash, S., Reddy, G.M.: High temperature corrosion studies on friction welded low alloy steel and stainless steel in air and molten salt environment at 650°. Materials and Design 34, 459–468 (2012)
[5] Davis: Nickel, Cobalt and their alloys. ASM International p. 267
[6] Ahila, S., Ramakrishna Iyer, S., Radhakrishnan, V.M.: Measurement of hot corrosion of 2.25Cr-1Mo steel-347H steel welded joint in K_2SO_4 - 60%NaCl mixture. Materials Letters 18, 243–245 (1994)
[7] Li, Y.S., Spiegel, M.: Models describing the degradation of FeAl and NiAl alloys induced by ZnCl2–KCl melt at 400 – 450°C. Corrosion Science 46(8), 2009–2023 (2004)

Microstructure and Mechanical Behaviour of Friction Stir Welded Copper

N. Srirangarajalu[1], G. Madhusudhan Reddy[2], S.R. Koteswara Rao[3], and A. Rajadurai[1]

[1] Madras Institute of Technology,
Anna University, Chennai - 600 044, India
{nsrirangarajulu,rajaduraianna}@gmail.com
[2] DMRL, Hyderabad - 500 058, India
[3] Tagore Engineering College, Chennai - 600 048, India

Abstract. The objective of this experimental study was analyzing the joining behavior of 6 mm thick cold rolled copper plate using Friction Stir Welding (FSW) technique. The role of tool rotational speed, travel speed and tool pin profiles on the weld quality, tensile and bend behaviors, hardness, and microstrucuture was investigated. Defect free weld was obtained at tool rotational speeds ranging between 1300 - 1600rpm and welding travel speeds ranging between 30-45mm/min. Tensile strength interms of joint efficiency was found to be 73% compare to the base material (BM). The average hardness of the nugget zone was lesser than the base material because of annealing of the cold rolled copper plates during welding. Different microstructure zones were revealed by optical microscopy (OM). The nugget zone (NZ) and heat affected zone (HAZ) were found to have fine equiaxed grains and fine elongated grains respectively.

Keywords: Friction Stir Welding, Copper plates, Mechanical Properties.

1 Introduction

Copper and its alloys are widely used in industrial applications due to their excellent electrical and thermal conductivities, good strength, corrosion and fatigue resistances [1]. The joining of copper and its alloys has acquired importance in recent years. The most suitable process in each case can be selected only after consideration of the properties required, such as corrosion resistance, conductivity and mechanical strength at ordinary and elevated temperatures. Welding of copper is usually difficult by conventional fusion welding techniques because of its high thermal diffusivity, which is 10-100 times higher than that of steels and nickel alloys. Hence, the heat input required for welding is much higher, resulting in quite low welding speeds [2]. Higher thermal conductivity and thermal expansion of copper result in greater weld distortion than steel [1].

During arc welding of copper and copper alloys, oxygen segregates on grain boundaries of metal. This can lead to embrittlement of the weld joint. Precipitation hardenable copper alloys may lose their alloying elements through oxidation during

S.G. Ponnambalam et al. (Eds.): IRAM 2012, CCIS 330, pp. 458–465, 2012.
© Springer-Verlag Berlin Heidelberg 2012

fusion welding and results in reduction in their strength. Copper welds frequently suffer from lack of fusion because of high thermal conductivity as it reduces the concentration of heat needed to melt critical mass of metal and ensures complete filling of the weld cavity [3]. Recently for few industrial applications, FSW has been successfully used for joining of copper. Eg. Such as heat exchangers, coolers and fabrication of the copper containment canister for nuclear waste [4]. The FSW process is executed while the materials are in a solid state, thus preventing many of the metallurgical problems that occur with conventional fusion welding, such as distortion, shrinkage, porosity and spatter [5]. The rapid dissipation of heat, much heat input is necessary during FSW of copper and therefore the welding processes were usually carried out with high rotation speed and low welding speed. The grain size decreased from 210μm for the base metal to 100μm for the nugget zone, but the hardness value decreased slightly due to the reduction in dislocation density relative to base metal [8]. In view of huge commercial importance of copper alloys, in this study, attempts were made to investigate the effect of FSW parameters viz. tool rotational speeds and welding speeds of cold rolled copper plates on mechanical properties and microstructure of friction stir weld joints.

2   Experimental Procedure

Among the four different tool profiles namely straight cylindrical (SC), Tapered Cylindrical (TC) ,Tapered Threaded Cylindrical (TTC) and Straight Threaded Cylindrical (STC). The different tool pin profiles are shown in Fig-1. The TTC alone resulted defect free weld joint. Whereas SC, TC and STC tool pin profiles resulted defects such as worm hole and lack of penetration. Hence detailed investigation was conducted on the joints made with TTC tool pin profile.

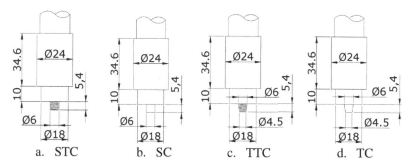

Fig. 1. Different tool pin profiles

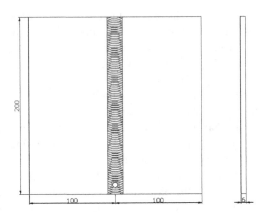

Fig. 2. Friction stir welding of copper plates

In this study, cold rolled copper plates of dimension 200mm in length, 100mm in width and 6mm in thickness was welded by FSW in Fig-2. The chemical composition of the cold rolled copper plate is given in Table-1.

Table 1. Chemical composition of cold rolled copper plate

Element	Zn	Pb	Sn	Fe	Ni	Si	Al	P	Cu
Wt %	0.010	0.011	0.010	0.005	0.044	0.005	0.002	0.020	99.863

Hardened and tempered M2 high speed tool steel of 55 HRC was used as tool material. The geometry of the pin affects the heat generation and the flow of the plastic material eventually, the pin can affect the metallurgical quality and the mechanical properties of the weld.

The welding speeds used in this study were 30mm/min and 45mm/min. The tool rotational speeds selected for this study were 1300, 1400 and 1600 rpm. The tool pin was tilted by an angle of 3^0 to the vertical axis and rotated in the clockwise direction.

FSW experiments were performed on a computer controlled FSW machine, wherein the specimens were firmly clamped. The rotating tool pin was initially plunged at one end of the intended weld line and a dwell time of 5 seconds was allowed to generate adequate heat. Then the work table along with the work piece was made to traverse along the weld line.

After FSW, the welds were visual examined to check the presence of visible surface defects. Microstructural examination was carried out on base material and few welded specimens to visualize the microstructural change at nugget zone and heat affected zone. The welded specimens without any visible defects were chosen and sliced into ASTME8 sub-size standard tensile test specimens in CNC wire EDM. Tensile tests were conducted in a tensile testing machine of 20 tons capacity with constant cross head traverse speed of 1 mm/min. The bend tests were carried out in 40 tons capacity computer controlled universal testing machine with a cross head speed of 1 mm/min. The micro hardness profile across the weld zone was measured on cross section and perpendicular to the welding direction using the Vickers indenter with 300 gmf load for 10 seconds. The microstructural examination was carried out on specimens which were mirror polished and etched with ferric chloride etchant.

3   Result and Discussion

3.1   Microstructure

Cold rolled copper plates were successfully welded in butt joint configuration by friction stir welding. Defect free weld joint was obtained at the tool rotational speed of 1300 – 1600 rpm and travel speed of 30-45mm/min. The microstructure of the base material ie cold rolled copper plate revealed the presence of elongated grains of length ranging between 20 - 30μm and width of about 10μm Fig-3(a). The microstructure of the nugget zone (NZ) and heat affected zone (HAZ) are shown in Fig-3 (b,c). Fig-3(b) shows the microstructure of the nugget zone of the copper plates welded with 1300rpm of tool rotational speed and traverse speed of 30mm/min. This revealed that no porosity or other defects are not present in the nugget zone of all the joints produced. The nugget zone reveals the presence of refined equiaxed grains of size 1-2 microns. This observation indicates the occurrence of a complete recrystallisation in the nugget zone. Fig-3(c) shows the microstructure of the HAZ, wherein a partial recrystallisation resulting in equiaxed grains of size ranging between 5-10μm could be seen. The friction stir welding resulted in a grain refinement within the nugget zone. The finest grain size was observed in the nugget zone of the joint produced with a traverse speed of 45mm/min and a rotational speed of 1300 rpm. Fine equiaxed grains were found to be distributed throughout the nugget zone and a small increment in grain size in HAZ was also noticed in Fig-3(c).

a)   Base Metal

Fig. 3. Microstructure of Copper to Copper Weld

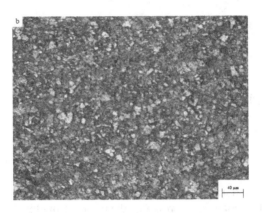

b)   Nugget Zone

c) Heat Affected Zone

Fig. 3. (*Continued*)

3.2   Tensile and Fracture Behavior

Tensile test results of the base metal and FSW specimens along with the joint efficiency calculated with reference to the UTS of base material are given in Table-2.

The best combination of mechanical properties was obtained for a tool rotational speed of 1300 rpm with a traverse speed of 30 mm/min in copper to copper weld. The ASTM E8 sub size tensile specimen shown in Fig-4. The weld efficiency was found to be 73%. The tensile strength and percentage of elongation of the copper base material were 333MPa and 17% respectively. Whereas the tensile strength and elongation of the FSW joint was observed to be 239MPa and 18% respectively. On increasing the spindle rotational speed and the traverse speed to 1600rpm and 45 mm/min, the joint efficiency and elongation were found to be 71% and 18% respectively. In this case, the fracture location of the weld joint was in the HAZ of the advancing side. Whereas in all other cases the fracture occurred along the weld line.

Table 2. The welding parameters and the results of tensile tests

Rotational Speed (rpm)	Welding Speed (mm/min)	Tool pin Profile used	Tensile Strength MPa	0.2% Proof stress MPa	Elongation %	Joint Efficiency %	Fracture Location
			333	326	17		Middle
1300	30	TTC	242	176	19	73	HAZ
1300	45	TTC	226	144	12	68	HAZ
1400	30	TTC	240	175	19	72	HAZ
1600	45	TTC	239	174	18	71	HAZ

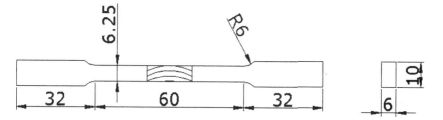

Fig. 4. ASTME8 sub-size standard tensile test specimen

3.3   Bend Test Behavior

The bend test specimen is shown in Fig-5. Both face and root bend tests were performed on the welded specimens for copper to copper. The samples showed that, face bend of the welded plate withstood a maximum load of 4.5kN. The cracks were observed on retreating side of HAZ.

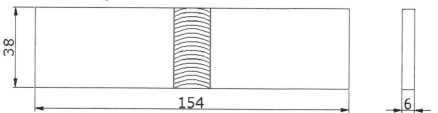

Fig. 5. ASTM B4 Bend test specimen

3.4   Microhardness

The microhardness of the BM, HAZ and NZ are shown in Fig-6. In friction stir welding of copper, to copper nugget zone softening and reduction of hardness in the nugget zone was observed. The hardness of base metal ranged from 120-125 VHN, However, the hardness near the nugget zone shows values from 85-92 VHN.

The weld centre has slightly lower hardness than that of the base metal in spite of small grain size. The low hardness of nugget zone could be attributed to the effect of annealing on the cold worked base material during welding.

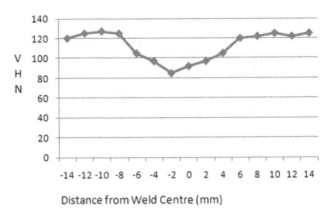

Distance from Weld Centre (mm)

Fig. 6. Copper to Copper Weld Microhardness

4   Conclusions

1. Nugget zone showed fine equiaxed grains of 1-2 micron size in comparison with the elongated grains of 20-30μm the base metal.
2. Hardness of the nugget zone was lower than that of base metal, because of annealing effect during welding.
3. Tensile strength and maximum joint efficiency obtained was 242 MPa and 73% respectively.
4. The percentage elongation was not affected in the welded plates.
5. The tensile fracture occurred in the HAZ at the advancing side of the weld due to the presence of few coarse grains. Similarly, the variations of the hardness values showed a relative correspondence to the fracture location.

References

1. ASM Hand Book, Welding, Brazing and Soldering, USA, vol. 6, pp 1872–1876 (1993)
2. Anderson, C.G.: Proceedings of the First International Symposium on Friction Stir welding. Thousand Oaks, California (2000)
3. Avula, D., Singh, R.K.R., Dwivedi, D.K., Mehta, N.K.: Effect of Friction Stir Welding on Microstructural and Mechanical Properties of Copper Alloy. World Academy of Science, Engineering and Technology 74 (2011)
4. Kokamoto, K., Doi, M., Hirano, S., Aota, K., Okamura, H., Aono, Y., Ping, T.C.: Proceedings of the Third International Symposium on Friction Stir Welding, Kobe, Japan (2001)
5. Hwang, Y.M., Fan, P.L., Lin, C.H.: Experimental study on Friction Stir Welding of copper metals. Journal of Material Processing Technology, 1667–1672 (2010)

6. Park, H.S., Kimura, T., Murakami, T., Nagano, Y., Nakata, K., Ushio, M.: Microstructures and mechanical properties of friction stir welds of 60% Cu-40% Zn copper alloy. Material Science and Engineering, 160–169 (2004)
7. Shen, J.J., Liu, H.J., Cui, F.: Effect of welding speed on microstructure and mechanical properties of friction stir welded copper. Material and Design, 3937–3942 (2010)
8. Sun, F.Y., Fujii, H.: Investigation of the welding parameter dependent microstructure and mechanical properties of friction stir welded pure copper. Materials Science and Engineering A 527, 6879–6886 (2010)

Self-healing Ability of Structural Ceramics – A Review

Madhan M. and Prabhakaran G.

Mechanical Engineering, Velammal Engineering College,
Chennai – 600 066, Tamilnadu, India
g_prabha2006@yahoo.com

Abstract. The development and characterization of self-healing structural ceramics have been inspired by researchers in which damage triggers an autonomic healing response. This is one of the emerging and fascinating areas of research that could significantly extend the working life and safety of the ceramic components at higher temperature. The structural ceramics are superior in strength to metal at high temperature, but they are brittle and sensitive to flaws. Due to this, the structural integrity of the ceramic components is seriously affected. There are few advantages in crack healing ability of materials (a) higher fabrication efficient at low cost, of the self-healing takes place after the machining is performed, (b) reliability of the material improves, when all the cracks are healed and (c) if the crack gets healed in service, the full strength of the material is recovered. In this paper, Overview of various self-healing concepts for structural ceramic materials; Literature crack healing ability and the Parameters that influence the crack healing are presented.

Keywords: Ceramics, Crack-healing.

1 Introduction

The heat resisting limit of the structural ceramics is greatly superior to that of the metallic materials. Structural ceramics are one of the prime materials used for manufacturing of high temperature apparatus such as gas turbines and fusion reactors. But the fracture toughness of the structural ceramics is fairly lower than the metallic materials, because they are sensitive to flaws. As a result, the structural integrity of a ceramic component is seriously affected. The various options for resolving this problems and limitations are furnished below.

Several investigators have found that the strength of the structural ceramics can be increased by heating them before testing [1-4]. Heat treatment of the ceramic materials containing cracks can result in complete or partial recovery of the strength of the specimen. This phenomenon is generally called "*self-healing*". The advantages of crack-healing in structural ceramics are (i) increase in the reliability, (ii) decrease in the machining cost, (iii) decrease in the maintenance cost, (iv) increase in strength, hardness and (v) increase in life time. Crack healing has been observed in many traditional heat sintering ceramics such as SiC [5], Si_3N_4 [6-7], mullite – SiC composites [8] and Si_3N_4 – SiC composites [9]. Crack healing happens by means of extra bonding force exerted by the glass phase on the crack wake by the reaction of the crack surface with the environment; mostly by oxidation [5].

S.G. Ponnambalam et al. (Eds.): IRAM 2012, CCIS 330, pp. 466–474, 2012.
© Springer-Verlag Berlin Heidelberg 2012

Table 1. Testing methods on cracks and their limitations

S. No:	Methods	Limitations
1.	✓ Conducting a non-destructive inspection before use to detect the cracks. ✓ Repairing dangerous cracks, if any.	✓ flaws occurred during usual machining like grinding, polishing, etc., are so small that is almost difficult to detect ✓ the structural ceramics are so brittle almost it is impossible to repair
2.	✓ Improving the fracture toughness of the material by microstructure control and fibre reinforcement	✓ many studies are made in fracture toughness of the material by fibre reinforcement
3.	✓ Conducting a proof test to prevent use of low reliability member	✓ the conduct of proof test is time consuming ✓ it decreases the fabrication efficiency ✓ increases the fabrication cost
4.	✓ Heal all the dangerous cracks and recover the components strength	✓ very few studies have been made

2   Evolution of Crack Healing Process

In 1966, Strengthening of ceramics by heat treatment was investigated by Heuer and Roberts [10]. The term "crack-healing" was first used by Lange and Gupta [11] while reporting the strengthening of Zinc Oxide and Magnesium Oxide by heat treatment. There are many reports found in strengthening of cracked ceramics. The crack-healing is categorized into (i) re-sintering, (ii) relaxation of tensile residual stress at the indentation site, (iii) cracks bonding by oxidation Re-sintering of the ceramic component commences with a degradation of the primary crack but generates the cylindrical voids in the immediate crack tip. In the second type, relaxation increases the strength recovery but it does not heal the crack. So the crack bonding by oxidation is first investigated by Lange [5]. He investigated the strength recovery of cracked silicon carbide (SiC) by heat treatment in air at 1673K. He found that the bending strength of the specimen increases 10% more than the smooth non-heat treated specimens after conducting heat treatment for 110 hours in air. In 1982, Easler et al [12] found the same crack-healing ability in silicon nitride.

3   Mechanism of Self-healing

Silicon carbide or silicon nitride particles embedded in ceramic matrices give rise to self-healing function in the structural ceramics operated at high temperature. In ceramic components, the brittle fracture occurs usually in rapid and catastrophic manner. This brittle fracture takes place because of the stress concentration at the crack tip. The components having Silicon carbide or silicon nitride particles can heal the surface crack produced during various machining operations. Surface cracks allow the silicon carbide or silicon nitride particles on the crack walls to contact the oxygen in the surrounding atmosphere. When the components are at high temperature, the oxygen contact would cause the oxidation as per the following equation,

$$SiC + \frac{3}{2}O_2 \rightarrow SiO_2 + CO \tag{1}$$

The oxidation induces almost two times volume expansion, such that space between the crack walls can be completely filled with the formed oxide. Since the component is at high temperature, a strong bonding between the ceramic matrices and the formed oxide will be established. By this, the degraded strength recovers completely and enhanced with high mechanical reliability. The schematic diagram of self crack-healing mechanism of SiC is shown in fig. 1.

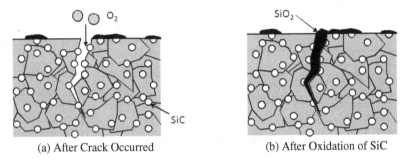

(a) After Crack Occurred   (b) After Oxidation of SiC

Fig. 1. Crack healing mechanism

4   Experimental Work

In the experimental work by Zhang at el [6] used a specimen with dimensions of 27mm x 4mm x 3mm for fracture toughness determination and a large specimen with dimensions of 54mm x 10mm x 4.5mm for fatigue crack growth tests. A crack starter was introduced on the top surface of a specimen using a Vickers hardness indentation with an applied load of 20kg. To produce a long through crack, specimen bars with crack starter were pre cracked using the bridge indentation method [17]. The specimens are heated at various temperatures at 1273 K, 1473 K and 1573 K in air for 1 hour. In 2009, Jung at al [18] investigated the crack produced by the grinding process in the Silicon Nitride specimen. They produced semicircular groove on the specimen by metal-bonded diamond grind stone. The dimensions of the specimens are 3mm x 4mm x 22mm. They compared the results of the sintered specimen with that of machined specimen. The specimens are heated at 1573 K in air for 1 hour. In most of the article, the cracks are introduced by the Vickers hardness indentation method and the specimens are heated in air for 1 hour [19-27]. Ando et al [6,7] observe while alumina/15 vol% 0.27 μm SiC particles composition containing indentation crack produced in Vickers hardness is heat-treated at 1573 K in air. The three point bending test and microstructure examination is performed using Scanning Electron Microscope and X-ray diffraction method.

5   Parameters

The various parameters that influence the self-healing process are (i) Composition (ii) SiC particle size (iii) Atmosphere (iv) Temperature (v)Stress.

5.1   Composition

The SiC volume fraction is the important factor in the self-healing ability of the ceramics. In 1998, Wu et al [13] reported that the crack length and bonding strength of alumina / 5 vol% of 0.2μm SiC particles composite increases after annealing at 1573 K for 2 hour in air. But Chou et al [3] in 1998 stated that a uniform reaction layer was not formed in the crack because of lower SiC content results in small quantity of oxide formation. Ando at al in 1999, found that, the similar crack healing in mullite $3Al_2O_3-2SiO_2$, Si_3N_4 [6-7] and alumina [14-17] based composites containing more than 15% SiC particles can recover the cracked strength completely. They have stated that the healed material is stronger than that the base ceramic material, and concluded that (i) by the crack healing reaction, mechanically stronger products should be formed, (ii) the crack-healing reaction fills the gap between the crack walls completely and   (iii) the bond between crack wall and the product should be strong enough. The table 2 shows the composition of alumina and mullite with SiC and their corresponding strength and fracture toughness.

Table 2. Strength and fracture toughness of various compositions of alumina & Mullite with Silicon Carbide

Matrix	Matric %	SiC Particle	SiC whiskers	Strength (MPa)	Fracture Toughness $(MPam^{1/2})$
Alumina	85	15		850	3.2
	75	30		1050	3.6
	80	-	20	970	4.8
	70	-	30	830	5.8
	70	10	20	980	5
Mullite	85	25	-	470	2.2
	85	-	15	710	2.8
	80	-	20	840	3.6
	75	-	25	820	4.2
	80	5	15	750	3.2
	75	10	15	740	3.5

5.2   SiC Particle Size

The particle size of the SiC also influences the crack-healing ability. Especially, SiC whiskers causes intrinsic changes to the micro mechanism of the crack healing. In 1995, Sato et al [28] have stated that the crack healed strength of $3Al_2O_32SiO_2/20$ vol% SiC composite is greater when the SiC particle size is 0-56 μm. They conducted the crack healing at 1573 K for 1hr in air. Ceramics containing SiC whiskers showed self-healing property, but there is a limitation in using SiC whiskers alone. SiC whiskers forms a barrier between the crack walls as shown in figure 2.

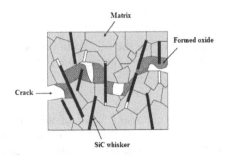

Fig. 2. Crack-healing mechanism by SiC whiskers

So, the amount of oxidation throughout the crack length is restricted by the whiskers. This is observed in the crack-healed zone of alumina/20 vol% SiC whiskers [29, 30]. Therefore composite containing SiC whiskers as well as SiC particles are examined by Nakao at al [31] in 2005, they investigated the Mullite /15 vol% of SiC whiskers/10vol% of SiC particle of size 0.27 μm shows greater strength than Mullite / SiC whiskers samples. It shows excellent self-healing ability.

5.3   Atmosphere

The annealing atmosphere is an important criterion in the self-healing process. The crack-healing is occurred due to the oxidation of SiC present in the components. So, the presence of O_2 in the atmosphere is a must for self-healing phenomenon. Most of the researchers have conducted the annealing in air that was produced better strength recovery than other environment. For example in 2003, Kim et al [32], looked into the influence of atmosphere on the crack healing behavior of Al_2O_3/15 vol% SiC. The bending strength of the sintered specimen is about 650 Mpa. After crack is introduced the bending strength reduced to 180 MPa at the decreasing rate of 73%. They conducted the crack healing test at 1573 K for 1 hr in air; the bending strength of crack healed specimen is 800 Mpa. The bending strength of crack healed specimen is larger than as-received by sintered specimen. When crack healing is done in N_2, Ar and Vacuum the bending strength is recovered at most 350 MPa.

5.4   Temperature

The structural ceramics are usually operated at high temperature. It is very important to know the temperature range for self-healing of different structural ceramics. Oxidation of SiC is a chemical reaction, the recovery of strength decreases with decrease in the temperature. For example, the alumina/15 vol% of 0.27 μm SiC particles requires to be heated at 1573 K in air for 1hr in air to heal the semi-elliptical crack of length 100 μm in surface length. The relation between the crack-healing temperature and the strength recovery rate follows Arrhenius' equation

$$\frac{1}{t_{HM}} = Q_0 \exp\left(\frac{-Q_H}{RT_{HL}}\right) \tag{2}$$

Where, t_{HM} = time, T_{HL} = temperature, Q_0 = proportional moduli of material and Q_H = activation energy. The table gives the relationship between the time t_{HM} required to heal a standard semi-elliptical crack completely and the crack healing temperature.

Table 3. Activation energy and proportional coefficient for various materials

Material	Activation Energy Q_H in KJ/mol	Proportional coefficient Q_0
Si_3N_4/SiC	277	4.2×10^{11}
Si_3N_4	150	5.3×10^{4}
Al_2O_3/SiC	334	1.7×10^{11}
Mullite/SiC	413	4.7×10^{23}

From the plot given below, we can find the time for which a standard semi-elliptical crack of 100 µm in surface length can be completely healed at several temperature. In 2009, Osada at al [33] investigated the alumina / 15% of 0.27 µm SiC in the temperature range of 1573 K to 1773 K and found the recovery of the strength and crack healing of semi-elliptical crack of 100 µm produced by vicker's indentation method. Jung at al [18] found the healing of cracks produced by the grinding process in Si_3N_4/SiC composite in the temperature range of 1473 K to 1673 K for 1hr in air.

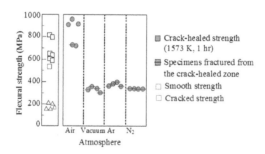

Fig. 3. Crack-healing behavior of alumina / 15 vol% 0.27 µm SiC particles composite under several atmosphere

Table 4. Temperature limit and range of various materials for crack healing

S. No.	Material	Temperature Limit in K	Temperature range of crack healing in K
1.	Si_3N_4 / 20 vol% SiC particle	1573	1073 - 1573
2.	Alumina / 15 vol% SiC particle	1573	1173 - 1573
3.	Mullite / 15 vol% SiC particle	1473	1273 – 1473
4.	SiC with Sc_2O_3 & AIN additives	1673	1473 - 1673

5.5   Stress

Stress applied on the material is also important factor for self-healing ability. When the applied stress exceeds the critical value, it will results in a catastrophic failure. In 2007, Nakao et al investigated the Al_2O_3 / SiC and Mullite / SiC composites. They found that the constant or cyclic stress for crack healing is a function of the bending strength of pre-cracked specimens. The proportional constants for the relationship between the threshold stress and bending strength of pre-cracked specimen is 64% for constant stress and 76% for cyclic stress. In 2010, Takahashi et al studied a hot-pressed SiC particle reinforced Si_3N_4 composite containing 20 vol% SiC particle and 8 vol% Yt_2O_3 as additive. A semi-elliptical crack is created by Vicker's indentation method. Then the crack healing tests at 1473 K for 5 hr under constant stress is carried out. They found that, the specimens crack healed under a constant stress of 200 MPa showed higher bending strength compared to that of the specimens crack-healed under no stress.

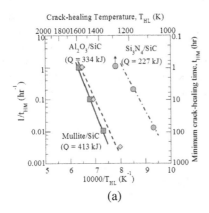

(a)

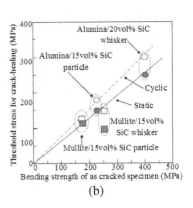

(b)

Fig. 4. (a) Arrhenius' plot for the various crack-healing ceramics [21]; (b) Relation between threshold stress during crack healing and the corresponding cracked strength

6   Conclusion

Structural ceramics are generally brittle which affects the reliability of the components. There are four ways to overcome this problem. They are (1) conducting a non-destructive inspection before use, and detect and repair any dangerous cracks are found, (2) improve the fracture toughness of the material by microstructure control and fibre reinforcement, (3) conduct a proof test to prevent use of low reliability member, (4) heal all the dangerous cracks and recover the components strength. In this paper, a special attention is focused on self-healing methods and the parameters which influence the self-healing. From the review it is concluded that the crack healing occurs in the structural ceramics

  i.   When the vol% of SiC particles is more than 10% with the matrix material.
 ii.   Combination of SiC particles and whiskers produce better strength when compared with the structural material containing SiC whiskers alone.

iii. When the annealing is occurred in air produce more bending strength when compared to other atmosphere like vacuum, Ar and N_2.

iv. The optimum temperature for crack healing in most of the structural ceramics is 1473 K to 1573K.

v. The stress in the healed component should not to be more than 200 MPa.

The crack-healing ability of structural ceramics is a very useful method for higher structural integrity and for reducing the machining and non-destructive inspection costs.

References

1. Gupta, T.K.: Crack Healing and Strengthening of Thermally Shocked Alumina. J. Am. Ceram. Soc. 59(5-6), 259–262 (1976)
2. Choi, S.R., Tikare, V.: Crack Healing Behavior of Hot Pressed Silicon Nitride Due to Oxidation. Scr. Metall. Mater. 26, 1263–1268 (1992)
3. Chou, A., Chan, H.M., Harmer, M.P.: Effect of Annealing Environment on the Crack Healing and Mechanical Behavior of Silicon Carbide-Reinforced Alumina Nanocomposites. J. Am. Ceram. Soc. 81(5), 1203–1208 (1998)
4. Kim, H.E., Song, H., Ha, J.: Effect of Oxidation on the Room-Temperature Flexural Strength of Reaction-Bonded Silicon Carbides. J. Am. Ceram. Soc. 82(6), 1601–1604 (1999)
5. Lange, F.F.: Healing of Surface Cracks in SiC by Oxidation. J. Am. Ceram. Soc. 53(5), 290 (1970)
6. Zhang, Y.H., Edwards, L., Plumbridge, W.J.: Crack Healing in a Silicon Nitride Ceramic. J. Am. Ceram. Soc. 81(7), 11861–11868 (1998)
7. Zhang, Y.H., Edwards, L.: Cyclic fatigue crack growth behaviour of silicon nitride at 1400°C. Material Science and Engineering 256, 144–151 (1998)
8. Thompson, M., Chan, H.M., Harmer, M.P.: Crack Healing and Stress Relaxation in Al2O3–SiC Nanocomposites. J. Am. Ceram. Soc. 78(3), 5671 (1995)
9. Ando, K., Furusawa, K., Chu, M.C., Hanagata, T., Tuji, K., Sato, S.: Crack Healing Behavior Under Stress of Mullite/Silicon Carbide Ceramics and the Resultant Fatigue Strength. J. Am. Ceram. Soc. 84(9), 2073–2078 (2001)
10. Heuer, A.H., Roberts, J.P.: The Influence of Annealing on the Strength of Corundum Crystals. Proc. Bri. Ceram. Soc. 6, 17–27 (1966)
11. Lange, F.F., Gupta, T.K.: Crack Healing by Heat Treatment. J. Am. Ceram. Soc. 53(1), 54–55 (1970)
12. Easler, T.E., Bradt, R.C., Tressler, R.E.: Strength Distribution of Sic Ceramics After Oxidation and Oxidation Under Load. J. Am. Cerum. Soc. 64(I2), 731–734 (1981)
13. Wu, H.Z., Lawrence, C.W., Roberts, S.G., Titchmarsh, J.M.: Strengthening alumina-silicon carbide nanocomposites by annealing. Acta Materialia 46(11), 3839–3848 (1998)
14. Liang, J., Wang, Y., Fang, G., Wang, G.: Influence of Oxidation Healing for Cracks on the Strength of Hot-Pressed ZrB_2–SiC–AlN Ceramics. International Journal of Applied Ceramic Society, 1–6 (2011)
15. Nakao, W., Mori, S., Nakamura, J., Takahashi, K., Ando, K.: Self-Crack-Healing Behavior of Mullite/SiC Particle/SiC Whisker Multi-Composites and Potential Use for Ceramic Springs. J. Am. Cerum. Soc. 89(4), 1352–1357 (2006)

16. Ando, K., Liu, S.-P.: Fatigue strength characteristics of crack-healing materials - Al_2O_3/SiC composite ceramics and monolithic $Al_2O_3/$. Journal of the Chinese Institute of Engineering 27(3), 395–401 (2004)

17. Ono, M., Nakao, W., Takahashi, K., Nakatani, M., Ando, K.: A new methodology to guarantee the structural integrity of Al_2O_3/SiC composite using crack healing and a proof test. Fatigue Fract. Engng. Mater. Struct. 30, 599–607 (2007)

18. Jung, Y., Guo, Y., Nakao, W., Takahashi, K., Ando, K., Saito, S.: Crack-healing behavior and resultant high-temperature fatigue strength of machined Si_3N_4/SiC composite ceramic. Fatigue Fract. Engng. Mater. Struct. 31, 2–11 (2007)

19. Takahashi, K., Kim, B.-S., Chu, M.-C., Sato, S., Ando, K.: Crack-healing behavior and static fatigue strength of Si_3N_4/SiC ceramics held under stress at temperature (800, 900, 1000°C). Journal of the European Ceramic Society 23, 1971–1978 (2003)

20. Ando, K., Chu, M.C., Matsushita, S., Sato, S.: Effect of crack-healing and proof-testing procedures on fatigue strength and reliability of Si_3N_4/SiC composites. Journal of the European Ceramic Society 23, 977–984 (2003)

21. Houjou, K., Ando, K., Liu, S.-P., Sato, S.: Crack-healing and oxidation behavior of silicon nitride ceramics. Journal of the European Ceramic Society 24, 2329–2338 (2004)

22. Lee, S.-K., Ando, K., Kim, Y.-W.: Effect of Heat Treatments on the Crack-Healing and Static Fatigue Behavior of Silicon Carbide Sintered with Sc_2O_3 and AlN. J. Am. Cerum. Soc. 88(12), 3478–3482 (2005)

23. Takahashi, K., Ando, K., Murase, H., Nakayama, S., Saito, S.: Threshold Stress for Crack-Healing of Si_3N_4/SiC and Resultant Cyclic Fatigue Strength at the Healing Temperature. J. Am. Cerum. Soc. 88(3), 645–651 (2005)

24. Ando, K., Furusawa, K., Takahashi, K., Sato, S.: Crack-healing ability of structural ceramics and a new methodology to guarantee the structural integrity using the ability and proof-test. Journal of the European Ceramic Society 25, 549–558 (2005)

25. Lee, S.-K., Ishida, W., Lee, S.-Y., Nam, K.-W., Ando, K.: Crack-healing behavior and resultant strength properties of silicon carbide ceramic. Journal of the European Ceramic Society 25, 569–576 (2005)

26. Ando, K., Chu, M.-C., Tsuji, K., Hirasawa, T., Kobayashi, Y., Sato, S.: Crack healing behaviour and high-temperature strength of mullite/SiC composite ceramics. Journal of the European Ceramic Society 22, 1313–1319 (2002)

27. Ando, K., Takahashi, K., Nakayama, S., Saito, S.: Crack-Healing Behavior of Si_3N_4/SiC Ceramics under Cyclic Stress and Resultant Fatigue Strength at the Healing Temperature. J. Am. Cerum. Soc. 85(9), 2268–2272 (2002)

28. Sato, S., Chu, M.C., Kobayashi, Y., Ando, K.: Strengthening of mullite by dispersion of carbide ceramics particles. Jpn. Soc. Mech. Eng. 61(585A), 1023–1030 (1995)

29. Takahashi, K., Yokouchi, M., Lee, S.-K., Ando, K.: Crack-Healing Behavior of Al_2O_3 Toughened by SiC Whiskers. Journal of American Ceramic Society 86(12), 2143–2147 (2003)

30. Zhang, X., Xu, L., Du, S., Han, W., Han, J.: Preoxidation and Crack-Healing Behavior of ZrB_2–SiC Ceramic Composite. J. Am. Cerum. Soc. 91(12), 4068–4073 (2008)

31. Nakao, W., Takahashi, K., Ando, K.: Self crack-healing behavior of Mullite/SiC particle/SiC whiskers multi-composite. Journal of Materials 1, 1–6 (2005)

32. Kim, B.S., Ando, K., Chu, M.C., Saito, S.: Crack-healing behavior of Liquid-phase sintered Silicon Carbide. Journal of the Society of Materials Science 52(6), 667–673 (2002)

33. Osada, T., Nakao, W., Takahashi, K., Ando, K.: Kinetics of Self-Crack-Healing of Alumina/Silicon Carbide Composite Including Oxygen Partial Pressure Effect. J. Am. Cerum. Soc. 92(4), 864–869 (2009)

Effect of Tool Nose Profile Tolerance on Surface Roughness in Precision Turning

Aun Naa Sung, Mani Maran Ratnam, and Wei Ping Loh

School of Mechanical Engineering, Engineering Campus,
Universiti Sains Malaysia, Seri Ampangan,
14300 Nibong Tebal, Penang, Malaysia
mmaran@eng.usm.my

Abstract. The effect of the tool nose profile deviations in cutting tool inserts on the surface roughness of the work piece produced based on the actual tool nose profile geometry is studied. The nose profile was detected from the tool nose image captured using the 3-D metrology system. A edge detection approach combining moment invariance operator with Sobel 2-D filter operator is proposed. A work piece surface profile is then generated by considering tool nose profile deviation, feed rate, nose radius and wedge angle to study the effect of the work piece geometry deviation on the roughness values. Based on the experimental results, the maximum differences from ideal and experimental results are 19.8% for R_t, 19.9% for R_a and 16.1% for R_q respectively.

Keywords: surface roughness, tool nose profile deviation, sub-pixel accuracy.

1 Introduction

Surface roughness of work piece is a common concern in machining. It is well-known that surface profile is formed by the repetitive tool nose profile geometry [1,2]. The. The tool condition such as tool nose radius and entering angle plays significant role in determining the surface roughness [3-5]. Neseli et al. [3] investigated the effect of tool nose radius on the surface roughness of AISI 1040 steel using response surface methodology and found that tool nose radius is the most significant factor on surface roughness. The tool nose radius increase causes to increases of surface roughness.

Singh and Rao [4] showed that feed is the dominant factor affecting the surface roughness, followed by the nose radius, cutting velocity and effective rake angle. Thomas et al. [5] analyzed the surface roughness data generated by lathe dry turning of mild carbon steel and reported that the feed rate and the tool nose radius are the factor that produces the most important effects on surface roughness. As the nose radius increased the surface roughness is decreased. In most of the past studies, however, a perfectly rounded tool nose is assumed. In practice, the tool nose have non-geometric profile due to manufacturing tolerances. Progressive wear of the tool also affects the surface roughness [6-8]. The effect of the tool nose radius deviation caused by manufacturing tolerances on surface finish of the work piece has not been studied.

S.G. Ponnambalam et al. (Eds.): IRAM 2012, CCIS 330, pp. 475–482, 2012.
© Springer-Verlag Berlin Heidelberg 2012

In this study, a tool nose optical measurement method is introduced based on machine vision measurement method with sub-pixel edge detection. This new approach combines the moment invariance method (sub pixel-level) with Sobel 2-D method (pixel-level) to detect the tool nose profile. The optimum nose radius is detected and nose profile was presented as a linear profile using polar-radius transformation. The maximum peak-to-valley roughness (R_t), R_a and root-mean-square roughness (R_q) were determined based on extracted tool nose profile.

2   Tool Nose Radius Measurement and Profile Extraction Method

The tool radius measurement method is based on the machine vision measurement method developed in the past [9]. The commercial 3-D optical metrology system (*InfiniteFocus-Alicona*) was used to capture the image of cutting tool. Table 1 shows the details of the tool for investigation. The lens 5x was selected to produce an image having resolution of 1.754 µm/pixel. Fig. 1 shows a sample tool image captured.

Fig. 1. Image captured by Alicona optical measurement system

Table 1. The details of tool and tool holder used

Tool Shape	Rhombic 55°	Tool holder model	DDNNN 2525M15
Tool Model	DNMG 150608	Hand of Tool	neutral
Nominal radius	0.8 mm	Inclination angle	-9°
Positive/negative insert shape	negative	Rake angle	-5°
Tool included angle	55°	Entering angle	62.5°
No of edge/inserts	4	Wedge angle	62.5°

Fig. 2 shows the flow chart of the algorithm for optimum nose radius detection and polar-radius transformation of the rounded tool-work piece engagement edge. In Stage 1, the tool nose image was pre-processed to clean up the image. The original image was read as a true color image and was converted to gray scale image in pixels. The image was eroded to remove pixels on the object boundaries, and then morphological reconstruction was performed for the eroded image under the original image. The reconstructed image was dilated using the same structuring element as used for erosion. The reconstruction was applied again for the complement of the dilated image. The tool nose image after pre-processing is in non-uniform illumination due to the contour of the insert. Thus, the common edge detector such as Sobel operator [10] is not applicable for the image. In Stage 2, a Sobel–moment invariance operator is proposed to detect the edge. The band consisting the edge was determined by the gradient magnitude in Eqn. (1).

$$\text{gradient magnitude} = \sqrt{G_x{}^2 + G_y{}^2} \ . \tag{1}$$

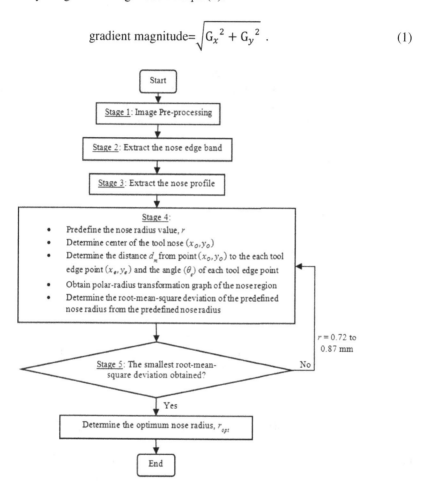

Fig. 2. The flow chart of the algorithm for optimum nose radius detection and polar-radius transformation graph

The gradient is high at the borders of the tool and mostly low at the background and inside the tool. A gradient threshold value is predefined to determine the nose edge band. The threshold value is selected to produce a smooth nose profile as in Fig. 3. In Stage 3, the nose edge band was used as the processing area to obtain the tool nose profile. To locate the nose profile, a moment invariance operator with sub pixel accuracy [11] was introduced. The detected nose profile location (x_e, y_e) is shown in Fig. 3.

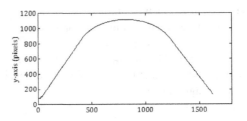

Fig. 3. The tool nose profile

In Stage 4, the center of the tool nose O (x_o, y_o) was calculated using the theory developed in the past [9]. This theory is further improved to increase the accuracy of results. A polar-radius graph shows the radial distance d_e against the angle θ_e measured counterclockwise from the nose profile center point is illustrated in Fig. 4.

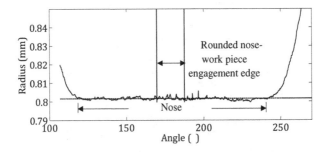

Fig. 4. The polar-radius graph for the tool nose

In Stage 5, Stages 4 was repeated for different radii to determine the optimum nose radius r_{opt}. The nose radius is predefined in the range of ±10% of the nominal radius. The radius that produces the smallest root-mean-square deviation from the radius will be the optimum nose radius.

3   Surface Roughness Prediction by Simulation Method

For surface roughness prediction the feed rate is chosen as 0.25 mm/rev for finishing operation, while the nose radius and wedge angle values were chosen as shown in Table 1. The tool was placed on the tool holder to produce the image. The flow chart of the algorithm for surface profile generation and to calculate R_t, R_a and R_q is shown in stages in Fig. 5. Stages 1 to 3 in Section 2 were repeated to detect the nose profile. In Stage 4, the tool in the image is rotated counterclockwise through an angle Ω to locate the tool to the appropriate wedge angle. The rotation angle Ω is shown as Eqn. (3),

$$\Omega = |\tan^{-1} g_2| - \beta_l \ . \tag{3}$$

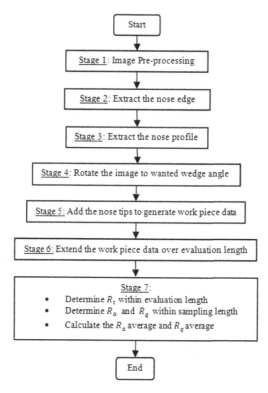

Fig. 5. The flow chart of the algorithm for surface roughness prediction based on the tool image captured

The tool nose profile (x_r, y_r) is calculated by Eqn. (4) since the points (x_e, y_e) are rotated in counterclockwise through the rotation angle Ω.

$$x_r = x_e \cos \Omega - y_e \sin \Omega, \; y_r = x_e \sin \Omega + y_e \cos \Omega \qquad (4)$$

In a turning operation the surface profile of the work piece consists of small and repetitive arcs produced by the geometry of the feed marks. In Stage 5, the work piece surface data is simulated by adding few 'nose tips' which are spaced out a feed rate apart. Consequently, the nose profile is crop to one feed length which represent the work piece produced by one feed cut. Since the work piece profile (x_r, y_r) have nonuniformly spaced vectors x_r, the work piece profile (x_r, y_r) is interpolated to calculate y_i the values of the underlying function y_r to fits to uniformly spaced vectors x_i to spacing 1. In stage 6, by duplicating the work piece profile (x_i, y_i) in a few feed rate lengths, the total length of the turned surface profile data is extended as shown in Fig. 6. In Stage 7, R_t, R_a and R_q were determined from the work piece profile. R_t is determined from the work piece profile within the evaluation length as 4.0 mm according to BS 1134:2010 [12]. The assessment of R_a and were made over five sampling lengths based on 0.8 mm interval in width.

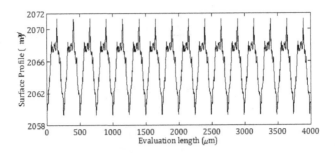

Fig. 6. Extended work piece surface profile data

4   Experimental Setup

The machine tool used was an Okuma CNC lathe machine. The AISI 304 alloy steel rods were machined using same inserts and tool holder in simulation inputs. The details of the tool and its holder are shown in Table 1. The work pieces were machined using feed rates 0.25 mm/rev, cutting speed 1550 rpm, depth-of-cut 0.2 mm.

A stylus type roughness tester (Mitutoyo Surftest SV 400) was used to measure the surface roughness at the initial machined segment on the work piece. The measurement process was repeated four times by rotating about its axis through 90°. The experimental results obtained by averaging the results from four measured data.

5   Results and Discussion

Fig. 7 shows the different polar-radius graphs for three different tool noses with nominal radius 0.80 mm. As shown, the tool profiles are not smooth and deviate from 0.80 mm. These tools will produce different surface roughness after turning operation. Fig. 8(a) shows the comparison of the actual and ideal nose radius. The maximum and average absolute mean difference of tool tolerances are 1.1% and 0.5% respectively which is complies with ISO 3685 standard which is lower than 10%[14]. Figs. 8(b) to 8(d) show the comparisons of the ideal, simulated and experimental results for R_t, R_a and R_q respectively.

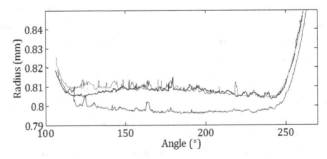

Fig. 7. The polar-radius graphs for three different tool noses

As shown in Figs. 8(b) to 8(d), the surface roughness data R_t, R_a and R_q from simulated surface profile using actual tool nose profile are different from ideal tool nose profile. The maximum differences from ideal and simulated tool nose profile are 47.7% for R_t, 10.7% for R_a and 14.5% for R_q respectively. The average absolute mean differences from ideal and simulated tool nose profile are 18.3% for R_t, 5.4% for R_a and 6.7% for R_q respectively. This reveals that although the tool tolerance is allowed in ISO 3685 standard, the tool will affect the work piece surface roughness significantly. For example, the actual radius for tool edge 1 is 0.803mm which is 0.4% difference from nominal radius, however, the absolute differences from ideal and simulated tool nose profile are 47.7% for R_t, 10.7% for R_a and 14.5% for R_q respectively.

As simulated results, the experimental results for R_t, R_a and R_q as shown in Figs. 8(a) to 8(d) also show deviations compare to ideal surface roughness. The average absolute mean differences from ideal and experimental results are 11.2% for R_t, 8.7% for R_a and 6.6% for R_q respectively. The maximum differences from ideal and experimental results are 19.8% for R_t, 19.9% for R_a and 16.1% for R_q respectively This proves that the tool tolerance is a factor affect surface roughness in real machining although all the cutting parameters are constant.

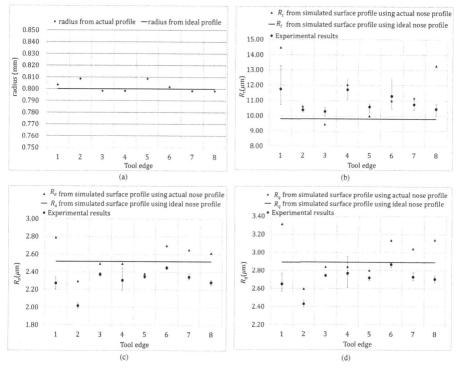

Fig. 8. (a)Nose radius from actual and ideal tool nose profiles. (b) R_t (c) R_a and (d) R_q from simulation (ideal and actual tool nose profile) and experimental results.

6   Conclusion

To fulfill the requirements of high accurately analysis of surface roughness, a simulation method has been proposed by combining the effect of feed rate, nose radius, wedge angle and tool tolerance. The surface roughness considering effect of tool tolerance was different with ideal surface roughness although the tool tolerance is less than 10%. This finding will be very significant for ongoing applications on precision engineering. The surface roughness can be predicted by considering feed rate, nose radius, wedge angle and tool tolerance and the best cutting edge can be determined before machining.

Acknowledgments. This research was partially funded by the USM RU grant (1001/PMEKANIK/814079).

References

1. Shahabi, H.H., Ratnam, M.M.: Assessment of flank wear and nose radius wear from work piece roughness profile in turning operation using machine vision. Int. Journal. Adv. Manuf. Tech. 43(1-2), 11–21 (2009)
2. Sung, A.N., Ratnam, M.M., Loh, W.P.: Simulation of surface roughness and topography in finish turning using digital image subtraction. In: ICCAIE-IEEE Conference on Computer Applications and Industrial Electronics, Penang, Malaysia, pp. 355–360 (2011)
3. Neseli, S., Yaldız, S., Türkes, E.: Optimization of tool geometry parameters for turning operations based on the response surface methodology. J. Measurement 44, 580–587 (2011)
4. Singh, D., Rao, P.V.: A surface roughness prediction model for hard turning process. Int. J. Adv. Manuf. Tech. 32, 1115–1124 (2007)
5. Thomas, M., Beauchamp, Y., Youssef, A.Y., Masounave, J.: Effect of tool vibration on surface roughness during lathe dry turning process. J. Comput. Ind. Eng. 31(3/4), 637–644 (1996)
6. Manna, A., Bhattacharayya, B.: Influence of machining parameters on the machinability of particulate reinforced Al/Si-MMC. Int. J. Adv. Manuf. Tech. 25(9-10), 850–856 (2005)
7. Pavel, R., Marinescu, I., Deis, M., Pillar, J.: Effect of tool wear on surface finish for a case of continuous and interrupted hard turning. J. Mater. Proc. Tech. 170(1-2), 341–349 (2005)
8. Kílíçkap, E., Çakír, O., Aksoy, M., Inan: A study of tool wear and surface roughness in machining of homogenized SiC-p reinforced aluminum metal matrix composite. J. Mater. Proc. Tech. 164-165, 862–867 (2005)
9. Chian, G.J., Ratnam, M.M.: Determination of tool nose radii of cutting inserts using machine vision. J. Sensor Rev. 31(2), 0260–2288 (2011)
10. Sobel: Neighbourhood coding of binary images fast contour following and general array binary processing. Comput. Graphics and Image Process. 8, 127–135 (1978)
11. Wang, W.H., Hong, G.S., Wong, Y.S.: Flank wear measurement by a threshold independent method with sub-pixel accuracy. Int.J. Mach. Tools Manuf. 46, 199–207 (2006)
12. BS 1134-2: Assessment of surface texture: guidance and general information, British Standard (2010)

Effects of Cutting and Vibration Parameters
on Transient Cutting Force
in Elliptical Vibration Cutting

Xinquan Zhang, A. Senthil Kumar, and Mustafizur Rahman

Deparment of Mechanical Engineering, National University of Singapore, Singapore

Abstract. As a novel vibration-assisted machining method, elliptical vibration cutting (EVC) technique has been found to be a better technique, compared to conventional cutting and conventional vibration cutting techniques. Due to the transient thickness of cut and continuous variation of tool velocity direction, its fundamental cutting mechanics is different from other cutting techniques. In the field of metal cutting, cutting force is usually considered as the most important indicator of machining state and quality. Analysis of the cutting force plays a vital role in determining and predicting various machining performances. In this study, a series of low-frequency orthogonal EVC tests were conducted to study the effects of three essential parameters on the transient cutting force values. It is found that the transient cutting force increases with the increment of speed ratio, the increment of tangential amplitude, and the decrement of thrust amplitude.

Keywords: Elliptical vibration cutting, Transient cutting force, Machining parameters.

1 Introduction

In the manufacturing industry, vibration-assisted machining has already been demonstrated as a well-known cost-effective method for machining various materials with superior cutting performance compared with the conventional cutting (CC) method [1]. As a novel two-dimension vibration-assisted machining method, elliptical vibration cutting (EVC) has received a lot of attention for its even better machining performance over the conventional vibration cutting (CVC) method [2]. Since EVC technique was introduced in 1994 [3], this technique has been proved to be a very promising technique to machine various difficult-to-cut brittle materials (e.g. hardened steel [4], tungsten carbide [5]) with lower cutting force and slower tool wear compared to the CC and CVC techniques.

Cutting force is considered as the most important indicator of machining state and quality. Analysis of the cutting force plays an important role in the determination of characteristics of machining performances like tool wear, surface quality, cutting energy, and machining accuracy. Hence, in order to investigate the fundamental cutting mechanics of the EVC process, researchers [3] have studied the transient cutting force at different vibration frequencies, and found that higher vibration frequency can reduce the transient cutting force. However, beside the vibration frequency, the effects of other cutting and vibration conditions on the transient cutting force have not been studied yet.

S.G. Ponnambalam et al. (Eds.): IRAM 2012, CCIS 330, pp. 483–490, 2012.

Speed ratio is considered as one of the most essential parameters in the EVC technique [6-7]. In the authors' recent study on machining hardened steel using PCD tools with the ultrasonic EVC technique, it was found that, compared to the feed rate and the depth of cut, the speed ratio has the most significant effects on cutting performances (e.g. time-averaged cutting force, tool wear and surface roughness). Tangential and thrust amplitudes are two key parameters in vibration-assisted machining technology [1]. Tangential amplitude is used to discriminate the CVC technique from the CC technique, and thrust amplitude is used to discriminate the EVC technique and the CVC technique. For the EVC technique, both the tangential and thrust amplitudes are larger than zero, and the tool tip vibrates in two dimension; for the CVC technique, the thrust amplitude is equal to zero, and the tool tip vibrates in only one dimension; while for the CC technique, both the tangential and thrust amplitudes are equal to zero, and the tool tip does not vibrates.

Unfortunately, the above three essential parameters' effects (speed ratio, tangential and thrust amplitudes) on the transient cutting force in the EVC process have not been studied yet. Therefore, an intensive experimental investigation to study their effects is necessary to enhance the understanding of fundamental material removal mechanism in the EVC process. In this paper, a series of low-frequency orthogonal EVC tests are conducted to study the effects of the three essential parameters on the transient cutting force.

2   Characteristics of EVC

The elliptical locus is generated by elliptical vibration of the tool tip and feed movement of the workpiece against the cutting tool. Fig. 1 shows a 3D section view of orthogonal EVC process, where the workpiece is fed rightward along the tangential cutting direction (x-axis). The orthogonal EVC is defined as a type of EVC process where the vibration modes, the cutting forces and the nominal cutting velocity are all perpendicular to the tool edge [6]. In Fig. 1, w represents the width of cut, and a_p represents the nominal uncut chip thickness.

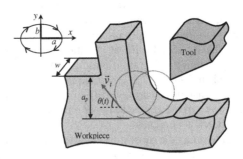

Fig. 1. Schematic 3D illustration of the orthogonal EVC process

When the tool is vibrated at an angular frequency ω ($\omega=2\pi f$, f is the tool vibration frequency), and the workpiece is fed at a nominal cutting speed v_c, the tool path with respect to the workpiece can be expressed by the x- and y- coordinates of the tool position as [3]:

$$\begin{cases} x(t) = a\cos(\omega t) - v_c t \\ y(t) = b\cos(\omega t + \phi) \end{cases} \tag{1}$$

where a and b represent the tangential and thrust directional vibration amplitudes, respectively, t is the time, and ϕ is the phase shift between the two vibration modes.

For the EVC technique, it is understood the variation of transient TOC (TOC_t) is a key characteristic in the EVC process [7]. The value of TOC_t gets continuously varied and is always smaller than a_p due to the overlapping cutting cycles. During each EVC cycle, the tool edge starts cutting from point A on the machined surface left by the previous cycle, reaches the bottom point B, passes the maximum TOC_t (symbolized as $(TOC_t)_m$) point D and the friction reversal point E [6], and finally ends this EVC cycle at the cutting-end point F. Fig. 2 (a) and (b) show the 2D view of the EVC process before and after the tool edge passes the $(TOC_t)_m$ point D, respectively. The point T represents the instant position of the tool edge, and the point P represents the contact location of the tool rake face on the surface machined by the previous cutting cycle.

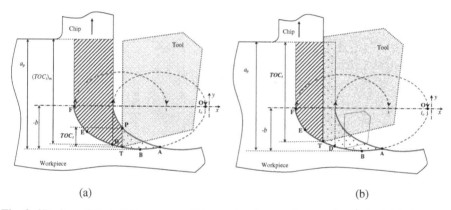

(a)   (b)

Fig. 2. 2D view of the EVC process at different time instants in a cutting cycle: (a) before the tool edge passes the $(TOC_t)_m$ point, (b) after the tool edge passes the $(TOC_t)_m$ point

3   Experimental Details

It is known that researchers usually apply high-frequency vibration (at ultrasonic level of about 20 kHz or more) to enhance the productivity and cutting performances in practical metal cutting with the EVC technique [2,5]. However, it is impossible to measure the transient force values with ultrasonic frequency using the state-of-the-art measurement technology, due to the low natural frequency (about 5 kHz or less) of common dynamometers. It is because the measurement system may act as a low pass filter [1], which is only able to measure the filtered time-averaged cutting force, but not the original transient force. Therefore, in order to study the transient cutting force in the EVC process, it is necessary to employ a low-frequency EVC method, instead of the ultrasonic EVC method.

In order to generate the low-frequency EVC motion, firstly, the ideal elliptical vibration loci are created using MATLAB software by using Equation (1) with desired cutting and vibration parameters. Secondly, to guarantee the fitting accuracy of the generated tool motion, the elliptical loci are fitted by sampling 360 points for each cutting cycle (i.e. every 2π phase of vibration). Thirdly, the coordinates of those derived points are used to generate the G-codes, which are then input into a CNC ultraprecision machine tool (*Toshiba ULG-100H³*). Finally, the EVC motion is generated by the combined movement of X- and Y- axes of the machine tool, which has a 10 nm linear resolution.

In this study, a series of orthogonal EVC tests were conducted on 6061 aluminum alloy workpiece. Fig. 3 shows a schematic illustration of the experimental setup for the cutting tests. The force signals were measured by a 3-component mini-dynamometer with 1 mN resolution mounted on the tool post and recorded with a real-time digitized recorder. In order to avoid the effect of tool edge geometry in this orthogonal EVC test, a flat-nose single crystal diamond tool was used, with a 0° rake angle and a 7° flank angle. Fig. 4 shows a microscope photograph of the flat nose diamond tool, which has a 760 μm nose width.

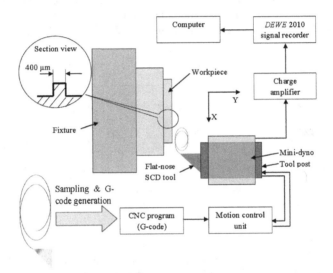

Fig. 3. Illustration of the experimental set-up for the low-frequency EVC tests

500.00 um/div

Fig. 4. Microscope photograph (X50) of the flat nose diamond tool

Table 1 shows the cutting and vibration conditions for the orthogonal EVC tests. The speed ratio R_s in this table represents the ratio of nominal cutting speed v_c to maximum vibration speed ($R_s = {v_c}/{2\pi a f}$), and its value is changed by varying the value of v_c. Four different speed ratios, five principal amplitudes and five thrust amplitudes were selected to study their effects on the transient cutting force, while keeping the other cutting and vibration conditions unvaried.

Table 1. Cutting and vibration conditions of the orthogonal elliptical vibration cutting tests

Tool	Flat nose diamond tool			
Workpiece	6061 aluminum alloy			
Width of cut, w [μm]	400			
Nominal uncut chip thickness, a_p [μm]	15			
Lubrication condition	Dry cutting			
Vibration frequency, f [Hz]	0.25			
Phase shift, ϕ [deg]	90			
Speed ratio, R_s	0.025	0.05	0.075	0.1
(Nominal cutting speed, v_c [mm/min])	(0.047)	(0.094)	(0.141)	(0.188)
Tangential amplitude, a [μm]	8	11	14	17	20
Thrust amplitude, b [μm]	2	5	8	11	14

4   Results and Analysis

4.1   Effect of Speed Ratio

Fig. 5(a) shows the recorded experimental values of the transient force components (the principal and thrust force) in an EVC cycle at two speed ratios (0.025 and 0.1) with 20 μm tangential amplitude and 5 μm thrust amplitude. Fig. 5(b) shows the values of the maximum resultant force R_{max} against different speed ratios.

From Fig. 5(a), it can be seen that the transient principal force starts increasing from zero, reaches the maximum value at some point, then decreases slightly, and finally drops to zero after the disengagement of tool and chip. The transient thrust force starts from zero and increases gradually, which is similar to the trend of transient principal force in the beginning portion. However, after reaching its maximum positive value, it starts decreasing and becomes negative. Then, as time goes on, the thrust force remains negative in the following portion of the EVC cycle until the tool is fully disengaged with the formed chip. It means that the thrust force is reversed in direction, and such reversal process is considered to be caused by the reversed direction of friction between the tool rake face and the formed chip, indicating that the tool is pulling the chip upward from the workpiece. From Fig. 5(b) It can be observed that the value of R_{max} increases gradually with the increment of R_s. The value of R_{max} is increased by more than 45% when the speed ratio is increased from 0.025 to 0.1.

According to Fig. 2(a) and (b), the values of TOC_t and $(TOC_t)_m$ against different speed ratios can be calculated. It will be found that both the values of TOC_t and $(TOC_t)_m$ increase with the increment of the speed ratio. Considering the direct proportion relationship between TOC_t and the transient cutting force, the variation of TOC_t can be treated as a major reason for the variation tendency found in Fig. 5(b).

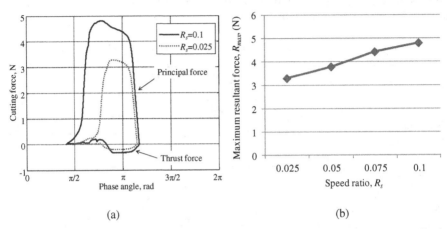

(a)   (b)

Fig. 5. The effect of speed ratio on: (a) the transient cutting force components, (b) the maximum resultant cutting force

4.2   Effect of Tangential Amplitude

In order to investigate the effect of tangential amplitude, the speed ratio is kept constant at 0.1 by changing the value of v_c accordingly, and the thrust amplitude is kept constant at 5 μm. Fig. 6 (a) and (b) show the effect of different tangential amplitudes on the transient cutting force and R_{max}. It can be seen from that the value of transient cutting force increases gradually with the increment of tangential amplitude, and the value of R_{max} is increased by 35% when the tangential amplitude is increased from 8 to 20.

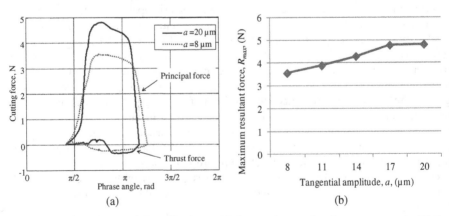

(a)   (b)

Fig. 6. The effect of tangential amplitude on: (a) the transient cutting force components, (b) the maximum resultant cutting force

Through calculating the values of TOC_t, it will be found that the value of TOC_t is identical at different tangential amplitudes. Accordingly, the value of $(TOC_t)_m$ does not change against the tangential amplitude. Hence, it can be concluded that the variation of TOC_t is not a reason for the variation tendency found in Fig. 6(a). The increment of transient cutting force with the increment of tangential amplitude may be caused by the increment of the friction reversal time, when the thrust force is reversed in direction.

4.3   Effect of Thrust Amplitude

Fig. 7 (a) and (b) show the effect of different thrust amplitudes on the transient cutting force and R_{max} with 20 μm tangential amplitude and 0.1 speed ratio. Unlike the case for the tangential amplitude, it can be observed that the value of R_{max} decreases with the increment of thrust amplitude, and the value of R_{max} is decreased by about 40% when the thrust amplitude is increased from 2 to 14. As TOC_t and $(TOC_t)_m$ gradually decrease with the increment of thrust amplitude, it can be concluded that the decrement of TOC_t contribute as one reason for the variation tendency of transient cutting force.

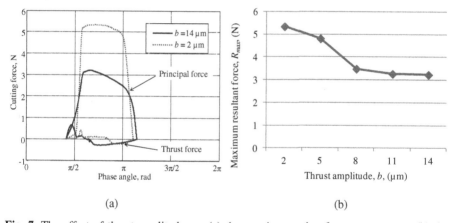

(a)   (b)

Fig. 7. The effect of thrust amplitude on: (a) the transient cutting force components, (b) the maximum resultant cutting force

5   Conclusion

In this study, the effects of three essential cutting and vibration parameters (speed ratio, tangential and thrust amplitudes) for the EVC technique were experimentally investigated by conducting a series of low-frequency EVC tests. Through analyzing the transient thickness of cut and the friction reversal time for every EVC test, the experimental results were analytically explained. According to the results and analysis, the following conclusions can be drawn:

i) The transient cutting force increases with the increment of speed ratio; and the maximum resultant force (R_{max}) is increased by more than 45% when the speed ratio is increased from 0.025 to 0.1.

ii) The transient force increases with the increment of tangential amplitude; and the value of R_{max} is increased by 35% when the tangential amplitude is increased from 8 to 20 µm.

iii) A larger value of thrust amplitude leads to a smaller value of transient cutting force; and R_{max} is decreased by about 40% when the thrust amplitude is increased from 2 to 14 µm.

References

1. Brehl, D.E., Dow, T.A.: Review of vibration-assisted machining. Precis. Eng. 32(3), 153–172 (2008)
2. Shamoto, E., Moriwaki, T.: Ultraprecision diamond cutting of hardened steel by applying elliptical vibration cutting. CIRP Ann. 48(1), 441–444 (1999)
3. Shamoto, E., Moriwaki, T.: Study on elliptical vibration cutting. CIRP Ann. 43(1), 35–38 (1994)
4. Zhang, X., Senthil Kumar, A., Rahman, M., Nath, C., Liu, K.: Experimental study on ultrasonic elliptical vibration cutting of hardened steel using PCD tools. J. Mater. Process. Technol. 211(11), 1701–1709 (2011)
5. Nath, C., Rahman, M., Neo, K.S.: Machinability study of tungsten carbide using PCD tools under ultrasonic elliptical vibration cutting. Int. J. Mach. Tools Manuf. 49(14), 1089–1095 (2009)
6. Shamoto, E., Suzuki, N., Hino, R.: Analysis of 3D elliptical vibration cutting with thin shear plane model. CIRP Ann. 57(1), 57–60 (2008)
7. Nath, C., Rahman, M., Neo, K.S.: Modeling of the effect of machining parameters on maximum thickness of cut in ultrasonic elliptical vibration cutting. ASME J. Manuf. Sci. Eng. 133(1), 011007 (2011)

Supplier Selection: Reliability
Based Total Cost of Ownership Approach
Using Cuckoo Search

G. Kanagaraj[1], S.G. Ponnambalam[1,*], and N. Jawahar[2]

[1] Monash University Sunway Campus, Bandar Sunway, Selangor, Malaysia
{kanagaraj.ganesan,sgponnambalam}@monash.edu
[2] Thiagarajar College of Engineering, Madurai, 625 015, India
jawahartce@yahoo.co.uk

Abstract. Traditional supplier selection methods are often based on the quoted price, which ignores the significant direct and indirect costs associated with quality, delivery, use and service cost. This paper proposes Reliability based total cost of ownership (RBTCO) model by incorporating the initial cost, replacement cost and downtime cost. The mathematical formulation of the RBTCO model for the supplier selection problem fits into the nonlinear integer programming problem, which belongs to the NP-hard category. A recently developed Cuckoo search algorithm is used to provide the optimal solutions. The performance of the algorithm is tested with numerical problems.

Keywords: Supplier selection, Total cost of ownership, Cuckoo search.

1   Introduction

The trend of globalization and increased outsourcing has resulted in greater dependence of companies on their suppliers for decreasing design costs, developing new and high quality products, providing on-time delivery and satisfactory after-sale services [1]. Supplier selection has become a very important area of consideration for purchasing managers in today's highly competitive environment. As the cost of raw materials purchased for production usually constitute a higher percentage of the total cost of finished products, it has become increasingly necessary for organizations to get the best value for money from suppliers [2]. Traditional supplier selection methods are often based on quoted price, which ignores significant direct and indirect costs associated with quality, delivery, use and service costs of purchased parts and materials. Products that are cheap, high in quality and excellent after-sale services are the basic necessities of a customer. This paper addresses Reliability based Total Cost of Ownership (RBTCO), which is the integration of quality, service and maintenance related costs along with the initial price of the product, has evolved as a supplier selection criterion.

Aissaoui et al [3] in their review on supplier selection and order lot sizing modeling indicated that the decision involved in selecting suppliers becomes the most important activity of an outsourcing process. Many experts believe that the supplier

---

[*] Corresponding author.

S.G. Ponnambalam et al. (Eds.): IRAM 2012, CCIS 330, pp. 491–501, 2012.
© Springer-Verlag Berlin Heidelberg 2012

selection is the most important activity of a purchasing department [4-6]. Hence, an efficient supplier selection process plays a pivotal role.

The supplier selection problem has received a considerable attention in academic research and literature. Dickson [6] identified over twenty attributes for supplier selection based on empirical data collected from 170 purchasing managers and members of National Association of Purchasing Managers. Hu [7] conducted a research on supplier selection process and concluded that price, quality, production capacity and delivery are the most important attributes of supplier evaluation techniques. Cost, quality and service have been identified as the prime decision criteria for supplier selection by many researchers [8-12]. The review reveals the following: Simply looking for suppliers offering the lowest prices is not the "efficient sourcing".

Carrubba [13] stated that TCO drives the manufacturer to look beyond the initial procurement cost for making decision on supplier selection and provides a meaningful way to integrate reliability and maintenance strategies with product sales and service offerings and concluded that one of the most important cost drivers in the TCO equation is product reliability, which significantly impacts maintenance costs, as well as fixed costs such as downtime. TCO attempts to quantify the costs related to the procurement of quality products or services offered by a supplier [14-18]. To the user of a product, reliability is measured by a long, failure free operation. To the supplier of a product, reliability is measured by completing a failure free warranty period under specified operating conditions with few failures during the design life of the product.

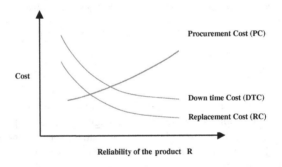

Fig. 1. Cost Vs reliability of the product

The major cost elements of TCO that have direct relationship with the reliability of the product are: Procurement Cost (PC), Replacement Cost (RC) and Down Time Cost (DTC). The relationship between the above costs of TCO and product reliability is shown in Figure 1. Concerning the above aspects, this paper introduces a reliability based total cost of ownership model, which incorporates procurement, maintenance and down time costs along with the practical constraints on product reliability and weight limitation for the supplier selection decisions. The rest of the paper is organized as follows. In section 2, describes the problem and elaborates the various cost elements of TCO with corresponding mathematical formulation. The proposed Cuckoo Search algorithm is illustrated numerically in section 3. Section 4, discusses the performance of the algorithm compared with enumeration technique. Finally, the conclusion and further research are discussed in section 5.

2   Problem Description

Fig. 2 shows the typical layout of a product or a system that consists of n elements arranged in series. For each element i, there are m_i number of suppliers available in the market with varying costs, reliabilities, weights and other characteristics. Let r_i^j, c_i^j and w_i^j be the reliability, cost and weight of element i of the supplier j, respectively. They differ from technologies/suppliers chosen and are known. Let x_i^j, defined as a binary variable (0 or 1), is considered as the decision variable that indicates the selection of supplier j for element i, i.e., for each element i, x_i^j is equal to 1 for the selected supplier j and is equal to 0 for all the non-selected suppliers for the element i. This implies that only one supplier is selected for an element.

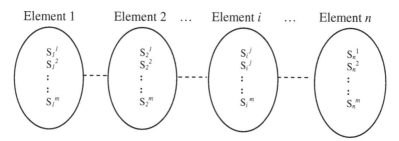

Fig. 2. Product/System configuration

2.1   Cost Elements of TCO

The framework for calculating TCO, which is development of TCO equation, depends on the problem environment. The three major cost elements of TCO model for supplier selection decision can be described as follows:

2.1.1 Procurement Cost
It is the sum of the cost of all n elements of the product. This depends on the selected suppliers for the elements and their corresponding cost. It is given as:

$$PC = \sum_{i=1}^{n} \sum_{j=1}^{m_i} c_i^j x_i^j \tag{1}$$

2.1.2 Replacement Cost
It is the sum of the cost of replacing the failed elements during the intended product life time t. It is assumed that the failure time of element i of supplier j follows negative exponential distribution with failure rate λ_i^j and the product is required to operate for a specified life time of t, then the reliability of the element i of supplier j is given by:

$$r_i^j = e^{-(\lambda_i^j)t} \tag{2}$$

The number of times the element i of supplier j fails during the product life N_i^j is equal to the multiplication of failure rate and life of the product.

$$N_i^j = (\lambda_i^j)t \tag{3}$$

$$r_i^j = e^{-N_i^j} \tag{4}$$

$$\ln r_i^j = -N_i^j \tag{5}$$

$$N_i^j = \ln\left(\frac{1}{r_i^j}\right) \tag{6}$$

The cost of element i of supplier j at the time of replacement would be different from the original cost c_i^j due to time value of money and individual replacement. Normally replacements lead to higher cost. A factor β_i^j is used here to account for the decrease in money value and the extra cost for replacement. The cost for the replacements of the element i of supplier j during the product life t becomes the multiplication of N_i^j, β_i^j and c_i^j. Hence, the total replacement cost (RC) for all the selected elements during the product life time t is derived as:

$$RC = \sum_{i=1}^{n}\sum_{j=1}^{m_i}\left\{\ln\left[\frac{1}{r_i^j}\right]\right\}\beta_i^j c_i^j x_i^j \tag{7}$$

2.1.3 Downtime Cost

It is the cost for the non-availability of the product. Failure of any one of the elements in the product leads to the non-availability of the product. Under the assumption that failure of the elements is independent (i.e. simultaneous failure of the elements does not occur) and the rectification/restoration time of element i of supplier j is known as DT_i^j, then the total downtime for an element i of supplier j becomes the multiplication of N_i^j and DTi^j. When the cost of non-availability of the product per unit time is given as DC, then the total downtime cost (DTC) for all the selected elements of the product becomes:

$$DTC = DC \sum_{i=1}^{n}\sum_{j=1}^{m_i}\left\{\ln\left[\frac{1}{r_i^j}\right]\right\}DT_i^j x_i^j \tag{8}$$

The total cost of ownership over the designed life of the product is obtained by adding the cost components given by equations (1), (7) and (8). Besides, the design specification warrants (i) a certain minimum required reliability of the product R_s and (ii) restriction on the maximum weight W_s. They become the constraints in the selection of suppliers for minimum TCO.

2.2   Problem Definition

Determination of optimal supplier selection X_{opt} (x_1^1, x_2^2,. x_i^j....x_n^m $\forall i$, $i=1$ to n; $\forall j$, $j=1$ to m_i) of the components of a product for minimum TCO subjected to minimum required product reliability R_s and limitation on maximum total weight W_s for the given input values of: Cost (c_i^j); Reliability (r_i^j); Weight (w_i^j) of element i of supplier j; Factor for individual replacement of element i of supplier j (β_i^j); Time required rectifying the defect of element i of supplier j (DT_i^j); Downtime cost of the product per unit time DC.

2.3   Mathematical Model

$$Min\ \textbf{TCO} = \sum_{i=1}^{n}\sum_{j=1}^{m_i} c_i^{\,j} x_i^{\,j} + \sum_{i=1}^{n}\sum_{j=1}^{m_i}\left\{\ln\left[\frac{1}{r_i^{\,j}}\right]\right\}\beta_i^{\,j} c_i^{\,j} x_i^{\,j} + DC\sum_{i=1}^{n}\sum_{j=1}^{m_i}\left\{\ln\left[\frac{1}{r_i^{\,j}}\right]\right\}DT_i^{\,j} x_i^{\,j} \qquad (9)$$

Subject to:

$$\prod_{i=1}^{n}\left(\sum_{j=1}^{m_i} x_i^{\,j} r_i^{\,j}\right)\geq R_s \qquad (10)$$

$$\sum_{i=1}^{n}\sum_{j=1}^{m_i} x_i^{\,j} w_i^{\,j} \leq W_s \qquad (11)$$

$$\sum_{j=1}^{m_i} x_i^{\,j} = 1 \qquad (12)$$

The equation 10 (first constraint) assures the minimum required reliability for the product. The equation 11 (second constraint) imposes the limitation on the permissible maximum total weight of the product. The equation 12 (third set of constraints) assures a single supplier selection for each element i among m_i number of available suppliers. The formulation of RBTCO model belongs to NP-hard category. Heuristic approaches are most often applied to computationally intractable NP-hard problems because solving these problems exactly can take an exponential amount of computation time. Hence, the Cuckoo search (CS) developed in 2009 by Yang and Deb [19], is proposed as the possible solution methodology for this RBTCO model.

3   Cuckoo Search Algorithm

Cuckoo search algorithm is inspired by the obligate brood parasitism of some cuckoo species by laying their eggs in the nests of other host birds of other species. It is more efficient than GA and PSO to adapt to wider class of optimization problems [19].

The CS is based on the following three idealized rules:

- Each cuckoo lays one egg at a time, and dumps it in a randomly chosen nest.
- The best nests with high quality of eggs (solutions) will carry over to the next generations.
- The number of available host nests is fixed, and a host can discover an alien egg with a probability Pa $\in$ [0, 1]. In this case, the host bird can either throw the egg away or abandon the nest so as to build a completely new nest in a new location.

For simplicity, this last assumption can be approximated by a fraction Pa of the n nests being replaced by new nests. For a maximization problem, the quality or fitness of a solution can simply be proportional to the objective function. Other forms of fitness can be defined in a similar way to the fitness function in GA. The basic steps of the CS can be summarized as the pseudo code as follows:

```
Begin
        Objective function f(x),  x =[ x₁¹, x₂²,. xⱼⁱ....xₙᵐ]ᵀ;
        Generate initial population of n host nests
While (t < Max Generation) or (stop criterion);
        Get a cuckoo (say i) randomly by Lévy flights;
            Evaluate its quality/fitness Fᵢ;
        Choose a nest among n (say j) randomly;
            if (Fᵢ > Fⱼ) then
                Replace j by a new solution
            end if
```

```
                    Abandon a fraction (P_a) of worse nests (and build new ones at new locations
                    via Levy flights);
              Keep the best solutions (or nests with quality solutions);
                 Rank the solutions and find the current best;
      end while
                  Post process results and visualization;
      end
```

When generating new solutions $x^{(t+1)}$ for, say cuckoo i, a Lévy flight is performed using the following equation:

$$x_i^{(t+1)} = x_i^t + \propto \oplus L\acute{e}vy\ (\lambda) \tag{13}$$

Where $\propto > 0$ is the step size which should be related to the scales of the problem of interest. The product $\oplus$ means entry-wise multiplication. The above equation is essentially the stochastic equation for random walk. In general, a random walk is a Markov chain whose next status/location only depends on the current location (the first term in the above equation) and the transition probability (the second term). The Lévy flight essentially provides a random walk while the random step length is drawn from a Lévy distribution which has an infinite variance with an infinite mean.

$$L\acute{e}vy \approx u = t^{-\lambda},\quad -1 < \lambda < 3 \tag{14}$$

Studies show that Lévy flights can maximize the efficiency of resource searches in uncertain environments [19]. Here the consecutive jumps/steps of a cuckoo essentially form a random walk process which obeys a power-law step-length distribution with a heavy tail. It is worth pointing out that, in the real world, if a cuckoo's egg is very similar to a host's eggs, then this cuckoo's egg is less likely to be discovered, thus the fitness should be related to the difference in solutions. Therefore, it is a good idea to do a random walk in a biased way with some random step sizes Yang & Deb [19].

4   Numerical Illustration

Table 1 shows the sample data set of an illustration problem. The data relevant to the first 4 elements from Table 1 is used to illustrate the CS algorithm.

4.1   Initialization

The CS parameters: the number of nests (n), step size parameter (α), discovering probability (pa) and maximum number of generation are set initially.

4.2   Generate Nests with Host Bird Egg

Generate $10*n$ number of nests with host bird (where n is the number of elements in a product). Each nest carries an egg (solution). The initial solution (egg) is generated randomly for all the nests. A solution (egg) is a row vector X ($x_1^{\ 1}$, $x_2^{\ 2}$... $x_i^{\ j}$....$x_n^{\ mi}$), represents a possible combination of single supplier selection for all elements of the product. The ith position of the vector denotes the supplier selected for the ith elementof the product. It is generated choosing random numbers, such that random number in the ith position lies between 1 to m_i. It is checked for the feasibility constraints with $x_i^{\ j}$ decoded from X. The decoding is done as follows;

$$x_i^j = \begin{cases} 1\ for\ j\ correspond\ ing\ to\ the\ random\ number\ found\ in\ the\ ith\ position \\ 0\ otherwise \end{cases}$$

Table 1. Sample data set of illustration problem

i	j	1	2	3	4	5	6	7	8	Rs	Ws
1	R_1^j	0.9	0.99	0.999	0.9999	0.99999	0.999999	0.9999999	0.99999999	0.90	300
	c_1^j	20	40	60	80	100	120	140	180		
	w_1^j	30	50 *	80	120	180	200	240	280		
	β_1^j	1.2	1.4	1.9	1.4	1.3	1.2	1.1	1.6		
	DT_1^j	4	7	9	8	6	8	9	4		
2	r_2^j	0.85	0.9775	0.9966	0.9995	0.9999					
	c_2^j	30	60	90	120	150					
	w_2^j	30	50	70	90	110					
	β_2^j	1.3	1.5	1.8	1.4	1.2					
	DT_2^j	5	8	6	4	2					
3	r_3^j	0.8	0.96	0.99	0.998	0.9997	0.9999	0.99999	0.999999		
	c_3^j	20	40	60	80	100	120	140	160		
	w_3^j	50	80	100	140	180	220	250	300		
	β_3^j	1.1	1.8	1.7	1.2	1.9	1.7	1.3	1.6		
	DT_3^j	5	9	4	6	8	3	6	7		
4	r_4^j	0.75	0.938	0.98	0.999	0.9999					
	c_4^j	30	40	50	60	70					
	w_4^j	20	40	100	60	90					
	β_4^j	1.5	1.8	1.4	1.2	1.3					
	DT_4^j	3	6	9	4	6					
5	r_5^j	0.85	0.99	0.999	0.9999	0.99998	0.999998	0.9999998	0.99999998		
	c_5^j	20	40	65	80	100	120	140	155		
	w_5^j	30	30	40	60	80	60	50	80		
	β_5^j	1.4	1.6	1.3	1.8	1.9	1.8	1.7	1.5		
	DT_5^j	6	8	9	7	4	5	6	8		
6	r_6^j	0.9	0.95	0.999	0.9999	0.999999				0.90	350
	c_6^j	20	30	50	70	90					
	w_6^j	30	50	70	90	110					
	β_6^j	1.3	1.5	1.8	1.4	1.2					
	DT_6^j	5	8	6	4	2					
7	r_7^j	0.95	0.99	0.997	0.9997	0.99997	0.999997	0.9999997	0.99999997	0.85	400
	c_7^j	40	60	80	100	120	140	160	180		
	w_7^j	50	80	100	140	180	220	250	300		
	β_7^j	1.1	1.8	1.7	1.2	1.9	1.7	1.3	1.6		
	DT_7^j	5	9	4	6	8	3	6	7		
8	r_8^j	0.85	0.995	0.999	0.9999	0.99999				0.85	500
	c_8^j	10	30	60	80	120					
	w_8^j	20	25	30	40	50					
	β_8^j	1.5	1.2	1.3	1.6	1.5					
	DT_8^j	6	8	4	5	9					
9	r_9^j	0.9	0.95	0.995	0.9995	0.99995	0.999995	0.9999995	0.99999995	0.85	550
	c_9^j	30	50	70	90	110	130	150	170		
	w_9^j	50	80	100	140	180	220	250	300		
	β_9^j	1.1	1.8	1.7	1.2	1.9	1.7	1.3	1.6		
	DT_9^j	5	9	4	6	8	3	6	7		
10	r_{10}^j	0.99	0.999	0.9999	0.99999	0.999999	0.9999999			0.85	600
	c_{10}^j	15	40	70	100	130	160				
	w_{10}^j	30	60	50	40	80	100				
	β_{10}^j	1.2	1.3	1.5	1.9	1.7	1.5				
	DT_{10}^j	7	5	6	9	8	12				
11	r_{11}^j	0.95	0.999	0.9998	0.99999	0.999998	0.9999999	0.99999997	0.999999999	0.85	600
	c_{11}^j	20	40	60	80	100	120	140	160		
	w_{11}^j	20	30	30	40	50	70	90	100		
	β_{11}^j	1.2	1.1	1.2	1.5	1.7	1.8	1.7	1.2		
	DT_{11}^j	5	2	6	8	9	2	5	7		
12	r_{12}^j	0.8	0.9	0.99	0.999	0.9999				0.85	700
	c_{12}^j	40	60	85	110	130					
	w_{12}^j	50	60	70	85	85					
	β_{12}^j	1.2	1.1	1.8	1.9	1.2					
	DT_{12}^j	6	4	5	2	8					
13	r_{13}^j	0.75	0.85	0.99	0.999	0.9996	0.99996	0.999996	0.9999996	0.85	700
	c_{13}^j	30	50	80	100	120	140	160	180		
	w_{13}^j	10	20	30	40	55	60	70	90		
	β_{13}^j	1.1	1.5	1.5	1.2	1.5	1.6	1.5	1.4		
	DT_{13}^j	8	7	5	9	6	4	8	5		
14	r_{14}^j	0.8	0.95	0.99	0.999	0.9999				0.85	800
	c_{14}^j	10	30	40	60	80					
	w_{14}^j	20	25	30	40	50					
	β_{14}^j	1.5	1.2	1.3	1.6	1.5					
	DT_{14}^j	6	8	4	5	9					
15	r_{15}^j	0.99	0.999	0.9999	0.99999	0.999999	0.9999999	0.99999998	0.999999995	0.80	800
	c_{15}^j	50	80	110	140	160	180	200	220		
	w_{15}^j	50	80	100	140	180	220	250	300		
	β_{15}^j	1.1	1.8	1.7	1.2	1.9	1.7	1.3	1.6		
	DT_{15}^j	5	9	4	6	8	3	6	7		

The process of generation, decoding and checking is repeated till a feasible solution (egg) is obtained for all nests. Table 2 shows the decoded information of the initial solution (egg) X (6 2 3 4).

Table 2. Decoded information of $x_i{}^j$ for the initial solution egg X (6 2 3 4)

i	j	1	2	3	4	5	6	7	8
1		0	0	0	0	0	1	0	0
2		0	1	0	0	0	-	-	
3		0	0	1	0	0	0	0	0
4		0	0	0	1	0	-	-	-

4.3   Generate New Cuckoos by Lévy Flights

All of the nests except for the best so far, are replaced in order of quality by new Cuckoo eggs produced with Lévy flights as

$$nest_i^{(t+1)} = nest_i^{(t)} + \propto \oplus \left(nest_i^{(t)} - nest_{best}^{(t)}\right) rand \qquad (15)$$

where $nest_i^{(t)}$ is the ith nest current position, α is the step size parameter; $\oplus$ is the Lévy flights vector as in Mantegna's algorithm ; *rand* is a random number from a standard normal distribution and $nest_{best}^{(t)}$ is the position of the best nest so far product of entry-wise multiplication.

4.4   Alien Eggs Discovery

The alien eggs discovery is performed for all of eggs but in term of probability matrix for each component of each solution such as: considered as algorithm's termination criterion.

$$P_{ij} = \begin{cases} 1 & if\ rand < p_a \\ 0 & if\ rand \geq p_a \end{cases} \qquad (16)$$

Where *rand* is a random number in [0, 1] interval and P_{ij} is is discovering probability for j^{th} variable of ith nest. Existing eggs are replaced considering quality by newly generated ones from their current position by random walks with step size such as:

$$\oplus = rand.\left[nests\left\{randperm(n),:\right\} - nests\left\{randperm(n),:\right\}\right] \qquad (17)$$

$$nest^{t+1} = nest^t + \oplus * P \qquad (18)$$

Where *randperm* is random permutation function is used for different rows permutation applied on nests matrix and P is the probability matrix.

4.5   Termination

The above steps are repeated until a termination criterion (20*n= 1000) is satisfied. The best solution of each generation corresponds to best egg is stored as the iteration best and replaces the global best if it is better than the previously stored global best solution. The optimal TCO obtained by CS is 302.05 corresponding solution (2 2 2 4).

5   Performance Comparison

The performance of CS is tested by comparing with the optimal solutions of 10 sample problems that are derived by complete enumeration. The database given in Table 1. Table 3 shows the results obtained for the ten sample problems by complete enumeration and CS. It is observed from the Table 3 that the proposed CS gives the optimum solution for all the cases. Table 4 compares the number of solutions to be evaluated (Feasible/infeasible) with the enumeration technique and the proposed CS. The comparison reveals that the computational effort needed for the enumeration grows exponentially as the size of the problem increases. On the other hand, with the parameters set for the proposed CS (i.e *pob_size* =5*n; *iter_no*=20*n; P_a=0.25), the number of evaluations is quite low. Hence it could be concluded that the proposed CS is capable of providing optimal or near optimal solution with reasonable computational effort.

Table 3. Results for ten sample problems

Problem No	No. of elements	No. of variables	TCO	
			Complete Enumeration	CS
1	6	39	367.05	367.05
2	7	47	435.28	435.28
3	8	52	454.84	454.84
4	9	60	527.44	527.44
5	10	66	549.65	549.65
6	11	74	589.89	589.89
7	12	79	681.46	681.46
8	13	87	767.69	767.69
9	14	92	812.24	812.24
10	15	100	867.81	867.81

Table 4. Computational efforts of enumeration and CS

Problem No	No. of elements	No. of variables	No of evaluations	
			Enumeration	CS
1	6	39	64000	3600
2	7	47	512000	4900
3	8	52	2560000	6400
4	9	60	20480000	8100
5	10	66	122880000	10000
6	11	74	983040000	12100
7	12	79	4915200000	14400
8	13	87	39321600000	16900
9	14	92	1.96608E+11	19600
10	15	100	1.57286E+12	22500

6   Conclusion

In this paper, RBTCO model was developed to choose the right suppliers for each element of a product by considering the major costs such as procurement cost, replacement cost and downtime cost. CS is proposed to obtain the optimal supplier selection decisions for the developed RBTCO model. The experimental study is also carried out by comparing the optimal solutions obtained by enumeration for fifteen problem instances. CS performed well in terms of the quality of the solutions. Computational tests showed that small-size instances can be solved by the enumeration in a fair amount of CPU time, but it is not possible for medium and large-size instances. Inspecting the CS algorithm carefully, there are essentially three components; selection of the best, exploitation by local random walk, and exploration by randomization via Levy flights globally. The following points may be considered in future research:

- The proposed RBTCO models consider only three costs; other cost such as labour cost and maintenance cost can also be included in the model.
- The model can be formulated as a multi-objective optimization problem by taking the constraints as objective functions.

References

1. Zhang, X., Lee, C.K.M., Chen, S.: Supplier evaluation and selection: a hybrid model based on DEAHP and ABC. International Journal of Production Research 50(7), 1877–1889 (2012)
2. Asamoah, D., Annan, J., Nyarko, S.: AHP Approach for Supplier Evaluation and Selection in a Pharmaceutical Manufacturing Firm in Ghana. International Journal of Business and Management 7(10), 49–62 (2012)
3. Aissaoui, N., Haouari, M., Hassini, E.: Supplier selection and order lot sizing modeling: a review. Computers and Operations Research 34(12), 3516–3540 (2007)
4. Dobler, D.W., Lee, L., Burt, N.: Purchasing and Materials Management: Text and Cases. McGraw-Hill, New York (1990)
5. Willis, H.T., Huston, R.C., Pohlkamp, F.: Evaluation measures of just in time supplier performance. Production and Inventory Management Journal 34(2), 1–5 (1993)
6. Dickson, G.W.: An analysis of vendor selection systems and decisions. Journal of Purchasing 2(1), 5–17 (1966)
7. Hu, J.: Supplier selection determination and centralized purchasing decisions, PhD paper, Washington State University (2004)
8. Pi, W.N., Low, C.: Supplier evaluation and selection via Taguchi loss functions and an AHP. International Journal of Advanced Manufacturing Technology 27(5-6), 625–630 (2006)
9. Celebi, D., Bayraktar, D.: An integrated neural network and data envelopment analysis for supplier evaluation under incomplete information. Expert Systems with Applications 35, 1698–1710 (2008)

10. Chan, F.T.S., Kumar, N., Tiwari, M.K., Lau, H.C.W., Choy, K.L.: Global supplier selection: a fuzzy – AHP approach. International Journal of Production Research 46(14), 3825–3857 (2008)
11. Garfamy, R.M.: A data envelopment analysis approach based on total cost of ownership for supplier selection. Journal of Enterprise Information Management 19(6), 662–678 (2006)
12. Degraeve, Z., Roodhooft, F.: Effectively selecting suppliers using cost of ownership. Journal of Supply Chain Management, 35(1), 5–9 (1999)
13. Carrubba, E.R.: Integrating life-cycle cost and cost of ownership in the commercial sector. In: Reliability and Maintainability Symposium, Annual Proceedings, January 21-23, pp. 101–108 (1992)
14. Ellram, L.M.: The total cost of ownership: an analysis approach for purchasing. International Journal of Physical Distribution & Logistics Management 25(8), 4–23 (1995)
15. Carr, L.P., Ittner, C.D.: Measuring the cost of ownership. Journal of Cost Management 6(3), 7–13 (1992)
16. Cavinato, J.L.: A total cost/value model for supply chain competitiveness. Journal of Business Logistics 13(2), 285–301 (1992)
17. Ellram, L.M.: A frame work of total cost of ownership. International Journal of Logistics Management 4(2), 49–60 (1993)
18. Ellram, L.M., Siferd, S.P.: Total cost of ownership: a key concept in strategic cost management decisions. Journal of Business Logistics 19(1), 55–76 (1998)
19. Yang, X.S., Deb, S.: Cuckoo search via Lévy flights. In: Proceedings of World Congress on Nature & Biologically Inspired Computing, India, pp. 210–214 (2009)

Enhancing Internal Quality
of the Software Using Intelligence Code Evaluator

M. Sangeetha[1], C. Arumugam[2], K.M. Senthil Kumar[3], and P.S. Alagirisamy[3]

[1] Department of CSE &IT, Coimbatore Institute of Technology, Coimbatore, India -641 014
[2] Department of Mechanical Engineering,
Coimbatore Institute of Technology, Coimbatore, India -641 014
[3] Department of Mechatronics Engineering,
Kumaraguru College of Technology, Coimbatore, India -641 014
{msangeethadr,kmscit}@gmail.com, carumugam@cit.edu.in

Abstract. Software quality is assessed by a number of variables. These variables can be divided into external and internal quality criteria. External quality is what a user experiences when running the software in its operational mode. Internal quality refers to aspects that are code-dependent, and that are not visible to the end-user. Internal quality   of the software is measured by software developer only. Developer fix the code complexity according to the problem. Minimum size of source code will leads to reduce debugging time and cost. This paper proposes a software quality support tool, a Java source code evaluator and a code profiler based on computational intelligence techniques to reduce schedule slippage of development activity. It gives a new approach to evaluate and identify inaccurate source code usage and transitively, the software product itself. The aim of this project is to provide the software development industry with a new tool to increase software quality by extending the value of source code metrics through computational intelligence.

Keywords: Software Quality Metrics Neural networks, clustering algorithms.

1   Introduction

Software Engineering is the application of systematic, disciplined and quantifiable approach to the development, operation, and maintenance of Software. It is a direct subfield of Computer Science and has some relations with Management Science. Software Requirements, Design, Construction, Testing, Maintenance and Quality are the major sub-disciplines of Software Engineering. Among these disciplines, Software Quality is the most important one, since the success of a Software Engineer relies on the development of failure free software.

In this modern era, society becomes more dependent on computer systems and hence there is more pressure on development teams to produce high-quality software. Many companies rely on program suites that analyze and evaluate the quality of software. Quality is the process of ensuring that software developed will satisfy customer requirements. Among the many software quality attributes like Functionality, Usability,

S.G. Ponnambalam et al. (Eds.): IRAM 2012, CCIS 330, pp. 502–510, 2012.

Capability, Maintainability and so on, Reliability is a major factor to ensure that software is failure free from failures. Software Reliability is the probability of failure-free software operation for a specified period of time in a specified environment. Informally it denotes a product's trustworthiness or dependability.

In the growing scenario, Software Reliability is difficult to achieve, because the complexity of a software tends to be high. Further, building good software quality models is very hard because many questions concerning the quality modeling are challenging and are adequately addressed. In spite of the several existing literature to tackle these challenges, still there arise a need to develop a new methodological and computational procedure for improving the quality of software through reliability growth models.

Software should meet requirements specifications. Best quality Software satisfies the need of the customer. Historically, the word "quality" has been adapted and has evolved together with the different technologies to which it has been applied. Each software should not contain compliance. It implies loss of quality or less trust on product. Inspection process goal was to avoid corrections through the identification of product deviations from requirement specification [2].

1.1   Software Quality

Software metrics can be classified into three categories: product metrics, process metrics, and project metrics. Product metrics describe the characteristics of the product such as size, complexity, design features, performance, and quality level Software industry focuses on the following principles: 1. Software requirements are the quality metric fundamental. Lack of compliance with requirements is a quality failure. 2. Standards establish development criteria. Absence of standards means, in many cases, low quality [5].3. Indirect measures (e.g. usability, maintainability, etc.) and direct measures (e.g. lines of code).

1.2   Strategic Methodologies

Effective quality programs and technical revisions implies strong management commitment. This provides success total quality management (TQM). Marginal profit of the company increases by using TQM and quality metrics.

1.3   Object Oriented Languages

Object paradigms language is reduced the bug levels in procedural languages. Software have defects such as: 1. A very ambitious scheduling. 2. Complex models. 3. Unbalanced module sizes. 4. Subtle code errors even when testing is over.[3]

1.4   Case Tools

The first problem encountered when attempting to understand program complexity is to define what it means for a program   to be complex. Basili defines complexity as a measure of the resources expended by a system while interacting with a piece of software to perform a given task [3]. If the interacting system is a computer, then complexity is defined by the execution time and storage required to perform the computation. If the interacting system is a programmer, then complexity is defined by the difficulty of performing tasks such as coding, debugging, testing, or modifying the software. The term software complexity is often applied to the interaction between a program and a programmer working on some programming task. Test case is mainly used to debug the defects. We cant assure like we will get bug free product after the unit testing .We can say only less than 30% of defects are identified. Test case does not provide correctness because there could be mistakes in the coding process. Maximum test cases are not original. It will leads to increase costs and does not optimize the use of resourses [3]. Cost is also increased because of software developers and reflect the additional test resources that are consumed due to inadequate testing tools and methods.

Despite the growing body of literature devoted to their development, analysis, and testing, software complexity measures have yet to gain wide acceptance. Early claims for the validity of the metrics have not been supported, and considerable criticism has been directed at the methodology of the experiments that support the measures. Nonetheless, new complexity measures continue to appear, and new support for old measures is earnestly sought. Complexity measures offer great potential for containing the galloping cost of software development and maintenance. Successful software-complexity measure development must be motivated by a theory of programming behavior. An integrated approach to metric development, testing, and use is essential as development should anticipate the demands of the measure's usage. Testing should be performed with specific pplications in mind, and where possible the test environment should simulate the actual use.

Our proposed tool prototype provides new source code metrics to model its content in context. Thresholds are set to obtain distances from the code style .Dataset is built by using Maximum Entropy Principle (MEP) data mining algorithm .Using that data source, we trained a neural network. Also uses the clusters algorithm to classify the source code as clusters. In a programmed self-tuning process, the prototype can adjust each cluster profile, determining a dynamic distinctive identity for every classification output (NN). The classification phase groups source code instances that share common attributes of their syntaxes. In those cases where the attribute reveals a sign of erroneous language handling, a recommendation phase is activated. An expert system pre-loaded with rules analyzes the classification results and identifies every inaccurate source code usage. The rule engine also builds a set of recommendations based on key features detected in the code. The analysis process is completed with a report-style output advising the author on convenient procedures to improve the source code.

2   Proposed System

Our Proposed System have core functions Fig. 1 shows component relations, storage units and external interfaces. Its design maximizes CPU load and reduces memory requirements. It is very reliable system. Thresholds are set to obtain distances from the preferred code style. A dataset built by Expectation Maximization (EM) data mining algorithm is the reference data source to train a neural network. A Multi Layer Perceptron (MLP) artificial neural network (NN) classifies the source code instances on clusters formerly established by the training set.

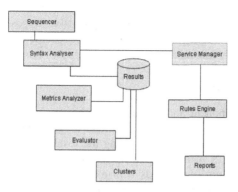

Fig. 1. Proposed System Architecture

It is a flexible and adaptable tool due to its design and XML configuration files. It could be used not only for scientific requirements but also to suit the needs of any firm. The whole tool is built on Enterprise Java technology platform; it runs on any JEE 1.5 servlet container. Its design maximizes CPU load and reduces memory requirements, enabling the quick analysis of large datasets. The following sections describe each module design and their main features.

2.1 Sequencer

Content Sequencer Module is an IJA extension of Java Collection API interface ApplicationProgramming Interface). It standardizes, encapsulates, and serializes source code files (SCF) content synchronically in order to process it in a transparent way. It can be configured to define specific word separator tokens.

2.2 Syntax Analyzer

The algorithm detects some reserved words, symbols structures and changes to a specific state. The IJA modular design makes it possible to extend all its functionalities to other

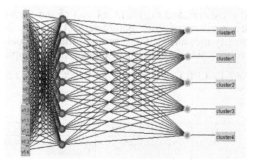

Fig. 2. IJA Neural Network

languages just by selecting a specific Syntax Analyzer module implementation each programming language. The IJA modular design makes it possible to extend all its functionalities to other languages just by selecting a specific Syntax Analyzer module implementation each programming language.

2.3   Metrics Analyzer

It is the calculus component and the analyst's chosen algebra operations translator. According to the actual XML configuration, it generates software metrics by executing mathematical operations and using the results obtained from the previous module. For example, a metric named v3 is the division between the quantity of methods and the quantity of methods with names starting with lowercase2.Besides some new metrics, the software also implements classical metrics.

Table 1. EM Cluster

cluster #	instances	%
0	9	1
1	127	13
2	102	10
3	149	15
4	572	57
5	4	4

2.4   Evaluator

The Results Evaluator module normalizes the specific numeric values for each metric between -1 and 1. There are predefined thresholds or quality class bounds to help evaluate the result quality. Each SCF is classified using the metric numeric results and the thresholds. Floating labels provide a code identification reference (ID) of the SCF accumulated in each sequence. Finally, the data is exported into an arff format so that the results (attribute-relation file format) are compatible. The EM algorithm stops when there is not significant quality increase. The quality is measured with:

$$r1.P(a) + r2.P(b) + r3.P(c) + r4.P(d) + r5.P(e) \qquad (1)$$

Being a, b, c, d and e clusters and r1, r2, r3, r4 and r5 the parameters, the algorithm uses the probability register of true parameters. Log likelihood stands for the willingness or credibility measure of these probabilities. It is obtained as the product of the conditional probabilities upon every instance i in the sample

$$r1.P(x1/a) + r2.P(x2/b) + r3.P(x3/c) + r4.P(x4/d) + r5.P(x5/e) \qquad (2)$$

Table 2.

metric	value	result	meaning
v1	-1	0.250503	A 25% of cluster classes have less than 100 LOC/class.
v1	0	0.26760563	Between 100 and 200 LOC/class.
v1	1	0.48189133	More than 200 LOC/clases

B. Neural Network Classification Accuracy

A general average, over 90%, confirms the strong correlation between SCF grouped in clusters by EM and the NN capability of distinguishing differences between attributes and of classifying them correctly [18]

3   Cluster Profiling

An automated algorithm to evaluate the meaning of each cluster was implemented. It depends on the instance SCF metric values. In this process each metric value of the cluster is compared to the total average (as a reference), and depending on a distance factor, a level of proximity is determined. This algorithm takes outputs from clustering and gets results from the following procedure:

    1. Inputs: the clusters characterized by the metrics: V1...Vn (discrete values [-1,0,1])

    The algorithm:
- a. Acquire an average for every metric and value, and select it as a reference (see Table).
- b. Select the value Vx with minimum distance to reference and categorize it comparing it with the same Vx of the other clusters (using relative values) (see Table).
- c. Set up a position (ranking) for the cluster, depending on the distance results (see Table).

2. Output clusters characterized by metrics. Using discrete numbers and classifications according to the proximity to reference (see Table). Demonstration for V1 (lines of code / number of classes)

Table 3. Reference Average Values

cluster #	metric	value	result	distance
0	v1	0	0.4326241	0.16501847
1	v1	-1	0.6369863	0.3864833
2	v1	0	0.4871795	0.21957386
3	v1	1	0.6551094 7	0.17321813
4	v1	0	0.4691358	0.20153016

Table 4. Distance to Reference

cluster #	instances	%
0	326	33
1	50	5
2	190	19
3	246	25
4	188	19

Table 5. Positions Defending on Distance Results

cluster #	metric	value	distance	position
0	v1	0	0.16501847	0
1	v1	-1	0.3864833	4
2	v1	0	0.21957386	3
3	v1	1	0.17321813	1
4	v1	0	0.20153016	2

Then, every numeric result with a high-grade position (0 or 1) is converted into a qualitative label where the profile that determines the identity of every cluster is obtained, for example the Cluster 0 profile:

Table 6. Cluster Profile

metric	value	position	meaning
v1	0	0	Between 100 and 200 LOC each class.
v2	1	1	Methods with more than 40 LOC on each block.
v4	1	1	Uppercased variable names.
v6	1	1	High usage of constant variables.
v10	1	0	High usage of inner and nested classes.
v11	1	1	Disproportionate usage of comments type.
v22	1	1	Most classes having just the default constructor.

Considering the information obtained through metrics and indicators, IJA uses an expert system which, according to the results of previous processes, proposes recommendations for the correction of any deficiencies found. The solution is generated by an expert system with pre-loaded rules in the knowledge base. Basically, each rule analyzes the classification created by a neuronal network and then makes a recommendation based on the cut values for each metric [17] (see Table)

Table 7. Recommendations as Metrics and Classification

metrics	meaning	intervals	recommendations
v1	Lines per class	0-100	No suggestion.
		101-200	It is suggested to decrement the number of LOC per class.
		201 or more	It is necessary to decrement the number of LOC per class.
v2	Methods per class	0-20	No suggestion.
		21-40	It is suggested to decrement the number of methods per class.
		40 or more	It is necessary to decrement the number of methods per class.
v22	Classes with default constructor	0	No suggestion.
		1	It is suggested to write constructors.
		More than 1	It is recommended to write the constructor for each class.

Performance shows the reducing unwanted LOC/FP from coding structure leads to better quality. Knowledge Base: The knowledge base that is part of the IJA expert system establishes a objective function between metrics and rules, that is to say, each metric that was evaluated has a specific rule associated to it. Every rule analyzes every classification result and metric value according to the following algorithm:

a. For the cluster where the SCF was classified, is that metric significant (ranking > 1)?

b. Does the value obtained agree with the one that was expected?

YES: No recommendation is necessary NO
Suggest a correction

The text for that suggestion is also different, considering the distance with respect to the expected value [22]. Significant deviations mean more relevant recommendations.

4   Future Work

The goal of the next stage of research is the intensive testing and subsequent tuning of the prototype by means of a statistical analysis that may validate the system or help make the required adjustments. In the same manner, more research will be done, taking into account the theory-practice framework that the results of the present work represent, in order to define new quality criteria for the evaluation of software.

5   Conclusion

This paper proposes a new approach to evaluate source code quality and source code profiling. In order to do so, it defines source code metrics and analyzes its internal behavior with data mining and machine learning procedures. In the process, a dataset created by a data mining algorithm is the reference classified data source to set up a neural network. The trained multilayer perception has shown excellent precision to classify this sort of data. An expert system analyzes the classification results and identifies every inaccurate source code usage. In order to test the prototype, a web user interface is being developed. Therefore, this feature will make community.

References

1. National Institute of Standards and Technology, The Economic Impacts of Inadequate Infrastructure for Software Testing, RTI (2002)
2. Roe and Lytle, p. 99 (1935)
3. Moore, p. 652 (1958)
4. Arthur, J.D.: Managing Software Quality: A Measurement Framework for Assessments and Prediction. Springer (2002)
5. ISO/IEC9126, http://www.cse.dcu.ie/essiscope/sm2/9/~126ref.html
6. Pressman, R.S.: Ingeniería del Software: Un Enfoque Práctico. Mc Graw Hill (1998)
7. Kan, S.H.: Metrics and Models in Software Quality Engineering. Addison - Wesley Professional (2002)
8. Jones, C.: Applied software measurement: assuring productivity and quality. Mc Graw Hill (1996)

9. National Institute of Standards and Technology, The Economic Impacts of Inadequate Infrastructure for Software Testing, RTI (2002)
10. Woods, W.A.: Transition Network Grammars for Natural Language Analysis. Communications of the ACM, 591–606 (1970)
11. Eckel, B.: Thinking in Patterns (2003)
12. Gosling, J., Joy, B., Steele, G., Brach, G.: The Java Language Specification, 3rd edn. Pretience Hall (2005)
13. López De Luise, D., Agüero, M.: Aplicación de Métricas Categóricas en Sistemas con Lógica Difusa, Revista IEEE América Latina (2007)
14. Winston, P.H.: Inteligencia Artificial, tercera edición. Addison Wesley, Iberoamericana (1992)
15. Witten, I.H., Frank, E.: Data Mining: Practical Machine Learning Tools and Techniques, p. 265. Morgan Kaufmann (2005)
16. Forgy, C.: Rete: A Fast Algorithm for the Many Pattern/Many Object Pattern Match Problem. Artificial Intelligence 19, 17–37 (1982)
17. Madou, F., Agüero, M., Esperón, G., López De Luise, D.: Sistemas Expertos en Evaluación de Calidad Java. In: CONESCAPAN (2009)
18. Agüero, M., Esperón, G., Madou, F., López De Luise, D.: Intelligent Java Analyzer. In: IEEE CERMA (2008)
19. CLIPS, http://clipsrules.sourceforge.net/
20. JESS, http://www.jessrules.com
21. DROOLS, http://www.jboss.org/drools/drools-expert.html
22. Madou, F., Agüero, M., Esperón, G., López De Luise, D.: Evaluador Inteligente de Código Java. In: CICA (2009)

Enhancing Quality Using FEAROM Model
for Finalizing a Casting Product Methods Design
in Preproduction Trials

T.A. Selvan[1], C. Jegadheesan[2], K.M. Senthil Kumar[3], and P.S. Alagirisamy[3]

[1] Department of Mechanical Engineering,
Sri Krishna College of Engineering and Technology Coimbatore, India - 641 014
[2] Department of Mechanical Engineering, Paavai Engineering College, Namakkal, India
[3] Department of Mechatronics Engineering,
Kumaraguru College of Technology, Coimbatore, India - 641 014

Abstract. In foundries, continuous quality improvement through failure investigation and identification is based on the traditional failure mode and effect analysis (FMEA) using Risk priority Number (RPN). Prioritize the failure modes through RPN produces the result which does not match in practice. This research paper addresses a novel model named FEAROM to prioritize the failure modes through FMEA. The most popular technique ANOVA has been used for testing the equality of RPN values mean data through a statistical software package. An experimental study was carried out for a cast component in a steel foundry using investment casting method to validate the proposed model. It has been found that application of the proposed FEAROM model resulted in sound castings.

1 Preliminary Considerations

During the recent years, foundries have been functioning under globally competitive environment. Hence foundries are required to enhance their performance to offer world class quality. One of the quality enhancement strategies is failure prevention [1, 2]. A widely used technique for failure prevention is Failure Mode and effects Analysis (FMEA) [4]. FMEA has stepped up since its inception in the aerospace industry in mid – 1960s [2, 4]. References [5, 6, 7, and 8] were proposed a modified FMEA using fuzzy logic, which eliminates the pitfalls in the traditional FMEA.

The aim of this paper is to introduce the new model named Failure Effects and Resolution of Modes (FEAROM) for prioritization of failure modes of moulds design. FEAROM is applied in preproduction trials during the development of cast components in foundries. It comprises fuzzy set and ANOVA. If two or more failure modes in methods design having the same RPN and the indexes occurrence (O), severity (S) and detection (D) are characterized by different level of importance, FEAROM model can be used. FEAROM methodology is based on the investigations cited in [6, 7].

S.G. Ponnambalam et al. (Eds.): IRAM 2012, CCIS 330, pp. 511–519, 2012.
© Springer-Verlag Berlin Heidelberg 2012

A typical format for FMEA sheet is illustrated in table 3. The characteristic failure mode indexes S,O and D are expressed on ordinal qualitative scales with the same scale levels of 1 to 10 (table 1). In traditional FMEA the RPN index is calculated as:

$$RPN = S \times O \times D \qquad (1)$$

Table 1. Rating for S, O, D indexes of failures

Rating	Severity [S]	Occurrence [O]	Ability to detect [D]
10	Safety issue and/or non-compliance with government regulation without warning	Almost every time	Almost no
9	Safety issue and/or non-compliance with government regulation with warning	1 in 2	Very remote
8	Operation down for a significant period of time and major financial impact; Loss of primary function	1 in 5	Remote
7	Serious disruption to operations, defects caught at customer site, requires major rework or scarp; Reduction in primary function	1 in 10	Very low
6	Major disruption to operations and requires light rework or scarp; Loss of comfort or convenience function	1 in 100	Low
5	Minor disruption to operations and requires light rework or scarp; Loss of comfort or convenience function	1 in 500	Moderate
4	Inconvenience to the process and requires minor rework; Returnable appearance and /or noise issue noticed by the most customers	1 in 1,000	Moderately High
3	Inconvenience to subsequent task and require minor rework; Non – returnable appearance and/or noise issue noticed by customers	1 in 5,000	High
2	Inconvenience to current task and requires minor rework; Non-returnable appearance and/or noise issue rarely noticed by customers	1 in 50,000	Very high
1	No discernable effect	Almost impossible	Almost certain

2   Methodology

The methodology begins with prioritization using traditional FMEA to find the rank order of moulds designs which possess least RPN value as first, next higher RPN value as second and so on. Next, FEAROM model followed which addresses the decision making criteria using fuzzy set and ANOVA. ANOVA is used to test whether the RPN means among two or more groups of methods designs data are differ, under the assumption that the RPN values are normally distributed. S, O, and D can be interpreted as evaluation criteria K_{ij} (with $j = 1, 2, 3$) while the methods design in preproduction trials during development stage as the alternatives 'M_i' (with $i = 1, …, n$) to be selected. Take, $1 \leq K_{ij} \leq 10$ for all i, j. The K_{ij}'s precisely takes the ranks from 1 to 10 in some order. Thus, the ranks 1, 2, 3… 10 for S, O, and D in table 1 are represented as general form in table 2 [7].

The FEAROM method suggests a three step procedure ;

Step 1: Risk Priority Code (RPC) [6]

$$\text{RPC } (M_i) = \frac{Max}{j} \left[Min\{(I\,(K_{ij}), g_j\,(M_i)\} \right] \qquad (2)$$

where $I(K_{ij})$ is the importance associated with each criterion g_j

Table 2. General form of methods design failure mode indexes and RPN

Methods design	S	O	D	RPN
M_1	K_{11}	K_{12}	K_{13}	R_1
M_2	K_{21}	K_{22}	K_{23}	R_2
.	.	.	.	.
.	.	.	.	.
.	.	.	.	.
M_n	K_{n1}	K_{n2}	K_{n3}	R_n

Step 2: Critical Failure Mode (CFM) [6]

$$\text{CFM } (M^*) = \frac{Min}{M_i \in A} \qquad (3)$$

where A is the set of methods design comprises failure modes

RPC (M_i) is defined on a new 10 point ordinal scale as those values utilized for expressing index evaluations

If two or more have the same critical failure mode consider the following indicator as "tie ranking" rule [6, 7]:

$$T\,(M_i) = N\,(M_i) \qquad (4)$$

Here N (M_i) is the number of places, in the row corresponding to M_i for which Kij < CFM (M^*). This term represents step 3 investigations for establishing a measure of dispersion of criteria, related to a specific failure mode, around the RPC index.

If still tie occurs, consider the low occurrence value to resolve. (5)

Step 3: Measure of dispersion and ANOVA [7]

Using ANOVA the data has to be tested for concluding RPN means are differ. Then mean and range can be used as a measure of dispersion of criteria to rank the methods design in preproduction trials through their failure modes.

Experimental Study

The study was carried out in an investment casting foundry located at Coimbatore city of India. They are the manufacturers and suppliers of investment casting products. Three methods design (figure 1) were used in the preproduction trials of a gas bonnet valve (figure 2) and S, O, D index values assigned by FMEA team members after brainstorming session (table 3).

<u>8 pieces / Tree and medium base runner</u>

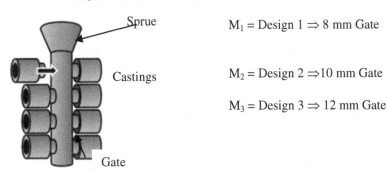

M_1 = Design 1 $\Rightarrow$ 8 mm Gate

M_2 = Design 2 $\Rightarrow$ 10 mm Gate

M_3 = Design 3 $\Rightarrow$ 12 mm Gate

Fig. 1. Methods design M_1, M_2 and M_3

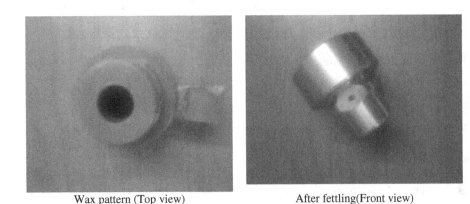

Wax pattern (Top view)   After fettling(Front view)

Fig. 2. Gas valve bonnet (photo)

The average values of the failure indexes for each methods design is depicted in Table 4.

Ranking Using Traditional FMEA

In traditional FMEA, it is appropriate to consider least RPN value as first; next higher RPN value as second and so on gives ranking order as M_1, M_2 and M_3 by referring column 5 in table 4.

Ranking Using FEAROM Method

Let us analyze four different situations.

Case (a): The same maximum importance (L_{10}) is assumed for all characteristics indexes which are similar to traditional FMEA. Hence:

$$I(S) = L_{10}; \qquad\qquad I(O) = L_{10}; \qquad\qquad I(D) = L_{10}$$

Calling M_1, M_2 and M_3 the three methods design, the aggregated RPC index calculation is performed as indicated by the equation (2) [see column six in table 4]:

Table 3. Failure Mode and Effects Analysis Worksheet

FMEA Team: Production manager, Methods engineers, Quality Assurance Manager

Team Leader: Technical Director

Component: Gas valve bonnet (An investment casting component)

S N o	Methods design/brief details	Potential Failure Mode	Potential Effect(s) of Failure	Severity	Potential Cause(s)/ Mechanism(s) of Failure	Occurrence	Detection method	Detection	RPN
1	METHOD 1 (M_1) Gate - Each 8 mm (Horizontal) Yield: 30% Pouring: Vertical orientation (8 pieces)	Gate shrinkage	Rejected at manufacturing plant	8	Tree assembly leading to variations in the cooling rate in different areas of the casting	5	Visual	3	
				7		6		2	
				6		7		4	
			Average	7		6		3	126
2	METHOD 2 (M_2) Gate - Each 10 mm (Horizontal) Yield: 45% Pouring: Vertical orientation (8 pieces)	Shrinkage at gate	Rejected at customer point	8	Tree assembly leading to variations in the cooling rate in different areas of the casting	4	After machining	8	
				7		3		7	
				9		2		6	
			Average	8		3		7	168
3	METHOD 3 (M_3) Gate - Each 12 mm (Horizontal) Yield: 42% Pouring: Vertical	Top face shrinkage	Rejected at customer point	6	Tree assembly leading to variations in the cooling rate in different areas of the casting	4	Radiography	7	
				7		5		6	
				8		3		8	
			Average	7		4		7	196

Table 4. Calculation of RPN and RPC indexes for the methods designs in preproduction trials of a bonnet valve investment casting

Methods Designs (Yield) (1)	Mean values of			RPN (5)	RPC [Case(a)] I(S) = L$_{10}$ I(O) = L$_{10}$ I(D) = L$_{10}$ (6)	Rank Order (7)	RPC [Case(b)] I(S) = L$_{10}$ I(O) = L$_8$ I(D) = L$_6$ (8)	Rank Order (9)	RPC [Case(c)] I(S) = L$_{10}$ I(O) = L$_5$ I(D) = L$_1$ (10)	Rank Order (11)	RPC [Case(d)] I(S) = L$_1$ I(O) = L$_5$ I(D) = L$_{10}$ (12)	Rank Order (13)
	S (2)	O (3)	D (4)									
M$_1$ (30%)	7	6	3	144	L$_7$	2	L$_7$	2	L$_7$	2	L$_5$	1
M$_2$ (45%)	8	3	7	168	L$_8$	3	L$_8$	3	L$_8$	3	L$_7$	3
M$_3$ (42%)	7	4	7	196	L$_7$ (*)	1	L$_7$ (*)	1	L$_7$ (*)	1	L$_6$	2

Note: I(S), I (O), I (D) are the importance associated with each index. RPC calculated for four different situations: (a), (b), (c), (d). When two or more methods designs have the same RPC index, the symbol (*) high lights the most preferable.

RPC (M$_1$) =Max [Min (L$_{10}$, L$_7$), Min (L$_{10}$, L$_6$), Min (L$_{10}$, L$_3$)] = Max [L$_7$, L$_6$, L$_3$] = L$_7$
RPC (M$_2$) = Max [L$_8$, L$_3$, L$_7$] = L$_8$
RPC (M$_3$) = Max [L$_7$, L$_4$, L$_7$] = L$_7$

From the result, the least preferable methods design is M$_2$.
   The Critical Failure Mode (CFM) is:

CFM (M*) = Min {RPC (M$_1$), RPC (M$_2$), RPC (M$_3$)} = RPC (M$_1$) = RPC (M$_3$) = L$_7$.

In this case the preferable methods designs are M$_1$ and M$_3$. Tie raking rule for M$_1$ and M$_3$ is:

T (M$_i$) = N (M$_i$) where N (M$_i$) is the number of places for which Kij < L$_7$

Therefore: T (M$_1$) = 2;   T (M$_3$) = 1

Since T (M$_3$) < T (M$_1$), M$_3$ is the most preferable methods design.
   Hence the order of methods designs is 2, 3, and 1 for M$_1$, M$_2$ and M$_3$ respectively (see column seven in table 4).
   In our application, it is essential to define a different level of importance for the three S, O and D indexes because of disagreed values for them were assigned by the team members. In this case we cannot use the traditional RPN approach. Hence the (S, O, D) sets (10, 8, 6), (10, 5, 1) and (1, 5, 10) have been considered by FMEA team. The corresponding decision results are shown in table 4 as case (b), case (c) and case (d).

ANOVA for randomized block design technique has been presented through SPSS (Statistical Package for Social Sciences) to compare the mean RPNs in table 5 associated with three methods design. Accordingly, the null hypothesis and alternate hypothesis would be:

H_o: All means are equal i.e., $\mu_{m1} = \mu_{m2} = \mu_{m3}$

H_a: RPN means differ at least for two methods design in preproduction trial

Test statistic: $F = MS_{Treatments}/MS_E$

Table 5. New approach for evaluation of RPN in preproduction trials

Methods	S	O	D	RPNs	RPN Mean	RPN Range
M_1 Yield: 30%	8	5	3	120, 80, 160, 105, 70, 140, 90, 60, 120	126	164
	7	6	2	144, 96, 192, 126, 84, 168, 108, 72, 144		
	6	7	4	168, 112, 224, 147, 98, 196, 126, 84, 168		
M_2 Yield: 45%	8	4	8	256, 224, 192, 224, 196, 168, 288, 252, 216	168	204
	7	3	7			
	9	2	6	192, 168, 144, 168, 147, 126, 216, 189, 162		
				128, 112, 96, 112, 98, 84, 144, 126, 108		
M_3 Yield: 42%	6	4	7	168, 144, 192, 196, 168, 224, 224, 192, 256	196	212
	7	5	6			
	8	3	8	210, 180, 240, 245, 210, 280, 280, 240, 320		
				126, 108, 144, 147, 126, 168, 168, 144, 192		

Table 6. ANOVA for data in table 5 (computer output)

Dependent Variable: RPN Values

Source	Type III Sum of Squares	df	Mean Square	F	Sig.
Corrected Model	146056.000[a]	28	5216.286	1.863	.026
Intercept	1920996.000	1	1920996.000	686.079	.000
RPN	19048.000	26	732.615	.262	1.000
Methods design	127008.000	2	63504.000	22.680	.000
Error	145598.000	52	2799.962		
Total	2212650.000	81			
Corrected Total	291654.000	80			

a. R Squared = .501 (Adjusted R Squared = .232)

From the standard tables of percentage points of the F distribution, we find $F_{0.05}$ = 3.18. SPSS software was used to analyze the data in table 5. The analysis confirmed the data is normally distributed. The methods design values in table 8 are significant because p = sig < 0.05 and the F ratio (highlighted in the table 6) is 22.68 > 3.18. We therefore reject the null hypothesis at α = 0.05 level of significance, concluding that at least two of the methods design RPN means differ in preproduction trial. Then, the measure of dispersion technique was applied to finalize the methods design. The details are presented in next section.

3   Results and Discussion

Analysis of the data in table 4 reveals that the method M_3 ranked as first in three cases out of four and hence the methods design M_3 was finalized. To ensure the selection of the methods design M_3, the measure of dispersion techniques was employed. The mean and range were determined as shown in table 5 to select the most significant methods design with different ranking scale. In the development of patterns, it is more appropriate to prioritize the methods design which possess higher RPN range as first, the next higher as second and so on [7]. Accordingly, M_3 is the most significant method compared to other methods results in less severity. The preproduction trials of the bonnet valve were made using the wax pattern of method M_3 and resulted in sound castings with 42% yield. Hence the same was adopted by the company for their batch production.

4   Conclusion

This paper demonstrates and substantiates the application of the novel model named FEAROM comprises fuzzy subset and ANOVA in steel foundries to prioritize the failure modes in preproduction trials. ANOVA for completely randomized design has been combined in data processing on the ordinal features of qualitative scales through SPSS software. Continuous quality improvement in investment casting components with shorter development time can be achieved through the FEAROM model. ✓

References

1. Ahmed, J.U.: Modern approaches to product reliability improvement. International Journal of Quality and Reliability Management 13(3), 27–41 (1996)
2. Banard, S.: Linkages between QFD and FMEA. ASI Quality Systems, QFD User Group (1996)
3. Teoh, P.C., Case, K.: Failure modes and effects Analysis through knowledge modeling. Journal of Material Processing Technology 153–154, 253–260 (2004)
4. Savick, F.: Current and future concepts in FMEA. In: IEEE Proceedings Annual Reliability and Maintainability Symposium, pp. 414–420 (1981)
5. Chang, C.-L., Wei, C.-C., Lee, Y.-H.: Failure mode and effects analysis using fuzzy method and grey theory. Kybernetes 28(9), 1072–1080 (1999)

6. Franceschini, F., Galetto, M.: A new approach for evaluation of risk priorities of failure modes in FMEA. International Journal of Production Research 39(13), 2991–3002 (2001)
7. Narayanagounder, S., Gurusami, K.: A New Approach for Prioritization of Failure Modes in Design FMEA using ANOVA. World academy of Science, Engineering and Technology 49, 524–531 (2009)
8. Zhang, Z.F., Chu, X.N.: Risk prioritization in failure mode and effects analysis under uncertainty. Expert Systems with Applications 38, 206–214 (2011)

Modeling and Analysis on Deformation Behavior for AA 6061 through Equal Channel Angular Pressing Die

R. Venkatraman[2], S. Raghuraman[1], and Raj Mohan R.[1]

[1] School of Mechanical Engineering, SASTRA University, Thanjavur, 613401, India
[2] Shanmuga Precision Forging, Thanjavur, 613401, India

Abstract. Equi-Channel Angular Pressing(ECAP) involves development of large simple shear which induces plastic deformation on the sample pressed through a die containing two intersecting channels of identical cross-section. The channel angle in ECAP die is having significant influence to induce the strain on the material during pressing. The strain imposed on the material increases while channel angle decreases. On another hand, the imparted strain increases with increase in hydrostatic pressure. The relation between hydrostatic pressure and channel angle is not communal because hydrostatic pressure decreases with increase in channel angle. Hence, it is clear that channel angle plays an influencing factor for inducing strain on the material and also hydrostatic pressure determination based on channel angle. Therefore a compromise solution has to be selected in determining the channel angle for achieving effective ECAP condition.The influence of channel angle on deformation behavior for AA 6061 Aluminum Alloy using ANSYS V12 was studied. The Analysis is carried out for different channel angles of 90°, 110° and 120° for different hydrostatic pressure conditions.

Keywords: Equal Channel Angular Pressing, Channel Angle, Hydrostatic Pressure, Imparted Strain.

1   Introduction

Equal channel angular pressing is one of the Severe Plastic Deformation(SPD) practice for producing ultra fine grains in submicron level to set up severe strain by simple shear by passing material through a uniform cross section L-shaped ECAP die without any reduction of the cross-sectional area of the sample. The current study dealt with the influence of channel angle on deformation behaviour for AA 6061 through analysis in ANSYS V12 for different channel angles of 90°, 110° and 120° with different hydrostatic pressure conditions.

Studies are carried on the influence of die structure and extruded materials on the effect of refining crystal, and found that the effect of extrusion was different with the die structure, especially the included angle of channels, ϕ, the die outer corner angle, ψ, and the radius of outer angle, R. The Influence of channel angle on the deformation behavior and strain homogeneity was studied by conducting the finite element simulations for a range of channel angles from $60 - 150°$ along with the consideration

S.G. Ponnambalam et al. (Eds.): IRAM 2012, CCIS 330, pp. 520–525, 2012.
© Springer-Verlag Berlin Heidelberg 2012

of friction and strain hardening of the material. The deformation behavior is more complicated and taking place in three stages with channel angles $\phi < 90°$. It is smooth and taking place in two stages with $\phi \geq 90°$. Comparatively thin and adequate length of plastic zone at the die diagonals is observable with $\phi = 90°$ and $105°$ by indicating the possibility of strain homogeneity. Effective strain contours across the width at the center of the sample show that strain homogeneity is greater with $\phi = 90°$ compared to all other channel angles, as proposed by ZHANG Xiao-Hua et al [1]. Nagasekhar et al [2] studied that the channel angle will vary from $60°$ to $150°$, this will influence strain homogeneity on the material. The greater strain homogeneity obtained in an angle closer to $90°$ compared to all other channel angles while keeping the outer corner angle as $10°$. The less sheared zone is the characteristics of the round corner die ECAP process due to the shorter length of the die outer part in $\psi > 0°$ than in the case of sharp corner ($\psi = 0°$). It should also be noted that the round die corner not only reduces the overall shear deformation but also intensify the strain inhomogeneity, as described by S.C. Yoon et al [3]. The strain imposed in ECAP increases with decreasing channel angle, it may be advantageous to perform the pressings using channel angles which are ϕ less than $90°$. Where, High pressures are required to successfully produce billets without the introduction of any cracking, as recommended by R. Ruslan et al [4].

The experimental research work carried out in various aluminum alloys through ECAP die at different channel angles focused on the die channel angle around $90°$ with zero inner radius and fillet in outer corner for aluminum alloys. In spite of a lot of recent research results little work has been carried on the ECAP die with channel angle more than $90°$ with inner and outer radius. Channel Angle with more than $90°$ facilitates the easy metal flow, constraints of metal blocking inside die is reduced; ejector pin is not required and also that the required pressure for ECAP is minimum when compared to the channel angle $90°$.

The work aims to formulate an effective ECAP condition for AA6061 Aluminum Alloy and obtain possible solution for processing the material from the following predictions through modeling and analysis. The relation between die geometry and deformation inhomogeneity is predicted and compared for the effects of channel angles $90°$, $110°$ and $120°$ respectively. The relation between channel angle, strain energy and imparted strain has been investigated under various hydrostatic pressure conditions.

2   Modeling and Analysis

The Die for Equal Channel Angular Pressing is designed with three different channel angles i.e. $90°$, $110°$, $120°$. Channel Angle 'ϕ' (Intersection of Two Channels) is $90°$, Inner Radius 'r' is 4 mm, and Outer Radius is 'R' is 16 mm, Length of inlet channel 'L_1' is 130 mm, Length of outlet channel 'L_2' is 161.19 mm and diameter of sample is 10 mm as shown in Fig. 1. a.

Channel Angle 'ϕ' (Intersection of Two Channels) is $110°$, Inner Radius 'r' is 4 mm, and Outer Radius is 'R' is 16 mm, Length of inlet channel 'L_1" is 130 mm, Length of outlet channel 'L_2' is 161.19 mm and diameter of sample is 10 mm as shown in Fig. 1. b. Channel Angle 'ϕ' (Intersection of Two Channels) is $120°$, Inner

Radius 'r' is 4 mm, and Outer Radius is 'R' is 16 mm, Length of inlet channel 'L₁" is 130 mm, Length of outlet channel 'L₂' is 161.19 mm and diameter of sample is 10 mm as shown in Fig. 1.c.

During pressing, the axial stress on the sample is being translated to hydrostatic pressure exerted on the inner surface of the inlet channel. From literature the maximum pressing load is taken to be around 10 ton that will cover the pressing of several aluminum alloys. In other words the die will be rated at 10 tons, as suggested by Ehab El-Danaf et al. [5]

Where Hydrostatic Pressure, P in Mpa

$$P = \frac{F}{A}$$

where 'A' sample cross section area is 10 mm and 'F' force in Ton, hydrostatic pressure is to be around 1269 MPa for 10 tons ie. 1 Ton = 9964 N. Increase of Hydrostatic Pressure leads to enhance the material deformation and resulted in accumulated strain increase up to samples failure.

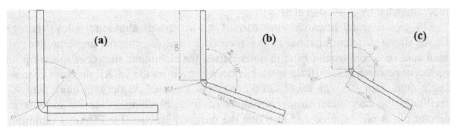

Fig. 1. (a) ECAP Die with Channel Angle 90°, (b) ECAP Die with Channel Angle 110°, (c) ECAP Die with Channel Angle 120°

2.1   Assumptions

Friction between the die channel inside and specimen assumed to be zero. The material is considered as isotropic and homogeneous. Heat generated due to deformation and friction was neglected. The von Mises flow rule is used.

2.2   Boundary Conditions

Body of the ECAP Die is considered as Rigid.This represents that displacement and rotation in x, y and z direction for all nodes in the die were arrested. Applying the Pressure on the top surface of the work-piece results in the movement of the work-piece through the channel angle.. Hence all nodes of top surface were given displacement. The displacement in the direction perpendicular to the plane and rotation about other two directions were arrested.

3   Result and Discussion

Average Equivalent Elastic Strain is calculated for three different channel angles i.e. 90° , 110° , 120° w.r.t. Various Hydrostatic pressure i.e. 127 Mpa , 381 Mpa , 635 Mpa, 888.5 Mpa , 1269 Mpa by using material AA 6061 as shown below in Fig.2. Average Strain Energy is calculated for three different channel angles i.e. 90° , 110° , 120° w.r.t. Various Hydrostatic pressure i.e. 127 Mpa , 381 Mpa , 635 Mpa, 888.5 Mpa , 1269 Mpa by using material AA 6061 as shown below in Fig.3. Average Imparted Strain is calculated for three different channel angles i.e. 90° , 110° , 120° w.r.t. Various Hydrostatic pressure i.e. 127 Mpa , 381 Mpa , 635 Mpa, 888.5 Mpa , 1269 Mpa by using material AA 6061 as shown below in Fig.4. Total deformation or displacement is obtained w.r.t various hydrostatic pressure for different channel angles were analysed. The deformation for Channel angles 90°, 110°, and 120° during the application of various hydrostatic pressure conditions as shown below in Fig.5.

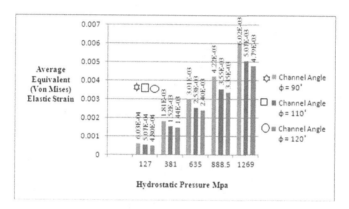

Fig. 2. Consolidated graph of average equivalent elastic strain for different channel angles

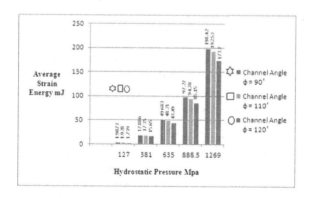

Fig. 3. Consolidated graph of average strain energy for different channel angles

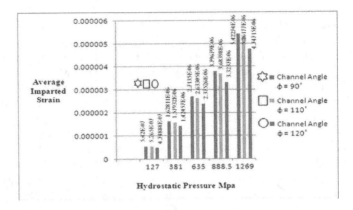

Fig. 4. Consolidated graph of imparted strain for different channel angles

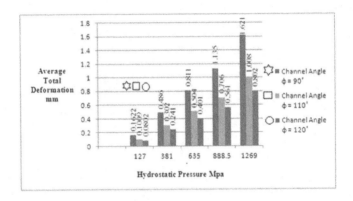

Fig. 5. Consolidated Total deformation of channel angle 90°, 110°, 120°

4   Conclusion

It was observed that influence of channel angle has significant effect on strain energy and imparted strain for the deformation of the material through ECAP. The strain energy and imparted strain decreases as the channel angle increases. Imparted strain and strain energy for channel angle 110° is close to channel angle 90°. In this case 110° is preferred than 90° because the hydrostatic pressure requirement is comparatively less in 110° than 90°.

Total deformation on the material is inhomogeneous irrespective of the channel angle 90°, 110°, and 120°. Displacement on the material decreases with increases in channel angle for different hydrostatic pressure conditions.

It is clear that channel angle plays an influencing factor for inducing strain on the material and also hydrostatic pressure determination based on channel angle. Therefore a compromise solution has to be selected in determining the channel angle for achieving effective ECAP condition.

4.1   Scope of the Future Work

- Analysis can be extended for different materials like copper, magnesium alloys and predicting corresponding deformation behaviour.
- During analysis Friction factor is to consider and predicting strain imposed on the material.
- Analysis will carried out with application of back pressure and predicts the corresponding behaviour.
- If Mesh Density differs, deformation differs. So, analysis will carried out with different mesh density.

References

1. Zhang, X.-H., Luo, S.-J., Du, Z.-M.: Uniformity and continuity of effective strain in AZ91D processed by multi-pass equal channel angular extrusion. Trans. Nonferrous Met. Soc. China 18, 92–98 (2008)
2. Nagasekhar, A.V., Tick-Hon, Y., Seow, H.P.: Deformation behavior and strain homogeneity in equal channel angular extrusion/pressing. Journal of Materials Processing Technology, 192–193, 449–452 (2007)
3. Yoon, S.C., Quang, P., Hong, S.I., Kim, H.S.: Die design for homogeneous plastic deformation during equal channel angular pressing. Journal of Materials Processing Technology, 187–188, 46–50 (2007)
4. Ruslan, R., Valiev, Z., Langdon, T.G.: Principles of equal-channel angular pressing as a processing tool for grain refinement. Progress in Materials Science 51, 881–981 (2006)
5. El-Danaf, E., Soliman, M., El-Rayes, M.: Design,Manufacturing and Preliminary Experimentation with an Equal Channel Angle Pressing Die. Research Center of King Saud University 3(426), 1–38 (2006)

Author Index